# WORLD WAR II

# MORE WILDSIDE CLASSICS

# WORLD WAR II

## A Cataloging Reference Guide

## by
## Buckley Barry Barrett

**WILDSIDE PRESS**

# WORLD WAR II

This edition published in 2006 by Wildside Press, LLC.
www.wildsidepress.com

# CONTENTS

# ACKNOWLEDGMENTS

Thanks to Nannette, Ross, and Elizabeth, for their patience and support during the six years needed to complete both the World War I and World War II phases of this project. Also, my appreciation goes to Ross and Rita Barrett for the encouragement and lodging given by them during my many visits to the Graduate Research Library at the University of California, Los Angeles, where I gathered much useful information for both titles.

INTRODUCTION

This guide seeks to improve the subject access to World War II information stored in most academic and public libraries in the United States. By describing and listing the classification or shelving schemes and controlled descriptors used by these libraries for cataloging the literature, I would hope to provide researchers with enough specific examples and overriding principles to find more materials than otherwise possible.

The scope of the work includes the Second World War as well as the preceding decades leading up to and pointing toward the conflict. Full cataloging coverage of World War I, its precedents, and related matters can be found in my volume on that conflict. Since this is mostly an historical tool, I have also included many of the countries involved and have rounded out the coverage with pertinent engineering, military, and naval concepts and facts.

Two main divisions make up the work: 1. Subject classification systems used for shelving and; 2. Controlled subject, biographical, and corporate headings used in electronic, card, or microform catalogs.

The first division contains two sections listing and describing Library of Congress and Dewey Decimal call numbers, with each section providing selected cross-references to the other system. Most academic or research libraries catalog by L.C., whereas public libraries tend toward the Dewey system. Numbers given in this guide concentrate heavily on the world war; but overall outlines of both schemes are given as well, for the sake of context and because the global war under study influenced or was influenced by matters of society, politics, economics, literature, and science in addition to history and other areas.

With a better comprehension of the major classification arrays utilized in the United States, researchers can look in a greater number of shelf locations and can find similar materials located in proximity. Certain library electronic or card catalogs may also allow for a type of remote subject browsing by call number or classification, which can prove a valuable complement to subject-term searching in the catalog.

The second primary section of the book contains Library of Congress subject headings along with proper biographical and corporate agency names. These are all placed in alphabetical order as might occur in libraries' separate subject or unified dictionary catalogs.

Most public and academic libraries in the United States look to the Library of Congress for authorized subject words and phrases; so, the search vocabulary need not change from library to library. The subject headings of this division of the book represent events, places, people, government departments, armies, navies, air forces, weapons, strategies, and other objective and subjective matters related to the war, its historical period, and the process of studying this era. Researchers may find that some of the biographical entries listed herein can be found in particular libraries as authors or topics. In a similar fashion one may find some of the government or other agency headings utilized as corporate authors or subjects.

I have given L.C. and/or Dewey call numbers or class ranges for a large sample of main and peripheral headings in order to assist with intelligent browsing of the stacks or shelf inventory records. The principal purpose here, however, is to improve catalog search results through the listing of a large volume of pertinent subject and corporate quasi-subject terms and types.

To summarize, this work attempts to provide readers with a library subject-control system for use in World War II research in both academic, public, and special libraries. With greater knowledge of both classified storage patterns and controlled indexing terminology, one can find a greater number of materials and can also pinpoint more specific items that might otherwise remain lost or buried.

# I. LIBRARY OF CONGRESS CLASSIFICATION SYSTEM (LC)

The Library of Congress classification system divides knowledge and history into groups of alphanumeric symbols. Single, double, or triple letters are followed by numbers from 1 through 9999. These numbers are sometimes broken down into more specialized topics by decimilization and/or letter-number symbols. Libraries finish LC call numbers with alphanumeric combinations generally derived from author's last names and sometimes from titles.

Each class letter section or schedule devised, published, and employed by LC represents a different discipline or area of information, and LC has developed each section more or less independently from the other sections through the years from around the early 20th Century.

As a result of this somewhat autonomous growth, patterns of usage vary from schedule to schedule. For example, the 'D' class covering Old World, Eastern, and Oceanic history featues double and even triple letters for certain areas. Great Britain is represented by 'DA' and Eastern Europe by 'DJK'. On the other hand, the 'E' and 'F' schedules cover North and South America without any multiple letters. Number spans also vary from class to class and even within. For instance, the 'VK' section of Naval Science ('V') goes up to around VK1660 or so in covering navigation and merchant marine, whereas 'VM' only reaches about VM990 in classifying naval architecture.

The LC system differs from the Dewey classification in a number of ways. The most obvious, of course, is the use of letters rather than numerals as the primary means of division. As will be seen in more detail in the next segment of this book, Dewey divides knowledge up into ten basic sets of 100 numbers each. For instance, history may often be found in the 900-999 section. Subdivisions are handled by the use of tens, digits, or decimals. Thus, much of the specific World War Two material may be in the 940.53-940.5499 area, while LC places equivalent items in the D731-D838 range in using letters followed by numbers in combination in order to separate different subjects or historical periods.

Call numbers built from either system can prove involved and lengthy, although complex DDC numbers may appear longer due to their general lack of breaks or pauses. LC schedules present more specific and more required choices, whereas DDC (Dewey Decimal Classification) specifies less and allows libraries to tack on one or more standardized decimal additions if desired for a more thorough description.

The Library of Congress array does not appear as essentially logical as the Dewey method because LC has neither the consistency nor the mnemonic hierarchy of its rival. LC's variable use of one, two, or three letters to begin different topical areas (e.g. 'D', 'DA-DX', and 'DJK' versus 'E' and 'F') does not stem from any pattern, and neither does its sometimes application of alphabetic subdivisions for greater subject detail (e.g. V858 for U.S. submarines as opposed to V859.G3 for German subs.).

In practice, LC brings similar titles together in useful groups just as well as Dewey, while usually allowing for more range expansion room and shorter, less crowded numbers. In some subject sections, LC has indeed left space for the future addition of entirely new and unused number sets out to 9999. For Dewey, however, new topics more often lead to longer, more awkward call numbers or to continued employment of the same old numbers but with new and unrelated meanings in mixed company.

Because of some of the reasons stated herein, most academic and some (generally larger) public libraries in the United States have chosen the Library of Congress system to catalog their resources. In summary, LC appears preferable for larger collections as well as for special ones due to its provision of more detail with less clutter.

This section of the guide first outlines the overall LC scheme and then gives a specific listing of the divisions most pertinent to world war and military research. LC alphanumerics are accompanied by descriptions and Dewey equivalents where feasible. Be aware of continuing changes and additions made to LC and Dewey in order to keep them as dynamic methods of classification. Some of these changes are noted as possible.

Both of the class systems allow for a certain amount of choice in matching topics with numbers, and yet each method also takes a somewhat different view of the universe and its knowledge. Hence, as in comparing and contrasting two languages, we see that each offers its own variety of internal synonyms and that these do not always exactly equal particular words in the other language.

A unified alphabetic index follows the conclusion of the Dewey class listing and contains both LC and Dewey numbers. Some topics do not have exact possibilities for call-number assignment and may seem to belong in more than one area, and sometimes perfectly equated LC/Dewey translations do not appear to exist. Accordingly, researchers should use the LC/Dewey index plus LC headings sections in order to determine the most classification numbers.

LC CLASS NUMBERS: DESCRIPTIONS: POSSIBLE DEWEY NUMBERS

| | | |
|---|---|---|
| A | General works (gen. almanacs, encyclopediae, etc.) | 000-099 |
| B | Philosophy, psychology, religion | 100-299 |
| C | History (auxiliary: civilization, gen. archaeology, heraldry, gen. biography) | 900-909, 920-929, 930-939+ |
| D | History (general, Eastern Hemisphere, Oceania) | 909, 930-969, 990, 996 |
| D-DX | World history, Europe, Africa, Asia, Oceania | 900-949, 990's |
| DA-DR | Europe and Turkey | 940's, 956.1 |
| D25 | Military history (world) | 355.48, 904.7, 909 |
| D501-680 | WORLD WAR I | 940.3-940.499 |
| D731-838 | WORLD WAR II | 940.53-940.5499 |
| E | America & North America (gen.), United States | 970, 973 |
| F | United States (local history), Canada, Latin America | 971-972, 974-989 |
| G | Geography, anthropology, sports, & recreation | 910-919, 301, 790's |
| H | Social sciences (economics, commerce, sociology, communism) | 300-319, 330-389 |
| J | Political science, international law | 320-329, 341 |
| K | Law | 340, 342-349 |
| L | Education | 370-379 |
| M | Music | 780-789 |
| N | Arts & architecture (visual, decorative & applied) | 700-709, 720-769 |
| P | Languages & literatures | 400-499, 800-899 |
| PN | Literature (gen. & gen. collections) | 800-809 |
| PR | English literature | 820-829 |
| PS | American literature in English | 810-819 |
| Q | Sciences (pure), math, & computer science | 500-599, 611-612 |
| R | Medicine, psychiatry, & nursing | 610-619, 649 |
| S | Agriculture, forestry, hunting | 630-639, 574, 581, 799 |
| T | Technology, photography, manufacturing, handicrafts, home, economics | 600-609, 620-629, 640-650, 660-699, 770-779 |
| U | Military science & engineering | 355-358, 623 |
| V | Naval science, navigation, & naval architecture | 359, 623, 629 |
| Z | Bibliography & library science (bibliog's. sometimes classed with A-Z subject #s) | 010-028+ |
| | | |
| D | History (general, Eastern Hemisphere, Oceania) | 909, 930-969, 990-996 |
| D25 | World military history | 355.48, 904.7, 909 |
| D51-838, D901+ | Europe (gen.) | 940-949 |
| D731-838 | WORLD WAR II | 940.53-940.5499 |
| DA | Great Britain | 941-942 |
| DB | Austria, Czechoslovakia, Hungary | 943.6-943.9 |
| DC | France | 944 |
| DD | Germany | 943 |
| DG | Italy | 945 |
| DJK | Eastern Europe (after about 1977-78) | 943.7-943.9, 947, 947.8, 949.6-949.84 |
| DK | Russia, Finland, Poland | |
| DL | Scandinavia | |
| DP | Iberian Peninsula | |
| DQ | Switzerland | 949.4 |
| DR | Balkan Peninsula, Eastern Europe (prior to about 1978-79) | 949.6-949.8, 943.7-943.9, 947, 947.8, 956 |

5

| | | |
|---|---|---|
| DS | Asia | 950-959 |
| DT | Africa | 960-969 |
| DU | Oceania, Australia, New Zealand | 990-996 |
| D1-1075+ | HISTORY (gen., world wars, Eur. overall, etc.) | 909, 940, 950 |
| D25 | Military history (world) | 355.48, 904.7, 909 |
| D25.A2 | Dictionaries, chronologies, etc. (military history: world) | |
| D27 | Naval history (world) | 359, 904.7 |
| D208 | Modern history (1453-) | 901.93, 909.8+, 940 |
| D215 | Naval history (1453-) | |
| D299 | Modern history (1789-) | 909.8+ |
| D358 | Modern history (1801-1914/20) | 909.81 |
| D359 | Europe (1801-1914) | 940.28 |
| D361 | Military history (1801-1914/20) | 355.033003+ |
| D362 | Naval history (1801-1914/20) | |
| D371-379 | Eastern question (1801-1914/20) | 949, 320.956, 327.41-42 |
| D410-460+ | WORLD HISTORY (20th c.: overall) | |
| D410 | Periodicals, associations, yearbooks (20th c.) | |
| D410.5 | Current events yrbks. (20th c.: nonserial: includes pictorial titles: by time then author) | |
| D411 | Primary sources (20th c.: collections) | |
| D412-412.8 | Biography (20th c.: memoirs and collective) | |
| D412 | Biography (20th c.: collective: gen.) | 920.02 |
| D412.5 | Women (20th c.: collective biography) | |
| D412.6 | Public figures (20th c.: collective biog.: men) | 920.02, 909.82, 940.50922 |
| D412.7 | Rulers, kings, etc. (20th c.: collective biography) | 929.7 |
| D412.8 | Queens, princesses, etc. (20th c.: collective biography) | |
| D413.A-Z | Biography (20th c.: individual or memoir by name) | |
| D414-415 | World history (20th c.: collected) | |
| D414 | World history (20th c.: several authors) | |
| D415 | World history (20th c.: single-author collections) | |
| D416 | Pamphlets, minor works (20th c.) | |
| D419 | Dictionaries (20th c. history) | 909.8203, 320.03, 320.904 |
| D421-425 | World history (20th c.: general titles) | |
| D421 | World history (20th c.: gen.) | 909.82 |
| D422 | Popular histories (20th c.) | |
| D424 | Europe (20th c.) | 940.288-5 |
| D425 | Popular histories (20th c.: Europe) | |
| D426 | Pictorial and graphic histories (20th c.) | 779.990194, 909.82 |
| D427 | Chronologies, outlines, syllabi, tables, etc. (20th c.) | 909.82, 940.28 |
| D429 | Civilization, customs, social life (20th c.: SEE ALSO CB415, GT146) | 940.5, 320.904, 327.09 |
| D431 | Military history (20th c.) | 355.020904, 355.009, 355.033+ |
| D436 | Naval history (20th c.) | 359.409, 904.7, 359.47 |
| D437 | Air warfare | 358.41409, 358.41447 |
| D440-460 | Politics and diplomacy (20th c.) | |
| D440 | Annual registers (20th c.: politics and diplomacy) | |
| D441 | Primary sources (20th c.: politics and diplomacy) | |
| D442 | Politics and diplomacy (20th c.: collected works) | |
| D443 | Politics and diplomacy (20th c.: gen.: world pol., Triple Alliance & Entente, etc.) | 940.5, 320.904, 327.09 |
| D445 | Politics and diplomacy (20th c.: gen. special: projected, possible wars, other polit. events) | |

| | |
|---|---|
| D446 | Anglo-Saxon supremacy |
| D447 | Pangermanism |
| D448 | Panlatinism |
| D448.5 | Panceltism |
| D449 | Panslavism |
| D450 | Pamphlets, minor works (20th c.: politics and diplomacy) |
| D451-457 | Diplomacy (20th c.) |
| D451 | Primary sources (20th c.: diplomacy) |
| D453 | Diplomacy (20th c.: gen.)        909.82, 327.3-9, 320.9 |
| D455 | Diplomacy (20th c.: gen. special) |
| D457 | Pamphlets, minor works (20th c.: diplomacy) |
| D458 | Triple Alliance (1882: SEE ALSO D397, D443, D511) |
| D459 | Triple Entente (1907: SEE ALSO D443, D511) |
| D460 | Little Entente (1919) |
| D461-475 | Eastern question (20th c.)        320.95, 956.03, 325.342 |
| D463 | Eastern question (20th c.: gen.) |
| D469.A-Z | Eastern question (20th c.: by country) |
| D471-72 | Central Asian question (20th c.) |
| D471 | Central Asian question (1914-) |
| D472.A-Z | Central Asian question (20th c.: by country) |
| D475 | Moroccan question (20th c.: PREFER DT317) |
| | |
| D501-680 | WORLD WAR I (1914-1918)        940.3-940.499 |
| D503 | Museums, exhibitions, etc. (WWI) |
| D505 | Primary sources, documents (WWI) |
| D510 | Dictionaries & encyclopedias (WWI: includes 'Times' index and chronology) |
| D511-520 | CAUSES, AIMS, RESULTS (WWI)        940.31-2 |
| D511 | Causes, aims, results (WWI: gen.)        940.311, .314 |
| D514 | Russia (WWI: causes, aims, results: includes Panslavism) |
| D515 | Germany (WWI: causes, aims, results) |
| D516 | France (WWI: causes, aims, results) |
| D517 | Great Britain (WWI: causes, aims, results) |
| D519 | Japan (WWI: causes, aims, results) |
| D520.I7 | Italy (WWI: causes, aims, results: includes Treaty of London, 1915) |
| D520.U6-7 | United States (WWI: causes, aims, results) |
| D521 | WORLD WAR I (GEN.)        940.3, 940.4 |
| D522 | Pictorials (WWI: SEE ALSO D527) |
| D522.23 | Movies (WWI) |
| D522.3 | Maps & atlases (WWI: PREFER G1037) |
| D522.42 | Historiography (WWI) |
| D522.7 | Juvenile works (WWI) |
| D526-526.7 | Poetry, satire, etc. (WWI: PREFER PQ-PT) |
| D526.2 | English poetry, satire, etc. (WWI: PREFER PR, PS) |
| D526.3 | French poetry, satire, etc. (WWI) |
| D526.5 | German poetry, satire, etc. (WWI) |
| D528 | Battlefield guides (WWI: gen.: SEE ALSO specific battles) |
| D528.5 | Mobilization and beginnings (WWI) |
| D529 | Reports, Official (WWI: military) |

| | | |
|---|---|---|
| D530-549 | WESTERN FRONT (WWI) | |
| D530 | MiILITARY OPS. (WWI: West: gen.) | 940.41+, .421, .424, .4272, .431, .434 |
| D531-538 | GERMAN MILITARY OPS. (WWI: West & overall) | |
| D531 | German military ops. (WWI: West & gen.: includes Hindenburg, Ludendorff memoirs) 940.343, .40943, .413+, 943.084-085 | |
| D538.5.A-Z | Local history (WWI: Ger.: by place) | |
| D544-549+ | Anglo-French & Allied military ops. (WWI) | |
| D544 | Allies & Allied military ops. (WWI: gen.) | 940.412+, .414, .42-3, 944.0814 |
| D546-547.8+ | BRITISH M ILITARY OPS., British Empire, & England (WWI) | |
| D546 | British military ops. (WWI: gen.) | 354.42066, 940.48341, .412+, 941.083 |
| D547.A-Z | British Empire & Britain (WWI: by place or name) | |
| D547.A1 | Colonies (WWI: G.B.: gen.) | |
| D547.A8 | Australia & Anzacs (WWI) | |
| D547.C2 | Canada (WWI) | |
| D547.I5 | India (WWI) | |
| D547.I6 | Ireland (WWI) | |
| D547.N5 | New Zealand (WWI) | |
| D547.8.A-Z | Local history (WWI: England: by place) | |
| D547.8.L7 | London, Eng. (WWI) | |
| D548-549 | French military ops. & France (WWI) | |
| D550-569 | EASTERN FRONT (WWI) | |
| D550 | Russian military ops. and Eastern Front (WWI: gen.) 940.4147, .40947 | |
| D551 | Russo-German conflict (WWI: gen.) | |
| D556 | Russo-Austrian conflict (WWI: gen.) | |
| D560-565 | Balkan conflict (WWI) | |
| D566-569 | Near East, Turkey, Italy, Greece (WWI) | |
| D568.2 | Egypt (WWI) | |
| D568.3 | Gallipoli & the Dardanelles (WWI) | |
| D568.7 | Palestine (WWI) | |
| D569 | Italy (WWI) 940.4145 | |
| D570-570.9+ | UNITED STATES MILITARY OPS. & U.S. (WWI) | 940.373, 41273, .40973, 327.73 |
| D570 | United States (WWI: gen.) 940.373 | |
| D570.A3 | Legislative compendia (WWI: U.S.) | |
| D570.A4 | Histories, Official (WWI: U.S.) | |
| D570.A5-Z | American military ops. & U.S. (WWI: gen. unofficial) | 940.373, 41273, .40973, 327.73 |
| D570.15 | Pamphlets, minor works (WWI: U.S.) | |
| D570.2-.79 | United States military ops. (WWI: organiz. units: land, sea, air: SEE D570.A4-Z, D545 etc. for overall participation, battles, etc.) | |
| D570.25-.358 | Armies etc. (WWI: U.S.) 940.412+, .44973, .45 | |
| D570.25.A-Z | General staff & headquarters (WWI: U.S.) | |
| D570.33 | Infantry (WWI: U.S.: newer bks. may use A1 or #'s as in D570.27) | |
| D570.348 | Marines (WWI: U.S.: inland ops.) | |
| D570.4-.5 | United States naval ops. (WWI: SEE ALSO D589.U5-8) | 940.45+, .41273 |
| D570.6 | United States aerial ops. (WWI: PREFER D606 for general works) | 940.44973 |

| | | |
|---|---|---|
| D570.8.A-Z | United States (WWI: special topics: SEE D639 for outside U.S.) | |
| D570.8.P7 | Political prisoners (WWI: U.S.) | |
| D570.8.S5 | Service flags (WWI: U.S.) | |
| D570.85.A-W | States of the U.S. (WWI) | 974-979 |
| D570.85.C21.A-Z | Local history (WWI: Calif.) | |
| D570.85.N4-5 | New York (WWI) | |
| D570.88.A-Z | Nationalities (WWI: U.S.) | |
| D571 | Japanese military ops. (WWI: gen.) | |
| D573-578 | Colonies (WWI) | |
| D577 | Pacific, Asiatic, & other colonies (WWI: Ger.: gen.) | |
| D578.N4 | New Guinea (WWI) | |
| D580-595 | NAVAL OPS. (WWI) | 940.45 |
| D580 | Freedom of the seas & naval ops. (gen.: WWI) | |
| D582.A-Z | British naval ops. & Anglo-German naval conflict (WWI: by battle, ship, etc.) | |
| D589.U5-8 | United States naval ops. (WWI: SEE ALSO D570.4-5) | |
| D590-595 | Submarine ops. & submarine chasers (WWI) | 940.451+ |
| D591 | German submarine ops. (WWI: gen.) | 940.4512 |
| D600-607 | AIR FORCE OPS. (WWI) | 940.44 |
| D602 | British aerial ops. (WWI) | 940.44941 |
| D603 | French aerial ops. (WWI) | 940.44944 |
| D604 | German aerial ops. (WWI) | 940.44943 |
| D605 | Russian aerial ops. (WWI) | |
| D606 | United States aerial ops. (WWI) | 940.44973 |
| D607.5 | Gas warfare (WWI: PREFER UG447) | |
| D608 | Tank warfare (WWI) | 358.18, 940.4+ |
| D609.A3-Z | Registers & lists (WWI: decorated, dead, wounded: by country) | |
| D610-621 | DIPLOMACY (WWI) | 940.32 |
| D610 | Diplomacy (WWI: gen.) | |
| D611 | Neutrality, other special diplomatic history (WWI) | |
| D614.A-Z | Treaties (WWI: misc. separate) | |
| D614.A2 | Treaties (WWI: misc. separate: collections) | |
| D614.B5 | Brest-Litovsk, Ukraine (WWI: treaty: 9 Feb. 1918) | |
| D614.B6 | Brest-Litovsk, Russia (WWI: treaty: 3 Mar. 1918) | |
| D617 | Italy & Italian neutrality (WWI: dipl. history) | |
| D619 | United States (WWI: neutrality & dipl. history) | 940.32273, .373 |
| D621.S3 | Scandinavia (WWI: dipl. hist.) | |
| D621.S45 | Norway (WWI: dipl. hist.) | |
| D621.S5 | Sweden (WWI: dipl. hist.) | |
| D622-639 | WORLD WAR I (SPECIAL TOPICS) | |
| D622 | Catholic Church (WWI) | |
| D623.A2 | Occupied territories (WWI: gen.: includes laws) | |
| D623.A3-Z | Occupied territories (WWI: by country) | |
| D625-626 | Atrocities, war crimes, trials (WWI) | |
| D626.G3 | Atrocities, war crimes, trials (WWI: Ger. & Central Powers) | |
| D627.A1 | Periodicals & associations (WWI: prisons) | 940.472+ |
| D627.A2 | Prisons & prisoners (WWI: gen.) | |
| D627.A3-Z | Prisons & prisoners (WWI: by country) | |
| D628-630 | MEDICAL SERVICES, HOSPITALS, RED CROSS (WWI) | |
| | | 940.475+, .477+ |
| D629.A-Z | Red Cross & medical services (WWI: by country) | |
| D629.G7 | Medical services & Red Cross (WWI: G.B.) | |
| D629.U6 | Medical services & Red Cross (WWI: U.S.: gen.) | |

| | | |
|---|---|---|
| D631 | Censorship, press, publicity (WWI: gen.: SEE ALSO D639.P6-7 for propaganda) | 940.315097 |
| D632 | Press, publicity, censorship (WWI: U.S.) | |
| D635 | Economic matters (WWI: commerce, finance, mail: SEE ALSO HC56, HF3030, HJ236,HJ8011) | |
| D636 | Alien enemies (WWI) | |
| D637 | Charities, refugees, relief work (WWI: gen.) | 940.477+ |
| D638.A-Z | Refugees, relief work, charities (WWI: by country or area) | |
| D638.U5 | Relief work, refugees, etc. (WWI: U.S.) | |
| D639.A-Z | WORLD WAR I (MISC. SPECIAL: SEE D570.8 for U.S.) | |
| D639.A65 | Animals (WWI: use of) | |
| D639.D4 | Dead (WWI: burial, cemeteries, etc.) | |
| D639.N4 | Blacks (WWI: Negroes) | |
| D639.P6 | Propaganda (WWI: gen.: SEE ALSO D631-633 for press) | 940.488+ |
| D639.P7.A-Z | Propaganda (WWI: by country) | |
| D639.P77 | Protest movements (WWI) | |
| D639.P87 | Public opinion (WWI: gen.) | |
| D639.P88.A-Z | Public opinion (WWI: by place) | |
| D639.R4 | Religion, Christianity (WWI) | 940.478 |
| D639.S2 | Science & technology (WWI) | |
| D639.S7-8 | Espionage, secret service, spies (WWI) | |
| D639.T8 | Transportation (WWI) | |
| D639.W7 | Women & women's work (WWI) | 940.315042 |
| D640 | Personal accounts (WWI: SEE ALSO D570.9 for U.S. soldiers) | |
| | | 940.481+ |
| D642-651 | PEACE (WWI) | 940.312, .3141 |
| D642 | Primary sources, documents (WWI: peace: collections) | |
| D643 | TREATIES (WWI: Allies-Central powers) | 940.3141 |
| D643.A2-A7 | Treaties (WWI: Ger.: 28 June 1919) | |
| D643.A2 | Treaty of Versailles (WWI: 28 June 1919: collected texts) | |
| D643.A5.1919+ | Treaty of Versailles (WWI: texts by date) | |
| D643.A67 | Resolution of peace (WWI: U.S. Congress by date) | |
| D643.A68 | Treaties (WWI: U.S.-Ger.) | |
| D643.A8-Z | Treaties (WWI: countries other than Ger.) | |
| D643.A8-A9 | Treaties (WWI: Austria: 10 Sept. 1919) | |
| D643.A8 | Treaty of St. Germain (WWI: texts by date) | |
| D643.A83 | Treaties (WWI: U.S.-Austria) | |
| D643.B5 | Treaties (WWI: Bulg.: 27 Nov. 1919) | |
| D643.B6 | Treaty of Neuilly-sur-Seine (WWI: texts) | |
| D643.H7-9 | Treaties (WWI: Hungary: 4 June 1920) | |
| D643.H7 | Treaty of Trianon (WWI: non-U.S. texts) | |
| D643.H8 | Treaties (WWI: U.S.-Hung.) | |
| D643.T8 | Treaties (WWI: Turkey: S`evres: 10 Aug. 1920) | |
| D644 | Peace (WWI: gen.) | 940.312 |
| D646 | Pamphlets, minor works (WWI: peace) | |
| D647.A2 | Peace commissions (WWI: gen.) | |
| D648 | Indemnity & reparations (WWI: gen.) | 940.31422 |
| D649.A-Z | Reparations & indemnity (WWI: by country) | |
| D649.G3 | Reparations (WWI: Ger.) | |
| D649.G3.A4-5 | Dawes Plan (WWI) | |
| D649.G3.A6-7 | Young Plan (WWI) | |

| | |
|---|---|
| D650.A-Z | Peace (WWI: other special topics) |
| D650.D5 | Disarmament (WWI: Ger.) |
| D650.I6 | Inter-allied Military Commission of Control in Germany (WWI) |
| D650.J4 | Jews (WWI: peace topic) |
| D650.M5 | Occupation, Military (WWI: Rhineland) |
| D650.T4 | Territorial questions (post-WWI: gen.: SEE D651 for specific places)        940.31424 |
| D651.A-Z | TERRITORIAL QUESTIONS (post-WWI: by place) |
| D651.A4 | Africa (post-WWI territorial ?s) |
| D651.A41 | German East Africa (post-WWI territorial ?s) |
| D651.A42 | German Southwest Africa (post-WWI territorial ?s) |
| D651.A5 | Albania (post-WWI territorial ?s) |
| D651.A95 | Austria (post-WWI territorial ?s) |
| D651.B2 | Baltic provinces (post-WWI territorial ?s) |
| D651.B3 | Belgium (post-WWI territorial ?s) |
| D651.B8 | Bulgaria (post-WWI territorial ?s) |
| D651.C4-7 | China (post-WWI territorial ?s) |
| D651.C5 | China (post-WWI relns.: U.S.) |
| D651.C6 | China (post-WWI relns.: Japan) |
| D651.C78 | Croatia (post-WWI territorial ?s) |
| D651.C8 | Cuba (post-WWI territorial ?s) |
| D651.C9 | Czechoslovakia (post-WWI territorial ?s) |
| D651.F5-7 | France (post-WWI territorial ?s) |
| D651.F5 | France (post-WWI territorial ?s: gen.) |
| D651.F6.A2-Z | France (post-WWI relns.: U.S.: inclu. defensive alliance bet. Fr., U.S., G.B.) |
| D651.G2 | Georgia, Transcaucasia (post-WWI territorial ?s) |
| D651.G3 | Germany (post-WWI territorial ?s) |
| D651.G5-7 | Great Britain (post-WWI territorial ?s) |
| D651.G5 | Great Britain (post-WWI territorial ?s: gen.) |
| D651.G6 | Great Britain (post-WWI relns.: U.S.: inclu. defensive alliance w. Fr., U.S.) |
| D651.G7 | Great Britain (post-WWI relns.: countries other than U.S.) |
| D651.G8 | Greece & unredeemed Greeks (post-WWI territorial ?s) |
| D651.H7 | Hungary (post-WWI territorial ?s) |
| D651.I6-8 | Italy (post-WWI territorial ?s: inclu. Fiume) |
| D651.I7 | Italy (post-WWI relns.: U.S.) |
| D651.J3-5 | Japan (post-WWI territorial ?s) |
| D651.J4 | Japan (post-WWI relns.: U.S.) |
| D651.N5 | Nicaragua (post-WWI territorial ?s) |
| D651.P2 | Pacific Islands, German (post-WWI territorial ?s) |
| D651.P3 | Palestine (post-WWI territorial ?s) |
| D651.P4 | Persia (post-WWI territorial ?s) |
| D651.P7 | Poland (post-WWI territorial ?s) |
| D651.P75 | Portugal (post-WWI territorial ?s) |
| D651.P89-9 | Prussia, East & West (post-WWI territorial ?s) |
| D651.R6 | Rumania (post-WWI territorial ?s) |
| D651.R8 | Russia (post-WWI territorial ?s) |
| D651.S13 | Saar Valley (post-WWI territorial ?s) |
| D651.S3 | Samoa, Western (post-WWI territorial ?s) |
| D651.S53 | Slovenia (post-WWI territorial ?s) |
| D651.S9 | Syria (post-WWI territorial ?s) |

| | | |
|---|---|---|
| D651.T8 | Transylvania (post-WWI territorial ?s) | |
| D651.T85 | Trieste (post-WWI territorial ?s) | |
| D651.T9 | Turkey (post-WWI territorial ?s) | |
| D651.T95 | Tyrol (post-WWI territorial ?s) | |
| D651.U6 | Ukraine (post-WWI territorial ?s) | |
| D651.Y8-9 | Yugoslavia (post-WWI territorial ?s) | |
| D652-659 | POST-WAR ERA & RECONSTRUCTION (WWI) | 940.3144, .34-39 |
| D653 | Reconstruction & post-war era (WWI: gen.) | |
| D659.A-Z | Reconstruction (WWI: countries outside U.S.) | |
| D659.F8 | France (WWI: Reconstruction) | |
| D663-680 | Monuments, memorials, celebrations (WWI) | 940.46+ |
| D675.A-Z | Monuments, memorials, celebrations (WWI: U.S.: by city) | |
| D680.G7 | Monuments, memorials, celebrations (WWI: G.B.) | |

| | | |
|---|---|---|
| D720-728 | World history (1919-39) | |
| D720 | Inter-war period (1919-39: gen.) | 940.5-.52 |
| D723 | Inter-war period (1919-39: special) | |
| D725 | Inter-war period (1919-39: essays, minor works) | |
| D726 | Civilization, customs, social life (1919-39: sometimes Europe alone) | |
| D726.5 | Fascism (1919-39: SEE ALSO JC481 and 'D' numbers for Italy, Ger.) | |
| | | 320.533, 321.94094 |
| D727 | Politics & diplomacy (1919-39) | 327.0904, .4, 909.822-23, 940.51-52 |
| D728 | Axis (Ger.-Italy: 1919-39) | 940.51-52 |

| | | |
|---|---|---|
| D731-838 | WORLD WAR II (1939-1945) | 940.53-940.5499 |
| D731 | Periodicals, serials, collections (WWII) | |
| D731.S73 | 'Stars and Stripes' (WWII: periodical) | |
| D732 | Associations, societies (WWII) | |
| D733 | Museums, exhibitions, etc. (WWII) | |
| D733.A1 | Museums, exhibitions, etc. (WWII: gen.) | |
| D733.A2-Z | Museums, exhibitions, etc. (WWII: by country) | |
| D733.5 | Collectibles, relics, trophies (WWII) | |
| D734 | CONFERENCES (WWII) | |
| D734.A1.A-Z | Conferences (WWII: gen. & multi.) | |
| D734.A2-Z999 | Conferences (WWII: single) | |
| D734.A7-8 | Atlantic Charter (Newfoundland: 14 Aug. 1941) | |
| D734.B4 | Conferences (1941: Berlin: Potsdam, Ger.) | |
| D734.C2 | Conferences (1943: Cairo, Eg.) | |
| D734.C25 | Conferences (1943: Casablanca, Mor.) | |
| D734.C7 | Conferences (1945: Crimea: Yalta, Rus.) | |
| D734.T4 | Conferences (1943: Tehran, Iran) | |
| D735 | Primary sources, documents (WWII: sometimes by gov. agency, A-Z) | |
| D735.A1 | Primary sources, documents (WWII: collection, preservation) | |
| D735.A7 | Atlantic Declaration (Charter': 14 Aug. 1941) | |
| D736 | Biography (collective: WWII: for individuals SEE DA-F class numbers for person's country: SEE ALSO D811 for personal narratives) 940.5481-5482 (ALSO country numbers ended sometimes by 0922-0924) | |
| D739 | World War II (collected works) | |
| D740 | Dictionaries & encyclopedias (WWII) | 940.5303 |

| | | |
|---|---|---|
| D741 | CAUSES, AIMS, RESULTS (WWII: gen.) | 940.5311, 327+ |
| D742.A-Z | Causes, aims, results (WWII: by country) | 940.534-539 |
| D742.C5 | China (WWII: causes, aims, results) | |
| D742.F8 | France (WWII: causes, aims, results) | |
| D742.G3 | Germany (WWII: causes, aims, results) | |
| D742.G7 | Great Britain (WWII: causes, aims, results) | |
| D742.J3 | Japan (WWII: causes, aims, results) | |
| D742.R9 | Russia (WWII: causes, aims, results) | |
| D742.U5-6 | United States (WWII: causes, aims, results) | |
| D743 | WORLD WAR II (GEN.) | 940.53, .54 |
| D743.2 | Pictorials (WWII: SEE ALSO D746) | |
| D743.22 | Documentary films, slides, etc. (WWII: catalogs: SEE ALSO D746.3 for older titles) | |
| D743.23 | Movies & movie propaganda (WWII) | 791.43+, 940.53+ |
| D743.25 | Posters (WWII: SEE D746.5 for older titles) | 769.4994+ |
| D743.27 | Collectibles (WWII) | |
| D743.3 | Maps & atlases (WWII: PREFER G1038) | |
| D743.4 | Instruction (WWII) | |
| D743.42 | Historiography (WWII) | |
| D743.5 | Chronologies, tables, outlines (WWII) | 940.530202 |
| D743.6 | Examinations, questions, etc. (WWII) | |
| D743.7 | Juvenile works (WWII) | |
| D743.9 | Pamphlets, minor works, sermons (WWII) | |
| D744 | World War II (gen. special: deception, strategy, psychological aspects, world politics, misc.) | |
| D744.4 | Ethics, religious questions (WWII) | |
| D744.5.A-Z | Religious & ethical questions (WWII: by country) | |
| D744.5.I8 | Italy (WWII: religious & ethical ?'s) | |
| D744.5.J3 | Japan (WWII: religious & ethical ?'s) | |
| D744.5.R9 | Russia (WWII: religious & ethical ?'s) | |
| D744.6 | Social aspects (WWII) | |
| D744.7.A-Z | Social aspects (WWII: by country) | |
| D745-745.7 | Poetry, satire, etc. (WWII: PREFER PQ-PT) | |
| D745 | Satire, poetry, etc. (WWII: gen.) | 940.5481, .5483, misc. 800 literature #'s |
| D745.2 | English poetry, satire, etc. (WWII: PREFER PR, PS) | |
| D745.3 | French poetry, satire, etc. (WWII) | |
| D745.5 | German poetry, satire, etc. (WWII) | |
| D745.7.A-Z | Poetry, satire, etc. (WWII: languages besides Eng., Fr., Ger.) | |
| D745.7.I8 | Italian poetry, satire, etc. (WWII) | |
| D745.7.R9 | Russian poetry, satire, etc. (WWII) | |
| D746 | Views (WWII: SEE ALSO D743.2+) | |
| D746.3 | Documentary films, slides, etc. (WWII: catalogs: SEE ALSO D743.22 for media catalogs of newer titles) | |
| D746.5 | Posters (WWII: SEE D743.25 for newer titles) | |
| D747 | Battlefield guides (WWII: gen.: particular battles at D756.5 etc.) | |

```
D748-754    DIPLOMACY (WWII)        940.532+, 327.+
D748        Diplomacy (WWII: gen.)
D749        Neutrality, small states, other special diplomatic history (WWII)
D749.5.A-Z  Treaties (WWII: separate: by name)
D749.5.A5   Anglo-Soviet Treaty (26 May 1942)
D750-754    Diplomacy (WWII: by place)        940.5322-5325
D750        Great Britain (WWII: dipl. history)   940.532241
D751        Germany (WWII: dipl. history)         940.532443
D752        France (WWII: dipl. history)          940.532244
D752.8      America & American neutrality (WWII: dipl. history)
D753-753.8  United States (WWII: dipl. hist., inclu. neutral years)    940.532573,
                                                                       .532273, 973.917
D753.2.A-Z  Mutual-aid agreements (WWII: U.S.: by country)
D753.2.G7   Lend-lease, mutual aid (WWII: U.S.-G.B.)
D753.2.R9   Lend-lease, mutual aid (WWII: U.S.-Rus.)
D753.3      Espionage, conspiracy, propaganda in U.S. (WWII)
D753.8      Japanese-Americans (WWII: SEE ALSO D769.8.A6)
D754.A-Z    Diplomacy (WWII: misc. countries or areas)
D754.A34    Africa (WWII: dipl. history)
D754.C95    Czechoslovakia (WWII: dipl. history)
D754.I5         Ireland (WWII: dipl. history: gen.)
D754.I6         Irish Free State (WWII: dipl. history)
D754.I7         Northern Ireland (WWII: dipl. history)
D754.I8         Italy (WWII: dipl. history)
D754.J3         Japan (WWII: dipl. history)        940.532452
D754.L4         Levant (WWII: dipl. history)
D754.N34    Near East (WWII: dipl. history)
D754.S29    Scandinavia (WWII: dipl. history)
D754.S8         Sweden (WWII: dipl. history)
D754.T8         Turkey (WWII: dipl. history)
D754.Y9         Yugoslavia (WWII: dipl. history)
D755-755.9  TIME PERIODS (WWII)
D755        World War II (Sept. 1939-Dec. 1941)
D755.1      World War II (Sept. 1939-May 1940)
D755.2      World War II (1940)
D755.3          World War II (1941)
D755.4          World War II (1942)
D755.5          World War II (1943)
D755.6      World War II (1944)
D755.7      World War II (1945)
D755.8      World War II (VE Day to VJ Day)
D756-763    WESTERN FRONT & Western Europe (WWII)        940.5421
D756        MILITARY OPS. (WWII: WEST: gen.)
D756.3      Military ops. (WWII: West: gen. special)
D756.5.A-Z  BATTLES, campaigns, sieges (WWII: WEST: by place)
D756.5.A7       Bulge, Battle of the (Ardennes: 1944-45)
D756.5.A78      Arras, Battle of (1940)
D756.5.B7       Britain, Battle of (1940)
D756.5.C2       Calais, Battle of (1940)
D756.5.D5   Dieppe Raid (1942)
D756.5.D8   Dunkirk, Battle of (1940)
D756.5.M4   Meuse, Battle of the (Monthermé: 1940)
D756.5.V3   Verdun, Battle of (WWII: 1940)
```

| | | |
|---|---|---|
| D757-757.9 | GERMANY & GERMAN MILITARY OPS. (WWII) | |
| D757 | German military ops. (WWII: gen.) | 940.5343, .54013, .5413, .5421, 943.086 |
| D757.1 | Armies (WWII: Ger.)  940.541343 | |
| D757.2 | Army corps (WWII: Ger.) | |
| D757.3 | Infantry (WWII: Ger.) | |
| D757.32.A-Z | Infantry (WWII: Ger.: by author, division, name, etc.) | |
| D757.39 | Mountain troops (WWII: Ger.) | |
| D757.4.A-5 | Artillery (WWII: Ger.) | |
| D757.4.A-53 | Anti-aircraft artillery (WWII: Ger.) | |
| D757.4.A-Z | Mountain troops (WWII: Ger.: by author, division, name, etc.) | |
| D757.54-57 | Panzer troops (WWII: Ger.) | |
| D757.54 | Panzer troops (WWII: Ger.: gen.) | |
| D757.55.A-Z | Panzer troops (by author, division, name, etc.) | |
| D757.55.R6 | Roten teufel, Die (WWII: Panzer troops) | |
| D757.56.1st- | Panzer divisions (by #) | |
| D757.57.1st- | Panzer regiments (by #) | |
| D757.6 | Airborne troops (WWII: Ger.) | |
| D757.63 | Parachute troops (WWII: Ger.) | |
| D757.65 | Signal Corps (WWII: Ger.: Nachrichten truppen) | |
| D757.8 | Engineers (WWII: Ger.) | |
| D757.83 | Nebeltruppe (WWII: Ger.) | |
| D757.85 | Waffen SS (WWII: Ger.: Waffenschutzstaffel) | |
| D757.855 | Technische Truppen (WWII: Ger.) | |
| D757.9.A-Z | Local history (WWII: Ger.: by place)  940.5343+, 943.1-9+ | |
| D757.9.B4 | Berlin, Ger. (WWII)  943.155086 | |
| D757.9.H3 | Hamburg, Ger. (WWII) | |
| D757.9.M9 | Munich, Ger. (WWII) | |
| D759-760 | GREAT BRITAIN & BRITISH MILITARY OPS. (WWII) | |
| D759 | British military ops. & Great Britain (WWII: gen.) | 940.54091, .5341-5342, 942.084 |
| D759.5.1st- | Armies etc. (WWII: G.B.: by #)  940.541241-541242 | |
| D759.5.51st | Highland Division (WWII: G.B.: 51st) | |
| D759.52 | Artillery (WWII: G.B.) | |
| D759.523 | Anti-aircraft Command (WWII: G.B.) | |
| D759.527 | Anti-aircraft, Light Artillery regiments (WWII: G.B.) | |
| D759.528 | Armored divisions etc. (WWII: G.B..) | |
| D759.53 | Infantry (WWII: G.B.) | |
| D759.54 | Cavalry (WWII: G.B.) | |
| D759.55 | Engineers (WWII: G.B.) | |
| D759.6 | Airborne troops (WWII: G.B.) | |
| D759.63 | Parachute troops (WWII: Brit.) | |
| D760.8.A-Z | LOCAL HISTORY (WWII: G.B.: by place) | 941.084, 942.084, 942.1-9+, 940.5341-5342+ |
| D760.8.B3 | Bath, Eng. (WWII) | |
| D760.8.B4 | Belfast, N. Ire. (WWII) | |
| D760.8.B7 | Bristol, Eng. (WWII) | |
| D760.8.C6 | Coventry, Eng. (WWII) | |
| D760.8.D6 | Dover, Eng. (WWII) | |
| D760.8.E3 | East Downing, Eng. (WWII) | |
| D760.8.E7 | Essex, Eng. (WWII) | |
| D760.8.E88 | Exeter, Eng. (WWII) | |
| D760.8.K4 | Kent, Eng. (WWII) | |

| | | |
|---|---|---|
| D760.8.L6 | Liverpool, Eng. (WWII) | |
| D760.8.L7 | London, Eng. (WWII) | 942.1084, 940.534421 |
| D760.8.M3 | Manchester, Eng. (WWII) | |
| D760.8.S75 | Stepney, Eng. (WWII: Middlesex) | |
| D760.A-Z | British military ops. (WWII: special by group or region) | 940.5412 |
| D760.A1 | Colonies (WWII: G.B.: gen.) | |
| D760.A8 | Auxiliary Territorial Service (WWII: G.B.) | |
| D760.D4 | Devonshire Regiment (WWII: G.B.) | |
| D760.I7 | Irish Guards (WWII: G.B.) | |
| D760.P5 | Pioneer Corps (WWII: G.B.) | |
| D760.R7 | Royal Armored Corps (WWII: G.B.) | |
| D761-762 | FRANCE & FRENCH MILITARY OPS. (WWII) | |
| D761 | French military ops. & France (WWII: gen.) | 940.5344, .540944, 944.0815-0816 |
| D761.1 | Armies (WWII: Fr.)    940.541244 | |
| D761.15 | Army corps (WWII: Fr.) | |
| D761.2 | Divisions (WWII: Fr.) | |
| D761.3 | Infantry (WWII: Fr.) | |
| D761.38 | Zouaves (WWII: Fr.: infantry) | |
| D761.5 | Chasseurs & Chasseurs Alpine (WWII: Fr.) | |
| D761.6 | Artillery (WWII: Fr.) | |
| D761.7 | Parachute troops (WWII: Fr.) | |
| D761.9.A-Z | French military ops. (WWII: misc.) | |
| D761.9.A1 | Colonies (WWII: Fr.: gen.) | |
| D761.9.F7 | Free French, France Combattante, French Volunteer Force (WWII) | |
| D761.9.P6 | Polish troops (WWII: French Army) | |
| D762.A-Z | Local history (WWII: Fr.: by place)    944.1-9+ | |
| D762.P3 | Paris, Fr. (WWII)    944.360816 | |
| D763.A-Z | WESTERN EUROPE (WWII: EXCEPT Ger., G.B., Fr.) | |
| D763.B4-42 | Belgium & Belgian military ops. (WWII)    940.3493, 949.3 | |
| D763.B4 | Belgian military ops. (WWII: gen.) | |
| D763.B41 | Divisions etc. (WWII: Bel.) | |
| D763.B42 | Local history (WWII: Bel.) | |
| D763.D4 | Denmark (WWII: gen.) | |
| D763.D42.A-Z | Local history (WWII: Den.: by place) | |
| D763.I8-82 | Italy & Italian military ops. (WWII)    940.40945, .41345, 945.091 | |
| D763.I8 | ITALIAN military ops. (WWII: gen.) | |
| D763.I81.1st- | Divisions etc. (WWII: Ital.: by #) | |
| D763.I813.A-Z | Divisions etc. (WWII: Ital.: by name or author) | |
| D763.I815-817 | Corpo Volontari Della Libert`a (WWII: Ital.) | |
| D763.I815 | Corpo Volontari Della Libert`a (WWII: Ital.: gen.) | |
| D763.I817.A-Z | Corpo Volontari Della Libert`a (WWII: Ital.: by name) | |
| D763.I82.A-Z | Local history (WWII: It.: by place) | |
| D763.L9 | Luxembourg (WWII: Grand Duchy) | |
| D763.M3 | Malta (WWII) | |
| D763.N4-42 | Netherlands & Dutch military ops. (WWII)    940.3492071, 949.207 | |
| D763.N4 | Dutch military ops. (WWII: gen.) | |
| D763.N41.1st- | Divisions etc. (WWII: Dutch: by #) | |
| D763.N42.A-Z | Local history (WWII: Neth.: by place) | |

| | | |
|---|---|---|
| D763.N6-62 | Norway & Norwegian military ops. (WWII) | 940.3481, 948.1041 |
| D763.N6 | Norwegian military ops. (WWII) | |
| D763.N61.1st- | Divisions etc. (WWII: Nor.: by #) | |
| D763.N613.A-Z | Divisions etc. (WWII: Nor.: by name or author) | |
| D763.N62.A-Z | Local history (WWII: Nor.: by place) | |
| D763.S5 | Sicily (WWII) | |
| D763.5 | Arctic areas (WWII: Greenland etc.) | |
| D764-766.7 | EASTERN FRONT (WWII) | |
| D764 | RUSSIA & Eastern Front (WWII: gen.) | 940.540947, .532247, .5347, .541247, 947.0842 |
| D764.3.A-Z | Battles, campaigns, sieges (WWII: Rus., Eastern front: by place) | |
| D764.3.L4 | Leningrad, Siege of (WWII) | |
| D764.3.S7 | Stalingrad, Battle of (1942-43) | |
| D764.5.1st- | Divisions etc. (WWII: Rus.: by #) | 940.541247 |
| D764.52 | Artillery (WWII: Rus.) | |
| D764.53 | Infantry (WWII: Rus.) | |
| D764.54 | Cavalry (WWII: Rus.) | |
| D764.6.A-Z | Russian military ops. (WWII: special: by region, name, author) | |
| D764.6.G7 | Gvardia (WWII: Rus.: gen.) | |
| D764.6.G8.1st- | Gvardia (WWII: Rus.: by #) | |
| D764.6.U82 | Ural Mts. (WWII) | |
| D764.7.A-Z | Local history (WWII: Rus.: by place) | |
| D764.7.K5 | Klintsy, Rus. (WWII) | |
| D764.7.M58 | Moscow, Rus. (WWII) | |
| D765-765.2+ | Poland & Polish military ops. (WWII) | |
| D765 | Polish military ops. (WWII: gen.) | 940.53438, .5409438, 943.8053 |
| D765.13 | Divisions etc. (WWII: Pol.) | |
| D765.2.A-Z | Local history (WWII: Pol.) | |
| D765.2.W3 | Warsaw, Pol. (WWII) | |
| D765.2.W7 | Wroclaw, Breslau, Pol. (WWII) | |
| D765.3-35 | Finland & Finnish military ops. (WWII) | 940.53471, 534897, .54094897, 948.97032 |
| D765.3 | Finnish military ops. (WWII: gen.) | |
| D765.32 | Divisions etc. (WWII: Fin.) | |
| D765.35.A-Z | Local history (WWII: Fin.) | |
| D765.4 | Austria (WWII: gen.) | 940.53436, 943.6052 |
| D765.45.A-Z | Local history (WWII: Austria) | |
| D765.45.V45 | Vienna, Austria (WWII) | |
| D765.45.V6 | Vorarlberg, Austria (WWII) | |
| D765.5-55 | Czechoslovakia & Czech military ops. (WWII) | 940.53437, 943.703 |
| D765.5 | Czech military ops. (WWII: gen.) | |
| D765.53 | Divisions etc. (WWII: Czech.) | |
| D765.55.A-Z | Local history (WWII: Czech.) | |
| D765.55.P7 | Prague, Cz. (WWII) | |
| D765.56 | Hungary (WWII: gen.) | 940.53439, 943.905 |
| D765.562.A-Z | Local history (WWII: Hung.) | |
| D765.562.B8 | Budapest, Hun. (WWII) | |

```
D766-766.79    Balkans, Near East, Eastern Mediterranean (WWII)
D766           NEAR EAST, BALKANS, E. MEDITERRANEAN (WWII: gen.)
                                        940.53495+, 949.5+, 956.03, 962.052
D766.3         Greece (WWII: gen.)       940.53495, 949.5074
D766.32.A-Z    Local history (WWII: Greece)
D766.32.A8     Athens, Gr. (WWII)
D766.32.C4     Cephalonia, Gr. (WWII)
D766.4-42      Rumania & Rumanian military ops. (WWII)    940.53498, 949.802
D766.4         Rumanian military ops. (WWII)
D766.413       Divisions etc. (WWII: Rum.)
D766.42.A-Z    Local history (WWII: Rum.)
D766.6-62      YUGOSLAVIA & Yugoslavian military ops. (WWII)    940.53497,
                                                                949.7022

D766.6         Yugoslavian military ops. (WWII)
D766.6.A1-5      Associations, societies (WWII: Yug.)
D766.6.A2        Yugoslavia (WWII: collections)
D766.61.1st-     Divisions etc. (WWII: Yug.: by #)
D766.613.A-Z     Divisions etc. (WWII: Yug.: by name)
D766.62.A-Z      Local history (WWII: Yug.)
D766.62.B4       Belgrade, Yug. (WWII)
D766.62.Z3       Zagreb, Yug. (WWII)
D766.7.A-Z     Balkans & Near East (WWII: misc. countries: by name)
D766.7.A4      Albania (WWII)
D766.7.B8      Bulgaria (WWII)
D766.7.C7      Crete (WWII)
D766.7.I55       Iran (WWII)
D766.7.I57       Iraq (WWII)
D766.7.I7        Palestine (WWII: Israel)
D766.7.S9-95     Syria (WWII)
D766.7.T8        Turkey (WWII)
D766.8-99      AFRICA(WWII)
D766.8         Africa (WWII: gen.)       940.536, .5423, 960.31
D766.82          North Africa (WWII)     940.5361, .5423, 961.03
D766.84          East Africa (WWII)          940.53676, 967.6
D766.9-99      Africa (WWII: by country)
D766.9           Egypt (WWII)            940.5423, .5362, 962.052
D766.92          Ethiopia & Ethiopian military ops. (WWII)        940.5423
D766.93          Libya (WWII)       940.5423, 961.203
D766.95          Belgian Congo (WWII)
D766.96        French Equatorial Africa (WWII)
D766.97        South Africa & South African military ops. (WWII)   940.5368, 540968,
                                                                   968.055
D766.99.A-Z    Africa (WWII: misc. countries: by name)
D766.99.A6     Algeria (WWII)
D766.99.M3     Madagascar (WWII)
D766.99.M8     Morocco (WWII)       940.5364, 964.04
D766.99.T7-8   Tunisia (WWII)       940.53611, 961.104
```

```
D767-767.99     ASIA & THE PACIFIC THEATRE
D767            Pacific Theatre & Asia (WWII: gen.)      940.5425-5426
D767.2-25       JAPAN & JAPANESE MILITARY OPS. (WWII)
D767.2          Japanese military ops. & Japan (WWII: gen.)      940.5352, .540952,
                                                                 .541352, 952.033

D767.23         Divisions etc. (WWII: Japan)
D767.25.A-Z     Local history (WWII: Japan: by place)
D767.25.H6      Hiroshima, Japan (WWII)
D767.25.N3      Nagasaki, Japan (WWII)
D767.25.T5-6    Tokyo, Japan (WWII)      952.135
D767.255        Korea (WWII)      940.53519
D767.3          CHINA & CHINESE MILITARY OPS. (WWII)      940.5351, .540951,
                                                          .5425, 951.042

D767.35-352     Cochin China (Vietnam: WWII)
D767.35         Vietnam (WWII: gen.)      940.53597, 959.703
D767.352.A-Z    Local history (WWII: Cochin China: by place)
D767.352.S3     Saigon, Viet. (WWII)
D767.4          Philippine Islands (WWII)      940.53599, .5409599, .5425-5426, 959.03
D767.45         French Indochina (WWII)      940.53597, 959.703
D767.47         Thailand (WWII)
D767.5          Malay Peninsula (WWII)      959.503
D767.55              Singapore (WWII)      959.5203
D767.6-63       India & Burma (WWII)      940.5425, .5354, 954.0359
D767.6          Burma & India (WWII)
D767.63         Free India (Azad Hind: WWII: 1943-45: includes Indian National Army)
D767.7          Dutch East Indies & Indonesia (WWII)      940.53598, .5425, 959.8022
D767.8-82       AUSTRALIA & AUSTRALIAN MILITARY OPS. (WWII)
D767.8          Australian military ops. & Australia (WWII: gen.)      940.532294, .5394,
                                                                       .540994, .541294, .5426, 994.042
D767.813        Divisions etc. (WWII: Australia)      940.541294
D767.82.A-Z     Local history (WWII: Australia: by place)      994.1-8
D767.82.M44     Melbourne, Australia (WWII)      994.51
D767.85-852     New Zealand (WWII)      940.53931, .5409931, .5426, 993.1032
D767.85         New Zealand military ops. (WWII)
D767.851        Divisions etc. (WWII: New Z.)      940.5412931
D767.852.A-Z    Local history (WWII: New Z.)
D767.852.W44    Wellington, N.Z. (WWII)      993.127
D767.9-99       OCEANIA OR PACIFIC ISLANDS (WWII)
D767.9          Pacific Islands (WWII: gen.)      940.5426, .54439, .544952,
                                                  .54539, .545952, .5352
D767.913        Aleutian Islands (WWII: PREFER D769.87.A4)
D767.917        Gilbert Islands (WWII)
D767.92         Hawaiian Islands (WWII)      940.539969, 996.903
D767.94         Midway Islands (WWII)
D767.95         New Guinea (WWII)      940.5426, .5395
D767.98         Solomon Islands (WWII: gen.)      940.53935, .5426
D767.982.A-Z    Solomon Islands (WWII: by specific is.: SEE ALSO D767.99.A-Z for
                     alternative #'s)
D767.982.B5     Bougainville (WWII)
D767.982.C4     Choiseul (WWII)
D767.982.G92    Guadalcanal (WWII)
D767.982.N34    New Georgia (WWII)
```

```
D767.99.A-Z        PACIFIC ISLANDS (WWII: misc. by name)
D767.99.B46            Bismarck Islands (WWII)
D767.99.B54            Bougainville (WWII)
D767.99.C3             Caroline Islands (WWII)
D767.99.E55            Ellice Islands (WWII)
D767.99.G38        Gilbert Islands (WWII)
D767.99.G88        Guadalcanal (WWII)
D767.99.G9         Guam (WWII)
D767.99.I9         Iwo Jima (WWII)
D767.99.M27        Mariana Islands (WWII: gen.)
D767.99.M272.A-Z   Mariana Islands (WWII: by specific is.: SEE ALSO D767.99.A-
                       Z for direct alternatives, e.g. D767.99.G9 for Guam)
D767.99.M272.G9    Guam (WWII)
D767.99.M3         Marshall Islands (WWII)
D767.99.N4         New Britain (WWII)
D767.99.N415.A-Z   Local history (WWII: New Britain)
D767.99.N415.R32   Rabaul, New Brit. (WWII)
D767.99.N42            New Caledonia (WWII)
D767.99.N44        New Georgia (WWII)
D767.99.N46        New Hebrides (WWII)
D767.99.N47        New Ireland (WWII)
D767.99.O45        Okinawa (WWII)
D767.99.P4             Palau Islands (Pelew Is.: WWII)
D767.99.R9             Ryukyu Islands (WWII)
D767.99.S3             Saipan (WWII)
D767.99.T3         Tarawa (WWII)
D767.99.T45        Tinian (WWII)
D767.99.T89        Truk (WWII)
D767.99.W35        Wake Is. (WWII)
D768-769           Americas (WWII)
D768               North & South America (WWII: gen.)
D768.15                Canada (WWII)      940.5371, .532271, .540971, .541271, 971.063
D768.18                Latin America (WWII)      940.538, .53228, .53248, .53258, 980.033
D768.2             Mexico (WWII)      940.5372
D768.3             Brazil (WWII)      940.5381, .544381, 981.061
D769-769.99        UNITED STATES MILITARY OPS. & U.S. (WWII)      940.532273,
                                       .5373, .540973, .541273, .5428
D769               United States (WWII: gen.)      940.532273, .5373, .540973,
                                       .541273, .5428
D769.A1-15         Associations, societies (WWII: U.S.)
D769.A2            United States (WWII: collections)
D769.A3            Legislative compendia (WWII: U.S.)
D769.A5-Z          United States & U.S. military ops. (WWII: gen.: SEE ALSO E806 for
                       internal, general U.S. history, 1939-45)      940.5373,
                                       .540973, .532273, 973.917
D769.1             United States (WWII: gen. special)
D769.15            Pamphlets, minor works (WWII: U.S.)
```

| | |
|---|---|
| D769.2-799 | United States military ops. (WWII: land,air, & sea: SEE D769.A5-Z for gen. works)                  940.541273, .544373, .544973 |
| D769.2-779 | United States military ops. (WWII: organiz. units: land, sea: D769.A5-Z, D756.5, D767 etc. for overall efforts, area campaigns, & battles) |
| D769.2 | United States military ops. (WWII: gen. special) |
| D769.25-4 | ARMIES ETC. (WWII: U.S.) |
| D769.25 | General staff & headquarters (WWII: U.S.) |
| D769.26 | Armies (WWII: U.S.: by # or author) |
| D769.27 | Army corps (WWII: U.S.) |
| D769.29-309 | Divisions etc. (WWII: U.S.) |
| D769.29 | Divisions etc. (WWII: U.S.: gen.) |
| D769.295.A-Z | Divisions etc. (WWII: U.S.: by name ) |
| D769.295.A5 | Americal Division (WWII: U.S.) |
| D769.3.1st- | Divisions etc. (WWII: U.S.: by #) |
| D769.305-307 | Armored divisions (WWII: U.S.) |
| D769.305 | Armored divisions (WWII: U.S.: gen.) |
| D769.3053 | Armored divisions (WWII: U.S.: by #) |
| D769.3055.1st- | Armored regiments (WWII: U.S.: by #) |
| D769.3058 | Reconnaisance battalions (WWII: U.S.) |
| D769.306.1st- | Tank battalions (WWII: U.S.: by #) |
| D769.307.1st- | Tank destroyer battalions (WWII: U.S.: by #) |
| D769.308 | Cavalry divisions (WWII: U.S.: 1st) |
| D769.309 | Civil Affairs Division (WWII: U.S. Army) |
| D769.31.1st- | Infantry (WWII: U.S.: regiments, combat teams, etc.: by #) |
| D769.32 | Cavalry (WWII: U.S.: gen.) |
| D769.325.1st- | Cavalry groups etc. (WWII: U.S.: by #) |
| D769.33 | Combat engineers (WWII: U.S.: gen.) |
| D769.335.1st- | Engineer battalions etc. (WWII: U.S.: by #) |
| D769.337.A-Z | Engineer battalions etc. (WWII: U.S.: by name) |
| D769.34.1st- | Field artillery groups etc. (WWII: U.S.: by #) |
| D769.342 | Anti-aircraft artillery (WWII: U.S.: gen.) |
| D769.343.1st- | Anti-aircraft artillery battalions (WWII: U.S.: by #) |
| D769.345 | Airborne troops (WWII: U.S.: gen.) |
| D769.346.1st- | Airborne troop battalions etc. (WWII: U.S.: by #) |
| D769.347 | Parachute troops (WWII: U.S.) |
| D769.35 | Chemical Corps (WWII: U.S.: gen.) |
| D769.353.A-Z | Chemical Corps battalions etc. (WWII: U.S.: by type, sub-arranged by # if applic.) |
| D769.36 | Signal Corps (WWII: U.S.: gen.) |
| D769.363.1st- | Signal Corps battalions etc. (WWII: U.S.: by #) |
| D769.369-372 | Marines (WWII: U.S.: land ops. only: SEE D767, D769.45, D774, D790, U-V for naval or aerial ops.) |
| D769.369 | Marine Corps (WWII: U.S.: gen.) |
| D769.37.1st- | Marine Corps divisions (WWII: U.S.: by #) |
| D769.372.1st- | Marine Corps regiments (WWII: U.S.: by #) |
| D769.375 | Chaplain Corps (WWII: U.S. Army) |
| D769.39 | WACS (Women's Army Corps: WWII: U.S.) |
| D769.4 | Armies etc. (WWII: U.S.: misc.) |

| | |
|---|---|
| D769.45-599 | UNITED STATES NAVAL OPS. & Coast Guard ops. (WWII: fleets, squadrons, bases, etc.: SEE D773-4, D783 for overall works, specific ships & engagements, submarines)    940.545973 |
| D769.45 | United States naval ops. (WWII: special topics: land batteries, defensive areas, Marine Corps except land, etc.) |
| D769.5-539 | Fleets, squadrons, etc. (WWII: U.S. Navy) |
| D769.5.1st- | Fleets (WWII: U.S. Navy: by #) |
| D769.52.A-Z | Naval forces & divisions (WWII: U.S.: by name) |
| D769.52.E7 | Escort carriers (WWII: U.S.)    940.545 |
| D769.53.1st- | Task forces (WWII: U.S.: by #) |
| D769.535 | Service squadrons (WWII: U.S.: gen.) |
| D769.537 | Service squadrons (WWII: U.S.: by #) |
| D769.54 | Naval bases (WWII: U.S.: gen.)    940.545373 |
| D769.542.A-Z | Naval bases (WWII: U.S.: by location) |
| D769.542.G9 | Guam (WWII: U.S. naval base) |
| D769.542.H38 | Hawaii (WWII: U.S. naval base) |
| D769.542.S345 | San Diego, Calif. (WWII: U.S. naval base) |
| D769.55-555 | Naval construction battalions (WWII: U.S.) |
| D769.55 | Seabees or naval construction battalions (WWII: U.S.: gen.) |
| D769.552.1st- | Seabees (WWII: U.S.: by battalion #) |
| D769.554 | Naval construction maintenance (WWII: U.S.: gen.) |
| D769.555.1st- | Naval construction maintenance units (WWII: U.S.:by#) |
| D769.585 | Coast Guard Reserve (WWII: U.S.: temporary inclu. U.S. Volunteer Port Security Force) |
| D769.59 | Naval Chaplain Corps (WWII: U.S.) |
| D769.597 | Naval Reserve & Women's Reserve (WAVES: WWII: U.S.) |
| D769.598 | Coast Guard Reserve & Women's Reserve (SPARS: WWII: U.S.) |
| D769.64 | Sino-American Cooperative Organization (WWII: for aerial ops. such as Flying Tigers SEE D790) |
| D769.72 | Transportation service (WWII: U.S.: gen.: PREFER D810.T8) |
| D769.73 | Transportation Corps (WWII: U.S.) |
| D769.73.1st- | Quartermaster depots (WWII: U.S.: by #) |
| D769.733.1st- | Transportation Corps battalions etc. (WWII: U.S.: by #) |
| D769.74 | Ordnance battalions etc. (WWII: U.S.: gen.) |
| D769.743.1st- | Ordnance battalions etc. (WWII: U.S.: by #) |
| D769.75 | Supply forces & army service forces (WWII: U.S.: gen.) |
| D769.76 | Technical intelligence service (WWII: U.S.) |
| D769.77 | Provost-Marshall-General's Bureau (WWII: U.S.: gen.) |
| D769.775 | Military Police (MP's: WWII: U.S.) |
| D769.8.A-Z | United States (WWII: special topics: SEE D810.A-Z for outside U.S.) |
| D769.8.A6 | Alien enemies (WWII: U.S.: inclu. Japanese relocation centers: SEE ALSO D753.8. For alien property custody SEE JX5313.U6)    940.5315+, .547273, .53163 |
| D769.8.C4 | Civil liberties & freedom of speech (WWII: U.S.: SEE UB342.U5 for conscientious objectors) |
| D769.8.F6 | Foreign population war effort (WWII: U.S.) |
| D769.8.F7.A-Z | Nationalities & the war (WWII: U.S.: by name: for Indians SEE D810.I5) |
| D769.8.L6 | Local government (WWII: U.S.) |
| D769.8.P7 | Political prisoners (WWII: U.S.: SEE ALSO D805.U5 for prisons & prisoners) |
| D769.8.S5 | Service flags (WWII: U.S.) |
| D769.8.T8 | Trophies, Military (WWII: U.S.) |

| | |
|---|---|
| D769.85-87 | World War II (gen. particip.: U.S.: by area or state) |
| D769.85.A-W | LOCAL HISTORY (WWII: U.S.: by state: SEE ALSO F1-951+) |
| D769.85.C2 | California (WWII: gen.)     979.4052 |
| D769.85.C21.A-Z | Local history (WWII: Calif.: by place) |
| D769.85.D6 | Washington, D.C. (District of Columbia: WWII) |
| D769.85.F5-51 | Florida (WWII) |
| D769.85.M7 | Mississippi (WWII) |
| D769.85.N33-34 | New Mexico (WWII) |
| D769.85.N4-5 | New York (WWII)     979.7042 |
| D769.85.W8-81 | Wyoming (WWII) |
| D769.87.A-Z | Territories (WWII: U.S.: by place) |
| D769.87.A4 | Aleutian Islands (WWII) |
| D769.87.H3 | Hawaiian Islands (WWII: SEE ALSO D767.92) |
| D769.87.P7 | Puerto Rico (WWII) |
| D769.88.A-Z | Nationalities (WWII: U.S.)     940.5315+ |
| D769.88.A7 | Armenians (WWII: U.S.) |
| D769.88.M4 | Mexican-Americans (WWII: as troops)     940.5404 |
| D769.9 | Personal accounts (WWII: U.S.: PREFER D811) |
| D770-784 | NAVAL & SUBMARINE OPS. (WWII)     940.545 |
| D770 | Battle of the Atlantic, freedom of the seas, general naval ops. (WWII)     940.545 |
| D771 | Anglo-German naval conflict & blockade (WWII: gen.)     940.545, .5452 |
| D772.3 | Russo-German naval conflict (WWII: Arctic areas & Baltic)     940.545947, .545943 |
| D772.A-Z | German-Anglo naval conflict & blockade (WWII: by battle, ship, etc.)     940.545941-43 |
| D772.A66 | Ark Royal (WWII: aircraft carrier) |
| D772.A7 | Athenia (WWII: steamship) |
| D772.B5 | Bismarck (WWII: battleship) |
| D772.F5 | Firedrake (WWII: destroyer) |
| D772.G7 | Graf Spee, Admiral (WWII: battleship) |
| D772.H6 | Hood (WWII: battle cruiser) |
| D772.P4 | Penelope (WWII: cruiser) |
| D772.S25 | San Demetrio (WWII: tanker) |
| D773-774 | UNITED STATES NAVAL OPS. (WWII: SEE ALSO D769.45-599 for specific fleets, squadrons, bases, units)     940.545973 |
| D773 | United States naval ops. (WWII: gen.: inclu. blockade, patrol)     940.545973 |
| D774.A-Z | United States naval ops. (WWII: by battle, ship, etc.) |
| D774.A7 | Arkansas (WWII: battleship) |
| D774.B48 | Bismarck Sea, Battle of (1943-44) |
| D774.B6 | Boise (WWII: cruiser) |
| D774.C57 | Coral Sea, Battle of (1942) |
| D774.E5 | Enterprise (WWII: aircraft carrier) |
| D774.E7 | Essex (WWII: aircraft carrier) |
| D774.H3 | Hancock (WWII: aircraft carrier) |
| D774.H4 | Helena (WWII: cruiser) |
| D774.H6 | Hornet (WWII: aircraft carrier) |
| D774.L4 | Lexington (WWII: aircraft carrier: 1st with name) |
| D774.M3 | Marblehead (WWII: cruiser) |
| D774.M35 | Maryland (WWII: battleship) |
| D774.M5 | Midway, Battle of (1942) |
| D774.N4 | New Orleans (WWII: cruiser) |
| D774.O3 | O'Bannon (WWII: destroyer) |

| | | |
|---|---|---|
| D774.P55 | Philippine Sea, Battle of (1944) | |
| D774.P7 | Princess (WWII: aircraft carrier) | |
| D774.S3 | Saratoga (WWII: aircraft carrier) | |
| D774.S318 | Savo Island, Battle of (1942) | |
| D774.S32 | Savo Island (WWII: aircraft carrier) | |
| D774.S45 | Solomons, Battle of the (1942-44) | |
| D774.S6 | South Dakota (WWII: battleship) | |
| D775 | Anglo-Italian naval conflict (WWII: gen.) | 940.545941, .545945 |
| D775.5.A-Z | Italian-Anglo naval conflict (WWII: by battle, ship, etc.) | |
| D775.5.S8 | Sydney (WWII: cruiser) | |
| D777 | JAPANESE NAVAL OPS. (WWII: gen.) | 940.545952, .5426 |
| D777.5.A-Z | Japanese naval ops. (WWII: by battle, ship, etc.) | |
| D779.A-Z | Naval ops. (WWII: misc. countries: by place) | |
| D779.A8 | Australian naval ops. (WWII) | 940.545994 |
| D779.C2-29 | Canadian naval ops. (WWII) | |
| D780-784 | SUBMARINE & ANTI-SUBMARINE OPS. (WWII) | 940.5451 |
| D780 | Antisubmarine & submarine ops. (WWII: gen.) | 940.54516 |
| D781 | German submarine ops. (WWII: gen.) | |
| D782.A-Z | German submarine ops. (WWII: by battle, ship, etc.) | |
| D782.M6 | Montevideo (WWII: steamship) | |
| D782.R6 | Robin Moor (WWII: steamship) | |
| D783 | United States submarine ops. (WWII: gen.) | |
| D783.5.A-Z | United States submarine ops. (WWII: by battle, ship, etc.) | |
| D783.5.C6 | Coast Guard Reserve Boat 3070 (WWII) | |
| D783.5.S4 | Seawolf (WWII: submarine) | |
| D783.5.S6 | Silversides (WWII: submarine) | |
| D783.5.S8 | Sturgeon (WWII: submarine) | |
| D783.6 | Japanese submarine ops. (WWII: gen.: SEE ALSO D784.J3) | |
| D783.7.A-Z | Japanese submarine ops. (WWII: by battle, ship, author, etc.) | |
| D784.A-Z | Submarine ops. (WWII: misc. countries: by place) | |
| D784.G7 | British submarine ops. (WWII: GB) | |
| D784.J3 | Japanese submarine ops. (WWII: SEE ALSO D783.6) | |
| D785-792 | AIR FORCE OPS. (WWII) | 940.544 |
| D785 | Aerial ops. (WWII: gen.) | 940.544 |
| D785.U57-63 | U.S. Strategic Bombing Survey reports (WWII) | |
| D785.U57 | Strategic Bombing Survey (WWII: U.S.: gen.) | |
| D785.U58.A-Z | Strategic Bombing Survey (WWII: U.S.: by industry attacked) | |
| D785.U6 | European aerial ops. (WWII: U.S. bombing survey) | |
| D785.U63 | Pacific aerial ops. (WWII: U.S. bombing survey) | |
| D786 | British aerial ops. (WWII) | 940.544941 |
| D787 | German aerial ops. (WWII) | 940.544943 |
| D788 | French aerial ops. (WWII) | 940.544944 |
| D790 | United States aerial ops. (WWII) | 940.544973 |
| D792.A-Z | Aerial ops. (WWII: misc. countries) | |
| D792.A8 | Australian aerial ops. (WWII) | 940.544994 |
| D792.C2-29 | Canadian aerial ops. (WWII) | |
| D792.I8 | Italian aerial ops. (WWII) | |
| D792.J3-39 | Japanese aerial ops. (WWII) | 940.544952 |
| D792.R9 | Russian aerial ops. (WWII) | |
| D793 | Tank warfare (WWII) | |
| D794 | Cavalry (WWII) | |
| D794.5 | Commando ops. (WWII) | |

| | |
|---|---|
| D795 | ENGINEERING OPS. (WWII) |
| D795.A2 | Engineering ops. (WWII: gen.) |
| D795.A3-Z | Engineering ops. (WWII: by country) |
| D795.G3 | German engineering ops. (WWII) |
| D795.G7 | British engineering ops. (WWII) |
| D795.J3 | Japanese engineering ops. (WWII) |
| D795.U6 | United States engineering ops. (WWII) |
| D796 | Medals, badges, decorations (WWII: inclu. individual s & lists: SEE ALSO D797 for older works) |
| D796.5.A-Z | Medals, badges, decorations (WWII: by country) |
| D797 | LISTS & REGISTERS (WWII: decorated, dead, wounded: SEE ALSO D796 for newer titles)          940.5467 |
| D797.A2 | Registers & lists (WWII: dead, wounded, decorated: gen.) |
| D797.A3-Z | Registers & lists (WWII: dead, wounded, decorated: by country) |
| D797.A8 | Dead, wounded, decorated (WWII: Australia) |
| D797.A83 | Dead, wounded, decorated (WWII: South Australia) |
| D797.U6 | Dead, wounded, decorated (WWII: U.S.: gen.)          940.546773 |
| D797.U62.C2 | Dead, wounded, decorated (WWII: U.S.: Calif.) |
| D797.U7 | Dead, wounded, decorated (WWII: U.S.: special) |
| D798-810 | WORLD WAR II (SPECIAL TOPICS) |
| D798-799 | PRESS, radio, censorship, propaganda & publicity (WWII: SEE ALSO D746.5 for posters, D753.3 for enemy propaganda in U.S., D810.P6-7 for propaganda elsewhere) |
| D798 | News media (WWII: gen.) |
| D799.A-Z | Censorship, news media, etc. (WWII: by country) |
| D799.G3 | News media, censorship, etc. (WWII: Ger.) |
| D799.G7 | News media, censorship, etc. (WWII: G.B.) |
| D799.U6 | News media, censorship, etc. (WWII: U.S.) |
| D800 | Economic matters (WWII: commerce, mail, finance, monetary & fiscal planning, etc. in gen.: SEE ALSO HC, HF, HJ for specific places) |
| D801 | Alien enemies (WWII)          940.5315, .53163 |
| D801.A2 | Alien enemies (WWII: gen.)          940.5315, .53163 |
| D801.A3-Z | Alien enemies (WWII: by country) |
| D801.F8 | Alien enemies (WWII: Fr.) |
| D802 | OCCUPIED TERRITORIES (WWII: events, laws, etc.) |
| D802.A2 | Occupied territories (WWII: gen.) |
| D802.A3-Z | Occupied territories (WWII: by country, area, etc.) |
| D802.A45 | Alsace-Lorraine (WWII: occupied terr.) |
| D802.B3 | Baltic States (WWII: occupied terr.) |
| D802.J3 | Japanese territories (WWII) |
| D802.L3 | Latvia (WWII: occupied terr.) |
| D802.M15 | Macedonia (WWII: occupied terr.) |
| D802.M2 | Malaya (WWII: occupied terr.) |
| D802.M25 | Manchuria (WWII: occupied terr.) |
| D802.M3 | Marshall Islands (WWII: occupied terr.) |
| D802.R8 | Russia (WWII: occupied terr.) |
| D802.R95 | Ruthenia (WWII: occupied terr.) |
| D802.S55 | Sicily (WWII: occupied terr.) |
| D802.S67 | Slovenia (WWII: occupied terr.) |
| D802.T7 | Tripolitania (WWII: occupied terr.) |

| | |
|---|---|
| D803-805 | CONCENTRATION CAMPS (WWII) |
| D803-804 | ATROCITIES, war crimes, trials (WWII) |
| D803 | War crimes, atrocities, concentration camps, trials (WWII: gen.) |
| D804.A-Z | Trials & concentration camps (WWII: atrocities, war crimes: by country accused) |
| D804.G3 | Concentration camps (WWII: Ger.) |
| D804.G4 | Atrocities, war crimes, trials (WWII: Ger.) |
| D804.G42 | Nuremberg Trial of Major German War Criminals (1945-46) |
| D804.G425.A-Z | Trials (WWII: atrocities, war crimes: Germ.: post-Nuremberg before American Military Tribunals, 1946-49: by main defendant) |
| D804.G43.A-Z | Trials (WWII: atrocities, war crimes: Germ.: post-Nuremberg: misc. by defendant) |
| D804.J3 | Trials (WWII: atrocities, war crimes: Jp.) |
| D804.J3 | Concentration camps (WWII: Jpn.) |
| D804.J32 | Tokyo Trials (1946-48) |
| D804.J33.A-Z | Trials (WWII: atrocities, war crimes: Jp. except Tokyo: by place or defendant) |
| D805 | PRISONS & PRISONERS (WWII: inclu. internment, extermination, & concentration camps)          940.5472+ |
| D805.A1 | Periodicals & associations (WWII: prison) |
| D805.A2 | Prisons & prisoners (WWII: gen.) |
| D805.A3-Z | Prisons & prisoners (WWII: by country) |
| D805.A3-Z.A1-19 | Periodicals (WWII: by country) |
| D805.F8 | French prisons & prisoners (WWII) |
| D805.G3 | German prisons & prisoners (WWII) |
| D805.G7 | British prisons & prisoners (WWII) |
| D805.R9 | Russian prisons & prisoners (WWII: SEE ALSO D805.S65 for Soviet)          940.547247 |
| D805.S65 | Soviet prisons & prisoners (WWII: SEE ALSO D805.R9) |
| D806-807 | MEDICAL SERVICES, HOSPITALS, RED CROSS (WWII) |
| D806 | Hospitals, medical services, etc. (WWII: gen.)          940.5475 |
| D807.A-Z | Red Cross & medical services (WWII: by country)          940.54764-69 |
| D807.A8 | Medical services & Red Cross (WWII: Australia) |
| D807.G7 | Medical services & Red Cross (WWII: G.B) |
| D807.H3 | Medical services & Red Cross (WWII: Hawaiian Islands) |
| D807.U6 | Medical services & Red Cross (WWII: U.S.: gen.)          940.547673 |
| D807.U6-89 | Medical services & Red Cross (WWII: U.S.) |
| D807.U62.A-W | United States medical services (WWII: by state) |
| D807.U62.C3 | United States medical services (WWII: Calif.) |
| D807.U72.1st- | Army hospitals (WWII: U.S.: general: by #) |
| D807.U722.1st- | Army hospitals (WWII: U.S.: evacuation: by #) |
| D807.U73.1st- | Field hospitals (WWII: U.S.: by #) |
| D807.U74.A-Z | Hospital ships (WWII: U.S.: by name) |
| D807.U85.1st- | Navy base hospitals (WWII: U.S.: by #) |
| D807.U87.1st- | Navy mobile base hospitals (WWII: U.S.: by #) |
| D808-809 | RELIEF WORK, REFUGEES, DISPLACED PERSONS, CHARITIES (WWII) |
| D808 | Refugees, relief work, charities (WWII: gen.)          940.5477 |
| D809.A-Z | Charities, refugees, relief work (WWII: by country)          940.54778+ |
| D809.B4 | Relief work, refugees, displaced persons, charities (WWII: Belgium) |
| D809.G7 | Relief work, refugees, displaced persons, charities (WWII: G.B.) |
| D809.U5 | Relief work, refugees, displaced persons, charities (WWII: U.S.: domestic & abroad) |

| | |
|---|---|
| D810.A-Z | WORLD WAR II ( MISC. SPECIAL: SEE D769.8.A-Z for U.S.) |
| D810.A53 | Aleuts (WWII) |
| D810.A6 | Anarchism & anarchists (WWII) |
| D810.A65 | Animals (WWII: inclu. use of dogs, horses, etc.) |
| D810.A7 | Art (WWII) |
| D810.A75 | Astrology (WWII) |
| D810.B3 | Germ warfare (WWII: bacterial) |
| D810.B66 | Bomb reconnaissance (WWII) |
| D810.B7 | Boy Scouts (WWII) |
| D810.C2 | Camouflage (WWII) |
| D810.C26 | Cartography (WWII) |
| D810.C35 | Chaplains (WWII: gen.)            940.5478 |
| D810.C36.A-Z | Chaplains (WWII: by country) |
| D810.C36.U6 | Chaplains (WWII: U.S.: SEE ALSO D769.375 & D769.59) |
| D810.C4 | Children & orphans (WWII) |
| D810.C5-68 | RELIGION (WWII: churches) |
| D810.C5 | Churches (WWII: gen.) |
| D810.C53 | Adventists (WWII) |
| D810.C56 | Baptists (WWII) |
| D810.C6 | Catholic Church (WWII) |
| D810.C62 | Christian Scientists (WWII) |
| D810.C63 | Church of the Brethren (WWII) |
| D810.C64 | Evangelical and Reformed Church (WWII) |
| D810.C65 | Quakers (WWII: Society of Friends) |
| D810.C66 | Lutheran Church (WWII) |
| D810.C665 | Mennonites (WWII) |
| D810.C67 | Methodist Church (WWII) |
| D810.C674 | Nihon Kirisuto Kyodan (WWII: churches) |
| D810.C6745 | Eastern Orthodox Church (WWII) |
| D810.C68 | Presbyterian Church (WWII) |
| D810.C69 | Civil defense (WWII: SEE UA926-929 for more technical works) |
| D810.C7 | Communications (WWII) |
| D810.C8 | Confiscation (WWII) |
| D810.C82 | Conscientious objectors (WWII) |
| D810.C83 | Cossacks (WWII) |
| D810.C88 | Cryptography (WWII) |
| D810.D4 | Dead (WWII: treatment, cemeteries, etc.) |
| D810.D5 | Deportation (WWII) |
| D810.D6 | Destruction & pillage (WWII: SEE ALSO D785.U58-63 for U.S. Strategic Bombing Survey) |
| D810.E2-5 | EDUCATION (WWII) |
| D810.E2 | Education (WWII: gen.) |
| D810.E3-46 | Education (WWII: U.S.) |
| D810.E3 | Education (WWII: U.S.: gen.) |
| D810.E4.A-W | Education (WWII: U.S.: by state) |
| D810.E4.M8-81 | Education (WWII: Missouri) |
| D810.E4.W6-61 | Education (WWII: Wisconsin) |
| D810.E45.A-Z | College, school, etc. (WWII: U.S.: by name) |
| D810.E45.H38 | Harvard Univ. (WWII) |
| D810.E46.A-Z | Fraternities (WWII: U.S. educ.: by name) |
| D810.E6 | Elks, Benevolent...Order of (WWII) |
| D810.E8 | Entertainment, recreation, hospitality (WWII: civilian services for military) |
| D810.F83 | Fuel supplies (WWII) |

| | | |
|---|---|---|
| D810.G57 | Girl Scouts (WWII) | |
| D810.G9 | Gypsies (WWII) | |
| D810.I5 | Indians (WWII) | |
| D810.J4 | Jews & the Holocaust (WWII) | |
| D810.L4 | Lawyers (WWII) | |
| D810.M6 or .M8 | Moslems or Muslims (WWII) | |
| D810.N2 | Naturalized subjects (WWII: in belligerent countries: gen.) | |
| D810.N3.A-Z | Naturalized subjects (WWII: in belligerent countries: by place: SEE D753.8 for Japanese-Am's. in U.S., D769.8.A6 for alien enemies in the U.S.) | |
| D810.N4 | Blacks (WWII: Negroes) | |
| D810.P4 | Photography (WWII) | |
| D810.P53 | Pigeons (WWII) | |
| D810.P6 | Propaganda (WWII: gen.: SEE ALSO D798-799 for press) | |
| D810.P7.A-Z | Propaganda (WWII: by country) | 940.54886-54889+ |
| D810.P7.G3 | Propaganda, German (WWII) | |
| D810.P7.U6 | United States propaganda (WWII) | |
| D810.P75 | Prophecies (WWII) | |
| D810.P76 | Protest movements (WWII) | |
| D810.P8 | Public opinion (WWII: gen.) | |
| D810.P85.A-Z | Public opinion (WWII: by country) | |
| D810.P85.G7 | British public opinion (WWII) | |
| D810.R3 | Race problems (WWII) | |
| D810.R33 | Radar, radio, etc. (WWII) | |
| D810.R6 | Rotary International (WWII) | |
| D810.S2 | Science & technology (WWII) | |
| D810.S42 | Search & rescue ops. (WWII: gen.) | |
| D810.S45.A-Z | Rescue & search ops. (WWII: by country) | |
| D810.S46 | Sex (WWII) | |
| D810.S47 | Shinto (WWII) | |
| D810.S5 | Slavs (WWII) | |
| D810.S6 | Socialism (WWII) | |
| D810.S7-8 | SECRET SERVICE, espionage, military intelligence (WWII: spies) | 940.5485-5487+ |
| D810.S7 | Espionage, secret service, intelligence (WWII: gen.: spies) | |
| D810.S8.A-Z | Spies (WWII: by name) | |
| D810.S8.D55 | Donovan, William, 1883-1959 (WWII: spy) | |
| D810.S8.S85 | Stephenson, William, Sir (WWII: spy) | |
| D810.S8.T65 | Trepper, Leopold (WWII: spy) | |
| D810.T4 | Temperance (WWII) | |
| D810.T8 | Transportation (WWII: inclu. merchant marine) | |
| D810.V45 | Veterinary service (WWII) | |
| D810.W7 | Women & women's work (WWII) | |
| D810.Y7 | Y.M.C.A., Y.W.C.A. (WWII) | |
| D810.Y74 | Youth (WWII) | |
| D811 | Personal accounts (WWII: SEE ALSO DA-F country #'s for biographies & memoirs) | 940.5481-5482+ |
| D811.A2 | Personal accounts (WWII: collections) | |
| D811.A3-Z | Personal accounts (WWII: individual: by name) | |
| D811.5.A-Z | Personal accounts (WWII: noncombatants: by name) | |
| D812 | Armistice (WWII: gen.) | 940.5314, .532+ |
| D813.A-Z | Armistice (WWII: by country) | 940.5314, .532+ |
| D813.F7 | Armistice (WWII: Fr.) | |
| D813.G3 | Armistice (WWII: Germ.) | |

| | | |
|---|---|---|
| D814-821 | Peace (WWII) | 940.5314, .532+ |
| D814 | PRIMARY SOURCES, documents (WWII: PEACE: collections: gen.) | |
| D814.1 | Surrender documents (WWII: Ger.) | |
| D814.2 | Surrender documents (WWII: It.) | |
| D814.3 | Surrender documents (WWII: Jp.) | |
| D814.4-47 | Council of Foreign Ministers (WWII) | |
| D814.4 | Council of Foreign Ministers (WWII: gen.) | |
| D814.413 | MEETINGS (Cncl. For. Min.: London: 1945: 11 Sept.-2 Oct.) | |
| D814.415 | Meetings (Cncl. For. Min.: Moscow: 1945: 16-26 Dec.) | |
| D814.42 | Meetings (Cncl. For. Min.: Paris: 1946: Apr.) | |
| D814.425 | Meetings (Cncl. For. Min.: Paris: 1946: 15 June-July) | |
| D814.43 | Meetings (Cncl. For. Min.: New York: 1946: Nov.-Dec.) | |
| D814.44 | Meetings (Cncl. For. Min.: Moscow: 1947: 10 Mar.-24 Apr.) | |
| D814.45 | Meetings (Cncl. For. Min.: London: 1947: 25 Nov.-16 Dec.) | |
| D814.46 | Meetings (Cncl. For. Min.: Paris: 1949: 23 May-20 June) | |
| D814.47 | Meetings (Cncl. For. Min.: Berlin: 1954: 25Jan.-18 Feb.) | |
| D814.55-9 | TREATIES (WWII: with Axis powers) | |
| D814.55 | Treaties (WWII: Axis powers: collections) | |
| D814.56 | Peace conferences (WWII: gen.) | |
| D814.565 | Conferences (Paris: 29 July-15 Oct. 1946) | |
| D814.6 | Treaties (WWII: Allies-Ger.) | |
| D814.7 | Treaties (WWII: Allies-It.) | |
| D814.8 | Treaties (WWII: Allies-Japan) | |
| D814.9.A-Z | Treaties (WWII: Allies-misc. Axis powers: by country) | |
| D814.9.B9 | Treaties (WWII: Allies-Bulg.) | |
| D815 | Peace (WWII: gen.) | |
| D816 | Peace (WWII: gen. spec.) | |
| D816.5 | Pamphlets, minor works (WWII: peace) | |
| D818 | Indemnity & reparations (WWII: gen.) | |
| D819.A-Z | Reparations & indemnity (WWII: by country) | |
| D819.G3 | Reparations (WWII: Ger.) | |
| D819.J3 | Reparations (WWII: Jp.) | |
| D820.A-Z | Peace (WWII: special topics) | |
| D820.D5 | Disarmament (WWII) | |
| D820.P7 | Nationalities (WWII: population transfers: gen.) | |
| D820.P7-72 | Population transfers (WWII) | |
| D820.P72.A-Z | Population transfers (WWII: by nationality) | |
| D820.P72.J | Population transfers (WWII: Jews) | |
| D820.T4 | TERRITORIAL QUESTIONS (post-WWII: gen.: SEE D821 for specific places) | |
| D821.A-Z | Territorial questions (post-WWII: by place) | |
| D821.L4 | Levant (post-WWII territorial ?s) | |
| D821.L5 | Lithuania (post-WWII territorial ?s) | |
| D821.P3 | Palestine (post-WWII territorial ?s) | |
| D821.R95 | Ruthenia (post-WWII territorial ?s) | |
| D821.T8 | Transylvania (post-WWII territorial ?s) | |
| D821.Y8 | Yugoslavia (post-WWII territorial ?s: inclu. Trieste) | |

| D824-829 | RECONSTRUCTION (WWII) |
|---|---|
| D824 | Primary sources, documents, collections (WWII: Reconstruction) |
| D825 | Reconstruction (WWII: gen.)        940.53144 |
| D826 | Pamphlets, minor works (WWII: Reconstruction) |
| D827 | United States (WWII: Reconstruction: gen.) |
| D828.A-W | United States (WWII: Reconstruction: by state) |
| D828.A8-81 | Arkansas (WWII: Reconstruction) |
| D828.C6-61 | Colorado (WWII: Reconstruction) |
| D828.N9-91 | North Dakota (WWII: Reconstruction) |
| D828.T4-41 | Texas (WWII: Reconstruction) |
| D828.V8-81 | Washington, D.C. (WWII: Reconstruction: Virginia) |
| D829.A-Z | Reconstruction (WWII: outside U.S.: by country, nationality, etc.) |
| D829.A33 | South Africa (WWII: Reconstruction) |
| D829.D8 | Dutch East Indies (WWII: Reconstruction) |
| D829.E2 | Far East (WWII: Reconstruction) |
| D829.J4 | Jews (WWII: Reconstruction) |
| D829.L5 | Lithuania (WWII: Reconstruction) |
| D829.P3 | Palestine (WWII: Reconstruction) |
| D830-838 | MONUMENTS, MEMORIALS, CELEBRATIONS (WWII: memorials dedicated to special divisions classed with them) |
| D830 | Memorials, monuments, celebrations (WWII: gen.)     940.5465 |
| D831 | Memorials, monuments, celebrations (WWII: misc.) |
| D833-836 | Memorials, monuments, celebrations (WWII: U.S.)     940.546573 |
| D833 | Celebrations, memorials, monuments (WWII: U.S.: gen.)   940.546573 |
| D835.A-Z | Monuments, memorials, celebrations (WWII: U.S.: by state) |
| | 940.546574-54679+ |
| D835.C2-21 | Monuments, memorials, celebrations (WWII: U.S.: Calif.) |
| | 940.5465794 |
| D835.D6 | Monuments, memorials, celebrations (WWII: U.S.: District of Columbia) |
| D835.I3-31 | Monuments, memorials, celebrations (WWII: U.S.: Ill.) |
| D835.N4-5 | Monuments, memorials, celebrations (WWII: U.S.: N.Y.) |
| D836.A-Z | Monuments, memorials, celebrations (WWII: U.S.: by city) |
| D836.L62 | Monuments, memorials, celebrations (WWII: U.S.: Los Angeles) |
| D836.N49 | Monuments, memorials, celebrations (WWII: U.S.: New York City) |
| D838.A-Z | Monuments, memorials, celebrations (WWII: outside U.S.: by place) |
| D838.A8 | Monuments, memorials, celebrations (WWII: Australia) |
| D838.F8 | Monuments, memorials, celebrations (WWII: Fr.: gen.) |
| D838.F8.P3 | Monuments, memorials, celebrations (WWII: Fr.: Paris) |
| D838.G3 | Monuments, memorials, celebrations (WWII: Ger.) |
| D838.G6 | Monuments, memorials, celebrations (WWII: G.B.: gen.) |
| D838.G7.A-Z | Memorials, monuments, celebrations (WWII: G.B.: local: by place) |
| D838.G7.L5 | Memorials, monuments, celebrations (WWII: G.B.: London) |
| D838.N45 | Monuments, memorials, celebrations (WWII: N.Z.) |
| D838.R9 | Monuments, memorials, celebrations (WWII: Rus.) |
| | |
| D839-845+ | HISTORY (1945-) |
| D839.5 | Biography (1945-: collective) |
| D839.7.A-Z | Biography (1945-: individual by name: SEE ALSO DA-F country & era #s) |
| D840 | Modern history (1945-)     909.824-825+ |
| D843 | Foreign relns. & politics (1945-) |
| D847 | Soviet Bloc (1945-) |
| D921 | Description & travel (Europe: 1901-1950)   914.045 |
| D1051+ | Europe (1945-)     940.55+ |

| | | |
|---|---|---|
| DA | GREAT BRITAIN | 941-942 |
| DA10-18 | British Empire & colonies (SEE ALSO JV1000-1099 for other collective works & D-F for specific colonies) | |
| DA11 | Description & travel (Brit. Empire) | |
| DA16 | British Empire (gen.) | 909.824+ |
| DA20-690 | England | |
| DA25 | Primary sources, documents (Eng.) | |
| DA30 | England (gen.) | 941, 942 |
| DA34 | Dictionaries, chronologies, etc. (G.B.) | |
| DA40 | Politics (Eng.: gen.) | |
| DA42 | Politics (Eng.: modern) | |
| DA45 | Diplomacy (G.B.: gen.) | 327.41+ |
| DA47 | Foreign relns. (G.B.-other countries) | 327.410+ |
| DA47.1 | Foreign relns. (G.B.-Fr.) | 327.41044 |
| DA47.2 | Foreign relns. (G.B.-Ger.) | 327.41043 |
| DA47.65 | Foreign relns. (G.B.-Rus.) | 327.41047 |
| DA47.9.A-Z | Foreign relns. (G.B.-misc. countries: SEE E183.8 for U.S.) | |
| DA50-69.3 | Military history (G.B.) | |
| DA50 | British military history (gen.) | 355.00941 |
| DA52 | Dictionaries, Military (G.B.) | |
| DA54 | Biography, Military (G.B.: collective) | |
| DA69 | Military history (G.B.: 20th. c.: gen.) | 355.00941, .033041, .033241, .033541 |
| DA69.3.A-Z | Biography, Military (G.B.: 20th c.: inclu. memoirs) | 355.3310922-24 |
| DA69.3.A1 | Biography, Military (G.B.: 20th c.: collective) | |
| DA69.3.A57 | Alexander, Harold Rupert (G.B.: 20th c. mil. biog.) | |
| DA69.3.M56 | Montgomery, Bernard Law Montgomery, 1st Viscount (G.B.: 20th c. mil. biog.) | |
| DA69.3.W37 | Wavell, Archibald Percival Wavell, 1st Earl of (G.B.: 20th c. mil. biog.) | |
| DA70-89 | Naval history (G.B.) | |
| DA70 | British naval history (gen.) | 359.00941 |
| DA72 | Dictionaries, Naval (G.B.) | |
| DA74 | Biography, Naval (G.B.: collective) | |
| DA89 | Naval history (G.B.: 20th c.) | 359.00941, .4741 |
| DA89.1.A-Z | Biography, Naval (G.B.: 20th c.: by name) | |
| DA89.1.A1 | Biography, Naval (G.B.: 20th c.: collective) | |
| DA89.5-6 | Air force history (G.B.) | |
| DA89.5 | British air force history (gen.) | 358.400941 |
| DA89.6.A-Z | Biography, Air force (G.B.: inclu. memoirs) | |
| DA89.6.A1 | Biography, Air force (G.B.: collective) | |
| DA89.6.J6 | Joubert de la Ferté, Philip Bennet, Sir (G.B.: air force biog.) | |
| DA300 | England (1485-) | |
| DA470 | England (1702-) | |

```
DA566-566.9    England (20th c.: misc. overall)
DA566          Great Britain (20th c.: gen.)              941.082
DA566.4        Civilization, customs, social life (G.B.: 20th c.)
DA566.5        Military & naval history (G.B.: 20th c.)
DA566.7        Foreign relns. & politics (G.B.: 20th c.)
DA566.8        Satire, caricature (G.B.: 20th c.)
DA566.9.A-Z    Biography (G.B.: 20th c.: inclu. memoirs)     941.0820922-24
DA566.9.A1         Biography (G.B.: 20th c.: collective)
DA566.9.B15        Baldwin, Stanley, 1st Earl (G.B.: 20th c.)
DA566.9.B2         Balfour, Arthur James Balfour, 1st Earl of (G.B.: 20th c.)
DA566.9.B37        Beaverbrook, William Maxwell Aitken, Baron (G.B.: 20th c.)
DA566.9.B5         Birkenhead, Frederick E. S., 1st Earl of (G.B.: 20th c.)
DA566.9.C43        Chamberlain, Austen, Sir (G.B.: 20th c.)
DA566.9.C5         Churchill, Winston Leonard Spencer, Sir (G.B.: 20th c.)
DA566.9.E28        Eden, Anthony (G.B.: 20th c.)
DA566.9.G8         Grey, Edward (G.B.: 20th c.)
DA566.9.L5         Lloyd George, David (G.B.: 20th c.)
DA566.9.M25        MacDonald, James Ramsay (G.B.: 20th c.)
DA566.9.N7         Northcliffe, Alfred C. W. Harmsworth, 1st Viscount (G.B.: 20th c.)
DA566.9.O7         Oxford and Asquith, Herbert Henry Asquith, 1st Earl of (G.B.:
                        20th c.)
DA567-570      England (1901-10: King Edward VII)          941.082
DA570          Great Britain (1901-10: gen.)
DA573-578      England (1910-36: King George V)            941.083
DA573          George V (G.B.: King: 1910-36)
DA574.A-Z      Biography (G.B.: 1910-36: inclu. memoirs)
DA574.A1          Biography (G.B.: 1910-36: collective)
DA574.A2-45       Biography (G.B.: 1910-36: various royalty)
DA574.A8          Astor, Nancy W. Langhorne, Viscountess (G.B.: 1910-36 era)
DA574.M6          Mosley, Oswald, Sir, Baronet (G.B.: 1910-36 biog.)
DA576          Great Britain (1910-36)
DA577          Great Britain (1914-19: WWI era)
DA578          Great Britain (1920-39)
DA580-583      England (1936: King Edward VIII)            941.084
DA580          Edward VIII (G.B.: King: 1936)
DA583          Great Britain (1936)
DA584-589      England (1937-52: King George VI)           941.084
DA584          George VI (G.B.: King: 1937-52)
DA585.A-Z      Biography (G.B.: 1937-52: inclu. memoirs)
DA585.A1          Biography (G.B.: 1937-52: collective)
DA585.A2          Elizabeth (G.B.:1937-52 royal biog.: Consort of George VI)
DA585.A5.A-Z      Biography (G.B.: 1937-52: misc. royalty)
DA586             Great Britain (1937-52)
DA587          Great Britain (1939-45: WWII era)
DA630          Description & travel (G.B.: 1901-45)     914.1-2, 914.10482
DA650          Guidebooks (G.B.)
```

| | | |
|---|---|---|
| DA670.A-Z | Local history (G.B.: counties, regions, etc.: by name) | 942+ |
| DA670.C4 | Channel Islands (G.B.) | 942.34 |
| DA675-689 | Local history (London, Eng.) | 942.1 |
| DA677 | London, Eng. (gen.) | 942.1 |
| DA679 | Guidebooks (London, Eng.) | 914.21 |
| DA684 | London, Eng. (1901-50) | 942.1082 |
| DA685.A-Z | London, Eng. (boroughs, streets, etc.) | |
| DA686-687 | Buildings (London, Eng.) | |
| DA687.A-Z | Buildings (London, Eng.: by name) | |
| DA687.D7 | Downing St. (London, Eng.: No. 10) | |
| DA688 | Social life, culture, customs (London, Eng.) | |
| DA689.A-Z | Scenic places (London, Eng.: bridges, parks, etc.) | |
| DA689.B8 | Bridges (London, Eng.: inclu. London Bridge) | |
| DA689.M7 | Monuments, statues, memorials (London, Eng.) | |
| DA689.P17 | Palaces (London, Eng.) | |
| DA689.P6 | Port of London (Eng.) | |
| DA690.A-Z | Local history (Eng.: towns besides London) | 942.2+ |
| DA690.C75 | Coventry, Eng. | |
| DA722 | WALES (19th & 20th c.) | 942.908+ |
| DA821 | SCOTLAND (20th c.) | 941.1082 |
| DA880.A-Z | Local history (Scotland: counties, regions, etc.) | |
| DA880.O5-6 | Orkney Islands (Scot.) | |
| DA880.S5 | Shetland Islands (Scot.) | |
| DA959 | IRELAND (20th c.) | 941.5082 |
| DA962 | Ireland (1914-21) | |
| DA963 | Ireland (1922-: Irish Free State, Eire, etc.) | |
| DA964.A-Z | Diplomacy (Ire.: 20th c.) | |
| DA964.A2 | Foreign relns. (Ire.: 20th c.: gen.) | |
| DA964.G3 | Foreign relns. (Ire.-Ger.: 20th c.) | |
| DA964.G7 | Foreign relns. (Ire.-G.B.: 20th c.) | |
| | | |
| DB | AUSTRIA, HUNGARY, CZECHOSLOVAKIA | 943.6-9 |
| DB1-860 | AUSTRIA | 943.6 |
| DB17 | Austria & Austro-Hungarian Empire (gen.) | |
| DB26 | Description & travel (Austria: 1901-45) | |
| DB38 | Austria (1801-) | 943.604 |
| DB46-49 | Politics & diplomacy (Austria) | |
| DB48 | Austrian question (20th c.) | |
| DB49.A-Z | Foreign relns. (Austria: by other country) | |
| DB86.7 | Austria (1914-18: WWI era) | |
| DB91 | Austria (20th c.: gen.) | |
| DB91-99+ | Austria (20th c.) | 943.605 |
| DB96 | Austria (1918-: Republic) | 943.6051 |
| DB98.A-Z | Biography (Austria: 20th c.: by name: inclu. memoirs) | |
| DB98.D6 | Dollfuss, Englebert (Austria) | |
| DB98.S3 | Schuschnigg, Kurt (Austria) | |
| DB99 | Austria (1938-1945: Ger. annex.) | 943.6052 |

| DB191-217 | CZECHOSLOVAKIA (PREFER DB2000-3150 for titles cataloged after 1979) | 943.7 |
|---|---|---|
| DB215 | Czechoslovakia (20th c.) | 943.7024-703+ |
| DB215.3 | Czechoslovakia (1939-1945: Ger. occup.) | 943.703 |
| DB250 | Bosnia & Bosnia-Herzegovina (20th c.) | |
| DB280 | Bukowina (20th c.) | |
| DB379 | Slavonia & Croatia (1918-) | |
| DB420 | Dalmatia (20th c.) | |
| DB500 | Galicia (20th c.) | |
| DB540 | Herzegovina (20th c.) | |
| DB540.5 | Liechtenstein (SEE ALSO DB881-898 for newer books) | |
| DB660 | Silesia (20th c.) | |
| DB679-679.3 | Slovakia (1918-45: PREFER DB2000+) | |
| DB780 | Tyrol & Vorarlberg (20th c.) | |
| DB847 | Vienna, Austria (gen. hist. & descr.) | |
| DB855 | Vienna (20th c.) | |
| DB861-975+ | HUNGARY, Liechtenstein | |
| DB872 | Budapest (20th c.) | |
| DB881-898 | LIECHTENSTEIN (SEE ALSO DB540.5 for older titles) | |
| DB886, 891 | Liechtenstein (gen. hist. & descr.) | |
| DB893 | Diplomacy (Liech.: gen.) | |
| DB894.A-Z | Foreign relns. (Liech.: by country) | |
| DB894.G3 | Foreign relns. (Liech.-Ger.) | |
| DB906 | HUNGARY (gen.) | 943.9 |
| DB925 | Hungary (gen.: pubn. dates 1801+) | |
| DB926 | Diplomacy (Hung.: gen.) | |
| DB926.3.A-Z | Foreign relns. (Hung.-other lands) | |
| DB926.3.G3 | Foreign relns. (Hung.-Ger.) | |
| DB926.3.S65 | Foreign relns. (Hung.-Sov. Un.) | |
| DB947-957+ | Hungary (20th c.) | 943.9043+ |
| DB947 | Hungary (20th c.: gen.) | |
| DB950.A-Z | Biography (Hung.: 20th c.: by name, inclu. memoirs) | |
| DB950.H6 | Horthy, Miklós (Hung.: 20th c.) | |
| DB953 | Hungary (1914-1918: WWI era) | 943.9043 |
| DB955 | Hungary (1918-1945) | 943.9051-2 |
| DB2000-3150+ | CZECHOSLOVAKIA (inclu. Bohemia, Moravia, Slovakia: SEE ALSO DB191-217 for earlier titles) | |
| DB2000-2299 | Czechoslovakia | 943.7+ |
| DB2011 | Czechoslovakia (gen.) | |
| DB2020 | Description & travel (Czech.: 1901-45) | |
| DB2062 | Czechoslovakia (1801-1976 pubns.) | |
| DB2078.A-Z | Foreign relns. (Czech.: by country) | |
| DB2185-2232+ | Czechoslovakia (1918-) | |
| DB2185 | Primary sources, documents (Czech.: 1918-) | |
| DB2186 | Czechoslovakia (1918-: gen.) | |
| DB2189 | Foreign relns. (Czech.: 1918-: gen.) | |
| DB2191.A-Z | Biography (Czech.: 1918-) | |
| DB2191.B45 | Benes, Edward (Czech.: era of 1918- ) | |
| DB2191.M37 | Masaryk, Jan (Czech.: era of 1918-) | |
| DB2191.M38 | Masaryk, Tomas G. (Czech.: era of 1918-) | |
| DB2195-2202 | Czechoslovakia (1918-39) | 943.703 |
| DB2196 | Czechoslovakia (1918-39: gen.) | |
| DB2199 | Foreign relns. (Czech: 1918-39) | |
| DB2200-2201.A-Z | Biography (Czech.: 1918-39) | |
| DB2202 | Munich Four-power Agreement | |

| | | |
|---|---|---|
| DB2205-2211 | Czechoslovakia (1939-45: Ger. occup.) | 943.703 |
| DB2206 | Czechoslovakia (1939-45: Ger. occup.: gen.) | |
| DB2208.7 | Politics (Czech.: 1939-45) | |
| DB2209 | Foreign relns. (Czech.: 1939-45) | |
| DB2211.A-Z | Biography (Czech.: 1939-45: inclu. memoirs) | |
| DB2211.H33 | Hácha, Emil (Czech.: 1939-45 period) | |
| DB2415-2421 | Moravia (20th c.) | |
| DB2416 | Moravia (20th c.: gen.) | |
| DB2629 | Prague, Cz. (20th c.) | |
| DB2795-2822+ | Slovakia (1800-1945) | |
| DB2805-2822+ | Slovakia (1918-: in Czech Republic) | |
| DB2806 | Slovakia (1918-) | |
| DB2809 | Foreign relns. (Slovakia: 1918-) | |
| DB2813 | Slovakia (1918-39) | |
| DB2815-2822 | Slovakia (1939-45) | |
| DB2816 | Slovakia (1939-45: gen.) | |
| DB2819 | Foreign relns. (Slovakia: 1939-45) | |
| DB2821.A-Z | Biography (Czech.: 1939-45: by name) | |
| DB2821.T57 | Tiso, Jozef (Czech.: 1939-45 era) | |
| DB2822 | Slovakia (1944: uprising) | |
| DB2826 | Slovakia (1945-68) | |
| | | |
| DC | FRANCE 944 | |
| DC3 | Primary sources, documents (Fr.) | |
| DC17 | France (gen. hist., culture) | |
| DC28 | Description & travel (Fr.: 1871-1945) | |
| DC33.7 | Civilization, customs, social life (Fr.: 1901-) | |
| DC38 | France (gen. hist.: pubn. 1815-) | |
| DC44-47 | Military history (Fr.) | |
| DC45 | French military history (gen.) | 355.00944, .033044 |
| DC47 | Military history (Fr.: 19th-20th c.) | |
| DC49-53 | Naval history (Fr.) | |
| DC50 | French naval history (gen.) | |
| DC53 | Naval history (Fr.: 19th-20th c.) | |
| DC55-59 | Politics & diplomacy (Fr.) | |
| DC55 | Diplomacy (Fr.: gen.) | |
| DC58 | Foreign relns. (Fr.: 19th-20th c.) | |
| DC59.8.A-Z | Foreign relns. (Fr.: by country) | 327.440+ |
| DC59.8.G3 | Foreign relns. (Fr.-Ger.) | 327.44043 |
| DC59.8.G7 | Foreign relns. (Fr.-G.B.) | 327.44041 |
| DC59.8.R9 | Foreign relns. (Fr.-Rus.) | |
| DC59.8.S65 | Foreign relns. (Fr.-Sov.Un.) | |
| DC110 | France (1515-) | |
| DC334-354+ | France (1871-1940: 3rd Repub.) | |
| DC334 | Primary sources, documents (Fr.: 1871-1940) | |
| DC335 | Third Republic (Fr.: 1871-1940) | |
| DC339 | Military history (Fr.: 1871-1940) | |
| DC342 | Biography (Fr.: 1871-1940: collective) | |
| DC342.8.A-Z | Biography (Fr.: 1871-1940: by name: inclu. memoirs & autobiog.) | |
| DC342.8.J6 | Joffre, Joseph J. (Fr.: 1871-1940 era) | |
| DC342.8.P4 | Pétain, Henri Philippe (Fr.: 1871-1940 era) | |

```
DC361-373   France (20th c.: overall)
DC361       France (20th c.: gen.)                944.081
DC365       Civilization, customs, social life (Fr.: 20th c.)
DC367       Military history (Fr.: 20th c.)
DC368       Naval history (Fr.: 20th c.)
DC369       Foreign relns. & politics (Fr.: 20th c.)        944.08
DC371          Biography (Fr.: 20th c.: collective)
DC373.A-Z      Biography (Fr.: 20th c.: by name)
DC373.B5       Blum, Léon (Fr.: 20th c.)
DC373.B7       Briand, Aristide (Fr.: 20th c.)
DC373.D3    Daladier, Édouard (Fr.: 20th c.)
DC373.G3    De Gaulle, Charles (Fr.: 20th c.)
DC373.L33   Lattre de Tassigny, Jean Joseph (Fr.: 20th c.)
DC373.L35      Laval, Pierre (Fr.: 20th c.)
DC373.M3       Maurras, Charles M. (Fr.: 20th c.)
DC373.R45      Reynaud, Paul (Fr.: 20th c.)
DC387       France (1914-18: WWI era)            944.0814
DC389-396      France (1919-40: Reconstruc.)
DC389          Reconstruction (Fr.: 1919-40)        944.0815
DC394       France (1924-31: Gaston Doumergue)
DC396       France (1932-40: Albert F. Lebrun)
DC397       France (1939-45: WWII period: inclu. Pétain collab.)     944.0816
DC601-609+     Local history (Fr.: north, east, Riviera, etc.)
DC611.A-Z      Local history (Fr.: regions, prov.'s, depts., etc.: by name)
DC611.B841-915    Brittany (Fr.)
DC611.C8-839  CORSICA (Fr.)
DC611.N841-899    Normandy (Fr.)
DC611.N899     Normandy (Fr.: 20th c.)
DC611.P981-992    PYRENEES (Fr.)
DC701-790+  Local history (Paris, Fr.)            944.36
DC707       Description & travel (Paris, Fr.: ALSO gen. hist.)
DC708       Guidebooks (Paris, Fr.)
DC715       Social life, culture, customs (Paris, Fr.)
DC736       Paris, Fr. (1914-21)
DC737+         Paris, Fr. (1922-)      944.360816
DC801.A-Z      Local history (Fr.: towns besides Paris)
DC801.B83      Brest, Fr.
DC801.C11      Caen, Fr.
DC801.D56         Dieppe, Fr.
DC801.L96-988     Lyons, Fr.
DC801.M34-38      Marseilles, Fr.
DC801.V45      Verdun, Fr.
DC801.V55-57   Versailles, Fr. (ALSO Trianon)
DC890          Colonies, French (PREFER D-F for individual colonies or JV1800-
                   1899 for collective works)
DC928       ANDORRA (modern hist.)
DC945       MONACO
DC989       Nice, Fr. (1860-)
```

| | | |
|---|---|---|
| DD | GERMANY & Prussia 943 | |
| DD16 | Guidebooks (Ger.) | |
| DD17 | Germany (gen. hist., culture, etc.) | |
| DD42 | Description & travel (Ger.: 1919-45) | 914.3009042 |
| DD67 | Civilization, customs, social life (Ger.) | |
| DD68 | German culture (in other lands: gen.) | |
| DD74 | Races & ethnography (Ger.) | |
| DD76 | National characteristics (Ger.) | |
| DD89 | Germany (gen.: pubn. 1801-) | |
| DD99-105 | Military history (Ger.) | |
| DD100.A2 | Biography, Military (Ger.: collective: gen.) | |
| DD100.A3-Z | Biography, Military (Ger.: collective: officers) | |
| DD101 | German military history (gen.) 355.00943 | |
| DD104 | Military history (Ger.: 20th c.) 355.00943, .033043, .033242, .033543 | |
| DD106 | Naval history (Ger.) 359.00943, .4743 | |
| DD110-120 | Politics & diplomacy (Ger.) | |
| DD110 | Primary sources, documents (Ger.: for. relns. & politics) | |
| DD112 | Diplomacy & politics (Ger.: gen.) 320.943, 327.43+ | |
| DD117 | Foreign relns. (Ger.: 19th-20th c.) 327.43+ | |
| DD119.3 | Germans (in other lands: gen.) | |
| DD119.5 | Propaganda, German | |
| DD120.A-Z | Foreign relns. (Ger.: by country) 327.430+ | |
| DD120.F8 | Foreign relns. (Ger.-Fr.) 327.43044 | |
| DD120.G7 | Foreign relns. (Ger.-G.B.) 327.43041 | |
| DD120.I6 | Foreign relns. (Ger.-Ire.) | |
| DD120.I8 | Foreign relns. (Ger.-It.) | |
| DD120.J3 | Foreign relns. (Ger.-Japan) 327.43052 | |
| DD120.R9 | Foreign relns. (Ger.-Rus.) 327.43047 | |
| DD120.S65 | Foreign relns. (Ger.-Sov. Un.) | |
| DD120.U6-7 | Foreign relns. (Ger.-U.S.) | |
| DD175 | Germany (1519-) | |
| DD228-231 | Germany (1888-1918: Kaiser Wilhelm II era) 943.084 | |
| DD228.6 | Diplomacy (Ger.: 1888-1918: gen.) 327.43+ | |
| DD228.7.A-Z | Foreign relns. (Ger.:1888-1918: by country) | |
| DD228.8 | Germany (1914-1918: WWI period) 943.08 | |
| DD231.A-Z | Biography (Ger.: 1888-1918+: by name) | |
| DD231.H5 | Hindenburg, Paul von (Ger.: 1888-1918+ period) | |
| DD232 | Germany (20th c.: gen.) | |
| DD233-251+ | Germany (1918-: revolution & Republic) 943.085 | |
| DD233 | Periodicals & associations (Ger.: 1918-) | |
| DD234 | Primary sources, documents (Ger.: 1918-) | |
| DD237 | Germany (1918-: revolution & Republic: gen.) | |
| DD239 | Civilization, customs, social life (Ger.: 1918-) | |
| DD240-241 | Diplomacy & politics (Ger.: 1918-) | |
| DD240 | Politics & diplomacy (Ger.: 1918-) | |
| DD241.A-Z | Foreign relns. (Ger.: 1918-: by country) | |
| DD241.A5 | Foreign relns. (Ger.-Albania: 1918-) | |
| DD241.A7 | Foreign relns. (Ger.-Argen.: 1918-) | |
| DD241.A9 | Foreign relns. (Ger.-Austria: 1918-) | |
| DD241.B4 | Foreign relns. (Ger.-Bel.: 1918-) | |
| DD241.B7 | Foreign relns. (Ger.-Brazil: 1918-) | |
| DD241.B8 | Foreign relns. (Ger.-Bulg.: 1918-) | |
| DD241.C2-29 | Foreign relns. (Ger.-Can.: 1918-) | |
| DD241.C95 | Foreign relns. (Ger.-Czech.: 1918-) | |
| DD241.D3 | Foreign relns. (Ger.-Den.: 1918-) | |

| | | |
|---|---|---|
| DD241.E3 | Foreign relns. (Ger.-Egypt: 1918-) | |
| DD241.F5 | Foreign relns. (Ger.-Fin.: 1918-) | |
| DD241.F8 | Foreign relns. (Ger.-Fr.: 1918-) | |
| DD241.G7 | Foreign relns. (Ger.-G.B.: 1918-) | |
| DD241.G8 | Foreign relns. (Ger.-Greece: 1918-) | |
| DD241.H9 | Foreign relns. (Ger.-Hung.: 1918-) | |
| DD241.I4 | Foreign relns. (Ger.-India: 1918-) | |
| DD241.I6 | Foreign relns. (Ger.-Ire.: 1918-) | |
| DD241.I8 | Foreign relns. (Ger.-It.: 1918-) | |
| DD241.J3 | Foreign relns. (Ger.-Japan: 1918-) | |
| DD241.N4 | Foreign relns. (Ger.-Neth.: 1918-) | |
| DD241.N8 | Foreign relns. (Ger.-Nor.: 1918-) | |
| DD241.P7 | Foreign relns. (Ger.-Pol.: 1918-) | |
| DD241.P8 | Foreign relns. (Ger.-Port.: 1918-) | |
| DD241.R8 | Foreign relns. (Ger.-Rum.: 1918-) | |
| DD241.R9 | Foreign relns. (Ger.-Rus.: 1918-) | |
| DD241.S7 | Foreign relns. (Ger.-Sp.: 1918-) | |
| DD241.S8 | Foreign relns. (Ger.-Swe.: 1918-) | |
| DD241.S9 | Foreign relns. (Ger.-Swit.: 1918-) | |
| DD241.S95 | Foreign relns. (Ger.-Syria: 1918-) | |
| DD241.T8 | Foreign relns. (Ger.-Tur.: 1918-) | |
| DD241.U6-69+ | Foreign relns. (Ger.-U.S.: 1918-) | |
| DD241.U7+ | Foreign relns. (Ger.-Uruguay: 1918-) | |
| DD241.Y8 | Foreign relns. (Ger.-Yug.: 1918-) | |
| DD243 | Biography (Ger.: 1918-48: group) | |
| DD244 | Public figures (Ger.: 1918-48: men) | |
| DD245 | Women (Ger.: 1918-48) | |
| DD247.A-Z | Biography (Ger.: 1918-48: inclu. memoirs: by name) | |
| DD247.B7 | Brüning, Heinrich (Ger.: 1918-48 era) | |
| DD247.E2 | Ebert, Friedrich (Ger.: 1918-48 era) | |
| DD247.G6 | Goebbels, Joseph (Ger.: 1918-48 era) | |
| DD247.G67 | Göring, Hermann (Ger.: 1918-48 era) | |
| DD247.H37 | Hess, Rudolf (Ger.: 1918-48 era) | |
| DD247.H5 | Hitler, Adolf (Ger.: 1918-48 era) | |
| DD247.P5 | Papen, Franz von (Ger.: 1918-48 era) | |
| DD247.R47 | Ribbentrop, Joachim von (Ger.: 1918-48 era) | |
| DD247.R58 | Rosenberg, Alfred (Ger.: 1918-48 era) | |
| DD247.S335 | Schacht, Hjalmar Horace Greeley (Ger.: 1918-48 era) | |
| DD247.S6-7 | Speer, Albert (Ger.: 1918-48 era) | |
| DD247.S8 | Strasser, Otto (Ger.: 1918-48 era) | |
| DD248 | Germany (1918: Revolution) | |
| DD249 | Germany (1919-25: Ebert period) | |
| DD251 | Germany (1925-34: Hindenburg era) | 943.085 |
| DD252-256 | Germany (1930-45, 1933-45: eras of Hitler & National Socialism) | |
| | | 943.086 |
| DD253 | Third Reich (Ger.: 1930+-45: contemporary works) | |
| DD253.A1 | Periodicals, associations, collections (Ger.: 1930-45) | |
| DD253.1st- | SS (Nazi Party: Ger.: by local #) | |

| | | |
|---|---|---|
| DD253.2-8 | Nazi Party (Ger.: 1930-45) | 329.43, 324.243+, 943.086 |
| DD253.2 | Periodicals & documents (Ger.: Nazi Party) | |
| DD253.25 | Nationalsozialistische Deutsche Arbeiter-Partei (Ger.: 1930-45: gen.) | |
| DD253.27 | Meetings (Nazi Party: Ger.: gen.) | |
| DD253.28.Date | Nazi Party meetings (Ger.: specific by date) | |
| DD253.28.1923 | Meetings (Nazi Party: Ger.: 1923) | |
| DD253.28.1926 | Meetings (Nazi Party: Ger.: 1926) | |
| DD253.28.1927 | Meetings (Nazi Party: Ger.: 1927) | |
| DD253.28.1929 | Meetings (Nazi Party: Ger.: 1929) | |
| DD253.28.1933-38 | Meetings (Nazi Party: Ger.: 1933-38) | |
| DD253.29-3 | Nazi Party (Ger.: admin. offices) | |
| DD253.39-45 | Nazi Party (Ger.: geog. divisions) | |
| DD253.46-73 | Nazi Party (Ger.: branches or gliederungen) | |
| DD253.49 | Deutsches Jungvolk (Nazi Party) | |
| DD253.5 | Hitler Youth (Hitlerjugend) | |
| DD253.58 | Nationalsozialistische Frauenschaft | |
| DD253.6-65 | SS (Nazi Party: Ger.) | |
| DD253.6 | Schutzstaffel (SS: Nazi Party: gen.) | |
| DD253.62.A-Z | SS (Nazi Party: by Ger. locality) | |
| DD254 | German propaganda (1933-45: in other countries: gen.) | |
| DD255.A-Z | Propaganda, German (1933-45: by place) | |
| DD255.F8 | Propaganda, German (1933-45: France) | |
| DD255.G7 | Propaganda, German (1933-45: Gt. Brit.) | |
| DD255.R9 | Propaganda, German (1933-45: Rus.: SEE ALSO DK272.7.G3) | |
| DD255.U6-7 | Propaganda, German (1933-45: United States) | |
| DD256 | Germany (1939-45: WWII period) | |
| DD256.3 | Resistance (Ger. vs. Nazis) | |
| DD256.5 | Germany (1930-45: postwar titles) | |
| DD257 | Germany (1945-: Allied occupation) | |
| DD257.25 | Germany (1945-: Reunification ?) | |
| DD448 | Prussia (1871-1918: gen.) | |
| DD452-454 | Prussia (1918-45) | |
| DD452 | Prussia (1918-45: gen.) | |
| DD453 | Prussia (1918-33) | |
| DD454 | Prussia (1933-45) | |
| DD491.A-Z | Local history (Prus.: provinces, regions, etc.) | |
| DD491.R4-52 | Rhine Province (Prus.) | |
| DD491.S3-39 | Saxony (Prus.) | |
| DD491.W4-52 | Westphalia (Prus.) | |
| DD701-800 | Local history (Ger.: large areas) | |
| DD791-800 | German Austria & Bavaria | |
| DD801.A-Z | Local history (Ger.: provinces, regions, states, etc.) | |
| DD801.A31-69 | Alsace-Lorraine (Ger.) | |
| DD801.B31-55 | Bavaria | 943.3 |
| DD801.B422 | Bavaria (1939-45) | |
| DD801.R7-76 | Rhine River (Ger.) | 943.4 |
| DD851-900 | Berlin, Ger. | |
| DD859 | Guidebooks (Berlin, Ger.) | |
| DD860 | Berlin, Ger. (gen.) | 943.155 |
| DD866 | Social life, culture, customs (Berlin, Ger.) | |
| DD879 | Berlin, Ger. (1914-21) | |
| DD880 | Berlin, Ger. (1922-45) | 943.155086 |
| DD883 | Berlin, Ger. (districts, sections) | |
| DD887 | Streets, bridges, etc. (Berlin, Ger.) | |
| DD896 | Buildings, Public (Berlin, Ger.) | |

| | | |
|---|---|---|
| DD901.A-Z | Local history (Ger.: areas, towns except Berlin) | |
| DD901.A25-28 | Aachen, Ger. (Aix-la-Chapelle) | |
| DD901.B4 | Bayreuth, Ger. | |
| DD901.B443 | Berchtesgaden, Ger. | |
| DD901.B65 | Brandenburg, Ger. | |
| DD901.B71-79 | Bremen, Ger. | |
| DD901.D2-29 | Danzig | |
| DD901.D28 | Danzig (19th-20th c.) | |
| DD901.D71-79 | Dresden, Ger. | |
| DD901.D95 | Düsseldorf, Ger. | |
| DD901.E75 | Essen, Ger. | |
| DD901.F71-79 | Frankfurt, Ger. | |
| DD901.H55-59 | Heidelberg, Ger. | |
| DD901.M71-95 | Munich, Ger. | |
| DD901.M77 | Munich, Ger. (gen.) | |
| DD901.M9 | Munich, Ger. (1871-1950) | |
| DD901.N91-97 | Nuremberg, Ger. | |
| DD901.S81-89 | Strassburg, Ger. | |
| DD901.S95-97 | Stuttgart, Ger. | |
| DD905 | Colonies, German (PREFER D-F #s for specific colonies or JV2000-2099 for collective titles) | |

| | | |
|---|---|---|
| DF | Greece | 949.5 |
| DF701-951+ | GREECE (Modern) | |
| DF751 | Greece (gen.) | 949.5 |
| DF765 | Military history (Greece) | |
| DF775 | Naval history (Greece) | |
| DF785 | Diplomacy (Greece: gen.) | |
| DF787.A-Z | Foreign relns. (Greece: by country) | |
| DF787.G3 | Foreign relns. (Greece-Ger.) | |
| DF787.G7 | Foreign relns. (Greece-G.B.) | |
| DF787.I8 | Foreign relns. (Greece-It.) | |
| DF833 | Greece (20th c.: gen.) | 949.507 |
| DF836.A-Z | Biography (Greece: 20th c.) | |
| DF838 | Greece (1914-18: WWI) | 949.506 |
| DF848 | Greece (1924-35: Republic) | |
| DF849 | Greece (1935-47: George II era) | 949.5074 |
| DF901.A-Z | Local history (Greece: regions, islands, provinces, etc.) | |
| DF901.C78-89 | Crete | |
| DF915-936 | Athens, Gr. | |
| DF925 | Athens, Gr. (1910-) | |

| | | |
|---|---|---|
| DG | ITALY, Sicily, Sardinia, Malta | 945 |
| DG48-84 | Military history (It.) | |
| DG401-579 | Italy (476-) | |
| DG403 | Primary sources, documents (It.) | |
| DG417 | Italy (gen. hist., culture, etc.) | |
| DG429 | Description & travel (It.: 1919-44) | |
| DG450 | Civilization, customs, social life (It.: 1816-1945) | |
| DG467 | Italy (gen.: titles dated after 1800) | |
| DG481 | Biography, Military (It.: collective) | |
| DG482 | Italian military history (gen.) | 355.00945 |
| DG484 | Military history (It.: 1792-20th c.) | |
| DG486 | Naval history (It.: gen.) | 359.00945 |

```
DG491-499      Diplomacy & politics (It.)
DG491          Politics & diplomacy (It.: gen.) 320.945, 327.45+
DG498          Foreign relns. (It.: 1861-1945)
DG499.A-Z      Foreign relns. (It.: by country) 327.450+
DG499.A5           Foreign relns. (It.-Alb.)
DG499.E7           Foreign relns. (It.-Eth.)
DG499.F8           Foreign relns. (It.-Fr.)
DG499.G3           Foreign relns. (It.-Ger.)
DG499.G7           Foreign relns. (It.-G.B.)
DG499.J3       Foreign relns. (It.-Japan)
DG499.R9       Foreign relns. (It.-Rus.)
DG499.S65      Foreign relns. (It.-Sov.Un.)
DG499.S9       Foreign relns. (It.-Swit.)
DG499.U6-7         Foreign relns. (It.-U.S.)
DG499.Y8           Foreign relns. (It.-Yug.)
DG555-575      Italy (1871-1947: United Italy: Monarchy)
DG555          Italy (1871-1947: gen.)              945.09
DG556.A-Z      Biography (It.: 1871-1941)
DG556.S6           Spaventa, Silvio (It.: 1871-1945 era)
DG566-575          Italy (1900-46: times of Vittorio Emanuele III, Umberto II)
DG566              Vittorio Emanuele III (It.: King, 1900-46: gen. inclu. times)
DG570          Italy (1914-18: WWI)              945.0814
DG571          Italy (1919-45: Fascism)          945.0815-0816
DG571.A1       Periodicals, associations, yearbooks (It.: 1919-45)
DG572          Italy (1939-45: WWII era)          945.0816
DG574          Biography (It.: 1871-1947: collec.)
DG575.A-Z      Biography (It.: 1900-46: by name, inclu. memoirs)
DG575.B2           Badoglio, Pietro (It.: 1900-46 period)
DG575.B3           Balbo, Italo (It. 1900-46 period)
DG575.C51          Ciano, Galeazzo, Conte (It.: 1900-46 period)
DG575.M8       Mussolini, Benito (It.: 1900-46 period)
DG575.N5       Nitti, Francesco (It. 1900-46 period)
DG600-980      Local history (It.: large areas, cities)
DG651-662          Lombardy & Milan, It.
DG660-662          Milan, It.
DG670-679          Venice, It. (city state & modern)
DG731-760          Tuscany & Florence, It.
DG760              Florence, It.
DG791-800+         PAPAL STATES
DG796              Papal States (modern)
DG799          Holy SEE (1870-)
DG800          Vatican City (1929-)
DG803-818          Rome, It. (modern era)
DG806              Description (Rome, It.: 1861-1950)
DG808          Rome, It. (476-: gen.)
DG812          Rome, It. (1527-)
DG813          Rome, It. (1871-)
DG840-855      Naples, It. (kingdom & later)
```

DG869          SICILY (20th c.)
DG869.2        Sicily (1900-45)
DG975.A-Z      Local history (It.: non-metro. towns, provinces, etc.)
DG975.S2       San Marino (Republic)
DG975.S29-33   SARDINIA
DG987-999      MALTA & Maltese Islands
DG990          Malta (gen.)
DG990.5        Military history (Malta)
DG990.7        Naval history (Malta)
DG991-991.6    Foreign relns. & politics (Malta)
DG992.7        Malta (1798-1964: Brit. era)
DG993          Malta (1802-1947)
DG994          Malta (20th c.)


DH-DJ          Low Countries
DH39           Description & travel (Bel. & Holl.: 1901-50)
DH401-925      Belgium & Luxembourg
DH418-811+     BELGIUM          949.3
DH433          Description & travel (Bel.: 1831-1945)
DH540          Military history (Bel.: gen.)
DH545          Military history (Bel.: 1815-)
DH566          Diplomacy & politics (Bel.: gen.)
DH569.A-Z      Foreign relns. (Bel.: by country)
DH569.F8       Foreign relns. (Bel.-Fr.)
DH569.G3       Foreign relns. (Bel.-Ger.)
DH677          Belgium (20th c.)          949.304
DH681          Belgium (1909-34: King Albert)      949.3041
DH682          Belgium (1914-18: WWI)
DH683          Belgium (1920-)
DH685.A-Z      Biography (Bel.: 1909-34)
DH687          Belgium (1934-51: reign of Leopold III)      949.3042
DH689.A-Z      Biography (Bel.: 1934-51)
DH801.A-Z      Local history (Bel.: provinces, regions, etc.)
DH801.A6-69    Antwerp area (Bel.)
DH801.F4-49    Flanders area (Bel.)
DH801.N2-29    Namur area (Bel.)
DH801.S6       Soignes Forest (Bel.)
DH802-809      Brussels, Bel.
DH807.5        Brussels, Bel. (20th c.)
DH811.A-Z      Local history (Bel.: towns except Brussels)
DH811.A55-68   Antwerp, Bel.
DH811.L5       Li`ege, Bel.
DH901-925      LUXEMBURG
DH905          Luxemburg (gen. hist., culture, etc.)
DH906          Description & travel (Lux.: to 1945)
DH908          Luxemburg (gen.)          949.35
DH908.5        Diplomacy & politics (Lux.)
DH908.6.A-Z    Foreign relns. (Lux.: by country)
DH908.6.G3     Foreign relns. (Lux.-Ger.)
DH916          Luxemburg (1815-)

| | | |
|---|---|---|
| DJ | NETHERLANDS (HOLLAND) | 949.2 |
| DJ39 | Description & travel (Neth.: 1901-45) | |
| DJ124 | Military history (Neth.) | |
| DJ142 | Politics & diplomacy (Neth.: gen.) | |
| DJ147 | Diplomacy & politics (Neth.: 1795-20th c.) | |
| DJ149.A-Z | Foreign relns. (Neth.: by country) | |
| DJ149.G3 | Foreign relns. (Neth.-Ger.) | |
| DJ281-287 | Holland (1890-1948: Queen Wilhelmina) | |
| DJ281 | Netherlands (1890-1948: gen. & biogs. of Queen Wilhelmina) | |
| | | 949.2071 |
| DJ283.A-Z | Biography (Neth.: by name) | |
| DJ285 | Netherlands (1914-18: WWI) | 949.2071 |
| DJ287 | Netherlands (1939-48: inclu. WWII period) | |
| DJ401.A-Z | Local history (Neth.: islands, provinces, regions, etc.) | |
| DJ411.A-Z | Local history (Neth.: towns, cities, etc.) | |
| DJ411.A5-59 | Amsterdam, Neth. | |
| DJ411.A8 | Arnhem, Neth. | |
| DJ500 | Colonies, Dutch (PREFER D-F #s for indiv. colonies or JV2500-2599 for collective) | |
| | | |
| DJK | EASTERN EUROPE (gen.: pubns. after about 1977-78: SEE DR for earlier & for specific countries) | |
| DJK17 | Description & travel (Eastern Europe: 1901-50) | |
| DJK38 | Europe, Eastern (gen.) | |
| DJK41 | Primary sources, documents (Eastern Europe: politics) | |
| DJK42 | Politics (Eastern Europe: gen.) | |
| DJK43-44 | Foreign relns. (Eastern Europe) | |
| DJK49 | Eastern Europe (1918-45) | |
| DJK61-66 | Black Sea region | |
| DJK71-75 | Carpathian Mts. region | |
| DJK76 | Danube River Valley (gen.) | |
| DJK77 | Pannonia | |
| | | |
| DK | Russia, Poland, Finland, Soviet Asia | |
| DK1-275+ | RUSSIA | 947 |
| DK3 | Primary sources, documents (Rus.) | |
| DK17 | Russia (gen.) | |
| DK27 | Description & travel (Rus.: 1901-44) | 914.70904 |
| DK32 | Civilization, customs, social life (Rus.: gen.) | |
| DK33 | Races & ethnography (Rus.) | |
| DK36 | Dictionaries, chronologies, etc. (Rus.) | |
| DK50-54 | Russian military history | |
| DK50.5-8 | Biography, Military (Rus.: collective) | |
| DK54 | Military history (Rus.: 1917-) | 355.00947, .033+ |
| DK59 | Naval history (Rus.: 1917-) | 359.00947 |

| | | |
|---|---|---|
| DK60-63 | Politics & diplomacy (Rus.) | |
| DK60 | Primary sources, documents (Rus.: politics & diplomacy) | |
| DK61 | Politics & diplomacy (Rus.: gen.) | 320.947 |
| DK63 | Politics & diplomacy (Rus.: 1894-1939) | |
| DK63.3 | Politics & diplomacy (Rus.: 1939-) | |
| DK65-69 | Diplomacy (Rus.) | |
| DK65 | Primary sources, documents (Rus.: for. relns.) | |
| DK66 | Foreign relns. (Rus.: gen.) | 327.47 |
| DK67-69 | Foreign relns. (Rus.: particular areas) | 327.470+ |
| DK67 | Foreign relns. (Rus.-Europe) | |
| DK67.3 | Foreign relns. (Rus.-Cath. Church) | |
| DK67.4 | Foreign relns. (Rus.-Balkan Penin.) | |
| DK67.5.A-Z | Foreign relns. (Rus.-specific Eur. countries) | |
| DK67.5.B8 | Foreign relns. (Rus.-Bulg.) | |
| DK67.5.C95 | Foreign relns. (Rus.-Czech.) | |
| DK67.5.F5 | Foreign relns. (Rus.-Fin.) | |
| DK67.5.F8 | Foreign relns. (Rus.-Fr.) | |
| DK67.5.G3 | Foreign relns. (Rus.-Ger.) | |
| DK67.5.G7 | Foreign relns. (Rus.-G.B.) | |
| DK67.5.G8 | Foreign relns. (Rus.-Greece) | |
| DK67.5.H9 | Foreign relns. (Rus.-Hung.) | |
| DK67.5.I8 | Foreign relns. (Rus.-It.) | |
| DK67.5.P7 | Foreign relns. (Rus.-Pol.) | |
| DK67.5.R8 | Foreign relns. (Rus.-Rum.) | |
| DK67.5.S8 | Foreign relns. (Rus.-Swe.) | |
| DK67.5.Y8 | Foreign relns. (Rus.-Yug.) | |
| DK68.A3-Z | Foreign relns. (Rus.-Asia: gen.: pubns. 1801-) | |
| DK68.7.A-Z | Foreign relns. (Rus.-particular Asian countries) | |
| DK68.7.C5 | Foreign relns. (Rus.-China) | 327.47051 |
| DK68.7.I4 | Foreign relns. (Rus.-India) | |
| DK68.7.I55 | Foreign relns. (Rus.-Iran) | |
| DK68.7.J3 | Foreign relns. (Rus.-Japan) | 327.47052 |
| DK68.7.T8 | Foreign relns. (Rus.-Tur.) | |
| DK69 | Foreign relns. (Rus.-U.S.: PREFER E183.8.R9) | 327.47073 |
| DK69.3.A-Z | Foreign relns. (Rus. & non-U.S. Am. countries) | |
| DK69.3.C2-29 | Foreign relns. (Rus.-Can.) | |
| DK69.3.M6 | Foreign relns. (Rus.-Mex.) | |
| DK246 | Russia (20th c.: gen.) | 947.084 |
| DK251-264 | Russia (1894-1917: Czar Nicholas II) | |
| DK254.A-Z | Biography (Rus.: 1894-1917: by name, inclu. memoirs) | |
| DK254.L3-46 | Lenin, Vladimir Ilich (Rus.: 1894-1917: biog. & works) | |
| DK254.L3.A2-219 | Lenin, Vladimir Ilich (Rus.: collected works by) | |
| DK254.L4-46 | Lenin, Vladimir Ilich (Rus.: biogs.) | |
| DK258-260 | Russia (1894-1917) | 947.083 |
| DK258 | Nicholas II (Rus.: Czar, 1894-1917) | |
| DK262 | Russia (1904-17: empire status) | |
| DK263-264.3 | Russian Revolution (1905-6) | |
| DK264.8 | Russia (1914-18: WWI era) | 947.083 |
| DK265-265.9+ | Russian Revolution (1917-21) | |
| DK265.A56-Z | Russian Revolution (1917-21: gen.) | |
| DK265.15 | Pictorials, satires, etc. (Rus. Rev., 1917-21) | |
| DK265.17 | Pamphlets, minor works, sermons (Rus. Rev., 1917-21) | |

| | |
|---|---|
| DK265.2 | Russian military ops. (Rev., 1917-21) |
| DK265.3 | Russian naval ops. (Rev., 1917-21) |
| DK265.4 | Russian Revolution (1917-21: Allied interventon, 1918-20) |
| DK265.42.A-Z | Allied intervention (Rus. Rev.: by country) |
| DK265.8.A-Z | Local history (Rus. Rev., 1917-21: by place) |
| DK265.8.L195 | Leningrad, Rus. (Rev., 1917-21) |
| DK265.8.M6 | Moscow, Rus. (Rev., 1917-21) |
| DK265.8.S5 | Siberia (Rev., 1917-21) |
| DK265.8.S63 | Central Asia (Rus, Rev., 1917-21) |
| DK265.8.U4 | Ukraine (Rev., 1917-21) |
| DK265.9.A-Z | Russian Revolution (1917-21: special topics) |
| DK265.9.A5 | Anarchists (Rus. Rev., 1917-21) |
| DK265.9.A6 | Politics (Rus. armed forces, 1917-21) |
| DK265.9.C62 | Cossacks (Rus. Rev., 1917-21) |
| DK265.9.E2 | Economic aspects (Rus. Rev., 1917-21) |
| DK265.9.F5 | Russian Revolution (1917-21: foreign particip.: gen.) |
| DK265.9.F52.A-Z | Foreign participation (Rus. Rev., 1917-21: by country) |
| DK265.9.K73 | Red Guard (Rus. Rev., 1917-21: Krasnaia Gvardiia) |
| DK265.9.S4 | Spies, secret service, etc. (Rus. Rev., 1917-21) |
| DK265.9.S6 | Soviets (Rus. Rev., 1917-21: councils) |
| DK265.9.W57 | Women (Rus. Rev., 1917-21) |
| DK266 | Soviet Union (1918-)    947.084 |
| DK266.A3 | Primary sources, documents (Rus.: 1918-) |
| DK266.A4-Z | Russia (1918-: gen.) |
| DK266.3 | Soviet Union (1918-: special inclu. espionage, sabotage) |
| DK266.5 | Soviet Union (1918-24: Lenin era)    947.0841 |
| DK267-273 | Soviet Union (1925-53: Stalin regime) |
| DK267 | Russia (1925-53: Stalin era: gen.)    947.0842 |
| DK267.3.1925-1953 | Pamphlets, minor works, addresses (Rus.: 1925-53) |
| DK268.A1 | Biography (Rus.: 1925-53: collective) |
| DK268.A2-Z | Biography (Rus.: 1925-53: inclu. memoirs: by name) |
| DK268.D9 | Dzerzhinsky, Feliks (Rus.: 1925-53 era) |
| DK268.L5 | Litvinov, Maksim M. (Rus.: 1925-53 era) |
| DK268.M64 | Molotov, Viacheslav M. (Rus.: 1925-53 era) |
| DK268.S75 | Stalin, Joseph (Rus.: works by) |
| DK268.S8 | Stalin, Joseph (Rus.: biogs.) |
| DK268.T75 | Trotsky, Leon (Rus.: 1925-53 era) |
| DK268.3 | Civilization, customs, social life (Rus.: 1925-53) |
| DK269 | Emigrés, Russian (1925-53) |
| DK269.5 | Propaganda, Russian (1925-53: internal) |
| DK270 | Soviet propaganda (1925-53: foreign: gen.) |
| DK272.A-Z | Propaganda, Soviet (1925-53: foreign: by country) |
| DK272.F8 | Propaganda, Soviet (1925-53: France) |
| DK272.G3 | Propaganda, Soviet (1925-53: Ger.) |
| DK272.G7 | Propaganda, Soviet (1925-53: G.B.) |
| DK272.J3 | Propaganda, Soviet (1925-53: Japan) |
| DK272.U6-7 | Propaganda, Soviet (1925-53: U.S.) |
| DK272.5 | Anti-Soviet propaganda (1925-53: gen.) |
| DK272.7.A-Z | Propaganda, Anti-Soviet (1925-53: by partic. country) |
| DK272.7.G3 | Propaganda, Anti-Soviet (1925-53: by Ger.: SEE ALSO DD255.R9) |
| DK272.7.J3 | Propaganda, Anti-Soviet (1925-53: by Japan) |
| DK273 | Soviet Union (1939-45: WWII period)    947.0842 |

| | |
|---|---|
| DK401-441+ | POLAND (SEE ALSO DK4010-4800 for newer titles from perhaps 1976 on)     943.8 |
| DK402 | Primary sources, documents (Pol.) |
| DK404 | Poland (gen. history, culture, etc.) |
| DK407 | Description & travel (Pol.: 1867-1945) |
| DK411 | Civilization, customs, social life (Pol.) |
| DK414.A3-Z | Poland (gen.: pubns. 1801+) |
| DK417 | Military history (Pol.: SEE ALSO DK4170+ for newer titles) |
| DK417.7 | Naval history (Pol.) |
| DK418 | Diplomacy & politics (Pol.) |
| DK418.5.A-Z | Foreign relns. (Pol.: by country) |
| DK418.5.F8 |    Foreign relns. (Pol.-Fr.) |
| DK418.5.G3 |    Foreign relns. (Pol.-Ger.) |
| DK418.5.G7 |    Foreign relns. (Pol.-G.B.) |
| DK418.5.R9 | Foreign relns. (Pol.-Rus.) |
| DK418.5.A-Z | Foreign relns. (Pol.: by country) |
| DK418.5.F8 | Foreign relns. (Pol.-Fr.) |
| DK418.5.G3 |    Foreign relns. (Pol.-Ger.) |
| DK418.5.G7 |    Foreign relns. (Pol.-G.B.) |
| DK418.5.R9 |    Foreign relns. (Pol.-Rus.) |
| DK434.9 | Poland (1795-1918)     943.803 |
| DK439 | Poland (1914-18: WWI)     943.803 |
| DK440 | Poland (1918-: Republic: inclu. wars of 1918-21)     943.804 |
| DK440.3 | Treaties (Pol., 1921: Riga) |
| DK440.5.A-Z | Biography (Pol.: 1918-: inclu. memoirs) |
| DK440.5.A1 | Biography (Pol.: 1918-: collective) |
| DK440.5.B4 |    Beck, Joseph (Pol.: 1918+ biog.) |
| DK440.5.P5 |    Pilsudski, Joseph (Pol.: 1918+ biog.) |
| DK440.5.S55 |    Sikorski, Wladyslaw (Pol.: 1918+ biog.) |
| DK441 | Poland (1939-45: WWII era)     943.8053 |
| DK443 | Poland (1945-) |
| DK445-465 | FINLAND (PREFER DL1002-1180+ for pubns. from around 1970 on)     948.97 |
| DK459 | Finland (20th c.: inclu. Revolution, 1917-18)     948.9703 |
| DK459.3 | Treaties (Fin.: 1918) |
| DK459.4 | Treaties (Fin.-Rus.: 1920) |
| DK459.45 | Finland (1939-)     948.97032 |
| DK459.5 | Russo-Finnish War (1939-40: SEE ALSO DL1095-1105)     947.0842, 948.97032 |
| DK461.A-Z | Biography (Fin.: 20th c.) |
| DK461.M32 | Mannerheim, Carl (Fin.: 20th c.) |
| DK501-973+ | Local history (Russia) |
| DK501 | Russia, Northern |
| DK502.3-505 | Baltic States |
| DK502.7 | Baltic States (gen.) |
| DK503 | Russia, Eastern & Estonia (SEE DK511.E4 for earlier pubns. on Estonia)     947.41 |
| DK503.73 | ESTONIA (1800-1918)     947.41 |
| DK503.74-746 |    Estonia (1918-40) |
| DK503.75-77 |    Estonia (1940+) |
| DK504 | LATVIA (SEE DK511.L15 for earlier pubns.)     947.43 |
| DK504.73 |    Latvia (1800-1918) |
| DK504.74-76 |    Latvia (1918-40) |
| DK504.77-79 | Latvia (1940+) |

```
DK505        LITHUANIA (SEE DK511.L2 for earlier pubns.)          947.5
DK505.73     Lithuania (1800-1918)
DK505.74-76    Lithuania (1918-40)
DK505.77-79    Lithuania (1940+)
DK507          White Russia (Western Russia)
DK508-508.9+   UKRAINE
DK508.54       Military history (Ukr.)
DK508.55     Cossacks (Ukr.)
DK508.554    Politics (Ukr.: gen.)
DK508.56     Diplomacy (Ukr.: gen.)
DK508.57       Foreign relns. (Ukr.: by country)
DK508.79-835   Ukraine (1917-44)
DK508.8        Ukraine (1917+: earlier pubns.)
DK508.812      Ukraine (1917-44: gen.)
DK508.833-835  Ukraine (1921-44)
DK508.9.A-Z    Local history (Ukraine: regions, oblasts, etc.)
DK508.9.C37    Carpathian Mts. (Uk.)
DK508.9.D64    Dnepropetrovsk (Uk.)
DK508.92-939   Kiev (Uk.)
DK508.95.A-Z   Local history (Ukraine: towns etc.)
DK508.95.I24   Yalta, Uk. (Jalta)
DK508.95.K54   Kiev, Uk. (Kyiv)
DK508.95.O33   Odessa, Uk.
DK508.95.S49   Sevastopol, Uk.
DK509        Russia, Southern (Black Sea, Caucasus, Armenia, etc.)
DK510        Russian S.F.S.R. (Russia)
DK510.7-72   Russian S.F.S.R. (1917-45)
DK511.A-Z      Local history (Eur. Russia, Poland: provinces, governments,
                   regions, etc.)
DK511.A5       Archangel (Rus.)
DK511.B2       Baku (Rus.)
DK511.C1-35    Caucasus area (Rus.)
DK511.C7       Crimea (Rus.)          947.717
DK511.D7       Don River Valley (Rus.)
DK511.E4-8     ESTONIA (SEE DK503 for later pubns.)          947.41
DK511.E6       Estonia (gen.)
DK511.G3-47    Georgia (Rus.: SEE DK670 for later pubns.)
DK511.L15-18   LATVIA (SEE DK504 for later pubns.)          947.43
DK511.L178        Latvia (1914-18: WWI)
DK511.L18         Latvia (1918-)
DK511.L195     Leningrad area (Rus.)
DK511.L2-28    LITHUANIA (SEE DK505 for later pubns.)     947.5
DK511.L26      Lithuania (1914-19)
DK511.L27      Lithuania (1919-)
DK511.M6       Moscow area (Rus.)
DK511.U7       Ural Mts. (Rus.)          947.87
DK511.V65      Volga River Valley (Rus.)
DK511.W5       White Russia (Belorussia)     947.65
DK541-579      Leningrad, U.S.S.R.     947.45
DK561          St. Petersburg, Rus. (gen.)
DK568          Petrograd, Rus. (1801-)
DK591-609      Moscow, Rus.     947.31
DK600          Social life, culture, customs (Moscow, Rus.)
DK601          Moscow, Rus. (to 1950)
```

| | |
|---|---|
| DK651.A-Z | Local history (Rus.: towns other than Moscow in Eur., Pol. areas) |
| DK651.K37 | Kiev, Rus. |
| DK651.M5 | Minsk, Rus. |
| DK651.O2 | Odessa, Rus. |
| DK651.R5 | Riga, Rus. |
| DK651.R7 | Rostov, Rus. |
| DK651.S45 | Sevastopol, Rus. |
| DK651.S65 | Smolensk, Rus. |
| DK651.S7 | Stalingrad, Rus.        947.4785 |
| DK651.T28 | Tallinn, Rus. (Reval) |
| DK651.W2 | Warsaw, Pol. |
| DK651.Y25 | Yalta, Rus. |
| DK670-679 | GEORGIA (Rus.: SEE DK511.G3 for earlier pubns.) |
| DK676.5-6 | Politics (Georgian S. S. R.: gen.) |
| DK677.4-6 | Georgian S. S. R. (1801-1921) |
| DK677.7-9+ | Georgian S. S. R. (1921+) |
| DK680-689 | ARMENIA (SEE ALSO DK509 for some gen. works, DS161-199 for earlier titles) |
| DK687+ | Armenian S. S. R. (1920+) |
| DK689 | Local history (Armenian S. S. R.) |
| DK690-699 | Azerbaijan S. S. R. |
| DK697.3-5 | Azerbaijan S. S. R. (1917+) |
| DK699.2-39 | Baku, Rus. |
| DK750-973+ | Russian Asia        957-958 |
| DK750 | Asia, Russian |
| DK751-781 | Siberia        957 |
| DK753 | Siberia (gen. hist., exploration, culture, etc.)        957 |
| DK755 | Description & travel (Siberia: 1801-1945) |
| DK761 | Siberia (gen.) |
| DK766 | Siberia (19th-20th c.)        957.08 |
| DK771.A-Z | Local history (Siberia: provinces, regions, etc.) |
| DK771.B3 | Lake Baikal (Sib.) |
| DK771.K2 | Kamchatka (Sib.) |
| DK771.S2 | Sakhalin (Siberia) |
| DK771.T8 | Transbaikalia (Sib.) |
| DK781.A-Z | Local history (Siberia: towns etc.) |
| DK781.V5 | Vladivostok, Rus. |
| DK845-973 | Asia, Soviet Central        958 |
| DK858 | Russian Central Asia (to 1920) |
| DK859 | Soviet Central Asia (1920+) |
| DK4010-4800 | POLAND (SEE ALSO DK401-441 for older titles prior to 1976-77) 943.8 |
| DK4040 | Poland (gen.) |
| DK4070 | Description & travel (Pol.: 1867-1944) |
| DK4110 | Social life, culture, customs (Pol.) |
| DK4120 | Races & ethnography (Pol.: gen.) |
| DK4121.5.A-Z | Races & ethnography (Pol.: by specific element) |
| DK4121.5.C9 | Czechs (in Pol.) |
| DK4121.5.G4 | Germans (in Pol.) |
| DK4121.5.T3 | Tatars (in Pol.) |
| DK4121.5.U4 | Ukrainians (in Pol.) |
| DK4121.5.W5 | White Russians (in Pol.) |
| DK4122 | Poles (in other lands) |
| DK4140 | Poland (gen.: pubn. dates 1801+) |

| | |
|---|---|
| DK4170-4178 | Military history (Pol.) |
| DK4170 | Polish military history (gen.: SEE ALSO DK417 for older works) |
| DK4173 | Military history (Pol.: 1795-1918) |
| DK4174 | Military history (Pol.: 1919-) |
| DK4177-4178 | Naval history (Pol.) |
| DK4178.5-4185 | Diplomacy & politics (Pol.) |
| DK4179 | Politics (Pol.) |
| DK4180 | Foreign relns. (Pol.: gen.) |
| DK4182 | Polish question |
| DK4185.A-Z | Foreign relns. (Pol.: with particular countries) |
| DK4185.F8 | Foreign relns. (Pol.-Fr.) |
| DK4185.G3 | Foreign relns. (Pol.-Ger.) |
| DK4185.R9 | Foreign relns. (Pol.-Rus.) |
| DK4380 | Poland (1864-1918)        943.803 |
| DK4382 | Poland (20th c.) |
| DK4390 | Poland (1914-18: WWI)      943.803 |
| DK4392 | Poland (1915-18: Austrian occupation) |
| DK4397 | Primary sources, documents (Pol.: 1918-45) |
| DK4397-4420 | Poland (1918-45)        943.804 |
| DK4400 | Poland (1918-45: gen.) |
| DK4402 | Politics & diplomacy (Pol.: 1918-45) |
| DK4402.5 | Foreign relns. (Pol.: 1918-45) |
| DK4403.5 | Poland (1918-26) |
| DK4404-4409 | Poland (1918-21: wars, inclu. Russo-Polish of 1919-20) |
| DK4405 | Russo-Polish War (1919-20: plus other Polish conflicts of the time) |
| DK4406 | Polish military ops. (1918-21, inclu. Russo-Polish conflict) |
| DK4406.5 | Personal accounts (Russo-Polish War, other Polish conflicts of 1918-21) |
| DK4407.3 | Treaties (Russo-Polish, other Polish conflicts: Riga: 1921) |
| DK4407.A-Z | Battles, campaigns, sieges (Russo-Polish, other Polish conflicts, 1918-21: by name) |
| DK4407.G3 | Galicia, Pol. (Polish wars, 1918-21) |
| DK4407.L9 | Lvov, Siege of (Polish wars, 1918-21) |
| DK4409.4 | Poland (1926: Coup) |
| DK4409.5 | Poland (1926-39) |
| DK4410-4420 | Poland (1939-45: WWII era)        943.8053 |
| DK4410 | Poland (1939-45: WWII era: gen., inclu. Ger. occup.) |
| DK4415 | Poland (1939-41: Russ. occup.) |
| DK4419 | Biography (Pol.: 1918-45: collec.) |
| DK4420.A-Z | Biography (Pol.: 1918-45: by name, inclu. memoirs) |
| DK4420.B4 | Beck, Josef (Pol.: 1918-45 era) |
| DK4420.P3 | Paderewski, Ignacy Jan (Pol.: 1918-45 era) |
| DK4420.P5 | Pilsudski, Jozef (Pol.: 1918-45 time) |
| DK4420.S5 | Sikorski, Wladyslaw (Pol.: 1918-45 period) |
| DK4600-4800 | Local history (Pol.) |
| DK4600.A-Z | Local history (Pol.: provinces) |
| DK4600.G34 | Galicia (Pol.) |
| DK4600.L63 | Lodz Voivodeship (Pol.) |
| DK4600.P67 | Pomerania (Pol.) |
| DK4600.P77 | Prussia, East (Pol.) |
| DK4600.S48 | Silesia Voivodeship (Pol.) |
| DK4600.V5 | Vistula River & Valley (Pol.: Wisla) |
| DK4610-4645 | Warsaw, Pol. |
| DK4630 | Warsaw, Pol. (gen.) |
| DK4633 | Warsaw, Pol. (1918-) |

| | | |
|---|---|---|
| DK4650-4685 | Danzig, Pol. (Gdansk) | |
| DK4670 | Gdansk, Pol. (Danzig: gen.) | |
| DK4673 | Danzig, Pol. (1919-45: time of free city) | |
| DK4700-4735 | Krakow, Pol. (Cracow) | |

| | | |
|---|---|---|
| DL | SCANDINAVIA, Northern Europe, Finland | |
| DL1-87+ | Europe, Northern (plus Scandinavia and Finland) | |
| DL10 | Description & travel (Scan., N. Eur., Fin.: 1901-50) | |
| DL52 | Military history (Scan., N. Eur., Fin.) | |
| DL53 | Naval history (Scan., N. Eur., Fin.) | |
| DL55 | Foreign relns. & politics (Scan., N. Eur., Fin.: gen.) | |
| DL83 | Northern Europe, Scandinavia, Finland (1901-45) | 948.08 |
| DL101-291+ | DENMARK | |
| DL103 | Primary sources, documents (Den.) | |
| DL109 | Denmark (gen.) 948.9 | |
| DL118 | Description & travel (Den.: 1901-50) | |
| DL154 | Military history (Den.) | |
| DL154.7 | Naval history (Den.: 19th-20th c.) | |
| DL159 | Diplomacy (Den.: gen.) | |
| DL159.5.A-Z | Foreign relns. (Den.-other lands) | |
| DL159.5.G3 | Foreign relns. (Den.-Ger.) | |
| DL159.5.G7 | Foreign relns. (Den.-G.B.) | |
| DL250 | Denmark (20th c.) 948.905 | |
| DL255-257 | Denmark (1912-47: time of Christian X) 948.9051 | |
| DL255 | Christian X (Den.: 1912-47 period: ALSO gen. histories of time) | |
| DL256 | Denmark (1914-18: WWI) | |
| DL256.5 | Denmark (1919+) | |
| DL257.A-Z | Biography (Den.: 1912-47) | |
| DL271.A-Z | Local history (Den.: counties, islands, regions) | |
| DL276 | Copenhagen, Den. | |
| DL291 | Local history (Den.: towns etc.) | |
| DL301-398+ | ICELAND 949.12 | |
| DL365 | Iceland (1801-1918) | |
| DL375 | Iceland (1918-) 949.1204 | |
| DL396-398 | Local history (Ice.) | |
| DL398.A-Z | Local history (Ice.: towns etc.) | |
| DL398.R5 | Reykjavik, Ice. | |
| DL401-596+ | NORWAY 948.1 | |
| DL403 | Primary sources, documents (Nor.) | |
| DL418 | Description & travel (Nor.) | |
| DL454 | Military history (Nor.) 355.009481 | |
| DL456 | Naval history (Nor.) | |
| DL458 | Diplomacy & politics (Nor.: gen.) | |
| DL459.A-Z | Foreign relns. (Nor.-other specific countries) 327.4810+ | |
| DL459.G3 | Foreign relns. (Nor.-Ger.) | |
| DL459.G7 | Foreign relns. (Nor.-G.B.) | |
| DL459.S8 | Foreign relns. (Nor.-Swe.) | |
| DL527 | Norway (20th c.) 948.104 | |
| DL529.A-Z | Biography (Nor.: 20th c.) | |
| DL529.A1 | Biography (Nor.: 20th c.: collective) | |
| DL529.Q5 | Quisling, Vidkun (Nor.: 20th c.) | |
| DL530-533 | Norway (1905-57: Haakon VII era) 948.1041-1045 | |
| DL530 | Haakon VII (Nor.: King, 1905-57) | |
| DL531 | Norway (1914-18) | |
| DL532 | Norway (1939-45) | |

| | | |
|---|---|---|
| DL576.A-Z | Local history (Nor.: counties, regions, etc.) | |
| DL576.B4 | Bergen (Nor.) | |
| DL576.S8 | Stavanger (Nor.) | |
| DL576.T4 | Telemark (Nor.) | |
| DL576.T9 | Trondheim (Nor.) | |
| DL581 | Oslo, Nor. (Christiana) | 948.2 |
| DL596.A-Z | Local history (Nor.: towns, villages, etc.) | |
| DL596.B4 | Bergen, Nor. | |
| DL596.M7 | Moss, Nor. | |
| DL596.S8 | Stavanger, Nor. | |
| DL596.T8 | Trondheim, Nor. | |
| DL596.V6 | Voss, Nor. | |
| DL601-991+ | SWEDEN | 948.5 |
| DL618 | Description & travel (Swe.: 1901-50) | |
| DL654 | Military history (Swe.) | |
| DL656 | Naval history (Swe.) | |
| DL658-659 | Diplomacy & politics (Swe.) | |
| DL658.A2 | Primary sources, documents (Swe.) | |
| DL658.A3-Z | Politics & diplomacy (Swe.: gen.) | 320.9485, 327.485 |
| DL658.8 | Foreign relns. (Swe.: 1818-20th c.) | |
| DL659.A-Z | Foreign relns. (Swe.-other lands: by name) | 327.485+ |
| DL659.F5 | Foreign relns. (Swe.-Fin.) | |
| DL659.G3 | Foreign relns. (Swe.-Ger.) | |
| DL659.G7 | Foreign relns. (Swe.-G.B.) | |
| DL659.N8 | Foreign relns. (Swe.-Nor.) | |
| DL659.R9 | Foreign relns. (Swe.-Rus.) | |
| DL659.S65 | Foreign relns. (Swe.-Sov. Un.) | |
| DL659.U6-7 | Foreign relns. (Swe.-U.S.) | |
| DL860 | Sweden (20th c.) | 948.505 |
| DL867 | Gustav V (Swe.: King, 1907-50) | |
| DL867-870 | Sweden (1907-50: Gustav V) | |
| DL867.5 | Diplomacy & politics (Swe.: 1907-50) | 948.5051-2 |
| DL868 | Sweden (1914-18: WWI era) | |
| DL868.5 | Sweden (1919-) | |
| DL869 | Biography (Swe.: 1907-50: collec.) | |
| DL870.A-Z | Biography (Swe.: 1907-50: by name) | |
| DL870.B47 | Bernadotte af Wisborg, Folke, greve (Swe.: 1907-50 period) | |
| DL971-991 | Local history (Swe.) | |
| DL976 | Stockholm, Swe. | |
| DL1002-1180+ | FINLAND (PREFER this but ALSO SEE DK445-465 for pre-1970 pubns. in some libs.) | 948.97 |
| DL1005 | Primary sources, documents (Fin.) | |
| DL1015.2 | Description & travel (Fin.: 1901-44) | |
| DL1015.3 | Description & travel (Fin.: 1945-80) | |
| DL1032 | Finland (gen.) | 948.97 |
| DL1036-1037 | Military history (Fin.) | 355.0094897 |
| DL1040-1042 | Naval history (Fin.) | |
| DL1046 | Diplomacy (Fin.: gen.) | 327.4897 |
| DL1048.A-Z | Foreign relns. (Fin. & other partic. lands) | |
| DL1048.G3 | Foreign relns. (Fin.-Ger.) | |
| DL1048.R9 | Foreign relns. (Fin.-Rus.) | |
| DL1048.S65 | Foreign relns. (Fin.-Sov. Un.) | |

| DL1065 | Finland (1809-1917: Russian control) | 948.9702 |

DL1065      Finland (1809-1917: Russian control)    948.9702
DL1066      Primary sources, documents (Fin.: 20th c.)
DL1066.5    Finland (20th c.)              948.9703
DL1084          Finland (1918-39)              948.97031
DL1088-1088.5   Biography (Fin.: 1918-39)
DL1090-1105+    Finland (1939-45)              948.97032
DL1090          Primary sources, documents (Fin.: 1939-45)
DL1092          Finland (1939-45: gen.)
DL1093-1093.5   Biography (Fin.: 1939-45)
DL1095-1105+    Russo-Finnish War (1939-40: might ALSO try DK459.5)
                                   948.97032, 947.0842
DL1095      Associations, periodicals, conferences (Russo-Fin. War, 1939-40)
DL1096      Primary sources, documents (Russo-Fin. War, 1939-40)
DL1097      Russo-Finnish War (1939-40: gen.)
DL1099          Military ops. (Russo-Fin. War, 1939-40)
DL1102          Personal accounts (Russo-Fin. War, 1939-40: collective)
DL1102.5        Personal accounts (Russo-Fin. War, 1939-40: individual)
DL1103.A-Z      Battles & local history (Russo-Fin. War, 1939-40)
DL1105.A-Z      Russo-Finnish War (1939-40: special topics)
DL1125      Finland (1945-)
DL1170.A-Z  Local history (Fin.: regions, provinces, etc.)
DL1175      Helsinki, Fin.                 948.971
DL1175.42       Helsinki, Fin. (gen.)
DL1175.48       Helsinki, Fin. (1917-)
DL1180.A-Z      Local history (Fin.: towns except Helsinki)

DP          Iberian Peninsula       946
DP1-402+    SPAIN       946
DP42        Description & travel (Sp.: 1901-50)
DP78.5      Military history (Sp.: 1808-20th c.)        355.00946
DP83-86     Diplomacy & politics (Sp.)
DP83        Primary sources, documents (Sp.: dipl. & polit. hist.)
DP84        Politics & diplomacy (Sp.)
DP85.8      Diplomacy (Sp.: 1814-20th c.)
DP86.A-Z    Foreign relns. (Sp.: with partic. countries)    327.460+
DP86.G3         Foreign relns. (Sp.-Ger.)        327.46043
DP86.I8         Foreign relns. (Sp.-It.)
DP86.R9         Foreign relns. (Sp.-Rus.)        327.46047
DP86.S65        Foreign relns. (Sp.-Sov. Un.)
DP233       Spain (1886-20th c.: gen.)        946.08
DP234-247   Spain (1886-1931: period of Alfonso XIII)
DP235-236   Biography (Sp.: 1886-1931)
DP238       Alfonso XIII (Sp.: King, 1886-1931)
DP240       Spain (1886-1931: gen.)
DP246       Spain (1914-18: WWI)
DP247       Spain (1918-31)        946.08
DP250-269   Spain (1931-39: 2d Repub.)              946.081
DP251       Primary sources, documents (Sp.: 1931-39)
DP254           Second Republic (Sp.: 1931-39: gen.)
DP257-258       Diplomacy & politics (Sp.: 1931-39)
DP257           Politics & diplomacy (Sp.: 1931-39: gen.)
DP258.A-Z   Foreign relns. (Sp.-specific lands: 1931-39)
DP258.F8    Foreign relns. (Sp.-Fr.: 1931-39)
DP258.G3    Foreign relns. (Sp.-Ger.: 1931-39)
DP258.I8        Foreign relns. (Sp.-It.: 1931-39)

| DP258.P8 | Foreign relns. (Sp.-Port.: 1931-39) | |
|---|---|---|
| DP258.R9 | Foreign relns. (Sp.-Rus.: 1931-39) | |
| DP258.S65 | Foreign relns. (Sp.-Sov. Un.: 1931-39) | |
| DP258.U6-7 | Foreign relns. (Sp.-U.S.: 1931-39) | |
| DP260 | Biography (Sp.: 1931-39: collective) | |
| DP264.A-Z | Biography (Sp.: 1931-39: by name: inclu. memoirs) | |
| DP264.F7 | Franco Bahamonde, Francisco (Sp.: 1931-39 period) | |
| DP267 | Spain (1931-36: Alcalá Zamora y Torres era) | |
| DP268 | Spain (1936-39: Azaña period) | |
| DP269-269.9+ | Spain (1936-39: Civil War) | 946.081 |
| DP269 | Spanish Civil War (1936-39) | 946.081 |
| DP269.A2-55 | Primary sources, documents (Sp.: 1936-39: Civil War) | |
| DP269.A56-Z | Military operations (Sp. Civil War, 1936-39: gen. titles on the war) | |
| DP269.15 | Pictorials, satires, etc. (Sp. Civil War, 1936-39) | |
| DP269.17 | Pamphlets, minor works, sermons (Sp. Civil War, 1936-39) | |
| DP269.2.A-Z | Battles, campaigns, sieges (Sp. Civil War, 1936-39: by name) | |
| DP269.2.A4 | Toledo, Siege of (Sp. Civil War: 1936: Alcazar) | |
| DP269.2.G8 | Guadalajara, Battle of (Sp. Civil War: 1937) | |
| DP269.23 | Spanish military ops. (Civil War, 1936-39: Loyalists) | |
| DP269.25 | Spanish military ops. (Civil War, 1936-39: Insurgents) | |
| DP269.27.A-Z | Local history (Sp. Civil War, 1936-39: by place name) | |
| DP269.27.C3 | Catalonia (Sp. Civil War, 1936-39) | |
| DP269.27.M3 | Madrid, Sp. (Civil War, 1936-39) | |
| DP269.3-35 | Naval ops. (Sp. Civil War, 1936-39) | |
| DP269.4 | Aerial ops. (Sp. Civil War, 1936-39) | |
| DP269.45 | Spanish Civil War (1936-39: foreign particip.: gen.) | |
| DP269.47.A-Z | Foreign participation (Sp. Civil War, 1936-39: by country) | |
| DP269.47.G3 | Foreign participation (Sp. Civil War, 1936-39: Ger.) | |
| DP269.47.I8 | Foreign participation (Sp. Civil War, 1936-39: It.) | |
| DP269.47.R8-9 | Foreign participation (Sp. Civil War, 1936-39: Rus.) | |
| DP269.47.U6-7 | Foreign participation (Sp. Civil War, 1936-39: U.S.) | |
| DP269.5-55 | Atrocities (Sp. Civil War, 1936-39) | |
| DP269.63-65 | Prisons & prisoners (Sp. Civil War, 1936-39) | |
| DP269.67 | Concentration camps (Sp. Civil War, 1936-39: outside Sp.) | |
| DP269.8.A-Z | Spanish Civil War (1936-39: special topics) | |
| DP269.8.E2 | Economic matters (Sp. Civil War, 1936-39) | |
| DP269.8.R4 | Religion (Sp. Civil War, 1936-39) | |
| DP269.8.S4 | Espionage, spies (Sp. Civil War, 1936-39) | |
| DP269.9 | Personal accounts (Sp. Civil War, 1936-39) | |
| DP270 | Spain (1939-) | 946.0824 |
| DP271.A-Z | Biography (Sp.: 1939-) | |
| DP302.A-Z | Local history (Sp.: provinces, regions, etc.) | |
| DP302.A41-55 | Andalusia (Sp.) | |
| DP302.C36-51 | Canary Islands | 964.9 |
| DP302.C57-69 | Catalonia (Sp.) | |
| DP302.G31-41 | GIBRALTAR | |
| DP302.G51-65 | Granada (Sp.) | |
| DP302.T51 | Toledo (Sp.) | |
| DP302.V11-25 | Valencia (Sp.) | |
| DP350-374 | Madrid, Sp. | 946.41 |
| DP361 | Madrid, Sp. (1801-1950) | |
| DP402.A-Z | Local history (Sp.: towns except Madrid) | |
| DP402.B2-3 | Barcelona, Sp. | |
| DP402.C2-3 | Cadiz, Sp. | |
| DP402.S3-32 | Saragossa, Sp. | |

```
DP402.S36-48    Seville, Sp.
DP402.T7-74       Toledo, Sp.
DP402.V15-25      Valencia, Sp.
DP501-900+      PORTUGAL       946.9
DP525           Description & travel (Port.: 1816-1950)
DP547           Military history (Port.)
DP551           Naval history (Port.)
DP555-557       Diplomacy & politics (Port.)        320.9469, 327.469+
DP555           Primary sources, documents (Port.: dipl. & polit. hist.)
DP556           Politics & diplomacy (Port.: gen.)
DP557.A-Z       Foreign relns. (Port.-other countries: by name)
DP557.G3          Foreign relns. (Port.-Ger.)
DP557.G7          Foreign relns. (Port.-G.B.)
DP557.S7          Foreign relns. (Port.-Sp.)
DP557.U6-7        Foreign relns. (Port.-U.S.)
DP670           Primary sources, documents (Port.: 20th c.)
DP672           Portugal (20th c.: gen.)       946.904
DP675           Portugal (1910-: Republic)     946.904
DP676.A-Z       Biography (Port.: 1910-)
DP677           Portugal (1914-18: WWI)        946.9041
DP678           Portugal (1919: Revolution)
DP680           Portugal (1919-)       946.9041-9042
DP702.A-Z       Local history (Port.: regions, provinces, areas)
DP702.A81-99    AZORES               946.99
DP702.A9          Azores (19th & 20th c.)     946.99
DP702.M11-23    Madeira Is.
DP752-776       Lisbon, Port.              946.942
DP764           Lisbon, Port. (1840-1950)
DP802.A-Z       Colonies, Portuguese (SEE ALSO D-F for indiv. places & JV4200-4299
                     for collective)

DQ              SWITZERLAND       949.4
DQ3             Primary sources, documents (Swit.)
DQ24            Description & travel (Swit.: 1901-50)
DQ36            Civilization, customs, social life (Swit.)
DQ59               Military history (Swit.)
DQ68-76           Diplomacy & politics (Swit.)        320.9494, 327.4940+
DQ68              Primary sources, documents (Swit.)
DQ69            Politics & diplomacy (Swit.: gen.)
DQ75            Diplomacy & politics (Swit.: 1798-20th c.)
DQ76.A-Z        Foreign relns. (Swit.-specific countries)       327.4940+
DQ76.F8         Foreign relns. (Swit.-Fr.)
DQ76.G3           Foreign relns. (Swit.-Ger.)       327.494043
DQ76.G7           Foreign relns. (Swit.-G.B.)
DQ76.I8           Foreign relns. (Swit.-It.)        327.494045
DQ76.R9         Foreign relns. (Swit.-Rus.)
DQ76.U6-7       Foreign relns. (Swit.-U.S.)       327.494073
DQ201           Switzerland (20th c.)       949.407
DQ206-207       Biography (Swit.: 20th c.)
DQ301-800       Local history (Swit.: cantons, cantonal capitals)
DQ401-420         Bern, Swit.       949.45
DQ441-460         Geneva, Swit.     949.45
DQ501-520         Lucerne, Swit.    949.45
DQ781-800         Zurich, Swit.     949.45
```

| | | |
|---|---|---|
| DQ820-829 | ALPS | 949.47 |
| DQ841.A-Z | Local history (Swit.: lakes, peaks, regions other than those in DQ820+ Alps #s) DQ841.L8 Lucerne, Lake (Swit.) | |
| DQ851.A-Z | Local history (Swit.: towns except cantonal capitals in DQ301-800) | |

| | | |
|---|---|---|
| DR | EASTERN EUROPE & Balkan Peninsula (SEE DJK for gen. bks. on E. Eur. after about 1977-78) 949.6-8 | |
| DR15 | Description & travel (E. Eur. & Balkan Penin.: 1901-50) | |
| DR45 | BALKAN PENINSULA & Eastern Europe (1901-: gen.) | |
| DR46 | Balkan War (1912-13) 949.6 | |
| DR47 | Balkan Peninsula (1913-19) | |
| DR48 | Balkan Peninsula (1919-45) | |
| DR51-98 | BULGARIA 949.77 | |
| DR52 | Primary sources, documents (Bulg.) | |
| DR60 | Description & travel (Bulg.: 1879-1950) | |
| DR70 | Military history (Bulg.) | |
| DR72 | Diplomacy & politics (Bulg.) | |
| DR73.A-Z | Foreign relns. (Bulg.-specific countries) | |
| DR73.G3 | Foreign relns. (Bulg.-Ger.) 327.4977043 | |
| DR73.R9 | Foreign relns. (Bulg.-Rus.) | |
| DR85 | Bulgaria (1879-1943) 949.7702 | |
| DR85.5.A-Z | Biography (Bulg.: 1879-1943: inclu. memoirs) | |
| DR87.7 | Bulgaria (1912-13: Balkan War period) | |
| DR87.8 | Bulgaria (1914-18: WWI) | |
| DR89 | Bulgaria (1918-43: Boris III era) | |
| DR90 | Bulgaria (1943-: inclu. regency of Simeon II, 1943-46) | |
| DR95-98 | Local history (Bulg.) | |
| DR97 | Sofia, Bulg. | |
| DR101-196+ | MONTENEGRO 949.76 | |
| DR109 | Description & travel (Montenegro: 1860-1950) | |
| DR117 | Montenegro (gen.) | |
| DR158 | Montenegro (1914-18: WWI) | |
| DR159 | Montenegro (1918-: part of Yug.) | |
| DR201-296 | RUMANIA 949.8 | |
| DR203 | Primary sources, documents (Rum.) | |
| DR209 | Description & travel (Rum.: 1866-1950) | |
| DR219 | Military history (Rum.) | |
| DR225 | Naval history (Rum.) | |
| DR226 | Diplomacy & politics (Rum.) | |
| DR229.A-Z | Foreign relns. (Rum. & partic. countries) | |
| DR229.G3 | Foreign relns. (Rum.-Ger.) 327.498043 | |
| DR229.R9 | Foreign relns. (Rum.-Rus.) | |
| DR250-266 | Rumania (1866-1944) | |
| DR250 | Rumania (1866-1944: gen.) | |
| DR258 | Rumania (1912-13: Balkan War era) | |
| DR260-263 | Rumania (1914-27: Ferdinand) 949.802 | |
| DR260 | Primary sources, documents (Rum.: 1914-27) | |
| DR261 | Ferdinand (Rum.: King, 1914-27: ALSO works on era) | |
| DR262.A-Z | Biography (Rum.: 1914-27) | |
| DR263 | Rumania (1914-18: WWI) | |
| DR264-266 | Rumania (1918-44) 949.802 | |
| DR265 | Michael (Rum.: regent period, 1927-3; King, 1940-47) | |
| DR266 | Carol II (Rum.: King, 1930-40) | |
| DR267 | Romania (1944-) | |

| | | |
|---|---|---|
| DR281-296 | Local history (Rum.) | |
| DR286 | Bucharest, Rum. | 949.82 |
| DR301-396 | YUGOSLAVIA (Serbia: SEE ALSO DR1202+ for later pubns.) | 949.7-71 |
| DR309 | Description & travel (Yug.: 1860-1944) | |
| DR317 | Yugoslavia (gen.) | |
| DR319 | Military history (Yug.) | |
| DR326 | Diplomacy & politics (Yug.) | |
| DR327.A-Z | Foreign relns. (Yug.-specific countries) | |
| DR357 | Yugoslavia (20th c.) | 949.702, .7102 |
| DR359.A-Z | Biography (Yug.: 20th c.) | |
| DR359.A2 | Biography (Yug.: 20th c.: collective) | |
| DR359.M5 | Mihailovi´c, Draza (Yug.: 20th c.) | |
| DR359.T5 | Tito, Josip Broz (Yug.: 20th c.) | |
| DR360-363 | Yugoslavia (1903-21: Peter I) | 949.701-702 |
| DR360 | Peter I (Yug.: King, 1903-21: ALSO covers era) | |
| DR363 | Yugoslavia (1914-18: WWI) | |
| DR364-369 | Yugoslavia (1918-45: inclu. Croatia, Serbia, Slovenia) | 949.7021- |
| | | 7022, 949.7102 (Serbia) |
| DR364 | Primary sources, documents (Yug.: 1918-45) | |
| DR366 | Yugoslavia (1918-45: gen.) | |
| DR367.A-Z | Diplomacy & politics (Yug.: 1918-45) | |
| DR367.A1 | Politics & diplomacy (Yug.: 1918-45: gen.) | |
| DR367.G3 | Foreign relns. (Yug.-Ger.: 1918-45) | |
| DR367.G7 | Foreign relns. (Yug.-G.B.: 1918-45) | |
| DR367.I8 | Foreign relns. (Yug.-It.: 1918-45) | |
| DR367.R9 | Foreign relns. (Yug.-Rus.: 1918-45) | |
| DR367.U6-7 | Foreign relns. (Yug.-U.S.: 1918-45) | |
| DR368 | Yugoslavia (1921-34: Alexander) | |
| DR369 | Yugoslavia (1934-45: Peter II) | 949.7022 |
| DR370 | Yugoslavia (1945-) | |
| DR381-396 | Local history (Yug.) | |
| DR381.A-Z | Local history (Yug.: provinces, regions, etc.) | |
| DR386 | Belgrade, Yug. | |
| DR401-741 | TURKEY & Albania (primarily Tur.) | |
| DR403 | Primary sources, documents (Tur.) | |
| DR428 | Description & travel (Tur.: 1901-50) | |
| DR448 | Military history (Tur.) | 355.009561 |
| DR451 | Naval history (Tur.) | |
| DR476 | Politics & diplomacy (Tur.: 1876-1918: inclu. Panislamism) | |
| DR477 | Diplomacy & politics (Tur.: 1918-) | 327.5610+, 320.9561 |
| DR479.A-Z | Foreign relns. (Tur.-particular countries) | |
| DR479.G3 | Foreign relns. (Tur.-Ger.) | |
| DR479.G7 | Foreign relns. (Tur.-G.B.) | |
| DR479.R9 | Foreign relns. (Tur.-Rus.) | |
| DR577 | Turkey (20th c.) | 956.102 |
| DR588 | Turkey (1914-18: WWI era) | |
| DR589 | Turkey (1918-22: Mohammed VI) | |
| DR590 | Turkey (1923-60: Republic) | 956.1024 |
| DR592.A-Z | Biography (Tur.: 1909-: inclu. memoirs) | |
| DR592.K4 | Kemal, Mustafa (Tur.: 'Atatürk': 1909- era) | |
| DR701.A-Z | Local history (Tur.: Eur. regions: by name) | |
| DR701.A5 | Aegean Sea | |
| DR701.D2 | Dardanelles (Tur.) | |
| DR701.G3 | Gallipoli (Tur.) | |

| | | |
|---|---|---|
| DR701.S49-86 | ALBANIA (Scutari: SEE ALSO DR941-979 for later titles) | 949.65 |
| DR701.S5 | Scutari (Albania: gen.) | |
| DR701.S6 | Albania (1914-17: Kingdom) | 949.6502 |
| DR701.S7 | Albania (1917-25) | 949.6502 |
| DR701.S8 | Albania (1925-39: Zog I) | 949.6502 |
| DR701.S85 | Albania (1939-43: Ital. rule) | 949.6502 |
| DR701.S86 | Albania (1946-: Republic) | |
| DR716-739 | Istanbul, Tur. (Constantinople) | 956.3 |
| DR941-979+ | ALBANIA (SEE ALSO DR701.S49-86 for earlier works) | 949.65 |
| DR941 | Albania (gen.) | |
| DR970-975 | Albania (1912-44) | |
| DR971 | Albania (1912-44: gen.) | |
| DR972 | Albania (1912-18: SEE ALSO DR46+ for Balkan War etc.) | |
| DR974 | Albania (1925-39) | 949.6501-6502 |
| DR975 | Albania (1939-44) | |
| DR977 | Albania (1944-) | 949.6502-6503 |
| DR1214-1307+ | YUGOSLAVIA (SEE ALSO DR301+ for earlier pubns.) | 949.7 |
| DR1214 | Yugoslavia (gen., descrip., culture, hist.) | 949.7 |
| DR1221 | Description & travel (Yug.: 1901-44) | 914.971+ |
| DR1245-1246 | Yugoslavia (gen. hist.) | 949.7 |
| DR1251 | Military history (Yug.: gen.) | |
| DR1257-1258 | Foreign relns. (Yug.: gen.) | |
| DR1280 | Yugoslavia (1914-18: WWI era: SEE ALSO DR301+ for earlier pubns.) | 949.7, .701 |
| DR1288-1298 | Yugoslavia (1918-45) | 949.702 |
| DR1288 | Primary sources, documents (Yug.) | |
| DR1289 | Yugoslavia (1918-45: gen.) | 949.702-7022 |
| DR1291 | Politics & diplomacy (Yug.: 1918-45) | |
| DR1292 | Foreign relns. (Yug.: 1918-45) | |
| DR1293-1294 | Biography (Yug.: 1918-45) | |
| DR1294.A-Z | Biography (Yug.: 1918-45: by name, inclu. memoirs) | |
| DR1294.M54 | Mihailovic, Draza (Yug.: 1918-45 era) | |
| DR1295 | Yugoslavia (1918-21: reign of Peter I) | |
| DR1296 | Yugoslavia (1921-34: Alexander I) | |
| DR1297-1298 | Yugoslavia (1934-45: time of Peter II) | |
| DR1297 | Peter II (Yug.: monarch, 1934-45) | |
| DR1298 | Yugoslavia (1941-45: Axis occup.) | 949.7022 |
| DR1300-1305 | Biography (Yug.: 1934-45+) | |
| DR1350.A-Z | Local history (Yug.: regions not limited to partic. sections or old republics) | |
| DR1350.A35 | Adriatic coast (Yug.) | |
| DR1350.D35 | Danube River Valley (Yug.) | |
| DR1350.D55 | Dinaric Alps (Yug.) | |
| DR1352-2285+ | Local history (Yug.: sections & old republics: Slovenia, Bosnia, Montenegro, etc.) | |
| DR1352-1485+ | SLOVENIA | 949.73 |
| DR1370, 1376 | Slovenia (gen.) | |
| DR1434 | Slovenia (1914-18: WWI) | |
| DR1435-1443 | Slovenia (1918-45) | |
| DR1436 | Slovenia (1918-45: gen.) | |
| DR1443 | Slovenia (1941-45: occupation) | |

| | | |
|---|---|---|
| DR1502-1645 | CROATIA | 949.72 |
| DR1510, 1535 | Croatia (gen.) | |
| DR1582 | Croatia (1914-18: WWI) | |
| DR1583-1591 | Croatia (1918-45) | |
| DR1584 | Croatia (1918-45: gen.) | |
| DR1591 | Croatia (1941-45: WWII) | |
| DR1620-1630 | Dalmatia (Yug.: local Croatia) | 949.72 |
| DR1620-1636+ | Local history (Croatia) | |
| DR1633-1636 | Slavonia (Yug.: local Croatia) | 949.72 |
| DR1652-1785 | BOSNIA & Hercegovina (Herzegovina: SEE ALSO DR357 etc.) | |
| | | 949.742 |
| DR1660, 1685 | HERZEGOVINA (Hercegovina) & Bosnia (gen.) | |
| DR1732 | Bosnia & Hercegovina (1914-18: WWI) | |
| DR1733-1741 | Bosnia & Hercegovina (1918-45) | |
| DR1734 | Hercegovina & Bosnia (1918-45: gen.) | |
| DR1741 | Bosnia & Hercegovina (1941-45: Axis occup.) | |
| DR1801-1928 | Montenegro (SEE ALSO DR357+, DR1214) | 949.745 |
| DR1810, 1835 | Montenegro (gen.) | |
| DR1878-1883 | Montenegro (1878-1918: Nicholas I) | |
| DR1883 | Montenegro (1912-18: Balkan wars & WWI) | |
| DR1884-1893 | Montenegro (1918-45) | |
| DR1885 | Montenegro (1918-45: gen.) | |
| DR1887 | Politics & diplomacy (Montenegro: 1918-45) | |
| DR1890-1891 | Biography (Montenegro: 1918-45) | |
| DR1893 | Montenegro (1941-45) | |
| DR1932-2125+ | SERBIA (SEE ALSO DR301+ & DR1202 areas) | 949.71-71022 |
| DR1940 | Serbia (gen., descrip., culture, history) | |
| DR1965 | Serbia (gen. histories) | |
| DR1970 | Military history (Serbia) | |
| DR1972 | Politics (Serbia: gen.) | |
| DR1975 | Diplomacy & politics (Serbia: gen.) | |
| DR1976.A-Z | Foreign relns. (Serbia-other specific places) | |
| DR2030-2032 | Serbia (1903-18: Peter I Karadordevic) | |
| DR2030 | Peter I Karadordevic (Serbia: ruler, 1903-18: ALSO gen. works on period) | |
| DR2031 | Biography (Serbia: 1903-18) | |
| DR2032 | Serbia (1914-18: WWI) | |
| DR2033-2040 | Serbia (1918-45: part of Yug.) | |
| DR2033 | Primary sources, documents (Serbia: 1918-45) | |
| DR2034 | Serbia (1918-45: gen.) | |
| DR2035 | Civilization, customs, social life (Serbia: 1918-45) | |
| DR2036 | Politics (Serbia: 1918-45) | |
| DR2038 | Biography (Serbia: 1918-45) | |
| DR2040 | Serbia (1941-45: WWII era) | |
| DR2075-2125 | Local history (Serbia) | |
| DR2106-2124 | Belgrade, Serbia (Yug.) | |
| DR2152-2285+ | MACEDONIA | 949.76 |
| DR2160, 2185 | Macedonia (gen., descrip., culture, hist.) | |
| DR2230 | Macedonia (1912-45) | |
| DR2237 | Macedonia (1912-19) | |
| DR2240 | Macedonia (1919-45) | |
| DR2242 | Macedonia (1941-45: WWII) | |

```
DS            ASIA        950-959
DS9           Description & travel (Asia: 1901-50)      915.044
DS19-23.1     Mongols (SEE ALSO DS793.M7 for Mongolia)
DS31          Dictionaries, chronologies, etc. (Asia)
DS33.3        Politics & diplomacy (Asia: gen.)      320.95, 327.5+
DS33.4.A-Z    Foreign relns. (Asia-particular other areas or countries)
DS35          Asia (20th c.)        950.4

DS41-329      MIDDLE EAST & Southwestern Asia        953, 955, 956
DS49          Description & travel (Mid. East, SW. Asia: 1901-50)      915.6044
DS52-53       Aegean islands        949.9
DS54          Cyprus        956.45
DS62          SOUTHWESTERN ASIA & Middle East (gen. histories)
DS62.4        NEAR EAST & Southwestern Asia (modern)
DS63          Politics & diplomacy (Middle East, SW. Asia)      320.956, 327.56+
DS63.2.A-Z    Foreign relns. (Mid. East, SW. Asia: by specific country)      327.560+
DS67-79       IRAQ        956.7
DS70.95       Diplomacy & politics (Iraq: gen.)
DS70.96.A-Z   Foreign relns. (Iraq-other specific places)
DS70.96.G3    Foreign relns. (Iraq-Ger.)
DS70.96.G7    Foreign relns. (Iraq-G.B.)
DS77          Iraq (1517-1918: Turkish period)      956.703
DS79          Iraq (1919-)        956.704
DS79.5        Iraq (1921-33: Faisal I)
DS79.52       Iraq (1933-39: Ghazi I)
DS79.53       Iraq (1939-58: Faisal II)      956.7042
DS79.8.A-Z    Biography (Iraq: 1919-: by name)
DS80-90       LEBANON        956.92
DS85          Lebanon (1861-1918: close of Turkish era)
DS86          Lebanon (1919-)        956.92034+
DS92-99       SYRIA        956.91
DS95          Syria (gen.)
DS95.5        Diplomacy & politics (Syria: gen.)
DS95.6.A-Z    Foreign relns. (Syria-other countries)      327.56910+
DS95.6.F8     Foreign relns. (Syria-Fr.)
DS95.6.G3     Foreign relns. (Syria-Ger.)
DS95.6.G7     Foreign relns. (Syria-G.B.)
DS97.5        Syria (1517-1918: Turkish period)      956.9103
DS98          Syria (1918-45: French mandate)      956.9104-91041
DS101-151     PALESTINE, Israel, & the Jews      956.94, 909.04924
DS102         Primary sources, documents (Palestine & the Jews)
DS107.3       Description & travel (Palestine: 1901-50)
DS109         Jerusalem, Pal.
DS109.93      Jerusalem, Pal. (1917-)
DS110.A-Z     Local history (Palestine: regions, towns, etc.)
DS110.J6      Jordan River (Pal.)
DS112-113     Civilization, customs, social life (Palestine & the Jews)
DS114         Dictionaries, chronologies, etc. (Palestine, the Jews)
DS117         Jews, Palestine, & Israel (gen. histories)
DS119-119.8   Politics & diplomacy (Palestine, Jews)
```

```
DS123          Israel (70 A.D.+)
DS125          Palestine (19th-20th c.)              956.9403-9404
DS125.3.A-Z       Biography (Palestine: 19th-20th c.)
DS125.3.A2        Biography (Palestine: 19th-20th c.: collective)
DS125.3.B37       Ben-Gurion, David (Palestine: 19th-20th c.)
DS125.3.W45       Weizmann, Chaim (Palestine: 19th-20th c.)
DS125.5           Palestine (1914-18: WWI)              956.9403-9404
DS126          Palestine (1919-48: Brit. control)       956.9404
DS126.3        Israel & the Jews (1939-45: WWII era: PREFER D810.J4 to cover
                             titles on ethnic group)
DS133-151      Jews (outside Palestine)
DS134          Jews (outside Israel: gen.)       909.04924
DS135.A-Z      Jews (by country or area)  Usually 004924 after Dewey place #s
DS135.E5-6        Jews (Eng. and G.B.)
DS135.E8-9        Jews (Eur.)        940.04924 (single '0' after decimal in this case)
DS135.F8-9        Jews (Fr.)         944.004924
DS135.G3-5        Jews (Ger.)        943.004924
DS135.G3.A5-Z    Jews (Ger.: gen.)
DS135.G33         Jews (Ger.: 19th-20th c.)
DS135.I8-9        Jews (It.)         945.004924
DS135.R9-95       Jews (Rus.)        947.004924
DS135.S8          Jews (S. Am.: PREFER E #s in most cases)
DS135.U6-7        Jews (U.S: PREFER E184.J5 in most cases)       973.004924
DS140-140.5       Jews (outside Israel: economic, political, social conditions)
DS141          Jewish question
DS143          Jews, Modern
DS145             Anti-Semitism
DS145.P49-7       Protocols of the Wise Men of Zion (WWI: anti-Semitism)
DS149-151         Zionism, Restoration, Judenstaat
DS153-154      JORDAN            956.95
DS154.4        Jordan (1517-1918: Turkish rule)          956.9503
DS154.5        Jordan (1919-)        956.9504
DS161-199      ARMENIA (SEE ALSO  DK509 for some gen. titles, DK680-689 for later
                             works)    956.62
DS195          Armenia (1901-)       956.6202
DS201-248      SAUDI ARABIA & Arabian Peninsula          953
DS207          Description & travel (Arabian Penin.: 1801-1950)
DS223          Arabian Peninsula (gen.)
DS227          Diplomacy & politics (Saudi Arabia: gen.)
DS228.A-Z         Foreign relns. (Saudi Arabia-specific countries)
DS228.G3          Foreign relns. (Saudi Arab. Penin.: Ger.)
DS228.G7          Foreign relns. (Saudi Arab. Penin.: G.B.)
DS244          Saudi Arabia (1914-: gen.)          953.04-05
DS244.53       Saudi Arabia (1932-: Ibn Saud)       953.052
DS247.A-Z      Local history (Arabian Penin.: regions, sultanates, etc.: by place)
DS247.A2          Aden
DS247.B2-28       Bahrein
DS247.K8-88       Kuwait
DS247.O6-68       Oman
DS247.Y4-48       Yemen
DS248.A-Z      Local history (Arabian Penin.: cities)
DS248.M4       Mecca, Saudi Arabia
```

```
DS251-325      IRAN (Persia)        955
DS251          Description & travel (Iran: 1801-1950)
DS274          Diplomacy & politics (Iran)
DS274.2.A-Z        Foreign relns. (Iran-other countries)        327.550+
DS274.2.G3         Foreign relns. (Iran-Ger.)        327.55043
DS274.2.G7         Foreign relns. (Iran-G.B.)        327.55042
DS274.2.R9         Foreign relns. (Iran-Rus.)        327.55047
DS274.2.U6-7       Foreign relns. (Iran-U.S.)        327.55073
DS298-316      Persia (1794-1925: Kajar dynasty)        955.04-051
DS298          Iran (1794-1925: Kajar dynasty: gen.)
DS315          Iran (1909-25: Ahmed era)        955.05-051
DS317          Iran (1925-41: Pahlavi family: Riza Shah)        955.052
DS318          Iran (1941-78?: Pahlavi: Mohammed Riza)        955.053
DS335-498          SOUTHERN ASIA & Indian Ocean Region        954, 958.1, 959.1
DS335              INDIAN OCEAN REGION & Southern Asia (gen.)
DS350-375          AFGHANISTAN        958.1
DS356          Afghanistan (gen.)        958.1
DS361          Afghanistan (19th-20th c.: gen.)        958.103-104
DS368          Afghanistan (1901-19: Habibullah)        958.103-104
DS369.4        Afghanistan (1933-: Muhammad Zahir Shah & others)        958.1043
DS376-498          INDIA, Pakistan, Ceylon, Burma, etc.        954, 959.1
DS401-498          PAKISTAN (pre-1947), India, Ceylon, Burma, etc.        954
DS401-481          India (overall) & pre-1947 Pakistan        954
DS403          Primary sources, documents (India, pre-1947 Pak.)
DS413          Description & travel (India, pre-1947 Pak.)
DS442.6        Military history (India: 1901-)
DS443          Naval history (India)
DS448          Diplomacy & politics (India, pre-1947 Pak.: 20th c.)
DS450.A-Z          Foreign relns. (India-other specific places)        327.540+
DS450.G3           Foreign relns. (India-Ger.)        327.54043
DS450.J3           Foreign relns. (India-Japan)        327.54052
DS463-480.83       India (1761-1947: Brit. rule)        954.03
DS463          India (1761-1947: Brit. rule: gen.)
DS480.4        India (1914-19)        954.0356-0357
DS480.45       India (1919-47)        954.035+
DS480.5        India (1916-21: Viscount of Chelmsford)
DS480.8        India (1931-36: Marquis of Willingdon)
DS480.82       India (1936-43: Marquis of Linlithgow)        954.0359
DS480.83       India (1943-47: Earl of Wavell)        954.0359
DS481.A-Z      Biography (India: 1901-: inclu. memoirs)
DS481.A1           Biography (India: 1901-: collective)
DS481.B6           Bose, Subhas Chandra (India: 1901+ era)
DS481.G3           Gandhi, Mohandas (India: 1901+ era)
DS481.N35          Nehru, Jawaharlal (India: 1901+ era)
DS481.S8           Sultan Muhammad Shah, Sir, Agha Khan (India: 1901+ era)
```

DS485-498    Local history (India, Pak., Burma, Ceylon, Indian Ocean islands, etc.)
DS485.A-Z        Local history (Indian region kingdom, states, etc.)
DS485.B39-492    Bengal (E. Pak.)
DS485.B39-493    Pakistan (Bengal: East & West)    954.14
DS485.B493       Bengal (W. Pak.)          954.14
DS485.B79-892    BURMA (SEE DS527-530 for later items)    959.1
DS485.B89        Burma (1851-1947)    959.104
DS486.A-Z        Local history (India, Burma, etc.)
DS486.B7             Bombay, India
DS486.C2             Calcutta, India
DS486.R25            Rangoon, Burma
DS488-490        CEYLON       954.93
DS489.5          Sri Lanka (Ceylon: gen.)
DS491.A-Z        INDIAN OCEAN ISLANDS
DS491.A5-6       Andaman & Nicobar Islands
DS491.M3         Maldive Islands

DS501-935+       FAR EAST, Eastern & Southeastern Asia        950-952, 958-959
DS503        Primary sources, documents (Far East, E. & SE.Asia)
DS504        Dictionaries, guidebooks, etc. (Far East, E. & SE.Asia)
DS508        Description & travel (Far East, E. & SE.Asia: 1901-50)       915.0441
DS516-517        Russo-Japanese War (1904-5)       952.031, 947.083
DS518-518.9      EASTERN ASIA (history & foreign relns.: inclu. SE. Asia)
DS518        Far East (1904-45: inclu. Far Eastern question: SEE ALSO DU29)
                                              327.5, 950.41
DS518.2      Far Eastern question (France)
DS518.3      Far Eastern question (Ger.)
DS518.4      Far Eastern question (G.B.)
DS518.5      Far Eastern question (Netherlands)
DS518.6          Far Eastern question (Port.)
DS518.7          Far Eastern question (Russia)
DS518.8          Far Eastern question (U.S.)
DS518.9.A-Z      Far Eastern question (misc. countries: SEE DS845 for Japan,
                     DS740.63 for China)
DS519            Yellow Peril
DS521-689    SOUTHEAST ASIA, Dutch East Indies, Philippines    959
DS521-605    Southeast Asia       959
DS521-560    INDOCHINA        959-959.7
DS521-526+       Asia, Southeast (newer titles)
DS521            Southeast Asia (newer titles: gen.)    959
DS522.4          Description & travel (SE. Asia: 1901-50: for earlier books SEE
                     DS525)       915.9045+
DS525        Southeast Asia (gen. histories: older titles have descrip. & travel)
DS526.6      Southeast Asia (1900-45)
DS527-530    BURMA (SEE DS485.B89 for earlier titles)
DS527.4          Burma (gen.)
DS527.6          Description & travel (Burma: 1824-1945)
DS530            Burma (1885-1945)

| | | |
|---|---|---|
| DS531-560 | FRENCH INDOCHINA | 959.4, 959.6-7 |
| DS532 | Primary sources, documents (Fr. Indoch.) | |
| DS534 | Description & travel (Fr. Indoch.: 1788-1950) | 915.97043 |
| DS541 | French Indochina (gen.) | |
| DS544 | Military history (Fr. Indoch.) | |
| DS545 | Naval history (Fr. Indoch.) | |
| DS549 | French Indochina (1884-1945) | 959.703 |
| DS554 | CAMBODIA (SEE ALSO DS557.C2 for older works) | 959.6 |
| DS554.5-58 | Foreign relns. (Cambodia: plus gen. hist.) | |
| DS554.7-73 | Cambodia (1863-1954) | 959.603 |
| DS555 | LAOS (SEE ALSO DS557.L2 for earlier titles) | 959.4 |
| DS555.5-58 | Foreign relns. (Laos: ALSO gen. hist.) | |
| DS555.7-73 | Laos (1893-1954) | 959.403+ |
| DS556 | VIETNAM (Annam) | 959.7 |
| DS556.2 | Primary sources, documents (Viet.) | |
| DS556.36 | Description & travel (Viet.: 1801-1954) | 915.97043 |
| DS556.5 | Annam (Vietnam: gen.) | |
| DS556.57 | Diplomacy (Viet.: gen.) | |
| DS556.58.A-Z | Foreign relns. (Viet.-other countries: by place) | |
| DS556.58.F8 | Foreign relns. (Viet.-Fr.) | |
| DS556.58.J3 | Foreign relns. (Viet.-Japan) | |
| DS557.A-Z | Local history (Fr. Indoch.: regions: earlier titles: by place) | |
| DS557.C2 | CAMBODIA (SEE DS554 for later works) | |
| DS557.L2 | LAOS (SEE DS555 for later titles) | |
| DS558.8 | Vietnam (1802-1954) | |
| DS558.82 | Biography (Viet.: collective) | |
| DS558.83.A-Z | Biography (Viet.: by name: inclu. memoirs: Ho Chi Minh at DS560.72.H6) | |
| DS558.A-Z | Local history (Fr. Indoch.: towns: earlier works) | |
| DS558.A6 | Angkor, Cam. | |
| DS558.H3 | Hanoi, Viet. (for later titles use DS560.92.H3) | |
| DS558.S3 | Saigon, Viet. (SEE DS559.93.S2 for later titles) | |
| DS559.92.A-Z | Local history (Viet.: regions, protectorates, etc.) | |
| DS559.92.A5 | Annam (Fr. protectorate only) | |
| DS559.93.A-Z | Local history (Viet.: cities, towns, etc.) | |
| DS559.93.S2 | Saigon, Viet. (for earlier works use DS558.S3) | 959.7 |
| DS560 | NORTH VIETNAM (1945-75) | 959.7 |
| DS560.6 | North Vietnam (gen.) | |
| DS560.68 | Diplomacy (N. Viet.) | |
| DS560.69.A-Z | Foreign relns. (N. Viet.-other countries) | |
| DS560.72.A-Z | Biography (N. Viet.: 1945-: inclu. memoirs) | |
| DS560.72.H6 | Ho Chi Minh (N. Viet.) | |
| DS560.9.A-Z | Local history (N. Viet.: regions etc.) | |
| DS560.92.A-Z | Local history (N. Viet.: cities etc.) | |
| DS560.92.H3 | Hanoi, N. Viet. (SEE DS558.H3 for earlier titles) | |
| DS561-589 | THAILAND (Siam) | 959.3 |
| DS565 | Description & travel (Thai.: 1801-1950) | |
| DS573 | Military history (Thai.) | |
| DS574 | Naval history (Thai.) | |
| DS575 | Politics & diplomacy (Thai.) | |
| DS575.5.A-Z | Foreign relns. (Thai.-other places) | |
| DS575.5.J3 | Foreign relns. (Thai.-Japan) | |
| DS578 | Thailand (19th-20th c.) | 959.303-304 |
| DS585 | Thailand (1935-46: time of Ananda Mahidol, or Rama VIII) | 959.3043 |

| | | |
|---|---|---|
| DS588-589 | Local history (Thai.) | |
| DS589.B2 | Bangkok, Thai. | |
| DS591-599 | MALAY PENINSULA, Malaya, & the Straits | 959.5 |
| DS596 | MALAYA & Malay Peninsula (gen.) | |
| DS596.5 | Malay Peninsula (to 1946) | 959.503 |
| DS598.A-Z | Local history (Malay Penin.: protectorates, regions, settlements) | |
| DS598.S7 | Singapore 959.52 | |
| DS599.A-Z | Local history (Malay Penin.: towns etc.) | |
| DS599.M3 | Malacca, Malay Penin. | |
| DS600-605 | MALAY ARCHIPELAGO & Indonesia | 959.8 |
| DS603 | Malay Archipelago (gen.) | |
| DS611-649 | DUTCH EAST INDIES & Indonesia | |
| DS613 | Primary sources, documents (Dutch E. Ind.) | |
| DS619 | Description & travel (Dutch E. Ind. & Indon.: 1801-1945) | |
| DS636 | Military history (Dutch E. Ind.) | |
| DS637 | Naval history (Dutch E. Ind.) | |
| DS638 | Politics & diplomacy (Indon.: gen.) | |
| DS640.A-Z | Foreign relns. (Indon.-other countries) | |
| DS640.J3 | Foreign relns. (Indon.-Japan) | |
| DS643 | INDONESIA (1798-1942: colonial era) | 959.8022 |
| DS643.5 | Indonesia (1942-45: Japanese occupation) | 959.8022 |
| DS646.1 | Sumatra (Indon.: gen.) 959.81 | |
| DS646.15.A-Z | Local history (Sumatra, Indon.) | |
| DS646.15.P3 | Palembang, Sumatra | |
| DS646.17-29 | Java (Indon.) 959.82 | |
| DS646.2 | Description & travel (Java, Indon.: 1801-1945) | |
| DS646.27 | Java (Indon.: gen. hist.) | |
| DS646.29.A-Z | Local history (Java, Indon.) | |
| DS646.29.B23 | Bandung, Java | |
| DS646.29.B3 | Batavia, Java (Djakarta) | |
| DS646.3-38 | BORNEO & the Dyaks 959.53-55, .83 | |
| DS646.3 | Dyak Islands & Borneo (gen.) 959.53, .83 | |
| DS646.33-34 | British North Borneo 959.53 | |
| DS646.335.A-Z | Local history (Br. N. Borneo) | |
| DS646.335.B24 | Balikpapan, Br. N. Borneo | |
| DS646.35 | Brunei 959.55 | |
| DS646.36-38 | Sarawak 959.54 | |
| DS646.4 | Celebes 959.84 | |
| DS646.5 | Timor 959.86 | |
| DS646.6 | Moluccas 959.85 | |
| DS647.A-Z | Local history (Dutch E. Ind.: islands, regions, etc.) | |
| DS647.B2 | Bali (Indon.) 959.86 | |
| DS648 | British East Indies (SEE DS646.3 for Borneo) | |
| DS649 | German East Indies | |
| DS651-689 | PHILIPPINE ISLANDS 959.9 | |
| DS653 | Primary sources, documents (Philip.) | |
| DS659 | Description & travel (Philip.: 1898-1945) | 915.99043 |
| DS663-664 | Civilization, customs, social life (Philip.) | |
| DS665-666 | Races & ethnography (Philip.) | |
| DS668.A3-Z | Philippine Islands (gen.: pubn. 1801+) | 959.9 |
| DS671 | Military history (Philip.) 355.009599 | |
| DS672 | Naval history (Philip.) | |

| | | |
|---|---|---|
| DS672.8 | Politics & diplomacy (Philip.: gen.) | 320.9599, 327.599 |
| DS673.A-Z | Foreign relns. (Philip.: by country) | 327.5990+ |
| DS673.J3 | Foreign relns. (Philip.-Japan) | 327.599052 |
| DS673.U6-7 | Foreign relns. (Philip.-U.S.) | 327.599073 |

DS682-684 Military & naval history (Philip.: inclu. battles vs. Sp. & U.S.: PREFER
E717.7 for Battle of Manila Bay [1898] & U.S.-Sp. naval
confront.)

| | | |
|---|---|---|
| DS685 | Philippine Islands (1901+) | 959.903 |
| DS686 | Philippine Islands (1935-46: Commonwealth) | 959.9035 |
| DS686.2.A-Z | Biography (Philip.: 1935-46: inclu. memoirs) | |
| DS686.2.A2 | Biography (Philip.: 1935-46: collective) | |
| DS686.2.L3 | Laurel, José P. (Philip.: 1935-46 period) | |
| DS686.2.R6 | Romulo, Carlos P. (Philip.: 1935-46 era) | |
| DS686.3 | Philippine Islands (1935-44: Manuel Quezon era) | 959.9035 |

DS686.4 Philippine Islands (1942-46: Japanese occup. [1942-45] & Osmeña
rule [44-46])

| | | |
|---|---|---|
| DS688.A-Z | Local history (Philip.: islands, provinces, regions) | |
| DS688.B2 | Bataan (Luzon, Philip.) | 959.91 |
| DS688.B6 | Bisayas (Visayan Islands, Philip.) | 959.95 |
| DS688.C4 | Cebu (Philip.) | 959.95 |
| DS688.C67 | Corregidor (Philip.) | 959.91 |
| DS688.D3 | Davao (Philip.) | |
| DS688.L9 | Luzon (Philip.) | 959.91 |
| DS688.M2 | Mindanao (Philip.) | 959.97 |
| DS688.M28 | Mindoro (Philip.) | 959.93 |
| DS688.M5 | Mountain Province (Philip.) | |
| DS688.N5 | Negros Islands (Philip.) | 959.95 |
| DS688.P15 | Palawan (Philip.) | 959.94 |
| DS688.P2 | Panay (Philip.) | 959.95 |
| DS688.S9 | Sulu Archipelago (Philip.) | 959.99 |
| DS689.A-Z | Local history (Philip.: towns & cities) | |
| DS689.B2 | Baguio, Philip. | |
| DS689.C5 | Cebu, Philip. (town) | |
| DS689.M2 | Manila, Philip. | 959.91 |

| | | |
|---|---|---|
| DS701-796+ | CHINA 951 | |
| DS710 | Description & travel (China: 1901-48) | 915.1043-1044 |
| DS721 | Civilization, customs, social life (China: gen.) | |
| DS730-731 | Races & ethnography (China) | |
| DS732 | Chinese (in other lands: gen.) | |
| DS733 | Dictionaries, chronologies, etc. (China) | |
| DS735.A3-Z | China (gen.: pubn. 1801+) | 951 |
| DS740.4 | Diplomacy (China: gen.) | 327.51 |
| DS740.5.A-Z | Foreign relns. (China & other lands: by name) | 327.510+ |
| DS740.5.G2-3 | Foreign relns. (China-Ger.) | 327.51043 |
| DS740.5.G5-6 | Foreign relns. (China-G.B.) | |
| DS740.5.G6.H6 | Foreign relns. (China-Hong Kong) | |
| DS740.5.G6.J3 | Foreign relns. (China-Japan) | 327.51052 |
| DS740.5.S65 | Foreign relns. (China-Sov. Un.) | 327.51047 |
| DS740.5.U6-7 | Foreign relns. (China-U.S.) [PREFER E183.8.C5] | 327.51073 |
| DS740.63 | Far Eastern question (China: 1861-1945) | |

| | | |
|---|---|---|
| DS761 | China (1861-1912) | |
| DS764.4-767.7 | Chinese-Japanese War (1894-5) | 951.03, 952.031 |
| DS765 | Sino-Japanese War (1894-5: gen.) | |
| DS770-772 | Boxer Rebellion (China: 1899-1901) | 951.03 |
| DS773.32-6 | Chinese Revolution (1911-12) | 951.03 |
| DS773.83-776 | China (1912-49 [Republic] & 20th c. overall) | 951.03-04 |
| DS773.83 | Primary sources, documents (China: 20th c. & 1912-49) | |
| DS774 | China (1912-49 [Republic] & 20th c. overall: gen.) | 951.04 |
| DS775.2 | Civilization, customs, social life (China: 20th c. & 1912-49) | |
| DS775.4 | Military history (China: 20th c. & 1912-49) | |
| DS775.5 | Naval history (China: 20th c. & 1912-49) | |
| DS775.7 | Politics (China: 20th c. & 1912-49) | |
| DS775.8 | Foreign relns. (China: 20th c. & 1912-49) | |
| DS776 | Biography (China: 20th c. & 1912-49: collective: SEE partic. era for indiv.) | |
| DS776.4 | China (1912-28: gen.) | 951.041 |
| DS777.A2-567 | Sun Yat Sen (China: 1912-49 era: writings of) | |
| DS777.A3 | Sun Yat Sen (China: 1912-49 era: autobiography) | |
| DS777.A597.A-Z89 | Sun Yat Sen (China: 1912-49 era: biograpy & criticism) | |
| DS777.15.A-Z | Biography (China: 1912-49 period: except Sun Yat Sen) | |
| DS777.2 | China (1913: 2d Rev.) | |
| DS777.43 | May 4th Movement (China: 20th c.) | |
| DS777.46 | Northern Expedition (China: 1926-28) | |
| DS777.462 | Tsinan, Ch. (N. Exped., 1926-28: incident) | |
| DS777.47-514 | China (1928-37: Nationalist rule) | 951.042 |
| DS777.47 | China (1928-37: gen.) | |
| DS777.487 | Biography (China: 1928-37 era: collective) | |
| DS777.488.A-Z | Biography (China: 1928-37 era: indiv. inclu. memoirs) | |
| DS777.488.C5 | Chiang Kai Shek (China: 1887-1975: SEE DS778.M3 for Mao Tse Tung) | |
| DS777.5 | Chinese-Japanese Conflict (1931-33) | 951.042, 952.033 |
| DS777.51 | Shanghai, Ch. (Ch.-Jpn. Confl.: 1932: invasion) | |
| DS777.5132-5139 | Long March (China: 1934-35: Communists) | |
| DS777.5134 | Long March (China: 1934-35: Communists: gen.) | |
| DS777.514 | Sian, Ch. (1936: incident) | |
| DS777.518 | China (1937-45) | 951.042 |
| DS777.5194-5 | Biography (China: 1937-45) | |
| DS777.52-533 | Sino-Japanese Conflict (1937-45) | 940.53, 951.042, 952.033 |
| DS777.52 | Primary sources, documents (Sino-Jpn. Confl., 1937-45) | |
| DS777.53 | Chinese-Japanese Conflict (1937-45: gen.) | 940.53, 951.042, 952.033 |
| DS777.5314 | Personal accounts (Sino-Jpn. Confl., 1937-45: collections) | |
| DS777.5315.A-Z | Personal accounts (Sino-Jpn. Confl., 1937-45: indiv. by name) | |
| DS777.5316.A-Z | Battles, campaigns, etc. (Sino-Jpn. Confl., 1937-45: by name) | |
| DS777.533.A-Z | Sino-Japanese Conflict (1937-45: misc. topics) | |
| DS777.533.I53 | Indemnity (Sino-Jpn. Confl., 1937-45) | |
| DS777.533.M3 | Marco Polo Bridge Incident (Sino-Jpn. Confl.: 1937) | |
| DS777.533.S65 | Spies, intelligence (Sino-Jpn. Confl., 1937-45) | |
| DS777.533.U53 | Underground movements (Sino-Jpn. Confl., 1937-45) | |
| DS777.534 | Southern Anhui (China: Sino-Jpn. Confl.: 1941: incident) | |
| DS777.535 | China (1945-49: Republic: gen.) | 951.042 |
| DS777.54 | Chinese Civil War (1945-49: gen.) | |
| DS778.A-Z | Biography (China: 1949+) | |
| DS778.M3 | Mao Tse Tung (China: 1893-1976: SEE DS777.488.C5 for Chiang Kai Shek) | |

```
DS781-784.2+   MANCHURIA        951.803-804
DS783.7        Manchuria (19th-20th c.)
DS783.7.L4-45  League of Nations Commission of Enquiry (Manchuria: Lytton
                  Commission)
DS783.7.L45    Lytton Commission (Manchuria: League of Nations Commission of
                  Enquiry: summary & var. reports)
DS783.8        Mukden, Manch. (Ch.-Jpn. Confl.:1931: incident)
DS784          Manchoukuo (1932-45: P'u-i era)
DS785.A5-Z     CENTRAL ASIA & Tibet (pubns. to 1950: gen.)  951.5, 958 (C. Asia)
DS786          TIBET & Central Asia (1951+ pubns.: gen.)
DS793.A-Z      Local history (China: dependencies, provinces, areas, etc.)
DS793.G6       Gobi (China)
DS793.H5       Honan (China)
DS793.H7       Hunan (China)
DS793.K4          Kiangsi (China)
DS793.K6          Kwangsi (China)
DS793.K7          Kwangtung (China)
DS793.K8          Kweichow (China)
DS793.L6          Lop-nor (China: lake)
DS793.M7       MONGOLIA (SEE ALSO DS19-23.1 for Mongols)       951.7
DS793.S8       Szechwan (China)
DS793.Y25      Yangtze River (China)       951.2
DS793.Y8       Yunnan (China)
DS795          Peiping, China (Peking)     951.156
DS796.A-Z      Local history (China: cities & towns)
DS796.C2          Canton, China
DS796.H3          Hankow, China
DS796.H7       HONG KONG        951.25
DS796.M2       MACAO            951.26
DS796.M8       Mukden, China
DS796.N2       Nanking, China
DS796.S2       Shanghai, China       951.132
DS796.T5       Tientsin, China
DS796.T7       Tsingtao, China
DS798.92-799.99+   FORMOSA (Taiwan: SEE ALSO DS895.F7-77 for many pre-
                      1970 pubns.)              951.249
DS799          TAIWAN (Formosa: gen. hist., culture, descrip.)
DS799.15       Description & travel (Formosa: to 1945)       915.1249044
DS799.5        Formosa (gen.)       951.249
DS799.625         Diplomacy (Formosa: gen.)
DS799.63.A-Z      Foreign relns. (Formosa-other places)
DS799.63.J3       Foreign relns. (Formosa-Japan)
DS799.69-72       Formosa (1895-1945)       951.24904
DS799.693         Primary sources, documents (Formosa: 1895-1945)
DS799.7           Taiwan (1895-1945: gen.)
DS799.714         Military history (Formosa: 1895-1945)
DS799.716         Politics (Formosa: 1895-1945)
DS799.718         Foreign relns. (Formosa: 1895-1945)
DS799.72.A-Z      Biography (Formosa: 1895-1945)

DS801-897+     JAPAN        952
DS803             Primary sources, documents (Japan)
DS805             Dictionaries, gazeteers, guidebooks (Japan)
DS806          Japan (gen. & cultural)
DS810          Description & travel (Japan: 1901-45)       915.2043
```

| | | |
|---|---|---|
| DS821 | Civilization, customs, social life (Japan: gen.) | |
| DS822.25 | Civilization, customs, social life (Japan: 1868+) | |
| DS822.4 | Civilization, customs, social life (Japan: 1912-45) | |
| DS827.A-Z | Civilization, customs, social life (Japan: by special topic) | |
| DS827.B98 | Bushido (Jpn. custom) | |
| DS827.D4 | Death (Jpn. custom) | |
| DS827.S3 | Samurai (Jpn. custom) | |
| DS833 | Dictionaries, chronologies, etc. (Japan) | |
| DS834 | Biography (Japan: collective) | |
| DS834.1 | Biography (Japan: Imperial family & rulers) | |
| DS835 | Japan (gen. history, descrip., culture) | |
| DS838 | Military history (Japan: overall) | 355.00952 |
| DS838.7 | Military history (Japan: 1868+) | 355.00952, .033052, .033252, .033552 |
| DS839 | Naval history (Japan: gen.) | 359.00952 |
| DS839.7 | Naval history (Japan: 1868+) | 359.00952, .4752 |
| DS840-849 | Diplomacy & politics (Japan) | 320.952, 327.52 |
| DS840 | Primary sources, documents (Japan) | |
| DS841 | Politics & diplomacy (Japan: gen.) | |
| DS844 | Pamphlets & minor works (Jpn. polit. & dipl. hist.) | |
| DS845 | Diplomacy (Japan: gen.) | 327.52 |
| DS847 | Pamphlets & minor works (Jpn. for. relns.) | |
| DS849.A-Z | Foreign relns. (Japan-other places) | 327.520+ |
| DS849.A75 | Foreign relns. (Japan-Asia) | 327.5205 |
| DS849.A8 | Foreign relns. (Japan-Australia) | 327.52094 |
| DS849.B9 | Foreign relns. (Japan-Burma) | |
| DS849.C15 | Foreign relns. (Japan-Cambodia) | |
| DS849.C5 | Foreign relns. (Japan-China) | 327.52051 |
| DS849.G3 | Foreign relns. (Japan-Ger.) | 327.52043 |
| DS849.G7 | Foreign relns. (Japan-G.B.) | 327.52041 |
| DS849.I4 | Foreign relns. (Japan-India) | |
| DS849.I45 | Foreign relns. (Japan-Indoch.) | |
| DS849.I5 | Foreign relns. (Japan-Indonesia) | |
| DS849.I8 | Foreign relns. (Japan-It.) | |
| DS849.K5 | Foreign relns. (Japan-Korea) | |
| DS849.M3 | Foreign relns. (Japan-Malayas) | |
| DS849.N45 | Foreign relns. (Japan-New Zea.) | |
| DS849.P5 | Foreign relns. (Japan-Philip.) | 327.520599 |
| DS849.R9 | Foreign relns. (Japan-Rus.) | 327.52047 |
| DS849.S65 | Foreign relns. (Japan-Sov. Un.) | 327.52047 |
| DS849.T4 | Foreign relns. (Japan-Thai.) | |
| DS849.U6-7 | Foreign relns. (Japan-U.S.) | 327.52073 |
| DS849.V5 | Foreign relns. (Japan-Viet.) | |
| DS881.85+ | Japan (1868+: modern era) | 952.03 |
| DS885 | Japan (20th c.) | 952.03-04 |
| DS885.5.A-Z | Biography (Japan: 20th c.: inclu. memoirs: SEE ALSO DS890) | |
| DS885.5.A1 | Biography (Japan: 20th c.: collective) | |
| DS885.5.K6 | Konoye, Fumimaro, Prince (Japan: 20th. c.) | |
| DS886 | Japan (1912-26: Taisho time: Yoshihito) | 952.032 |
| DS887 | Japan (1914-18: WWI era) | 952.032 |
| DS888 | Japan (1912-26: special topics: inclu. large earthquakes like 1923) | |
| DS888.15-DS890 | Japan (1926-1989: Showa period: Hirohito rule) | 952.033 |
| DS888.15 | Japan (1926-1989: Hirohito rule: collected, non-serial works) | |
| DS888.2 | Japan (1926-1989: Hirohito rule: gen.) | |
| DS888.5 | Japan (1926-45) | 952.033 |
| DS889 | Japan (1945+: may ALSO cover 1926+) | 952.04 |

| | | |
|---|---|---|
| DS889.2 | Japanese propaganda (1926-89: in other lands: gen.) | |
| DS889.3.A-Z | Propaganda, Japanese (1926-89: abroad: by place) | |
| DS889.3.C5 | Propaganda, Japanese (1926-89: China) | |
| DS889.3.G7 | Propaganda, Japanese (1926-89: G.B.) | |
| DS889.3.I5 | Propaganda, Japanese (1926-89: Indonesia) | |
| DS889.3.P5 | Propaganda, Japanese (1926-89: Philip.) | |
| DS889.3.U6 | Propaganda, Japanese (1926-89: U.S.) | |
| DS889.7-9 | Biography (Japan: 1926-89: royal family) | |
| DS889.8 | Hirohito (Japan: Emperor, 1926-89) | |
| DS890.A-Z | Biography (Japan: 1926-89: inclu. memoirs: SEE ALSO DS885.5) | |
| DS890.A1 | Biography (Japan: 1926-89: collective) | |
| DS890.N23 | Nagumo, Chuichi, Vice Adm. (Japan: 1926-89 period) | |
| DS890.T64 | Tojo, Hideki, Gen., 1884-1948 (Japan: 1926-89 era) | |
| DS890.Y25 | Yamamoto, Isoroku, Adm., 1884-1943 (Japan: 1926-89 era) | |
| DS895.A-Z | Local history (Japan: islands, provinces, regions) | |
| DS895.B6 | Bonin Islands (Japan) | 952.85 |
| DS895.F7-77 | FORMOSA (Taiwan: SEE ALSO DS799 for many post-1969 pubns.) | |
| | | 951.249 |
| DS895.F72 | Taiwan (Formosa: gen.) | |
| DS895.F75 | Formosa (19th-20th c.) | 951.24903-24904 |
| DS895.H6 | Hokkaido (Japan) | 952.4 |
| DS895.K9 | Kurile Islands (Japan) | 957.7 |
| DS895.O4 | Okinawa (Japan) | 952.81 |
| DS895.R9 | Ryukyu Islands (Japan) | 952.81 |
| DS896 | Tokyo, Japan (SEE DS897.T6 for earlier works) | 952.135 |
| DS896.6 | Tokyo, Japan (gen.) | |
| DS896.64 | Tokyo, Japan (1867-1945) | 952.13503 |
| DS897.A-Z | Local history (Japan: towns & cities) | |
| DS897.H48 | Hiroshima, Japan | 952.19 |
| DS897.K8 | Kyoto, Japan | 952.191 |
| DS897.N285 | Nagasaki, Japan | 952.2 |
| DS897.O8 | Osaka, Japan | 952.183 |
| DS897.T6 | Tokyo, Japan (SEE DS896 for later pubns.) | 952.135 |
| DS901-935+ | KOREA | 951.9 |
| DS901 | Primary sources, documents (Korea) | |
| DS907 | Korea (gen.) | |
| DS910 | Politics & diplomacy (Korea) | |
| DS910.2.A-Z | Foreign relns. (Korea-other lands) | 327.5190+ |
| DS910.2.C5 | Foreign relns. (Korea-China) | 327.519051 |
| DS910.2.J3 | Foreign relns. (Korea-Japan) | 327.519052 |
| DS910.2.R9 | Foreign relns. (Korea-Rus.) | |
| DS916 | Korea (20th c.) | 951.903-904 |
| DS916.5.A-Z | Biography (Korea: 20th c.: inclu. memoirs) | |
| DS916.5.R5 | Rhee, Syngman (Korea: 20th c.) | |
| DS917 | Korea (1945+) | |

| | | | |
|---|---|---|---|
| DT | AFRICA | 960-969 | |
| DT1-38 | Africa (overall) | 960 | |
| DT12 | Description & travel (Africa: 1901-50) | | 916.0431-0432 |
| DT29 | Africa (1884-1945: gen.) | | 960.23-31 |
| DT31-38 | Politics & diplomacy (Africa: inclu. colonialism) | | 320.96, 327.6 |
| DT31.5 | Diplomacy & politics (Africa: 19th-20th c.: gen.) | | |
| DT32.5 | Foreign relns. (Africa-G.B.: 19th-20th c.) | | 960.23-3, 325.3+ |
| DT33.5 | Foreign relns. (Africa-Fr.: 19th-20th c.) | | |
| DT34.5 | Foreign relns. (Africa-Ger.: 19th-20th c.) | | |
| DT35.5 | Foreign relns. (Africa-It.: 19th-20th c.) | | |

| | | | |
|---|---|---|---|
| DT43-154 | EGYPT & the Egyptian Sudan | 962 | |
| DT43 | Primary sources, documents (Egypt) | | |
| DT55 | Description & travel (Egypt & Egyp. Sudan: 1901-50) | | 916.2044-2045 |
| DT77 | Egypt (gen.) | | |
| DT81 | Military history (Egypt) | | |
| DT82 | Politics & diplomacy (Egypt: gen.) | | |
| DT82.5.A-Z | Foreign relns. (Egypt & various countries) | | 327.620+ |
| DT82.5.G3 | Foreign relns. (Egypt-Ger.) | 327.62043 | |
| DT82.5.G7 | Foreign relns. (Egypt-G.B.) | 327.62041 | |
| DT107 | Egypt (1879-1952) | 962.03-052 | |
| DT107.2.A-Z | Biography (Egypt: 1879-1952) | | |
| DT107.7 | Egypt (1914-17: Hussein Kamil) | 962.04 | |
| DT107.8 | Egypt (1917-36: Fuad I) | 962.04-051 | |
| DT107.82 | Egypt (1936-52: Faruk I) | 962.052 | |
| DT108 | EGYPTIAN SUDAN (inclu. Anglo-Egyptian: for newer titles SEE DT154.1-159) | | 962.4 |
| DT108.6 | Anglo-Egyptian Sudan (1899-1955) | 962.403 | |
| DT124 | Nile River (20th c.: descrip. & travel) | 962.044-045 | |
| DT137.A-Z | Local history (Egypt: provinces, regions, etc.) | | |
| DT137.A7 | Arabian Desert (Egypt) | | |
| DT139-152 | Cairo, Egypt | 962.16 | |
| DT143 | Cairo, Egypt (gen. hist. & descrip.) | | |
| DT154.1-159 | SUDAN & Anglo-Egyptian Sudan (SEE DT108 for older works) | | |
| DT154.A-Z | Local history (Egypt: cities, towns, other) | | |
| DT154.A4 | Alexandria, Egypt | | |
| DT154.K63 | Khartoum, Egypt | | |
| DT154.S9 | Suez Canal (Egypt: inclu. Isthmus) | | 962.15 |
| DT155.6 | Sudan (gen.) | | |
| DT156.7 | Sudan (1900-1955) | | |
| DT160-177 | NORTH AFRICA (Egypt & Barbary States) | 961-962 | |
| DT165 | Description & travel (N. Africa: 1901-50) | | 916.2043 |
| DT176 | North Africa (19th-20th c.) | 961.023-03+ | |
| DT181-346 | BARBARY STATES | 961.1-2, 964-965, 966 | |
| DT190 | Description & travel (Barbary States: 1901-50) | | |
| DT204 | Barbary States (19th-20th c.) | 961.023-03+ | |
| DT211-239 | LIBYA | 961.2 | |
| DT220 | Description & travel (Libya: 1901-50) | | |
| DT227 | Politics & diplomacy (Libya: gen.) | | |
| DT227.5.A-Z | Foreign relns. (Libya & other particular places) | | |
| DT227.5.G3 | Foreign relns. (Libya-Ger.) | | |
| DT227.5.I8 | Foreign relns. (Libya-It.) | | |
| DT235 | Libya (1912-45) 961.203 | | |

| | | |
|---|---|---|
| DT238-239 | Local history (Libya) | |
| DT239.A-Z | Local history (Libya: towns etc.) | |
| DT239.T7 | Tripoli, Libya | |
| DT241-269 | TUNISIA | 961.1 |
| DT250 | Description & travel (Tunisia: 1901-50) | |
| DT257 | Politics & diplomacy (Tunisia: gen.) | |
| DT257.5.A-Z | Foreign relns. (Tunisia-other lands: by name) | |
| DT257.5.I8 | Foreign relns. (Tunisia-It.) | |
| DT264 | Tunisia (1881-1957: Fr. Protectorate) | 961.104 |
| DT271-299 | ALGERIA | 965 |
| DT280 | Description & travel (Algeria: 1901-50) | |
| DT294.5-295.3 | Algeria (1901-62: for older titles use DT295) | |
| DT294.5-7 | Algeria (1901-45) | 965.04 (1900-62) |
| DT295 | Algeria (1901+: for newer works SEE DT294.5-295.3) | 965.04+ |
| DT299.A-Z | Local history (Algeria: towns etc.) | |
| DT299.A5 | Algiers, Alg. | 965.3 |
| DT299.O7 | Oran, Alg. | |
| DT301-330 | MOROCCO | 964 |
| DT310 | Description & travel (Morocco: 1901-50) | |
| DT317 | Politics & diplomacy (Morocco: gen.) | |
| DT317.5.A-Z | Foreign relns. (Morocco-other specific places) | |
| DT317.5.F8 | Foreign relns. (Morocco-Fr.) | |
| DT317.5.G3 | Foreign relns. (Morocco-Ger.) | |
| DT324 | Morocco (19th-20th c.) | 964.03-04 |
| DT329.A-Z | Local history (Morocco: cities, towns, etc.) | |
| DT329.C3 | Casablanca, Mor. | 964.3 |
| DT329.T16 | Tangier Zone, Mor. | 964.2 |
| DT330 | SPANISH MOROCCO | 964.2 |
| DT331-346 | SAHARA DESERT | 966 |
| DT333 | Sahara Desert (gen. hist., descrip. etc.) | |
| DT351-364 | CENTRAL AFRICA | 967 |
| DT365-469 | EAST AFRICA | 967.6, 963 |
| DT365.7 | East Africa (1884-1960: gen.) 967.6 | |
| DT367 | ITALIAN EAST AFRICA & Northeast Africa | 963 |
| DT367.75 | NORTHEAST AFRICA (1900-74) | 963.05+ |
| DT371-390 | ETHIOPIA (Abyssinia) | 963 |
| DT378 | Description & travel (Ethiopia: 1901-50) | |
| DT386 | ABYSSINIA (19th -20th c.) | 963.03-05+ |
| DT387-387.6 | Ethiopia (1889-1928: inclu. 1895-6 conflict w. Italy) | 963.043-054 |
| DT387.7 | Ethiopia (1928-74: Haile Selassie) 963.055-06 | |
| DT387.8 | Italo-Ethiopian War (1935-6) | 963.056 |
| DT387.8.A1-7 | Primary sources, documents (Italo-Eth. War, 1935-6) | |
| DT387.8.A8-Z | Italo-Ethiopian War (1935-6: gen.) 963.056 | |
| DT390.A-Z | Local history (Ethiopia: kingdoms, regions, towns, etc.) | 963.056 |
| DT390.A3 | Addis Ababa, Eth. | |
| DT391-398 | ERITREA 963.5 | |
| DT401-420 | SOMALILAND | 967.7 |
| DT406 | BRITISH SOMALILAND 967.73-7305+ | |
| DT411 | FRENCH SOMALILAND (Djibouti or Afars & Issas) | 967.71-7104+ |
| DT416 | ITALIAN SOMALILAND 967.73-7305+ | |

| | | |
|---|---|---|
| DT421-435 | BRITISH EAST AFRICA & East Africa | 967.6 |
| DT431 | EAST AFRICA (to 1960) | |
| DT433.5-434 | KENYA (newer books) | |
| DT433.57-433.577 | Kenya (1895-1963: Brit. era) | |
| DT433.575 | Kenya (1920-63) | |
| DT434.E2 | Kenya (older books) | |
| DT434.Z3 | ZANZIBAR (Brit. colony: SEE DT449.Z2+ for newer) | |
| DT435 | Zanzibar (island & coast) | |
| DT436-449 | TANGANYIKA (German East Africa) | 967.82 |
| DT444 | German East Africa (gen.: later Tanganyika) | |
| DT447 | Tanganyika (to 1960: newer titles) | |
| DT449.Z2-Z29 | ZANZIBAR (SEE DT434.Z3 & DT435 for older titles) | |
| DT449.Z28 | Zanzibar (1890-1963) | |
| DT451-465 | MOZAMBIQUE (Portuguese East Africa) | 967.9 |
| DT469.A-Z | East African islands | |
| DT469.M21-38 | MADAGASCAR | 969.1 |
| DT471-720 | WEST AFRICA | 966-967, 968.8 |
| DT491-518 | BRITISH WEST AFRICA | 966, 966.4-51, .7, .81, .9 |
| DT521-553 | FRENCH WEST AFRICA | 966, 966.1-3, .52, .68, .81 |
| DT561-584 | CAMEROONS (German West Africa) & Togoland 966.6695, .81, 967.1 |
| DT591-617 | ANGOLA (Portuguese West Africa) | 967.3 |
| DT641-665 | BELGIAN CONGO | 967.5 |
| DT671.A-Z | West African islands | |
| DT671.C2 | CAPE VERDE ISLANDS | 966.58 |
| DT701-720 | SOUTHWEST AFRICA (German Southwest Africa) | 967.1, 968.8 |
| DT730-995 | SOUTHERN AFRICA | 968 |
| DT751-848 | BRITISH SOUTH AFRICA | 968-968.7 |
| DT769 | Military history (S. Afr.) | 355.00968 |
| DT779 | SOUTH AFRICA (1909-: Union) | 968.05+ |
| DT779.5 | South Africa (1914-18: WWI period) | |
| DT779.6 | South Africa (1919-39) | 968.05-054 |
| DT779.7 | South Africa (1939-45: WWII era) | 968.055 |
| DT855 | BRITISH CENTRAL AFRICA (1901-52) | 968.97 |
| DT858-865 | NYASALAND (Malawi, Brit. Cent. Afr. Protec.) | |
| DT946-965 | RHODESIA | |
| | | |
| DU | OCEANIA (Pacific Ocean) | 990-996, 909.0964 |
| DU22 | Description & travel (Pacific: 1898-1950) | |
| DU28 | Civilization, customs, social life, races (Pacific) | |
| DU28.3 | PACIFIC OCEAN (Oceania: gen.) | 990, 990.09, 909.0964 |
| DU29 | Diplomacy & politics (Pacific: gen.: inclu. colonial rule) | |
| DU30 | Foreign relns. (Pacific-U.S.) | |
| DU40 | Foreign relns. (Pacific-G.B.) | |
| DU50 | Foreign relns. (Pacific-Fr.) | |
| DU60 | Foreign relns. (Pacific-Ger.) | |
| DU65 | Foreign relns. (Pacific-Sp.) | |
| | | |
| DU80-480 | AUSTRALIA, New Zealand, Tasmania | |
| DU80-398 | AUSTRALIA | 994 |
| DU80 | Primary sources, documents (Australia) | |
| DU104 | Description & travel (Australia: 1901-50) | 919.4044 |
| DU107 | Civilization, customs, social life (Australia) | |
| DU110 | Australia (gen.) | 994 |
| DU112.3 | Military history (Australia) | 355.00994, .033094 |
| DU112.4 | Naval history (Australia) | 359.00994 |

| | | |
|---|---|---|
| DU113 | Diplomacy (Australia: gen.) 327.94 | |
| DU113.5.A-Z | Foreign relns. (Australia-other specific lands) | 327.940+ |
| DU113.5.G7 | Foreign relns. (Australia-G.B.) | 327.94041 |
| DU113.5.J3 | Foreign relns. (Australia-Japan) | 327.94052 |
| DU113.5.U6-7 | Foreign relns. (Australia-U.S.) | 327.94073 |
| DU114.A2 | Biography (Australia: collective) | |
| DU114.A3-Z | Biography (Australia: by name: SEE ALSO DU116.2 for later works) | |
| DU114.B52 | Blamey, Thomas, Sir (Australia) | |
| DU116 | Australia (1901-45: Commonwealth) 994.04 | |
| DU116.2 | Biography (Australia: 1901-45: SEE DU114 for earlier pubns.) | |
| DU120-122 | Races & ethnography (Australia) | |
| DU145-398 | Local history (Australia) | |
| DU145 | Canberra, Australia (inclu. Capital Territory) | |
| DU150-180 | New South Wales (Australia) 994.4 | |
| DU161 | New South Wales (Australia: 1837-1950: gen.) | |
| DU178 | Sydney, Australia 994.41 | |
| DU180.A-Z | Local history (New S. Wales, Aust.: towns, regions, etc. except Sydney) | |
| DU200-230 | Victoria (Australia) 994.5 | |
| DU212 | Victoria (Australia: 1851-1950: inclu. descrip.) | |
| DU228 | Melbourne, Australia 994.51 | |
| DU230.A-Z | Local history (Victoria, Aust.: all except Melbourne) | |
| DU250-280 | Queensland (Australia) 994.3 | |
| DU260-270 | Queensland (Australia: gen.: inclu. descrip.) | |
| DU278 | Brisbane, Australia 994.31 | |
| DU280.A-Z | Local history (Queens., Aust.: all except Brisbane) | |
| DU280.C3 | Cape York Peninsula (Queens., Aust.) | |
| DU280.M7 | Moreton Bay (Queens., Aust.) | |
| DU280.T7 | Torres Strait (Queens., Aust.) | |
| DU300-330 | South Australia 994.23 | |
| DU310-320 | South Australia (gen. & descrip.) | |
| DU328 | Adelaide, Australia 994.231 | |
| DU330.A-Z | Local history (S. Australia except Adelaide) | |
| DU350-380 | Western Australia 994.1 | |
| DU360-370 | Western Australia (gen. & descrip.) | |
| DU378 | Perth, Australia 994.11 | |
| DU380.A-Z | Local history (W. Australia except Perth) | |
| DU380.F8 | Fremantle. Australia | |
| DU390 | Central Australia 994.2 | |
| DU392-398 | Northern Australia 994.29 | |
| DU395-396 | Northern Australia (gen. & descrip.) | |
| DU398.A-Z | Local history (N. Australia: regions, towns, etc.) | |
| DU398.D3 | Darwin, Australia 994.295 | |
| DU400-430 | NEW ZEALAND 993.1 | |
| DU411 | Description & travel (N. Zea.: 1840-1950) 919.31042-310435 | |
| DU420 | New Zealand (gen.) 993.1-1037+ | |
| DU420.5 | Military history (N. Zea.) 355.009931 | |
| DU421 | Politics & diplomacy (N. Zea.: gen.) | |
| DU421.5.A-Z | Foreign relns. (N. Zea.-other specific places) 327.9310+ | |
| DU421.5.J3 | Foreign relns. (N. Zea.-Japan) 327.931052 | |
| DU421.5.U6-7 | Foreign relns. (N. Zea.-U.S.) 327.931073 | |
| DU422.A-Z | Biography (N. Zea.: inclu. memoirs: by name) | |
| DU423 | Races & ethnography (N. Zea.) | |
| DU428 | Wellington, N.Z. 993.127 | |

| | | |
|---|---|---|
| DU430.A-Z | Local history (N. Zea.: regions, towns, dependencies, etc. except Wellington) | |
| DU430.A8 | Auckland, N.Zea. | 993.122 |
| DU430.C5 | Christchurch, N. Zea. | 993.155 |
| DU430.C6 | COOK ISLANDS | 996.23-24 |
| DU450-480 | TASMANIA (Van Diemen's Land) | 994.6 |
| DU460-470 | Van Diemen's Land (Tasmania: gen. & descrip.) | |
| DU480.A-Z | Local history (Tasmania: regions, towns, etc.) | |
| DU480.H6 | Hobart, Australia (Tasmania) | 994.61 |
| | | |
| DU490 | MELANESIA (gen.: SEE DU520-950 for specific islands, groups, atolls, etc.) | 993, 993.2-7, 996.1 |
| DU500 | MICRONESIA (gen.: SEE DU520-950 for particular islands, island groups, atolls, etc.) | 996.5-68 |
| DU510 | POLYNESIA (gen.: SEE DU520-950 for specific island groups, individual islands, atolls, etc.) | 996, 996.1-4, .9 |
| DU520-950 | SOUTH SEAS (Oceanica: islands, chains, groups, etc.) | |
| DU520 | ADMIRALTY ISLANDS | 993.7 |
| DU550 | BISMARCK ARCHIPELAGO (gen.) | 993.6 |
| DU553.A-Z | Local history (Bismarck Arch.: islands, groups, etc. by name) | |
| DU553.N35 | New Britain (Bismarck Arch.: inclu. Rabaul) | |
| DU553.N4 | New Ireland (Bismarck Arch.) | |
| DU560-568 | CAROLINE ISLANDS | 996.6 |
| DU563 | Description & travel (Caroline Islands) | |
| DU565 | Caroline Islands (gen.) | |
| DU567 | Caroline Islands (modern hist.) | |
| DU568.A-Z | Local history (Caroline Islands: islands, groups, towns, etc.) | |
| DU568.P7 | Ponape (Carolines) | |
| DU568.T7 | Truk Islands (Carolines) | |
| DU568.U5 | Ulithi (Carolines) | |
| DU568.Y3 | Yap (Carolines) | |
| DU590 | ELLICE ISLANDS | 996.81 |
| DU600 | FIJI ISLANDS | 996.11 |
| DU615 | GILBERT ISLANDS (inclu. Tarawa & Makin Atolls) | 996.81 |
| DU620-629 | HAWAIIAN ISLANDS | 996.9 |
| DU623 | Description & travel (Hawaiian Is.: to 1950) | 919.69043 |
| DU625 | Hawaiian Islands (gen.) | 996.9 |
| DU627.4 | Hawaiian Islands (annex. to U.S.) | |
| DU627.5.A1-5 | Primary sources, documents (Hawaiian Is.: 1900-59) | |
| DU627.5.A6-Z | Hawaii (1900-59: U.S. Territory) | 996.903 |
| DU627.7.A-Z | Biography (Hawaii: 1891-1959: inclu. memoirs) | |
| DU628.A-Z | Local history (Hawaii: islands, counties, etc.) | |
| DU628.H25 | Hawaii (island) | 996.91 |
| DU628.K3 | Kauai (Haw. Is.) | 996.94 |
| DU628.L3 | Lanai (Haw. Is.) | 996.923 |
| DU628.M3 | Maui (Haw. Is.) | 996.921 |
| DU628.M5 | Midway Islands (Haw. Is.) | 996.99 |
| DU628.M7 | Molokai (Haw. Is.) | 996.924 |
| DU628.O3 | Oahu (Haw. Is.) | 996.93 |
| DU629.A-Z | Local history (Hawaii: towns, volcanoes, etc.) | |
| DU629.H5 | Hilo, Haw. | |
| DU629.H7 | Honolulu, Haw. | 996.931 |

```
DU640-648   MARIANA ISLANDS (Ladrones)      996.7
DU645       Ladrone Islands (Marianas: gen.)
DU647       Guam (Mariana Is.)        996.7
DU648.A-Z      Local history (Mariana Is.: islands, towns, etc.)
DU648.S35      Saipan (Mariana Is.)
DU648.ST4      Tinian (Mariana Is.)
DU700       MARQUESAS ISLANDS         996.31
DU710       MARSHALL ISLANDS (inclu. Kwajalein Atoll)      996.83
DU720       NEW CALEDONIA       993.2, .97
DU740-746   NEW GUINEA      995
DU740       Papua & New Guinea (gen.: inclu. Brit. terr. & Port Moresby, Owen
                  Stanley Mts., Lae, Salamaua, etc.)      995, 995.3
DU742       German New Guinea (N.E.: SEE ALSO DU550+ for Bismarck Arch.)
                                                    993.6, 995
DU744-744.5    DUTCH NEW GUINEA (West)   995.1
DU760          NEW HEBRIDES        993.4
DU810-819      SAMOAN ISLANDS    996.13-14
DU817.A6-Z     Samoa (modern hist.)
DU819.A1       American Samoa          996.13
DU819.A2       Western Samoa (was Ger. Samoa)      996.14
DU819.A3-Z     Local history (Samoan Is.: partic. islands, towns, etc.)
DU819.P3       Pago Pago, Samoa
DU840       SANTA CRUZ ISLANDS        993.5
DU850       SOLOMON ISLANDS (inclu. Guadalcanal, New Georgia, Choiseul,
                  Savo, Florida, Bougainville, etc.)      993.5
DU870       SOCIETY ISLANDS (inclu. Tahiti, Bora Bora, etc.)      996.21
DU880       TONGA ISLANDS       996.12
DU950.A-Z      Pacific Islands (smaller misc.: by name)
DU950.W28      WAKE ISLAND         996.5

DX1-301     GYPSIES
DX145       Gypsies in Europe (gen. & elsewhere)
DX211-275   European Gypsies (by place)
DX222       Gypsies in Czechoslovakia
DX229       Gypsies in Germany
DX241       Gypsies in Russia (inclu. Poland & Lith.)

E           WESTERN HEMISPHERE (gen.) & United States          970
E1-143      AMERICA (gen.)        970
E18.185        America (1901-)         970.05
E31-45      NORTH AMERICA           970
E45         North America (gen.)
E77-99      Indians (N. Am.)      970.00497, .1-5, 973.0497
E98.M5      Military skill (Indians of N. Am.)

E151-860+   UNITED STATES         973-979.9+
E151        United States (gen. & cultural, serials, societies, etc.)
E161        Civilization, customs, social life (U.S.: gen.)
E169        Description, travel, civilization, customs (U.S.: 1914-45)      917.3049
E169.1      Americanization, civilization, etc. (U.S.)
E171        Periodicals & yearbooks (U.S.)
E172        Associations, societies (U.S.)
E173        Primary sources, documents (U.S.)
E174        Dictionaries & encyclopedias (U.S.)      973.03
E174.5      Chronologies (U.S.)
```

| | | |
|---|---|---|
| E178 | United States (gen. hist.) | 973 |
| E181 | Military history (U.S.) | 355.00973, .033073 |
| E182 | Naval history (U.S.) | 359.00973, .4773 |
| E183 | Politics (U.S.: gen.) | 320.973 |
| E183.7 | Diplomacy (U.S.: gen.) | 327.73 |
| E183.8.A-Z | Foreign relns. (U.S.-other places) | 327.730+ |
| E183.8.C5 | Foreign relns. (U.S.-China) | 327.73051 |
| E183.8.F8 | Foreign relns. (U.S.-Fr.) | 327.73044 |
| E183.8.G3 | Foreign relns. (U.S.-Ger.) | 327.73043 |
| E183.8.G7 | Foreign relns. (U.S.-G.B.) | 327.73041 |
| E183.8.I8 | Foreign relns. (U.S.-It.) | 327.73045 |
| E183.8.J3 | Foreign relns. (U.S.-Japan) | 327.73052 |
| E183.8.R9 | Foreign relns. (U.S.-Russia) | 327.73047 |
| E183.8.S65 | Foreign relns. (U.S.-Sov.Un.) | 327.73047 |
| E184.A-Z | Races, ethnography, religious groups (U.S.) | 973.04+ |
| E184.A1 | Races, ethnography, religious groups (U.S.: gen.) | |
| E184.B7 | British (in U.S.) | |
| E184.F8 | French (in U.S.) | |
| E184.G3 | Germans (in U.S.) | |
| E184.I8 | Italians (in U.S.) | |
| E184.J3 | Japanese (in U.S.) | |
| E184.J5 | Jews (in U.S.) | |
| E184.O6 | Orientals (in U.S.) | |
| E184.R9 | Russians (in U.S.) | |
| E185 | Blacks (in U.S.) | 973.0496 |
| E185.63 | Blacks as soldiers & seamen (U.S.) | |
| E660-738 | United States (1865-1900+) | 973.8-89 |
| E660.A-Z | Statesmen (U.S.: collected works: inclu. some working through 1921: SEE E742.5 for rest of 20th c.) | |
| E660.W7-75 | Wilson, Woodrow (U.S.: 1865-1900 era: works) | |
| E664.A-Z | Biography (U.S.: 1865-1900: by name) | |
| E664.L7 | Lodge, Henry Cabot (U.S.: 1865-1900 era) | |
| E714-735 | Spanish-American War (1898) | 973.89-898 |
| E717.7 | Philippine Islands (Sp.-Am. War, 1898: ALSO Battle of Manila Bay) 973.8937 | |
| E740-749 | United States (20th c.: overall) | 973.9 |
| E740 | Associations, periodicals, societies (U.S.: 20th c.) | |
| E740.5 | Primary sources, documents (U.S.: 20th c.) | |
| E741 | United States (20th c.: gen.) | 973.9 |
| E742.5.A-Z | Statesmen (U.S.: collected works: 20th c.: SEE E660 for up to 1921) | |
| E742.5.I25 | Ickes, Harold (U.S.: 20th c.: works) | |
| E742.5.R5-7 | Roosevelt, Franklin Delano (U.S.: 20th c.: works) | |
| E742.5.W3 | Wallace, Henry A. (U.S.: 20th c.: works) | |
| E743 | Politics (U.S.: 20th c.) | 320.973, .904 |
| E743.5 | Subversive activities (in U.S.: propaganda, espionage, 5th column, etc.) | |
| E744 | Foreign relns. (U.S.: 20th c.: gen.) | 327.73 |
| E745 | Military history (U.S.: 20th c.: inclu. biog.: more than 1 war) 355.00973, .033073, .033273, .033573 | |
| E746 | Naval history (U.S.: 20th c.) | 359.00973, .4773 |

| | | |
|---|---|---|
| E747 | Biography (U.S.: 20th c.: collective) | |
| E748.A-Z | Biography (U.S.: 20th c.: by name) | |
| E748.B32 | Baruch, Bernard (U.S.: 20th c.) | |
| E748.D48 | Dewey, Thomas (U.S.: 20th c.) | |
| E748.F24 | Farley, James (U.S.: 20th c.) | |
| E748.G23 | Garner, John Nance (U.S.: 20th c.) | |
| E748.H67 | Hopkins, Harry (U.S.: 20th c.) | |
| E748.H93 | Hull, Cordell (U.S.: 20th c.) | |
| E748.I28 | Ickes, Harold (U.S.: 20th c.) | |
| E748.K55 | Knox, W. Frank (U.S.: 20th c.) | |
| E748.S895 | Stimson, Henry (U.S.: 20th c.) | |
| E748.W23 | Wallace, Henry A. (U.S.: 20th c.) | |
| E748.W7 | Willkie, Wendell (U.S.: 20th c.) | |
| E765-783 | United States (1913-21: Woodrow Wilson period) | 973.913 |
| E766 | United States (1913-21: gen.) | |
| E767 | Wilson, Woodrow (U.S.: Pres., 1913-21) | |
| E768 | Foreign relns. (U.S.: 1913-21) | |
| E772 | Woodrow Wilson Foundation | |
| E780 | United States (1914-18: WWI era: internal) | 973.913 |
| E783 | Politics (U.S.: 1920 Pres. campaign) | |
| E784 | United States (1919-33: inclu. Roaring Twenties) | 973.913-916 |
| E785 | United States (1921-3: Warren G. Harding era: gen.: SEE JX235 ALSO for arms limitation conference, Pacific possessions treaty, etc.) 973.914 | |
| E791 | United States (1923-9: Calvin Coolidge period: gen.: SEE ALSO JX1952 & JX1987 for Kellogg-Briand Pact of 1928) 973.915 | |
| E801 | United States (1929-33: Pres. Herbert Hoover: inclu. London & 3-Power naval conferences & treaties: SEE ALSO JX1974) 973.916 | |
| E802 | Hoover, Herbert (U.S.: Pres., 1929-33) | |
| E805-812 | United States (1933-45: Pres. Franklin D. Roosevelt) | 973.917 |
| E805 | Politics (U.S.: Pres. campaign, 1932) | |
| E806 | United States (1933-45: gen.) | |
| E807 | Roosevelt, Franklin D. (U.S.: Pres., 1933-45) | |
| E807.1 | Roosevelt, Franklin D. (U.S.: Pres., 1933-45: family, inclu. Eleanor) | |
| E810 | Politics (U.S.: Pres. race, 1936) | |
| E811 | Politics (U.S.: Pres. race, 1940) | |
| E812 | Politics (U.S.: Pres. race, 1944) | |
| E813-815 | United States (1945-53: Pres. Harry S Truman) | 973.918 |
| E813 | United States (1945-53: gen.) | |
| E814 | Truman, Harry S (U.S.: Pres., 1945-53) | |
| E836 | Eisenhower, Dwight D. (U.S.: 1953-61) | 973.9210924, 940.540973, 355.0024 |
| | | |
| F | UNITED STATES (local), Canada, Newfoundland, Mexico, Central & South America 974-79+, 971-2, 980-89 | |
| F1-975+ | United States (local: regions, states, towns, etc.) | 974-79 |
| F1-15 | New England (overall) 974 | |
| F4 | New England (gen. hist.) 974 | |
| F6-105 | New England states 974.1-6 | |
| F9 | New England (1865-1950) 974.04-042 | |
| F16-30 | Maine 974.1 | |
| F19 | Maine (gen.) | |
| F25 | Maine (1865-1950) | |

| | | |
|---|---|---|
| F61-75 | Massachusetts | 974.4 |
| F70 | Massachusetts (1865-1950: SEE D570.85.M4-41 for war years, 1914-18 & D769.85.M4-41 for 1939-45) | 974.404-043 |
| F73.5 | Boston, Mass. (1865-1950) | |
| F106 | Atlantic Coast (U.S.: Maine to Flor.) | 974-975 |
| F116-205 | Middle Atlantic states & District of Columbia | |
| F116-130 | New York | 974.7 |
| F119 | New York (gen.) | |
| F124 | New York (1865-1950: SEE D570.85.N4-5 for 1914-18 war years & D769.85.N4-5 for 1939-45) | 974.704 |
| F127.A-Z | Local history (New York: regions, counties, etc.) | |
| F127.H8 | Hudson River (N.Y.) | |
| F127.L8 | Long Island (N.Y.) | |
| F128 | New York City, N.Y. | 974.71 |
| F128.3 | New York City, N.Y. (gen.) | |
| F128.5 | New York City area (N.Y.: 1901-50) | 974.7104-043 |
| F128.67.A-Z | New York City, N.Y. (streets, bridges, railroads) | |
| F128.68.A-Z | New York City, N.Y. (sections, suburbs, rivers) | |
| F129.A-Z | Local history (N.Y.: cities, towns, etc. except N.Y.C.) | |
| F129.A3 | Albany, N.Y. | |
| F129.B8 | Buffalo, N.Y. | |
| F130.A-Z | Races, ethnography, religious groups (N.Y.) | |
| F130.G3 | Germans (in N.Y.) | |
| F130.I8 | Italians (in N.Y.) | |
| F130.J5 | Jews (in N.Y.) | |
| F131-145 | New Jersey | 974.9 |
| F139 | New Jersey (1865-1950: SEE D570.85.N3-31 for 1914-18 war years & D769.85.N3-31 for 1039-45) | |
| F146-160 | Pennsylvania | 974.8 |
| F154 | Pennsylvania (1865-1950) | |
| F158 | Philadelphia, Penn. | 974.811 |
| F191-205 | District of Columbia | 975.3 |
| F194 | Washington, D.C. (gen.) | |
| F196 | Social life & politics (Washington, D.C.) | |
| F199 | Washington, D.C. area (1878-1950) | 975.303-304 |
| F203 | Local history (Washington, D.C.: cemeteries, churches, hotels, statues, parks, circles, streets, etc.) | |
| F203.4.A-Z | Monuments, statues, memorials (Washington, D.C.) | |
| F203.7.A-Z | Washington, D.C. (streets, bridges, railroads) | |
| F203.7.P4 | Pennsylvania Ave. (Washington, D.C.) | |
| F204.A-Z | Buildings (Washington, D.C.) | |
| F204.W5 | White House (Washington, D.C.) | |
| F206-220 | South Atlantic states & the South (U.S.: covers south of Mason-Dixon Line) | 975-976 |
| F215 | South & South Atlantic states (1865-1950) | 975.04, 976.04 |
| F221-235 | Virginia | 975.5 |
| F232.A-Z | Local history (Virginia: regions, counties, etc.) | |
| F232.C43 | Chesapeake Bay region (Va.) | |
| F234.A-Z | Local history (Virginia: towns etc.) | |
| F234.A7 | Arlington National Cemetery (Arlington, Va.) | |
| F234.N8 | Norfolk, Va. | |
| F251-265 | North Carolina | 975.6 |
| F259 | North Carolina (1865-1950) | |
| F281-295 | Georgia | 975.8 |

| | | |
|---|---|---|
| F296-395 | Gulf states, Mississippi Valley, Middle West, & Texas | 975.9-976.4, 976.7-9 |
| F296 | Gulf states (U.S.: gen.) 976 | |
| F306-320 | Florida 975.9 | |
| F316 | Florida (1865-1950) 975.906 | |
| F317.A-Z | Local history (Florida: regions, counties, etc.) | |
| F317.G8 | Gulf Coast (Florida) | |
| F317.M7 | Florida Keys (Monroe County, Fl.) | |
| F319.A-Z | Local history (Florida: towns etc.) | |
| F319.P4 | Pensacola, Florida | |
| F321-335 | Alabama 976.1 | |
| F326 | Alabama (to 1950) | |
| F336-350 | Mississippi 976.2 | |
| F351-355 | Mississippi Valley & the Midwest 976-977 | |
| F354 | Middle West & Mississippi River Valley (1865-1950) 977.03 | |
| F366-380 | Louisiana 976.3 | |
| F381-395 | Texas 976.4 | |
| F391 | Texas (1846+: SEE D570.85.T4-41 for 1914-18 war years & D769.85.T4-41 for 1939-45) 976.405-406 | |
| F392.A-Z | Local history (Texas: regions, counties, etc.) | |
| F392.G9 | Gulf Coast (Texas) | |
| F394.A-Z | Local history (Texas: towns etc.) | |
| F394.D2 | Dallas, Texas | |
| F394.E4 | El Paso, Texas | |
| F394.H8 | Houston, Texas 976.41411 | |
| F396-475 | Southwest (Old) & lower Mississippi Valley (Ark., Tenn., Ken., Missouri) 976.7-9, 977, 977.8 | |
| F461-475 | Missouri 977.8 | |
| F474.S2 | St. Louis, Mo. 977.866 | |
| F476-590 | Northwest (U.S.: Old) 977 | |
| F484.5 | Old Northwest (U.S.: 1865-1950) 977.03 | |
| F486-500 | Ohio 977.1 | |
| F536-550 | Illinois 977.3 | |
| F546 | Illinois (1865-1950) 977.303 | |
| F548 | Chicago, Ill. 977.311 | |
| F548.5 | Chicago, Ill. (1892-1950) 977.31103-033 | |
| F551-556 | Great Lakes (U.S.) 977 | |
| F561-575 | Michigan 977.4 | |
| F591-705 | West (U.S.) & Trans-Mississippi 978 | |
| F595 | Trans-Mississippi & the West (1880-1950) 978.02-033 | |
| F601-615 | Minnesota 977.6 | |
| F631-645 | North Dakota 978.4 | |
| F676-690 | Kansas 978.1 | |
| F691-705 | Oklahoma 976.6 | |
| F721-785 | Rocky Mts. area (Mont., Idaho, Wyo., Colo.) 978 | |
| F726-740 | Montana 978.6 | |
| F771-785 | Colorado 978.8 | |
| F786-850 | Southwest (New: New Mex., Ariz., Utah, Nev.) 978.9-979.3, 979 | |
| F791-805 | New Mexico 978.9 | |
| F801 | New Mexico (1848-1950) | |
| F804.A-Z | Local history (New Mex.: towns etc.) | |
| F804.L6 | Los Alamos, New Mex. | |

| F851-915+ | Pacific States & Alaska | 979 |
| F852 | Pacific Northwest (1859-1950) | 979.5 |

F851-915+   Pacific States & Alaska        979
F852        Pacific Northwest (1859-1950)        979.5
F856-870    California        979.4
F861        California (gen.)        979.4
F866        California (1869-1950: SEE D570.85.C2-21 for 1914-18 war years
                    & D769.85.C2-21 for 1939-45)        979.404-4053
F867        Southern California        979.49
F868.A-Z    Local history (Calif.: regions, counties, etc.)
F868.L8         Los Angeles County (Calif.)        979.493
F868.S156       San Francisco Bay area (Calif.)        979.46
F868.S23        Santa Barbara County (Calif.)        979.491
F869.A-Z    Local history (Calif.: towns etc.)
F869.L8         Los Angeles, Calif.        979.494
F869.S22        San Diego, Calif.        979.498
F869.S3         San Francisco, Calif.        979.461
F870.A-Z    Races, ethnography, religious groups (Calif.)
F870.A1         Races, ethnography, religious groups (Calif.: gen.)
F870.G3         Germans (in Calif.)
F870.J3         Japanese (in Calif.)
F870.J5         Jews (in Calif.)
F870.O6         Orientals (in Calif.)
F886-900    Washington (state)        979.7
F891        Washington (state: to 1950)
F897.A-Z    Local history (Wash. state: regions, counties, etc.)
F897.P9     Puget Sound (Wash.)
F899.A-Z    Local history (Wash. state: towns etc.)
F899.S4     Seattle, Wash.        979.777
F901-951    Alaska area        979.8
F909        Alaska (1894-1959)        979.803-804
F951        Aleutian Islands & Bering Sea (SEE D769.87.A4 for 1939-45 & Jpn.
                    occupation)        979.84, 940.096451, 909.096451824
F965        Territories (U.S.: inclu. Alaska & Hawaii: SEE ALSO DU620-629
                    for Haw.)
F970        Territories (U.S.: island types in gen.: SEE ALSO DU647 for Guam &
                    DU620-629 for Haw.)

F1001-1140+     CANADA        971
F1015           Description & travel (Can.: 1867-1950)        917.1045-1063
F1026           Canada (gen.)
F1027           French Canadians
F1028       Military history (Can.)        355.00971
F1028.5     Naval history (Can.)        359.00971
F1029       Diplomacy (Can.: gen.)        327.71
F1029.5.A-Z     Foreign relns. (Can.-other places)        327.710+
F1029.5.F8      Foreign relns. (Can.-Fr.)        327.71044
F1029.5.G3      Foreign relns. (Can.-Ger.)        327.71043
F1029.5.G7      Foreign relns. (Can.-G.B.)        327.71041
F1029.5.I8      Foreign relns. (Can.-It.)
F1029.5.J3      Foreign relns. (Can.-Japan)
F1029.5.R9      Foreign relns. (Can.-Rus.)        327.71047
F1029.5.U6-7    Foreign relns. (Can.-U.S.)        327.71073
F1033       Canada (1867+)        971.05+
F1034       Canada (1914+: SEE ALSO D768.15 for 1939-45 war years)        971.061+

```
F1035.A-Z    Races, ethnography, religious groups (Can.)
F1035.G3     Germans (in Can.)
F1035.J3     Japanese (in Can.)
F1035.8      Maritime Provinces (Can.: Atlantic coast)      971.5-8
F1036-1040        Nova Scotia    971.6
F1041-1045        New Brunswick    971.5
F1056-1059.7      Ontario (Can.)    971.3
F1075-1080        Alberta        971.23
F1086-1089.7      British Columbia  971.1
F1088             British Columbia (gen. hist.)
F1089.5.A-Z       Local history (Br. Colum.: towns, cities, etc.)
F1089.5.V22       Vancouver, B.C.      971.134
F1121-1139        Newfoundland        971.8, .803 (1934-49)
F1135-1139        Labrador
F1170        Saint Pierre & Miquelon    971.88

F1201-3799+      LATIN AMERICA & the West Indies       972, 980-989
F1201-1392       MEXICO        972-972.7
F1215            Description & travel (Mex.: 1867-1950)        917.2048+
F1227.5      Military & naval history (Mex.)
F1228        Diplomacy (Mex.: gen.)
F1228.5.A-Z      Foreign relns. (Mex.-other places)       327.720+
F1228.5.G3       Foreign relns. (Mex.-Ger.)      327.72043
F1228.5.J3       Foreign relns. (Mex.-Japan)      327.72052
F1228.5.R9       Foreign relns. (Mex.-Rus.)      327.72047
F1228.5.S65      Foreign relns. (Mex.-Sov.Un.)  327.72047
F1228.5.U6-7     Foreign relns. (Mex.-U.S.)      327.72073
F1234        Mexico (1910-46)        972.081-082
F1386        Mexico City area (Mex.)    972.53
F1391.A-Z    Local history (Mex.: cities, towns, etc. except for Mex. City)
F1392.A-Z    Races, ethnography, religious groups (Mex.)
F1392.G4         Germans (in Mex.)
F1392.J4         Jews (in Mex.)
F1401-1419   Latin America (gen.)        980
F1409        Description & travel (Latin Am.: 1811-1950)        918.042-043
F1414        Latin America (1898-)        980.032+
F1415        Diplomacy (Latin Am.: gen.)      327.8
F1416.A-Z    Foreign relns. (Latin Am. & other places except U.S.) 327.80+
F1416.F8     Foreign relns. (Latin Am.-Fr.)
F1416.G3         Foreign relns. (Latin Am.-Ger.)        327.8043
F1416.G7         Foreign relns. (Latin Am.-G.B.)
F1416.I8         Foreign relns. (Latin Am.-It.)
F1416.J3         Foreign relns. (Latin Am.-Japan)      327.8052
F1416.R9         Foreign relns. (Latin Am.-Rus.)
F1418        Foreign relns. (Latin Am.-U.S.)        327.8073
F1421-1577       CENTRAL AMERICA        972, 972.8+
F1438        Central America (1821-1950)        972.804-805
F1440.A-Z    Races, ethnography, religious groups (C.Am.)
F1440.G3     Germans (in C.Am.)
F1561-1577       PANAMA        972.87
F1566.5      Panama (1903-52)        972.8705-052
F1569.A-Z    Local history (Pan.: provinces, regions, etc.)
F1569.C2     CANAL ZONE & Panama Canal        972.875
```

```
F1601-2175+    WEST INDIES    972.9
F1611              Description & travel (W.Ind.: 1810-1950)    917.29044-045
F1621          West Indies (gen. hist.)
F1621.5        Diplomacy (W.Ind.: gen.)
F1622              Foreign relns. (W.Ind.-U.S.)
F1622.5.A-Z       Foreign relns. (W.Ind.-partic. places)
F1622.5.G3        Foreign relns. (W.Ind.-Ger.)
F1622.5.G7        Foreign relns. (W.Ind.-G.B.)
F1623          West Indies (1898-)    972.904-905
F1629.A-Z         Races, ethnography, religious groups (W.Ind.)
F1630-1640        BERMUDA ISLANDS    972.99
F1636-1637        Bermuda (gen. hist.)
F1650-1660        BAHAMA ISLANDS    972.96
F1656-1657        Bahamas (gen. hist.)
F1741-1991  GREATER ANTILLES (Cuba, Haiti, Puerto Rico, Jamaica, etc.)
                                                     972.9, .91-95
F1741          Antilles (Greater: gen. hist. of the chain)    972.9
F1751-1849     CUBA        972.91
F1765             Description & travel (Cuba: 1898-)    917.291046
F1776          Cuba (gen.)
F1776.1        Military & naval history (Cuba)
F1776.2        Diplomacy (Cuba: gen.)
F1776.3.A-Z    Foreign relns. (Cuba-other places)
F1776.3.G3     Foreign relns. (Cuba-Ger.)
F1776.3.G7     Foreign relns. (Cuba-G.B.)
F1776.3.U6-7   Foreign relns. (Cuba-U.S.)
F1788          Cuba (1933-)        972.91063
F1789.A-Z      Races. ethnography, religious groups (Cuba)
F1789.J4       Jews (in Cuba)
F1791-1799        Havana Province (Cuba)
F1799.A-Z         Havana, Cuba    972.9123
F1861-1896        JAMAICA         972.92
F1871          Description & travel (Jam.: 1811-1950)
F1881          Jamaica (gen.)
F1886          Jamaica (1810-1953)    972.92034-9205
F1891.A-Z      Local history (Jam.: regions, islands, etc.)
F1895.A-Z      Local history (Jam.: towns etc.)
F1895.K5          Kingston, Jam.
F1895.M6          Montego Bay, Jam.
F1895.P6          Port Royal, Jam.
F1896.A-Z         Races, ethnography, religious groups (Jam.)
F1900-1940        HAITI        972.94
F1927             Haiti (1915-50)    972.9405-9406
F1931-1941        DOMINICAN REPUBLIC    972.93
F1951-1983        PUERTO RICO    972.95
F1965          Description & travel (Puerto R.: 1898-)
F1971          Puerto Rico (gen.)
F1975          Puerto Rico (1898-1952)    972.9504-9505
F1981.A-Z         Local history (Puerto R.: regions, towns, etc.)
F1981.S2          San Juan, P.R.
```

| F2001-2151 | LESSER ANTILLES & Caribbes | 972.9, .97-98 |
|---|---|---|
| F2001 | Antilles (Lesser: gen.) | 972.9 |
| F2006 | LEEWARD ISLANDS (inclu. St. Thomas, Virgin Islands, etc.) | 972.97 |
| F2011 | WINDWARD ISLANDS (inclu. Barbados, St. Lucia. etc.) | 972.98 |
| F2016 | Venezuelan coast islands (Aruba, Curaçao, Tobago, Trinidad, etc.) | 972.98 |
| F2033-2129 | Lesser Antilles (indiv. islands in alphab. order) | |
| F2131-2151 | Lesser Antilles (by political group) | |
| F2131-2133 | BRITISH WEST INDIES | 972.9, .973 |
| F2136 | VIRGIN ISLANDS (U.S.) | 972.9722 |
| F2141 | DUTCH WEST INDIES | 972.986 |
| F2151 | FRENCH WEST INDIES | 972.976 |
| F2161-2175 | CARIBBEAN SEA AREA | 972.9, 909.096365 |
| F2171 | Description & travel (Carib. Sea: 1811-) | |
| F2175 | Caribbean Sea area (1811-) | 972.904-905 |

| F2201-3799+ | SOUTH AMERICA | 980-989 |
|---|---|---|
| F2212-2217 | Local history (S.Am.: regions) | |
| F2212 | ANDES | |
| F2213 | Pacific Coast (S.Am.) | |
| F2214 | Atlantic Coast (S.Am.) | 980.009821, .009636 |
| F2216 | South America (northern: Brazil, Ven., Peru, etc.) | |
| F2217 | South America (southern: Arg., Chile, Uru., etc.) | |
| F2223 | Description & travel (S.Am.: 1811-1950) | |
| F2231 | South America (gen.) | 980 |
| F2236 | South America (1830-) | 980.03 |
| F2237 | South America (1939-) | 980.033+ |
| F2239.A-Z | Races, ethnography, religious groups (S.Am.) | |
| F2239.B8 | British (in S.Am.) | |
| F2239.F8 | French (in S.Am.) | |
| F2239.G3 | Germans (in S.Am.) | |
| F2239.I8 | Italians (in S.Am.) | |
| F2239.J5 | Jews (in S.Am.) | |
| F2251-2299 | COLOMBIA | 986.1+ |
| F2277 | Colombia (1904-46) | 986.1062-10631 |
| F2301-2349 | VENEZUELA | 987 |
| F2321 | Venezuela (gen.) | |
| F2321.2 | Diplomacy (Venez.: gen.) | |
| F2321.3.A-Z | Foreign relns. (Venez. & other places) | |
| F2321.3.G3 | Foreign relns. (Venez.-Ger.) | |
| F2326 | Venezuela (1935-) | 987.0632 |
| F2351-2471 | GUIANA (Brit., Dutch, & Fr.) | 988 |
| F2501-2659 | BRAZIL | 981 |
| F2515 | Description & travel (Brazil: 1890-1950) | 918.1045-1061 |
| F2521 | Brazil (gen.) | |
| F2522 | Military & naval history (Brazil) | |
| F2523 | Diplomacy (Brazil: gen.) | 327.81 |
| F2523.A-Z | Foreign relns. (Brazil-other lands) | |
| F2523.G3 | Foreign relns. (Brazil-Ger.) | |
| F2523.G7 | Foreign relns. (Brazil-G.B.) | |
| F2535 | Brazil (1822-) | 981.04+ |
| F2537 | Brazil (1889-) | 981.05+ |
| F2538 | Brazil (1930-54) | 981.06-061 |

| | | |
|---|---|---|
| F2541-2636+ | Local history (Brazil: regions, states, etc.) | |
| F2611 | Rio de Janeiro (Brazil: state) | |
| F2646 | Rio de Janeiro, Br. | 981.53 |
| F2659.A-Z | Races, ethnography, religious groups (Brazil) | |
| F2659.A5 | Americans (in Brazil) | |
| F2659.F8 | French (in Brazil) | |
| F2659.G3 | Germans (in Brazil) | |
| F2659.J3 | Japanese (in Brazil) | |
| F2659.J5 | Jews (in Brazil) | |
| F2659.P8 | Portuguese (in Brazil) | |
| F2661-2699 | PARAGUAY | 989.2 |
| F2681 | Paraguay (gen.) | |
| F2682 | Diplomacy (Paraguay) | |
| F2682.A-Z | Foreign relns. (Paraguay-other places) | |
| F2682.G3 | Foreign relns. (Paraguay-Ger.) | 327.892043 |
| F2689 | Paraguay (1938-) | 989.2071-2072 |
| F2699.A-Z | Races, ethnography, religious groups (Paraguay) | |
| F2699.G3 | Germans (in Paraguay) | |
| F2699.I8 | Italians (in Paraguay) | |
| F2701-2799 | URUGUAY | 989.5 |
| F2721 | Uruguay (gen.) | |
| F2722 | Diplomacy (Urug.: gen.) | |
| F2722.5.A-Z | Foreign relns. (Urug. & other partic. places: by name) | |
| F2722.5.G3 | Foreign relns. (Urug.-Ger.) | 327.895043 |
| F2722.5.I8 | Foreign relns. (Urug.-It.) | |
| F2728 | Uruguay (1904-) | 989.5061-5063 |
| F2781 | Montevideo, Urug. | 989.513 |
| F2799.A-Z | Races, ethnography, religious groups (Urug.) | |
| F2799.F7 | French (in Urug.) | |
| F2799.G3 | Germans (in Urug.) | |
| F2799.J4 | Jews (in Urug.) | |
| F2801-3021 | ARGENTINA | 982 |
| F2815 | Description & travel (Arg.: 1806-1950) | 918.2043-2062 |
| F2831 | Argentina (gen.) | |
| F2832 | Military & naval history (Arg.) | |
| F2833 | Diplomacy (Arg.: gen.) | |
| F2833.5.A-Z | Foreign relns. (Arg.-partic. lands) | 327.820+ |
| F2833.5.F8 | Foreign relns. (Arg.-Fr.) | |
| F2833.5.G3 | Foreign relns. (Arg.-Ger.) | 327.82043 |
| F2833.5.G7 | Foreign relns. (Arg.-G.B.) | |
| F2833.5.I8 | Foreign relns. (Arg.-It.) | |
| F2833.5.J3 | Foreign relns. (Arg.-Japan) | |
| F2833.5.U6-7 | Foreign relns. (Arg.-U.S.) | |
| F2846 | Argentina (1810-) | 982.03+ |
| F2848 | Argentina (1910-43) | 982.06 |
| F2849 | Argentina (1943-: Inclu. Perón regime & biog.) | 982.061-062 |
| F2850-2991 | Local history (Arg.: provinces, regions, etc.: alphab. order) | |
| F2861 | Buenos Aires (Arg.: province) | |
| F3001 | Buenos Aires, Arg. | 982.11 |
| F3011.A-Z | Local history (Arg.: towns etc.) | |

| | | |
|---|---|---|
| F3021.A-Z | Races, ethnography, religious groups (Arg.) | |
| F3021.A1 | Races, ethnography, religious groups (Arg.: gen.) | |
| F3021.A5 | Americans (in Arg.) | |
| F3021.B86 | British (in Arg.) | |
| F3021.F8 | French (in Arg.) | |
| F3021.G3 | Germans (in Arg.) | |
| F3021.I8 | Italians (in Arg.) | |
| F3021.J5 | Jews (in Arg.) | |
| F3021.U5 | Ukrainians (in Arg.) | |
| F3031 | FALKLAND ISLANDS | 997.11 |
| F3051-3285 | CHILE | 983 |
| F3063 | Description & travel (Chile: 1810-1950) | 918.3044-30643 |
| F3081 | Chile (gen.) | |
| F3083 | Diplomacy (Chile: gen.) | |
| F3083.5.A-Z | Foreign relns. (Chile-other places) | |
| F3083.5.G3 | Foreign relns. (Chile-Ger.) | |
| F3083.5.J3 | Foreign relns. (Chile-Japan) | |
| F3083.5.U6-7 | Foreign relns. (Chile-U.S.) | |
| F3099 | Chile (1921-) | 983.063-064+ |
| F3285.A-Z | Races, ethnography, religious groups (Chile) | |
| F3285.G3 | Germans (in Chile) | |
| F3285.J4 | Jews (in Chile) | |
| F3301-3359 | BOLIVIA | 984 |
| F3326 | Bolivia (1938-) | 984.051 |
| F3359.A-Z | Races, ethnography, religious groups (Bolivia) | |
| F3359.G3 | Germans (in Bolivia) | |
| F3401-3619 | PERU | 985 |
| F3423 | Description & travel (Peru: 1820-1950) | |
| F3431 | Peru (gen.) | |
| F3433 | Diplomacy (Peru: gen.) | |
| F3434.A-Z | Foreign relns. (Peru-other places) | |
| F3434.G3 | Foreign relns. (Peru-Ger.) | |
| F3434.J3 | Foreign relns. (Peru-Japan) | |
| F3434.U6-7 | Foreign relns. (Peru-U.S.) | |
| F3448 | Peru (1919-) | 985.0631-0632 |
| F3619.A-Z | Races, ethnography, religious groups (Peru) | |
| F3619.A5 | Americans (in Peru) | |
| F3619.G3 | Germans (in Peru) | |
| F3619.J3 | Japanese (in Peru) | |
| F3701-3799 | ECUADOR | 986.6 |
| F3737 | Ecuador (1895-1944) | 986.607-6072 |

| | | |
|---|---|---|
| U | Military science (gen.) | 355 |
| U-UH | MILITARY SCIENCE, MILITARY ENGINEERING, & AIR FORCES | |
| | | 355-359, 623 |
| UA | Armies (organization, descrip., status) | |
| UB | Administration, Military | |
| UC | Maintenance & transportation, Military | |
| UD | Infantry | |
| UE | Cavalry (armored & mechanized) | |
| UF | Artillery | |
| UG | Military engineering & air forces | |
| UH | Military science (misc. services: medical etc.) | |

| | | |
|---|---|---|
| U1-900+ | MILITARY SCIENCE (GEN.) | 355 |
| U1 | Periodicals & associations (military: in English) 355.005-006 | |
| U9 | Almanacs, annuals, etc., Military (U.S.) | |
| U10.A-Z | Almanacs, annuals, etc., Military (countries besides U.S.) | |
| U10.G7 | Almanacs, annuals, etc., Military (G.B.) | |
| U13.A-Z | Museums, Military (inclu. exhibitions) | 355.0074 |
| U13.A1 | Military museums & exhibitions (gen.) | |
| U13.A2-Z | Exhibitions & museums, Military (by country) | 355.00740+ |
| U13.F8 | Museums, Military (Fr.) | |
| U13.G7 | Museums, Military (G.B.) | |
| U13.G72.L69 | Imperial War Museum (London, G.B.) | |
| U13.S65 | Museums, Military (Sov.Un.) | |
| U13.U6-7 | Museums, Military (U.S.) | 355.0074073 |
| U21.75 | Women & the military (sociology) | |
| U24-25 | Dictionaries & encyclopedias (mil. sci.) | 355.003 |
| U27-45 | Military science (history) | |
| U27 | Military science (history: gen.) | 355.009 |
| U39 | Military science (modern: 1800-) | |
| U41 | Military science (19th c.) | |
| U42 | Military science (20th c.) | 355.00904 |
| U43.A-Z | Military science (history: by country or area) | |
| U51-55 | Biography, Military (SEE ALSO D-F war & country #s) | |
| | | 355.3310922-0924, .00922-00924 |
| U52 | Military biography (U.S.: collective) | |
| U53.A-Z | Biography, Military (U.S.: individual) | 355.330973 |
| U54.A-Z | Biography, Military (except U.S.: group by place) | |
| U55.A-Z | Biography, Military (except U.S.: individual) | |
| U56 | Military clubs (U.S.) | |
| U58 | Clubs, Military (G.B.) | |
| U59.A-Z | Clubs, Military (by place, except U.S. & G.B.) | |
| U102 | Military science (gen. titles: pubn. date 1789-) | 355, .43 |
| U110-145 | Handbooks & manuals, Soldiers' | 355.00202 |
| U110 | Soldiers' handbooks & manuals (gen.) | |
| U113 | Manuals & handbooks, Soldiers' (U.S.) | |
| U115.A-Z | Handbooks & manuals, Soldiers' (by place except U.S.) | |
| U130-135 | Handbooks, Officers' | |
| U150-155 | Military planning | |
| U153 | Planning, Military (U.S.) | |
| U162 | Strategy (mil. sci.: pubn. 1789-) | 355.43 |
| U162.6 | Deterrence | |
| U165 | Tactics, Military (pubn. 1811-) | 355.42 |

| | | |
|---|---|---|
| U167.5.A-Z | Military tactics (special topics: by name) | |
| U167.5.A35 | Advanced guard | |
| U167.5.D4 | Desert warfare | |
| U167.5.E57 | Envelopment (mil. sci.) | |
| U167.5.F6 | Forest fighting | |
| U167.5.H3 | Hand-to-hand fighting | |
| U167.5.J8 | Jungle warfare | |
| U167.5.L5 | Blitzkrieg (lightning war) | |
| U167.5.M3 | Machine-gun warfare | |
| U167.5.M6 | Motorized units (mil. sci.) | |
| U167.5.N5 | Night fighting | |
| U167.5.R34 | Raids (mil. sci.) | |
| U167.5.S7 | Street fighting | |
| U167.5.W5 | Winter warfare | |
| U168 | Logistics (mil. sci.) | 355.411 |
| U170-175 | Field service (mil. sci.) | |
| U180-185 | Encampments | 355.412 |
| U200 | Landing maneuvers & debarkation | |
| U215 | Rearguard action | |
| U220 | Reconnaisance & patrols | 355.413, 358.45 |
| U225 | Survival (combat: escape & evasion) | |
| U240 | Guerrilla warfare & small wars | 355.02184, 356.15 |
| U241 | Anti-guerrilla warfare | |
| U250-255 | Maneuvers (mil. sci.) | |
| U250 | Maneuvers (mil. sci.: gen.) | 355.52 |
| U253 | Maneuvers (mil. sci.: U.S.) | |
| U255.A-Z | Maneuvers (mil. sci.: places besides U.S.) | |
| U260 | Combined ops. (joint: air, army, navy) | |
| U261 | Amphibious ops. | 359.83, .96 |
| U262 | Commando tactics | 355.425 |
| U264 | Atomic weapons (SEE ALSO UG1282.A8) | |
| U265 | Military expeditions | |
| U290 | Drill camps, instruction bases, maneuver grounds (gen.) | |
| U293 | Instruction camps, maneuver grounds, etc. (U.S.) | |
| U294.5.A-Z | Drill camps, maneuver grounds, etc. (U.S.: by name) | |
| U300-305 | Artillery & rifle ranges | |
| U303 | Rifle & artillery ranges (U.S.) | |
| U310 | War games | 355.5 |
| U311 | Models, Military | |
| U312 | Map maneuvers & problems | |
| U320-325 | Physical training (mil. sci.) | 355.54+ |
| U323 | Training, Physical (mil. sci.: U.S.) | |
| U327 | Sports, Military (gen.) | |
| U328.A-Z | Military sports (by place) | |
| U390-395 | Research, Military | 355.07 |
| U393 | Military research (U.S.) | |

| | | |
|---|---|---|
| U400-714 | EDUCATION, MILITARY | 355.07 |
| U400 | Military education & training (gen.) | 355.07 |
| U403 | Training & education, Military (modern hist.) | |
| U405 | Education, Military (gen.: pubns. 1801+) | |
| U407-439 | Education, Military (U.S.) | |
| U408 | Military education (U.S.: gen.) | 355.0071073 |
| U408.3 | U.S. military education (gen. special) | |
| U410.A-R3+ | U.S. Military Academy (West Point) | 355.0071173 |
| U410.C3-H8 | U.S. Military Academy (admin.) | |
| U410.E1 | Reports, Official (U.S. Mil. Acad. Superinten.: annual) | |
| U410.E5 | Reports, Congressional (U.S. Military Academy: by date) | |
| U410.H2 | Rosters, Officers' (U.S. Mil. Acad.) | |
| U410.H3-4 | Registers, Official (U.S. Mil. Acad.) | |
| U410.H5 | Cullum's Register (U.S. Mil. Acad.) | |
| U410.H5-8 | U.S. Military Academy (registers, unoff.) | |
| U410.L1 | U.S. Military Academy (gen. hist.) | |
| U410.L1.A1-5 | West Point (U.S. Mil. Acad.: official hist's.) | |
| U410.L3 | Pictorials (U.S. Mil. Acad.) | |
| U410.M1.A1-Z | Biography (U.S. Mil. Acad.: by name) | |
| U410.M1.P1 | West Point (descrip. & life) | |
| U412 | National War College (U.S.: Wash., D.C.) | |
| U413 | Army War College (U.S.) | |
| U415 | Military education (U.S.: Command & Gen. Staff Coll.) | |
| U428.5 | Reserve Officers' Training Corps (U.S.: R.O.T.C.) | |
| U440-444 | Military education (Can.) | |
| U505-630 | Education, Military (Eur.) | 355.007104+ |
| U505 | Military education (Eur.: gen.) | |
| U510-549.3 | Education, Military (G.B.) | |
| U510 | Military education (G.B.: gen.) | |
| U511 | British military education (special time periods) | |
| U518.A-Z | Royal Military Academy (Woolwich: div'd like U410.A-Z) | |
| U518.L1 | Royal Military Academy (Woolwich: gen. hist's.) | |
| U520.A-Z | Royal Military College (Sandhurst) | |
| U520.L1 | Sandhurst (Royal Mil. Coll.: descrip. & life) | |
| U565-569 | Education, Military (Fr.) | |
| U570-574 | Education, Military (Ger.) | 355.0071043 |
| U570 | Military education (Ger.: gen.) | |
| U571 | German military education (special times) | |
| U572.A-Z | Military education (Ger.: special topics) | |
| U574.A-Z | Training, Military (Ger.: by school location) | |
| U585-589 | Education, Military (It.) | |
| U590-594 | Education, Military (Nor.) | |
| U600-604 | Education, Military (Rus.) | 355.0071047 |
| U625 | Education, Military (Balkan States) | |
| U635-660 | Education, Military (Asia) | |
| U635 | Military education (Asia: gen.) | |
| U640-644 | Education, Military (China) | 355.0071051 |
| U640 | Military education (China: gen.) | |
| U650-654 | Education, Military (Japan) | 355.0071052 |
| U650 | Military education (Japan: gen.) | |
| U651 | Japanese military education (special periods) | |
| U700-704 | Education, Military (Australia) | 355.0071094 |
| U705-709 | Education, Military (New Z.) | |

| | | |
|---|---|---|
| U719-740+ | Observations, Military | |
| U719 | Military observations (collected: 2 or more wars) | |
| U735 | Observations, Military (Russo-Jpn. War, 1904-5) | |
| U738 | Observations, Military (WWI) | |
| U739.5 | Observations, Military (Sp. Civil War, 1936-9) | |
| U739.8 | Observations, Military (Sino-Jpn. War, 1937-45) | |
| U740 | Observations, Military (WWII) | |
| U750-773 | MILITARY LIFE & CUSTOMS | 355.1 |
| U750 | Customs, Military (gen.) | |
| U765 | Life & customs, Military (modern: gen.) | 355.1 |
| U766 | Military life & customs (modern: U.S.) | 355.10973 |
| U767 | Military life & customs (modern: G.B.) | 355.10941 |
| U768 | Military life & customs (modern: Fr.) | |
| U769 | Military life & customs (modern: Ger.) | 355.10943 |
| U770 | Military life & customs (modern: It.) | |
| U771 | Military life & customs (modern: Rus.) | 355.10947 |
| U773 | Military life & customs (modern: misc. countries besides U766-771) | |
| U790 | Curiosities, Military (inclu. collector's hdbks.) | |
| U799-897 | ARMS & ARMOR (Hist.) | |
| U799 | Periodicals & associations (arms & armor: hist.) | |
| U800.A3-Z | Arms (gen.: pubn. dates 1801+) | 355.8, 623.4 |
| U804 | Museums, exhibitions, etc. (arms) | |
| U804.A2-Z | Museums, exhibitions, etc. (arms: by country) | |
| U815 | Armament (modern: gen.) | |
| U818 | Armament (modern: U.S.) | |
| U820.A-Z | Armament (modern: Eur.: by place) | |
| U820.G3 | British armament (modern) | |
| U820.G7 | German armament (modern) | |
| U821.A-Z | Armament (modern: Asia: by country) | |
| U821.J3 | Japanese armament (modern) | |
| U880 | Guns (gen.) | 623.4 |
| U884 | Small arms (gen.) | |
| U889 | Small arms (19th-20th c.) | |
| U897.A-Z | Small arms (by region or country) | |
| | | |
| UA | ARMIES (organiz. & world status) | 355 |
| UA10 | Military status (world: gen.) | 355.03 |
| UA10.5 | National security (gen.) | |
| UA11 | Policy, Military (gen.) | |
| UA14 | Colonial troops | |
| UA15 | Armies & navies (of the world) | |
| UA16 | Military missions | |
| UA17 | Costs, Military | 355.622 |
| UA17.5.A2 | Manpower (gen.) | 355.22, .61 |
| UA17.5.A3-Z | Manpower (by country) | |
| UA18.A2 | Mobilization, Industrial (gen.) | 355.28 |
| UA18.A3-Z | Industrial mobilization (by country: SEE ALSO D-F for specific wars) | |

89

| UA21-876+ | MILITARY STATUS (worldwide: place by place) | 355.0330+ |
| UA21-645 | MILITARY STATUS (W. Hemis.) | |
| UA21 | America (mil. status: gen.) | 355.03301812 |
| UA22-602 | MILITARY STATUS (N. Am.) | |
| UA22 | North America (mil. status: gen.) | 355.03307 |
| UA23-585 | MILITARY STATUS (U.S.) | 355.033273 |
| UA23.A1.A-Z | Periodicals & associations (military: U.S.) | |
| UA23.A2-Z | United States (mil. status: gen.) | |
| UA23.2-6 | U.S. Dept. of Defense | 353.6-7 |
| UA23.2 | Reports, Official (U.S. Dept. Defense: formerly War Dept.) | |
| UA23.6 | U.S. Dept. of Defense (gen. hist.) | |
| UA24-39 | U.S. Army | |
| UA24.A1-7 | Reports, Official (U.S. Army: War Dept., Dept. o/t Army, Adj. Gen., Inspec. Gen., etc.: annual) | |
| UA24.A1-149 | U.S. War Dept. (ann. reports) | |
| UA25 | U.S. Army (gen.) | 355.00973, .30973, .310973 |
| UA26.A1-6 | Army posts (U.S.: gen.) | |
| UA26.A7-Z | Army posts (U.S.: by place) | |
| UA27.3.1st- | Armies (U.S.: by #/author) | |
| UA27.5.1st- | Divisions (U.S.: by #/author) | |
| UA27.A-Z | Divisions (U.S. Army: by place) | |
| UA27.P5 | Division of the Philippines (U.S. Army) | |
| UA28 | Infantry (U.S.: gen.) | 356.10973 |
| UA29.1st- | Infantry regiments (U.S.: by #/author) | |
| UA30 | Armored units & cavalry (U.S.: inclu. mechanized: gen.) | 357.10973 |
| UA31.1st- | Cavalry & armored regiments (U.S.: by #/author) | |
| UA32 | Artillery (U.S.: gen.) | 358.10973, .120973 |
| UA33.1st- | Artillery batteries (U.S.: by #/author) | |
| UA34.A-Z | U.S. Army (special troops: by name) | |
| UA37 | Lists & registers (U.S. Army: vets.) | |
| UA42-560 | RESERVES, ARMY (U.S.: Nat. Guard, militia, volunteers, etc.) | |
| UA42.A1-59 | Reports, Official (army reserves: U.S.) | |
| UA42.A6.A-Z | Associations, periodicals, societies (U.S.: army reserves) | E740 |
| UA42.A7-Z | U.S. National Guard (gen.) | |
| UA45 | Women's reserves (U.S.) | |
| UA50-549 | MILITIA (U.S.: inclu. Nat. Guard etc.: state by state) | |
| UA90-99 | Reserves, Army (U.S.: Calif.) | |
| UA90 | California National Guard (gen.) | |
| UA91 | Primary sources, documents (Calif. army reserves) | |
| UA92 | Lists & registers (Calif. Nat. Guard) | |
| UA93-94 | Infantry (U.S.: Calif. reserves) | |
| UA96 | Artillery (U.S.: Calif. reserves: gen., inclu. field) | |
| UA97-97.5 | Coast artillery (U.S.: Calif. reserves) | |
| UA97.7-75 | Antiaircraft artillery (U.S.: Calif. army reserves) | |
| UA159.1-9 | Reserves, Army (U.S.: Hawaii) | |
| UA170-179 | Volunteers (Nat. Guard, militia, etc.: Illinois) | |
| UA290-299 | Reserves, Army (U.S.: Missouri) | |

| | | |
|---|---|---|
| UA360-369 | Reserves, Army (U.S.: N.Y.: militia, volunteers, Nat. Guard, etc.) | |
| UA360 | New York National Guard (gen.) | |
| UA361 | Primary sources, documents (N.Y. army reserves) | |
| UA362 | Lists & registers (N.Y. Nat. Guard) | |
| UA363-364 | Infantry (U.S.: N.Y. reserves) | |
| UA366-367.75 | Artillery (U.S.: N.Y. reserves) | |
| UA366 | Field artillery (U.S.: N.Y. reserves: ALSO gen. artil.) | |
| UA367-367.5 | Coast artillery (U.S.: N.Y. reserves) | |
| UA367.7-75 | Antiaircraft (U.S.: N.Y. army reserves) | |
| UA420-429 | Reserves, Army (U.S.: Penn.) | |
| UA470-479 | Reserves, Army (U.S.: Texas) | |
| UA565.A-Z | Auxiliaries, Army (U.S.) | |
| UA565.W6 | WACS (Women's Army Corps: U.S.) | |
| UA600-602 | Military status (Can.) | |
| UA600 | Canada (mil. status: gen.) | 355.033271, .033571, .033071 |
| UA602.3 | Latin America (mil. status: gen.) | 355.03328, .03308 |
| UA603-605 | Mexico (mil. status) | |
| UA606-608 | Military status (Central Am.) | |
| UA607.A-Z | Central America (mil. status: by country) | |
| UA607.P3 | Panama (mil. status) | |
| UA609-611 | West Indies (mil. status) | |
| UA612-645 | Military status (S.Am.) | |
| UA612 | South America (mil. status: gen.) | 355.03308, .03328 |
| UA613-615 | Argentina (mil. status) | 355.033082 |
| UA619-621 | Brazil (mil. status) | |
| UA622-624 | Chile (mil. status) | |
| UA634-636 | Paraguay (mil. status) | 355.0330892 |
| UA637-639 | Peru (mil. status) | |
| UA640-642 | Uruguay (mil. status) | 355.0330895 |
| UA643-645 | Venezuela (mil. status) | |
| UA646-829 | MILITARY STATUS (Eur.) | |
| UA646 | Europe (mil. status) | 355.03304, .03324, .03354 |
| UA646.53 | Baltic Sea (mil. status) | 355.033016334, .4716334, 359.4716334 |
| UA646.55 | Mediterranean Sea (mil. status) | 355.03301638, 359.471638 |
| UA646.6 | North Sea (mil. status) | 355.033016336 |
| UA646.7 | Scandinavia (mil. status) | 355.033048, .033248, .033548 |
| UA646.85 | Northern Europe (mil. status) | 355.033048 |
| UA647-668 | Military status (G.B.) | 355.033041-033042, .033241, .033541 |
| UA647 | Great Britain (mil. status) | 355.033041 |
| UA648 | Primary sources, documents (G.B.: War Dept., Parliament, other re military) | |
| UA649-668 | G.B. Army | |
| UA649 | G.B. Army (gen.) | 355.00941, .310941 |
| UA650-653 | Infantry (G.B.) | |
| UA650 | Infantry (G.B.: gen.) | 356.10941 |
| UA651.A-Z | Infantry regiments (G.B.: by name) | |
| UA651.C6 | Coldstream Guards (G.B.) | |
| UA654-657 | Cavalry (G.B.) | 357.10941 |
| UA658 | Artillery (G.B.) | 358.10941, .120941 |
| UA663 | Welsh troops (G.B.) | |
| UA664 | Scottish troops (G.B.) | |
| UA665 | Irish troops (G.B.) | |
| UA668 | Colonial troops (G.B.: inclu. natives: gen.) | |

| | | |
|---|---|---|
| UA670-679 | Military status (Austria & Austria-Hung.) | |
| UA670 | Austria & Austria-Hungary (mil. status) | 355.0330436 |
| UA672 | Austria-Hungary. Army (gen.) | 355.309436 |
| UA673 | Infantry (Austria & Austria-Hung.) | |
| UA674 | Cavalry (Austria & Austria-Hung.) | |
| UA680-689 | Belgium (mil. status) | 355.0330493 |
| UA690-699 | Denmark (mil. status) | 355.0330489 |
| UA700-709 | Military status (Fr.) | |
| UA700 | France (mil. status: gen.) | 355.033044 |
| UA702 | France. Army (gen.) | 355.00944, .30944 |
| UA702.3 | Army posts (Fr.: gen.) | |
| UA702.32.A-Z | Army posts (Fr.: by place) | |
| UA703-705 | France. Army (infantry, cavalry, armor, artillery) | |
| UA709 | Colonial troops (Fr.) | |
| UA710-719 | Military status (Ger.) | |
| UA710 | Germany (mil. status: gen.) | 355.033043, .033243, .033543 |
| UA712 | Germany. Army (gen.) | 355.00943, .30943, .310943 |
| UA713.A1-Z9.A-Z | Infantry (Ger.) | 356.10943 |
| UA713.A1-5 | Primary sources, documents (Ger. infantry) | |
| UA713.A6-Z4 | Infantry (Ger.: gen.) | |
| UA713.Z6.1st- | Infantry (Ger.: by regiment #) | |
| UA713.Z9.A-Z | Infantry (Ger.: by group name) | |
| UA714 | Armored units & cavalry (Ger.) | 357.10943, .50943, 358.180943 |
| UA715 | Artillery (Ger.) | |
| UA716.A-Z | Germany. Army (special units: by name) | |
| UA717 | Militia (Ger.) | |
| UA718.A-Z | Germany. Army (local) | |
| UA719 | Colonial troops (Ger.) | |
| UA720-729 | Greece (mil. status) | 355.0330495 |
| UA730-739 | Netherlands (mil. status) | 355.0330492 |
| UA740-749 | Military status (It.) | |
| UA740 | Italy (mil. status) | 355.033045 |
| UA742 | Italy. Army (gen.) | 355.30945 |
| UA743 | Infantry (It.) | |
| UA744 | Armored units & cavalry (It.) | |
| UA745 | Artillery (It.) | |
| UA745.5 | Swiss Guards (Papal Guards) | |
| UA750-759 | Military status (Norway) | |
| UA750 | Norway (mil. status) | 355.0330481 |
| UA760-769 | Portugal (mil. status) | |
| UA770-779 | Military status (Rus. or Sov.Un.) | |
| UA770 | Russia (mil. status) | 355.033047, .033247, .033547 |
| UA771 | Primary sources, documents (Rus. military) | |
| UA772 | Russia. Army (gen.) | 355.30947, .00947 |
| UA773.A1-Z9.A-Z | Infantry (Rus.) | |
| UA773.A1-5 | Primary sources, documents (Rus.) | |
| UA773.A6-Z4 | Infantry (Rus.: gen.) | |
| UA773.Z6.1st- | Infantry (Rus.: by regiment #) | |
| UA773.Z9.A-Z | Infantry (Rus.: by group name) | |
| UA774 | Armored units & cavalry (Rus.) | |
| UA775 | Artillery (Rus.) | |
| UA780-789 | Spain (mil. status) | 355.033046 |
| UA790-799 | Sweden (mil. status) | 355.0330485 |
| UA800-809 | Switzerland (mil. status) | 355.0330494 |

```
UA810-819    Military status (Tur.)
UA810        Turkey (mil. status)      355.0330561
UA820-827    Military status (Balkan States)
   UA820        Balkan States (mil. status: gen.)    355.0330496
   UA822        Balkan States (mil. status: descrip. & hist.)
   UA824        Bulgaria (mil. status)      355.03304977
   UA826        Rumania (mil. status)       355.0330498
   UA827        Yugoslavia (mil. status)    355.0330497
UA829.A-Z    Military status (misc. Eur. countries)
UA829.C95    Czechoslovakia (mil. status)       355.0330437
UA829.H9     Hungary (mil. status)      355.0330439
UA829.P7     Poland (mil. status)       355.0330438
UA830-853    MILITARY STATUS (Asia)
UA830        Asia (mil. status: gen.)        355.03305, .03325, .03355
UA835-839    Military status (China)
UA835        China (mil. status)             355.033051, .033251, .033551
UA837        China. Army (gen.)              355.30951, .00951
UA840-844    India (mil. status)             355.033054
UA845-849    Military status (Japan)
UA845        Japan (mil. status: gen.)    355.033052, .033252, .033552
UA846        Primary sources, documents (Jpn. military)
UA847        Japan. Army (gen.)           355.00952, .30952, .310952
UA848.A-Z       Japan. Army (service branches by name)
UA849.A-Z       Japan (mil. status: states, provinces, etc.)
UA853.A-Z    Military status (Asia: by country except India, China, Japan)
UA853.B9     Burma (mil. status)
UA853.I5     Indonesia (mil. status)
UA853.M3     Malaya (mil. status)
UA853.P5        Philippines (mil. status)    355.0330599
UA853.V5        Vietnam (mil. status)
UA855-868    Military status (Africa)
UA855        Africa (mil. status: gen.)    355.03306
UA856           South Africa (mil. status)        355.00968, .033068
UA858        Algeria (mil. status)    355.033065
UA859           Cameroon (mil. status)
UA860        Ethiopia (mil. status)      355.033063
UA860.5      Kenya (mil. status)         355.03306762
UA865        Egypt       355.033062
UA867           Morocco (mil. status)        355.033064
UA867.5      Tunisia (mil. status)       355.0330611
UA868        Libya (mil. status)         355.0330612
UA870-874    Military status (Australia)
UA870        Australia (mil. status)        355.033094, .033294, .033594
UA871        Primary sources, documents (Australia: military status)
UA872        Australia. Army (descrip. & hist.)      355.00994, .30994, .310994
UA873.A-Z       Australia. Army (special branches by name)
UA874.A-Z       Australia (mil. status: states, territories, localities)
UA874.3-7    Military status (New Z.)
UA874.3         New Zealand (mil. status: gen.)       355.0330931
UA874.5         New Zealand. Army (descrip. & hist.)     355.309931
UA874.6.A-Z     New Zealand. Army (special sections)
UA875-876    Military status (Pacific islands)
UA875           Oceania (mil. status)       355.03309
UA876.A-Z       Pacific Islands (mil. status: by island or group name)
```

| UA910-915 | Mobilization | |
|---|---|---|
| UA910 | Mobilization (gen.) | 355.28 |
| UA913 | Mobilization (U.S.) | 355.280973 |
| UA915.A-Z | Mobilization (except U.S.: by name of place) | |
| UA915.G7 | Mobilization (G.B.) | 355.280941 |
| UA917.A2 | Demobilization (gen.) | 355.29 |
| UA917.A3-Z | Demobilization (by country) | |
| UA920 | Attack & defense plans (gen.) | 355.0330+, .0332+, .0335+, .4+ |
| UA923 | Defense & attack plans (U.S.) | 355.033073, .4773 |
| UA925.A-Z | Plans, Attack & defense (countries except U.S.) | |
| UA926.A3-Z | Civil defense (gen.: SEE ALSO numbers within wars, such as D810.C69 for WWII) | |
| UA926.5 | Bomb shelters (plus other special civil defense topics like psych. aspects) | |
| UA927 | Civil defense (U.S.: gen.) | |
| UA928-928.5.A-Z | Defense, Civil (U.S. states, cities, etc.) | |
| UA929.A-Z | Civil defense (countries besides U.S.) | |
| UA929.G7 | Civil defense (G.B.) | |
| UA929.S65 | Civil defense (Sov.Un.) | |
| UA929.5 | Industrial defense (gen.) | 355.28, .26 |
| UA929.6-8 | Defense, Industrial (U.S.) | |
| UA929.9.A-Z | Industrial defense (places besides U.S.) | |
| UA929.95.A-Z | Industrial defense (by specific industry: SEE ALSO H industry #s) | |
| UA929.95.A35 | Agriculture (defense) | |
| UA929.95.C5 | Chemical industry (defense) | |
| UA929.95.E4 | Electric plants (defense) | |
| UA929.95.G7 | Grain industry (defense) | |
| UA929.95.P4 | Petroleum industry (defense) | |
| UA929.95.P93 | Public utilities (defense) | |
| UA929.95.R3 | Railroads (defense) | |
| UA929.95.T4 | Telecommunication (defense) | |
| UA929.95.T7 | Transportation (defense) | |
| UA929.95.W3 | Waterworks (defense) | |
| UA930 | Strategic lines, bases, etc. | 355.43 |
| UA940 | Military communications (gen.) | 355.27, .41, .6 |
| UA943-944 | Communications, Military (U.S.) | |
| UA945.A-Z | Military communications (except U.S.: by country) | |
| UA950-979 | Communication routes (mil. sci.) | |
| UA950 | Travel routes (mil. sci.: gen.) | |
| UA953-954 | Communication routes (U.S.) | |
| UA955.A-Z | Communication routes (except U.S.) | |
| UA960 | Roads & highways (gen.) | |
| UA963-964 | Highways (U.S.) | |
| UA965.A-Z | Roads (places outside U.S.) | |
| UA970-975 | Waterways | |
| UA975.A-Z | Waterways (outside U.S.) | |
| UA975.G3 | Waterways (Ger.) | |
| UA979 | Travel routes (misc.) | |
| UA985-997 | Military geography | 355.47+, .0330+, 359.47+ |
| UA990 | Geography, Military (gen. inclu. Eur.) | 355.47 |
| UA993 | Military geography (U.S.) | 355.4773, 359.4773 |
| UA995.A-Z | Military geography (except U.S.) | |
| UA997 | Preservation of maps & charts | |

| UB | ADMINISTRATION, MILITARY (command, intelligence, law, etc.) |
| | 355, .6 |

| | |
|---|---|
| UB1 | Periodicals (mil. admin.) |
| UB15 | Administration, Military (gen. hist.) |
| UB21-124 | MILITARY ADMINISTRATION (by country) |
| UB23-25 | Military administration (U.S.)      353.6, 355.60973 |
| UB23 | Administration, Military (U.S.: gen.) |
| UB24.A-W | Military administration (U.S.: by state) |
| UB26-27 | Military administration (Can.) |
| UB27.5-54 | Military administration (Lat.Am.) |
| UB55-95 | Military administration (Eur.) |
| UB55 | Administration, Military (Eur.: gen.) |
| UB57-64 | Military administration (G.B.) |
| UB57 | Administration, Military (G.B.: gen.)      355.60941, 354.41066 |
| UB58.1900+ | Military administration (G.B.: by time period) |
| UB59 | Military administration (G.B.: Eng. & Wales) |
| UB61 | Military administration (G.B.: Scot.) |
| UB67-68 | Military administration (Belg.) |
| UB69-70 | Military administration (Den.) |
| UB71-72 | Military administration (Fr.)      354.44066 |
| UB73-74 | Military administration (Ger.)      354.43066, 355.60943 |
| UB75-76 | Military administration (Greece) |
| UB79-80 | Military administration (It.) |
| UB81-82 | Military administration (Norway) |
| UB85-86 | Military administration (Rus.: Eur.)      354.47066 |
| UB86.5 | Military administration (Scan.: gen.) |
| UB87-88 | Military administration (Sp.) |
| UB95.A-Z | Military administration (misc. Eur. lands) |
| UB95.P7 | Military administration (Pol.) |
| UB99-113 | Military administration (Asia) |
| UB99 | Administration, Military (Asia: gen.) |
| UB101-102 | Military administration (China)      354.51066 |
| UB103-104 | Military administration (India |
| UB105-106 | Military administration (Japan)      354.52066, 355.60952 |
| UB109-110 | Military administration (Rus.: Asia & Sib.) |
| UB113.A-Z | Military administration (misc. Asian lands) |
| UB115-119 | Military administration (Africa) |
| UB121-122 | Military administration (Australia)      354.94066 |
| UB122.5 | Military administration (New Z.) |
| UB123-124 | Military administration (Pac. islands) |
| UB145 | Military administration (gen.: pubn. 1801-1970)      355.6 |
| UB146 | Military administration (gen.: pubn. 1971+)      355.6 |
| UB147 | Military service as a profession |
| UB160-165 | Accounting & accounts, Military (inclu. records, muster rolls, etc.) |
| UB160 | Muster rolls & accounts, Military (gen.: inclu. gen. corresp.: admin.) |
| UB170-175 | Adjutant generals' offices |
| UB180-197 | Military administration (civil sections) |
| UB180 | Civilian personnel (mil. admin.: gen.)      355.23 |
| UB193 | Personnel, Civilian (mil. admin.: U.S.) |

| | | |
|---|---|---|
| UB200-245 | Command control | 355.41, .33, .6 |
| UB200 | Generals, marshals, commanders (admin.: duties etc.) | 355.331 |
| UB210 | Leadership, Military | |
| UB212 | Command & control systems | |
| UB220-225 | Staffs, Army | |
| UB220 | Staffs, Military (gen.) | |
| UB223 | Army staffs (U.S.) | |
| UB225.A-Z | Military staffs (countries besides U.S.) | |
| UB230-235 | Headquarters, Military | |
| UB230 | Military headquarters ops. (gen.: inclu. aides, adjutants, etc.) | |
| UB240-245 | Inspection, Military | |
| UB246-249 | Security (defense info.) | |
| UB246 | Information security (mil. data: gen.) | |
| UB247 | Military information (security: U.S.) | |
| UB248.A-Z | Military information (security: besides U.S.) | |
| UB249 | Security, Industrial (defense purposes) | |
| UB250-271 | Intelligence, Military | |
| UB250 | Military intelligence (gen.) | 355.3432 |
| UB251.A-Z | Intelligence, Military (by country) | |
| UB251.G3 | Military intelligence (Ger.) | 355.34320943 |
| UB251.G7 | Military intelligence (G.B.) | |
| UB260 | Attachés, Military | |
| UB270-271 | Espionage & spies (mil. admin.) | |
| UB270 | Spies (mil. admin.) | 327.12 |
| UB271.A-Z | Espionage (by country responsible: SEE D-F #s for other cases in particular countries or particular wars) | |
| UB271.G3 | German espionage (gen.) | 327.120943 |
| UB271.G32.A-Z | Spies, German (by name) | |
| UB271.G7 | British espionage (gen.) | 327.120941 |
| UB271.R9 | Russian espionage (gen.) | 327.120947 |
| UB271.R92.A-Z | Spies, Russian (by name) | |
| UB271.U6 | Espionage (U.S.: gen.) | 327.120973 |
| UB271.U62.A-Z | Spies, United States (by name) | |
| UB273 | Sabotage (mil. sci.: gen.) | 355.3437 |
| UB274 | Sabotage equipment (mil. sci.) | |
| UB275 | Propaganda & psych. warfare (mil. sci.: gen.: SEE ALSO BF1045.M55 & HM263 for indiv. & social aspects) | 355.3434 |
| UB276 | Propaganda & psych. warfare (U.S.) | 355.34340973 |
| UB277.A-Z | Psychological warfare & propaganda (countries except U.S.) | |
| UB277.G3 | Propaganda & psych. warfare (Ger.) | 355.34340943 |
| UB277.J3 | Propaganda & psych. warfare (Japan) | 355.34340952 |
| UB277.R9 | Propaganda & psych. warfare (Rus.) | 355.34340947 |
| UB277.S65 | Propaganda & psych. warfare (Sov.Un.) | 355.34340947 |
| UB280-285 | Orders, passes, field correspondence (mil. sci.) | |
| UB280 | Passes, orders, field correspondence (mil. sci.: gen.) | |
| UB290 | Cryptography & ciphers | 358.24 |
| UB320-325 | Recruitment, enlistment, promotion, discharge (mil. sci.) | |
| UB320 | Promotion, discharge, recruitment, enlistment (mil. sci.: gen.) | 355.2, .61 |
| UB323 | Enlistment, recruitment, promotion, discharge (mil. sci.: U.S) | 355.20973 |
| UB325.A-Z | Discharge, promotion, recruitment, enlistment (mil. sci.: countries besides U.S.) | |
| UB330-336 | Medical & mental examinations (mil. recruits) | |
| UB330 | Mental & medical examinations (mil. recruits: gen.) | 355.2236 |

| UB337 | Classification, Military | |
|---|---|---|
| UB340-345 | Conscription & exemption (mil. service) | |
| UB340 | Induction & exemption (mil.) | 355.22363, .225 |
| UB341 | Conscientious objectors (gen.) | 355.224 |
| UB342.A-Z | Conscientious objectors (by country) | |
| UB343-344 | Draft & exemption (mil.: U.S.) | 355.2236306073 |
| UB345.A-Z | Compulsory service & exemption (mil.: besides U.S.) | |
| UB345.G3 | Exemption & draft (mil.: Ger.) | |
| UB345.J3 | Draft & exemption (mil.: Japan) | |
| UB350-355 | Universal service | |
| UB356-405 | Veterans' benefits & services | 355.115 |
| UB356 | Veterans' education, employment, etc. (gen.) | 355.1152, .1154 |
| UB357-358 | Education & employment of veterans (U.S.) | 355.1150973 |
| UB359.A-Z | Employment & education of veterans (countries except U.S.) | |
| UB360 | Rehabilitation of disabled veterans (gen.) | 355.1156, .1154 |
| UB363-364 | Disabled veterans (U.S.: rehab.) | |
| UB365.A-Z | Veterans' rehabilitation (places besides U.S.) | |
| UB366.A-Z | Occupational rehabilitation of veterans (by occup.) | |
| UB368-369 | Medical care of veterans | 355.115 |
| UB370-375 | Pensions, Veterans' | 355.64, .1151 |
| UB380-385 | Veterans' homes & hospitals | |
| UB380 | Soldiers' & sailors' homes | |
| UB382-384 | U.S. Veterans' Administration | |
| UB383 | National Home & Vets' Admin. (U.S.: gen.) | |
| UB384.A-W | Soldiers' & sailors' homes (U.S.: state) | |
| UB385.A-Z | Veterans' homes & hospitals (besides U.S.) | |
| UB390-397 | Cemeteries & graves, Military | |
| UB400-405 | Pensions, Survivors' (mil.) | |
| UB407-409 | Warrant officers (mil.) | |
| UB407 | Officers, Warrant (mil.: gen.) | |
| UB410-415 | Officers, Military (inclu. appt., promo., retire.) | |
| UB410 | Rank, appointment, promotion, retirement, etc. (mil. officers: gen.) 355.332 | |
| UB412-414 | Officers, Military (U.S.) | 355.3320973 |
| UB415.A-Z | Military officers (except U.S.: by country) | |
| UB415.G3 | Officers, Military (Ger.) | 355.3320943 |
| UB415.G7 | Officers, Military (G.B.) | 355.3320941 |
| UB416 | Minorities & women in the armed forces (gen.) | 355.22 (women), .3 |
| UB417 | Women & minorities in the armed forces (U.S.: gen.) | |
| UB418.A-Z | Minorities & women in the armed forces (U.S.: by group name) | |
| UB418.A47 | Afro-Americans (armed forces) | |
| UB418.B69 | Boys (armed forces) | |
| UB418.H57 | Hispanic-Americans (armed forces) | |
| UB418.W65 | Women (armed forces: U.S.) | |
| UB419 | Minorities & women in the armed forces (places besides U.S.) | |
| UB420-425 | Furloughs | |
| UB430-435 | Military decorations, medals, rewards, etc.   355.1342 | |
| UB430 | Decorations, Military (gen.) | |
| UB433 | Medals, decorations, etc. (mil.: U.S.) | |
| UB440-445 | Retired military | 355.1342 |
| UB448-449 | Medical care for retired military | |

| UB461-736 | MILITARY LAW |
| UB465 | Law, Military (gen.: pubn. 1801+)      343.01 |
| UB481 | International military law (PREFER JX areas)      341.6 |
| UB485 | Customs & laws of war (inclu. treatment of prisoners: SEE ALSO JX) |
| UB500-504 | Military law (U.S.: PREFER KF7201-7755)      343.010973, .0106073 |
| UB505-509 | Military law (Can.) |
| UB590-684 | European military law |
| UB590 | Military law (Eur.: gen.) |
| UB600-604 | Military law (Austria) |
| UB615-619 | Military law (Fr.) |
| UB620-624 | Military law (Ger.)      343.010943 |
| UB625-629 | Military law (G.B.: PREFER KD6000-6355)      343.010941 |
| UB655 | Military law (Rus.: gen.)      343.010947 |
| UB655.A2 | Military law (Rus.: statutes & compil's.) |
| UB655.A7-Z | Law, Military (Rus.: commentaries, digests, etc.) |
| UB655.9-656.5 | Regulations, Army (Rus.) |
| UB657 | General orders (Rus. military: collections) |
| UB657.A5 | Orders, General (Rus. military: offic. compil's.) |
| UB657.A6-7 | Orders, Special (Rus. military: collec's. & compil's.) |
| UB680-683 | Military law (Balkan states) |
| UB685-710 | Asian military law |
| UB685 | Military law (Asia ) |
| UB690-694 | Military law (China) |
| UB700-704 | Military law (Japan)      343.010952 |
| UB705-709 | Military law (Phil. Islands) |
| UB730-734 | Military law (Australia) |
| UB734.5 | Military law (New Z.) |
| UB780-789 | Offenses & crimes, Military |
| UB780 | Crimes, Military (gen.)      355.1334 |
| UB783 | Military crimes (U.S.: SEE ALSO KF7615-7618) |
| UB785.A-Z | Military crimes (countries outside U.S.) |
| UB787 | Mutiny (mil.) |
| UB788 | Desertion (mil.) |
| UB789 | Looting & other mil. crimes |
| UB790-795 | Military discipline      343.014, .13325 |
| UB793 | Discipline, Military (U.S.: SEE ALSO KF7590) |
| UB800 | Military prisons & prisoners (gen.)      365.48, 355.13325, 344.03548 |
| UB803 | Prisons, Military (U.S.: SEE ALSO KF7675) |
| UB805.A-Z | Military prisons (outside U.S.) |
| UB810 | Corporal punishment & flogging (mil. sci.: gen.) |
| UB813 | Punishment, Corporal (U.S.) |
| UB815.A-Z | Flogging & corp. punish. (countries besides U.S.) |
| UB820 | Military police (gen.)      355.13323 |
| UB825.A-Z | Police, Military (by country) |
| UB840 | Military justice (admin.: gen.)      343.0143, .133 |
| UB845.A-Z | Judiciary, Military (by country except U.S., for which SEE KF7601-7679) |
| UB850 | Courts-martial, Military (gen.)      343.0146, 355.13325 |
| UB855.A-Z | Courts-martial, Military (besides U.S., for which SEE KF7625-7659) |
| UB857.A-Z | Cases (courts-martial, mil.: by place: for U.S. SEE KF7642, 7652, etc.) |
| UB860 | Courts of inquiry, Military (gen.) |
| UB865.A-Z | Inquiry, Courts of (mil.: by country) |
| UB867.A-Z | Cases (courts of inquiry: by place: SEE KF7642 etc. for U.S.) |
| UB870 | Commissions, Military (gen.) |
| UB875.A-Z | Military commissions (by country except U.S., for which SEE KF7661) |

| UC | MAINTENANCE & TRANSPORT, MILITARY |
|---|---|
| UC10 | Military maintenance & transport (gen.)      355.6-8 |
| UC12 | Transport & maintenance (mil. sci.: gen. spec.) |
| UC15 | Requisitions, Military |
| UC20-258 | ORGANIZATION (mil. maint. & transport: by country) |
| UC20-88 | Maintenance & transport (mil.: U.S.) |
| UC20 | Military maintenance & transport (U.S.: gen.) |
| UC23 | Maintenance & transport (mil.: U.S.: by time period) |
| UC23.1917-1918 | Military maintenance & transport (U.S.: WWI era) |
| UC23.1941-1945 | Military maintenance & transport (U.S.: WWII era) |
| UC30-34 | Quartermaster's Dept. (U.S.)      355.8 |
| UC40-44 | Subsistence Dept. (U.S. Army) |
| UC45 | Construction Div. (U.S. Army) |
| UC46 | Military construction (U.S.: gen.: SEE ALSO UG for engineer., VC420+ |
| | & VG590+ for naval)      358.22 |
| UC70-75 | Paymaster's Dept. (U.S. Army) |
| UC90-93 | Maintenance & transport (mil.: Can.) |
| UC158-233 | Maintenance & transport (mil.: Eur.) |
| UC158 | Military maintenance & transport (Eur.: gen.) |
| UC180-183 | Maintenance & transport (mil.: Ger.) |
| UC184-187 | Maintenance & transport (mil.: G.B.) |
| UC184 | Supply & transport depts. (mil.: G.B.) |
| UC185 | Pay & allowances (mil.: G.B.) |
| UC208-211 | Maintenance & transport (mil.: Rus.) |
| UC234-245 | Maintenance & transport (mil.: Asia) |
| UC234 | Military maintenance & transport (Asia: gen.) |
| UC241 | Maintenance & transport (mil.: Japan) |
| UC255 | Maintenance & transport (mil.: Australia) |
| UC256.5 | Maintenance & transport (mil.: New Z.) |
| UC257-258 | Maintenance & transport (mil.: Pac. islands) |
| UC260-267 | Supplies & stores, Military (inclu. procure., storage, specs., |
| | surplus, etc.) |
| UC260 | Military supplies & stores (gen.) |
| UC263-264 | Stores & supplies, Military (U.S.) |
| UC265.A-Z | Procurement (mil. supplies: countries besides U.S.) |
| UC267 | Contracts, Military (supplies) |
| UC270-360 | Transport, Military      358.25, .44, 355.27 |
| UC270 | Transportation, Military (gen.)      358.25 |
| UC273-274 | Military transport (U.S.) |
| UC275.A-Z | Transport, Military (besides U.S.: by place) |
| UC277 | Packing & shipment (mil. supplies) |
| UC310 | Railroads (mil. transp.: gen.)      623.63, 355.83 |
| UC313 | Military railroads (U.S.: gen.)      355.830973 |
| UC314.A-Z | Railroads (mil. transp.: U.S. regions or states) |
| UC315.A-Z | Transport, Railroad (mil.: places besides U.S.) |
| UC320-325 | Waterways & troopships (mil. transp.)      359.3264 |
| UC320 | Troopships & waterways (mil. transp.: gen.) |
| UC330-335 | Air transport, Military      358.44 |
| UC333-334 | Military air transport (U.S.)      358.440973 |
| UC340-345 | Motor transport (mil. sci.)      355.83 |
| UC343 | Transport, Motor (mil. sci.: U.S.) |
| UC347 | Motorcycles (mil. transp.)      623.7472 |
| UC349 | Coolies (mil. transp.) |
| UC350 | Camels, elephants, etc. (mil. transp.) |
| UC355 | Dogs (mil. transp.: SEE ALSO UH100)      355.424 |

| UC360 | Snowshoes, skis, skates, etc. (mil. transp.) | |
|---|---|---|
| UC400-440 | Camps & barracks, Military | |
| UC400 | Barracks & camps, Military (gen.) | 355.412, .7 |
| UC403-404 | Military barracks & camps (U.S.) | 355.70973 |
| UC405.A-Z | Military quarters & camps (besides U.S.) | |
| UC410 | Billeting | |
| UC415 | Furnishings (mil. qtrs.) | |
| UC420 | Fuel & light (mil. qtrs.) | |
| UC425 | Fires (mil. qtrs.) | |
| UC430 | Latrines & sewers (mil. qtrs.) | |
| UC440 | Laundries, Military | |
| UC460-535 | Clothing & equipment, Military | |
| UC460 | Equipment & clothing, Military (gen.) | |
| UC463-464 | Military clothing & equipment (U.S.) | |
| UC465.A-Z | Clothing & equipment, Military (places besides U.S.) | |
| UC480 | Uniforms, Military (gen.) | 355.14 |
| UC483-484 | Military uniforms (U.S.) | 355.140973 |
| UC485.A-Z | Uniforms, Military (besides U.S.) | |
| UC490-495 | Shoes, footwear, gloves (mil.) | |
| UC493 | Military footwear (U.S.) | |
| UC500-505 | Helmets, hats, etc. (mil.) | |
| UC500 | Military headgear | |
| UC520 | Equipment, Military (gen.) | 355.8 |
| UC523-524 | Military equipment (U.S.) | 355.80973 |
| UC525.A-Z | Equipment, Military (countries except U.S.) | |
| UC529.A-Z | Equipment, Military (special: by name) | |
| UC529.C2 | Canteens (mil. equip.) | |
| UC529.K6 | Knapsacks (mil. equip.) | |
| UC530-535 | Badges, insignia, etc. (mil.: SEE ALSO UB430+ for decorations) | |
| UC533 | Insignia, badges, etc. (mil.: U.S.) | |
| UC540-585 | Field kits & equip. (mil.) | |
| UC540 | Military kits & field equip. (gen.) | 355.81 |
| UC543-544 | Field kits & equip. (mil.: U.S.) | |
| UC550-555 | Bunks & bedding (mil.) | |
| UC570-585 | Tents, Military | |
| UC590-595 | Flags, colors, standards (mil.) | |
| UC590 | Military flags, colors, standards (gen.) | 355.15 |
| UC593-594 | Colors, flags, standards (mil.: U.S.) | |
| UC595.A-Z | Standards, colors, flags (mil.: places besides U.S.) | |
| UC600-695 | Horses & mules, Military | |
| UC700-780 | Food, cooking, water, etc. | 355.65-66, .81 |
| UC700 | Subsistence (mil.: gen.) | |
| UC703-704 | Subsistence (mil.: U.S.) | |
| UC705.A-Z | Subsistence (mil.: countries besides U.S.) | |
| UC710-715 | Rations (mil.) | |
| UC720 | Cooking (mil.: gen.) | |
| UC723 | Messing (mil.: cooking: U.S.) | |
| UC730-735 | Bakeries (mil.) | |
| UC730 | Field ovens (mil.) | |
| UC740-745 | Clubs, Officers' (mil.) | |
| UC743 | Officers' clubs & messes, Military (U.S.) | |
| UC750-755 | Post exchanges & canteens, Military | |
| UC753 | Canteens & post exchanges, Military (U.S.) | |

| | |
|---|---|
| UC760 | Refrigerators, Military |
| UC770 | Slaughterhouses, Military |
| UC780 | Water supplies, Military |
| | |
| UD | INFANTRY (tactics, use, gen. hist's.: SEE ALSO UA for specific armies)    356 |
| UD1 | Periodicals & associations (infantry) |
| UD7 | Infantry (collections) |
| UD10 | Organization (infantry: gen.) |
| UD15 | Infantry (gen. hist.)    356.09, 109, 355.009 |
| UD21-124 | INFANTRY (hist.: by area or country regardless of specific unit: SEE ALSO UA) |
| UD23 | Infantry (U.S.)    356.10973 |
| UD26 | Infantry (Can.) |
| UD55-95 | Infantry (Eur.) |
| UD55 |    European infantry (gen.)    356.1094 |
| UD57-64 |    Infantry (G.B.) |
| UD57 |    British infantry (gen.)    356.10941 |
| UD58 |    Infantry (G.B.: by date) |
| UD71 | Infantry (Fr.)    356.10944 |
| UD73 | Infantry (Ger.)    356.10943 |
| UD79 | Infantry (It.)    356.10945 |
| UD85 | Infantry (Rus.: Eur.)  356.10947 |
| UD99-113 | Infantry (Asia) |
| UD99 | Asian infantry (gen.)  356.1095 |
| UD101 |    Infantry (China)    356.10951 |
| UD105 |    Infantry (Japan)    356.10952 |
| UD109 |    Infantry (Rus.: Asian) |
| UD121 | Infantry (Australia)    356.10994 |
| UD122.5 | Infantry (New Z.) |
| UD145 | Infantry (gen.: pubn. 1801+)   356.1 |
| UD150-155 | Manuals, Infantry |
| UD150 | Infantry manuals (gen.)    356.10202 |
| UD153 | Handbooks, Infantry (U.S.) |
| UD155.A-Z | Manuals, Infantry (places besides U.S.) |
| UD157-302 | TACTICS, MANEUVERS, & DRILLS (infantry) |
| UD157 | Maneuvers, drills, & tactics (infantry: gen.)    356.18, 355.42 |
| UD160-162 |    Drills, tactics, & maneuvers (infantry: U.S.) |
| UD160 |    Infantry tactics & maneuvers (U.S.: gen.) |
| UD161 |    Drill regulations (infantry: U.S. reserves) |
| UD215-269 | Tactics, maneuvers, & drills (infantry: Eur.) |
| UD215 | Infantry tactics & maneuvers (Eur.: gen.) |
| UD219-221 | Tactics, maneuvers, & drills (infantry: Australia) |
| UD228-230 | Tactics, maneuvers, & drills (infantry: Fr.) |
| UD231-233 | Tactics, maneuvers, & drills (infantry: Ger.) |
| UD234-236 |    Tactics, maneuvers, & drills (infantry: G.B.) |
| UD243-245 |    Tactics, maneuvers, & drills (infantry: It.) |
| UD252-254 |    Tactics, maneuvers, & drills (infantry: Rus.) |
| UD270-280 | Tactics, maneuvers, & drills (infantry: Asia) |
| UD270 | Infantry tactics & maneuvers (Asia: gen.) |
| UD271-273 |    Tactics, maneuvers, & drills (infantry: China) |
| UD277-279 |    Tactics, maneuvers, & drills (infantry: Japan) |
| UD295-298 | Tactics, maneuvers, & drills (infantry: Australia & New Z.) |

| UD310 | Marching & guides (mil.: gen.) |
|---|---|
| UD313-314 | Guides & marching (mil.) |
| UD315.A-Z | Marching & guides (countries except U.S.) |
| UD315.G3 | German marching (mil.) |
| UD317 | River & stream crossing (infantry) |
| UD320-325 | Arms manuals (infantry) |
| UD323-324 | Manual of arms (infantry: U.S.) |
| UD330 | Firing or sharpshooting (infantry: gen.) |
| UD333-334 | Sharpshooting (infantry: U.S.) |
| UD340-345 | Bayonet drill |
| UD370-375 | Equipment, Infantry |
| UD380-425 | Small arms (infantry)  355.824+, 623.44 |
| UD380 | Arms, Small (infantry: gen.) |
| UD382 | Inspection (small arms: infantry) |
| UD383-384 | Infantry arms (small: U.S.) |
| UD385.A-Z | Small arms (infantry: countries besides U.S.) |
| UD390-395 | Rifles, carbines, etc. (infantry)  355.82425, 623.4425 |
| UD390 | Carbines, rifles, etc. |
| UD395.A-Z | Rifles (infantry: by type) |
| UD395.G4 | Garand rifle |
| UD395.M17 | M1 rifle |
| UD395.M3 | Mauser rifle |
| UD395.S8 | Springfield rifle |
| UD395.U6 | United States magazine rifle |
| UD396 | Shotguns |
| UD400 | Bayonets |
| UD410 | Pistols & revolvers (gen.)  355.8243, 623.443 |
| UD413-414 | Revolvers & pistols, Infantry (U.S. models) |
| UD420-425 | Swords |
| UD430 | Reserves & militia, Infantry |
| UD440-445 | Field service, Infantry |
| UD450 | Mounted infantry (gen.) |
| UD453-454 | Infantry, Mounted (U.S.) |
| UD460-465 | Mountain warfare & troops  356.164 |
| UD470-475 | Ski troops  356.164 |
| UD475.A-Z | Ski troops (by country)  356.16409+ |
| UD475.G3 | German ski troops  356.1640943 |
| UD480-485 | Airborne & parachute troops  356.166 |
| UD480 | Parachute & airborne troops (gen.) |
| UD483-484 | Troops, Airborne (U.S.)  356.1660973 |
| | |
| UE | ARMOR & CAVALRY (SEE ALSO UA for specific armies)  357-358.1 |
| UE1 | Periodicals & associations (armor & cavalry) |
| UE7 | Cavalry & armor (collections) |
| UE10 | Organization (armor & cavalry: gen.) |
| UE15 | Armor & cavalry (gen. hist.: inclu. several countries)  357.09, .109, 358.1809 |
| UE21-124 | CAVALRY & ARMOR (by place: SEE ALSO UA for specific units) |
| UE23 | Armor & cavalry (U.S.)  357.0973 |
| UE55-95 | Armor & cavalry (Eur.) |
| UE55 | Cavalry & armor (Eur.: gen.)  357.094 |
| UE57-64 | Armor & cavalry (G.B.) |
| UE57 | Cavalry & armor (G.B.: gen.)  357.0941 |
| UE58 | Armor & cavalry (G.B.: by date) . |
| UE71 | Armor & cavalry (Fr.)  357.0944 |

| | | |
|---|---|---|
| UE73 | Armor & cavalry (Ger.) | 357.0943 |
| UE79 | Armor & cavalry (It.) | |
| UE85 | Armor & cavalry (Rus.: Eur.) | 357.0947 |
| UE99-113 | Armor & cavalry (Asia) | |
| UE99 | Cavalry & armor (Asia: gen.) | 357.095 |
| UE101 | Armor & cavalry (China) | |
| UE105 | Armor & cavalry (Japan) | 357.0952 |
| UE109 | Armor & cavalry (Rus.: Asia) | |
| UE121-122.5 | Armor & cavalry (Australia & New Z.) | 357.099+ |
| UE145 | Horse cavalry (pubn. 1801+) | 357.1 |
| UE147 | Mechanized & armored cavalry | 357.5, 358.18 |
| UE149 | Armor & cavalry (essays & speeches) | |
| UE150-155 | Manuals, Armor & Cavalry | |
| UE153-154 | Armor & Cavalry manuals (U.S.) | |
| UE157-302 | TACTICS, MANEUVERS, & DRILLS (armor & cavalry) | |
| UE159 | Tactics, maneuvers, & drills (armored & mechanized cavalry) | |
| UE160-302 | MANEUVERS & TACTICS (armor & cavalry: by place) | |
| UE160 | Tactics, maneuvers, & drills (armor & cavalry: U.S.: gen.) | |
| UE161 | Drill regulations (armor & cavalry: U.S. reserves) | |
| UE215-269 | Drills, tactics, & maneuvers (armor & cavalry: Eur.) | |
| UE215 | Tactics, maneuvers, & drills (armor & cavalry: Eur.: gen.) | |
| UE228 | Tactics, maneuvers, & drills (armor & cavalry: Fr.) | |
| UE231 | Tactics, maneuvers, & drills (armor & cavalry: Ger.) | |
| UE252 | Tactics, maneuvers, & drills (armor & cavalry: Rus.) | |
| UE270-280 | Maneuvers & tactics (armor & cavalry: Asia) | |
| UE270 | Tactics, maneuvers, & drills (armor & cavalry: Asia: gen.) | |
| UE271 | Tactics, maneuvers, & drills (armor & cavalry: China) | |
| UE277 | Tactics, maneuvers, & drills (armor & cavalry: Japan) | |
| UE295 | Tactics, maneuvers, & drills (armor & cavalry: Australia) | |
| UE360 | Reconnaisance, Cavalry | 355.413, 358.45 |
| UE400-405 | Firing (armor & cavalry) | |
| UE420-425 | Sword exercises (cavalry) | |
| UE430 | Training camps (armor & cavalry: gen.) | |
| UE433-434 | Camps, Training (armor & cavalry: U.S.) | |
| UE435.A-Z | Training camps (armor & cavalry: places besides U.S.) | |
| UE460-475 | Horses, Cavalry | |
| UE460 | Cavalry horses (gen.) | |
| UE500 | Camel troops & camelry | |
| | | |
| UF | ARTILLERY (SEE ALSO UA for specific armies & units) | 358.1+, 355.82+ |
| UF1 | Periodicals & associations (artillery) | |
| UF6 | Museums, Artillery (inclu. exhibitions) | |
| UF6.A1.A-Z | Artillery museums & exhibitons (gen.) | 358.12 |
| UF6.A2-Z | Museums, Artillery (by country or region) | |
| UF6.x2.A-Z | Museums, Artillery (by city within area, whose 1st letter & shelf # are shown by 'x' in 'x2') | |
| UF7 | Artillery (titles in collections) | |
| UF9 | Dictionaries & encyclopedias (artillery) | 358.1203 |
| UF10 | Organization (artillery forces) | |
| UF15 | Artillery (gen. hist.) | 358.109, .1209, 355.82, .821 |

| | |
|---|---|
| UF21-121 | ARTILLERY (by place: SEE ALSO UA for particular armies) |
| UF23 | Artillery (U.S.)    358.120973, .10973, 355.820973 |
| UF57 | Artillery (G.B.: gen.)    358.120941 |
| UF58 | Artillery (G.B.: by date periods) |
| UF58.1939-45 | Artillery (G.B.: WWII) |
| UF71 | Artillery (Fr.)    358.120944 |
| UF73 | Artillery (Ger.)    358.120943 |
| UF79 | Artillery (It.) |
| UF81 | Artillery (Norway) |
| UF85 | Artillery (Rus.: Eur.) |
| UF99-113 | Artillery (Asia) |
| UF99 | Artillery (Asia: gen.) |
| UF101 | Artillery (China) |
| UF105 | Artillery (Japan)    358.120952 |
| UF121-122.5 | Artillery (Australia & New Z.) |
| UF130-135 | Laws, Ordnance |
| UF133 | Ordnance laws (U.S.: PREFER KF7335 |
| UF145 | Artillery (pubn. 1801+)    358.12 |
| UF148 | Exercises, problems, etc. (artillery) |
| UF150-155 | Manuals (artillery)    358.120202 |
| UF153-154 | Artillery manuals (U.S.) |
| UF157-302 | TACTICS, MANEUVERS, & DRILLS (artillery) |
| UF157 | Maneuvers, drills, & tactics (artillery: gen.) |
| UF160-302 | DRILLS, MANEUVERS, & TACTICS (artillery: by place) |
| UF160 | Tactics, maneuvers, & drills (artillery: U.S.: gen.) |
| UF162.A-W | Drill regulations (artillery: U.S. reserves: by state) |
| UF163 | Tactics, maneuvers, & drills (artillery: Can.) |
| UF215-269 | Maneuvers & tactics (artillery: Eur.) |
| UF215 | Tactics, maneuvers, & drills (artillery: Eur.: gen.) |
| UF228 | Tactics, maneuvers, & drills (artillery: Fr.) |
| UF231 | Tactics, maneuvers, & drills (artillery: Ger.) |
| UF234 | Tactics, maneuvers, & drills (artillery: G.B.) |
| UF243 | Tactics, maneuvers, & drills (artillery: It.) |
| UF252 | Tactics, maneuvers, & drills (artillery: Rus.) |
| UF270-280 | Maneuvers & tactics (artillery: Asia) |
| UF270 | Tactics, maneuvers, & drills (artillery: Asia: gen.) |
| UF271 | Tactics, maneuvers, & drills (artillery: China) |
| UF277 | Tactics, maneuvers, & drills (artillery: Japan) |
| UF295-298 | Tactics, maneuvers, & drills (artillery: Australia & New Z.) |
| UF320 | Stream & river crossing (artillery) |
| UF340-345 | Target practice |
| UF356 | Reserves, Artillery |
| UF370 | Horses, Artillery |
| UF380-385 | Wagons & carts, Artillery |
| UF390 | Motor transport, Artillery |
| UF400 | Field artillery (gen.)    358.12 |
| UF403-404 | Artillery, Field (U.S.) |
| UF405.A-Z | Field artillery (places besides U.S.) |
| UF405.G3 | German field artillery |
| UF410 | Horse artillery |
| UF420 | Camel batteries |
| UF430 | Elephant batteries |

| | | |
|---|---|---|
| UF440-445 | Mountain artillery | |
| UF443-444 | Artillery, Mountain (U.S.) | |
| UF450-455 | Seacoast artillery | |
| UF450 | Coast artillery (gen.) | |
| UF453-454 | Artillery, Seacoast (U.S.) | |
| UF460-465 | Siege artillery | |
| UF460 | Artillery, Siege (gen.) | |
| UF470-475 | Howitzers & mortars | |
| UF473 | Mortars & howitzers (U.S.: gen.) | |
| UF475.A-Z | Artillery, Howitzer & mortar (places besides U.S.) | |
| UF475.F8 | Howitzers & mortars (Fr.) | |
| UF475.G7 | Howitzers & mortars (G.B.) | |
| UF475.J3 | Howitzers & mortars (Japan) | |
| UF480 | Garrison & fortress artillery (gen.) | |
| UF483 | Fortress & garrison artillery (U.S.: gen.) | |
| UF490 | Railroad artillery (gen.) | |
| UF493 | Artillery, Railway (U.S.: gen.) | |
| UF495.A-Z | Railway artillery (countries besides U.S.) | |
| UF495.F8 | Railway artillery (Fr.) | |
| UF495.G3 | Railway artillery (Ger.) | |
| UF500-505 | Weapons systems (artillery) | |
| UF520-537 | Ordnance & small arms | 355.82, 623.4+, .44 |
| UF520 | Small arms & ordnance (gen.) | 355.82 |
| UF523 | Ordnance & small arms (U.S.) | 355.820973 |
| UF525.A-Z | Small arms & ordnance (besides U.S.: by place) | |
| UF526 | Research, Ordnance & small-arms | |
| UF526.3 | Ordnance & small-arms research (U.S.) | |
| UF526.5.A-Z | Small-arms & ordnance research (places besides U.S.) | |
| UF527 | Instruction (ordnance & small arms) | |
| UF530 | Manufacture (ordnance & small arms: gen.) | 623.4+, 338.476234 |
| UF533 | Small arms & ordnance (manufacture: U.S.: gen.) | 338.4762340973 |
| UF534.A-W | Manufacture (small arms & ordnance: U.S.: by state) | |
| UF537.A-Z | Manufacturers (small arms & ordnance) | |
| UF540 | Armories, arsenals, magazines (gen.) | |
| UF543 | Arsenals, armories, etc. (U.S.: gen.) | |
| UF545.A-Z | Magazines, armories, etc. (countries except U.S.) | |
| UF550 | Ordnance stores, accounts, etc. (gen.) | |
| UF553 | Stores, Ordnance (U.S.: gen.) | |
| UF560-780 | ORDNANCE PROPER | |
| UF560-565.A-Z.A-Z(II-IV) etc. | Ordnance material (by type, mark #, ed. date, etc.) | |
| UF560-565... .B.L | Breech-loading ordnance | |
| UF560-565... .H | Hotchkiss ordnance | |
| UF560-565... .M.L | Muzzle-loading ordnance | |
| UF560-565... .N | Nordenfelt ordnance | |
| UF560-565... .Q.F | Quick-firing ordnance | |
| UF560 | Ordnance material (gen.) | 355.82+, 623.4+ |
| UF563 | Ordnance material (U.S.: gen.) | 355.820973, 623.40973 |

| | | |
|---|---|---|
| UF563.A4-8 | Handbooks, Gun (U.S.: artillery) | |
| UF563.A4.1+ | Gun handbooks (U.S.: by mm. or cm. then date) | |
| UF563.A5 | Handbooks, Gun (U.S.: by inches) | |
| UF563.A5.2.95in.Mt. | Mountain guns (U.S.: handbooks: 2.95) | |
| UF563.A6 | Handbooks, Gun (U.S.: by pounds) | |
| UF563.A7-8 | Handbooks, Gun (U.S.: by class or type: sometimes use | |

UF563.A4-6 with measure. & alphab. symbol: e.g.
UF563.A5.12 in.M for 12 mortar... or ... Mt. for mountain)

| | | |
|---|---|---|
| UF563.A7 | Coast guns (U.S.: handbooks) | |
| UF563.A75 | Mortars (U.S.: handbooks) | |
| UF563.A76 | Railway gun matériel (U.S.: handbooks) | |
| UF563.A8 | Subcaliber guns (U.S.: handbooks) | |
| UF563.A9-Z | United States ordnance (gen.) | |
| UF565.A-Z | Ordnance material (countries besides U.S.) | |
| UF565.F8 | Ordnance material (Fr.) | |
| UF565.G3 | Ordnance material (Ger.) | |
| UF565.G7 | Ordnance material (G.B.) | |
| UF565.J3 | Ordnance material (Japan) | |
| UF565.R9 | Ordnance material (Rus.) | |
| UF620.A2 | Machine guns (gen.) | 623.4424 |
| UF620.A3-Z | Machine guns (specific types) | |
| UF620.B6 | Browning machine guns | |
| UF620.C6 | Colt machine guns | |
| UF620.G3 | Gatling machine guns | |
| UF620.G6 | Goriunov machine guns | |
| UF620.H8 | Hotchkiss machine guns | |
| UF620.L5 | Lewis machine guns | |
| UF620.M4 | Maxim machine guns | |
| UF620.N8 | Nordenfelt machine guns | |
| UF620.S8 | Sten machine guns | |
| UF620.T5 | Thompson machine guns | |
| UF620.U6 | United States automatic machine guns | |
| UF620.V4 | Vickers machine guns | |
| UF625 | Antiaircraft guns & defenses (SEE ALSO UG730+) | 358.13 |
| UF628 | Antitank guns | 623.42, .44, .4518 |
| UF630 | Guns (misc. types: mil. sci.) | |
| UF640 | Gun carriages, caissons, limbers, etc. (gen.) | 623.43 |
| UF643 | Caissons, gun carriages, etc. (U.S.: gen.) | |
| UF650 | Gun carriages, Disappearing | |
| UF652 | Gun carriages, Self-propelled (plus track-layer tractors & other self-contained) | |
| UF655 | Railway gun cars (SEE ALSO UF563.A76, UF565) | 358.22 |
| UF660 | Cupolas, Revolving (& other portable gun shelters) | |
| UF670-675 | Firing instructions, Artillery | |
| UF700 | Ammunition, Artillery | 358.825, 623.45 |
| UF740-745 | Cartridges | 623.455 |
| UF750-770 | Projectiles, Artillery | 623.451 |
| UF750 | Artillery projectiles (gen.) | |
| UF753 | Projectiles, Artillery (U.S.) | |
| UF760 | Shells & shrapnel | 623.4513-4518 |
| UF765 | Grenades | 623.45114 |
| UF767 | Bombs & projectiles, Aircraft (inclu. std. & nuclear) | 623.451 |
| UF770 | Bullets | 623.455 |
| UF780 | Firing devices (primers, percussion caps, etc.) | |
| UF800 | Gunnery, Artillery (gen.) | 623.55 |

| UF805 | Aerial observations (artillery) |
| UF810 | Firing tests (artillery) |
| UF820-830 | Ballistics    623.51+ |
| UF820 | Projectile velocities & motions (gen.)    623.51 |
| UF823 | Ballistics, Interior    623.513 |
| UF825 | Ballistics, Exterior    623.514 |
| UF830.A-Z | Ballistic instruments |
| UF840 | Photography, Ballistic (inclu. photochronography) |
| UF845 | Binoculars & telescopes, Military |
| UF848-856 | Fire control, Artillery (inclu. instruments) |
| UF848 | Artillery fire control (inclu. instruments: gen.)    623.558 |
| UF849-856 | Instruments, Artillery (specific types) |
| UF849 | Optical instruments & tools, Artillery |
| UF850.A2 | Range finders, Artillery (gen.)    623.46 |
| UF850.A3-Z | Artillery range finders (particular types) |
| UF850.A9 | Azimuth instrument (artillery) |
| UF850.D4 | Depression range finder |
| UF850.W3 | Watkin range finder |
| UF853 | Position finders (artillery)    623.46 |
| UF854 | Sights, Firearm |
| UF855 | Telescopic sights (artillery) |
| UF856.A-Z | Artillery instruments (misc.) |
| UF857 | Range tables, Artillery |
| UF860-880 | Military explosives, unguided rockets, etc. |
| UF860 | Explosives, Military (gen.)    623.452 |
| UF870 | Explosions, powder force, etc. |
| UF880 | Rockets, Unguided (mil. sci.: SEE UG1310-1315 for guided rockets)    623.4543 |
| UF890 | Tests, Ordnance |
| UF900 | Resistance to projectiles (artillery) |
| UF910 | Bulletproof clothing, materials, etc. |
| | |
| UG | MILITARY ENGINEERING, AIR FORCES, & AIR WARFARE    358.2, 623, 358.4 (air forces etc.) |
| UG1-620 | ENGINEERING, MILITARY |
| UG1 | Periodicals & associations (mil. engineering) |
| UG6 | Museums & exhibitions (mil. engineering) |
| UG7 | Military engineering (collections) |
| UG15 | Engineering, Military (gen. hist.)    358.2, .209 |
| UG21-124 | Engineering, Military (by country or area) |
| UG23-25 | Engineering, Military (U.S.)    358.20973 |
| UG23 | Military engineering (U.S.: gen.) |
| UG55-95 | Engineering, Military (Eur.)    358.2094 |
| UG55 | Military engineering (Eur.: gen.) |
| UG57 | Engineering, Military (G.B.) |
| UG57.Z6.1st+ | Military engineering (G.B.: by #'d regiment) |
| UG71 | Engineering, Military (Fr.) |
| UG73 | Engineering, Military (Ger.) |
| UG73.Z6.1st+ | Military enginering (Ger.: by #'d regiment) |
| UG85 | Engineering, Military (Rus.: Eur.) |

| UG99-113 | Engineering, Military (Asia) | |
| UG99 | Military engineering (Asia: gen.) | |
| UG101 | Engineering, Military (China) | |
| UG105 | Engineering, Military (Japan) | |
| UG105.Z6.1st+ | Military engineering (Japan: by #'d regiment) | |
| UG121-122.5 | Engineering, Military (Australia + New Z.) | |
| UG125.1st+ | Military engineering (U.S.: by #'d regiment) | |
| UG127 | Biography, Military engineering (collective) | |
| UG128.A-Z | Biography, Military engineering (indiv.: SEE ALSO UG21-124) | |
| UG130-135 | Laws (engineer corps) | |
| UG133 | Laws (engineer corps: U.S.: PREFER KF7335.E5) | |
| UG145 | Engineering, Military (gen.: pubn. 1801+) | |
| UG150-155 | Manuals (mil. engineering) | |
| UG153 | Military engineering manuals (U.S.) | |
| UG156 | Engineering, Military (essays & lectures) | |
| UG157 | Instruction (mil. engineering) | |
| UG160-302 | TACTICS & REGULATIONS (mil. engineering: by place) | |
| UG160 | Tactics & regulations (mil. engineering: U.S.) | |
| UG163 | Tactics & regulations (mil. engineering: Can.) | |
| UG215-269 | Tactics & regulations (mil. engineering: Eur.) | |
| UG215 | Regulations & tactics (mil. engineering: Eur.: gen.) | |
| UG228 | Tactics & regulations (mil. engineering: Fr.) | |
| UG231 | Tactics & regulations (mil. engineering: Ger.) | |
| UG234 | Tactics & regulations (mil. engineering: G.B.) | |
| UG252 | Tactics & regulations (mil. engineering: Rus.) | |
| UG270-280 | Tactics & regulations (mil. engineering: Asia) | |
| UG270 | Regulations & tactics (mil. engineering: Asia: gen.) | |
| UG271 | Tactics & regulations (mil. engineering: China) | |
| UG277 | Tactics & regulations (mil. engineering: Japan) | |
| UG295-298 | Tactics & regulations (mil. engineering: Australia & New Z.) | |
| UG320-325 | Maneuvers (mil. engineering) | |
| UG323 | Military engineering maneuvers (U.S.) | |
| UG330 | Roads (mil. engineering) | 623.62 |
| UG335 | Bridges (mil. engineering) | 623.67 |
| UG340 | Tunnels (mil. engineering) | 623.68 |
| UG343 | Ice excavation, tunnels, rooms, etc. (mil. engineering) | |
| UG345 | Railroads, armored trains, etc. (mil. engineering) | 623.63 |
| UG350 | Harbors, canals, dams (mil. engineering) | 623.64 |
| UG360-390 | Field engineering (mil.) | |
| UG360 | Military engineering (field: gen.) | |
| UG365 | Camp-making (mil. sci.) | 355.412, .544, .71 |
| UG370 | Demolitions (mil. engineering) | 623.4545, 358.23 |
| UG375 | Obstacles (mil. engineering) | 355.544 |
| UG380 | Intrenching tools (mil.) | |
| UG385 | Ferrying (mil. engineering) | |
| UG390 | Field engineering (misc. topics) | |

| | | |
|---|---|---|
| UG400-442 | Fortification | |
| UG401 | Fortification (gen.: pubn. 1801+) | 355.544, 623.1 |
| UG403 | Field fortification | |
| UG405 | Fortification, Permanent | |
| UG407 | Entanglements & misc. fortification | |
| UG408-409 | Steel & iron land defenses | |
| UG410-442 | Fortifications (by place) | 623.19+, 355.45-47+ |
| UG410-412 | Fortified defenses (U.S.) | 623.1973, 355.4773 |
| UG410 | Defenses, Fortified (U.S.: gen.) | 623.1973, 355.4773 |
| UG411.A-Z | Fortifications (U.S.: by state or region) | 623.1974-1979+, 355.450974+, .4774+ |
| UG411.P2 | Pacific Coast (U.S.: fortifications) | |
| UG412.A-Z | Fortifications (U.S.: by town or place) | |
| UG412.K4 | Key West, Fl. (fortifications) | |
| UG412.N5 | New York City (fortifications) | |
| UG412.P3 | Panama Canal (fortifications) | |
| UG412.S3 | San Diego, Calif. (fortifications) | |
| UG413-415 | Fortified defenses (Can.) | |
| UG422-424 | Fortified defenses (W. Indies) | |
| UG428-430 | Fortified defenses (Eur.) | |
| UG428 | Defenses, Fortified (Eur.: gen.) | 623.194, 355.474 |
| UG429.A-Z | Fortifications (Eur.: by region or country) | |
| UG429.G3 | Fortified defenses (Ger.) | |
| UG430.A-Z | Fortifications (Eur.: by town or place) | |
| UG431-433 | Fortified defenses (Asia) | 623.195 |
| UG432.A-Z | Fortifications (Asia: by country) | |
| UG432.J3 | Fortified defenses (Japan) | 623.1952 |
| UG432.P5 | Fortified defenses (Philip.) | |
| UG437-439 | Fortified defenses (Australia) | |
| UG440-442 | Fortified defenses (Pacific islands) | |
| UG443-449 | Attack, defense, & siege | |
| UG444 | Defense, attack, & siege (gen.: pubn. 1789+) | 355.4+ |
| UG446 | Trench warfare 355.44 | |
| UG446.5 | Tanks, armored cars, etc. (attack, defense, & siege: SEE ALSO UE159-302 for armored cavalry) 355.422, 357.5, 358.18 | |
| UG447-447.6 | Chemical warfare (inclu. flames) | 623.4516 |
| UG447 | Flame & chemical weapons (gen.) | 358.34 |
| UG447.5.A-Z | Gas warfare (by chem. name) | 623.4516 |
| UG447.5.M8 | Mustard gas 623.4516 | |
| UG447.6 | Gas masks (mil.) | |
| UG447.65 | Incendiary weapons | |
| UG447.7 | Smoke screens & tactics | |
| UG447.8 | Biological & bacterial warfare | |
| UG448 | Coast defenses (SEE UG410-442 for specific places) 358.16, 355.45 | |
| UG449 | Camouflage (SEE ALSO V215 for naval) 358.3, 623.77 | |
| UG450 | Mechanical engineering (mil. applications) | |
| UG455 | Weights & measures (mil. metrology) | |
| UG465-465.5 | Geology & seismology, Military | |
| UG460 | Architecture, Military 623.1 | |
| UG467 | Meteorology, Military | |
| UG468 | Hydrology, Military | |
| UG470-474 | Military surveying, mapping, & topography | |
| UG470 | Surveying, mapping, & topography (military: gen.) 623.71 | |
| UG472 | Mapping & surveying, Military (U.S.) | |
| UG473.A-Z | Topography & mapping, Military (places except U.S.) | |

| | | |
|---|---|---|
| UG475 | Surveillance, Military | 355.413, 358.45 |
| UG476 | Photography, Military | 623.72 |
| UG480 | Electricity (mil. uses) | 623.76 |
| UG485 | Electronics, Military | 623.732+ |
| UG490 | Mines, Land (inclu. countermeasures) | 623.45115 |
| UG500-565 | Technical troops & other special corps | |
| UG500 | Technical troops & artificers (gen.) | 358.2-3 |
| UG503 | Artificers, Military (U.S.: ALSO tech. troops) | |
| UG503 | Sappers & bridge troops (U.S.) | |
| UG505.A-Z | Military artificers & technical troops (places besides U.S.) | |
| UG510 | Bridge troops & sappers (gen.) | |
| UG520-525 | Railroad troops | |
| UG530-535 | Pioneer troops | |
| UG550-555 | Mining & torpedo troops | |
| UG550 | Torpedo & mining troops | |
| UG560-565 | Electricians, Military | |
| UG570-582 | Signaling, Military | 358.24, 623.73+, 355.85 |
| UG570-575 | Signal corps & troops | |
| UG573 | Signal corps & troops (U.S.) | |
| UG580 | Military signaling (gen.) | |
| UG582.A-Z | Signaling, Military (particular types) | |
| UG582.H2 | Hand signaling (mil.) | |
| UG582.H4 | Heliograph (mil. signal.) | |
| UG582.S4 | Semaphores (mil.) | |
| UG582.S68 | Sound signaling (mil.) | |
| UG582.V5 | Visual signaling (mil.) | |
| UG590-613.5 | Telecommunications, Military | |
| UG590 | Telephone, radio, & telegraph (military: gen.) | 623.732-7345 |
| UG600-605 | Telegraph, Military (inclu. telegraph troops) | |
| UG603 | Military telegraph & troops (U.S.) | |
| UG607 | Submarine cables (mil.) | |
| UG610 | Telephone, Military (gen.) | |
| UG610.3 | Military telephone (U.S.) | |
| UG610.5.A-Z | Telephone, Military (places besides U.S.) | |
| UG611 | Radio, Military (gen.) | |
| UG611.3 | Military radio (U.S.) | |
| UG612 | Radar, Military (gen.) | 623.7348 |
| UG612.3 | Military radar (U.S.) | |
| UG612.5.A-Z | Radar, Military (places except U.S.) | |
| UG612.5.G7 | Radar, Military (G.B.) | |
| UG615 | Motor vehicles, Military (gen.) | 623.747, 355.83, 357.5+ |
| UG618 | Vehicles, Motor (mil.: U.S.) | |
| UG620.A-Z | Military motor vehicles (places besides U.S.) | |

| | | |
|---|---|---|
| UG622-1425 | AIR FORCES & AIR WARFARE | 358.4, 623.74-746 |
| UG622 | Periodicals & associations (air forces) | 358.005-006 |
| UG623 | Conferences (air forces) | |
| UG623.3.A1 | Museums, Air force (inclu. exhibitions: gen.) | 623.74074, 358.40074 |
| UG623.3.A2-Z | Air museums & exhibitions (by country or area) | |
| UG623.3.x2.A-Z | Exhibitions & museums, Air force (by place within country) | |
| UG624 | Air warfare & forces (collected works: gen.) | |
| UG625 | Air forces & warfare (hist.: gen.) | 358.4009 |
| UG626 | Biography, Air force (collective) | 358.400922 |
| UG626.2.A-Z | Biography, Air force (individual) | 358.400924 |
| UG627 | Air forces & warfare (essays & lectures) | |
| UG628 | Dictionaries & encyclopedias (air forces & warfare) | 358.4003 |
| UG630 | Air warfare & forces (gen.) | 358.4 |
| UG633 | Air forces (U.S.: gen.) | 358.400973 |
| UG634.5.A-Z | Air bases & fields (U.S.: by name) | |
| UG634.A-W | Air forces (U.S.: by state) | |
| UG635.A-Z | Air forces (places besides U.S.) | |
| UG635.A8 | Air forces (Australia) | |
| UG635.F8 | Air forces (Fr.) | |
| UG635.G3 | Air forces (Ger.) | |
| UG635.G322.T3 | Tempelhof Airfield (Berlin, Ger.) | |
| UG635.G7 | Air forces (G.B.) | |
| UG635.I8 | Air forces (It.) | |
| UG635.J3 | Air forces (Japan) | |
| UG635.R9 | Air forces (Rus.) | |
| UG635.S65 | Air forces (Sov.Un.) | |
| UG635.x2.A-Z | Airfields & bases (countries besides U.S.: by name of base) | |
| UG637-639 | Education & training, Air force | 358.415+ |
| UG637 | Training & education, Air force (gen.) | |
| UG638-638.8 | Air force training & education (U.S.) | |
| UG638 | Flight training, Air force (U.S.: gen.: inclu. other educ.) | 358.4150973 |
| UG639.A-Z | Training & education, Air force (places besides U.S.) | |
| UG640 | Research, Aeronautical (mil.: gen.) | 358.407, .40072+ |
| UG643 | Aeronautical research, Military (U.S.: gen.) | 358.4070973 |
| UG643.5.A-W | Military research, Aeronautical (U.S.: by state of origin) | |
| UG644.A-Z | Research, Aeronautical (mil.: by company or establishment) | |
| UG645.A-Z | Research, Aeronautical (mil.: places besides U.S.) | |
| UG645.G3 | Aeronautical research, Military (Ger.) | |
| UG670 | Manuals & regulations, Air force (gen.) | |
| UG673 | Regulations & manuals, Air force (U.S.) | |
| UG675.A-Z | Air force manuals & regulations (places except U.S.) | |
| UG675.G3 | Air force regulations & manuals (Ger.) | |
| UG700-705 | Tactics, Air warfare (bombing, strafing, dog fighting, air mining, etc.) | 358.4142, .43 |
| UG700 | Air force tactics (gen.) | |
| UG703 | Bombing, dog fighting, other air tactics (U.S.) | |
| UG705.A-Z | Dog fighting, bombing, other air tactics (countries besides U.S.) | |
| UG730-735 | Defenses, Air (SEE ALSO UF625 for antiaircraft & UA926+ for civil defense) | 358.4145, .13 |
| UG733 | Air defenses (U.S.) | 358.41450973 |
| UG735.A-Z | Defenses, Air (places besides U.S.) | |
| UG760-765 | Reconnaisance, Aerial | 358.45 |
| UG763 | Aerial reconnaisance (U.S.) | |

111

| UG770-1045 | ORGANIZATION (air forces) | |
|---|---|---|
| UG770-775 | Administration (air forces: structure & personnel: gen.) | 358.41, .413, .416+ |
| UG773 | Personnel & administration (air forces: U.S.) | |
| UG790 | Officers, Air force (gen.)  358.41331-41332 | |
| UG793 | Officers, Air force (U.S.) | |
| UG795.A-Z | Air force officers (countries except U.S.) | |
| UG795.G3 | Officers, Air force (Ger.) | |
| UG820-825 | Airmen & non-commissioned air officers  358.41338 | |
| UG823 | Officers, Non-commissioned (air: U.S.: inclu. airmen) | |
| UG825.A-Z | Non-commissioned officers, Air force (countries besides U.S.) | |
| UG850-855 | Reserves, Air force | |
| UG853 | Air National Guard (U.S.) | |
| UG880-885 | Recruiting, enlistment, etc. (air forces) | |
| UG880 | Enlistment, recruiting, etc. (air forces: gen.) | |
| UG940-945 | Pay & benefits (air forces)  358.41135, .4164 | |
| UG943 | Benefits, pay, allowances (air forces: U.S.) | |
| UG970 | Leaves, furloughs, etc. (air forces: gen.) | |
| UG973 | Furloughs, leaves, etc. (air forces: U.S.) | |
| UG980-985 | Medical services (air forces)  358.41345 | |
| UG990-995 | Recreation, social work, etc. (air forces) | |
| UG990 | Social work, recreation, etc. (air forces: U.S.) | |
| UG1000-1005 | Chaplains, Air force | |
| UG1020-1025 | Police, Air force | |
| UG1040-1045 | Prisons, Air force | |
| UG1100-1425 | EQUIPMENT & SUPPLIES (air force) | |
| UG1100-1105 | Supplies & equipment (air force: gen.)  358.418 | |
| UG1120 | Procurement & contracts, Air force (gen.)  358.41621 | |
| UG1123 | Contracts & procurement, Air force (U.S.) | |
| UG1130-1185 | Personnel, Air force | |
| UG1130-1135 | Air force personnel (gen.)  358.4161 | |
| UG1140-1145 | Barracks & quarters, Air force  358.4171 | |
| UG1143 | Quarters & barracks, Air force (U.S.) | |
| UG1160-1165 | Uniforms, Air force  358.4114 | |
| UG1180-1185 | Insignia, badges, etc. (air force) | |
| UG1200-1405 | Operational equipment, Air force (airplanes, bombs, guns, vehicles) | |
| UG1200 | Air force equipment (gen.: planes, bombs, etc.)  358.418, .412 | |
| UG1203 | Equipment, Air force (gen.: planes, bombs, etc.: U.S.)  358.4180973 | |
| UG1220 | Airships or dirigibles (gen.)  623.743 | |
| UG1225.A-Z | Dirigibles (places outside U.S.) | |
| UG1225.G3 | Dirigibles (Ger.) | |
| UG1230-1235 | Helicopters, Military  623.746047 | |
| UG1240-1245 | Airplanes, Military  623.746, 358.418 | |
| UG1240 | Airplanes (air force: gen.) | |
| UG1242.A-Z | Airplanes (air force: by type) | |
| UG1242.A25 | Antisubmarine aircraft | |
| UG1242.A28 | Attack planes | |
| UG1242.B6 | Bombers (air force)  623.7463, 358.42 | |
| UG1242.F5 | Fighter planes  623.7464, 358.43 | |
| UG1242.R4 | Reconnaisance planes  623.7467, 358.45 | |
| UG1242.S3 | Seaplanes (air force)  629.133347, 623.7466-7467 | |
| UG1242.T7 | Transport planes (air force) | |

| UG1243 | Air force planes (U.S.: PREFER UG1242 for particular types) |
|---|---|
| | 358.40973, .4140973, .414773, 623.740973, .7460973 |
| UG1245.A-Z | Air force planes (countries besides U.S.) |
| UG1245.F8 | Air force planes (Fr.) 358.400944 |
| UG1245.G3 | Air force planes (Ger.) 358.400943, .414743, 623.740943 |
| UG1245.G7 | Air force planes (G.B.) 358.400941, .414741-414742, |
| | 623.740941, .7460941 |
| UG1245.I8 | Air force planes (It.) 358.400945 |
| UG1245.J3 | Air force planes (Japan) 358.400952, .414752, 623.740952 |
| UG1245.R9 | Air force planes (Rus.) 358.400947 |
| UG1270-1275 | Ordnance, Air force (gen.) 358.4182, 623.45+ |
| UG1273 | Air force ordnance (gen.: U.S.) |
| UG1280-1285 | Bombs, Air force 358.418251, 623.451 |
| UG1282.A-Z | Air force bombs (by specific type) |
| UG1282.A8 | Atomic bombs (SEE ALSO U264) 358.41825119, 623.45119 |
| UG1282.F7 | Fragmentation bombs (aerial) 623.4514 |
| UG1282.I6 | Incendiary bombs (aerial) 623.4516 |
| UG1310-1315 | Rockets & missiles, Air force 623.451, .4519, .4543 |
| UG1312.A-Z | Missiles & rockets, Air force (by particular type) |
| UG1312.V2 | V-2 rocket |
| UG1313 | Rockets, Air force (U.S.) |
| UG1315.A-Z | Rockets, Air force (places except U.S.) |
| UG1315.G3 | Rockets, Air force (Ger.) |
| UG1340-1345 | Guns, Aircraft 623.7461 |
| UG1340 | Aircraft guns & small weapons (gen.) |
| UG1370-1375 | Balloons & kites, Air force 623.741-744 |
| UG1400-1405 | Vehicles, Motor (air force: ground) |
| UG1420 | Radar & electronics, Air force (gen.) 623.7348, .7467 |
| UG1423 | Electronics & radar, Air force (U.S.) |
| UG1425.A-Z | Air force radar & electronics (places besides U.S.) |
| UG1425.G7 | Radar & electronics, Air force (G.B.) |
| | |
| UH | MILITARY SERVICES (misc.) |
| UH20 | Chaplains or religious officials, Military (gen.) 355.347 |
| UH23 | Chaplains, Military (U.S.) 355.3470973 |
| UH25.A-Z | Religious officials, Military (countries except U.S.) |
| UH30-35 | Cyclists, Military |
| UH30 | Bicyclists, Military (gen.) 357.52 |
| UH40-45 | Bands & music, Military |
| UH40 | Music & bands, Military (gen.) |
| UH60-65 | Banking services, Military |
| UH80-85 | Postal service, Military 355.69 |
| UH87-100 | Animals, Military |
| UH87 | Military animals (gen.) 355.24 |
| UH90 | Pigeons, Military (for communications: SEE ALSO D639.P45 for WWI & |
| | D810.P53 for WWII) |
| UH100 | Dogs, Military |
| UH201-570 | MEDICAL & RELIEF SERVICES, MILITARY |
| UH201-515 | SANITARY & MEDICAL SERVICES, MILITARY |
| UH201 | Periodicals & associations (military medical services) |
| UH206 | Museums, Military medical (inclu. exhibitions) |

UH215-324   MEDICAL SERVICES, MILITARY (hist., statistics, etc.: gen. & by
                 place)
UH215         Military medical services (hist., statistics, etc.: includes sanitary
                       services: gen.)        355.345
UH223-225            Medical services, Military (U.S.)        355.3450973
UH223.A1-29          Reports, Official (military medical: U.S.: serial)
UH223.A1-49             Medical services, Military (U.S.: official reports)
UH223.A3-39             Reports, Official (military medical: U.S.: monographic)
UH223.A4-49             Statistics, Official (military medical: U.S.)
UH223.A5             Statistics (militray medical: U.S.: unofficial)
UH223.A6-Z          Medical services, Military (U.S.: unofficial)
UH224                Military medical services (U.S.: by time period or date: SEE ALSO
                       particular wars)
UH224.1917-18   Medical services, Military (U.S.: WWI)
UH224.1941-45   Medical services, Military (U.S.: WWII)
UH226-227        Medical services, Military (Can.)
UH255-295        Medical services, Military (Eur.)
UH255                   Medical services, Military (Eur.: gen.)    355.345094
UH256                   Military medical services, Military (Eur.: by date or period)
UH256.1914-18          Medical services, Military (Eur.: WWI)
UH256.1939-45          Medical services, Military (Eur.: WWII)
UH257                   Medical services, Military (G.B.: gen.)    355.3450941
UH258                   Military medical services (G.B.: by period or date)
UH271-272        Medical services, Military (Fr.)
UH273-274        Medical services, Military (Ger.)      355.3450943
UH285-286        Medical services, Military (Rus.)
UH286.5          Medical services, Military (Scandin.)
UH299-313   Medical services, Military (Asia)
UH299      Military medical services (Asia: gen.)
UH301-302        Medical services, Military (China)
UH305-306        Medical services, Military (Japan)   355.3450952
UH309-310        Medical services, Military (Rus.: Asia)
UH313.A-Z        Medical services, Military (misc. Asian lands)
UH313.P5         Medical services, Military (Philippines)
UH315-319   Medical services, Military (Africa)
UH317-318   Medical services, Military (Egypt)
UH321-322   Medical services, Military (Australia)
UH322.5     Medical services, Military (New Z.)
UH323-324   Medical services, Military (Pac. islands)
UH341         Biography, Military medical (collective, inclu. nurses)
                                                                        355.3450922
UH347.A-Z   Medical biography, Military (indiv.: by name)        355.3450924
UH390-396   Medicine, Military (gen., hdbks., etc.)
UH390         Military medicine (gen.: inclu. hdbks., manuals, etc.)      616.98023
UH393            Medicine, Military (U.S.: official manuals etc.)
UH394            Medicine, Military (U.S.: unofficial manuals etc.)
UH395.A-Z        Medicine, Military (places besides U.S.: manuals etc.)
UH396      First-aid manuals, Soldiers' (SEE ALSO UH393-395)
UH398      Medical schools, Army (U.S.: gen.)
UH398.5.A-Z      Army medical schools (U.S.: by region or state)
UH399.5-7        Research & laboratories, Medical (mil.)
UH399.A-Z        Medical schools, Army (places besides U.S.)
UH400-485   Organization (mil. medical: inclu. services)
UH400         Military medical services (gen.: inclu. organization, surgeons, etc.)
UH420-425   Pharmacy services, Military

| | |
|---|---|
| UH430-435 | Dentistry, Military |
| UH440-445 | Supplies, Medical & surgical (mil.)    355.88 |
| UH450-455 | Bacteriology, Military (inclu. vaccination) |
| UH460-485 | Hospital services, Military |
| UH470 | Hospitals, Military (gen.)    355.72 |
| UH473-474 | Military hospitals (U.S.: SEE ALSO D629.U6-8 & D807.U6-87 for WWI & II) |
| UH475.A-Z | Hospitals, Military (except U.S.) |
| UH487 | Cookery & diet, Medical (mil.) |
| UH490 | Nurses & nursing, Military (gen.)    355.345 |
| UH493 | Military nursing (U.S.) |
| UH495.A-Z | Nursing & nurses, Military (besides U.S.) |
| UH500-505 | Ambulances, Military (plus transport)    623.74724 |
| UH500 | Transport, Medical (mil.: gen.) |
| UH510-515 | Equipment, Medical corps |
| UH510 | Medical corps equipment (gen.) |
| UH520-560 | Relief societies (mil.: inclu. care of sick & wounded)    361.05, .77 |
| UH520 | Wounded, Care of (mil.: inclu. relief societies: gen.)    361.05, .77, .9, 940.477+ |
| UH523 | Sick & wounded, Care of (mil.: relief societies, etc.: U.S.: gen.) |
| UH524.A-Z | Relief societies (mil.: U.S. by state or region) |
| UH525.A-Z | Relief societies (mil.: besides U.S.: by place) |
| UH531-533 | Geneva & Hague conventions (PREFER JX5136 & JX5243) 341.6+, .65 |
| UH531 | Hague & Geneva conventions (official works: by date: PREFER JX5136 & JX5243) |
| UH533 | Treatment of prisoners (Geneva & Hague conven.: unofficial: PREFER JX5136 & JX5243) |
| UH534 | Congresses, International (relief, sick, wounded, etc.: misc.: by date) |
| UH535 | Red Cross (gen.: wartime)    940.4771, .54771 |
| UH537.A | American Red Cross |
| UH537.A-Z | Red Cross (by country or region) |
| UH543-545 | Relief associations (besides U.S.) |
| UH560 | Employment for crippled soldiers & sailors (PREFER UB360-366) 355.1154-1156 |
| UH570 | Dead, Treatment of |
| UH600-629 | Hygiene & sanitation, Military |
| UH600 | Sanitation & hygiene, Military |
| UH603 | Military hygiene & sanitation (U.S.) |
| UH605.A-Z | Hygiene & sanitation, Military (besides U.S.) |
| UH611 | Tropical hygiene (mil. sci.) |
| UH623 | Handbooks & manuals (mil. hygiene: Eng. & Am.) |
| UH625 | Manuals & handbooks (mil. hygiene: not Eng. or Am.) |
| UH627 | Research, Physiological (mil. hygiene) |
| UH629 | Mental health, psychiatry, etc. (mil.: gen.) |
| UH629.3 | Psychiatry, Military (U.S.: inclu. mental health) |
| UH629.5.A-Z | Hygiene, Mental (besides U.S.) |
| UH630 | Moral & health protection (mil.: alcoholism, drug abuse, prostitution, venereal diseases, etc. & work vs.) |
| UH650-655 | Veterinary services (mil.)    355.345 |
| UH700-705 | Press & public relns. (mil.) |
| UH700 | Media & public relns. (mil.: gen.)    070.433, .449, 355.342 |
| UH703 | War correspondents & public relns. (mil.: U.S.) |
| UH705.A-Z | Public relations & press (mil.: places besides U.S.) |
| UH705.G3 | Radio, media, & public relns. (mil.: Ger.) |
| UH705.J3 | Newspapers, media, & public relns. (mil.: Japan) |

| | | |
|---|---|---|
| UH720-725 | Nonmilitary use of armed forces | |
| UH723 | Civic programs (armed forces: U.S.) | |
| UH750 | Social work, Military (gen.) | 355.34, .346-347 |
| UH755 | Welfare services, Military (U.S.: gen.) | |
| UH760 | Social welfare services, Military (U.S. Army) | |
| UH769.A-Z | Military social & welfare services (countries besides U.S.) | |
| UH800-910 | Recreation & information services, Military | |
| UH800 | Military recreation & information services (gen.) | 355.346 |
| UH805 | Information & recreation, Military (U.S.: gen.) | 355.3460973 |
| UH810-815 | Recreation & information services, Military (U.S. Army) | |
| UH819.A-Z | Recreation & information services, Military (besides U.S.) | |
| UH820 | Movie services, Military (gen.) | |
| UH825 | Motion-picture services, Military (U.S.: gen.: inclu. armed forces) | |
| UH826 | Military movie services (U.S. Army) | |
| UH829.A-Z | Movie services, Military (by place except U.S.) | |
| UH850 | Radio services, Military (gen.) | |
| UH855 | Radiobroadcasting services, Military (U.S.: gen., inclu. armed forces) | |
| UH857 | Military radio services (U.S. Army) | |
| UH859.A-Z | Radio services, Military (by place except U.S.) | |
| UH859.F8 | Radiobroadcasting, Military (Fr.) | |
| UH859.G3 | Radiobroadcasting, Military (Ger.) | |
| UH859.J3 | Radiobroadcasting, Military (Japan) | |
| UH900-910 | Recreation, Military (off-post) | |
| UH905 | Canteens (Off-post mil. recreation: U.S.) | |

| | | |
|---|---|---|
| V | Naval science (gen.) | 359, 623, 629 |
| V-VM | NAVAL SCIENCE, NAVIGATION, & SHIPBUILDING | |
| VA | Navies (organiz. & world status) | |
| VB | Naval administration | |
| VC | Maintenance, Naval | |
| VD | Seamen, Naval | |
| VE | Marines | |
| VF | Ordnance, Naval | |
| VG | Naval science (misc. services: medical etc.) | |
| VK | Navigation & merchant marine | |
| VM | Naval architecture & shipbuilding | |

| | | |
|---|---|---|
| V1-995+ | NAVAL SCIENCE (gen.) | 359, 623.8 |
| V1 | Periodicals & associations (naval: in English) | 359.005, .006+ |
| V7 | Conferences (naval sci.) | 359.0060+, .0063 |
| V9 | Almanacs, Naval (official) | 359.00202 |
| V10 | Yearbooks, Naval (unofficial) | |
| V11.A-Z | Yearbooks, Naval (official: ALSO lists: by country: SEE ALSO VA #s if dept. reports involved) | 359.0025+, .005 |
| V11.U6 | Lists, Naval (U.S.: ALSO official yearbooks) | |
| V13.A1 | Museums, Naval (gen.: inclu. exhibitions) | 359.0074 |
| V13.A2-Z | Naval museums & exhibitions (by country) | 359.00740+ |
| V13.x2.A-Z | Exhibitions & museums, Naval (by country then city) | |
| V15-17 | Naval science (collected works: monographic) | |
| V19 | Speeches & essays (naval sci.: gen.) | |
| V23 | Dictionaries & encyclopedias (naval sci.: gen.) | 359.003 |
| V24 | Dictionaries (naval sci.: multi-ling.) | |

| | | |
|---|---|---|
| V25-64 | Naval science (history, antiquities, & biog.: gen., during peace & war: SEE ALSO D-F #s for specific countries, wars, etc.) | |
| V25 | Philosophy, Naval (e.g. theory of naval sea power) | |
| V27 | Navies (gen. hist.) | 359.009, .409, .47 |
| V29-41 | Naval science (ancient hist.) | 359.00901 |
| V43-46 | Naval science (medieval hist.) | 359.00902 |
| V47-53+ | Naval science (modern hist.: 17th-20th c.) | 359.00903 |
| V51 | Naval science (19th c.) | 359.009034 |
| V53 | Naval science (20th c.) | 359.00904, .40904 |
| V55.A-Z | Naval science (by region or country) | 359.47+ |
| V55.A65 | Navies (America) | 359.477, .1812 |
| V55.A75 | Navies (Asia) | 359.475 |
| V55.E8 | Navies (Europe) | 359.474 |
| V61-64 | Biography, Naval (SEE ALSO D-F #s for indiv. biog's. from particular countries) | |
| V61 | Naval biography (collective) | 359.00922 |
| V62 | Naval biography (U.S.: collective) | 359.00922 |
| V63.A-Z | Biography, Naval (U.S.: by name) | 359.00924, .3310924, 940.410924, .450924, .540924, .5420924, .5450924 |
| V64.A-Z | Biography, Naval (places besides U.S.: by place) | |
| V64.x2.A-Z | Naval biography (places except U.S.: by person's name after country name) | |
| V66 | Navy clubs (U.S.) | |
| V67.A-Z | Clubs, Navy (Am. besides U.S.) | |
| V68 | Clubs, Navy (G.B.) | |
| V69.A-Z | Clubs, Navy (besides U.S. & G.B.: by country) | |
| V101 | Naval science (gen.: pubn. thru 1800) | |
| V103 | Naval science (gen.: pubn. 1801+) | |
| V107 | Naval science (pop. works) | 359 |
| V110-145 | Handbooks, Naval | |
| V110 | Handbooks, Seamen's (gen.) | 359.00202 |
| V113 | Seamen's handbooks (U.S. Navy) | |
| V115.A-Z | Naval handbooks (seamen's: places besides U.S.) | |
| V115.G3 | Seamen's handbooks (Ger.) | |
| V115.G7 | Seamen's handbooks (G.B.) | |
| V115.J3 | Seamen's handbooks (Japan) | |
| V115.R9 | Seamen's handbooks (Rus.) | |
| V120-125 | Handbooks, Petty officers' | |
| V120 | Petty officers' handbooks (gen.) | |
| V123 | Naval petty officers' handbooks (U.S.) | |
| V130-135 | Handbooks, Naval officers' | 359.3320202 |
| V133 | Naval officers' handbooks (U.S.) | |
| V135.A-Z | Officers' handbooks, Naval (places besides U.S.) | |
| V140-145 | Handbooks, Naval reserve | |
| V160 | Strategy, Naval (gen.: pubn. thru 1800) | |
| V163 | Naval strategy (gen.: pubn. 1801+) | 359.03, .43 |
| V165 | Naval strategy (gen. special) | |
| V167 | Tactics, Naval (gen.) | 359.42 |
| V169 | Naval tactics (gen. particular) | |
| V175 | Landing ops. & field service tactics (naval: inclu. shore srvc., small arms instruc., etc.) | 355.41, .422 |
| V178 | Boat attack (naval tactics) | 359.32, .42 |
| V179 | Logistics, Naval | 359.41 |
| V180 | Blockades, Naval | 355.44, 359.42-43, 940.452, .5452 |
| V182 | Convoys, Naval | 359.4-43 |

| | | |
|---|---|---|
| V185 | Security, Naval | |
| V190 | Patrols & reconnaisance, Naval | 359.413 |
| V200 | Coast defense, Naval (SEE ALSO UG410-442) | 359.45 |
| V210 | Submarine warfare (gen.) | 359.3257, .42-43 |
| V214 | Antisubmarine warfare | 359.3254, .42-43 |
| V215 | Camouflage, Marine | 623.77 |
| V220 | Bases, ports, & docks (naval: gen.: SEE ALSO VA67-750 for specific<br>countries) | 359.7 |
| V230 | Yards, Navy (gen.: SEE ALSO VA67-750 for particular places)<br>                                                                            359.7 | |
| V240 | Coaling stations, Naval (gen.: SEE ALSO VA67-750) | |
| V245 | Maneuvers, Naval (SEE U260-262 for combined — army, navy, air<br>forces — or amphibious warfare ops.)           359.52 | |
| V250 | War games, Naval | 359.52 |
| V252 | Training, Simulated (navies) | |
| V253 | Imaginary naval battles & wars | 359.47 |
| V260 | Training, Physical (navies: gen.) | 359.54 |
| V263-264 | Physical training (navies: U.S.) | |
| V265.A-Z | Training, Physical (navies: countries besides U.S.) | |
| V267-268 | Sports in navies | |
| V270 | Orders, Transmission of (navies) | 359.27, .85 |
| V280-285 | Signaling, Naval (gen.) | 359.27, .983 |
| V283 | Naval signaling (U.S.) | |
| V300 | Flags, Naval & marine (gen.: SEE ALSO VK385) | 359.15 |
| V303 | Naval flags (U.S.: inclu. marine) | |
| V305.A-Z | Flags, Naval & marine (besides U.S.) | |
| V305.G7 | Naval flags (G.B.) | |
| V305.J3 | Naval flags (Japan) | |
| V310 | Ceremonies, honors, & salutes (navies: gen.) | 359.17, .1349 |
| V380-385 | Safety measures, Naval (inclu. educ.) | |
| V390 | Research, Naval (gen.) | 359.07 |
| V393 | Research, Naval (U.S.: gen.) | 359.070973 |
| V393.5.A-W | Naval research (U.S.: by state) | |
| V394.A-Z | Naval research (U.S.: by special establishment locale) | |
| V395.A-Z | Research, Naval (countries besides U.S.) | |
| V396 | Oceanography, Military (gen.) | 359.982, 551.46, 620.4162 |
| V396.3-4 | Military oceanography (U.S.) | |
| V396.5.A-Z | Oceanography, Military (places besides U.S.) | |
| V400-695 | EDUCATION, NAVAL | |
| V400 | Naval education & training (gen.) | 359.007 |
| V401 | Education, Naval (hist.: gen.) | |
| V404 | Training & education, Naval (modern hist.: gen.) | |
| V409 | Education, Naval (hist.: 20th c.) | |
| V411-438 | Education, Naval (U.S.) | |
| V411 | Naval education (U.S.: gen.) 359.0071073, .0071173, .50973, .550973 | |
| V415.A1 | U.S. Naval Academy (Act of incorp.: PREFER KF7353.55) | |
| V415.A1-R4+ | U.S. Naval Academy (Annapolis) | 359.0071173 |
| V415.C3-6 | Regulations (U.S. Naval Acad.) | |
| V415.C3-H5 | U.S. Naval Academy (admin.) | |
| V415.E1-4 | Reports, Official (U.S. Naval Acad. Superinten.: annual) | |
| V415.E5 | U.S. Naval Academy (Cong. docs.: gen.: by date) | |
| V415.E9 | Hazing (U.S. Naval Acad.: Cong. docs.) | |
| V415.F3.A-Z | Commencement addresses (U.S. Naval Acad.: by speaker) | |
| V415.F5.A-Z | Speeches (U.S. Naval Acad.: misc.: by speaker) | |
| V415.F7 | Reports, Official & unoff. (U.S. Naval Acad.) | |

| | |
|---|---|
| V415.H3-39 | Registers, Official (U.S. Naval Acad.: annual) |
| V415.H5 | U.S. Naval Academy (registers, unoff.) |
| V415.J1-7 | Student publications (U.S. Naval Acad.) |
| V415.K1-4 | Publications, Graduate (U.S. Naval Acad.) |
| V415.K4 | Class histories (U.S. Naval Acad.: by date) |
| V415.L1 | Annapolis (U.S. Naval Acad.: gen. hist's. & other titles) |
| V415.L1-P1 | U.S. Naval Academy (hist. & descrip.) |
| V415.L3 | Pictorials (U.S. Naval Acad.) |
| V415.M1.A-Z | Biography (U.S. Naval Acad.: by name) |
| V415.P1 | Annapolis (U.S. Naval Acad.: life & conditions) |
| V415.R1-4 | Examinations (U.S. Naval Acad.) |
| V420 | Naval War College (U.S.)    359.550973, .0071173 |
| V425.A-Z | Training schools, Naval (misc.) |
| V426 | Naval Reserve Officers' Training Corps (U.S.: N.R.O.T.C.)   359.2232 |
| V430 | Schools, Private naval (U.S.) |
| V433 | Training stations, Naval (U.S.: gen.)    359.50973, .70973 |
| V434.A-Z | Naval training stations (U.S.: by place) |
| V434.G7 | Great Lakes Naval Training Station (Ill.) |
| V434.H2 | Hampton Roads Naval Training Station (Va.) |
| V435 | Training ships (U.S. Navy: gen.) |
| V436.A-Z | Naval training ships (U.S.: by name) |
| V437 | Training & education, Naval (U.S. Coast Guard)    359.9707 |
| V440-444 | Education, Naval (Can.) |
| V500-623 | Education, Naval (Eur.) |
| V500 | Naval education (Eur.: gen.) |
| V510-530 | Education, Naval (G.B.) |
| V510 | Naval education (G.B.: gen.)   359.0071141, .50941, .550941, .007041 |
| V511-512 | British naval education (special topics) |
| V513 | Examinations (G.B. Royal Navy) |
| V515.A1 | Dartmouth (Royal Naval College: Act of incorp.) |
| V515.A1-R1+ | Royal Naval College (Dartmouth) |
| V515.C1-K3 | G.B. Royal Naval College, Dartmouth (admin.) |
| V515.E1-49 | Reports, Official (Royal Naval Coll., Dart.: annual) |
| V515.F3.A-Z | Speeches (Royal Naval Coll., Dart.: by speaker) |
| V515.H1-5 | Registers, Official & unoff. (Royal Naval Coll., Dart.) |
| V515.K3 | Class histories (Royal Naval Coll., Dart.: by date) |
| V515.L1 | Royal Naval College (Dartmouth: hist.) |
| V515.M1.A-Z | Biography (Royal Naval Coll., Dart.: by name) |
| V515.P1 | Royal Naval College (Dartmouth: life, pictorials, etc.) |
| V520.A1-R1+ | Royal Naval College (Greenwich: set up like V515) |
| V522-525 | Training & education, Naval (G.B.: stations, ships, engin. schools, etc.) |
| V522.5.A-Z | Training stations, Naval (G.B.: by place) |
| V522.5.P6 | Portsmouth, Eng. (Royal Naval Barracks) |
| V565-569 | Education, Naval (Fr.) |
| V570-574 | Education, Naval (Ger.) |
| V570 | Naval education (Ger.: gen.)    359.007043, .50943 |
| V574.A-Z | Schools, Naval (Ger.) |
| V574.A2-65 | German naval education (main school) |
| V574.A7-Z | Naval schools (Ger.: by name or place) |
| V585-589 | Education, Naval (It.) |
| V600-604 | Education, Naval (Rus.) |

| V625-650 | Education, Naval (Asia) |
| V625 | Naval education (Asia: gen.) |
| V630-634 | Education, Naval (China) |
| V640-644 | Education, Naval (Japan) |
| V640 | Naval education (Japan: gen.) 359.007052, .0071152, .50952, .550952 |
| V650.A-Z | Education, Naval (Asia: misc. countries) |
| V650.P5 | Education, Naval (Philippines) |
| V690-694 | Education, Naval (Australia)   359.007094 |
| V694.1-5 | Education, Naval (New Z.) |
| V701-716 | Naval observations (wartime: PREFER D-F areas) |
| V713 | Observations, Naval (Russo-Japanese War, 1904-5)      952.031, 359.4752, .4747 |
| V715 | Observations, Naval (WWI)   940.45-453 |
| V716 | Observations, Naval (WWII)   940.545-5459 |
| V720-743 | Naval life & customs |
| V720 | Customs, Naval (gen.)   359.1 |
| V735-743 | Naval life & customs (modern) |
| V735 | Life & customs, Naval (modern: gen.)   359.10904 |
| V736 | Naval life & customs (modern: U.S.)   359.10973 |
| V737 | Naval life & customs (modern: G.B.)   359.10941 |
| V739 | Naval life & customs (modern: Ger.)   359.10943 |
| V741 | Naval life & customs (modern: Rus.)   359.10947 |
| V743.A-Z | Naval life & customs (modern: misc. countries) |
| V743.J3 | Naval life & customs (modern: Japan) |
| V745 | Curiosities, Naval   359.00207, .002 |
| V750-995+ | WARSHIPS (construction, armament, types, etc.: SEE VA for status & organiz. of specific navies around the world) |
| V750 | Ships, Naval (gen.: SEE here for earlier works on battleships & V815 for later works) |
| V765-767 | Vessels, Naval war (modern period)   623.80904 |
| V799 | Construction of warships (1860-1900: armored vessels) |
| V800 | Construction of warships (1901+)   623.825, 359.325+ |
| V805 | Construction of warships (materials: gen.) |
| V805.3 | Construction of warships (materials: U.S.) |
| V805.5.A-Z | Construction of warships (materials: besides U.S.) |
| V810 | Damage control (warships)   623.888 |
| V815-895 | Warships (types)   623.825-826, 359.83, .325-326 |
| V815 | Battleships (gen.: construc., armament, etc.: SEE V750 for earlier titles)   623.8252, .81252, 359.3252 |
| V815.3 | Battleships (U.S.)   623.82520973, 359.32520973 |
| V815.5.A-Z | Battleships (besides U.S.: by place) |
| V815.5.G3 | Battleships (Ger.)   623.82520943 |
| V815.5.G7 | Battleships (G.B.)   623.82520941 |
| V815.5.J3 | Battleships (Japan)   623.82520952 |
| V820 | Cruisers (gen.: tech. info.)   623.8253, .81253, 359.3253 |
| V820.3 | Cruisers (U.S.) |
| V820.5.A-Z | Cruisers (besides U.S.) |
| V820.5.G7 | Cruisers (G.B.) |
| V825 | Destroyers (gen.)   623.8254, .81254, 359.3254 |
| V825.3 | Destroyers (U.S.) |
| V825.5.A-Z | Destroyers (besides U.S.: by place) |
| V825.5.J3 | Destroyers (Japan) |
| V826 | Frigates & corvettes (gen.)   623.8254 |
| V826.3 | Frigates (U.S.) |
| V826.5.A-Z | Corvettes & frigates (besides U.S.) |

| V830-838 | Torpedo boats    623.8258, 359.3258 |
| V830 | P.T. boats (gen.) |
| V833 | Torpedo boats (U.S.) |
| V835.A-Z | Torpedo boats (places besides U.S.) |
| V835.G3 | Torpedo boats (Ger.) |
| V837-838 | Torpedo boat service |
| V840 | Torpedo boat destroyers    623.8254 |
| V850 | Torpedoes (gen.: inclu. propelling or launching devices)    623.4517, 359.82517 |
| V855.A-Z | Torpedoes (types or devices: by name) |
| V855.G7 | Graydon aerial torpedo thrower |
| V855.W5 | Whitehead torpedo |
| V856 | Minelaying, minesweeping, submarine mines, etc. (gen.)    623.2, .26, .263, .36, .45115, .8262, 359.825115, .3262 |
| V856.5.A-Z | Minesweeping, minelaying, sub. mines, etc. (by place) |
| V856.5.U6-7 | Submarine mines, minelaying, minesweeping, etc. (U.S.) |
| V857 | Submarines (gen.: SEE ALSO V210-14 for sub warfare & VM365-7 for construc.)    623.8257, .82572, .81257, 359.3257 |
| V858 | Submarines (U.S.)    623.82570973, 359.32570973 |
| V859.A-Z | Submarines (besides U.S.) |
| V859.G3 | Submarines (Ger.)    623.82570943 |
| V859.J3 | Submarines (Japan)    623.82570952 |
| V860 | Turrets, Revolving (naval sci.: inclu. monitors) |
| V865 | Naval vessels (auxiliary: fleet trains, repair & supply ships, etc.)    623.826, 359.326 |
| V870 | Naval vessels, Unarmored |
| V874 | Aircraft carriers (gen.)    623.8255, 359.3255 |
| V874.3 | Aircraft carriers (U.S.)    623.82550973, .81255, 359.32550973 |
| V874.5.A-Z | Carriers, Aircraft (besides U.S.) |
| V874.5.G7 | Aircraft carriers (G.B.)    623.82550941 |
| V874.5.J3 | Aircraft carriers (Japan)    623.82550952 |
| V875.A-Z | Aircraft carriers (special topics) |
| V875.A36 | Aircraft launching & recovery equipment (carriers) |
| V875.F5 | Flight decks (aircraft carriers) |
| V880 | Vedettes, scout & dispatch boats, other minor craft (gen.) |
| V885 | Minesweepers (SEE ALSO V856)    623.8262 |
| V890 | Floating batteries |
| V895 | Naval vessels (misc., non-major: inclu. landing craft) |
| V900-925 | Armor plate (naval sci.) |
| V900 | Armor plate (naval sci.: gen.)    623.81821, .8251 |
| V903 | Armor, Naval (U.S.)    623.82510973 |
| V905.A-Z | Naval armor (places besides U.S.) |
| V907.A-Z | Plating, Armor (naval sci.: special type) |
| V907.K7 | Krupp armor plating (naval sci.) |
| V910-915 | Testing (naval armor: SEE ALSO VF540) |
| V913 | Naval armor testing (U.S.) |
| V950 | Armament, Naval (gen.)    623.8251 |
| V960 | Naval armament (installation) |
| V980 | Equipment, Naval (misc.) |

```
VA          NAVIES (organiz. & world status)
VA10        Naval status (world: gen.)      359, .03
VA20-25     Costs, Naval (budgets etc.)
VA25        Budgets, Naval (gen.)           359.622
VA40            Navies (of the world: gen.)      359, .03, .009, 623.82509
VA41            World navies (pop. works)
VA42            Pictorials (world navies)
VA45        Reserves, Naval (gen.)          359.37+
VA48        Mobilizaton, Naval (gen.)       359.28
VA49-750+   NAVAL STATUS (worldwide: place by place)
VA49        Periodicals & associations (naval: U.S.)      359.005-007+
VA50        Naval status (U.S.: gen.)       359.030973, .4773
VA52-395    NAVAL STATUS (U.S.)
VA52-79         U.S. Navy (SEE ALSO E182)
VA52.A1-89      Reports, Official (U.S. Navy Dept.)
VA52.A1-19      U.S. Navy Dept. (official docs.: gen.)
VA52.A2-29      Secretary of the Navy (U.S.: official docs.)
VA52.A6-67      Reports, Official (U.S. Navy Bur's. of Navigation, Personnel)
VA52.A68-69     Material, Naval (U.S. Navy. Office of: reports)
VA52.A7-79      Naval ops. (U.S. Navy. Office of: reports)
VA53        Reports, Congressional (U.S. Navy: official & others)
VA54        Speeches (U.S. Navy)
VA55        U.S. Navy (gen.)            359.00973, .30973, .4773
VA58        U.S. Navy (gen.: 1881-1970 coverage)      359.00973
VA59        Pictorials (naval: U.S.)        359.3250973
VA60        Budgets, Naval (U.S.)           359.6220973
VA61        Ships (U.S. Navy: lists)        359.32, .320222
VA62-74     U.S. Navy (placement & stations)
VA62        U.S. Navy (distribution: gen.)      359.4773, .31
VA62.5          Naval districts (U.S.: gen.)      359.70973
VA62.7.1st+     Naval districts (U.S.: by #)
VA63.A-Z    Fleets, squadrons, etc. (U.S. Navy: by name)      359.310973
VA63.A83        Atlantic Fleet (U.S.)
VA63.N8         North Atlantic Fleet (U.S.)
VA63.P2         Pacific Fleet (U.S.)
VA65.A-Z    Ships (U.S. Navy: by name)      359.32520973-.32560973
VA65.A75    Arizona (battleship: U.S.)
VA65.C3     California (battleship: U.S.)
VA65.M8         Missouri (battleship: U.S.)      359.32520973
VA65.S28        Saratoga (aircraft carrier: U.S.)      359.32550973
VA66.A-Z    U.S. Navy (misc. units: by name)
VA66.C6-65  Construction Battalions (U.S. Navy)      359.33+, .90973
VA67-68     Naval bases, ports, docks, etc. (U.S.)
VA67        Ports, bases, docks, etc. (U.S. Navy: gen.)      359.70973,
                940.4530973 (WWI), .54530973 (WWII), .545973 (WWII)
VA68.A-Z    Bases, ports, etc. (U.S. Navy: by place)
VA69        Naval yards & stations (U.S.: gen.)      359.70973, 623.830973
VA70.A-Z    Yards & stations, Naval (U.S.: by place)
VA70.N5     New London Naval Station (U.S.: Conn.)
VA70.N7     Norfolk Navy Yard (U.S.: Va.)
VA70.P5     Philadelphia Navy Yard (U.S.: Penn.)
VA70.P8     Portsmouth Navy Yard (U.S.: N.H.)
VA73        Naval coaling stations (U.S.: gen.)      359.70973, .750973
VA77        Mobilization (U.S. Navy)        359.280973
```

| | |
|---|---|
| VA79 | Supply vessels, transports, service craft, etc. (U.S. Naval Auxiliary Service) |
| VA80-390 | RESERVES, NAVAL (U.S.) |
| VA80 | Naval reserves (U.S.: gen.)   359.370973 |
| VA90-387 | MILITIA, NAVAL (U.S.: state by state) |
| VA100-107 | Reserves, Naval (U.S.: Calif.) |
| VA100 | Naval reserves (U.S.: Calif.: gen.)   359.3709794 |
| VA101 | Reports, Official (naval reserves: U.S.: Calif.) |
| VA102 | Registers & lists (naval reserves: U.S.: Calif.) |
| VA103.1st+ | Reserves, Naval (U.S.: Calif.: special groups by #) |
| VA104.A-Z | Reserves, Naval (U.S.: Calif.: special groups by name) |
| VA105.A-Z | Ships (Calif. naval reserves: by name) |
| VA107 | Reserves, Naval (U.S.: Calif.: misc. topics) |
| VA140-147 | Reserves, Naval (U.S.: Florida) |
| VA158-158.7 | Reserves, Naval (U.S.: Hawaii) |
| VA160-167 | Reserves, Naval (U.S.: Ill.) |
| VA240-247 | Reserves, Naval (U.S.: Mississ.) |
| VA250-257 | Reserves, Naval (U.S.: Missouri) |
| VA280-287 | Reserves, Naval (U.S.: N.Y.) |
| VA350-357 | Reserves, Naval (U.S.: Texas) |
| VA370-377 | Reserves, Naval (U.S.: Wash.) |
| VA380-387 | Reserves, Naval (U.S.: Wisc.) |
| VA390 | Waves (U.S. naval reserves for women & other non-local U.S. naval res.) |
| VA400-402 | Naval status (Can.) |
| VA400 | Canada (naval status: gen.)   359.030971, .4771 |
| VA402.5 | Latin America (naval status) |
| VA415-445 | Naval status (S.Am.) |
| VA415 | South America (naval status: gen.)   359.03098 |
| VA416 | Argentina (naval status)   359.030982 |
| VA440 | Uruguay (naval status) |
| VA450-619 | NAVAL STATUS (Eur.) |
| VA450 | Europe (naval status: gen.)   359.03094, .474 |
| VA452-467 | Naval status (G.B.) |
| VA452 | Periodicals & associations (naval: G.B.) |
| VA453 | Primary sources, documents (naval: G.B.) |
| VA454 | G.B. Royal Navy (gen.)   359.0309441, .30941, .4741-4742, .00941 |
| VA455 | Budgets, Naval (G.B.) |
| VA456 | Ships (G.B. Royal Navy: lists)   359.325+, .320941 |
| VA457.A-Z | Fleets, squadrons, etc. (G.B.: by name)   359.310941 |
| VA458.A-Z | Ships (G.B. Royal Navy: by name)   359.320941, .3252+-.326+ |
| VA458.A7 | Ark Royal (aircraft carrier: G.B.) |
| VA458.H6 | Hood (battle cruiser: G.B.) |
| VA458.I55 | Invincible (aircraft carrier: G.B.) |
| VA458.P75 | Prince of Wales (battleship: G.B.) |
| VA459 | Naval bases, ports, docks, etc. (G.B.) |
| VA459.A1 | Ports, bases, docks, etc. (G.B. Royal Navy: gen.)   359.70941, 940.4530941 (WWI), .54530941 (WWII) |
| VA459.A3-Z | Bases, ports, etc. (G.B. Royal Navy: by place) |
| VA459.H55 | Hong Kong Naval Base (Royal Navy) |
| VA459.S5 | Singapore Naval Base (Royal Navy)   940.5453095952, .5453095957(WWII) |
| VA460 | Naval yards & stations (G.B.)   359.70941 |
| VA463 | Mobilization, Naval (G.B.)   359.280941 |
| VA464 | Reserves, Naval (G.B.) |

```
VA480-489    Belgium (naval status)
VA490-499    Denmark (naval status)
VA500-509    Naval status (Fr.)
VA503.A1-49      Ships (Fr. Navy: lists)        359.320944, .3250944
VA503.A5-Z       France (naval status: gen.)    359.030944, .4744
VA510-519    Naval status (Ger.)
VA510        Periodicals & associations (naval: Ger.)
VA511        Budgets, Naval (Ger.)
VA512        Primary sources, documents (naval: Ger.)
VA513.A1-49      Ships (Ger. Navy: lists)       359.320943, .3250943
VA513.A5-Z       Germany (naval status: gen.)   359.030943, .00943, .30943, .4743
VA514.A-Z    Fleets, squadrons, etc. (Ger.: by name)    359.310943
VA515.A-Z        Ships (Ger. Navy: by name)     359.320943, .3252+-.326+
VA515.B4         Bismarck (battleship: Ger.)
VA515.G          Graf Spee, Admiral (cruiser, armoured: Ger.)
VA515.P73        Prinz Eugen (cruiser, heavy: Ger.)     359.32530943
VA515.S          Scharnhorst (battle cruisers: Ger.: WWI & II)
VA516.A1     Naval bases, ports, docks, etc. (Ger.: gen.)    359.70943,
                 940.4530943 (WWI), .54530943 (WWII)
VA516.A3-Z   Ports, bases, docks, etc. (Ger. Navy: by name)
VA516.K4     Kiel Naval Base (Ger.)
VA518        Mobilization, Naval (Ger.)     359.290943
VA519        Reserves, Naval (Ger.)         359.370943
VA520-529        Greece (naval status)
VA530-539        Netherlands (naval status)
VA540-549    Naval status (It.)
VA543.A5-Z       Italy (naval status: gen.)     359.030945, .00945, .30945, .4745
VA550-559        Norway (naval status)          359.0309481
VA570-579    Naval status (Rus.)
VA573.A5-Z   Russia (naval status: gen.)    359.030947, .00947, .4747
VA580-589    Spain (naval status)
VA590-599    Sweden (naval status)
VA620-667    NAVAL STATUS (Asia)
VA620        Asia (naval status: gen.)      359.03095
VA630-639        China (naval status)       359.030951
VA650-659        Naval status (Japan)
VA653.A1-49      Ships (Japan. Imper. Navy: lists)      359.30952, .320952,
                                                        .3252+-326+
VA653.A5-Z   Japan (naval status: gen.)     359.030952, .00952, .30952, .4752
VA654.A-Z    Fleets, squadrons, etc. (Japan: by name)    359.310952
VA655.A-Z        Ships (Japan. Imper. Navy: by name)    359.320952, .3252+-.326+
VA655.A43        Akagi (aircraft carrier: Japan)
VA655.Y25        Yamato (battleship: Japan)     359.32520952
VA656        Naval bases, ports, docks, etc. (Japan. Imper. Navy)    359.70952,
                                                          940.54530952 (WWII)
VA658        Mobilization, Naval (Japan)    359.280952
VA667.A-Z    Naval status (Asia: misc. countries)
VA667.P5     Philippines (naval status)     359.0309599
VA670-700    Africa (naval status)
VA690        Egypt (naval status)           359.030962
VA700.S52    South Africa (naval status)    359.030968
```

| VA710-719 | Naval status (Australia) | |
| VA713.A1-49 | Ships (Australia. Navy: lists) | 359.30994, .320994, .3250994 |
| VA713.A5-Z | Australia (naval status: gen.) | 359.030994, .00994, .4794 |
| VA715.A-Z | Ships (Australia. Navy: by name) | 359.32520994-.3260994 |
| VA716 | Naval bases, ports, docks, etc. (Australia) | 359.70994 |
| VA720-729 | Naval status (New Z.) | |
| VA723.A1-49 | Ships (New Z. Navy: lists) | 359.309931 |
| VA723.A5-Z | New Zealand (naval status: gen.) | 359.0309931, .009931, .47931 |

| VB | ADMINISTRATION, NAVAL (command, personnel, law, etc.) | |
| VB15 | Administration, Naval (gen. hist.) | 359.6, .1-3 |
| VB21-124 | NAVAL ADMINISTRATION (by country) | |
| VB23 | Naval administration (U.S.) | 359.60973 |
| VB26 | Naval administration (Can.) | |
| VB55-96 | Naval administration (Eur.) | |
| VB55 | Administration, Naval (Eur.: gen.) | 359.6094 |
| VB57 | Naval administration (G.B.) | 359.60941, .30941 |
| VB71 | Naval administration (Fr.) | 359.60944 |
| VB73 | Naval administration (Ger.) | 359.60943, .30943 |
| VB79 | Naval administration (It.) | 359.60945 |
| VB85 | Naval administration (Rus.) | 359.60947 |
| VB99-113 | Naval administration (Asia) | |
| VB99 | Administration, Naval (Asia: gen.) | 359.6095 |
| VB105 | Naval administration (Japan) | 359.60952, .30952 |
| VB121 | Naval administration (Australia) | 359.60994 |
| VB122.5 | Naval administration (New Z.) | |
| VB145 | Naval administration (gen.: pubn. 1801-1970) | 359.6, .3 |
| VB170-187 | Naval administration (civil sections) | |
| VB170 | Civil depts. (naval admin.: gen.) | |
| VB180-187 | Civilian personnel (naval admin.) | |
| VB180 | Personnel, Civilian (naval admin.: gen.) | |
| VB183 | Employees, Civilian (naval admin.: U.S.) | |
| VB185.A-Z | Civilian personnel (naval admin.: places besides U.S.) | |
| VB190 | Admirals, commanders, etc. (admin.: inclu. duties) | |
| VB200-205 | Naval command and leadership | |
| VB200 | Command of ships (naval admin.: gen.) | 359.33, .6, 158.4, 350.00323 |
| VB203 | Leadership (naval admin.: U.S.) | |
| VB205.A-Z | Leadership (naval admin.: besides U.S.) | |
| VB210 | Headquarters, Naval (ops. inclu. aides) | |
| VB220-225 | Inspection, Naval (inclu. inspectors) | |
| VB230-254 | Intelligence, Naval | |
| VB230 | Naval intelligence (gen.) | 359.3432 |
| VB231.A-Z | Intelligence, Naval (by country) | 359.343209+ |
| VB231.G3 | Naval intelligence (Ger.) | 359.34320943 |
| VB231.G7 | Naval intelligence (G.B.) | 359.34320941 |
| VB231.U6-7 | Naval intelligence (U.S.) | 359.34320973 |
| VB240 | Attachés, Naval | |
| VB250 | Espionage & spies (naval admin.) | 359.3432-3433 |
| VB252 | Propaganda & psych. warfare (naval sci.: gen.) | 359.3434 |
| VB253 | Propaganda & psych. warfare (naval sci.: U.S.) | 359.34340973 |
| VB254.A-Z | Psychological warfare & propaganda (naval sci.: places besides U.S.) | |
| VB255 | Orders, passes, field correspondence (naval admin.) | |
| VB257 | Personnel administration (naval sci.: gen.) | 359.61 |
| VB258 | Naval personnel (admin.: U.S.) | 359.610973 |
| VB259 | Career guidance (naval sci.) | |

| VB260-275 | Enlisted personnel (naval sci.: inclu. recruitment, enlistment, promotion, discharge, etc.) | |
| VB260 | Recruitment, enlistment, promotion, discharge (naval sci.: enlisted personnel: gen.) | 359.223, .338, .11+ |
| VB263 | Promotion, discharge, recruitment, enlistment (naval sci.: enlisted personnel: U.S.) | 359.2230973, .3380973 |
| VB264.A-Z | Enlistment, recruitment, promotion, discharge (Naval sci.: U.S.: by region or state) | |
| VB265.A-Z | Discharge, promotion, recruitment, enlistment (naval sci.: places besides U.S.) | |
| VB265.G3 | Enlisted personnel (naval sci.: Ger.: inclu. enlistment, promotion, etc.) | 359.2230943 |
| VB270-275 | Recruits, Naval (inclu. medical & mental examinations) | 359.2236 |
| VB277 | Demobilization, Naval (inclu. civil employ.) | 359.29, .1154 |
| VB278 | Crippled sailors, Employment of (PREFER UB360-366) | |
| VB280-285 | Pensions, disability benefits, etc. (naval admin.) | 359.115-1156 |
| VB283 | Disability benefits, pensions, etc. (naval admin.: U.S.) | |
| VB290-295 | Homes, Sailors' (SEE ALSO UB380-385) | |
| VB300-305 | Cemeteries (naval) | 351.86, .866 |
| VB303-304 | Naval cemeteries (U.S.) | |
| VB307 | Warrant officers (naval: gen.) | 359.332 |
| VB308 | Officers, Warrant (naval: U.S.) | 359.3320973 |
| VB309.A-Z | Naval warrant officers (besides U.S.) | |
| VB310-315 | Officers, Naval (inclu. appt., promo., rank, retire., etc.) | |
| VB310 | Rank, appointment, promotion, retirement, etc. (naval officers: gen.) | 359.332, .331 |
| VB313 | Officers, Naval (U.S.: gen.) | 359.3320973, .3310973 |
| VB314.A-Z | Biography, Naval (U.S.: by name) | 359.3310973, .3310924 |
| VB314.H25 | Halsey, William F., 'Bull', Admiral (U.S. Navy) | |
| VB315.A-Z | Naval officers (except U.S.) | |
| VB315.G7 | Officers, Naval (G.B.) | 359.3320941 |
| VB315.J3 | Officers, Naval (Japan) | |
| VB315.R9 | Officers, Naval (Rus.) | |
| VB320-325 | Minorities & women (navies) | |
| VB320 | Women & minorities (navies: gen.) | 359.22 |
| VB323 | Women & minorities (U.S. Navy: gen.) | |
| VB324.A-Z | Minorities (U.S. Navy: by group) | |
| VB324.A47 | Afro-Americans (U.S. Navy) | |
| VB324.I5 | Indians (U.S. Navy: native-Am's.) | |
| VB324.W65 | Women (U.S. Navy) | |
| VB330-335 | Badges, brevets, medals of honor, rewards, etc. (navies) | |
| VB330 | Medals, badges, brevets, etc. (navies: gen.) | 359.1342 |
| VB333 | Brevets, badges, medals, etc. (U.S. Navy: inclu. Navy Cross) | 359.13420973 |
| VB335.A-Z | Rewards, badges, brevets, medals (navies: except U.S.) | |
| VB340-345 | Pensions, Survivors' (naval) | |
| VB350-785 | NAVAL LAW | |
| VB350 | Law, Naval (gen.) | 359.13, 343.01+ |
| VB353 | International naval law | |
| VB360-785 | NAVAL LAW (by area or country) | |
| VB360-369 | Naval law (U.S.: PREFER KF7345-7375) | |
| VB360 | Law, Naval (U.S.) | 343.7301 |
| VB363 | Regulations, Naval (U.S.) | |
| VB365 | General orders (naval: U.S.) | |
| VB370-379 | Naval law (Can.) | |

| VB530-699 | European naval law |
|---|---|
| VB530 | Naval Law (Eur.: gen.) |
| VB570-579 | Naval Law (FR.) |
| VB580-589 | Naval Law (Ger.) |
| VB590-599 | Naval Law (G.B.: PREFER KD6128-6158)   343.4101 |
| VB650-659 | Naval law (Rus.) |
| VB700-799 | Asian naval law |
| VB700 | Naval law (Asia: gen.) |
| VB710-719 | Naval law (China) |
| VB730-739 | Naval law (Japan)   343.5201 |
| VB775 | Naval law (Australia) |
| VB777 | Naval law (New Z.) |
| VB790-925 | Naval justice (admin. of) |
| VB790 | Justice, Naval (gen.: inclu. judiciary)   343.014, .0146 |
| VB793 | Judiciary, Naval (U.S.: inclu. overall naval justice) |
| VB795.A-Z | Naval justice (places besides U.S.) |
| VB800 | Courts-martial, Naval (gen.)   343.0146 |
| VB803 | Courts-martial, Naval (U.S.: PREFER KF7646-7650) |
| VB805.A-Z | Courts-martial, Naval (besides U.S.: by place) |
| VB806 | Cases (courts-martial, naval: U.S.: PREFER KF7646-7650) |
| VB807.A-Z | Cases (courts-martial, naval: besides U.S.: by place) |
| VB810-815 | Courts of inquiry, Naval   343.0143 |
| VB813 | Inquiry, Courts of (naval: U.S.: PREFER KF7646-7650) |
| VB814.A-Z | Cases (courts of inquiry, naval: U.S.: PREFER KF #s) |
| VB815.A-Z | Courts of inquiry, Naval (besides U.S.) |
| VB840-845 | Naval discipline   359.13 |
| VB843 | Discipline, Naval (U.S.)   359.130973 |
| VB845.A-Z | Discipline, Naval (besides U.S.) |
| VB845.G7 | Discipline, Naval (G.B.) |
| VB850-880 | Offenses & crimes, Naval |
| VB850 | Crimes, Naval (gen.)   359.1334 |
| VB853 | Naval crimes (U.S.) |
| VB855.A-Z | Naval crimes (except U.S.) |
| VB855.G3 | Naval crimes (Ger.) |
| VB855.G7 | Naval crimes (G.B.) |
| VB855.J3 | Naval crimes (Japan) |
| VB860 | Mutiny (naval: gen.)   359.1334 |
| VB863 | Mutiny (naval: U.S.) |
| VB865.A-Z | Mutiny (naval: except U.S.) |
| VB867.A-Z | Naval mutiny (by ship) |
| VB870-875 | Desertion (naval)   359.1334 |
| VB873 | Naval desertion (U.S.) |
| VB880 | Looting & other naval crimes |
| VB890-910 | Prisoners, prisons, punishments (naval) |
| VB890 | Naval prisons & prisoners (gen.)   344.03548 |
| VB893 | Prisons & prisoners, Naval (U.S.)   344.035480973 |
| VB895.A-Z | Prisons & prisoners, Naval (except U.S.: by place) |
| VB895.G7 | Prisons & prisoners, Naval (G.B.) |
| VB895.R9 | Prisons & prisoners, Naval (Rus.) |
| VB910 | Corporal punishment (naval)   364.67, 343.0146, 359.13325 |

| | | |
|---|---|---|
| VB920 | Shore patrol (gen.) | 359.13323, .34 |
| VB923 | Shore patrol (U.S.) | |
| VB925.A-Z | Police, Naval (besides U.S.) | |
| VB925.G3 | Shore patrol (Ger.) | |
| VB925.G7 | Shore patrol (G.B.) | |
| VB955 | Administration, Naval (misc. topics) | |

| | | |
|---|---|---|
| VC | MAINTENANCE, NAVAL | 359.6-8 |
| VC10 | Naval maintenance (gen.) | 359.6 |
| VC20-258 | ORGANIZATION (naval maintenance: by place) | |
| VC20-65 | Maintenance, Naval (U.S.) | |
| VC20 | Naval maintenance (U.S.: gen.) | 359.60973 |
| VC25-38 | Reports, Official (naval maint.: U.S.) | |
| VC39 | Reports, Unofficial (naval maint.: U.S.) | |
| VC40-41 | Reserves, Naval (U.S.: maint. & organ.) | 359.370973 |
| VC50-65 | Pay & allowances (U.S. Navy) | 359.135, .640973 |
| VC54-60 | Handbooks & tables (naval pay & allowances: U.S.) | |
| VC54 | Allowances & pay (U.S. Navy: tables inclu. interest) | |
| VC60 | Handbooks & manuals (U.S. Navy: Pay & allowances) | |
| VC64 | Reports, Unofficial (naval pay etc.: U.S.) | |
| VC90-93 | Maintenance, Naval (Can.) | |
| VC160-229 | Maintenance, Naval (Eur.) | |
| VC160 | Naval maintenance (Eur.: gen.) | |
| VC176-179 | Maintenance, Naval (Fr.) | |
| VC180-183 | Maintenance, Naval (Ger.) | 359.60943 |
| VC180 | Supplies, Naval (Ger.) | 359.80943 |
| VC181 | Pay & allowances (Ger. Navy) | |
| VC182 | Reserves, Naval (Ger.: maint. & organ.) | 359.370943 |
| VC183.A-Z | Maintenance, Naval (Ger.: by region or area) | |
| VC184-187 | Maintenance, Naval (G.B.) | 359.60941 |
| VC196-199 | Maintenance, Naval (It.) | |
| VC208-211 | Maintenance, Naval (Rus.) | |
| VC230-245 | Maintenance, Naval (Asia) | |
| VC230 | Naval maintenance (Asia: gen.) | |
| VC235 | Maintenance, Naval (China) | |
| VC241 | Maintenance, Naval (Japan) | 359.60952 |
| VC255-256 | Maintenance, Naval (Australia) | 359.60944 |
| VC256.5 | Maintenance, Naval (New Z.) | |
| VC260-268 | Supplies & stores, Naval (inclu. stds., procure., storage, etc.) | |
| VC260 | Naval supplies & stores (gen.) | 359.8, .62 |
| VC263-264 | Stores & supplies, Naval (U.S.) | 359.80973 |
| VC265.A-Z | Procurement (naval supplies: except U.S.) | |
| VC265.G7 | Naval stores & supplies (G.B.) | |
| VC266 | Supplies & stores, Naval (management methods) | 359.62 |
| VC267.A-Z | Contracts & claims, Naval (supplies: by place) | |
| VC267.U6-7 | Naval contracts (supplies: U.S.) | |
| VC268.A-Z | Commandeering, compensation, etc. (naval: by country or place) | |
| VC270-279 | Equipment, fuel, supplies, etc. (ships) | |
| VC270 | Naval equipment & supplies (gen.: for ships) | 359.8 |
| VC273-274 | Ships' stores & equipment (U.S.) | |
| VC275.A-Z | Ships' stores & equipment (except U.S.) | |
| VC276 | Fuel supplies & costs, Naval | |
| VC276.A1 | Naval fuel (gen.: ALSO costs etc.) | 359.83, 623.874, .415 |
| VC276.A3-49 | Fuel, Naval (U.S.) | 359.83 |
| VC276.A5-Z | Fuel, Naval (other than U.S.) | |

| | | |
|---|---|---|
| VC279.A-Z | Supplies & stores, Naval (misc.) | |
| VC279.C3 | Cables (naval supplies) | |
| VC279.H45 | Hemp (naval supplies) | |
| VC279.R6 | Rope (naval supplies) | |
| VC279.R8 | Rubber (naval supplies) | |
| VC279.T5 | Timber (naval supplies) | |
| VC279.T6 | Tools (naval supplies) | |
| VC280-345 | Clothing, Naval (inclu. related items) | |
| VC280-285 | Naval clothing & personal equipment (overall) | |
| VC300-345 | Naval uniforms, badges, shoes, etc. | |
| VC300 | Uniforms, Naval (gen.) | 359.14, .81 |
| VC303 | Naval uniforms (U.S.: gen.) | 359.140973, .81 |
| VC305.A-Z | Uniforms, Naval (besides U.S.) | |
| VC307 | Foul-weather gear, Naval (plus other special clothing) | 359.81 |
| VC310 | Shoes & footwear, Naval | |
| VC320 | Headgear, Naval | |
| VC330 | Tailoring (naval clothing) | |
| VC340 | Binoculars (naval clothing: inclu. other misc. accessories) | |
| VC345 | Insignia & badges (naval clothing) | 359.1342 |
| VC350-410 | Subsistence & provisions, Naval (inclu. rations, galleys, water, etc.) | |
| VC350 | Provisions & subsistence, Naval (gen.) | 359.81 |
| VC353-354 | Naval provisions & subsistence (U.S.) | 359.810973 |
| VC355.A-Z | Naval provisions & subsistence (countries besides U.S.) | |
| VC355.G3 | Provisions & subsistence, Naval (Ger.) | |
| VC355.J3 | Provisions & subsistence, Naval (Japan) | |
| VC355.R9 | Provisions & subsistence, Naval (Rus.) | |
| VC360-365 | Rations, Naval | |
| VC370-375 | Cookery, Naval | 359.81 |
| VC380-385 | Officers' clubs & messes, Naval | |
| VC380 | Messes & clubs, Naval officers' (gen.) | 359.346 |
| VC383 | Naval officers' clubs (U.S.) | 359.3460973 |
| VC384.A-W | Naval officers' clubs (U.S.: by state) | |
| VC390-395 | Canteens & ship exchanges | |
| VC390 | Ship exchanges & canteens (gen.) | 359.341 |
| VC398 | Galleys & equipment (naval sci.) | |
| VC400 | Refrigeration (naval sci.) | 623.8535 |
| VC410 | Water supplies, Naval (inclu. preservation, purification, etc.: SEE VM503 for onboard storage) | 623.854 |
| VC412-425 | Navy yards, shore facilities, stations, etc. | |
| VC412 | Shore facilities, yards, stations (navies: gen.) | 359.7, 623.83 |
| VC414 | Yards, stations, shore facilities (navies: U.S.: gen.) | 359.70973 |
| VC415.A-W | Stations, shore facilities, yards (navies: U.S.: by state) | |
| VC415.C2 | Naval stations & shore facilities (U.S.: Calif.) | |
| VC415.F5 | Naval stations & shore facilities (U.S.: Fl.) | |
| VC415.H2 | Naval stations & shore facilities (U.S.: Haw.) | |
| VC416.A-Z | Naval stations & shore facilities (countries besides U.S.) | |
| VC416.G3 | Naval stations & shore facilities (Ger.) | |
| VC417 | Maintenance & repair, Naval (yards etc.) | |
| VC417.5 | Sanitation & refuse (naval sci.) | |
| VC418 | Power systems, Electric (naval sci.) | |
| VC420-425 | Barracks, quarters, housing (naval) | |
| VC420 | Quarters & barracks, Naval (gen.) | 359.71 |
| VC423-424 | Naval quarters & barracks (U.S.) | |
| VC425.A-Z | Housing & barracks, Naval (places besides U.S.) | |
| VC430 | Laundries, Naval | |

| | | |
|---|---|---|
| VC500-505 | Accounting & accounts, Naval (inclu. ships' records) | 359.622 |
| VC503-504 | Ships' records & accounts (U.S.) | |
| VC530-580 | Transport, Naval | |
| VC530-535 | Transportation, Naval (gen.) | 359.83, .27 |
| VC533 | Naval transport (U.S.) | |
| VC537 | Shipment & packing (naval sci.) | |
| VC550-555 | Personnel transport (navies) | |
| VC553 | Transport, Personnel (navies: U.S.) | |
| VC570-575 | Motor transport (naval sci.) | |
| VC573 | Transport, Motor (navies: U.S.) | |
| VC580 | Railroads (naval transp.) | |
| | | |
| VD | SEAMEN, NAVAL (enlisted personnel in gen.: drill, way of life, etc.) | |
| VD7 | Enlisted personnel, Naval (gen.: nonperiodical collections) | |
| VD15 | Naval seamen (gen. hist.: enlisted way of life etc.) | 359.338, .12 |
| VD21-124 | NAVAL SEAMEN (by area or country) | |
| VD23-25 | Sailors, Navy (U.S.) | |
| VD23 | Seamen, Naval (U.S.: gen.) | 359.3380973, .120973 |
| VD24.A-W | Naval seamen (U.S.: by state) | |
| VD25.A-Z | Enlisted personnel, Naval (U.S.: by city) | |
| VD26-27 | Sailors, Navy (Can.) | |
| VD55-96 | Sailors, Navy (Eur.) | |
| VD55 | Seamen, Naval (Eur.: gen.) | 359.338094, .12094 |
| VD57-64 | Sailors, Navy (G.B.) | |
| VD57 | Seamen, Naval (G.B.: gen.) | 359.3380941, .120941 |
| VD59 | Naval seamen (G.B.: Eng. & Wales) | |
| VD61 | Naval seamen (G.B.: Scot.) | |
| VD63 | Naval seamen (G.B.: N. Ire.) | |
| VD64.A-Z | Enlisted personnel, Naval (G.B.: by city or other div.) | |
| VD71-72 | Sailors, Navy (Fr.) | 359.3380944 |
| VD73-74 | Sailors, Navy (Ger.) | |
| VD73 | Seamen, Naval (Ger.: gen.) | 359.3380943, .120943 |
| VD74.A-Z | Naval seamen (Ger.: by locality) | |
| VD76.5 | Sailors, Navy (Ire.) | |
| VD85-86 | Sailors, Navy (Rus.) | 359.3380947 |
| VD99-113 | Sailors, Navy (Asia) | |
| VD99 | Seamen, Naval (Asia: gen.) | 359.338095, .12095 |
| VD101 | Sailors, Navy (China) | |
| VD105-106 | Sailors, Navy (Japan) | |
| VD105 | Seamen, Naval (Japan: gen.) | 359.3380952, .120952 |
| VD121-122 | Sailors, Navy (Australia) | 359.3380994 |
| VD122.5 | Sailors, Navy (New Z.) | |
| VD145 | Seamen, Naval (gen.: pubn. 1801-1970) | |
| VD146 | Sailors, Navy (gen.: pubn. 1970+) | |
| VD150 | Manuals (naval seamen: gen.: SEE ALSO V110+ & V120+) | |
| | 359.00202, .40202 | |
| VD153 | Manuals (naval seamen: U.S.) | 359.402020973 |
| VD155.A-Z | Manuals (naval seamen: places except U.S.) | |
| VD157 | Tactics & maneuvers, Naval (PREFER V167-178 & V245) | |
| | 359.415, .4152 | |

```
VD160-302   NAVAL DRILLS (seamen: by country or area: includes watch, station,
                quarter, fire)
VD160-162   Drills, Naval (U.S.)
VD160       Watch drills, Naval (U.S.: gen.: ALSO quarter, station, other)
                                       359.50973, .1330973, .133220973
VD163       Quarter drills, Naval (Can.: ALSO watch, station, other)
VD215-269   Drills, Naval (Eur.)
VD215       Station drills, Naval (Eur.: gen.: ALSO quarter, watch, etc.)
VD228       Fire drills, Naval (Fr.: ALSO quarter, watch, station, etc.)
VD231       Drills, Naval (Ger.)       359.50943
VD234       Drills, Naval (G.B.)       359.50941
VD252       Drills, Naval (Rus.)
VD270-280      Drills, Naval (Asia)
VD270          Naval drills (Asia: gen.)
VD271          Drills, Naval (China)
VD277          Drills, Naval (Japan)       359.50952
VD295       Drills, Naval (Australia)   359.50994
VD298       Drills, Naval (New Z.)
VD320       Manual of arms (naval seamen)   359.5470202, .8240202
VD330-335   Shooting (naval seamen: inclu. marksmanship, regs., etc.)
VD333       Marksmanship (naval seamen: U.S.)
VD340-345      Bayonet drill (naval seamen)
VD350-355      Equipment (naval seamen)
VD360-365      Arms, Small (navies: gen. & by place)   359.824, .8242
VD360-390   Small arms (navies)
VD363       Naval small arms (U.S.)        359.8240973
VD370       Rifles, carbines, etc. (navies)    359.82425
VD380       Bayonets (navies)              359.8241
VD390       Revolvers & pistols (navies)   359.8243
VD400-405   Small boat service (inclu. armament)    359.3258
VD430       Seamen, Naval (misc. subjects)


VE          MARINES        359.96
VE7         Marines (collected, nonserial titles)
VE15        Marines (gen. hist.)        359.96, .9609
VE21-124    MARINES (by geographic area)
VE21        Marines (Am.)
VE22        Marines (N. Am.)
VE23        U.S. Marine Corps    359.960973
VE23.A1.A-Z    Periodicals (U.S. Marines)    359.96097305
VE23.A13-14    U.S. Marine Corps League
VE23.A2-79     Reports, Official (U.S. Marines)
VE23.A2        Reports, Official (U.S. Marines: annual)
VE23.A25    Regulations, Marine (U.S.)
VE23.A3-32  U.S. Marine Corps (official hist's.)
VE23.A33    Registers (U.S. Marines)
VE23.A48    Manuals (U.S. Marines)
VE23.A5     U.S. Marine Corps (official monographs)
VE23.A6     Recruiting literature (U.S. Marines: by date)
VE23.A8-Z      U.S. Marine Corps (gen.)
VE23.22.1st+   Divisions (U.S. Marines: by #)
VE23.25.1st+   Marine regiments (U.S.: by #)
VE23.3      Reserves, Marine (U.S.)
VE23.4      Women's reserve, Marine (U.S.)
VE25        Biography (U.S. Marines: PREFER E #s)
```

| | | |
|---|---|---|
| VE26 | Marines (Can.) | |
| VE55-96 | Marines (Eur.) | |
| VE55 | European marines (gen.) | |
| VE57-64 | Marines (G.B.) | |
| VE57 | British marines (gen.) | 359.960941 |
| VE59 | Marines (Eng. & Wales) | |
| VE61 | Marines (Scot.) | |
| VE73 | Marines (Ger.) | |
| VE79 | Marines (It.) | |
| VE85 | Marines (Rus.) | |
| VE99-113 | Marines (Asia) | |
| VE99 | Asian marines (gen.) | |
| VE105 | Marines (Japan) | 359.960952 |
| VE121-122.5 | Marines (Australia & New Z.) | |
| VE145 | Marines (gen.: pubn. 1801-1970) | 359.9609 |
| VE146 | Marines (gen.: pubn. 1970+) | 359.9609 |
| VE150 | Manuals & handbooks (marines: gen.) | 359.960202 |
| VE153 | Handbooks & manuals (marines: U.S.) | |
| VE155.A-Z | Manuals & handbooks (marines: places besides U.S.) | |
| VE155.G7 | Handbooks & manuals (marines: G.B.) | |
| VE157 | Maneuvers & tactics (marines) | 359.9642, .9652 |
| VE160-302 | MARINE DRILLS (by place) | |
| VE160-162 | Drill regulations, Marine (U.S.) | |
| VE160 | Drills, Marine (U.S.: gen.) | 359.965, .9654 |
| VE215-269 | Drills, Marine (Eur.) | |
| VE215 | Marine drills (Eur.: gen.) | |
| VE231 | Drills, Marine (Ger.) | |
| VE234 | Drills, Marine (G.B.) | |
| VE270-280 | Drills, Marine (Asia) | |
| VE270 | Marine drills (Asia: gen.) | |
| VE277 | Drills, Marine (Japan) | |
| VE295 | Drills, Marine (Australia) | |
| VE320 | Manual of arms (marines) | 359.968240202 |
| VE330-335 | Shooting (marines: inclu. marksmanship, training, etc.) | |
| VE330 | Training (shooting: marines: gen.) | 359.96547 |
| VE333 | Marksmanship (marines: U.S.) | 359.96547 |
| VE340 | Bayonet drill (marines) | 359.96547 |
| VE350-355 | Equipment (marines) | |
| VE360-390 | Small arms (marines) | |
| VE360 | Arms, Small (marines: gen.) | 359.96824, 623.44 |
| VE370 | Rifles (marines) | 359.9682425, 623.4425 |
| VE380 | Bayonets (marines) | 623.441 |
| VE390 | Pistols & revolvers (marines) | 359.968243 |
| VE400-405 | Uniforms, Marine | 359.9614 |
| VE403 | Marine uniforms (U.S.) | 359.96140973 |
| VE410 | Shore service (marines) | |
| VE420-425 | Barracks & quarters, Marine | |
| VE420 | Marine barracks & quarters (gen.) | 359.961292, .9671 |
| VE422 | Quarters & barracks, Marine (U.S.: gen.) | 359.96710973 |
| VE424.A-Z | Barracks & quarters, Marine (U.S.: by place) | |
| VE424.C2 | Barracks & quarters, Marine (U.S.: Calif.) | 359.967109794 |

| VE430-435 | Training camps, Marine | 359.967+ |
| VE432 | Marine training camps (U.S.: gen.) | 359.9670973 |
| VE434.A-Z | Camps, Marine training (U.S.: by place) | |
| VE434.C2 or P... | Camp Pendleton (Calif.: U.S. Marines) | |
| VE434.S6 | Marine camps (South Carolina: training) | 359.96709757 |
| VE480 | Records & accounting (marines) | |
| VE490 | Pay & allowances (marines) | 359.9664 |
| VE500 | Marines (misc. subjects: not A-Z) | |

| VF | ORDNANCE, NAVAL | 359.82, 623.8251 |
| VF1 | Periodicals & associations (naval ordnance) | |
| VF6.A1 | Museums & exhibitions (naval ordnance: gen.) | |
| VF6.A2-Z | Exhibitions & museums (naval ordnance: by place or country) | |
| VF7 | Naval ordnance (nonperiodical collections) | |
| VF15 | Ordnance, Naval (gen. hist's.) | 359.8209 |
| VF21-124 | NAVAL ORDNANCE (by country or place) | |
| VF23 | Ordnance, Naval (U.S.) | 359.820973, 623.82510973 |
| VF55-96 | Ordnance, Naval (Eur.) | 359.82094 |
| VF55 | Naval ordnance (Eur.: gen.) | |
| VF57 | Ordnance, Naval (G.B.) | 359.820941 |
| VF71 | Ordnance, Naval (Fr.) | |
| VF73 | Ordnance, Naval (Ger.) | 359.820943 |
| VF79 | Ordnance, Naval (It.) | |
| VF85 | Ordnance, Naval (Rus.) | |
| VF99-113 | Ordnance, Naval (Asia) | |
| VF99 | Naval ordnance (Asia: gen.) | |
| VF105 | Ordnance, Naval (Japan) | 359.820952 |
| VF121 | Ordnance, Naval (Australia) | |
| VF145 | Ordnance, Naval (gen. pubns. 1801+) | 359.82 |
| VF147 | Naval ordnance (special overall) | |
| VF150-155 | Handbooks & manuals (naval ordnance) | |
| VF150 | Ordnance, Naval (handbooks & manuals: gen.) | |
| VF153 | Manuals & handbooks (naval ordnance: U.S.) | |
| VF155.A-Z | Manuals & handbooks (naval ordnance: places besides U.S.) | |
| VF160-302 | NAVAL ORDNANCE DRILLS (by place) | |
| VF160 | Drills, Naval ordnance (U.S.: gen.) | |
| VF215-269 | Drills, Naval ordnance (Eur.) | |
| VF215 | Ordnance drills, Naval (Eur.: gen.) | |
| VF228 | Drills, Naval ordnance (Fr.) | |
| VF231 | Drills, Naval ordnance (Ger.) | |
| VF234 | Drills, Naval ordnance (G.B.) | |
| VF252 | Drills, Naval ordnance (Rus.) | |
| VF270-280 | Drills, Naval ordnance (Asia) | |
| VF277 | Drills, Naval ordnance (Japan) | |
| VF295 | Drills, Naval ordnance (Australia) | |
| VF310-315 | Target practice, Naval | |
| VF310 | Naval target practice (gen.) | 623.553 |
| VF313 | Gunnery practice, Naval (U.S.) | 623.5530973 |
| VF315.A-Z | Naval gunnery practice (places except U.S.) | |
| VF315.G7 | Gunnery practice, Naval (G.B.) | 623.5530941 |
| VF320-325 | Artillery equipment, Naval | |
| VF323 | Naval artillery equipment (U.S.) | |
| VF325.A-Z | Equipment, Naval artillery (places other than U.S.) | |
| VF330-335 | Shore service | |

VF346-348    Weapons systems, Naval
VF347        Naval weapons systems
VF350-375    Ordnance & arms, Naval (in sum)
VF350-355    Arms & ordnance, Naval (gen.)        359.82, 623.418
VF350        Naval ordnance & arms (gen.)
VF353        Naval arms & ordnance (gen.: U.S.)
VF357        Instruction (naval ordnance)
VF360        Research (naval ordnance: gen.)        359.82072
VF360.3          Ordnance research, Naval (U.S.)
VF360.5.A-Z      Naval research (ordnance: places besides U.S.)
VF370-375        Ordnance & arms, Naval (manufacture)
VF370            Manufacture (naval ordnance & arms: gen.)
VF373            Naval ordnance & arms (manufacture: U.S.)
VF380-385    Ordnance magazines & facilities (navies)
VF380            Magazines, Ordnance (navies: gen.)        359.75
VF390-395    Ordnance proper (navies)
VF390        Naval ordnance material (gen.)        623.418
VF393        Ordnance material (navies: U.S.)
VF393.A1-3       Ordnance proper (navies: U.S.: documents)
VF393.A4-6       Manuals, Naval ordnance (U.S.: by mm., cm., inches, or lbs.)
VF393.A5.5       5 in. guns, Naval (U.S.: manuals)
VF393.A7-Z       Ordnance proper (navies: U.S.: gen.)
VF395.A-Z        Naval ordnance material (besides U.S.)
VF410.A2     Machine guns, Naval (gen.)        623.4424
VF410.A3-Z   Naval machine guns (special by name)
VF418        Antiaircraft guns, Naval        359.981
VF420        Ordnance material (misc.)
VF430        Gun carriages, Naval        623.43
VF440        Turrets & cupolas, Naval
VF450-455    Firing instructions, Naval
VF460        Ammunition, Naval        359.825, 623.45
VF470            Cartridges, Naval        359.8255
VF480-500        Projectiles, Naval
VF480            Naval projectiles (gen.)        359.8251, 623.451
VF490            Shells & shrapnel, Naval
VF500            Bullets (navies)        359.8255, 623.455
VF509        Depth charges, Naval        623.45115, .4517
VF520-530    Fire control, Naval gunnery (inclu. instruments)
VF520        Instruments, Naval gunnery        623.558
VF530        Radar equipment, Naval        623.557
VF540        Tests, Ordnance & firing (navies)
VF550        Range tables, Naval ordnance        623.5530212
VF580        Ordnance, Naval (misc. topics)

VG           NAVAL SERVICES (misc.)
VG20-25      Chaplains or religious officials, Naval
VG20         Naval chaplains (gen.)        359.347
VG23         Chaplains, Naval (U.S.)        359.3470973
VG25.A-Z     Religious officials, Naval (places besides U.S.)
VG30-35      Bands & music, Naval (SEE ALSO ML1300-1354)
VG33         Music & bands, Naval (U.S.)        359.340973, .170973
VG50-55      Coast guard & coast signal service        359.97
VG50         Signal service, Coast (plus coast guard: gen.)
VG53         U.S. Coast Guard        359.970973
VG55.A-Z     Coast guard & coast signal service (places besides U.S.)

| | | |
|---|---|---|
| VG60-65 | Postal service, Naval | 359.341 |
| VG70-85 | Telecommunications, Naval | 359.415, .85, 623.856, .73 |
| VG70-75 | Telegraph, Naval | |
| VG73 | Naval telegraph (U.S.) | 359.4150973 |
| VG76-78 | Telegraph, radar, & radio communications (navies: wireless) | |
| VG76 | Communications, Naval (inclu. radio, radar, wireless telegraph: gen.) | |
| | | 623.8564, .734 |
| VG77 | Radio, radar, & wireless telegraph (navies: U.S.) | 623.85640973 |
| VG78.A-Z | Radar, radio, & wireless telegraph (navies: besides U.S.) | |
| VG80-85 | Telephone, Naval | 623.85645 |
| VG83 | Naval telephone (U.S.) | |
| VG86-88 | Underwater demolition teams (navies) | |
| VG86 | Frogmen (navies: gen.) | 359.984 |
| VG87 | Naval underwater teams (U.S.: inclu. demolition) | 359.9840973 |
| VG88.A-Z | Navy frogmen (besides U.S.) | |
| VG90-95 | Air forces & warfare, Naval | 359.94, 358.4 |
| VG90 | Air warfare & forces, Naval (gen.) | 358.4, 359.3255, 623.746 |
| VG93-94 | Naval aviation (U.S.) | 358.40973 |
| VG93 | Aviation, Naval (U.S.: gen.) | |
| VG94.A-Z | Air forces, Naval (U.S.: by area or state) | |
| VG94.5.A-Z | Air fields & stations, Naval (U.S.: by name) | |
| VG94.5.P4 | Pensacola Naval Air Station (Flor.) | |
| VG94.6.A-Z | Units, Naval air (U.S.: by name: inclu. organizations) | |
| VG94.7.A-Z | Air reserves, Naval & marine (U.S.) | |
| VG95.A-Z | Aviation, Naval (places besides U.S.) | |
| VG95.G3 | Naval aviation (Ger.) | |
| VG95.J3 | Naval aviation (Japan) | |
| VG100-475 | MEDICAL SERVICES, NAVAL (SEE ALSO UH201-515) | |
| VG100 | Periodicals & associations (naval medical services) | |
| VG115 | Naval medical services (gen.) | 359.345, .72, 616.98024 |
| VG121-224 | NAVAL MEDICAL SERVICES (by place) | |
| VG123 | Medical services, Naval (U.S.) | 359.3450973 |
| VG155-196 | Medical services, Naval (Eur.) | |
| VG157 | Medical services, Naval (G.B.) | |
| VG173 | Medical services, Naval (Ger.) | |
| VG185 | Medical services, Naval (Rus.) | |
| VG199-213 | Medical services, Naval (Asia) | |
| VG205 | Medical services, Naval (Japan) | |
| VG221 | Medical services, Naval (Australia) | |
| VG226 | Biography, Naval medical (gen.) | |
| VG227.A1 | Medical biography, Naval (U.S.: collective) | |
| VG227.A2-Z | Naval medical biography (U.S.: indiv.) | |
| VG228.A-Z | Biography, Naval medical (places besides U.S.) | |
| VG230-235 | Instruction (naval medicine) | |
| VG240-245 | Research & laboratories, Naval medical | |
| VG260-265 | Surgeons, Naval | 359.345, 616.98024, 617.99 |
| VG263 | Naval surgeons (U.S.) | |
| VG270-275 | Dispensaries, Naval | |
| VG280-285 | Dentistry, Naval | |
| VG290-295 | Supplies, Medical & surgical (navies) | |
| VG310-325 | Hospital corps, Naval | |
| VG310 | Naval hospital corps (gen.) | |
| VG320 | Hospital corps, Naval (U.S.) | |
| VG325.A-Z | Hospital corps, Naval (places besides U.S.) | |

| VG350-355 | Nurse corps, Naval |
|---|---|
| VG350 | Naval nurse corps (gen.)    359.345, 610.7349, .7361, 616.98024 |
| VG353 | Nurse corps, Naval (U.S.) |
| VG410-450 | Hospital services & hospitals, Naval (SEE ALSO D #s for particular wars) |
| VG410 | Hospital services, Naval (gen.)    359.72 |
| VG420-425 | Hospital services, Naval (U.S.) |
| VG420 | Hospitals, Naval (gen.) |
| VG424.A-Z | Naval hospitals (U.S.: by area or state) |
| VG425.A-Z | Hospitals, Naval (U.S.: by town) |
| VG430.A-Z | Naval hospitals (places except U.S.) |
| VG450 | Hospital ships    623.8264, 359.3264 |
| VG457 | Red Cross at sea |
| VG460-466 | Handbooks, Medical & surgical (navies) |
| VG460 | Medical & surgical handbooks (navies: gen.)    359.3450202, 610.0202, 617.0260202 |
| VG463 | Surgical & medical handbooks (navies: U.S.) |
| VG465.A-Z | Manuals, medical & surgical (navies: besides U.S.) |
| VG466 | First-aid handbooks, Naval |
| VG470-475 | Health, hygiene, & sanitation (navies) |
| VG470 | Naval health, hygiene, & sanitation (gen.) |
| VG471 | Hygiene, health, & sanitation (navies: special: tropics, drinking water, alcohol problem, venereal diseases, diet, etc.) |
| VG473 | Health, hygiene, & sanitation (navies: U.S.) |
| VG475.A-Z | Sanitation, health, & hygiene (navies: places besides U.S.) |
| VG478 | Rehabilitation of disabled sailors (PREFER UB360+) |
| VG500-505 | Press & public relns. (navies) |
| VG500 | Media & public relns. (navies: gen.)    359.342, 070.433, .439 |
| VG503 | War correspondents & public relns. (navies: U.S.) |
| VG505.A-Z | Newspapers, media, & public relns. (navies: besides U.S.) |
| VG590-595 | Civil engineering (navies: SEE ALSO VA66.C6+) |
| VG590 | Engineering, Civil (navies: gen.) |
| VG593 | Naval engineering (civil: U.S.) |
| VG600-605 | Artisans, Naval (carpenters' mates, painters, etc.) |
| VG600 | Artificers, Naval (gen.: inclu. carpenters' mates etc.) |
| VG603 | Carpenters & other naval artisans (U.S.) |
| VG610-615 | Aerographers (naval weather & surf forecaster) |
| VG610 | Weather forecaster, Naval (gen.) |
| VG613 | Forecaster, Weather (navies: U.S.) |
| VG800-805 | Machinists, Naval |
| VG900-905 | Yeomen & clerks, Naval |
| VG903 | Clerks & yeomen, Naval (U.S.) |
| VG920-925 | Surveyors, draftsmen, & engineering aids (navies) |
| VG920 | Draftsmen & surveyors, Naval (gen.) |
| VG950-955 | Boatswains |
| VG953 | Boatswains' mates (U.S.) |
| VG1010-1015 | Photographers, Naval |
| VG1020 | Photographic interpretation (navies) |
| VG1030-1035 | Instrumentmen, Naval |

| | |
|---|---|
| VG2000-2005 | Social welfare services, Naval |
| VG2000 | Social work, Naval (gen.) |
| VG2003 | Welfare services, Naval (U.S.) |
| VG2005.A-Z | Naval welfare services (places besides U.S.) |
| VG2020-2029 | Recreation & information services, Naval |
| VG2020 | Naval recreation & information services (gen.)  359.346 |
| VG2025-2026 | Information & recreation services, Naval (U.S.: gen.) 359.3460973 |
| VG2029 | Recreation & information services, Naval (places besides U.S.) |
| | |
| VK | MARINE NAVIGATION & MERCHANT MARINE |
| VK1 | Periodicals & associations (marine navig. & merch. marine) |
| VK5 | Conferences (marine navig. & merch. marine) |
| VK6 | Museums & exhibitions (marine navig. & merch. marine) |
| VK7-8 | Nautical almanacs & yearbooks |
| VK7 | Almanacs & yearbooks, Nautical (American: inclu. abridged) |
| VK8 | Yearbooks & almanacs, Nautical (non-American) |
| VK15 | Merchant marine & navigation (gen. hist's.) |
| VK18 | Navigation, Marine (gen. hist's.: modern: inclu. merch. marine) |
| VK20 | Merchant marine & navigation (20th c.: hist. & conditions) |
| VK21-124 | Merchant marine & navigation (hist. & conditions: by area or country) |
| VK139-140 | Biography (merch. marine) |
| VK145 | Marine navigation & merchant marine (gen.: pubn. 1801+)  623.89 |
| VK147 | Merchant marine & navigation (gen. special) |
| VK149 | Nautical life (merchant marine: pop. titles) |
| VK155 | Handbooks & manuals (marine navig. & merch. marine)  623.890202 |
| VK160 | Merchant marine (occupation)  387.0023 |
| VK199 | Accidents, Marine |
| VK200 | Safety, Marine |
| VK205 | Masters' manuals (merch. marine: inclu. command of ships) |
| VK221 | Manning of vessels (merch. marine) |
| VK233 | Watch duty (merch. duty) |
| VK321-369+ | Harbors & ports  387.1+ |
| VK358 | Terminals, Marine (bunkers, coal supplies, repairs, etc.) |
| VK371-378 | Collisions & avoidance, High seas |
| VK381-397 | Signaling, Merchant marine (flags, lights, codes, radio, etc.) |
| VK383 | Fog signals (merch. marine) |
| VK385 | Flag signals (merch. marine) |
| VK387 | Light signals (merch. marine) |
| VK391 | Code signals (merch. marine) |
| VK397 | Wireless signals (merch. marine) |
| VK401-529 | Instruction (merch. marine) |
| VK401 | Merchant marine & navigation (study & teaching: gen.) |
| VK421-524 | Marine navigation (instruction: by locale: inclu. merch. marine) |
| VK423 | Merchant marine & navigation (instruction: U.S.) |
| VK457 | Navigation, Marine (instruction: G.B.: inclu. merch. marine) |
| VK531-537 | Training (marine navig. & merch. marine) |
| VK541-547 | Seamanship (marine navig. & merch. marine)  623.88 |
| VK545 | Warship handling (plus other seamanship topics)  623.8825 |

| | | |
|---|---|---|
| VK549-572 | Marine navigation science | |
| VK549 | Navigation, Marine (science: hist.) | 527.094, 387.155 |
| VK555 | Science of marine navigation (gen.: pubn. 1801+) | 623.81 |
| VK560 | Electronics, Marine navigation | 623.893 |
| VK561.A1 | Loran tables (marine navig.: ca. 1932+: gen.) | |
| VK561.A2-Z | Loran tables (marine navig.: by region) | |
| VK561.A6 | Coasts, Asian (Loran tables) | |
| VK561.A7 | Atlantic Ocean (Loran tables) | |
| VK561.P3 | Pacific Ocean (Loran tables) | |
| VK561.U5 | Coasts, United States (Loran tables) | |
| VK561.U53-54 | East Coast (U.S.: Loran tables) | |
| VK561.U57 | West Coast (U.S.: Loran tables) | |
| VK563-567+ | Tables, Nautical | 623.8920212 |
| VK563 | Nautical tables (gen.: inclu. azimuth) | |
| VK565 | Latitude & longitude (marine navig.: inclu. tables) | |
| VK567 | Longitude & time at sea (marine navig.: inclu. tables) | |
| VK570 | Optimum ship routing | |
| VK571 | Great circle routing (marine navig.) | |
| VK572 | Dead reckoning (naut. navig.) | 623.8923 |
| VK573-587 | Instruments, Nautical | |
| VK573 | Nautical instruments (gen.) | 623.894, .863 |
| VK575-584 | Instruments, Nautical (special) | |
| VK575 | Chronometers, Nautical (PREFER QB107) | |
| VK577 | Compasses (sea, air, or land: inclu. gyro type) | 623.82 |
| VK579 | Distance finders (inclu. tables etc.) | |
| VK581 | Logs, Nautical | |
| VK583 | Sextants & quadrants | 527.028, 623.894 |
| VK584.A-Z | Nautical instruments (misc.) | |
| VK584.A7 | Artificial horizon | |
| VK584.A8 | Automatic pilot (marine navig.) | |
| VK584.G8 | Gyroscopic devices (marine navig.) | |
| VK584.S6 | Sounding apparatus | |
| VK587 | Chart use, Nautical (plus other misc. topics on naut. instruments) | |
| VK588-597 | Hydrography, Marine | |
| VK591 | Marine hydrography & surveying (gen.) | |
| VK593 | Surveying, Hydrographic (gen. special) | |
| VK600-794 | TIDE & CURRENT TABLES | |
| VK602 | Current & tide tables (gen.: pubn. 1801+) | 623.8949 |
| VK603 | Tables, Tide & current (collections) | |
| VK607-794 | TIDE & CURRENT TABLES (by area) | |
| VK610-680 | Atlantic Ocean (all & east: tide & current tables) | |
| VK610 | Tide & current tables (Atlantic Ocean: all & east: gen.) | 623.894909163 |
| VK611 | North Atlantic (tide & current tables) | 623.8949091631 |
| VK615-626 | North Sea & Baltic (tide & current tables) | |
| VK627-638 | British Isles (tide & current tables) | |
| VK639-644 | English Channel (tide & current tables) | |
| VK645 | Coasts, French (gen. & Eng. Ch.: tide & current tables) | |
| VK651 | Gibraltar Strait (tide & current tables) | |
| VK653-674 | Mediterranean Sea (tide & current tables) | |
| VK685-701 | Indian Ocean (tide & current tables) | |
| VK702-711 | Coasts, Asian (tide & current tables) | |
| VK702 | Asian coasts (tide & current tables) | |
| VK709 | Japanese Islands (tide & current tables) | |
| VK710 | Malaysia & Singapore (tide & current tables) | |
| VK711 | Philippine Islands (tide & current tables) | |

```
VK715-756   Pacific Ocean & islands (tide & current tables)
VK715       Tide & current tables (Pac. Ocean & islands: gen.)    623.894909164
VK717       Current & tide tables (North Pacific)
VK725       Tide & current tables (South Pacific)
VK747       West Coast (U.S.: tide & current tables)    623.8949091643
VK759-792   Current & tide tables (Atlantic Ocean: west)
VK771-777       Caribbean Sea & Gulf of Mexico (tide & current tables)
VK775           Gulf of Mexico (tide & current tables)
VK777           Florida Keys & Strait & Windward Passage (tide & current tables)
VK781           East Coast (U.S.: tide & current tables)    623.8949091634
VK793       Coasts, United States (tide & current tables)
VK798-997   SAILING DIRECTIONS & PILOT GUIDES
VK799       Tables, Nautical navigation (distances etc.)    623.8920212
VK802       Pilot guides & sailing directions (gen.: pubn. 1801+)    623.8922, .8929+
VK803       Sailing & pilot guides (official: British)
VK804-997   PILOT & SAILING GUIDES (by area)
VK804       American waters (gen.: pilot & sailing guides)    623.89297
VK810-880   Atlantic Ocean (all & east: pilot & sailing guides)
VK810       Pilot & sailing guides (Atl. Ocean: all & east: gen.)    623.8929163
VK811-814.5     North Atlantic (pilot & sailing guides)
VK813           Convoy lanes (N. Atlantic: pilot & sailing guides)
VK815-826       North Sea & Baltic (pilot & sailing guides)
VK827-84        British Isles & English Channel (pilot & sailing  guides)
                                    623.892916336, .8929422
VK845       Coasts, French (gen. & Eng. Ch.: pilot & sailing guides)
                                    623.8929442 (Normandy)
VK851       Gibraltar Strait (pilot & sailing & guides)    623.8929448, .89294689
VK853-874   Mediterranean Sea (pilot & sailing guides)    623.89291638, .8929448
VK881       East Indies (pilot & sailing guides: Eng. to India etc.)
VK885-901   Indian Ocean (pilot & sailing guides)
VK902-911   Coasts, Asian (pilot & sailing guides)
VK902           Asian coasts (pilot & sailing guides: gen.)
VK909           Japanese Islands (pilot & sailing guides)    623.892952
VK911           Philippine Islands (pilot & sailing guides)    623.8929599
VK915-956   Pacific Ocean & islands (pilot & sailing guides)
VK915       Pilot & sailing guides (Pac. Ocean & islands: gen.)    623.8929164
VK917       North Pacific (pilot & sailing guides)    623.89291644-89291646
VK925       South Pacific (pilot & sailing guides)    623.89291646-89291649
VK927-929   Australia & New Zealand (pilot & sailing guides)
VK931       East Indies & Indonesia (pilot & sailing guides: from U.S.)
VK933.A-Z   Pilot & sailing guides (Pac. islands: misc.)
VK933.C27       Caroline Islands (pilot & sailing guides)
VK933.H3        Hawaiian Islands (pilot & sailing guides)
VK933.M27       Mariana Islands (pilot & sailing guides)
VK933.S65       Solomon Islands (pilot & sailing guides)
VK933.T79       Truk Islands (pilot & sailing guides)
VK941-956   West Coast (Am.: plus E. Pac.: pilot & sailing guides)
VK941       Pilot & sailing guides (E. Pac. & Am. W. Coast: gen.)
VK943       Bering Strait & Alaska coast (pilot & sailing guides)
VK945       Canada (W. coast: pilot & sailing guides)
VK947       West Coast (U.S.: pilot & sailing guides)    623.892916432
VK951-952       Central America (pilot & sailing guides)
VK959-992   Atlantic Ocean (West: pilot & sailing guides)
VK959           Pilot & sailing guides (W. Atlantic: gen.)
VK961-968       South American coasts (gen. & east: pilot & sailing guides)
```

| VK969-970 | Mexican & Central American coasts (pilot & sailing guides) |
|---|---|
| VK970.A-Z | Pilot & sailing guides (C. Am.: by locality) |
| VK970.P2 | Panama Canal (pilot & sailing guides) |
| VK971-973 | Caribbean Sea & West Indies (pilot & sailing guides) |
| VK973.A-Z | West Indies (pilot & sailing guides: by island[s]) |
| VK975-977 | Gulf of Mexico (pilot & sailing guides) |
| VK977 | Florida Keys & Strait & Windward Passage (pilot & sailing guides) |
| VK981 | East Coast (U.S.: pilot & sailing guides) |
| VK985 | Canada (E. coast: pilot & sailing guides) |
| VK993 | Coasts, United States (pilot & sailing guides) |
| VK1000-1249 | LIGHTHOUSES, BEACONS, FOGHORNS, ETC. (inclu. buoys & lightships) |
| VK1010 | Beacons, foghorns, lighthouses, etc. (gen.)    623.8942, 387.155 |
| VK1015 | Foghorns, beacons, lighthouses, etc. (hist's.) |
| VK1021-1124 | LIGHTHOUSES, BEACONS, FOGHORNS, ETC. (by area) |
| VK1023-1025 | United States (lighthouses, beacons, foghorns, etc.) |
| VK1024 | Lighthouses, beacons, foghorns, etc. (U.S.: by area) |
| VK1055-1096 | Europe (lighthouses, beacons, foghorns, etc.) |
| VK1055 | Lighthouses, beacons, foghorns, etc. (Eur.: gen.) |
| VK1057-1064 | Great Britain (lighthouses, beacons, foghorns, etc.) |
| VK1071-1072 | France (lighthouses, beacons, foghorns, etc.) |
| VK1073-1074 | Germany (lighthouses, beacons, foghorns, etc.) |
| VK1079-1080 | Italy (lighthouses, beacons, foghorns, etc.) |
| VK1085-1086 | Russia (Eur.: lighthouses, beacons, foghorns, etc.) |
| VK1086.5 | Scandinavia (lighthouses, beacons, foghorns, etc.) |
| | 623.89420948 |
| VK1099-1113 | Asia (lighthouses, beacons, foghorns, etc.) |
| VK1101-1102 | China (lighthouses, beacons, foghorns, etc.) |
| VK1105-1106 | Japanese Islands (lighthouses, beacons, foghorns, etc.) |
| | 623.89420952 |
| VK1109-1110 | Russia (Asia: lighthouses, beacons, foghorns, etc.) |
| VK1111-1112 | Turkey & Asia Minor (lighthouses, beacons, foghorns, etc.) |
| VK1115-1119 | Africa (lighthouses, beacons, foghorns, etc.) |
| VK1121-1122 | Australia (lighthouses, beacons, foghorns, etc.)    623.89420994 |
| VK1122.5 | New Zealand (lighthouses, beacons, foghorns, etc.) |
| | 623.894209931 |
| VK1123-1124 | Pacific Ocean & islands (lighthouses, beacons, foghorns, etc.) |
| | 623.8942099+, .894209164+ |
| VK1150-1249 | LISTS (beacons, foghorns, lighthouses, etc.) |
| VK1150 | Beacons, foghorns, lighthouses, etc. (lists: gen.: inclu. Br. Admiralty)    623.8944 |
| VK1151-1185 | Europe (lighthouses, beacons, foghorns, etc.: lists) |
| VK1151 | Lighthouses, beacons, foghorns, etc. (Eur.: gen.: lists) |
| | 623.8944094 |
| VK1153-1159 | Great Britain & Ireland (lighthouses, beacons, foghorns, etc.: lists) |
| | 623.89440941 |
| VK1173 | France (lighthouses, beacons, foghorns, etc.: lists) |
| | 623.89440944 |
| VK1176 | Mediterranean Sea (lighthouses, beacons, foghorns, etc.: lists) |
| | 623.8944091638 |
| VK1190-1199 | Africa (lighthouses, beacons, foghorns, etc.: lists) |
| VK1198 | Egypt (lighthouses, beacons, foghorns, etc.: lists) |
| VK1203-1209 | Asia (lighthouses, beacons, foghorns, etc.: lists) |
| VK1207 | Japanese Islands (lighthouses, beacons, foghorns, etc.: lists) |
| | 623.89440952 |

| VK1211-1212 | Australia & New Zealand (lighthouses, beacons, foghorns, etc.: lists) 623.89440993-89440994 |
| VK1214-1223 | Pacific Ocean & islands (lighthouses, beacons, foghorns, etc.: lists) 623.894409164 |
| VK1239-1240 | West Indies (lighthouses, beacons, foghorns, etc.: lists) |
| VK1241-1246 | Lighthouses, beacons, foghorns, etc. (N. Am.: lists) 623.8944097 |
| VK1243 | United States (lighthouses, beacons, foghorns, etc.: lists) |
| VK1250-1299 | SHIPWRECKS & FIRES (PREFER D-F #s for specific wars) |
| VK1250 | Fires & shipwrecks (gen.)          910.453 |
| VK1255.A-Z | Shipwrecks (by name) |
| VK1257.A-Z | Fires, Nautical (by name of ship) |
| VK1259 | Abandoning ship (plus other misc. marine topics of disaster) |
| VK1265 | Disasters, Submarine |
| VK1270-1294 | Shipwrecks (by area) |
| VK1270-1273 | Shipwrecks (U.S.) |
| VK1280-1282 | Shipwrecks (Eur.) |
| VK1286 | Shipwrecks (Asia) |
| VK1289-1294 | Shipwrecks (Australia & Oceania) |
| VK1299 | Icebergs |
| VK1300-1491 | SAVING LIFE & PROPERTY (marine navig.) |
| VK1300-1481 | Lifesaving, Marine |
| VK1315 | Marine lifesaving (hist's.) |
| VK1321-1424 | Nautical lifesaving (by area) |
| VK1445-1447 | Survival after shipwrecks (plus other misc. lifesaving topics) 623.865 |
| VK1460-1481 | Lifesaving apparatus & stations (marine navig.) |
| VK1460-1461 | Equipment, Lifesaving (marine navig.: gen.)          623.865 |
| VK1462-1463 | Lifesaving on ships |
| VK1473 | Lifeboats          623.829 |
| VK1477 | Life preservers |
| VK1479 | Rockets, signal (marine lifesaving) |
| VK1481.A-Z | Lifesaving equipment (special: by name) |
| VK1481.S4 | Shark protection |
| VK1491 | Salvage, Marine |
| VK1500-1661 | PILOTS & PILOTING, NAUTICAL |
| VK1515 | Nautical pilots & piloting (gen. hist's.)          623.8922, .892209 |
| VK1521-1624 | PILOTING & PILOTS, NAUTICAL (by area)          623.291-89299 |
| VK1523-1525 | Piloting, Nautical (U.S.)          623.2973 |
| VK1555-1596 | Piloting, Nautical (Eur.)          623.294 |
| VK1599-1613 | Piloting, Nautical (Asia) |
| VK1621-1624 | Piloting, Nautical (Australia & the Pac.) |
| VK1645-1661 | Pilots & piloting, Nautical (gen.) |
| | |
| VM | NAVAL ARCHITECTURE & MARINE ENGINEERING |
| VM1-565 | NAVAL ARCHITECTURE & SHIPBUILDING (SEE ALSO V750-995+ for construction & armament of warships) |
| VM1 | Periodicals & associations (naval architec.: Eng.) |
| VM5 | Conferences (naval architec.) |
| VM6 | Museums & exhibitions (naval architec.) |
| VM7 | Architecture, Naval (collected, nonperiodical works) |
| VM12 | Directories (naval architec.) |

| | | |
|---|---|---|
| VM15-124 | Naval architecture (hist.) | |
| VM15 | Shipbuilding, Naval (gen. hist.) | |
| VM18 | Naval architecture (hist.: modern: gen.) | |
| VM19 | Naval architecture (hist.: 19th c.) | |
| VM20 | Naval architecture (hist.: 20th c.) | |
| VM21-124 | Naval shipbuilding (hist.: by area or country) | |
| VM23-25 | Shipbuilding, Naval (hist.: U.S.) | 623.80973 |
| VM55-96 | Shipbuilding, Naval (hist.: Eur.) | |
| VM55 | Naval shipbuilding (hist.: Eur.: gen.) | 623.8094 |
| VM57-64 | Shipbuilding, Naval (hist.: G.B.) | 623.80941 |
| VM71-72 | Shipbuilding, Naval (hist.: Fr.) | 623.80944 |
| VM73-74 | Shipbuilding, Naval (hist.: Ger.) | 623.80943 |
| VM79-80 | Shipbuilding, Naval (hist.: It.) | 623.80945 |
| VM85-86 | Shipbuilding, Naval (hist.: Rus.) | 623.80947 |
| VM99-113 | Shipbuilding, Naval (hist.: Asia) | |
| VM99 | Naval shipbuilding (hist.: Asia: gen.) | 623.8095 |
| VM105-106 | Shipbuilding, Naval (hist.: Japan) | 623.80952 |
| VM121-122 | Shipbuilding, Naval (hist.: Australia) | 623.80994 |
| VM122.5 | Shipbuilding, Naval (hist.: New Z.) | |
| VM139-140 | Biography (naval architec.) | |
| VM142-148 | Naval architecture (gen.) | 623.81 |
| VM142-145 | Wooden ships (naval architec.) | 623.81 |
| VM146-147 | Metal ships (naval architec.) | 623.8182 |
| VM148 | Concrete ships (naval architec.) | |
| VM151 | Handbooks, tables, etc. (ship calculations: naval architec.) | |
| | 623.810202, .810212 | |
| VM153 | Tonnage tables (naval architec.) | |
| VM155 | Measurement of ships (naval architec.) | |
| VM156-163 | Theory & principles (naval architec.) | |
| VM165-276 | Instruction (naval architec.) | |
| VM165 | Naval shipbuilding (instruc.: gen.) | 623.8107 |
| VM171-274 | Instruction (naval architec.: by place) | |
| VM173 | Shipbuilding, Naval (instruc.: U.S.) | |
| VM205 | Shipbuilding, Naval (instruc.: Eur.: gen.) | |
| VM207 | Shipbuilding, Naval (instruc.: G.B.) | |
| VM223 | Shipbuilding, Naval (instruc.: Ger.) | |
| VM255 | Shipbuilding, Naval (instruc.: Japan) | |
| VM271 | Shipbuilding, Naval (instruc.: Australia) | |
| VM275-276 | Schools (naval architec.: special) | |
| VM293 | Standards (naval architec.) | |
| VM295-296 | Contracts & specifications (naval architec.) | |
| VM295 | Specifications & contracts (naval architec.: gen.) | |
| VM297 | Designs, drawings, blueprints (naval architec.) | 623.812 |
| VM297.5 | Blueprints, drawings, designs (naval architec.: laying out) | |
| VM298 | Models, Ship | 623.8201, 745.5928 |
| VM298.5-301. | Shipbuilding industry | |
| VM298.5 | Industry, Shipbuilding (gen.) | 338.476238, 387.5+ |
| VM298.6 | Shipbuilding industry (U.S.) | 387.50973 |
| VM298.7.A-Z | Shipbuilding industry (places besides U.S.) | |
| VM298.7.G7 | Shipbuilding industry (G.B.) | |
| VM301.A-Z | Shipyards & shipbuilding companies (by name) | |
| VM307 | Pictorials (ships) | 387.2+ |
| VM308 | Figureheads, ornaments, decorations on ships | |

| | | |
|---|---|---|
| VM321-349 | Small craft | |
| VM321 | Small craft (gen.) | |
| VM321.5 | Boatyards, Small craft (gen.) | |
| VM321.52.A-Z | Boatyards, Small craft (by name) | |
| VM322 | Maintenance & repair (small craft) | |
| VM331 | Yachts (small craft: gen.) | |
| VM341 | Motorboats & launches (small craft: gen.) | |
| VM351 | Rowboats, small sailboats, etc. | |
| VM365-367 | Submarine boats | |
| VM365 | Submarine boats (gen.) | 359.3257, 623.8257 |
| VM367.A-Z | Equipment (submarine boats: special) | |
| VM367.P4 | Periscopes (submarine architec.) | |
| VM367.S7 | Batteries, Storage (submarine architec.) | |
| VM378-466 | Vessels (naval architec.: by use) | |
| VM380 | Warships (naval architec.: PREFER V750-995+) | 623.825, 359.32 |
| VM381-383 | Passenger ships (naval architec.) | |
| VM383.A-Z | Liners, Passenger (by name) | |
| VM383.B7 | Bremen (pass. ship) | |
| VM383.N6 | Normandie (pass. ship) | |
| VM383.Q4 | Queen Mary (pass. ship) | |
| VM385.A-Z | Steamship lines (by co. name) | |
| VM391-395 | Freighters (naval architec.) | 623.8245, 387.544 |
| VM397 | Coast guard vessels (naval architec.: by type) | 623.8245, 359.9732 |
| VM451 | Icebreakers (naval architec.) | 623.828 |
| VM455 | Tankers (naval architec.) | 623.8245, 387.544 |
| VM457 | Ore carriers | 623.8245, 387.544 |
| VM469.5 | Pontoons & pontoon gear (naval architec.) | |
| VM471-479 | Electricity (naval architec. & engin.) | 623.8503, .852, .8726 |
| VM473 | Electricity (naval architec. & engin.: U.S. Navy) | |
| VM480 | Electronics, Marine (radar, radio, sonar, etc.: naval architec. & engin.) | |
| | 623.8504, .734+, .8564-85648 | |
| VM480.3 | Radar, radio, sonar, etc. (naval architec.: U.S. Navy) | |
| VM480.5.A-Z | Sonar, radio, radar, etc. (naval architec.: places except U.S.) | |
| VM480.5.G7 | Radio, radar, sonar, etc. (naval architec.: G.B.) | |
| VM481-482 | Heating, ventilation, & sanitation (naval architec. & engin.) | |
| VM481 | Sanitation, heating, & ventilation (naval architec. & engin.) | 623.853-54 |
| VM483 | Disinfection & fumigation (naval engin.) | |
| VM485 | Cold storage (naval architec. & engin.) | |
| VM491-493 | Lighting (naval architec. & engin.) | |
| VM501 | Plumbing (naval architec. & engin.) | |
| VM503-505 | Water supply (naval architec. & engin.) | 623.854 |
| VM511 | Hammocks, berths, etc. (naval architec.) | |
| VM521 | Propulsion (naval architec. & engin.: gen.) | 623.87 |
| VM565 | Steerage, Nautical | |
| VM600-989 | MARINE ENGINEERING | |
| VM600-605 | Engineering, Marine (gen.) | 623.87 |
| VM607 | Handbooks, tables, etc. (marine engin.) | 623.870202 |
| VM615 | Marine engineering (hist.: gen.) | |
| VM621-724 | Engineering, Marine (hist.: by place) | |
| VM623-625 | Marine engineering (hist.: U.S.) | |
| VM655 | Marine engineering (hist.: Eur.) | |
| VM657 | Marine engineering (hist.: G.B.) | 623.870941-870942 |
| VM671 | Marine engineering (hist.: Fr.) | |
| VM673 | Marine engineering (hist.: Ger.) | 623.870943 |
| VM679 | Marine engineering (hist.: It.) | |

| | | |
|---|---|---|
| VM685 | Marine engineering (hist.: Rus.) | |
| VM699 | Marine engineering (hist.: Japan) | 623.870952 |
| VM721 | Marine engineering (hist.: Australia) | |
| VM725-728 | Instruction (marine engin.) | 623.8707 |
| VM727 | Marine engineering (instruction: U.S.) | |
| VM728.A-Z | Instruction (marine engin.: places except U.S.) | |
| VM731-779 | Marine engines | |
| VM731 | Engines, Marine (gen.) | 623.872 |
| VM740 | Turbines, Marine | 623.87233 |
| VM741-750 | Boilers, Marine | 623.873 |
| VM751-759 | Propulsion & resistance (marine engin.) | |
| VM751 | Resistance & propulsion (marine engin.: gen.) | |
| VM753-757 | Propellers (marine engin.) | 623.81473 |
| VM770 | Diesel, oil, & gas engines (marine engin.) | 623.8723 |
| VM773 | Electric propulsion (marine engin.) | 623.8726 |
| VM779 | Fuels, Marine engine | 623.874 |
| VM781-861 | Ships' appliances (engin.) | |
| VM781 | Appliances, Ships' (engin.: gen.) | 623.86 |
| VM791 | Anchors, cables, etc. (marine engin.) | |
| VM815 | Lights, Ships' (engin.) | |
| VM821 | Pumps, Marine (engin.) | |
| VM841-845 | Steering gear, Marine (engin.) | |
| VM851 | Hatchways, ladders, other special fittings (marine engin.) | |
| VM880 | Ship trials (gen.) | |
| VM881.A-Z | Trials, Ship (by name of vessel) | |
| VM901-965 | Maintenance & building devices & procedures, Marine (engin.) | |
| VM901 | Shipbuilding & maintenance appliances & activities (engin.: gen.: SEE TC361 & 363 for dry & floating docks) | |
| VM951 | Fouling, corrosion, etc. (marine engin.) | |
| VM961 | Scraping, painting, etc. (marine engin.) | |
| VM965 | Welding & cutting, Underwater (marine engin.) | |
| VM975-989 | Diving (marine engin.: SEE GV840.S78 for skindiving) | |
| VM977 | Diving (marine engin.: hist.) | 627.7209, 623.8257 (subs.), 359.3257 (subs.—naval ops.), 797.23 (scuba) |
| VM980 | Biography (divers: marine engin.) | |
| VM981 | Diving (marine engin.: gen.) | 627.72 |
| VM985-989 | Diving (marine engin.: special types) | |
| | | |
| Z | BIBLIOGRAPHY | 010 |
| Z1236 | Bibliographies (U.S.: hist.) | 016.97309 |
| Z1244 | Bibliographies (U.S.: hist.: 1900-45) | 016.9730904, .97309044 (WWII) |
| Z1249.M5 | Bibliographies (mil. hist.: U.S.) | 016.3550973, .35500973, |
| Z1249.N3 | Bibliographies (naval hist.: U.S.) | 016.3590973, .35900973, .35930973, .3593310924 |
| Z2016-2020+ | Bibliographies (G.B.: hist.) | 016.941-942 |
| Z2021.N3 | Bibliographies (naval hist.: G.B.) | 016.3590941 |
| Z2237 | Bibliographies (Ger.: hist.) | 016.94309 |
| Z2241.M5 | Bibliographies (mil. hist.: Ger.) | 016.3550943 |
| Z2506-2510+ | Bibliographies (Rus.: hist.) | 016.94709 |
| Z3306-3308 | Bibliographies (Japan: hist.) | 016.95209 |
| Z3308.M5 | Bibliographies (naval hist.: Japan) | 016.3590952 |
| Z6207.E8 or .W7 | Bibliographies (WWI) | 016.9403 |
| Z6207.W8 | Bibliographies (WWII) | 016.94053-94054, .36 |
| Z6616 | Bibliographies (naval sci. & hist.) | 016.35909, .35900722 |
| Z6724 | Bibliographies (mil. sci. & hist.) | 016.35509, 355.009, .0009 |

## II. DEWEY DECIMAL CLASSIFICATION SYSTEM (DDC)

Dewey Decimal Classification numbers consist of three digits followed in some instances by a decimal point and one or more digits beyond the decimal. These added numerals may represent divisions of the higher subject unique to that class. They may ALSO be repeating subdivisions taken from the ends of other specified numbers or from certain standard or geographic tables. The complete call numbers end with a letter and number usually for the author's last name.

The basic concept of the Dewey class system is to divide all knowledge into 1000 hierarchical categories running from 000 through 999. Each group of 100 numbers then represents a related area of research. For instance, the 900's belong to the class of History and Geography. Within each set of 100 or 10 or even within single numbers users can find associated material extending out to the third digit and beyond the decimal point as well.

Dewey numbers differ from Library of Congress numbers in several ways, some of which are discussed in the LC introduction. DDC uses digits sometimes succeeded by decimalized numbers for the classification scheme, whereas LC employs letters followed by numerals possibly followed by more letter-number subject subdivisions. Dewey has fewer basic numbers and tries to keep allied material closer together in a tighter overall schema. Further, DDC call numbers utilized in many libraries tend to have fewer identification lines than LC but may well have longer ones if many numbers past the decimal are applied. Incidentally, remember to look at the earlier digits past the decimal to keep proper order rather than going by total number of digits. Therefore, 355.34 shelves AFTER 355.338.

Since many DDC libraries try to avoid overlong numbers traveling six or more digits past the decimal, one can generally count on Dewey numbers to show less specificity in practice than their LC counterparts. The obvious hierarchical nature of the Dewey system, however, makes it more mnemonic for some people and may appear to bring related titles more closely together on the shelves.

Because of its relatively tight character, DDC has not always comfortably incorporated new subject concepts or historical developments. The hierarchical logic of the scheme and its available subdivisions has nevertheless made it a popular model of both sophistication and simplicity. Basic Dewey numbers are definitely easier than LC numbers to remember.

Most public libraries utilize the Dewey system of classification and shelving. In addition, some academic libraries use Dewey or have a split collection, with newer titles probably ordered by LC.

This part of the classification section consists of an outline of the primary Dewey groups followed by an extensive listing of pertinent military, engineering, and historical areas. Brief descriptions of each number are given, and similar Library of Congress numbers follow when available or relevant.

A single index to both Dewey and LC class numbers can be found after the Dewey listings. As mentioned before, certain topics do not easily translate from LC to DDC. Also, while each book or resource item can obviously receive only one call number in the cataloging process, every item may well receive several subject or other headings. Furthermore, subject and corporate headings may provide the greatest focus for certain specific matters. Therefore, readers should check the overall classification index as well as the LC headings section after it in order to find the most leads.

DEWEY CLASS NUMBERS: DESCRIPTIONS: POSSIBLE LC CLASS NUMBERS

| | | |
|---|---|---|
| 000-099 | General works | |
| 010 | Bibliography | Z; sometimes D-F, U-V, or other subject classes |
| 016 | Bibliographies (specific subjects) | Z; sometimes D-F, U-V, or other subject classes |
| 100-199 | Philosophy & psychology | B-BD, BH-BJ, BF |
| 200-299 | Religion | BL-BX |
| 300-399 | Social sciences | G-H, J-L, U-V |
| 355-358 | Military science | U |
| 359 | Naval science | V |
| 400-499 | Language | P |
| 500-599 | Sciences (pure) & math | Q |
| 600-699 | Technology, medicine, engineering, agriculture, management | T, R, QA76, S, H |
| 620 | Engineering | T |
| 623 | Military & marine engineering | UG, VM |
| 629.13 | Aeronautics | |
| 700-799 | Arts, architecture, music, sports, & recreation | N, NB-NX, NA, M, GV |
| 800-899 | Literature | P |
| 900-999 | Geography & history | G, D-F |
| 940.3-.499 | European War (1914-18) | D501-680 |
| 940.53-5499 | World War II (1939-45) | D731-838 |

| | | |
|---|---|---|
| 010-019 | Bibliographies (inclu. partic. kinds, subjects, etc.) | Z |
| 016 | BIBLIOGRAPHIES [SEE ALSO subject #'s like 359+, 940+, etc.] | |
| 016.355 | Bibliographies (mil. sci. & hist.) | Z6724 |
| 016.359 | Bibliographies (naval sci. & hist.) | Z6616 |
| 016.9403 | Bibliographies (WWI) | Z6207.E8 or .W7 |
| 016.94053-94054 | Bibliographies (WWII) | Z6207.W8 |
| 016.94109 | Bibliographies (G.B.: hist.) | Z2016-2020+ |
| 016.94309 | Bibliographies (Ger.: hist.) | Z2237 |
| 016.94709 | Bibliographies (Rus.: hist.) | Z2506-2510+ |
| 016.95209 | Bibliographies (Japan: hist.) | Z3306-3308 |
| 016.97309 | Bibliographies (U.S.: hist.) | Z1236-1245+ |

| | | |
|---|---|---|
| 300-399 | Social sciences | G-H, J-L, U-V |
| 300-309 | Social sciences (gen.) | H1-99 |
| 320-329 | Political science | J |
| 330-339 | Economics | HB-HJ |
| 340-349 | Law | K |
| 350-359 | Public administration | H-J |
| 355-359 | Military & naval science | U, V |
| 370-379 | Education | L |
| 380-389 | Commerce, communications, & transport | HF, HE |

| | | |
|---|---|---|
| 355-358 | Military forces & science | U |
| 356-359 | Warfare & military forces (types) | UD-UG, V |
| 358.41 | Air warfare (gen.) | |
| 359 | Naval science | V |

| 355 | MILITARY SCIENCE & ORGANIZATION (ALSO armed forces, | |
|---|---|---|
| | ground forces, etc.: officers' hdbks. here at 355) | U, U21+ |

| 355.003 | Dictionaries & encyclopedias (mil. sci.) | U24-25 |
|---|---|---|
| 355.0082 | Women in armed forces | |
| 355.0092 | Biography, Military | U51-55 |
| 355.02 | War & warfare | U21, U21.2, U102 |
| 355.021 | Warfare (summary topics) | U161-162, UA10 |
| 355.0213 | Militarism & antimilitarism (inclu. mil.-indus. complex) | JX1952, JX1963, UA23, U21.5, JF195.C5 |
| 355.0215 | Limited war (ALSO older titles on total war) | UA11+, U21+, UA11 |
| 355.022 | Sociological factors of war [SEE ALSO 303.66 & 306.2] | |
| 355.023 | Economic factors of war [PREFER 355.02] | HB195, HC65, JX1953 |
| 355.027 | War (causes) | U21.2, HB195, JX1952 |
| 355.0272 | Causes of war (political) | |
| 355.0273 | Causes of war (economic) | HB195 |
| 355.0274 | Causes of war (sociological) | |
| 355.0275 | Causes of war (psychological) | |
| 355.028 | War (aftermath: occupation, reconstruc., etc.) | |
| 355.03 | Military status (gen.: inclu. policy) | |
| 355.031 | Alliances, Military | |
| 355.032 | Military missions & attachés | |
| 355.033 | Military status (gen. hist.) | D25, U21+, U27, UA15 |
| 355.033001-033005 | Military status (hist. periods) | |
| 355.033004 | Military status (20th c.) | U42 |
| 355.0330041 | Military status (1900-1919) | |
| 355.0330043 | Military status (1930-39) | |
| 355.0330044 | Military status (1940-49) | |
| 355.03301-03309 | Military status (by area or country) | |
| 355.03304 | Europe (mil. status) | |
| 355.033043 | Germany (mil. status) | |
| 355.033052 | Japan (mil. status) | UA845+ |
| 355.033073 | United States (mil. status) | UA23 |
| 355.033094 | Australia (mil. status) | UA870+ |
| 355.0332+ | Military capability | |
| 355.033244 | France (mil. capabil.) | |
| 355.033251 | China (mil. capabil.) | |
| 355.033273 | United States (mil. capabil.) | |
| 355.0335+ | Policy, Military | |
| 355.033541-033542 | Great Britain (mil. policy) | UA647+, UA647-668 |
| 355.033543 | Germany & Central Europe (mil. policy) | UA710+, UA710-719 |
| 355.033547 | Russia (mil. policy) | UA770+ |
| 355.033551 (China)-033552 (Japan) | Japan & China (mil. policy) | UA830, UA835+, UA845+ |
| 355.033573 | United States (mil. policy) | |
| 355.033594 | Australia (mil. policy) | UA870-874 |
| 355.07 | Research & development, Military | |

| 355.1 | MILITARY LIFE, CUSTOMS, & POSTMILITARY BENEFITS | U750, U22 |
|---|---|---|
| 355.11 | Military life (service periods, promotion, vet. benefits, etc.) | |
| 355.112 | Promotion & demotion (mil.) | UB320+ |
| 355.113 | Leaves, furloughs, other inactive periods (mil.) | |
| 355.114 | Discharge, retirement, other termination (mil.) | UB320+ |
| 355.115 | Veterans' benefits | UB356-405, UB356-358 |
| 355.1151 | Pensions, Veterans' [PREFER now 331.25291355] | |

| | | |
|---|---|---|
| 355.12 | Living conditions, Military | U750-773, U750, U765 |
| 355.123 | Morale, Military | U22 |
| 355.129 | Military living conditions (partic. situations) | U765+ |
| 355.1292 | Basic training (mil. living conditions: ALSO regular quarters) | |
| 355.1293 | Transport & maneuvers (mil. living conditions) | |
| 355.1294 | Combat conditions (mil. life) | |
| 355.1295 | Military prison life (SEE ALSO 365.48) | |
| 355.1296 | Prisoner-of-war camps (mil. life: SEE ALSO 365.45) | UB800-805 |
| 355.13 | Conduct & rewards, Military | U765+ |
| 355.133 | Discipline & conduct, Military (regulation) | |
| 355.1332 | Punishment & enforcement, Military | |
| 355.13323 | Military police & conduct enforcement | |
| 355.13325 | Military prisons (SEE ALSO 365.48) | UB800-805 |
| 355.1334 | Mutinies & military offenses (SEE 364.138 for war crimes) | UB780+ |
| 355.1336 | Etiquette, Military | U765+ |
| 355.134 | Rewards & privileges, Military | UB430-435 |
| 355.1342 | Medals, decorations, badges, etc. (mil. rewards) | |
| 355.1349 | Gun salutes & other military rewards (misc.: USE 355.134 with 1989+ pubns.) | |
| 355.135 | Salaries, Military (SEE ALSO 355.64) | UC70-75 (U.S.), UC91-258 (other places), UC180-183 (Ger.), UC184-187 (G.B.), UC241 (Japan) |
| 355.14 | Uniforms, Military (inclu. insignia, etiquette of, etc.) | UC480-535, UC483 (U.S.) |
| 355.15 | Colors & standards, Military | UC590-595, U360-365 |
| 355.16 | Celebrations & commemorations, Military | |
| 355.17 | Ceremonies, Military | U350-355 |
| | | |
| 355.2 | RESOURCES, MILITARY | UA18, UA10 |
| 355.21 | Military resources (prep., review, preserv.) | |
| 355.22 | Human resources (mil.) | UA17.5, UB320+, UB340+ |
| 355.223 | Recruitment & enlistment, Military | |
| 355.2232 | Training, Reserve | |
| 355.2234 | Qualifications, Service (mil.) | |
| 355.2236 | Commissioning, registration, classification, exams, etc. (mil. manpower procure.) | UB330+, U400+ |
| 355.22362 | Enlistment, Military | UB320-325, UB323 (U.S.) |
| 355.22363 | Draft, Military | UB340-345, UB343 (U.S.) |
| 355.224 | Conscientious objectors | UB341-342 |
| 355.225 | Universal service & training (mil. resources) | UB350-355 |
| 355.23 | Civilian personnel (mil. resources) | |
| 355.24 | Raw materials (mil. resources) | HC110.A-Z, UA18, UA929.5+ |
| 355.242 | Metals (mil. raw materials) | |
| 355.243 | Minerals (non-metal: mil. raw materials) | |
| 355.245 | Agricultural products (mil. raw materials) | UA929.95.A35 |
| 355.26 | Industrial resources (mil. use) | UA18, UA929.5+, HC106+ |
| 355.27 | Communication & transport (mil. resources) | UA940-945, UA929.95.T7, UC10+, UC270-275 |
| 355.28 | Mobilization (mil. resources: inclu. requisition, commandeering, voluntary, etc.) | UA910-915, UA913 (U.S.) |
| 355.29 | Demobilization (mil. resources: gen.) | UA917 |

| 355.3 | MILITARY PERSONNEL (inclu. organization; readiness of partic. groups)     UA15+, UA23-39+ (U.S.) |
|---|---|
| 355.309 | Organization (mil. personnel: hist. & geog. treatment) |
| 355.31 | Military units (types: armies, div's., regiments, co's., mil. districts, etc.) UA, UA23-39+ (U.S.), UA646-829 (Eur.), UA830-853 (Asia), UA870-876 (Australia-Pac.) |
| 355.33 | Hierarchy, Military (mil. personnel)     UA, UB410-415, UB210 |
| 355.33041 | Line functions (mil. organiz.) |
| 355.33042 | Staff functions (mil. organiz.) |
| 355.331 | General & flag officers (above army col. or navy capt.)     UB200, UB210 |
| 355.332 | Officers, Commissioned & warrant     UB407-415 |
| 355.338 | Enlisted personnel (inclu. non-coms)     UB320, U765+ |
| 355.34 | Noncombat services (mil.: inclu. soc. srvcs., dependent srvcs., civil activ's., etc.) |
| 355.341 | Supply & administrative services, Military (canteens, post-ex's., messes, etc.: SEE ALSO 355.6 & .71)     UC, UC750-755, UH80-85 |
| 355.342 | Public information & relations (mil.) UH700-705, UH703 (U.S.) |
| 355.343 | Espionage & unconventional warfare (mil.: SEE ALSO 327.12) UB250-290 |
| 355.3432 | Intelligence & military espionage (inclu. cryptanalysis, data analysis, etc.)     UB250-251, UB251.A-Z (by country), UB270-271, UB271.A-Z (by place), UB271.x2.A-Z (by spy), UB271.R92.S565 (R. Sorge) |
| 355.3433 | Counterintelligence (mil.) |
| 355.3434 | Psychological warfare & propaganda (mil.: ALSO use 355.34 for propag.)     UB275-277, UB276 (U.S.), UB277.A-Z (except U.S.) |
| 355.3437 | Subversion & sabotage (mil.)     UB273-274UB275-277, UB276 (U.S.), UB277.A-Z (except U.S.) |
| 355.345 | Medical & health services, Military     UH201-629, UH215, UH223-225 (U.S.) |
| 355.346 | Recreation services, Military (inclu. sports, arts, music, libraries, clubs, etc.)     UH800-910, UH800, UH805 (U.S.) |
| 355.347 | Religious & counseling services, Military     UH20-25 |
| 355.348 | Women's military units     UA565.W6 (U.S. Wac's) |
| 355.35 | Combat units (by service field)     UA |
| 355.351 | Home guards & frontier troops     UA42 (U.S. Nat. Guard) |
| 355.352 | Expeditionary & colonial forces     UA14, UA668 (G.B.), UA709 (Fr.), UA719 (Ger.), UA849 (Jp.) |
| 355.356 | Allied forces (inclu. various multi-nat. & combined ops.)     UA12 (U.S.), UA15, U260 (comb. ops.) |
| 355.357 | International forces (PERHAPS PREFER 355.356) |
| 355.359 | Foreign legions |
| 355.37 | Reserves, Army     UA, UA42 (U.S.), UA50-549 (U.S.: by state), UA661 (G.B.) |
| | |
| 355.4 | STRATEGY & MILITARY OPS. (plans, attack, defense, etc.)     UA11, UA23 (U.S.), U27, U42-43, U102, U161-167 |
| 355.409 | Military ops. (hist's. & types of persons: SEE ALSO 355.47 for geog. treat.)     U27-43 |
| 355.41 | Support & logistics, Military (logistics, camouflage, p.o.w. care, etc.) U168, UC260-270 |
| 355.411 | Logistics & troop movement |

| 355.412 | Encampments | U180-185 |
| 355.413 | Reconnaisance & patrols | U220 |

355.415 Troop support (communication, supply, medical, p.o.w.'s, etc.:
        ALSO use 355.41 for newer titles on p.o.w. care)
                              UC260-267, UA940-945

355.42    Tactics, Military    U164-167.5, U165
355.422       Military tactics (partic. kinds: commando, retreats, blitz, landings,
           attacks & counters, etc.)
355.423       Tactics, Military (in different terrains, climates, weathers)
           U167.D4 (desert), .F6 (forest), .J8 (jungle), .W5 (winter)
355.424       Animals, Use of (mil. sci.)
355.425       Guerrilla tactics (SEE 355.0218 for guer. war)    U240
355.426       Urban warfare tactics           U167.5.S7
355.43    Nuclear ops., Military (also gen. strategy: USE 355.4 for post-'88 titles
           on gen. strategy)           U161-163
355.44    Siege warfare      UG443-449
355.45    Home defense (coasts, frontiers, other valuable redoubts)
           UA (gen.), UG410-442 (fortific's.), UG410-412 (U.S.),
           UG428-430 (Eur.), UG429.G7 (G.B.)
355.46    Combined ops., Military (2 or more types of forces)
355.47    Geography, Military (tactical & strategic)    UA985-997
355.473       United States (mil. geog.)     UA993
355.474       Europe (mil. geog.)      UA990, UA995.E ·
355.4741-4742   Great Britain (mil. geog.)   UA995.G7
355.4743    Germany & Central Europe (mil. geog.)    UA995.G3
355.4747    Russia (mil. geog.)     UA995.R9
355.4751   China (mil. geog.)    UA995.C
355.4752   Japan (mil. geog.)    UA995.J2
355.47599     Philippines (mil. geog.)
355.4761-4762   Tunisia & Egypt (mil. geog.)
355.477287    Panama (mil. geog.: SEE ALSO .47862)
355.478       South America (mil. geog.)
355.4793   Melanesia & New Zealand (mil. geog.)
355.47935   Solomon Islands (mil. geog.)   UA995.S
355.4794   Australia (mil. geog.)    UA995.A
355.4795   New Guinea (mil. geog.)
355.4796   Micronesia & Polynesia (mil. geog.)
355.47966     Caroline Islands
355.47967     Mariana Islands (mil. geog.)    UA995.M
355.47969     Hawaiiian Islands (mil. geog.)    UA995.H
355.48    Analysis, Military (real & mock events)    UA719-740+, U161-167+
355.49    Occupation & government, Military    D802 (WWII)

355.5     TRAINING & EDUCATION, MILITARY    U400-717, U400 (gen.),
        U403 (modern), U408 (U.S.), U410 (West Pt.), U510-549 (G.B.)
355.50973   Education & training, Military (U.S.)
355.52    Military maneuvers    U250-255
355.54    Basic training (mil.: inclu. drills, survival exercises, etc.)
           U400-717, U765-773, U320-325
355.544       Encampment & field training (mil.)    U180-185, UG400-409+
355.547       Small arms & bayonet training    UD380-415, U169
355.548       Hand-to-hand combat & self-defense (training: inclu. unarmed &
           knife fighting)     U167.5.H3, U262
355.55    Training, Officer (mil. sci.)    U400-717 (educ.)
355.56    Training, Technical (mil. sci.)

| | | |
|---|---|---|
| 355.6 | MILITARY ADMINISTRATION | UB-UC |
| 355.61 | Personnel administration, Military (civilian & mil.) | UB160-165, |
| | UB180-197, UB410-415 (officers), UB320-338 | |
| 355.62 | Administration, Military supply & finance | UC260-267, UA |
| 355.621 | Supply administration (mil.) | UC260-267 |
| 355.6211 | Contract administration (mil.) | UC267 |
| 355.6212 | Procurement (mil. supplies) | UC263-267, HD3858-3860 |
| 355.6213 | Supplies, Military (use & disposal) | |
| 355.622 | Financial administration (mil.) | UB150-155, UC263-267, |
| | UA21-876, UA910-915 | |
| 355.63 | Military inspection | UB240-245 |
| 355.64 | Salaries & wages, Military (admin.: SEE ALSO 355.135) | UC70-75 |
| 355.65-66 | Clothing, food, & equipment (mil. admin.: PREFER 355.81) | |
| | UC460-535, UC700-735 | |
| 355.67 | Housing administration (mil.: SEE ALSO 355.71 & .12 [gen.]) | |
| | UC400-440 | |
| 355.693 | Mail, Military | |
| 355.699 | Graves registration & military burial | |
| | | |
| 355.7 | MILITARY INSTALLATIONS & LAND (inclu. bases, forts, camps, posts, | |
| | etc.) | UA26+ (U.S.), UC400-405, UA600-876 |
| 355.709 | Military bases, camps, forts, reservations, etc. (geog. & hist. applic.) | |
| 355.71 | Quarters, Military (barracks, p.o.w. camps etc. on-site) | UC400-405 |
| 355.72 | Medical installations, Military | UH470-475 |
| 355.73 | Artillery installations (arsenals, depots, target ranges, schools, etc.) | |
| | UF540-545 | |
| 355.74 | Engineering installations, Military | |
| 355.75 | Supply depots, Military | UC260-269 |
| 355.79 | Land (mil. bases, reservations, etc.) | |
| | | |
| 355.8 | EQUIPMENT & SUPPLIES, MILITARY | U800+, UC260-267 |
| 355.81 | CLOTHING, FOOD, CAMP EQUIPMENT, ETC. (SEE ALSO .65-66) | |
| | UC460-465+, UC700-705 | |
| 355.82 | Ordnance | UF520-780, U800-823+ |
| 355.821 | Artillery (gen.) | |
| 355.8212 | Artillery, Field | UF400-405 |
| 355.8217 | Artillery, Coast | UF450-455 |
| 355.8218 | Artillery, Naval (SEE ALSO 359.8218) | VF320-325 |
| 355.822 | Artillery (specific pieces) | |
| 355.823 | Gun mounts | |
| 355.824 | Small arms | UF520-537+ |
| 355.82424 | Automatic firearms (rifles, machine guns, etc.) | UF620 |
| 355.82425 | Rifles | UD390-395 |
| 355.8243 | Revolvers & pistols | UD410-415 |
| 355.825 | Bombs, ammunition, etc. | |
| 355.82511 | Grenades, mines, etc. | |
| 355.825114 | Grenades, Hand & rifle | UF765 |
| 355.825115 | Mines (mil. equip.) | UG490 |
| 355.825119 | Nuclear weapons | UG1282.A8 |
| 355.82516 | Chemical & biological weapons (projectiles etc.) | UG447-447.8 |
| 355.8252 | Explosives | UF860-880 |
| 355.82542 | Detonators | |
| 355.82543 | Rockets, Tactical | |
| 355.82545 | Demolition charges | |
| 355.8255 | Ammunition, Small arms | |

| 355.82594 | Biological agents (mil.) |
|---|---|
| 355.826 | Sighting apparatus & other ordnance access.  UF848-856 |
| 355.83 | Transport equipment & supplies, Military (vehicles, fuel, trains, etc.) |
| | UC270-360, UC270-275, UC340-345, UC260-267, UG615-620 |
| 355.85 | Communication equipment, Military  UG570-613, UA940-945 |
| 355.88 | Medical supplies  UH440-445 |

| 356-357 | Land forces warfare  UD-UF |
|---|---|
| 356 | FOOT FORCES WARFARE  UD, U14-43, UA |
| 356.1 | INFANTRY  UD, UD15, UD21-124 (by place), UD144-145+, UA |
| 356.11 | Motorized infantry (pubns. before 1989 may inclu. regular infan. also) |
| | U167.5.M6, UD15, UD21-124+, UA |
| 356.15 | Irregular troops (guerrillas, brigands, etc.)  U240, U167.5.A-Z |
| 356.16 | Troops, Special-purpose  U167.5.A-Z |
| 356.162 | Snipers, bazookamen, machine-gunners, & other special-weapon |
| | troops  U167.5.A-Z, UD390+, UF620 |
| 356.164 | Troops, Ski & mountain  UD470-475, U167.5.W5 |
| 356.166 | Paratroops  UD480-485, UD483 (U.S.), UG630-635 |
| 356.167 | Rangers & commandos  U262 |
| 356.18 | Infantry (gen.)  UD160-302, UD160 (U.S.) |
| 356.181 | Life & customs (infantry) |
| 356.1814 | Uniforms, Infantry |
| 356.183 | Tactics & operations, Infantry |
| 356.184 | Training (infantry)  U400-714 (educ.), U320-325 |
| 356.186 | Equipment & supplies (infantry)  UD380+, UC260-267, UC460+ |
| 356.187 | Installations, Infantry  UC400-405, U180-185 |
| 356.189 | Organization & personnel (infantry) |

| 357 | MOUNTED FORCES & WARFARE  UE, UE15, UE21-124, |
|---|---|
| | UE23 (U.S.), UE57 (G.B.), UE65 (Austria), UD450-455 |
| 357.043 | Organization & personnel (cavalry: inclu. specific units) |
| 357.1 | CAVALRY, HORSE  UE15, UE21-124, UE150+, UA |
| 357.184 | Horse cavalry (gen. & ops.)  UE150-475, UE150+, UE157+ |
| 357.5 | CAVALRY, MECHANIZED  UE147-149, UE150-155 (manuals), |
| | UE159, UE160-302 (by place) |
| 357.52 | Bicycle troops (mech. cav.)  UH30-35 |
| 357.53 | Motorcycle troops (mech. cav.)  UC347 |
| 357.54 | Mechanized cavalry (jeep, truck, other large-motor vehicle troops) |
| | UC340-345, UG615-620 |
| 357.58 | Mechanized cavalry (gen. & ops.)  UE147-155, UE159, |
| | UE160-302 (by place) |

| 358 | SPECIALIZED FORCES & WARFARE (armored land, technical land, & |
|---|---|
| | air)  UE-UG |
| 358.1 | ARTILLERY, LAND MISSILE FORCES, & ARMORED WARFARE |
| | UF, UF15, UF21-124, UE147, UA32-33 (U.S.), UA |
| 358.12 | Army artillery (inclu. field & antitank)  UF400-405, UF15, |
| | UF21-124 (by place), UF150-157+ (manuals & tactics) |
| 358.13 | Artillery, Antiaircraft (land)  UF625 |
| 358.16 | Artillery, Coast  UF450-455 |
| 358.17 | Missile forces & warfare (land: may be mostly post-WWII) |
| | UG1310-1315 |
| 358.171 | Guided missile forces (land: gen.) |
| 358.175 | Rocket forces (land: types) |
| 358.18 | Armored forces & warfare (tanks, armored cav., etc.)  UG446.5, UE147 |

| | | |
|---|---|---|
| 358.2 | ENGINEER FORCES, ARMY | UG15, UG21-124 (by place), UG23 (U.S.),UG500-620 |
| 358.22 | Construction & maintenance (army engineers) | UG360-390+, UG15-124 |
| 358.23 | Bomb disposal & demolition (army engineers) | UG370, UG550-555 |
| 358.24 | Communications, signaling, & cryptography forces (mil. engineers) | UG570-611.5, UA940-945, UB290 (cryp.) |
| 358.25 | Transportation services (mil. engineers) | UC270-275, UG345 (rail) |
| 358.3 | TECHNICAL FORCES (chem., biol., & radiation warfare: pre-1989 titles may cover camouflage construc. & war matériel manufac.) | |
| 358.34 | Chemical warfare | UG447-447.6 |
| 358.38 | Biological warfare | UG447.8 |
| 358.39 | Nuclear warfare | UF767, U162, U165, UA |
| | | |
| 358.4 | AERIAL WARFARE & AIR FORCES (inclu. naval av. for works prior to 1989--SEE 359.94 after 1988) | UG622-1425, UG630, UG633-634 (U.S.), UG635.A-Z (places besides U.S.), VG90-95 (naval av.) |
| 358.403 | Air forces (policy & status) | UG630-635, UA |
| 358.407 | Research & development (air forces equip. & supplies) | |
| 358.41 | Air warfare (gen.) | |
| 358.411 | Air force life & customs | U750-773, UG770-775, UG1130-1135 |
| 358.41112 | Promotion & demotion (air forces) | UB320-325, UB410-415 |
| 358.4112 | Living conditions (air forces) | |
| 358.4113 | Conduct, discipline, & reward (air forces: etiquette, enforcement, punishments, etc.) | UB790-795, UB430-435 |
| 358.4114 | Uniforms, Air force | UG1160-1165 |
| 358.412 | Resources, Air force | UG630+, UG1100+ |
| 358.4122 | Human resources (air forces: enlistment etc.) | UG880-885 |
| 358.4124-4126 | Industrial resources & raw materials (air forces) | UG1100-1105, UG630+ |
| 358.4127 | Communication & transport (air force resources) | UC330-335, UA940-945 |
| 358.413 | Structure & personnel, Air force | UG770-775, UG1130-1135 |
| 358.4131 | Air force units (types) | |
| 358.4133 | Hierarchy, Air force | UG770-775 |
| 358.41331 | General officers (air forces) | UG790-795 |
| 358.41332 | Commissioned & warrant officers, Air force | UG820-825 |
| 358.41338 | Enlisted personnel & non-coms, Air force | UG820-825 |
| 358.4134 | Noncombat services (air forces) | |
| 358.41343 | Unconventional warfare (air forces: intelligence, propaganda, etc.) | |
| 358.41345 | Medical & health services, Air force | UH201-655 |
| 358.41348 | Women in air forces | |
| 358.41356 | Allied forces (air) | UG625, UG630+ |
| 358.4137 | Reserves, Air force | UG850-855 |
| 358.414 | Air force ops. (gen.) | UG630, UG633-635, UG700-765 |
| 358.41409 | Air warfare (hist.: gen.) | UG625 |
| 358.4141 | Logistics & support, Air force | UG1100-1105 |
| 358.41415 | Troop support (air forces) | UG700-705, UG260 |
| 358.4142 | Tactics, Air force | UG700-705 |
| 358.4143 | Strategy, Air force | U162-163, UG633-635 |
| 358.4145 | Home defense, Air force | UG730-735, UG630-635 |
| 358.4147 | Geography, Air warfare | UG633-635, UA |
| 358.41474 | Europe (air war geog.) | |
| 358.414741 | Great Britain (air war geog.) | UG635.G7 |
| 358.414743 | Germany (air war geog.) | UG635.G3 |
| 358.414747 | Russia (air war geog.) | |

| 358.41475 | Asia (air war geog.) |
| 358.414751 | China (air war geog.) |
| 358.414752 | Japan (air war geog.) |
| 358.414773 | United States (air war geog.)   UG633 |
| 358.41479 | Pacific (air war geog.) |
| 358.4148 | Analysis, Air warfare (real & imagined)   UG630-635 |
| 358.415 | Training & education, Air force   UG637-639 |
| 358.4152 | Maneuvers, Air force (training) |
| 358.4155 | Training, Officer (air forces) |
| 358.4156 | Training, Technical (air forces) |
| 358.416 | Air force administration   UG770-775, UG1100-1135, UG630-635 |
| 358.4161 | Air force personnel   UG1130-1135 |
| 358.4162 | Finances & supplies (air force admin.)   UG1100-1105, UG1100-1425 |
| 358.416212 | Equipment & supply procurement (air forces)   UG1120-1125, UG1123 (U.S.) |
| 358.4164 | Wages & salaries, Air force   UG940-945, UC74 (U.S.), UC90+ |
| 358.4165-4166 | Clothing, food, & equipment (air forces)   UG1100-1105, UG1160-1165, UC460-465, UC700-705 |
| 358.4167 | Housing administration (air forces)   UG1140-1145 |
| 358.417 | Bases & fields, Air force   UG634.5.A-Z (U.S.: by name), UG635.A-Z (other countries) |
| 358.4171 | Barracks & quarters, Air force   UG1140-1145 |
| 358.418 | Matériel & equipment, Air force   UG1100-1425+, UG1100-1105 |
| 358.4182 | Ordnance, Air force   UG1270-1275 |
| 358.4183-4184 | Combat & support aircraft   UG1240-1245, UG1242.A-Z (by type), UG1243 (U.S.), UG633-635, VG90-95 (naval), TL685+ |
| 358.42 | Bomber forces & ops.   UG1242.B6, UG633-635, UG633 (U.S.), TL685.3, TL686.A-Z (by co. or name) |
| 358.43 | Pursuit & fighter forces & ops. (air)   UG1242.F5, UG633 (U.S.), UG635.A-Z (places except U.S.), TL685.3, TL686.A-Z (by co. or name) |
| 358.44 | Transport groups (air forces)   UC330-335, UG633-635, UG1242.T |
| 358.45 | Reconnaissance forces, Air (inclu. antisub. work)   UG760-765, UG1242.R4 |
| 358.46 | Air force communications & ops.   UA940-945, UG611-612.5 |
| 358.47 | Engineering services (air forces) |
| | |
| 359 | NAVAL FORCES & WARFARE   V-VM, V27-55, V101-109 |
| 359.001 | Theory & philosophy (naval warfare) |
| 359.003 | Dictionaries & encyclopedias (naval forces)   V23 |
| 359.009+ | Sea forces & warfare (hist.)   VA, D-F, VA10, VA25-55 |
| 359.00941-00942 | Great Britain (naval hist.)   VA452-467, DA70-89 |
| 359.00943 | Germany (naval hist.)   VA510-519 |
| 359.00952 | Japan (naval hist.)   VA650-659 |
| 359.0092 | Biography, Naval   V61-64, V63.A-Z (U.S.: by name), V64.A-Z (other countries) |
| 359.00973 | United States (naval hist.)   VA49-395, VA50-70, E182, E746 (20th c.) |
| 359.03+ (country #s follow) | Policy & status, Naval   VA |
| 359.030941 | Great Britain (naval policy & status) |
| 359.030952 | Japan (naval policy & status) |
| 359.030973 | United States (naval policy & status) |
| 359.07 | Research & development (naval equip. & supplies)   V390-395 |

| 359.1 | LIFE & CUSTOMS, NAVAL | V720-743, V110-145 |
|---|---|---|
| 359.11 | Service periods (navies) | |
| 359.112 | Promotion & demotion (navies) | |
| | | VB260-275, VB307-315 |
| 359.113 | Furloughs, leaves, other inactive periods (navies) | |
| | | VB260-275, VB307-315 |
| 359.114 | Retirement, resignation, other service termination (navies) | |
| 359.12 | Living conditions (navies) | V720-743, V720 (gen.), V735 (modern), |
| | | V736 (U.S.), V737 (G.B.) |
| 359.123 | Morale (navies) | |
| 359.129 | Living conditions (navies: partic. situations) | |
| 359.1292 | Naval living conditions (training or perm. bases) | |
| 359.1294 | Battle conditions, Naval | |
| 359.13 | Conduct & rewards, Naval | VB840-845, VB843 (U.S.) |
| 359.133 | Regulation of conduct, Naval | |
| 359.1332 | Discipline & enforcement (naval conduct) | VB850-855, VB890-925 |
| 359.13323 | Enforcement (naval conduct) | |
| 359.13325 | Punishments (naval conduct) | |
| 359.1334 | Mutiny & other naval offenses | VB850-880 |
| 359.1336 | Etiquette, Naval | V720-743, VB260-265, VB307-315 |
| 359.134 | Rewards (navies: inclu. privileges, citations, medals, etc.) | |
| | | VB330-335 |
| 359.1342 | Medals, decorations, other reward insignia (navies) | |
| 359.14 | Naval uniforms (insignia, service, etiquette, etc.) | VC300-345 |
| 359.15 | Colors & standards (navies) | V300-305 |
| 359.16 | Commemorations & celebrations (navies) | V310 |
| 359.17 | Naval ceremonies | V310 |

| 359.2 | RESOURCES, NAVAL | |
|---|---|---|
| | | VB, VB21-124 (by place), VB23 (U.S.), VB144-146, |
| | | VA49-750 (by place), VA50-80+ (U.S.) |
| 359.21 | Naval resources (preparation, eval., preserv.) | |
| 359.22 | Human resources (navies) | |
| 359.223 | Recruitment & enlistment (navies) | VB260-315 |
| 359.2232 | Training, Naval reserve | V400-695 |
| 359.2234 | Qualifications (naval personnel) | |
| 359.2236 | Commissioning, draft, examination, registration, other methods of | |
| | naval personnel procurement | VB260-275 (enlisted pers.), |
| | | VB307-315 (officers) |
| 359.22362 | Voluntary enlistment (navies) | |
| 359.22363 | Conscription or draft (navies) | |
| 359.229 | Women in naval forces | VA49-750, VA390.W (U.S. Waves) |
| 359.23 | Civilian personnel (navies) | VB170-187 |
| 359.24 | Raw materials (naval resources) | VC260-267, VF390+ |
| 359.26 | Industrial resources (navies) | |
| 359.27 | Communication & transport (naval resources) | VC530-580 (trans.), |
| | | VB255, VG70-85, V270 |
| 359.28 | Naval mobilization | VA48, VA77-750, VA77 (U.S.) |
| 359.29 | Naval demobilization | VB277, UA917 |

| 359.3 | ORGANIZATION & PERSONNEL, NAVAL | VA, VA50 (U.S.), VB21-124 |
|---|---|---|
| 359.31 | Squadrons, fleets, flotillas, etc. (naval units) | VA, VA63.A-Z (U.S.), VB200-205 |
| 359.32 | Ships & crews (naval forces) | V750-895, V750, VA (indiv. ships) |
| 359.325 | Ships, Powered (as units: group op. in squadrons etc., crew duties & life, hist's. of indiv. ships in most cases: SEE ALSO 359.83 & .835-836 for ships as equip.: PREFER .325+ when in doubt) | V750, V765-767, V799-800 |
| 359.3251 | Naval armor & ordnance | V900-905, V950-980, VF, VF23 (U.S.) |
| 359.3252 | Battleships (units) | V750, V765-767, V799-800, VA, VA65.A-Z (U.S.: by name) |
| 359.3253 | Cruisers (in units) | V820-820.5, VA65.A-Z (U.S.: by name) |
| 359.3254 | Destroyer escorts & destroyers (units) | V825-825.5, VA65 (U.S.) |
| 359.3255 | Aircraft carriers (units: SEE ALSO 359.9435 for pubns. after 1988) | V874-875, V874.3 (U.S.), V874.5.A-Z (other places), VA65.A-Z (U.S.: by name) |
| 359.3256 | Landing craft (navies: units) | V895 |
| 359.3257 | Naval submarines (units: SEE ALSO 359.933 after 1988) | V857-859, V858 (U.S.), V859.A-Z (other countries), VA65.A-Z (U.S.: by name), VM365-367 (construc.) |
| 359.32572 | Submarines, Diesel & electric (navies: units) | |
| 359.3258 | Combat vessels, Small (P.T.'s etc.: units) | V830-840, V880-885 |
| 359.326 | Support vessels, Naval (units) | V865 |
| 359.3262 | Minesweepers & minelayers (navies: units) | V885, V856+ |
| 359.3263 | Coast guard vessels (units) | VM397 |
| 359.3264 | Military transport vessels & hospital ships (units: SEE ALSO 359.9853 for transp. ships on pubns. after 1988) | VA79 (transports), VG450 (hosp. ships) |
| 359.3265 | Military supply ships (freighters, tankers, etc.: units: SEE ALSO 359.9853 after 1988) | VA79 |
| 359.33 | Hierarchy, Naval | V110-145, VA, VB21-124, VB23 (U.S.), VB257-258.5, VB203 |
| 359.33041 | Line positions (naval hier.) | |
| 359.33042 | Staff positions (naval hier.) | |
| 359.331 | Flag officers, Naval (above captain) | VB190, VB200-205, VB310-315 |
| 359.332 | Officers, Commissioned & warrant (navies) | VB307-315 |
| 359.338 | Enlisted personnel & non-coms, Naval | VB260-275 |
| 359.34 | Non-combat services, Naval | VG1-2029+, VC10-580+ |
| 359.341 | Supply services, Naval (canteens, post exch's, messes, etc.) | VC, VC10, VC20-258 (overall by place), VC20-65 (U.S.), VC260-410 |
| 359.342 | Public relations & information (navies) | VG500-505 |
| 359.343 | Unconventional warfare (navies) | VB230-250 |
| 359.3432 | Intelligence, Naval | VB230-250, VB230, UB250-271 |
| 359.3433 | Counterintelligence, Naval | |
| 359.3434 | Naval propaganda & psychological warfare | UB275-277 |
| 359.3437 | Sabotage, Naval | VG86-88 (underwater demolition), UB273-274 |
| 359.345 | Medical & nursing services (navies) | VG100-475, VG115, VG121-224 (overall by place), VG123 (U.S.), VG350-355 (nurse corps) |
| 359.346 etc.) | Recreation services, Naval (sports, arts, music, dancing, libraries, | VG2020-2029, UH800-910 |
| 359.347 | Religious & counseling services, Naval | VG20-25, VG2000 |
| 359.348 | Women's naval units (gen.) | VA |
| 359.351 | Home guard naval forces | VA45 |
| 359.356 | Allied naval forces (inclu. various coalition forces) | VA40-42, VA, U260 |
| 359.37 | Reserves, Naval | VA45, VA, VA80+ |

| 359.4 | STRATEGY & NAVAL OPS. (SEE ALSO 359.43 for strategic works | |
| | prior to1989) | V27-55, V101-107, VA, VA10, VA50-750 |
| 359.409 | Naval ops. (hist's.: gen.) | V27-55 |
| 359.41 | Support & logistics, Naval | V179, VC10 |
| 359.411 | Logistics, Naval | V179 |
| 359.413 | Reconnaissance, Naval | V190 |
| 359.415 | Troop support, Naval | |
| 359.42 | Tactics, Naval | V167-178 |
| 359.43 | Strategy, Naval (PREFER 359.4 with titles after 1988) | V160-165 |
| 359.45 | Home defense, Naval | VA45, V200 |
| 359.46 | Combined ops., Naval (2 or more types of forces) | |
| 359.47 | Geography, Naval (strategic & tactical) | UA985-997, VA160-178, VA49-750 (by place) |
| 359.474 | Europe (naval geog.) | VA450 |
| 359.4741-4742 | Great Britain (naval geog.) | VA452-467, VA454 (gen.) |
| 359.4743 | Germany (naval geog.) | VA510-519, VA513 (gen.) |
| 359.4744 | France (naval geog.) | VA500-509 |
| 359.4745 | Italy (naval geog.) | VA540-549 |
| 359.4747 | Russia (naval geog.) | VA570-579 |
| 359.4748 | Scandinavia (naval geog.) | VA619.S, VA590599 (Sweden) |
| 359.4749 | Europe (naval geog.: misc. areas: Greece etc.) | |
| 359.475 | Asia (naval geog.) | VA620-639 |
| 359.4751 | China (naval geog.) | VA630-639 |
| 359.4752 | Japan (naval geog.) | 650-659 |
| 359.47598 | Indonesia & Borneo (naval geog.) | VA667.I or .B |
| 359.47599 | Philippines (naval geog.) | VA667.P, VA750.P |
| 359.477287 | Panama (naval geog.) | VA407.P |
| 359.47729 | West Indies (naval geog.) | VA409-410 |
| 359.4773 | United States (naval geog.) | VA49-395, VA50 (gen.) |
| 359.4774-4779 | United States (naval geog.: partic. states) | VA90-387 |
| 359.47759 | Florida (naval geog.) | VA140-147 |
| 359.4779 | Pacific Coast (naval geog.) | VA50 |
| 359.47794 | California (naval geog.) | VA100-107 |
| 359.479 | Pacific (naval geog.) | VA710-750, VA730 |
| 359.4793 | New Zealand (naval geog.) | VA720-729 |
| 359.47935 | Solomon Islands (naval geog.) | VA750.S |
| 359.47936 | Bismarck Islands (naval geog.) | VA750.B |
| 359.4794 | Australia (naval geog.) | VA710-719 |
| 359.4795 | New Guinea (Papua: naval geog.) | VA750.N, VA667.N |
| 359.47965 | Micronesia (naval geog.) | VA750.M |
| 359.47969 | Hawaiian Islands (naval geog.) | VA750.H, VA158-158.7 |
| 359.48 | Analysis, Naval warfare (real & imagined battles, campaigns, etc.) | V25-55,V160-178 |
| | | |
| 359.5 | TRAINING & EDUCATION, NAVAL | V400-695 (by place), V411-438 (U.S.), V260-265 |
| 359.52 | Maneuvers, Naval (training) | V245 |
| 359.54 | Basic training (naval) | V260-265 |
| 359.55 | Training, Officer (navies) V400-695, V411-438 (U.S.: Annapolis etc.), | VB307-315 |
| 359.56 | Training, Technical (navies) | |

| 359.6 | ADMINISTRATION, NAVAL | VB, VB15, VB21-124 (by place), |
|---|---|---|

359.6      ADMINISTRATION, NAVAL      VB, VB15, VB21-124 (by place),
                                       VB23 (U.S.), VC (maint.), VC10,
                               VC20-258 (by place), VC20-65 (U.S.)
359.61     Personnel administration, Naval (civilian & mil.)   VB257-258.5
359.62     Administration, Naval supply & finance   VC10, VC20-258 (by place),
                                                     VC20-65 (U.S.)
359.621        Supply administration (navies)    VC260-267, VC263 (U.S.)
359.6211       Contract administration (navies)    VC267
359.6212       Procurement (naval supples &equip.)
359.622        Financial administration (navies)    VC20-258, VC500-505, VA
359.63     Naval inspection    VB220-225
359.64     Salary & wage administration, Naval    VC50-258, VC50-65 (U.S.)
359.65-66  Food, clothing, & equipment (naval admin.: SEE ALSO 359.81)
                               VC280-285+, VC283 (clothing: U.S.),
                               VC350-355 (food etc.), VC353 (U.S.)
359.67     Housing administration (navies)    VC420-425
359.69     Burial services, graves registration, & naval military mail
359.693        Mail, Military (navies)
359.699        Graves registration & burial services (navies)

359.7      BASES & STATIONS, NAVAL    V220 (gen.), VA67-750 (by place),
                   VA69-70 (U.S.), VA459-461 (G.B.), VA516-517 (Ger.), VA576-
                   577 (Rus.), VA656-657 (Japan), VC412-425 (maint.: gen.)
359.709+       Naval installations (hist. & geog. works)
359.70941-70942    Naval bases & stations (in G.B.)
359.70943      Naval bases & stations (in Ger.)
359.70944      Naval bases & stations (in Fr.)
359.70945      Naval bases & stations (in It.)
359.70947      Naval bases & stations (in Rus.)
359.70952      Naval bases & stations (in Japan)
359.709599     Naval bases & stations (in Philip.)
359.70973      Naval bases & stations (in U.S.)
359.70993      Naval bases & stations (in New Z.)
359.71     Quarters, barracks, etc. (navies)    VC420-425
359.72     Medical facilities, Naval    VG410-450, VG420 (U.S.), VG430 (G.B.)
359.73     Ordnance facilities, Naval    VF380-385
359.74     Engineering facilities, Naval    VM621-724, VM623 (U.S.), VC590-595
359.75     Supply depots, Naval    VC260-265
359.79     Land (naval bases etc.)    VC412-416

359.8      EQUIPMENT & SUPPLIES, NAVAL (develop., procure., issue, util.,
                   shipping, etc.)    VC, VF, VC10, VC20-258, VC20 (U.S.: gen.),
                   VC260-267, VF145, VF21-124, VF23 (ordnance: U.S.),
                   VF57 (G.B.), VF73 (Ger.), VF105 (Japan), VF71 (Fr.)
359.81     Clothing, equipment, food, & office supplies (navies: SEE ALSO
                   359.65-66)    VC280-345 (clothing & equip.), VC350-410 (food etc.)
359.82     Ordnance, Naval
359.8218   Artillery, Naval
359.825    Ammunition (navies)
359.8251   Delivery or charge-holding devices (naval ammun.)
359.825115     Mines (naval ammun.)
359.82513      Shells, Naval artillery
359.8254   Depth charges
359.826    Sighting & range apparatus (naval ordnance)

| 359.83 | Transport equipment & supplies, Naval (inclu. fuel, vehicles, ships [gen.], etc.) VC530-580, VC270-279, VC276, V750-895, UC320-325 |
| 359.835-836 | Warships (as equip.: develop., operation, tech. effectiveness: SEE ALSO 359.32+ for ships as units or indiv. ships) |
| 359.8351 | Armor & weapons, Naval |
| 359.8352 | Battleships (as equip.) |
| 359.8353 | Cruisers (as equip.) |
| 359.8354 | Destroyers (as equip.) |
| 359.8355 | Carriers, Aircraft (as equip.: SEE ALSO 359.94835 with works after 1988) |
| 359.8357 | Submarines, Naval (as equip.: SEE ALSO 359.93832 for titles after 1988) |
| 359.85 | Communication equipment, Naval VG70-85 |
| 359.88 | Medical supplies, Naval VG290-295 |
| | |
| 359.9 | SPECIALIST FORCES, NAVAL |
| 359.93 | Submarine forces & warfare |
| 359.933 | Submarines, Naval (as units: SEE 359.3257 for titles prior to 1989) |
| | |
| 359.938 | Equipment & supplies (naval submarines) |
| 359.93832 | Submarines, Conventionally-powered (navies: as equip.: SEE 359.8357 for works before 1989) |
| 359.94 | Naval air forces & warfare (SEE 358.4 for titles before 1989) VG90-95 |
| 359.943 | Naval aviation units |
| 359.9434 | Flights, groups, squadrons, wings, etc. (naval aviation) |
| 359.9435 | Carriers, Aircraft (as units: SEE 359.3255 for works before 1989) |
| 359.948 | Equipment & supplies (naval aviation) |
| 359.94834 | Aircraft, Naval |
| 359.94835 | Aircraft carriers (as equip.: SEE ALSO 359.8355 on titles before 1989) |

359.96 (add to .96 those #s after 355 in 355.1-.8)

| | MARINES & marine warfare VE, VE7-500+, VE15 (gen.), VE21-124 (by place), VE23 (U.S.), VE57 (G.B.), VE145-146, VG90-95 (aviation) |
| 359.961 | Life & customs (marines) VE, VE21-124, V735-743 |
| 359.9612 | Living conditions (marines) VE420-425 |
| 359.962 | Resources (marines) VA-VC |
| 359.963 | Organization & personnel (marines) VB21-124 |
| 359.9631 | Military units (marines) |
| 359.9633 | Hierarchy (marines) |
| 359.964 | Marine military ops. VE21-124 (by place) |
| 359.9642 | Tactics (marines) VE157 |
| 359.9643 | Strategy (marines) VE21-124 (by place), VE144-146 |
| 359.9647+ | Geography, Marine military (strategic & tactical) VE21-124, VA |
| 359.96479+ | Pacific (marine mil. geog.) VE123, VA730 |
| 359.965 | Training (marines) VE430-435, V411-695, V422 (U.S.) |
| 359.966 | Administration (marines) VB21-124 |
| 359.967 | Bases & camps (marines) VE21-124, VE23-25 (U.S.), VA67-68, VG90-95 (marine av.) |
| 359.968 | Matériel & equipment (marines) VE350-390, VF (ordnance) |

| | | |
|---|---|---|
| 359.97 | Coast guard (SEE ALSO 363.286 for U.S.C.G.)   VG50-55, VG53 (U.S.) | |
| 359.98 | Technical forces, Naval (engineering, communic's., etc.) | |
| 359.9812 | Artillery services, Naval | |
| 359.982 | Engineering services, Naval | |
| 359.983 | Communications services, Naval       VG70-85 | |
| 359.984 | Underwater reconnaissance & demolition (navies: inclu. frogmen) | |
| | VG86-88 (demo.), VG190 (recon.) | |
| | | |
| 600-699 | Technology, medicine, engineering, agriculture, management | |
| | T, R, QA76, S, H | |
| 620 | Engineering     T | |
| 623 | Military & marine engineering    UG, VM | |
| 623.8 | Naval engineering & seamanship    VM, VK | |
| 629.13 | Aeronautics | |
| | | |
| 623 | ENGINEERING, MILITARY & NAUTICAL        UG, VM (naval), V, | |
| | UG15 (mil.: gen.), UG21-124 (mil.: by place), | |
| | UG23 (U.S.), V750-895 (vessels) | |
| 623.003 | Dictionaries & encyclopedias (mil. & naut. engineering: SEE ALSO 603) | |
| | UG144-147 | |
| 623.009+ | Military & nautical engineering (hist. & biog. works: overall) | |
| | UG400-401 | |
| 623.04 | Military & nautical engineering (overall topics) | |
| 623.042 | Engineering, Military & nautical (optical)      UG476, UG487 | |
| 623.043 | Engineering, Military & nautical (electronic)   UG480-485 | |
| 623.044 | Engineering, Military & nautical (nuclear) | |
| 623.045 | Engineering, Military & nautical (mechanical)      UG450 | |
| 623.047 | Engineering, Military & nautical (construction)    UG460 | |
| 623.1 | Fortifications (mil. engineering)    UG400-442 | |
| 623.1-7 | Military engineering     UG | |
| 623.12 | Military fortifications, Permanent (engineering: for titles after 1988 SEE | |
| | ALSO 623.1)                UG405 | |
| 623.15 | Military fortifications, Temporary (engineering)    UG403 | |
| 623.19 | Fortifications (mil. engineering: by place: for works prior to 1989 SEE | |
| | ALSO 623.109)               UG410-442 | |
| 623.1944 | Maginot Line (Fr.: fortific's.: engineering)    UG429.F, UG430.M | |
| 623.262 | Mine laying & sweeping (mil. engnrg.: land)    UG490 | |
| 623.263 | Mine sweeping & laying (mil. engineering: marine)    V856-856.5 | |
| 623.27 | Demolition (mil. engineering)      UG37 | |
| 623.3 | Engineering, Defense     UG400-442 | |
| 623.31 | Defenses, Direct-invasion (barriers, flooding, traps, etc.) | |
| | UG375, UG403, UG407-409, UG448 (coast) | |
| 623.36 | Countermining (defense engineering: SEE ALSO 623.3)    UG490 | |
| 623.37 | Warning systems (defense engineering: SEE 623.737 for titles | |
| | after 1988) | |
| 623.38 | Bunkers, caves, shelters (defense engineering: protective construc.) | |
| 623.4 | ORDNANCE (engineering & design)          UF520-910+, | |
| | UF520-525 (gen.), UF523 (U.S.), VF (naval), VF1-580, | |
| | VF21-124 (by place), VF23 (U.S.) | |
| 623.41 | Artillery (design)      UF, UF1-910+, UF15 (gen.), UF144-145 (gen.), | |
| | UF21-124 (by place), UF23 (U.S.), VF320-325 (naval) | |
| 623.412 | Field  & rail artillery (design)    UF400-405, UF490-495 (rail) | |
| 623.417 | Coastal artillery (design)      UF450-455 | |
| 623.418 | Naval artillery (design)      VF320-325, VF323 (U.S.) | |
| 623.419 | Artillery (misc.: design: for space artil. after 1988) | |

| 623.42 | Cannons, howitzers, mortars, small rockets, other specific artillery (design) |
|---|---|
| 623.43 | Gun mounts (design) |
| 623.44 | Side arms & misc. weapons (design)      UD380-425 |
| 623.441 | Knives, bayonets, swords, etc. (design)      UD420-425, UD400 (bayonets) |
| 623.442 | Firearms, Portable (design)      UG520-525, UD380-385+ |
| 623.4424 | Automatic weapons (machine & submach. guns, auto. rifles, etc.: design)      UD390-395, UF620 (mach. g's.) |
| 623.4425 | Rifles & carbines (design)      UD390-395 |
| 623.4426 | Bazookas, grenade & rocket launchers, etc. (design)      UF628-630 |
| 623.443 | Military pistols & revolvers (design)      UD410-415 |
| 623.444 | Sidearms, Modern (design: SEE ALSO 623.441 or .44)      UD420-425, UD400 |
| 623.445 | Flame throwers, tear-gas devices, smoke mortars, other chemical weapons (design)      UG447-447.5 |
| 623.45 | Ammunition & other ruinous media (design)      UF700-770 |
| 623.451 | Shells, bombs, missiles, other delivery units with charges (design)      UF750-755 |
| 623.4511 | Grenades, mines, nuclear weapons (design) |
| 623.45114 | Grenades, Hand or rifle (design)      UF765 |
| 623.45115 | Mines (design)      UG490, V856-856.5 (naval) |
| 623.45119 | Nuclear weapons (design)      UF767, UG1282.A8 or .H, QC773.A1 or .H |
| 623.4513 | Artillery shells & other projectiles (design)      UF750-760, VF480 (naval) |
| 623.4514 | Shrapnel & other antipersonnel devices (design) UF760-765, VF490 |
| 623.4516 | Chemical & biological weapons (design)      UG447-447.6 (chem.), UG447 (gen.), UG447.5.A-Z (type gas), UG447.8 (bio.) |
| 623.4517 | High-explosive devices (torpedoes, blockbusters, etc.: design)      V850-855 (torpedoes), UF860-870 |
| 623.4518 | Armor-piercing shells & devices (design) |
| 623.4519 | Guided missiles (design)      UG1310-1315 |
| 623.45195 | Missiles, Surface-to-surface (design) |
| 623.452 | Explosives (design)      UF860-870 |
| 623.4526 | Gunpowder, cordite, & other explosives (design: inclu. propellant types)      UF870 |
| 623.4527 | High explosives (design: inclu. dynamite, nitro, TNT)      TP285, TP270-295 |
| 623.4542 | Detonators (design: fuses, percus. caps, primers, etc.)      UF780, VF510 |
| 623.4543 | Rockets (tactical: design)      UF880 |
| 623.4544 | Charges, Demolition (destructors, bangalore torpedoes, etc.: design)      UG370, UF860 |
| 623.455 | Small-arms ammunition (bullets, bazooka rockets, etc.: design)      UF700, UF740-745, UF770, TS538, VF500 |
| 623.459 | Nonexplosive agents (tear gas etc.: design)      UF780 |
| 623.4592 | Gases, poisons, other chemical agents (design) |
| 623.4594 | Biological agents (ammunition: design) |
| 623.4595 | Heat or other radiations (ammunition: design) |
| 623.46 | Ranging & sighting apparatus (ordnance: design)      UF848-856, VF520 |
| 623.48 | Maintenance & repair (ordnance)      UF350-355, UF550-560 |

| | | |
|---|---|---|
| 623.5 | BALLISTICS & GUNNERY (engineering) | UF800-830, UF820 |
| 623.51 | Ballistics (engineering) | UF820-830 |
| 623.513 | Ballistics, Interior (within bore) | UF823 |
| 623.514 | Ballistics, Exterior (environmental) | UF825 |
| 623.516 | Ballistics, Terminal (effects on targets) | |
| 623.55 | Gunnery (engineering) | UF800-805, VF144-302 |
| 623.551 | Gunnery, Land (engineering) | UF800-805 |
| 623.553 | Gunnery, Naval (engineering) | VF144-302, VF145 (gen.), VF150- |

623.553 Gunnery, Naval (engineering)	VF144-302, VF145 (gen.), VF150-
155 (hdbks.), VF160-302 (drill bks.), VF160 (U.S.)
623.555	Gunnery, Aircraft (engineering)
623.557	Target detection & selection (inclu. radar & other methods: engineering:
USE 623.46 for ranging & siting apparatae)
623.558	Firing & fire control (mil. engineering)	UF848-856, UF848 (gen.),
UF850.A-Z (range finders), VF520-530 (naval)
623.57	Recoil (mil. engineering)
623.6	MILITARY TRANSPORT ENGINEERING	UC, UC10, UC270-360,
UC270-275 (gen.)
623.61	Land transport (mil. engineering)
623.62	Construction, Road (mil. engineering)	UG330
623.63	Military railroads & rolling stock (engineering)	UC310-315,
UF490-495 (r.r. artil.), UG345 (engnrg.)
623.64	Naval facilities (bases, docks, artificial harbors, etc.: design)
V220-230, VA69-750 (by place), VA67-70 (U.S.), VM301
623.66	Air force facilities	UG633-635, UG21-124 (engnrg. by place),
UG360-390 (field engnrg.)
623.6613	Air bases (mil. design)	UG633-634.5 (U.S.), UG635 (other lands)
623.663	Runways (mil. airfields: design)
623.666	Air traffic control (mil. engineering)
623.668	Fire-fighting (mil. airfields)
623.67	Military bridges (design)	UG335, UC320-325
623.68	Military tunnels (design)	UG340
623.7	MILITARY ENGINEERING (misc.)
623.71	Reconnaisance & intelligence topography (mil. engineering) UG470-474
623.72	Photography, Military (mil. engineering)	UG476
623.73	Communications technology (mil. engineering)	UG590-613.5, UG580,
UG590, UG570-575
623.731	Signals, Visual (mil. engineering)	UG582.V5
623.7312	Semaphore, flag signals, & heliograph (mil. engineering)
UG582.S4, UG580, UG582, VK385, V300-305
623.7313	Pyrotechnic signal devices (mil. engineering)	UG580, UF860
623.7314	Blinkers & electrooptical signal devices (mil. engineering)
UG580, UG614-614.5, VK387
623.732	Telegraphy, Wire (mil. engineering)	UG600-607
623.733	Telephony, Wire (mil. engineering)	UG610-610.5
623.734	Radio & radar (mil. engineering)	UG611-612.5
623.7341	Shortwave radio (mil. engineering)
623.7342	Radiotelegraphy (mil. engineering)	UG600-607, VG76-78
623.7345	Telephones, Radio (mil. engineering)	UG611 (gen.), UG611.3 (U.S.),
UG611.5.A-Z (other lands), VG76-85
623.7348	Radar (mil. engineering)	UG612 (gen.), UG612.3 (U.S.),
UG612.5.A-Z (other places), UG612.5.G7 (G.B.), VG76-78
623.735	Television (mil. engineering)	UG613-613.5
623.737	Air-raid warning systems (design: SEE 623.37 for titles prior to 1989)
UG730-735

| 623.74 | Vehicles, Military (design: inclu. combat & support v's. & neces. ordnance) UC270-275+ |
| 623.741 | Aircraft (lighter-than-air: mil. design) UG1310-1375 |
| 623.742 | Balloons, Military (design) UG1370-1375 |
| 623.743 | Dirigibles (mil. engineering) TL659, UG1220-1225 |
| 623.7435 | Airships, Rigid (mil. engineering) |
| 623.7436-7437 | Airships, Semirigid & nonrigid (mil. engineering) |
| 623.744 | Barrage ballons & nets (design) UG1370-1375, UG730-735, UF625 |
| 623.746 | Aircraft (heavier-than-air: mil. engineering) UG1240-1245, UG630-635, TL685.3, VG90-95 |
| 623.746042 | Prop-driven aircraft (mil. design) |
| 623.746044 | Jet aircraft (mil. design) |
| 623.746047 | Helicopters, Military (design) TL716 |
| 623.746048 | Piloting (gen.: mil. engineering: SEE ALSO 623.7463 [bombers] or other types) TL710+, UG670-675 (manuals), UG700-705 (tactics) |
| 623.746049 | Aircraft components (cabins, engines, fuselages, instruments, wings, etc.) TL672-683 |
| 623.7461 | Ordnance, Aircraft (design) UG1270-1275, UF530-537 |
| 623.7462 | Training planes (design) |
| 623.7463 | Bombers & fighter-bombers (mil. engineering) TL685.3, TL686.A-Z (by manufac. or model), UG1242.B6 |
| 623.7464 | Planes, Fighter (design) TL685.3, TL686.A-Z (by manufac. or model), UG1242.F5 |
| 623.7465 | Cargo & personnel transport planes (design) TL685.7 |
| 623.7466 | Rescue aircraft (mil. engineering) |
| 623.7467 | Planes, Reconnaisance (mil. design) UG1242.R4 |
| 623.7469 | Guided aircraft (pilotless: mil. design) UG1310-1315 |
| 623.747 | Land vehicles, Motorized (mil. design) UC270-275, UC340-345 |
| 623.7472 | Personnel transport vehicles (land: mil. design) |
| 623.74722 | Jeeps (mil. design) |
| 623.74723 | Buses (mil. design) |
| 623.74724 | Ambulances (mil. design) UH500-505 |
| 623.7474 | Supply transport vehicles (land: mil. design) |
| 623.7475 | Armored cars & other combat vehicles (land: design) |
| 623.74752 | Tanks (design) UG446.5 |
| 623.75 | Safety & sanitation (mil. engineering) UH600-629.5, U380-385, VC417.5, VG470-475, VM481-482, V380-386 |
| 623.751 | Water supply (mil. engineering) UC780, VC410, VM503-505 |
| 623.753 | Sewage disposal (mil. design) UC430, VM481, VM503 |
| 623.754 | Garbage disposal (mil. engineering) |
| 623.76 | Electrical engineering (mil.) UG480, VM471-479 |
| 623.77 | Engineering, Camouflage (mil.) UG449, UG1240-1245 (air forces), V215 (ships) |
| 623.8 | NAUTICAL ENGINEERING & SEAMANSHIP VM (architec.), VK (navig.) |
| 623.81 | Naval design VM, V750-995 (warships), VM15-20 (hist.), VM21-124 (by place), VM23 (U.S.), VM57 (G.B.), VM146 (metal ships), VM156 (theory), V750, V765, V800 |
| 623.812 | Ships (design) VM297, V765 |
| 623.812045 | Submersibles (naval design) |
| 623.8125 | Warships (powered: design) V750, V765-767, V799-800 |
| 623.81255 | Carriers, Aircraft (design) V874-875 |
| 623.81257 | Submarines (naval: design) V858-859, VM365-367 |

| | | |
|---|---|---|
| 623.814 | Naval design (components & details) | VM, VM156 |
| 623.8144 | Hull design (naval architec.) | VM156 |
| 623.8147 | Powerplants (naval design) | VM731+ |
| 623.817 | Structural theory & design (naval architec.) | VM156-163 |
| 623.818 | Structural design (naval architec.: specific materials) | |
| 623.81821 | Structural design (naval architec.: steel) | VM146 |
| 623.819 | Tests (naval architec.) | |
| 623.82 | Nautical craft & types | VM, VM145 |
| 623.82001 | Theory & philosophy (nautical craft) | VM156 |
| 623.8201 | Model ships | |
| 623.8202 | Small craft (naut. engineering) | VM320-361, VM321, VM331, VM341 |
| 623.8205 | Submersibles (naut. engineering) | VM365-367 |
| 623.8208 | Maintenance & repair (naut. engineering: SEE ALSO 623.00288 after 1988) | VM763 (engines) |
| 623.821-829 | Seacraft, Modern (specific types: engineering) | |
| 623.823 | Power-driven craft (naut. engineering) | VM315 |
| 623.824 | Merchant ships, Powered (engineering) | |
| 623.8243 | Passenger ships (engineering) | VM381-385, VM383.A-Z (by ship name), VM385.A-Z (by co.) |
| 623.8245 | Cargo ships, freighters, & tankers (engineering) | VM391-395, VM455-459, VM455 (tankers) |
| 623.825 | Warships, Fuel-powered (engineering) | V750, V765, V797-799 |
| 623.8251 | Naval ordnance (engineering) | VF, VF21-124 (by place), VF23 (U.S.), VF350-355 |
| 623.8252 | Battleships (engineering) | V750 |
| 623.8253 | Cruisers (naval engineering) | V820-820.5 |
| 623.8254 | Destroyer escorts (d.e.'s) & destroyers (naval engineering) | V825-825.3 |
| 623.8255 | Aircraft carriers (engineering) | V874-874.5 |
| 623.8256 | Landing craft (naval engineering) | V895 |
| 623.8257 | Submarines, Naval (engineering) | VM365-367, V857-859 |
| 623.82572 | Naval submarines (diesel- & electric-powered: engineering) | |
| 623.8258 | Combat craft, Light (torpedo boats etc.: engineering) | V830-835 (p.t.'s), V880 |
| 623.826 | Support ships (naval engineering) | V865 |
| 623.8262 | Minelayers & minesweepers (naval engineering) | V885 (sweepers), V856-856.5 (both) |
| 623.8263 | Coast guard craft (engineering: also police boats, revenue cutters, etc.) | VM397 |
| 623.8264 | Transport ships & hospital ships (naval engineering) | UC320-325, VG450 (hosp. ships) |
| 623.8265 | Supply ships (naval engineering) | V865 |
| 623.828 | Lightships, icebreakers, other misc. ships (engineering) | VM451 (icebreakers) |
| 623.829 | Lifeboats & other manually-driven vessels (engineering) | VK1473, VM351, VM360 (inflatable) |
| 623.83 | Dry docks, shipyards, etc. (naval engineering) | VM301 |
| 623.84 | Ship hulls (naut. engineering) | VM156 |
| 623.848 | Hulls (special construc.: anti-fire & -shock, corrosion-resistant, etc.) | |
| 623.85 | Engineering systems (naut. craft: mech., electric, water, etc.) | VM471-505 |
| 623.8501 | Mechanical systems (naut. craft: engineering) | |
| 623.8503 | Electrical systems (naut. craft: engineering) | VM471-475 |
| 623.8504 | Electronic systems (naut. craft: engineering) | VM480-480.5 |
| 623.852 | Electric lighting (naut. craft: engineering) | VM491-493 |

| 623.853 | Cooling & heating (naut. craft: engineering) | VM481 |
| 623.854 | Water & sanitation (naut. craft: engineering) | VM503-505 (water), VM481-483 (san.) |

| 623.8542 | Water, Potable (naut. craft: engineering) | |
| 623.8543 | Water, Sea (naut. craft: engineering) | |
| 623.8546 | Sanitation (naut. craft: engineering) | VM481-483 |
| 623.856 | Communications systems, Naval (engineering) | VG70-85, VB255 |
| 623.8561 | Communication systems, Naval (visual: design) | V280-305 |
| 623.85612 | Communication systems, Naval (flag & semaphore: design) | V280-285, V300-305 (flags), VK385 |
| 623.85613 | Communication systems, Naval (pyrotechnical: design) | |
| 623.85614 | Communication systems, Naval (blinkers & electrooptical: design) | |
| 623.8564 | Communication systems, Naval (radar & radiocommun.: design) | VG76-78, UG610 |
| 623.85641 | Communication systems, Naval (shortwave radio: design) | |
| 623.85642 | Communication systems, Naval (radio telegraph: design) | VG70-75 |
| 623.85645 | Communication systems, Naval (radio telephone: design) | VG80-85 |
| 623.85648 | Communication systems, Naval (radar: design) | UG612-612.5, UG612.3 (U.S.) |
| 623.86 | Gear, equipment, & outfitting (nautical: engineering) | VM781-861, VM781 (gen.) |
| 623.862 | Rigging & gear, Nautical (anchors, masts, rope, rudders, sails, etc.: design) | VM791 (anchors), VC279.R6 (rope) |
| 623.863 | Instruments, Nautical (design) | VK573-587 |
| 623.865 | Safety equipment, Nautical (fire-fighting, life-saving, etc.: design) | VK1258, VK1460-1481 |
| 623.866 | Furniture (naut. design) | |
| 623.87 | Power plants (marine engineering) | VM600-779, VM600, VM623 (U.S.), VM657 (G.B.), VM673 (Ger.), VM705 (Japan) |
| 623.872 | Engines, Marine (types: design) | VM731-779, VM731 |
| 623.8722 | Steam engines (marine engineering) | VM741-749, TJ735-740 |
| 623.8723 | Internal combustion engines (marine engineering) | VM770 |
| 623.87233 | Gas-turbine engines (marine engineering) | VM740, TJ778 |
| 623.87234 | Spark-ignition engines (marine engineering) | |
| 623.87236 | Diesel engines (marine engineering) | VM770 |
| 623.87237 | Cylinders, valves, etc. (internal combustion engines: marine engineering) | VM769 |
| 623.8726 | Electric engines (marine engineering) | VM773 |
| 623.873 | Engine auxiliaries (marine engineering: boilers, blowers, pumps, propellers, etc.) | VM753-757 (propellers), VM741-750 (boilers), VM821 (pumps), VM781+ |
| 623.874 | Engine fuels, Marine | VM779 |
| 623.88 | Seamanship | VK1-587+, VK541-547 |
| 623.881 | Handling of nautical craft (gen.) | VK541 |
| 623.8812 | Small craft (naut. handling) | VK543, GV811 |
| 623.8814 | Handling of nautical craft (powered) | VK541, VK145, VK205, VB200-205 |
| 623.8825 | Warships, Fuel-powered (handling) | VB200-205 |
| 623.88252 | Battleships (handling) | V750 |
| 623.88253 | Cruisers (handling) | V820-820.5 |
| 623.88254 | Destroyers (handling) | V825-825.5 |
| 623.88255 | Aircraft carriers (handling) | V874-875 |
| 623.88257 | Submarines (navies: handling) | V857-859, V210-214 |

| 623.888 | Safety technology, Marine (plus other misc. topics) | |
| 623.8881 | Loading & unloading nautical craft (plus cargo handling) | VK235 |
| 623.8882 | Knots & splices (naut. ropes & cables) | VM533 |
| 623.8884 | Collision & grounding, Nautical (prevention) | VK371-378 |
| 623.8885 | Wrecks, Nautical (research) | VK1250+ |
| 623.8886 | Fire-fighting, Nautical (technology) | VK1258 |
| 623.8887 | Rescue ops., Nautical VK1321-1424, VK1323 (U.S.), VK1445 (gen.) | |
| 623.89 | Course navigation (marine: inclu. celestial) | VK549-572+ |
| 623.892 | Geonavigation, Marine | |
| 623.8920212 | Tables, formulae, statistics (marine geonavigation) | |
| 623.8922 | Piloting & pilot guides, Nautical VK1500-1661, VK1523- 1525 (U.S.), VK1645 (gen.), VK798-803 | |
| 623.8923 | Dead reckoning (naut. navig.) | VK572 |
| 623.8929 | Harbor piloting (inclu. approach) | VK321-369.8 |
| 623.89291-89299 | Pilot guides (geog. treatment) VK804-997 | |
| 623.892941-892942 | British Isles (pilot guides) VK827-838.5 | |
| 623.892943 | Germany (pilot guides) VK822, VK824 | |
| 623.892947 | Russia (pilot guides) VK809, VK821, VK870, VK910 (Siberia) | |
| 623.892951 | China (pilot guides) VK902-907 | |
| 623.892952 | Japan (pilot guides) VK909 | |
| 623.892973 | United States (pilot guides: gen.) VK993 | |
| 623.892974-892979 | United States (pilot guides: specific areas) VK947-948 (W. Coast), VK981-982 (E. Coast) | |
| 623.8929759 | Florida (pilot guides: Key West etc.) VK977 | |
| 623.893 | Navigational aids, Marine (electronic) VK560 | |
| 623.8932 | Navigational aids, Marine (radio: beacons, compasses, loran, radio, etc.) VK560-561, VG76-85 | |
| 623.8933 | Navigational aids, Marine (radar & microwave) VK560-561, VG76-78 | |
| 623.8938 | Navigational aids, Marine (sonar & other sound-ranging) VK388, VK560, VM480-480.5 | |
| 623.894 | Geonavigational aids, Marine (misc. non-electronic) | |
| 623.8942 | Lighthouses VK1000-1249 (gen. & by place), VK1010, VK1021-1124, VK1023-1025 (U.S.), VK1243 (U.S.: lists) | |
| 623.8943 | Lightships VK1010, VK1021-1124 | |
| 623.8944 | Beacons, buoys, etc. (marine navig.) VK1000-1249, VK1010, VK1021-1124, VK1023-1025 (U.S.) | |
| 623.8945 | Light lists (marine navig.) VK1150-1246, VK1150, VK1151-1185 (Eur.), VK1203-1209 (Asia), VK1211-1223 (Australia & Pac.), VK1241-1246 (N.Am.) | |
| 623.8949 | Tide & current tables VK600-794, VK602 (gen.), VK610- 650 (Atl.: E.), VK628-644 (Brit. Isles & Eng. Ch.), VK653- 674 (Medit.), VK702-711 (China, Japan, Asian coasts), VK715-756 (Pac.), VK727-733 (Australia & Oceania), VK741 (Am. W. Coast), VK759-792 (Atl: W., U.S., Carib.) | |

| 629.13 | AERONAUTICS |
| 629.1309 | Flight (gen. hist.) |
| 629.13091+ | Transoceanic flights |
| 629.130915 | Trans-Pacific flights |
| 629.13092 | Fliers (biog.) |
| 629.132 | Aeronautics (principles) |
| 629.1323 | Aerodynamics |
| 629.1324 | Meteorology, Aviation |

```
629.1325       Flying
629.13251          Navigation, Aerial
629.13252          Piloting, Aerial
629.1325212        Takeoff (aviation)
629.1325213        Landing (aviation)
629.133+       Aircraft (types)
629.13324          Dirigibles
629.13334          Airplanes
629.133343         Propeller-driven airplanes
629.133347         Seaplanes
629.133348         Amphibious planes
629.133349         Jet airplanes
629.133352         Helicopters
629.134        Aircraft parts & components
629.13432      Wings, Aircraft
629.13434      Fuselages, Aircraft
629.134351             Fuels, Aircraft
629.134352-134354+      Engines, Aircraft
629.1346                Maintenance & repair, Aircraft
629.135                 Instrumentation, Aircraft
629.1351       Navigational instruments (air.)
629.1352       Flight instruments
629.136        Airports
629.1363       Runways, Airport
629.1366       Air traffic control systems
629.1368       Fire-fighting equipment, Airport


900-999+       HISTORY & GEOGRAPHY       G (geog.), D-F
900-909        Geography & history (gen.)     G, C-D
910-919        Geography & travel       G, D-F
920-929        Biography (sometimes placed with country #s or topical #s in 930-999 or
                   000 999)                    C-F
930-939        Ancient history      C-F
940-949        Europe      D-DR
940.3-.499         Great War (1914-18)      D501-680
940.53-5499        Second World War (1939-45)       D731-838
950-959        Asia      DS
960-969        Africa      DT
970-979        North America & America   E-F
980-989        South America    F
990-999        History (misc. areas: Oceania, Atlantic islands, Arctic, extraterr.
                   worlds, etc.)       C-F, G, Q
993-996            Oceanica    DU


900-909        GEOGRAPHY & HISTORY (gen.)       G, C-D
903            Dictionaries & encyclopedias (history: gen.)      D9
909.8          World history (gen.: 1800-)       D299, D395
909.82         1900-1999 (20th c.: gen. hist.)       D421, D443
909.821            1900-1919 (gen. hist.)       D421, D521 (WWI: gen.)
909.822            1920-1929 (gen. hist.)       D653, D655-659, D720,
                                                D723-728 (1919-39)
909.823            1930-1939 (gen. hist.)     D720, D723-728
909.824            1940-1949 (gen. hist.)     D743 (WWII: gen.), D825, D840
```

| | | |
|---|---|---|
| 910-919 | TRAVEL & GEOGRAPHY     G (geog.), D-F (descr. & travel) | |
| 912 | MAPS & ATLASES     G | |
| 912.4 | Europe (maps & atlases) | G1796+ |
| 912.5 | Asia (maps & atlases) | G2200+ |
| 912.73 | United States (maps & atlases)     G1200+, G1201 | |
| 912.9 | Pacific Ocean area (maps & atlases)     G2860-3012 | |
| 913-919 | GEOGRAPHY & TRAVEL (by locale) | |
| 914 | EUROPE (geog. & travel)     D901-980, D907 (gen.), D921 (1901-50) | |
| 914.1 | Great Britain & Ireland (geog. & travel)     DA11, DA600-668, DA969-987 (Ire.) | |
| 914.2 | England (geog. & travel)     DA600-668, DA600 (gen.), DA630 (1901-45) | |
| 914.3 | Central Europe & Germany (geog. & travel)     DD21-43, DB21-27, D901-980 | |
| 914.31-35 | Germany (geog. & travel)     DD21-43, DD42 (1919-45) | |
| 914.36 | Austria (geog. & travel)     DB21-27, DB26 (1901-45) | |
| 914.37 | Czechoslovakia (geog. & travel)     DB191 (titles prior to 1979-80), DB2020 | |
| 914.38 | Poland (geog. & travel)     DK407 (1867-1945) | |
| 914.39 | Hungary (geog. & travel)     DB916-917 | |
| 914.4 | France (geog. & travel)     DC28-45 | |
| 914.5 | Italy (geog. & travel)     DG428-429 | |
| 914.581-582 | Sicily (geog. & travel)     DG864 | |
| 914.585 | Malta (geog. & travel)     DG989 | |
| 914.6 | Spain & Portugal (geog. & travel)     DP42, DP525 (Port.) | |
| 914.7 | Soviet Union & Eur. Russia (geog. & travel)     DK27 | |
| 914.76 | White Russia & Western U.S.S.R. (geog. & travel) | |
| 914.77 | Black Sea area (geog. & travel)     DK511.C7 | |
| 914.771 | Ukraine (geog. & travel) | |
| 914.79 | Caucasus (geog. & travel) | |
| 914.8 | Scandinavia (geog. & travel)     DL10 | |
| 914.81-84 | Norway (geog. & travel)     DL418 | |
| 914.891-895 | Denmark (geog. & travel)     DL118 | |
| 914.897 | Finland (geog. & travel: SEE ALSO 914.71 for earlier works)     DK450, DL1015.2 (books cataloged after 1969-70) | |
| 914.92 | Holland (geog. & travel)     DJ39 | |
| 914.931-934 | Belgium (geog. & travel)     DH433 | |
| 914.94 | Switzerland (geog. & travel)     DQ24 | |
| 914.95 | Greece (geog. & travel)     DF726 | |
| 914.96 | Balkan Peninsula (geog. & travel)    DR15, DR1221 (later works) | |
| 914.965 | Albania (geog. & travel)     DR701.S5, DR917 (later books) | |
| 914.971-976 | Yugoslavia (geog. & travel)     DR309, DR1221 (later books) | |
| 914.977 | Bulgaria (geog. & travel)     DR60 (1879-1950) | |
| 914.98 | Rumania (geog. & travel)     DR209 (1866-1950) | |
| 914.99 | Crete & Aegean Islands (geog. & travel)     DF901.C8 (Crete), .C9 (Cyclades), DS52-53, DS53.A-Z (by island), DS53.R4-6 (Rhodes) | |
| 915 | ASIA (geog. & travel)     DS9 (1901-50) | |
| 915.1 | China (geog. & travel)     DS710 (1901-48) | |
| 915.18 | Manchuria (geog. & travel)     DS784 | |
| 915.19 | Korea (geog. & travel)     DS902 | |
| 915.2 | Japan (geog. & travel)     DS810 (1901-45) | |
| 915.3 | Arabian Peninsula (geog. & travel)     DS207 | |
| 915.4 | India, Pakistan, & Ceylon (geog. & travel)     DS335, DS413 | |
| 915.5 | Persia (geog. & travel)     DS258 | |

| | | |
|---|---|---|
| 915.6 | Middle East (geog. & travel) DS49-49.5 | |
| 915.61-66 | Turkey & Cyprus (geog. & travel) | DR428, DS54 (Cyprus) |
| 915.67 | Iraq (geog. & travel) DS70.6, DS79+ | |
| 915.69 | Mediterranean, Eastern (geog. & travel) | DS44, DS49, D972-973 |
| 915.691 | Syria (geog. & travel) DS94 | |
| 915.694 | Palestine (geog. & travel) DS107.3 | |
| 915.7 | Siberia & Asiatic Russia (geog. & travel) | DK755, DK584 (C.Asia) |
| 915.9 | Southeast Asia (geog. & travel) DS508 | |
| 915.91 | Burma (geog. & travel) DS485.B74-892, DS527.6 (later bks.) | |
| 915.97 | Vietnam (geog. & travel) DS556.36 | |
| 915.98 | Indonesia (geog. & travel) DS619 | |
| 915.99 | Philippines (geog. & travel) DS659 | |
| 915.991 | Luzon (geog. & travel) DS688.L9 | |
| 915.997 | Mindanao (geog. & travel) DS688.M2 | |
| 916 | AFRICA (geog. & travel) DT55 (1901-50) | |
| 916.1 | Tunisia & Libya (geog. & travel) | |
| 916.2 | Egypt & Sudan (geog. & travel) DT55 (Egypt), DT124 | |
| 916.3 | Ethiopia (geog. & travel) DT378 | |
| 916.4 | Africa, Northwest (geog. & travel: Morocco, Canary Islands, etc.) | |
| | | DT165, DT310 (Mor.) |
| 916.5 | Algeria (geog. & travel) DT280 | |
| 917 | NORTH AMERICA (geog. & travel) E41, E27 | |
| 917.1 | Canada (geog. & travel) F1015 | |
| 917.2 | Mexico & Central America (geog. & travel) | F1215 (Mexico), |
| | | F1432 (C.Am.) |
| 917.29 | Bermuda & West Indies (geog. & travel) F1611 | |
| 917.3 | United States (geog. & travel: overall) E169 (1914-45) | |
| 917.4-9 | United States (geog. & travel: states, areas, & towns) | |
| 917.4 | New England & Middle Atlantic states (geog. & travel) | F2.3, F4, |
| | | F9 (1865-1950), F106 (Mid.Atl.) |
| 917.5 | South Atlantic states & Florida (geog. & travel) | F106, |
| | | F207.3 (S.Atl.), F309.3 (Fla.) |
| 917.53 | District of Columbia (geog. & travel) F192.3, F194, F199 | |
| 917.59 | Florida (geog. & travel) F309.3, F316 | |
| 917.6 | Gulf Coast & South Central states (geog. & travel) | F296 (Gulf), F396 |
| 917.64 | Texas (geog. & travel) F384.3, F391 | |
| 917.7 | Great Lakes & North Central states (geog. & travel) F477.3 (Old NW.), | |
| | | F551 (Lakes area in gen.), F484.5 |
| 917.8 | Great Plains & American West (geog. & travel) F591 | |
| 917.9 | Pacific Coast & Far West (U.S.: geog. & travel) F851 | |
| 917.94 | California (geog. & travel) F859.3, F861, F866 (hist.: 1869-1950) | |
| 918 | SOUTH AMERICA (geog. & travel) F2211, F2223, F2236-2237 | |
| 919 | PACIFIC OCEAN & MISC. (geog. & travel) DU22 | |
| 919.31 | New Zealand (geog. & travel) DU411 | |
| 919.32-37 | Melanesia (geog. & travel) | |
| 919.35 | Solomon Islands (geog. & travel) | |
| 919.36 | Bismarck Archipelago (geog. & travel) | |
| 919.4 | Australia (geog. & travel) DU104 | |
| 919.5 | New Guinea (geog. & travel) DU740 | |
| 919.6 | Pacific Ocean areas (misc.: geog. & travel) | |
| 919.65 | Micronesia (geog. & travel) DU500 | |
| 919.66-67 | Caroline & Mariana Islands (geog. & travel) | |
| 919.68 | Gilbert, Marshall, & related islands (geog. & travel) | |
| 919.69 | Hawaiian Islands (geog. & travel) DU623 | |

| 920-929 | BIOGRAPHY & GENEALOGY        CT (gen. or collec.), D-F, other specific classes for specialists or famous people in those areas |
| 920 | BIOGRAPHY (gen.: SOMETIMES '92' or 'B' are used, followed by particular individuals in alphabetical order by last name. These may also be placed in specific discipline number areas followed by the standard subdivision, '092'. So, 355.0092 is for mil. biog.) |
| 923 | BIOGRAPHY (social sciences: gov., law, commerce, etc.) |
| 923.1 | HEADS OF STATE (biog.) |
| 923.14 | Europe (biog.: heads of state)        D107 |
| 923.141-142 | Great Britain (biog.: heads of state) |
| 923.143 | Germany (biog.: heads of state) |
| 923.144 | France (biog.: heads of state) |
| 923.145 | Italy (biog.: heads of state) |
| 923.147 | Russia (biog.: heads of state) |
| 923.15 | Asia (biog.: heads of state)        DS32 (collective) |
| 923.151 | China (biog.: heads of state) |
| 923.152 | Japan (biog.: heads of state) |
| 923.173 | United States (biog.: heads of state)        E176.1 (Presidents: collective) |
| 923.5 | MILITARY BIOGRAPHY (SEE ALSO 355.0092, 940.3+, .53+, etc.) |
|  | U51-55 |
| 923.54 | Biography, Military (Eur.) |
| 923.541-542 | Military biography (G.B.)        DA54 (collec.), DA69.3.A-Z (20th c.: indiv.), DA89.1.A-Z (naval: 20th c.: indiv.), U55.G7 |
| 923.543 | Military biography (Ger.)        DD100 (group) |
| 923.547 | Military biography (Rus.)        DK50.5-8 |
| 923.55 | Military biography (Asia) |
| 923.551 | Military biography (China)        DS738 (group) |
| 923.552 | Military biography (Japan)        DS838-839 |
| 923.573 | Military biography (U.S.)        E181 (mil.: collec.), E182 (naval: collec.), U52-53 |
| 929 | GENEALOGY |
| 929.7 | Royal houses (genealogy) |
| 929.72 | Genealogy (royal houses: G.B.: hist. treatment poss. or in 941+)        DA28.1-.35, CS418-424 |
| 940-949 | EUROPE & THE WORLD WARS        D-DR, D501-651, D731-838 |
| 940 | EUROPE & W. EUROPE (gen.)        D-DR |
| 940.092 | Biography (Eur.: group)        D106-110 (group) |
| 940.2 | Western Europe & Europe (1453+)        D208, D217 |
| 940.28 | Europe (1789-1914)        D299, D359 (1801-1914) |
| 940.288 | Europe (1900-14)        D424, D443 (pol. & dipl.) |
| 940.3-.499 | WORLD WAR I (1914-18)        D501-680 |
| 940.3 | European War (1914-18: gen.)        D521 |
| 940.31 | First World War (econ., polit., social hist.)        D443, D453, D511-523, D610 |
| 940.311 | Causes (WWI)        D511 |
| 940.3112 | Causes (WWI: polit. & dipl.)        D610-621, D610 |
| 940.3113 | Causes (WWI: econ.)        D635 |
| 940.3114 | Causes (WWI: psychological & social) |
| 940.312 | Peace efforts (WWI: preserve or restore)        D613, D641-644+ (armistice) |

| 940.314 | Results (WWI: dipl., econ., & polit.: SEE ALSO specific country #s) |
| | D511-20, D511, D610-611, D643-644+ |
| 940.3141 | Conferences & treaties (WWI)    D642-647 |
| 940.3142 | Treaties (WWI: results)    D511-20 |
| 940.31422 | Reparations (WWI)    D648-649 |
| 940.31424 | Post-WWI territorial questions  D650, D651.A-Z |
| 940.31426 | Mandates (post-WWI)    D651 |
| 940.3144 | Post-WWI reconstruction  D652-659, D653 (gen.), D657-658 (U.S.), |
| | D659.A-Z (other places) |
| 940.315 | Social groups (WWI)    D639.A-Z |
| 940.31503 | Ethnic or racial groups (WWI) |
| 940.315042 | World War I & women    D639.W7, JX1965 |
| 940.3152 | Religious groups & officials (WWI)  D639.R4, D622 (Cath. Church) |
| 940.3155 | Scientists (WWI)    D639.S2 |
| 940.3159 | Refugees (WWI)    D637, D638.A-Z (by place) |
| 940.316 | Noncombatants, pacifists, sympathizers, etc. (WWI) |
| 940.3161 | Orphans, children, similar noncombatants (WWI)    D639.C4 |
| 940.3162 | Pacifists (WWI)    D613, UB342.A-Z (by place) |
| 940.3163 | Sympathizers, Enemy (WWI)    D570.8.A6 (U.S.), D636.A-Z (by locale) |
| 940.32 | Diplomatic history (WWI)    D610-621, D610 (gen.) |
| 940.322 | Allies & associates (WWI: dipl. hist.)    D511, D459 (Triple Entente) |
| 940.324 | Central Powers (WWI: dipl. hist.)    D511, D458 (Triple Alliance) |
| 940.325 | Neutrals (WWI: dipl. hist.)    D611, D639.N |
| 940.332 | Allies (WWI: gen. particip.)    D544 |
| 940.334 | Central Powers (WWI: gen. particip.)    D531 |
| 940.335 | Neutrals (WWI: gen. particip.)    D639.N, D615 (Belgium), |
| | D611 |
| 940.34-39 | World War I (gen. particip.: by country: inclu. mobilization) |
| 940.341-342 | World War I (gen. particip.: G.B.)    D546, DA577 |
| 940.343 | World War I (gen. particip.: Ger.)    D531, DD228.8 |
| 940.344 | World War I (gen. particip.: Fr.)    D548, DC387 |
| 940.345 | World War I (gen. particip.: It.)    D569, DG570 |
| 940.347 | World War I (gen. particip.: Rus.)    D550, DK264.8 |
| 940.371 | World War I (gen. particip.: Can.)    D547.C2 |
| 940.373-379 | World War I (gen. particip.: U.S.)    D570 |
| 940.3931 | World War I (gen. particip.: New Z.: SEE ALSO 940.393 for titles |
| | after 1988)    D547.N5 |
| 940.394 | World War I (gen. particip.: Australia)    D547.A8 |
| 940.4 | Military history (WWI)    D521 (gen.), D529-608 |
| 940.4003 | Encyclopedias & dictionaries (WWI) |
| | D510, D521, D523 |
| 940.4005 | Magazines & serial pubns. (WWI)    D501 |
| 940.4006 | Societies & associations (WWI) |
| | D502, D504 (congresses) |
| 940.40074 | Exhibitions, museums, etc. (WWI)    D503 |
| 940.401 | Strategy (WWI)    D521, D530, D550 |
| 940.4012 | Strategy (WWI: Allies)    D544, D570 |
| 940.4013 | Strategy (WWI: Central Powers)    D531 |
| 940.402 | World War I (mobilization: SEE 940.34-39 for particular countries) |
| 940.403 | Racial minorities (WWI: soldiers)    D547.N4 (blacks: G.B.), |
| | D570.8.l6 (Indians: U.S.), D639.N4 (blacks) |
| 940.405 | Repression & atrocities (WWI)    D625 (gen.), |
| | D626.A-Z (by place) |

| 940.409 | Military history (WWI: by place) | |
|---|---|---|
| 940.40941-40942 | Great Britain (WWI: mil. hist.) | D546-547 |
| 940.40943 | Germany & Austria (WWI: mil. hist.) | D531-538 (Ger.), |
| | | D531 (gen.), D539 (Austria) |
| 940.40944 | France (WWI: mil. hist.) | D548-549 |
| 940.40945 | Italy (WWI: mil. hist.) | D569 |
| 940.40947 | Russia (WWI: mil. hist.) | D550 |
| 940.409571 | Military history (WWI: Can.) | D547.C2 |
| 940.40973 | Military history (WWI: U.S.) | D570 |
| 940.40993 | Military history (WWI: New Z.: SEE ALSO 940.409931 for titles | |
| | earlier than 1989) | D547.N5 |
| 940.40994 | Military history (WWI: Australia) | D547.A8 |
| 940.41 | World War I (mil. units & ops.: gen.) | D521 |
| 940.412-413+ | Military history (WWI: units & ops.: by country: inclu. structure, | |
| | hist., registers, etc.) | D532-578, D608 |
| 940.412+ | World War I (Allies & associates: mil. units & ops.) | D544-550, |
| | | D569-570 |
| 940.41241 | Military history (WWI: units & ops.: G.B.) | D546-546.55+, D547 |
| 940.413+ | World War I (Central Powers: mil. units & ops.) | D531-540, D566 |
| 940.41343 | Military history (WWI: units & ops.: Ger.) | D531-538 |
| 940.414 | Fronts (WWI: Eur.) | D521, D530 (W.), D550 (E.) |
| 940.4147 | Fronts (WWI: Rus. & E. in gen.) | D550, D551 (Rus.-Ger.-Austrian), |
| | | D556 (Rus.-Austrian), D560 (Balkan) |
| 940.42 | Battles & campaigns, Land (WWI: 1914-16) | |
| 940.43 | Battles & campaigns, Land (WWI: 1917-18) | |
| 940.439 | World War I (Armistice) | D641 |
| 940.44 | Battles & campaigns, Aerial (WWI) | D600-607 |
| 940.449 | Aerial ops. (WWI: particular countries) | |
| 940.44941 | Aerial ops. (WWI: G.B.) | D602 |
| 940.44943 | Aerial ops. (WWI: Ger.) | D604 |
| 940.44973 | Aerial ops. (WWI: U.S.) | D606, D570.6-7 (squadrons) |
| 940.45 | Battles & campaigns, Naval (WWI) | D580-595, D580 (gen.) |
| 940.451 | World War I (submarine ops.) | D590-595, D590 (gen.) |
| 940.4512 | Submarine ops. (WWI: Ger.) | D591 (gen.), |
| | | D592.A-Z (by ship, battle, etc.) |
| 940.4513 | Submarine ops. (WWI: Allies) | D590 |
| 940.4516 | World War I (antisub. ops.) | D580-589, D590 |
| 940.452 | Blockades & blockade-running (WWI) | D581 |
| 940.453+ | Naval bases (WWI) | D581-589 |
| 940.45341 | Naval bases (WWI: in G.B.) | |
| 940.459 | World War I (naval ops.: particular countries) | D580-589 |
| 940.45941 | Naval ops. (WWI: G.B.) | D581-582, VA458 |
| 940.45943 | Naval ops. (WWI: Ger.) | D581-582 |
| 940.45973 | Naval ops. (WWI: U.S.) | D589.U5-8 |
| 940.45994 | Naval ops. (WWI: Australia) | D589.A |
| 940.46 | Commemorations, celebrations, & memorials (WWI: gen.) | |
| | | D663-680, D663 (gen.) |
| 940.465 | Cemeteries & monuments (WWI) | D639.D4 (cem's.), |
| | D663-680 (mon's.), D675.W2 (Tomb of Unkn. Soldier: Wash. D.C.) | |
| 940.46547 | Monuments & cemeteries (WWI: Rus.) | D680.R |
| 940.467 | Rolls of honored & dead (WWI) | D609, D609.A2 (gen.) |
| 940.46741 | Honored & dead (WWI: G.B.: rolls) | D609.G7 |
| 940.46743 | Honored & dead (WWI: Ger.: rolls) | D609.G3 |

| | | |
|---|---|---|
| 940.47 | Social services, prisons, & medical services (WWI) | |
| 940.472 | Prisoner-of-war camps & internment (WWI) | D627 |
| 940.47241-47242 | P.O.W. camps & internment centers (WWI: in G.B.) | D627.G7 |
| 940.47243 | P.O.W. camps & internment centers (WWI: in Ger.) | D627.G3 |
| 940.47247 | P.O.W. camps & internment centers (WWI: in Rus.) | D627.R9 |
| 940.47273 | Internment centers & P.O.W. camps (WWI: in U.S.) | D627.U6+ |
| 940.475 | World War I (medical srvcs.) | D628 (gen.), D629.A-Z (by country), D630.A-Z (biog.) |
| 940.4752 | Sanitary control (WWI: med. srvcs.) | |
| 940.47547 | Medical services (WWI: Rus.) | D629.R9 |
| 940.47573 | Medical services (WWI: U.S.) | D629.U6-8 |
| 940.4763+ | Hospitals (WWI: in particular places) | D629.A-Z |
| 940.4764-4769 | Hospitals (WWI: operated by particular countries) | |
| 940.477 | Welfare & relief services (WWI) | D637-638 |
| 940.4778+ | Welfare & relief services (WWI: provided by specific countries) | D638.A-Z |
| 940.477841 | Welfare & relief services (WWI: by G.B.) | D638.G7 |
| 940.4779+ | Welfare & relief services (WWI: in specific places) | D638.A-Z, D657-658 (Reconstruc. in U.S.), D659.A-Z (by place) |
| 940.477943 | Relief & welfare services (WWI: in Ger.) | D638.G3, D659.G3 |
| 940.477947 | Relief & welfare services (WWI: in Rus.) | D638.R9, D659.R9 |
| 940.48 | World War I (misc. topics) | |
| 940.481+ | Personal accounts, Allied (WWI) | D640, D570.9 (U.S.) |
| 940.482+ | Personal accounts, Central Power (WWI) | D640, D531-540 |
| 940.483+ | Allies (WWI: mil. & naval life & customs) | D544 |
| 940.48373 | Military & naval life & customs (WWI: U.S.) | D570, D589.U6-7 (naval), D606 (aerial) |
| 940.484 | Central Powers (WWI: mil. & naval life & customs) | |
| 940.48443 | Military & naval life & customs (WWI: Ger.) | D532-538, D581-582 (naval), D604 (aerial) |
| 940.485 | Unconventional warfare (WWI: espionage, intell., infilt., sabotage, etc.) | D639.S7-8 |
| 940.486 | Unconventional warfare, Allied (WWI: espionage, intell., infilt., sabotage, etc.) | |
| 940.48641 | Intelligence, espionage, & unconventional warfare (WWI: G.B.) | |
| 940.487 | Unconventional warfare, Central Power (WWI) | |
| 940.48743 | Intelligence, espionage, & unconventional warfare (WWI: Ger.) | D619.3-5 (in U.S.) |
| 940.488 | News & propaganda (WWI) | D639.P6-7, D631-633, D619.3 |
| 940.4886 | Propaganda, Allied (WWI) | |
| 940.488673 | Propaganda, American (WWI: U.S.) | D632, D639.P7.U5+ |
| 940.4887 | Propaganda, Central Power (WWI) | |
| 940.488743 | Propaganda, German (WWI) | D639.P7.G3, D619.3 (in U.S.) |
| 940.4889+ | News & propaganda (WWI: in specific countries) | |
| 940.488943 | News & propaganda (WWI: in Ger.) | |
| 940.488947 | News & propaganda (WWI: in Rus.) | |
| | | |
| 940.5 | Europe (20th c. or 1918-) | D424-425, D720 (1919-39), D431-443, D551, D720-728 |
| 940.51 | Europe (1918-29) | |
| 940.52 | Europe (1930-39) | |

| 940.53-5499 | WORLD WAR II (1939-45) | D731-838 |
| 940.53 | World War II (1939-45: gen.: inclu. overall works on Sino-Japanese War [1937-45]) | D743 |
| 940.531 | Second World War (econ., polit., social hist.) | D421, D443, D720-728, D743, D748 |
| 940.5311 | Causes (WWII: gen.) | D741 (gen.), D742.A-Z (by country), D720-728 |
| 940.53112 | Causes (WWII: dipl. & polit.) | D741-742, D443, D727, D748 |
| 940.53113 | Causes (WWII: econ.) | D741-742, D720-728, D421, D800 |
| 940.53114 | Causes (WWII: psychological & social) | D741-742, D726, D421 |
| 940.5312 | Peace efforts (WWII: preserve or restore) | D749, D748-754 |
| 940.5314 | Results (WWII: dipl., econ, & polit.: SEE ALSO specific country #s) D743, D748-754, D825-829 (Reconstruction), D814-821 (peace, reparations, terr. ?s, etc.), D840+ | |
| 940.53141 | Conferences & treaties (WWII) | |
| 940.53142 | Treaties (WWII: results) | |
| 940.531422 | Reparations (WWII) | |
| 940.531424 | Post-WWII territorial questions | |
| 940.531425 | New countries (post-WWII: formation) | |
| 940.531426 | Mandates (post-WWII) | |
| 940.53144 | Post-WWII reconstruction D824-829, D825 (gen.), D827-828 (U.S.), D829.A-Z (by country, nationality, etc.) | |
| 940.5315+ | Social groups (WWII) | |
| 940.531503 | Ethnic or racial groups (WWII) | |
| 940.531503924 | Jews (WWII: SEE ALSO 940.5315296) | D810.J4, D804.G4, D829.J4, DS135 |
| 940.53150396073 | Afro-Americans (WWII) | E185, D810.N4 |
| 940.5315042 | World War II & women | D810.W7 |
| 940.5315062 | Wealthy & upper classes (WWII) | D800 |
| 940.5315097 | Journalists & publishers (WWII) | D798 (gen.), D799.A-Z (by place) |
| 940.53152 | Religious groups & officials (WWII) | D810.C5-68 |
| 940.5315296 | Jewish groups (WWII: SEE ALSO 940.531503924) | D810.J4 |
| 940.5315355 | Military personnel (WWII) | |
| 940.5315372 | Teachers (WWII) | D810.E2-5 |
| 940.53155 | Scientists (WWII) | D810.S2 |
| 940.53156 | Scientists, Applied (WWII) | |
| 940.531562 | Engineers (WWII) | D795 |
| 940.531563 | Farmers (WWII) | HD9006 (U.S.) |
| 940.53157 | Artists (WWII) | D810.A7 |
| 940.531578 | Musicians (WWII) | D810.A7 or .M |
| 940.5315791-5315793 | Entertainers (WWII) | D810.E8 |
| 940.5315796 | Athletes (WWII) | D810.E8 |
| 940.53158 | Writers (WWII) | D810.A7 |
| 940.53159 | Refugees (WWII) | D808, D809.A-Z (by place) |
| 940.5316 | Noncombatants, pacifists, sympathizers, etc. (WWII) | |
| 940.53161 | Orphans, children, similar noncombatants (WWII) | D810.C4 |
| 940.53162 | Pacifists (WWII) | D810.C82, UB342.A-Z (by place) |
| 940.53163 | Sympathizers, Enemy (WWII) | D769.8.A6 (U.S.), D801.A2 (gen.), D801.A3-Z (by place except U.S.) |

| | |
|---|---|
| 940.5317 | Concentration camps, internment centers, labor camps (WWII) |
| 940.531709+ | Internment centers, labor & concentration camps (WWII: geog. treatment: by controlling country: SEE 940.5472+ for works prior to 1989 on intern. ctrs.) |
| 940.53170943 | Labor camps, internment centers, concentration camps (WWII: Ger.) |
| 940.53174-53179 | Concentration camps & internment centers (WWII: by location) |
| 940.5317438 | Auschwitz Concentration Camp (Poland) |
| 940.531779487 | Manzanar Internment Camp (Calif.) |
| 940.5318 | Holocaust (WWII: inclu. exterm. camps) |
| 940.532 | World War II (dipl. hist.)        D748-754, D748 (gen.) |
| 940.5322+ | Allies & anti-Axis exile govs. or nat. groups (WWII: dipl. hist.)        D748 |
| 940.532241 | Diplomacy (WWII: G.B.)        D750 |
| 940.532244 | Diplomacy (WWII: Fr.)        D752 |
| 940.532247 | Russia (WWII: dipl. hist.)        D754.R9 or .S65 (Sov. U.) |
| 940.5322481 | Norway (WWII: dipl. hist.)        D754.N8 |
| 940.5322493 | Belgium (WWII: dipl. hist.)        D754.B |
| 940.5322495 | Greece (WWII: dipl. hist.)        D754.G |
| 940.5322497 | Diplomacy (WWII: Yug.)        D754.Y |
| 940.532251 | China (WWII: dipl. hist.)        D754.C5 |
| 940.532254 | India (WWII: dipl. hist.)        D754.I4 |
| 940.5322599 | Philippines (WWII: dipl. hist.: puppet gov. might be with Axis Powers at 940.5324599)        D754.P5 |
| 940.532268 | South Africa (WWII: dipl. hist.)        D754.S |
| 940.532271 | Canada (WWII: dipl. hist.)        D754.C2 |
| 940.532273 | Diplomacy (WWII: U.S.)        D753 |
| 940.532282 | Argentina (WWII: dipl. hist.)        D754.A |
| 940.5322892 | Paraguay (WWII: dipl. hist.: might ALSO be with Neutrals at 940.5325892)        D754.P |
| 940.5322931 | New Zealand (WWII: dipl. hist.: titles after 1988 may be at 940.532293)        D754.N45 |
| 940.532294 | Australia (WWII: dipl. hist.)        D754.A8 |
| 940.5324+ | Axis Powers (WWII: dipl. hist.)        D748 |
| 940.532443 | Diplomacy (WWII: Ger.)        D751 |
| 940.532444 | Vichy France (WWII: dipl. hist.: perhaps ALSO 940.532544)        D752 |
| 940.532445 | Italy (WWII: dipl. hist.)        D754.I8 |
| 940.5325 | Neutrals (WWII: dipl. hist.) |
| 940.5325415 | Diplomacy (WWII: Ire.: could ALSO be at 940.5322415 with Allies or at .5324415 with Axis)        D754.I5-7 |
| 940.5325485 | Diplomacy (WWII: Sweden)        D754.S8 |
| 940.5325494 | Switzerland (WWII: dipl. hist.)        D754.S9 |
| 940.532572 | Mexico (WWII: dipl. hist.: could be with Allies at 940.532272)        D754.M |
| 940.532581 | Brazil (WWII: dipl. hist.)        D754.B |
| 940.532582 | Argentina (WWII: dipl. hist.: might ALSO be at 940.532482 with Axis)        D754.A7 |
| 940.5325895 | Uruguay (WWII: dipl. hist.: could ALSO be at 940.5324895 with Axis)        D754.U |

| | | |
|---|---|---|
| 940.533 | World War II (gen. particip.: country groups, inclu. nat. groups, pro- & anti-Axis nat. groups, mobilization) | |
| 940.5332 | United Nations (WWII: Allies: gen. particip.) | D743, D748 |
| 940.5334 | Axis (WWII: gen. particip.) | D743, D748 |
| 940.5335 | Neutral nations (WWII: gen. particip.) | D743, D749 |
| 940.5336 | Occupied countries (WWII: gen. particip.) | D802.A2 |
| 940.5337 | Captured nations (WWII: Axis-occup'd.: gen. particip.) | |
| 940.5338 | Captured nations (WWII: Allied-occup'd.: gen. particip.) | |
| 940.534-539 | World War II (gen. particip.: by country: inclu. exile govs., undergr. move's., pro- & anti-Axis nat. groups, mobilization, etc.) | |
| 940.5341-5342 | British Isles (WWII: gen. particip.) | |
| 940.5341 | World War II (gen. particip.: G.B.) | D750, D759, DA587 |
| 940.53411 | Scotland (WWII: gen. particip.) | |
| 940.53415 | Ireland (WWII: gen. particip.) | |
| 940.5342 | England & Wales (WWII: gen. particip.) | |
| 940.53421 | World War II (gen. particip.: London, Eng.) | D760.8.L7, DA684 |
| 940.534234 | Channel Islands (Eng.: WWII: gen. particip.) | DA670.C4, .J5 (Jersey), .G8-9 (Guernsey) |
| 940.5343 | World War II (gen. particip.: Ger.) | D751, D757, DD253-256.5 |
| 940.53436 | World War II (gen. particip.: Austria & Liech.) | D765.4 (Austria), DB99, D765.45.L (Liech.), DB540.5 |
| 940.53437 | Czechoslovakia (WWII: gen. particip.) | D765.5, DB215.3, DB2205-2211, DB2206 |
| 940.53438 | Poland (WWII: gen. particip.) | D765, DK441 |
| 940.53439 | World War II (gen. particip.: Hungary) | D765.56, DB955 |
| 940.5344 | World War II (gen. particip.: Fr. & Monaco) | D752, D761, DC397 |
| 940.534436 | World War II (gen. particip.: Paris, Fr. area) | D762.P3, DC737+ |
| 940.5345 | World War II (gen. particip.: It.) | D763.I8, DG571-572 |
| 940.5345634 | Vatican City (Rome: WWII: gen. particip.) | D763.I82.V or .R, D810.C6, DG800 |
| 940.5346 | Spain (WWII: gen. particip.) | D754.S7, DP270-271 |
| 940.53469 | Portugal (WWII: gen. particip.) | D754.P8, DP680 |
| 940.5347 | World War II (gen. particip.: Rus.) | D764, D754.R9 or .S65, DK267-273, DK273 |
| 940.53481 | World War II (gen. particip.: Nor.) | D763.N6-62, DL532 |
| 940.53485 | Sweden (WWII: gen. particip.) | D754.S8, DL868.5-870 |
| 940.53489 | World War II (gen. particip.: Denmark & Fin.) | D763.D4-42, DL256 (Den.) |
| 940.534897 | World War II (gen. particip.: Finland: SEE ALSO 940.53471 for some works before 1980) | D754.F5, D765.3, DK459.45+, DL1090-1105+ (works after about 1980), DL1090, DL1097 |
| 940.53492 | Holland (WWII: gen. particip.) | DL763.N4-42, DJ287 |
| 940.53493 | World War II (gen. particip.: Belgium) | D763.B4-42, DH687 |
| 940.534935 | World War II (gen. particip.: Luxemb.) | D763.L9, DH916 |
| 940.53494 | Switzerland (WWII: gen. particip.) | D754.S9, DQ201 |
| 940.53495 | World War II (gen. particip.: Greece) | D766.3-32, DF726 |
| 940.534965 | World War II (gen. particip.: Albania) | D766.7.A4, DR701.S8-86, DR974 (later works after 1980?) |
| 940.53497 | World War II (gen. particip.: Yug.) | D766.6-62, DR366, DR1289 (later works after 1980?) |
| 940.534977 | World War II (gen. particip.: Bulg.) | D766.7.B8, DR89-90 |
| 940.53498 | World War II (gen. particip.: Rumania) | D766.4, DR264-267 |
| 940.53499 | Greek Isles (WWII: gen. particip.) | DF901.C9 (Cyclades) |
| 940.534998 | World War II (gen. particip.: Crete) | D766.7.C7, DF901. C86 |

| 940.535 | World War II (gen. particip.: Asia) | |
|---|---|---|
| 940.5351 | World War II (gen. particip.: China) | D767.3, DS777.518-533 |
| 940.53512 | Hong Kong (WWII: gen. particip.) | DS796.H7 |
| 940.5351249 | Formosa (WWII: gen. particip.) | DS895.F75, |
| | | DS799.69-72 (pubns. 1970+) |
| 940.53517 | Mongolia (WWII: gen. particip.) | DS793.M7 |
| 940.53518 | Manchuria (WWII: gen. particip.) | DS784 |
| 940.53519 | Korea (WWII: gen. particip.)    DS916 | |
| 940.5352 | World War II (gen. particip.: Japan) | D767.2-25, DS888.5-889 |
| 940.5354 | World War II (gen. particip.: India) | D767.6, D767.63 (Free India), |
| | | DS413 |
| 940.5355 | World War II (gen. particip.: Iran) | D766.7.I55, DS317-318 |
| 940.53561 | Turkey (WWII: gen. particip.) | D766.7.T8, DR590 |
| 940.535645 | Cyprus (WWII: gen. particip.) | DS54.8 |
| 940.53567 | World War II (gen. particip.: Iraq) | D766.7.I57, DS79.53 |
| 940.53569 | World War II (gen. particip.: Syria) | D766.7.S9, DS98 |
| 940.535694 | World War II (gen. particip.: Israel) | D766.7.P (Palestine), D766.7.I7 |
| 940.5357 | Siberia (WWII: gen. particip.: more likely with Russia at 940.5347) | |
| | | D764, D767, DK766 |
| 940.53591 | World War II (gen. particip.: Burma) | D767.6, DS485.B89, |
| | | DS530 (later titles post 1970?) |
| 940.53593 | Thailand (WWII: gen. particip.) | DS585 |
| 940.53594 | Laos (WWII: gen. particip.) | DS555.36 |
| 940.535951 | Malaysia (WWII: gen. particip.) | D767.5, DS596, |
| | | DS598-599 (local, A-Z) |
| 940.535952 | World War II (gen. particip.: Singapore: SEE 940.535957 for later titles) | |
| | | D767.5, DS598.S7 |
| 940.5359527 | Singapore (WWII: gen. particip.: SEE 940.535952 for earlier titles) | |
| | | D767.5, DS598.S7 |
| 940.53597 | Vietnam (Annam: WWII: gen. particip.) | D767.45, DS556.36, |
| | | DS549 (earlier works) |
| 940.53598 | Indonesia & Malay Archipelago (WWII: gen. particip.) | |
| | | D767.7 (Dutch E. Indies), DS643.5, DS643 |
| 940.535983 | Borneo (WWII: gen. particip.) | D767.7, DS646.3 |
| 940.53599 | World War II (gen. particip.: Philippines) | D767.4, DS686.3-4 |
| 940.53611 | World War II (gen. particip.: Tunisia) | D766.99.T8, DT264 |
| 940.53612 | World War II (gen. particip.: Libya) | D766.93, DT235 |
| 940.5362 | World War II (gen. particip.: Egypt) | D766.9, DT107.82 |
| 940.5364 | World War II (gen. particip.: Morocco) | D766.99.M8, DT324 |
| 940.5365 | World War II (gen. particip.: Algeria) | D766.99.A4-6, DT295 |
| 940.5368 | World War II (gen. particip.: S. Africa) | D766.97, DT779.7 |
| 940.5371 | World War II (gen. particip.: Can.) | D768.15, F1034 |
| 940.5373 | World War II (gen. particip.: U.S.) | D769, E806-813, E806 (gen.) |
| 940.5374-5379 | United States (WWII: gen. particip.: by area or state) | |
| | | D769.85.A-Z, D769.87-88, F1-951+ |
| 940.53747 | World War II (gen. particip.: U.S.: N.Y.) | D769.85.N4-5, F124 |
| 940.53794 | California (WWII: gen. particip.) | D769.85.C2-21, F866 |
| 940.5393 | Melanesia (WWII: gen. particip.) | DU940 |
| 940.53931 | World War II (gen. particip.: New Z.: SEE ALSO 940.5393 for works | |
| | after 1988) | D767.85-852, DU411 |
| 940.53932 | New Caledonia (WWII: gen. particip.) | DU720 |
| 940.53934 | New Hebrides (WWII: gen. particip.) | DU760 |
| 940.53935 | World War II (gen. particip.: Solomon Is.) | D767.98, DU850 |
| 940.53936 | Bismarck Archipelago (WWII: gen. particip.) | DU550-553 |
| 940.5394 | World War II (gen. particip.: Australia) | D767.8-82, DU116 |

| 940.5395 | World War II (gen. particip.: New Guinea) | D767.95, DU740-746 |
| 940.53965 | Micronesia (WWII: gen. particip.) | DU500 |
| 940.53966 | World War II (gen. particip.: Caroline Is.) | DU565-567 |
| 940.53967 | World War II (gen. particip.: Guam & the Marianas) | D767.G or .M, |
| | | DU647 (Guam), DU645 (Marianas) |
| 940.53968 | Micronesia, Eastern (Ellice, Gilbert, Marshall Is.: WWII: gen. particip.) | |
| | D767.917 (Gilb's.), D767.99.M3 (Marshalls), DU500 (Micro.), | |
| | DU590 (Ell. Is.), DU615 (Gilb's.), DU710 (Marshalls) | |
| 940.54 | Military history (WWII) | D743 |
| 940.54003 | Encyclopedias & dictionaries (WWII) | D740 |
| 940.54005 | Magazines & serial pubns. (WWII) | D731 |
| 940.54006 | Societies & associations (WWII) | D732, D734 |
| 940.5401 | Strategy (WWII) | D743 |
| 940.54012 | Strategy (WWII: Allies) | |
| 940.54013 | Strategy (WWII: Axis) | |
| 940.5402 | World War II (mobilization: SEE 940.534-539 for particular countries) | |
| | | D800, HC, HF, HJ |
| 940.5403 | Afro-Americans & American Indians as troops (WWII) | |
| | | D810.N4, D810.I5 |
| 940.5404 | Minorities, Ethnic (WWII: as troops) | D769.88.A-Z, |
| | | D769.88.M4 (Mex.-Am's.) |
| 940.5405 | Repression & atrocities (WWII) | D803, D804.A-Z (by country) |
| 940.54094-54099 | Military history (WWII: by place) | D757-769 |
| 940.540941-540942 | Military history (WWII: G.B.) | D759-760 |
| 940.540943 | Military history (WWII: Ger.) | D757 |
| 940.5409436 | Military history (WWII: Austria) | D765.4 |
| 940.5409437 | Czechoslovakia (WWII: mil. hist.) | D765.5 |
| 940.5409438 | Poland (WWII: mil. hist.) | D765 |
| 940.5409439 | Military history (WWII: Hungary) | D765.56 |
| 940.540944 | Military history (WWII: Fr.) | D761 |
| 940.540945 | Military history (WWII: It.) | D763.I8-817 |
| 940.540947 | Military history (WWII: Rus.) | D764 |
| 940.5409471 | Military history (WWII: Fin.: SEE 940.54094897 for newer | |
| | titles) | D765.3 |
| 940.5409481 | Military history (WWII: Norway) | D763.N6-613 |
| 940.5409489 | Military history (WWII: Denmark) | D763.D4 |
| 940.54094897 | Finnish military history (WWII: SEE ALSO 940.5409471 for | |
| | earlier works) | D765.3 |
| 940.5409492 | Holland (WWII: mil. hist.) | D763.N4-41 |
| 940.5409493 | Military history (WWII: Belgium) | D763.B4 |
| 940.54094935 | Military history (WWII: Luxemb.) | D763.L9 |
| 940.5409495 | Military history (WWII: Greece) | D766.3 |
| 940.5409497 | Military history (WWII: Yug.) | D766.6-613 |
| 940.54094977 | Military history (WWII: Bulg.) | D766.7.B8 |
| 940.5409498 | Military history (WWII: Rumania) | D766.4 |
| 940.540951 | Military history (WWII: China) | D767.3 |
| 940.540952 | Military history (WWII: Japan) | D767.2 |
| 940.540954 | Military history (WWII: India) | D767.6, |
| | | D767.63 (Free India, 1943-45) |
| 940.5409561 | Military history (WWII: Turkey) | D766.7.T8 |
| 940.5409591 | Military history (WWII: Burma) | D767.6 |
| 940.5409595 | Malaysia (WWII: mil. hist.) | D767.5 |
| 940.54095957 | Military history (WWII: Singapore) | |
| 940.5409598 | Indonesia (WWII: mil. hist.) | D767.7 |
| 940.5409599 | Military history (WWII: Philip. Is.) | D767.4 |

| | | |
|---|---|---|
| 940.540962 | Military history (WWII: Egypt) | D766.9 |
| 940.540968 | Military history (WWII: S. Africa) | D766.97 |
| 940.540971 | Military history (WWII: Can.) | D768.15 |
| 940.540973 | Military history (WWII: U.S.) | D769, D769.25-4 (armies, div's., regt's.), D769.45-598 (naval particip., units, ops.) |
| 940.54097308664 | Homosexuals (WWII: U.S.: armed forces) | |
| 940.5409931 | Military history (WWII: New Z.: SEE ALSO 940.540993 for titles prior to 1989) | D767.85 |
| 940.540994 | Military history (WWII: Australia) | D767.8 |
| 940.541 | World War II (mil. units & ops.: gen.) | D743 |
| 940.5412-5413+ | Military history (WWII: units & ops.: by country: inclu. structure, history, registers, & service records) | |
| 940.5412+ | World War II (Allies & United Nations: mil. units & ops.) | |
| 940.541241 | Military history (WWII: units & ops.: G.B.) | D759.5-760.A-Z |
| 940.5412411 | Military history (WWII: units & ops.: Scot.) | D760.S |
| 940.541242 | England (WWII: mil. units & ops.) | D759.5-63+, D760.A-Z |
| 940.541244 | Military history (WWII: units & ops.: Fr.) | D761.1-9 |
| 940.5412481 | Military history (WWII: units & ops.: Norway) | D763.N61-613 |
| 940.5412493 | Military history (WWII: units & ops.: Belgium) | D763.B4 |
| 940.5412495 | Military history (WWII: units & ops.: Greece) | D766.3 |
| 940.5412497 | Military history (WWII: units & ops.: Yug.) | D766.61-613 |
| 940.541251 | Military history (WWII: units & ops.: China) | D767.3 |
| 940.541254 | Military history (WWII: units & ops.: India) | |
| | | D767.6, D767.63 (Free India, 1943-45) |
| 940.5412591 | Military history (WWII: units & ops.: Burma) | D767.6 |
| 940.5412599 | Military history (WWII: units & ops.: Phil. Is.) | D767.4 |
| 940.541268 | Military history (WWII: units & ops.: S. Africa) | D766.97 |
| 940.541271 | Military history (WWII: units & ops.: Can.) | D768.15 |
| 940.541273 | Military history (WWII: units & ops.: U.S.) | |
| | | D769.25-4, D769.5-555 (naval), D769.585-598 (Coast Guard etc.), D769.73-76+ (transport, ordnance, supplies) |
| 940.541274-541279 | Military history (WWII: units & ops.: U.S.: particular areas or states) | D769.85.A-Z |
| 940.5412931 | Military history (WWII: units & ops.: New Z.: SEE ALSO 940.541293 for works before 1989) | D767.85 |
| 940.541294 | Military history (WWII: units & ops.: Australia) | D767.8 |
| 940.5413+ | World War II (Axis Powers: mil. units & ops.) | |
| 940.541343 | Military history (WWII: units & ops.: Ger.) | D757.1-.85 |
| 940.541345 | Military history (WWII: units & ops.: It.) | D763.I81-813, |
| | | D763.I815-817 (Corpo Volontari Della Liberta) |
| 940.54134897 | Military history (WWII: units & ops.: Fin.) | D765.3 |
| 940.5413498 | Military history (WWII: units & ops.: Rum.) | D766.4 |
| 940.541352 | Military history (WWII: units & ops.:Japan) | D767.2 |
| 940.542 | Battles & campaigns (WWII: by theatre) | D756-769 |
| 940.5421 | Theatres, Battle (WWII: Eur.) | D743, D756 (W.), D764 (E.) |
| 940.5423 | Theatres, Battle (WWII: Afr. & Mid. E.) | D766.8 (Afr.), |
| | | D766 (Balkans, E. Medit., Near E.) |
| 940.5425 | Theatres, Battle (WWII: E. Ind., S.E. Asian, E. Asia: SEE ALSO 951.042 for pre-1941 Sino-Jpn. conflict) | D767, D767.6 (India-Burma), D767.35 & D767.45 (Cochin China, Fr. Indoch.) |
| 940.5426 | Theatres, Battle (WWII: Pacific) | D767 (gen.), D767.9+ (Pac. Is.) |
| 940.5428 | Theatres, Battle (WWII: Am.) | D768 (gen.), D768.18-3 (Latin Am.), D769 (U.S.) |
| 940.5429 | Theatres, Battle (WWII: misc.) | |

| 940.544 | Battles & campaigns, Aerial (WWII: inclu. comb. air & naval ops. as well as antiaircraft defenses)   D785-792, D785 (gen.) |
|---|---|
| 940.5441 | Aerial ops. (WWII: particular srvcs.: scouting, artil. supp., bombing, close air supp., antisub. ops., balloon barrage, coast patrols, etc.) |
| 940.5442 | Air battles & campaigns (WWII)   D785+ |
| 940.5443+ | Air bases (WWII: by area or place) |
| 940.544342 | Air bases (WWII: in Eng.)   D786 |
| 940.544343 | Air bases (WWII: in Ger.)   D787 |
| 940.544347 | Air bases (WWII: in Rus.) |
| 940.544351 | Air bases (WWII: in China) |
| 940.544352 | Air bases (WWII: in Japan)   D792.J3 |
| 940.544373 | Air bases (WWII: in U.S.)   D790 |
| 940.544394 | Air bases (WWII: in Australia) |
| 940.5449+ | Aerial ops. (WWII: by country: inclu. specific craft, units, fliers) |
| 940.544941-544942 | Aerial ops. (WWII: G.B.: R.A.F. etc.)   D786 |
| 940.544943 | Aerial ops. (WWII: Ger.: Luftwaffe etc.) D787 |
| 940.544945 | Aerial ops. (WWII: It.)   D792.I8 |
| 940.544947 | Aerial ops. (WWII: Rus.)   D792.R9 or .S65 |
| 940.544951 | Aerial ops. (WWII: China)   D792.C5 |
| 940.544952 | Aerial ops. (WWII: Japan)   D792.J3 |
| 940.544971 | Aerial ops. (WWII: Can.) |
| 940.544973 | Aerial ops. (WWII: U.S.: Army Air Corps, Navy, Marines, etc.)   D790 |
| 940.544994 | Aerial ops. (WWII: Australia)   D792.A8 |
| 940.545 | Battles & campaigns, Naval (WWII: SEE ALSO 940.542 for ops. by theatre)   D770-784, D770 (gen.), D773 (U.S.: gen.), D774.A-Z (U.S.: by ship, battle, etc.), D769.45-598 (U.S.: by fleet, squadron, base, etc.) |
| 940.5451+ | World War II (submarine ops.: SEE ALSO 940.542 for ops. by theatre)   D780-784, D780 (gen.), D781-782 (Ger.), D783 (U.S.), D784.A-Z (other lands) |
| 940.54516 | World War II (antisub. ops.)   D780, D770-784 |
| 940.5451941 | Submarine ops. (WWII: G.B.)   D784.G7 |
| 940.5451943 | Submarine ops. (WWII: Ger.)   D781-782 |
| 940.5451945 | Submarine ops. (WWII: It.)   D784.I8 |
| 940.5451952 | Submarine ops. (WWII: Japan)   D784.J3 |
| 940.5451973 | Submarine ops. (WWII: U.S.)   D783 |
| 940.5452 | Blockades & blockade-running (WWII)   D770, D771 (Anglo-Grmn.), D773 (U.S.) |
| 940.5453+ | Naval bases (WWII)   D769.54-542 (U.S.), D770-784 (other lands) |
| 940.545341 | Naval bases (WWII: in G.B.) |
| 940.5453411 | Scapa Flow Naval Base (G.B.: Scot.: WWII) |
| 940.545343 | Naval bases (WWII: in Ger.) |
| 940.545344 | Naval bases (WWII: in Fr.) |
| 940.545345 | Naval bases (WWII: in It.) |
| 940.545352 | Naval bases (WWII: in Japan) |
| 940.545373 | Naval bases (WWII: in U.S.) |
| 940.5453755 | Naval bases (WWII: in U.S.: Va.) |
| 940.5453794 | Naval bases (WWII: in U.S.: Calif.) |
| 940.54537946 | Naval bases (WWII: in U.S.: Calif.: S.F. Bay Area) |
| 940.5453794985 | Naval bases (WWII: in U.S.: Calif.: San Diego) |

| 940.5459+ | World War II (naval ops.: particular countries) | D770-784 |
|---|---|---|
| 940.545941-545942 | Naval ops. (WWII: G.B. Royal Navy) | D771-772, D767 |
| | (Pac.), DA89, DA89.1.A-Z (biog's.), DA566.5 (20th c.) | |
| 940.545943 | Naval ops. (WWII: Ger.) | D771-772, DD106 |
| 940.545944 | Naval ops. (WWII: Fr.) | D779.F8, DC53, DC368 |
| 940.545945 | Naval ops. (WWII: It.) | D775, DG486 |
| 940.545952 | Naval ops. (WWII: Japan) | D777, VA653, DS890.A-Z (biog.) |
| 940.545971 | Naval ops. (WWII: Can.) | D779.C2, F1028.5 |
| 940.545973 | Naval ops. (WWII: U.S.: U.S.N., Marines, Coast Guard) | |
| | D773-774, D769.45-598 (fleets etc.), E746 | |
| 940.5459931 | Naval ops. (WWII: New Z.: SEE ALSO 940.545993 for earlier titles | |
| | prior to 1989) | D779.N45 |
| 940.545994 | Naval ops. (WWII: Australia) | D779.A8, DU112.4 |
| 940.546 | Commemorations, celebrations, & memorials (WWII: gen.) | D830-838 |
| 940.5465 | Cemeteries & monuments (WWII) | D833-838 (celebrations, |
| | monuments, etc.), D810.D4 (dead, cemeteries, etc.) | |
| 940.546542 | Cemeteries & monuments (WWII: Eng.) | D838.G6 (gen.), |
| | .G7.A-Z (local, by place) | |
| 940.546543 | Monuments & cemeteries (WWII: Ger.) | D838.G3 |
| 940.546544 | Monuments & cemeteries (WWII: Fr.) | D838.F8 |
| 940.546547 | Monuments & cemeteries (WWII: Rus.) | D838.R9 or .S65 |
| 940.546551 | Monuments & cemeteries (WWII: China) | D838.C5 |
| 940.546552 | Monuments & cemeteries (WWII: Japan) | D838.J3 |
| 940.546573 | Cemeteries & monuments (WWII: U.S.) | D833-836, |
| | D833 (gen.), D835.A-W (by state), D836.A-Z (by town) | |
| 940.5465753 | Monuments & cemeteries (WWII: U.S.: Wash. D.C.) | |
| | D835.D6, D836.W | |
| 940.546594 | Monuments & cemeteries (WWII: Australia) | D838.A8 |
| 940.5465969 | Monuments & cemeteries (WWII: Hawaiian Is.) | |
| | D835.H, D838.H | |
| 940.5467 | Rolls of honored & dead (WWII) | D797 |
| 940.546741 | Honored & dead (WWII: G.B.: rolls) | D797.G7 |
| 940.546743 | Honored & dead (WWII: Ger.: rolls) | D797.G3 |
| 940.546744 | Honored & dead (WWII: Fr.: rolls) | D797.F8 |
| 940.546747 | Honored & dead (WWII: Rus.: rolls) | D797.R9 |
| 940.546752 | Honored & dead (WWII: Japan: rolls) | D797.J3 |
| 940.546773 | Honored & dead (WWII: U.S.: rolls) | D797.U6-7 |
| 940.547 | Social services, prisons, & medical services (WWII) | |
| | D805-809 | |
| 940.5472+ | Prisoner-of-war camps & internment centers (WWII: SEE ALSO | |
| | 940.5317+ for post-1988 titles on internment camps) | D805 |
| 940.547241 | P.O.W. camps & internment centers (WWII: run by G.B.) | D805.G7 |
| 940.547243 | P.O.W. camps & internment centers (WWII: run by Ger.) | D805.G3 |
| 940.547247 | P.O.W. camps & internment centers (WWII: run by Rus.) | D805.R9 |
| 940.547252 | P.O.W. camps & internment centers (WWII: run by Japan) | |
| | D805.J3 | |
| 940.547273 | P.O.W. camps & internment centers (WWII: run by U.S.) | |
| | D805.U5-6 | |
| 940.5473 | Prisoner exchanges (WWII) | D805 |

| | | |
|---|---|---|
| 940.5475 | World War II (medical srvcs.) | D806-807, D806 (gen.) |
| 940.54752 | Sanitary control (WWII) | |
| 940.54753 | Ambulance services (WWII) | |
| 940.54754-54759 | Medical services (WWII: particular countries) | D807.A-Z |
| 940.547541 | Medical services (WWII: G.B.) | D807.G7 |
| 940.547543 | Medical services (WWII: Ger.) | D807.G3 |
| 940.547547 | Medical services (WWII: Rus.) | D807.R9 |
| 940.547552 | Medical services (WWII: Japan) | D807.J3 |
| 940.547573 | United States medical services (WWII) | D807.U6-87, |

.U6 (gen.), .U62.A-Z (by state),
.U72-73 (Army hospitals), .U85-87 (Navy hospitals)

| | | |
|---|---|---|
| 940.5476 | Medical services (WWII: hospitals) | D806 |
| 940.547634-547639 | Hospitals (WWII: in particular places) | D807.A-Z |
| 940.5476341-5476342 | Hospitals (WWII: in G.B.) | D807.G7 |
| 940.5476343 | Hospitals (WWII: in Ger.) | D807.G3 |
| 940.5476344 | Hospitals (WWII: in Fr.) | D807.F8 |
| 940.5476351 | Hospitals (WWII: in China) | D807.C5 |
| 940.5476352 | Hospitals (WWII: in Japan) | D807.J3 |
| 940.5476373 | Hospitals (WWII: in U.S.) | D807.U6-87 |
| 940.5476394 | Hospitals (WWII: in Australia) | D807.A8 |
| 940.54764-54769 | Hospitals (WWII: operated by particular countries) | D807.A-Z |
| 940.547641 | Medical services (WWII: hospitals, British) | D807.G7 |
| 940.547643 | Medical services (WWII: hospitals, German) | D807.G3 |
| 940.547647 | Medical services (WWII: hospitals, Russian) | D807.R9 |
| 940.547652 | Medical services (WWII: hospitals, Japanese) | D807.J3 |
| 940.547673 | Medical services (WWII: hospitals, United States) | D807.U6-87 |
| 940.5477 | Welfare & relief services (WWII) | D808-809 |
| 940.54771 | Red Cross (WWII) | D806-807 |
| 940.547784-547789 | Welfare & relief services (WWII: provided by specific | |
| | countries) | D809.A-Z |
| 940.5477841 | Welfare & relief services (WWII: by G.B.) | D809.G7 |
| 940.5477873 | Welfare & relief services (WWII: by U.S.) | D809.U5 |
| 940.5477894 | Welfare & relief services (WWII: by Australia) | D809.A8 |
| 940.547794-547799 | Welfare & relief services (WWII: in particular countries) | |
| | | D809.A-Z |
| 940.5477943 | Relief & welfare & services (WWII: in Ger.) | D809.G3 |
| 940.5477944 | Relief & welfare & services (WWII: in Fr.) | D809.F8 |
| 940.5477947 | Relief & welfare & services (WWII: in Rus.) | D809.R9 |
| 940.5477951 | Relief & welfare & services (WWII: in China) | D809.C5 |
| 940.5477952 | Relief & welfare & services (WWII: in Japan) | D809.J3 |
| 940.54779599 | Relief & welfare & services (WWII: in Philip. Is.) | D809.P5 |
| 940.5478 | Religious services (WWII) | D810.C35-6 (chaplains), |

.C5 (churches: gen.), .C53-68 (alphab. by denom.)

| | | |
|---|---|---|
| 940.548 | World War II (misc. topics) | |
| 940.5481+ | Personal accounts, Allied (WWII) | D811 |
| 940.548141 | Personal accounts, British (WWII) | |
| 940.548142 | Personal accounts, English (WWII) | |
| 940.548144 | Personal accounts, French (WWII) | |
| 940.548147 | Personal accounts, Russian (WWII) | |
| 940.548173 | Personal accounts, American (WWII: U.S.) | |
| 940.548194 | Personal accounts, Australian (WWII) | |
| 940.5482+ | Personal accounts, Axis (WWII) | D811 |
| 940.548243 | Personal accounts, German (WWII) | |
| 940.548245 | Personal accounts, Italian (WWII) | |
| 940.548252 | Personal accounts, Japanese (WWII) | |

| | | |
|---|---|---|
| 940.5483+ | Allies (WWII: mil. & naval life & customs) | U750, U765+, V720 (naval), V735+ |
| 940.548341 | Military & naval life & customs (WWII: G.B.) | U767, V737 |
| 940.548347 | Military & naval life & customs (WWII: Rus.) | U771, V741 |
| 940.548373 | Naval & military life & customs (WWII: U.S.) | U766, V736 |
| 940.5484+ | Axis (WWII: mil. & naval life & customs) | U750, U765+, V720 (naval), V735+ |
| 940.548443 | Military & naval life & customs (WWII: Ger.) | U769, V739 |
| 940.548452 | Military & naval life & customs (WWII: Japan) | U773, V743.J3 |
| 940.5485 | Unconventional warfare (WWII: inclu. espionage, infilt., intelligence, subversion) D810.S7 (gen.), .S8.A-Z (by spy), D802(underground), D802.F8 (Fr. undergr.), UB250-274, UB273-274 (sabo.), UB251.A-Z (intell., by country), UB271.A-Z (espion., by country respons.), VB230-250 (naval intell. & espionage) | |
| 940.5486+ | Unconventional warfare, Allied (WWII: inclu. espionage, infilt., intelligence, subversion) | |
| 940.548641 | Intelligence, espionage, & unconventional warfare (WWII: G.B.) D810.S7, UB251.G7, UB271.G7, VB230-250 | |
| 940.548644 | Sabotage, espionage, & unconventional warfare (WWII: Fr.) D802.F8 (underground), D810.S7+, UB271.F8 | |
| 940.548647 | Infiltration, espionage, & unconventional warfare (WWII: Rus.) UB251.R9, UB271.R9 | |
| 940.548673 | Intelligence, espionage, & unconventional warfare (WWII: U.S.) D810.S7+, UB251.U5, UB271.U5, VB230-250 (naval) | |
| 940.548694 | Espionage, intelligence, & unconventional warfare (WWII: Australia) | |
| 940.5487+ | Unconventional warfare, Axis (WWII: inclu. espionage, intelligence, infiltration, subversion) | |
| 940.548743 | Intelligence, espionage, & unconventional warfare (WWII: Ger.) D810.S7+, UB251.G3, UB271.G3 | |
| 940.548745 | Espionage, intelligence, & unconventional warfare (WWII: It.) | |
| 940.548752 | Espionage, intelligence, & unconventional warfare (WWII: Japan) UB251.J3, UB271.J3, VB230-250 | |
| 940.5488 | News & propaganda (WWII) D810.P6 (gen.), .P7.A-Z (by country) | |
| 940.54886 | Propaganda, Allied (WWII) | |
| 940.5488641 | Propaganda, British (WWII) D810.P7.G7 | |
| 940.5488644 | Propaganda, French (WWII) D810.P7.F8 | |
| 940.5488647 | Propaganda, Russian (WWII: after 21 June 1941) D810.P7.R9 or .S65 | |
| 940.5488673 | Propaganda, American (WWII: U.S.) D810.P7.U6 | |
| 940.54887+ | Propaganda, Axis (WWII) | |
| 940.5488743 | Propaganda, German (WWII) D810.P7.G3 | |
| 940.5488744 | Propaganda, French (WWII: Vichy) D810.P7.F8 | |
| 940.5488745 | Propaganda, Italian (WWII) D810.P7.I8 | |
| 940.5488747 | Propaganda, Russian (WWII: prior to 22 June 1941) D810.P7.R9 | |
| 940.5488752 | Propaganda, Japanese (WWII) D810.P7.J3 | |

| 940.54889+ | News & propaganda (WWII: in specific places) | |
|---|---|---|
| 940.5488941-5488942 | News & propaganda (WWII: in G.B.) | |
| 940.5488943 | News & propaganda (WWII: in Ger.) | |
| 940.5488944 | News & propaganda (WWII: in Fr.) | |
| 940.5488945 | News & propaganda (WWII: in It.) | |
| 940.5488947 | News & propaganda (WWII: in Rus.) | |
| 940.5488951 | News & propaganda (WWII: in China) | |
| 940.5488952 | News & propaganda (WWII: in Japan) | |
| 940.54889599 | News & propaganda (WWII: in Philip. Is.) | |
| 940.5488972 | News & propaganda (WWII: in Can.) | |
| 940.5488973 | News & propaganda (WWII: in U.S.)  D753.3 | |
| 940.5488994 | News & propaganda (WWII: in Australia) | |
| 940.549 | Humor, comics, pictorials, & miscellanea (WWII)  D743.9, D745 | |
| 940.5494 | Anecdotes (WWII)  D743.9 | |
| 940.5496-5497 | Comics, caricatures, humor (WWII) | |

| 941 | BRITAIN & BRITISH ISLES  DA | |
|---|---|---|
| 941.003 | Encyclopedias & dictionaries (G.B.)  DA34 | |
| 941.081 | Britain (19th c. & Victorian era of 1837-1901)  DA550-566, DA550 (gen.) | |
| 941.082 | Britain (20th c. & Edward VII era of 1901-1910)  DA567-570 (Ed. VII), DA570 (gen.), DA566 (20th c.: gen.) | |
| 941.083 | Britain (1910-36: George VI)  DA573-578, DA576 (gen.), DA577 (WWI era), DA578 (1920-39) | |
| 941.084 | Britain (1936-45: WWII era)  DA580-587, DA586 (gen.), DA587 (WWII period) | |
| 941.1 | SCOTLAND  DA750-890, DA760 (gen.) | |
| 941.1083 | Scotland (1910-36)  DA821 | |
| 941.1084 | Scotland (1936-45))  DA821 | |
| 941.34 | Edinburgh, Scot.  DA890.E2-4 | |
| 941.5 | IRELAND (overall)  DA900-995, DA910 (gen.) | |
| 941.508 | Ireland (19th-20th c.)  DA950-965+ | |
| 941.5082 | Ireland (20th c.)  DA959-965 | |
| 941.50821 | Ireland (1900-20)  DA960 | |
| 941.50822 | Ireland (1921-49)  DA963 | |
| 941.6 | Northern Ireland  DA990.U45-46 | |
| 941.7 | Eire (Republic of Ireland)  DA963 | |

| 942 | ENGLAND & WALES  DA20-745, DA20-690 (Eng.), DA700-45 (Wales) | |
|---|---|---|
| 942.083 | England (1910-36)  DA576 | |
| 942.084 | England (1936-45)  DA586-587 | |
| 942.1 | London, Eng.  DA675-689, DA677 (gen.) | |
| 942.1084 | London, Eng. (1936-45)  DA684 | |
| 942.34 | Channel Islands (G.B.)  DA670.C4 | |
| 942.341 | Jersey (G.B.: island) | |
| 942.342 | Guernsey (G.B.: island) | |
| 942.9 | Wales | |

| 943 | GERMANY & CENTRAL EUROPE | DD (Ger.), DB (Austria, Hung., Czech.), DK401-441 & DK4010-4800 (Pol.) |

943      GERMANY & CENTRAL EUROPE      DD (Ger.), DB (Austria, Hung., Czech.), DK401-441 & DK4010-4800 (Pol.)

943.0004924     Jews (Central Eur.)

943.004924     Jews (Ger.)      DS135.G3-5

943.084     Germany (1888-1918: Fred. & William II eras)     DD224-232, DD228 (gen.), DD228.8 (WWI era), DD448 (Prussia)

943.085     Weimar Republic (Ger.: 1918-33)     DD233-251, DD237 (gen.), DD251 (Hindenb. era), DD453 (Prussia)

943.086     Germany (1933-45: 3rd Reich)     DD253-256, DD256 (WWII period), DD256.5 (gen.: post-war pubn. dates), DD454 (Prussia)

943.155     Berlin, Ger.     DD851-900, DD860 (gen.)

943.155086     Berlin, Ger. (1933-45)     DD880

943.3     Bavaria     DD801.B31-55

943.4     Rhine River Valley     DD801.R7-76

943.42     Saar (Ger.)     DD801.S13

943.48     Black Forest (Ger.)     DD801.B63-65

943.6     AUSTRIA     DB1-170+

943.605     Austria (20th c. & 1919-)     DB91 (20th c.), DB96 (1918-)

943.6051     Austrian Republic (1919-38)     DB96-98

943.6052     Anschluss & WWII Period (Austria: 1938-55)     DB99 (1938-45), DB99.1 (Allied occup., 1945-55)

943.613     Vienna, Austria     DB841-860, DB847 (gen.)

943.648     LIECHTENSTEIN     DB540.5

943.7     CZECHOSLOVAKIA     DB191-217 (older works), DB2000-3150 (newer)

943.7024     Czechoslovakia (19th c.: 1815-1918)     DB214, DB2176

943.703     Czechoslovakia (1918-45)     DB215-215.3, DB2186-2211, DB2186 (gen.), DB2196 (1918-39), DB2206 (1939-45)

943.8     POLAND     DK401-441 (older titles), DK4010-4800 (titles 1970+?), DK414, DK4140

943.803     Poland (1795-1918: foreign rule)     DK434.9, DK4349, DK439

943.804     Polish Republic (1918-39)     DK440, DK4400

943.805     Poland (1939-)     DK441

943.8053     Poland (1939-45: WWII era)     DK441, DK4410

943.84     Warsaw, Pol. (area)     DK651.W2, DK4610-4645

943.9     HUNGARY     DB901-975+, DB906, DB925

943.905     Hungary (20th c.: 1918-)     DB947-950, DB947 (gen.), DB950.A-Z (biog.)

943.9051     Hungary (1918-41)     DB955

943.9052     Hungary (1942-56)     DB956


944     FRANCE     DC

944.08     France (1870- & 20th c.: 3d, 4th, 5th Repub's.)     DC289+, DC335+

944.081     France (1870-1945: 3d Repub.)     DC335

944.0814     France (1914-18: WWI era)     DC387

944.0815     France (1918-39)     DC389-396

944.0816     France (1939-45: WWII period)     DC397

944.1     Brittany     DC611.B841-915

944.2     Normandy area (Fr.)     DC611.N841-899

944.36     Paris, Fr. (area)     DC701-790, DC707 (gen.), DC735 (1871-1914), DC737 (1914-)

944.89     Pyrenees region     DC611.P981-992

944.949     MONACO     DC941-947

```
945          ITALY  DG
945.09       Italy (1870- & 20th c.)      DG555-575+, DG555, DG570 (WWI era)
945.091        Italy (1918-46: SEE ALSO 963.056 for Italo-Eth. War of 1935-6)
                     DG566-575, DG571, DG571-572 (Fascist period),
                     DG572 (WWII time)
945.632        Rome, It.      DG803-818, DG808, DG813 (1871-)
945.634        Vatican City    DG800
945.8        Sicily        DG869
945.85       MALTA         DG994


946          IBERIAN PENINSULA & SPAIN
                        DP, DP1-402+ (Sp.), DP501-900+ (Port.)
946.08       Spain (1868-)      DP222 (1868-86), DP233 (1886- & 20th c.)
946.081      Spain (1931-39: 2d Repub.: inclu. Civil War, 1936-39)      DP250-269,
                        DP254 (gen.), DP269 (Civil War)
946.082      Spain (1939-75: Franco period)      DP270
946.0824     Spain (1939-49)
946.41         Madrid, Sp. (area)     DP350-374, DP361
946.79       ANDORRA        DC921-930
946.89       GIBRALTAR (Br. colony)      DP302.G31-41
946.9        PORTUGAL      DP501-900+
946.904        Portugal (1910-)    DP675
946.9042       Portugal (1926-68)    DP680
946.942        Lisbon, Port.    DP752-776, DP764
946.99         Azores     DP702.A81-99, .A9 (19th-20th c.)


947          UNION OF SOVIET SOCIALIST REPUBLICS (Russia)
                        DK, DK1-275, DK501-973+
947.08       Russia (1855-)      DK219+, DK220-221
947.083      Russia (1894-1918: Nicholas II: perhaps SEE ALSO 952.031 for Russo-
                 Jpn. War)        DK251-264.3, DK258, DK260-262,
                        DS516-517 (R-J War)
947.084      Russia (20th c. & 1917-: Communist period)      DK246
947.0841     Soviet Union (1917-24: Rev. period & Lenin era)      DK265 (Rev.),
                        DK265-266.5+
947.0842     Soviet Union (1924-53: Stalin era: might ALSO try 948.97032 for
                 Russo-Finnish War)       DK267-273, DK267 (gen.),
                 DK459.5 (R-F War), DL1095-1105 (R-F War: later works)
947.1        FINLAND (SEE ALSO 948.97 for works after 1970 or so)
                        DK445-465, DL1002-1180+ (pubns. 1970+)
947.23       Archangel, Rus.
947.31       Moscow, Rus.     DK591-609, DK601 (hist. to 1950)
947.45       Leningrad, Rus.     DK541-579, DK568 (1801-)
947.65       Belorussia      DK511.W5 (White Russia)
947.7        Black Sea region (Rus.)    DK509
947.71         Little Russia (Ukraine)    DK508
947.717        Odessa & Crimea areas (Rus.)      DK511.C7
947.85       Volgograd, Rus. (ALSO Tsaritsyn or Stalingrad)      DK651.S7
947.87       Ural Mts. region (Rus.)    DK511.U7
947.9        Caucasus area (Rus.)    DK511.C1-35
947.95       Georgian Republic (U.S.S.R.)     DK511.G3-47, .G47 (gen. hist., 1917-)
```

| 948 | NORTHERN EUROPE & Scandinavia | DL |
|---|---|---|
| 948.08 | Scandinavia & N. Europe (20th c.: 1905-) | DL83-87+ |
| 948.081 | Scandinavia & N. Europe (1905-19) | DL83 |
| 948.082 | Scandinavia & N. Europe (1920-29) | DL83 |
| 948.083 | Scandinavia & N. Europe (1930-39) | DL83 |
| 948.084 | Scandinavia & N. Europe (1940-49) | DL83 (1901-45) |
| 948.1 | NORWAY    DL401-596, DL448 (gen.) | |
| 948.104 | Norway (20th c.: 1905-)    DL527+ | |
| 948.1041 | Norway (1905-45)    DL530-532 | |
| 948.2 | Oslo, Nor. (area)  DL581 | |
| 948.4 | Norway, Central & Northern | |
| 948.5 | SWEDEN    DL601-991+, DL648 | |
| 948.505 | Sweden (20th c.: 1905-)    DL860+ | |
| 948.5051 | Sweden (1905-45)    DL860-868 | |
| 948.7 | Stockholm, Swe. (area)    DL976 | |
| 948.9 | DENMARK & FINLAND | |
| 948.9 | DENMARK (overall)    DL101-291+, DL148 | |
| 948.905 | Denmark (1906-)    DL250 (20th c.) | |
| 948.9051 | Denmark (1906-45)    DL253-257 | |
| 948.97 | FINLAND    DK445-465 (mostly pre-1970 pubns.), | |
| | DL1002-1180+ (1970+ titles) | |
| 948.9702 | Finland (1809-1917)    DK458, DL1065 | |
| 948.9703 | Finland (1917-)    DK459, DL1066.5 | |
| 948.97031 | Finland (1917-39)    DK459, DL1084 | |
| 948.97032 | Finland (1939-45: WWII era: inclu. Russo-Finnish War: SEE ALSO | |
| | 947.0842 for R-F War)    DK459.45-5+, DL1090-1105+, | |
| | DL1090 (gen.) | |
| 948.971 | Helsingfors, Fin. (Helsinki: area)    DK465.H5, DL1175, | |
| | DL1175.48 (1917-) | |
| 948.977 | Lapland (Fin.)    DL971.L2, DL1170.L2 | |
| | | |
| 949 | EUROPE (misc. areas: Iceland, Belg., Switz., Greece, etc.) | |
| 949.12 | ICELAND    DL301-398+, DL375 (1918-) | |
| 949.2 | HOLLAND (NETHERLANDS)    DJ, DJ109 (gen.) | |
| 949.207 | Holland (20th c.)  DJ216 (19th-20th c.) | |
| 949.2071 | Holland (1890-1948: Q. Wilhelmina era)    DJ281-287, | |
| | DJ281 (gen.), DJ285 (WWI time), DJ287 (WWII | |
| era) | | |
| 949.3 | BELGIUM    DH401-811+, DH521 | |
| 949.304 | Belgium (1909-)    DH677 (20th c.) | |
| 949.3041 | Belgium (1909-34: Albert I)    DH681-685, DH681, DH682 (WWI) | |
| 949.3042 | Belgium (1934-51: Leopold III)    DH687-689, DH687 | |
| 949.35 | LUXEMBOURG    DH901-925, DH916 (1815-) | |
| 949.4 | SWITZERLAND    DQ, DQ54 | |
| 949.407 | Switzerland (20th c.)    DQ201 | |
| 949.4072 | Switzerland (1918-45) | |
| 949.47 | Alpine region (Switz.)    DQ820-841, DQ823 | |
| 949.5 | GREECE    DF, DF757 | |
| 949.506 | Greece (1821-1924: Monarchy)    DF802 | |
| 949.507 | Greece (20th c.: 1924-)    DF833 (20th c.), DF838 (WWI) | |
| 949.5073 | Greece (1924-35: Republic)    DF848 | |
| 949.5074 | Greece (1935-67: Monarchy)    DF849 | |
| 949.512 | Athens, Gr.    DF915-936, DF925 (1901-) | |
| 949.55 | Ionian Sea islands    DF901.I57-69 | |

| | | |
|---|---|---|
| 949.6 | BALKAN PENINSULA (inclu. Balkan Wars of 1912-13) | DR1-48, DR45 (20th c.), DR46 (Balkan Wars) |
| 949.65 | ALBANIA DR701.S49-86 (known as Scutari for earlier works), DR701.S5, DR941-979+ (for later works), DR941 (gen.) | |
| 949.6502 | Albania (1912-46) DR701.S6 (1914-17), .S85 (1939-43), DR971, DR972 (WWI), DR975 (WWII) | |
| 949.7 | YUGOSLAVIA (overall) DR301-396+ (earlier books), DR1202-1307+ | |
| 949.7+ | YUGOSLAVIA & BULGARIA | |
| 949.701 | Yugoslavia (to 1918) DR317, DR1274 | |
| 949.702 | Yugoslavia (20th c. & 1918-) DR357, DR1274, DR1282 | |
| 949.7021 | Yugoslavia (1918-39: Kingdom) DR366, DR1289 | |
| 949.7022 | Yugoslavia (1939-45: WWII era) DR369, DR1297-1298) | |
| 949.71 | SERBIA (inclu. Belgrade) DR301-396, DR1932-2125+ | |
| 949.71015 | Serbia (1878-1918: Independence) DR351-363, DR2006-2032 | |
| 949.7102 | Serbia (1918-) DR366, DR2034 | |
| 949.72 | CROATIA (inclu. Dalmatia, Istria, Slavonia) DB361-380, DR1502-1645 | |
| 949.73 | Slovenia DR381.S6, DR1352-1485+ | |
| 949.74 | Yugoslavia (central republics: Bosnia, Herzegovina, Montenegro) | |
| 949.742 | HERCEGOVINA (Herzegovina) & BOSNIA DB231-250 (Bos.), DB521-540 (Her.), DR1652-1785 | |
| 949.745 | MONTENEGRO DR101-196, DR1802-1928 | |
| 949.76 | MACEDONIA DR701.M13-42, DR2152-2285+ | |
| 949.77 | BULGARIA DR51-98 | |
| 949.7702 | Bulgaria (1878-1946) DR85-93, DR89 (1918-43) | |
| 949.8 | ROMANIA (Rumania) DR201-296 | |
| 949.802 | Romania (1861-1947: Monarchy) DR250-266, DR250, DR263 (1914-18), DR264 (1918-44) | |
| 949.9 | Aegean Sea islands DS52 | |
| 949.98 | CRETE DF901.C78-89, .C86 (1898-) | |
| | | |
| 950-959 | Asia DS | |
| 950 | ASIA (gen.) DS, DS5, DS33 | |
| 950.3 | Asia (1480-1905) DS33 | |
| 950.4 | Asia (20th c.) DS35 | |
| 950.41 | Asia (1905-45) DS35 | |
| | | |
| 951 | CHINA (plus surrounding areas) DS701-796+, DS706, DS735 | |
| 951.003 | Dictionaries & encyclopedias (China) DS705 | |
| 951.03 | China (1644-1912: inclu. Sino-Japanese War, 1894-5: SEE ALSO 952.03 for Sino-Jpn. War of 1894-5) DS764.4-767.7 | |
| 951.04 | China (1912-49) DS773.83-777.544, DS774 | |
| 951.041 | China (1912-27) DS776.4-777.462, DS776.4 | |
| 951.042 | China (1927-49: Nationalist rule: inclu. Sino-Jpn. conflict of 1937-45: SEE ALSO 940.53 for Sino-Jpn. War of 1937-45) DS777.47-544, DS777.47 | |
| 951.13 | Kiangsu Province (China: inclu. Nanking & Shanghai) DS793.K | |
| 951.156 | Peking, China DS795 | |
| 951.222 | Kiangsi Province (China) | |
| 951.245 | Fukien Province (China) | |
| 951.249 | FORMOSA (Taiwan) DS895.F7-77 (books prior to about 1970), DS798.92-799.99+ | |
| 951.24904 | Formosa (1895-1945: Japanese period) DS895.F75, DS799.69-72, DS799.7 (gen.) | |
| 951.25 | HONG KONG DS796.H7 | |
| 951.2504 | Hong Kong (1843-1945) DS796.H757 | |

| 951.3 | China (Southwestern) |
| 951.35 | Yunnan Province (China) |
| 951.38 | Chungking, China (plus Szechwan Province) |
| 951.38 | Szechwan Province (China: inclu. Chungking) DS793.S8 |
| 951.5 | TIBET DS785 |
| 951.7 | MONGOLIA DS793.M7 |
| 951.8 | MANCHURIA DS781-784+, DS784 (1932-45) |
| 951.9 | KOREA DS901-935, DS916 (20th c.) |

| 952 | JAPAN DS801-897+ |
| 952.03 | Japan (1868-1945: Imperial power) DS881.9 |
| 952.032 | Japan (1912-26: Taisho or Yoshihito era) DS885.8-888, DS886 (gen.) |
| 952.033 | Japan (1926-88: Showa or Hirohito period: inclu. Sino-Jpn. conflict of 1937-41: PREFER 951.042 for Sino-Jpn. War of 1937-41) DS888.15-890+, DS888.2, DS888.5 (1926-45) |
| 952.1 | Honshu (Japan) |
| 952.135 | Tokyo, Japan DS896, DS896.64 (1867-1945), DS897.T6 (for earlier works) |
| 952.19 | Hiroshima, Japan |
| 952.191 | Kyoto, Japan: USE 952.1864 with books after about 1988) |
| 952.3 | Shikoku (Japan) |
| 952.4 | Hokkaido (Japan) |
| 952.7 | Kurile Islands (Japan or Russia) |
| 952.81 | Ryukyu Islands (Japan: inclu. Okinawa: try 952.29 for titles after 1988) |
| 952.85 | Bonin Islands (Japan: SEE 952.28 for works after 1988) |

| 953 | ARABIAN PENINSULA DS201-248+, DS244 (1914-) |
| 954 | Southern Asia & India DS335-498+ |
| 954 | INDIA (overall) DS436 |
| 954.03 | India (1785-1947: British rule) DS463-480, DS463 (gen.) |
| 954.0356 | India (1905-16) DS480.2-3 |
| 954.0357 | India (1916-26) DS480.4-6 |
| 954.0358 | India (1926-36) DS480.7-8 |
| 954.0359 | India (1936-47: Gov'ships. of Linlithgow, Wavell, Mountbatten) DS480.82-83 |
| 954.14 | Calcutta, India (area) DS486.C2 |
| 954.93 | Ceylon DS488-490, DS489.5 (gen. hist.) |

| 955 | PERSIA (Iran) DS251-325, DS272 |
| 955.05 | Iran (1906-) DS298, DS313-318+ |
| 955.051 | Iran (1906-25) DS315-316 |
| 955.052 | Iran (1925-41: Reza Shah era) DS317 |
| 955.053 | Iran (1941-ca. 1978) DS318 |
| 956 | MIDDLE EAST (NEAR EAST) DS41-326 |
| 956.02 | Near East (1900-18) DS62.4 |
| 956.03 | Middle East (1918-45) DS62.4 |
| 956.1 | TURKEY & CYPRUS DR401-741, DS47-53, DS54 (Cyp.) |
| 956.1 | TURKEY (overall) DR440 |
| 956.102 | Turkey (1918-45) DR589-590 |
| 956.1024 | Turkey (1923-38: Kemal Ataturk era) DR590, DR592 (biogs.), DR592.K4(Ataturk) |
| 956.1025 | Turkey (1938-50: Ismet Inonu rule) DR590, DR592 |
| 956.45 | CYPRUS DS54 |
| 956.4503 | Cyprus (1878-1960: British rule) DS54.8 |

| 956.7 | IRAQ       DS67-79, DS70.9 |
| 956.703 | Iraq (1553-1920: Ottoman rule)       DS77 |
| 956.704 | Iraq (1920-: Mandate & independence)   DS79 |
| 956.9 | MEDITERRANEAN REGION (EASTERN)       DS80-151+, DS62 |
| 956.91 | SYRIA       DS92-99, DS95.5 |
| 956.9103 | Syria (1516-1920: time of Ottomans)       DS97.5-6 |
| 956.9104 | Syria (1920-: Mandate & independence)       DS98+ |
| 956.94 | ISRAEL & PALESTINE       DS101-131+, DS116-117, DS123 |
| 956.9403 | Palestine (640-1917)       DS124-125, DS125.5 (WWI yrs.) |
| 956.9404 | Israel (1917-48: Brit. rule)       DS126, DS126.3 (WWII era) |
|  |  |
| 957 | SIBERIA    DK751-781, DK761 |
|  |  |
| 959 | SOUTHEAST ASIA       DS521-689+, DS518 (1904-45: Far E. ?), |
|  | DS525, DS541 |
| 959.05 | Asia, Southeast (20th c.)       DS526.6-7+ |
| 959.051 | Southeast Asia (1900-41)       DS518, DS526.6 (newer titles), DS549 |
| 959.052 | Southeast Asia (1941-45: Japanese occup.)       DS549, DS526.6 |
| 959.1 | BURMA       DS485.B79-892, DS527-530 (newer works), DS528.5 |
| 959.104 | Burma (1886-1948: British rule)       DS485.B89, DS530-530.32 |
| 959.3 | SIAM (THAILAND)       DS561-589, DS571 |
| 959.304 | Siam (20th c.)       DS578 |
| 959.3043 | Siam (1935-46: time of Rama VIII)       DS585 |
| 959.4 | LAOS    DS555, DS557.L2 (earlier books) |
| 959.5 | MALAYSIA       DS591-599, DS592, DS596 |
| 959.503 | Malaysia (to 1946)       DS596, DS596.6 |
| 959.52 | SINGAPORE       DS598.S7 |
| 959.5203 | Singapore (to 1946) |
| 959.6 | CAMBODIA       DS554, DS554.7 |
| 959.7 | FRENCH INDOCHINA & VIETNAM       DS531-558 |
| 959.703 | French Indochina (to 1949)       DS556.8-83 |
| 959.8 | INDONESIA & MALAY ARCHIPELAGO       DS611-649 |
| 959.802 | Indonesia (1602-1945: Dutch period)       DS642-643 |
| 959.8022 | Indonesia (1798-1945)       DS643 |
| 959.81 | Sumatra (Indon.)       DS646.1-15, DS646.129 |
| 959.82 | Java (Indon.)       DS646.17-29, DS646.2 |
| 959.83 | BORNEO       DS646.3-38, DS646.3 |
| 959.9 | PHILIPPINE ISLANDS       DS651-689, DS655, DS668 |
| 959.903 | Philippine Islands (1898-1946: U.S. era)       DS679-686.4, DS685 |
| 959.9032 | Philippine Islands (1901-35)       DS685 |
| 959.9035 | Philippine Islands (1935-46: Commonwealth))       DS686-686.4 |
| 959.91 | Luzon (Philip.: inclu. Manila & Bataan)       DS688.L9 |
| 959.95 | Visayan Islands (Philip.: inclu. Cebu, Leyte, Negros, etc.) |
|  | DS688.B6 (Bisayas) |
| 959.98 | Mindanao (Philip.)       DS688.M2 |
|  |  |
| 960-969 | Africa       DT |
| 960 | AFRICA (gen.)       DT, DT3 (gen.), DT20 (gen. hist.) |
| 960.31 | Africa (1900-45)       DT29 |
|  |  |
| 961 | NORTH AFRICA       DT160-346 |
| 961.03 | North Africa (1830-1950: Eur. era)       DT176 |
| 961.1 | TUNISIA       DT241-269, DT254 |
| 961.104 | Tunisia (1881-1956)       DT264 |

| 961.2 | LIBYA | DT211-239, DT224 |
|---|---|---|
| 961.203 | Libya (1911-52: Ital. rule) | DT235 |
| 962 | EGYPT & SUDAN | DT43-159 |
| 962 | EGYPT (overall) | DT43-107, DT115-154, DT77 |
| 962.04 | Egypt (1882-1922: Brit. protec.) | DT107-107.8, DT107 (gen.) |
| 962.05 | Egypt (1922-: Independence) | DT107.8+ |
| 962.051 | Egypt (1922-36: Fuad I) | DT107.8 |
| 962.052 | Egypt (1936-52: Faruk I) | DT107.82 |
| 962.4 | SUDAN | DT108 (older works), DT154.1-159 |
| 963 | ETHIOPIA (Abyssinia) | DT371-398, DT381 |
| 963.05 | Ethiopia (1896-1941 & 20th c.) | DT386-387.9, DT386 |
| 963.055 | Ethiopia (1930-74: Haile Selassie era) | DT387.7-387.92 |
| 963.056 | Ethiopia (1935-6: Italo-Eth. War: SEE ALSO 945.091 for Italo-Eth. War of 1935-6) | DT387.8 |
| 963.057 | Ethiopia (1936-41: Ital. rule) | DT387.9 |
| 963.06 | Ethiopia (1941-: Independence) | DT387.9 |
|  |  |  |
| 964 | NORTHWEST AFRICA, Morocco, & offshore islands | |
| 964 | MOROCCO (in sum) | DT301-330, DT305, DT314 |
| 964.04 | Morocco (1900-56) | DT324 |
| 964.3 | Casablanca, Mor. (area) | DT329.C3 |
| 964.8 | SPANISH WEST AFRICA | |
| 964.9 | CANARY ISLANDS | DP302.C36-51 |
| 965 | ALGERIA | DT271-299, DT275, DT284 |
| 965.04 | Algeria (1900-62: last of Fr. rule) | DT295 (older titles), DT294.5-295.3 |
| 966 | SAHARA DESERT & West Africa | |
| 967.6 | EAST AFRICA (Uganda & Kenya) | DT421-435+ (newer titles), DT431 |
| 967.62 | KENYA | DT434.E2, DT433.5-434, DT433.522, DT433.557 |
| 967.6203 | Kenya (1895-1963: Brit. rule) | DT433.57-577 |
| 967.8103 | ZANZIBAR (1890-1963) | DT435, DT449.Z2-29 (newer works), DT449.Z28 |
| 967.8202 | GERMAN WEST AFRICA (1884-1916) | DT444, DT447 (newer books) |
| 967.8203 | Tanganyika (1916-61: Brit. era) | DT444, DT447 |
| 968 | AFRICA, SOUTHERN | DT730-990+, DT732-733 |
| 968 | SOUTH AFRICA (overall) | DT751-944, DT766 |
| 968.05 | South Africa (1910-61: Union) | DT779 |
| 968.052 | South Africa (1910-19: Louis Botha) | DT779.5 |
| 968.055 | South Africa (1939-48: Jan Christiaan Smuts: 2d era) | DT779.7 |
| 968.9 | NORTHERN RHODESIA (Zambia), Rhodesia (Zimbabwe), & Nyasaland (Malawi) | DT858-865 (Malawi, Nyasaland, Br. Central Afr. Protec.), DT946-965 (Rhodesia), DT963 (Zambia) |
| 969.1 | MADAGASCAR | DT469.M21-38 |

| | | |
|---|---|---|
| 970-979 | North America & America | E-F |
| 970 | NORTH AMERICA (gen.) | E-F1392+, E11-45, E31-45 |
| 970.05 | North America (1900-) | E45, E18.85 |
| 970.051 | North America (1900-18) | |
| 970.052 | North America (1918-45) | |

| | | |
|---|---|---|
| 971 | CANADA | F1001-1140 |
| 971.06 | Canada (20th c. & 1911-) | F1034 |
| 971.061 | Canada (1911-21) | |
| 971.062 | Canada (1921-35) | |
| 971.063 | Canada (1935-57) | |
| 971.0632 | Canada (1935-48: 2d prime min'ship. of Wm. Lyon Mackenzie King) | |
| 971.1 | British Columbia | F1086-1089.7, F1089 (gen.) |
| 971.3 | Ontario (Can.) | F1056-1059.7, F1058 (gen.) |
| 971.4 | Quebec | F1051-1055 |
| 971.6 | Nova Scotia | F1036-1040, F1038 (gen.) |
| 971.8 | Newfoundland | F1121-1139 |

| | | |
|---|---|---|
| 972 | CARIBBEAN, MEXICO, & CENTRAL AMERICA | F1201-1392 (Mex.), F1421-2175 |
| 972 | MEXICO (overall) | F1201-1392, F1208, F1226 |
| 972.082 | Mexico (1917-64) | F1234-1235 |
| 972.8 | CENTRAL AMERICA | F1421-1577, F1436 |
| 972.805 | Central America (1900-) | F1438-1439 |
| 972.87 | PANAMA | F1561-1577, F1566 |
| 972.87051 | Panama (1904-45) | F1566.5 |
| 972.875 | Panama Canal & Zone | F1569.C2 |
| 972.9 | WEST INDIES | F1601-2175+, F1608, F1621 |
| 972.9051 | West Indies (1902-45) | F1623 |
| 972.91 | CUBA | F1751-1849, F1758, F1776 |
| 972.9106 | Cuba (1899-) | F1787-1788 |
| 972.92 | JAMAICA | F1861-1896, F1881 |
| 972.95 | PUERTO RICO | F1951-1983, F1971 |
| 972.983 | TRINIDAD & TOBAGO | F2016 (Windward Is.), F2116 (Tob.), F2121 (Trin.) |

| | | |
|---|---|---|
| 973 | UNITED STATES | E-F975+, E178 (gen.) |
| 973.03 | Encyclopedias & dictionaries (U.S.) | E174 |
| 973.05 | Serials & periodicals (U.S.) | E171 |
| 973.06 | Clubs & societies (U.S.) | E172 |
| 973.9 | United States (20th c.) | E740-749, E741 |
| 973.91 | United States (1901-53) | E741, E740-816 |
| 973.913 | United States (1913-21: Woodrow Wilson) | E765-783, E766, E780 (WWI era) |
| 973.914 | United States (1921-23: Warren G. Harding era) | E783-786, E785 |
| 973.915 | United States (1923-29: Calvin Coolidge) | E791-796, E791 |
| 973.916 | United States (1929-33: Herbert C. Hoover) | E796-805, E801 |
| 973.917 | United States (1933-45: Franklin D. Roosevelt) | E805-812, E806 |

| | | |
|---|---|---|
| 974-979 | UNITED STATES (local: regions, states, towns, etc.: note that Hawaii is placed at 996.9) | F1-900+ |
| 974 | New England & Middle Atlantic states | F1-105 (New Eng.), F106-205 (Mid. At.), F1-15, F106 |
| 974.042 | New England & Middle Atlantic states (1918-45) | F9 (New Eng.), F106 (Mid. At.) |
| 974.1 | Maine F16-30, F19 (gen.), F25 (1865-1950) | |
| 974.4 | Massachusetts F61-75, F64 | |
| 974.7 | New York F116-130, F119 | |
| 974.7042 | New York (1918-45) F124 (1865-1950) | |
| 974.71 | New York City, N.Y. F128, F128.3 | |
| 974.721 | Long Island, N.Y. F127.L8 | |
| 974.8 | Pennsylvania F146-160, F149 | |
| 974.811 | Philadelphia, Penn. F158 | |
| 974.9 | New Jersey F131-145 | |
| 975 | South Atlantic states F206-295, F206-220, F209, F215 (1865-) | |
| 975.3 | District of Columbia F191-205, F194 | |
| 975.303 | Washington, D.C. (1865-1933) F198-199 | |
| 975.304 | Washington, D.C. (1933-) F199+ | |
| 975.5 | Virginia F221-235, F226, F231 (1865-1950) | |
| 975.8 | Georgia F281-295, F286 | |
| 975.9 | Florida F306-320, F311 | |
| 975.9062 | Florida (1918-45) F316 | |
| 975.9381 | Miami, Florida F319.M6 | |
| 975.941 | Florida Keys F317.M7 (Monroe Co.) | |
| 976 | South Central states & Gulf Coast F296-475, F296-395 (Gulf), F296-301, F396-475 (Old S.W.), F396 | |
| 976.3 | Louisiana F366-380, F369 | |
| 976.4 | Texas F381-395, F386 | |
| 976.4062 | Texas (1918-45) F391 | |
| 976.4139 | Galveston, Texas (area) F392.G25 | |
| 976.496 | El Paso, Texas (area) F392.E45, F394.E4 | |
| 976.7 | Arkansas F406-420 | |
| 976.9 | Kentucky F446-460 | |
| 977 | North Central states F476-705, F476-590 (Old N.W.), F476-485, F591-705 (Trans-Miss.), F591-596 | |
| 977.1 | Ohio F486-500, F491 | |
| 977.3 | Illinois F536-550, F541, F546 (1865-1950) | |
| 977.311 | Chicago, Ill. F548 | |
| 977.4 | Michigan (inclu. Lakes Mich. & Huron) F561-575, F566 | |
| 977.49 | Lake Superior & Upper Peninsula (Mich.) F572.N8 (N. Penin.), F552 (Lake Sup.) | |
| 977.8 | Missouri F461-475, F466 | |
| 978 | Western states F591-785, F591-596, F591 | |
| 978.1 | Kansas F676-690 | |
| 978.4 | North Dakota F631-645 | |
| 978.6 | Montana F726-740 | |
| 978.8 | Colorado F771-785, F776 | |
| 978.883 | Denver, Colo. F784.D4 | |
| 978.9 | New Mexico F791-805, F796 | |

| | | |
|---|---|---|
| 979 | Great Basin & Pacific Coast states | F786-915, F786-850 (New S.W.), F786-788, F851-915 (Pac. states), F851 |
| 979.03 | Pacific Coast & Great Basin (U.S.: 20th c.) | F786, F852 |
| 979.1 | Arizona F806-820 | |
| 979.3 | Nevada F836-850 | |
| 979.4 | California F856-870, F861 (gen.) | |
| 979.405 | California (1900-) F866 (1869-1950) | |
| 979.4052 | California (1918-45) F866 | |
| 979.454 | Sacramento, Calif. F869.S12 | |
| 979.46 | San Francisco Bay area F868.S156 | |
| 979.461 | San Francisco, Calif. F869.S3 | |
| 979.49 | California, Southern F867 | |
| 979.491 | Santa Barbara County (Calif.) F868.S23 | |
| 979.493 | Los Angeles County (Calif.) F868.L8 | |
| 979.494 | Los Angeles, Calif. F869.L8 | |
| 979.495 | San Bernardino County (Calif.) F868.S14 | |
| 979.498 | San Diego County (Calif.) F868.S15 | |
| 979.5 | Oregon F871-885 | |
| 979.7 | Washington F886-900, F891 | |
| 979.77 | Puget Sound area (Wash.) F897.P9 | |
| 979.777 | Seattle, Wash. (area) F897.K4, F899.S4 | |
| 979.8 | Alaska F901-915 | |
| 979.804 | Alaska (1912-59: U.S. Territory) F909 | |
| 979.84 | Aleutian Islands & Southwestern Alaska F951 | |
| | | |
| 980-989 | South America F | |
| 980 | SOUTH AMERICA (overall: inclu. Latin Am. in gen.) | F2201-3799+, F2201-2239, F2231 (GEN.) |
| 980.033 | South America (1918-49) F2236, F2237 (1939-) | |
| 981 | BRAZIL F2501-2659, F2521 | |
| 981.061 | Brazil (1930-54) F2538 | |
| 982 | ARGENTINA F2801-3021+, F2831 (gen.) | |
| 982.06 | Argentina (20th c.) F2847-2849+ | |
| 982.061 | Argentina (1910-46) F2848 | |
| 982.11 | Buenos Aires, Arg. (area) F3001 | |
| 983 | CHILE F3051-3285, F3081 (gen.) | |
| 985 | PERU F3401-3619, F3431 | |
| 987 | VENEZUELA F2301-2349, F2321 | |
| 989.2 | PARAGUAY F2661-2699 | |
| 989.5 | URUGUAY F2701-2799, F2721 (gen.) | |
| 989.5063 | Uruguay (1933-51) F2728 | |
| 989.513 | Montevideo, Urug. F2781 | |

| | |
|---|---|
| 990-999 | History (misc. areas: Oceania, Atlantic islands, Arctic, extraterr. worlds, etc.)          C-F, G, Q |
| 990 | OCEANICA & other misc. areas (SEE ALSO 995 for gen. works after about 1988)       DU, DU28.3 |
| 993-996 | OCEANIA       DU |

| | |
|---|---|
| 993 | NEW ZEALAND & MELANESIA (overall: SEE ALSO 993.1 for N.Z. titles before 1989, 995 for Mel. after about 1988)     DU400-490+ |
| 993.03 | New Zealand (1908-: Dominion: SEE ALSO 993.103 for works before 1989) |
| 993.032 | New Zealand (1918-45: SEE ALSO 993.1032 for titles before about 1989) |
| 993.1 | NEW ZEALAND (PREFER 993 after 1988)      DU400-430 |
| 993.103 | New Zealand (1908-: Dominion: PREFER 993.03+ for titles after 1988)       DU420-421 |
| 993.1031 | New Zealand (1908-18) |
| 993.1032 | New Zealand (1918-45) |
| 993.12 | North Island (New Z.) |
| 993.122 | Auckland, New Z. (area)     DU430.A79 |
| 993.15 | South Island (New Z.) |
| 993.155 | Christchurch, New Z. (area)     DU430.C5 |

| | |
|---|---|
| 993.2-993.7 | MELANESIA (PREFER 995 after 1988)     DU490 (gen.) |
| 993.2 | NEW CALEDONIA (try ALSO 993.97 after 1988)     DU720 |
| 993.4 | NEW HEBRIDES (SEE ALSO 995.95 for books after 1988)     DU760 |
| 993.5 | SOLOMON ISLANDS (ALSO try 995.93 for works dated after 1988)            DU850 |
| 993.6 | BISMARCK ARCHIPELAGO (inclu. New Britain [Rabaul] & New Ireland: PREFER 995.8 for pubn. dates after 1988)     DU550-553, DU553.N35 (New Brit.) |
| 993.95 | VANUATU (New Hebrides: SEE ALSO 993.4 to find works on New Hebrides prior to 1989)     DU760 |
| 993.97 | NEW CALEDONIA (SEE ALSO 993.2 for works before 1989)     DU720 |

| | |
|---|---|
| 994 | AUSTRALIA       DU80-398, DU450-480, DU110 (gen.) |
| 994.04 | Australia (1901-45)     DU116 |
| 994.041 | Australia (1901-22) |
| 994.042 | Australia (1922-45) |
| 994.1 | Australia, Western     DU350-380 |
| 994.11 | Perth, Australia (area)     DU378 |
| 994.2 | Australia, Central     DU300-330, DU390+ |
| 994.29 | Northern Territory (Australia)     DU392-398 |
| 994.295 | Darwin & N. District (Australia)     DU398.D3 |
| 994.3 | Queensland (Australia: inclu. Great Barrier Reef)     DU250-280 |
| 994.31 | Brisbane, Australia     DU278 |
| 994.4 | New South Wales (Australia)     DU150-180, DU170 |
| 994.41 | Sydney, Australia (area)     DU178 |
| 994.5 | Victoria (Australia)     DU200-230, DU220 |
| 994.51 | Melbourne, Australia     DU228 |
| 994.6 | Tasmania     DU450-480, DU470 |
| 994.7 | Capital Territory (Australia)     DU145 |
| 994.71 | Canberra, Australia     DU145 |

# III. INDEX TO LIBRARY OF CONGRESS & DEWEY CLASSIFICATION

Following is a unified index to both of the preceding classification sections--
Library of Congress and Dewey. Words and phrases are followed by either
LC, Dewey, or sometimes both kinds of numbers. Since this listing was
generated by alphabetizing a combined LC/Dewey database, one might find
either form given first. Entries missing one or the other of the types do so
because exact translations could not be found or do not exist. A similar
warning as in other sections: do not use this part of the book alone for
complete knowledge of a topical area. Class index entries, class numbers and
ranges, and subject/corporate phrases from the different sections should all
be consulted for the most thorough group of control points.

INDEX WORDS/PHRASES: POSSIBLE CLASS NUMBERS (LC AND/OR DEWEY)

5 in. guns, Naval (U.S.: manuals)   VF393.A5.5
1900-1999 (20th c.: gen. hist.)     909.82       D421, D443
1900-1919 (gen. hist.)     909.821     D421, D521 (WWI: gen.)
1920-1929 (gen. hist.)     909.822     D653, D655-659, D720, D723-728 (1919-39)
1930-1939 (gen. hist.)     909.823     D720, D723-728
1940-1949 (gen. hist.)     909.824     D743 (WWII: gen.), D825, D840

AACHEN, Ger. (Aix-la-Chapelle)    DD901.A25-28
Abandoning ship (plus other misc. marine topics of disaster)    VK1259
Abyssinia (19th -20th c.)        DT386    963.03-05+
Accidents, Marine      VK199
Accounting & accounts, Military (inclu. records, muster rolls, etc.)    UB160-165
Accounting & accounts, Naval (inclu. ships' records)    VC500-505    359.622
Addis Ababa, Eth.      DT390.A3
Adelaide, Australia     DU328       994.231
Aden             DS247.A2
Adjutant generals' offices      UB170-175
Administration (air forces: structure & personnel: gen.)    UG770-775    358.41,
                                                                    .413, .416+
Administration (marines)      359.966     VB21-124
ADMINISTRATION, MILITARY       UB
Administration, Military (Asia: gen.)      UB99
Administration, Military (command, intelligence, law, etc.)    UB    355, .6
Administration, Military (Eur.: gen.)      UB55
Administration, Military (G.B.: gen.)      UB57    355.60941, 354.41066
Administration, Military (gen. hist.)      UB15
Administration, Military supply & finance    355.62   UC260-267, UA
Administration, Military (U.S.: gen.)      UB23
ADMINISTRATION, NAVAL          359.6       VB, VB15, VB21-124 (by place),
              VB23 (U.S.), VC (maint.), VC10, VC20-258 (by place), VC20-65 (U.S.)
Administration, Naval (Asia: gen.)      VB99     359.6095
Administration, Naval (command, personnel, law, etc.)    VB
Administration, Naval (Eur.: gen.)      VB55     359.6094
Administration, Naval (gen. hist.)      VB15     359.6, .1-3
Administration, Naval (misc. topics)      VB955
Administration, Naval supply & finance      359.62     VC10, VC20-258 (by
                                                   place), VC20-65 (U.S.)

Admirals, commanders, etc. (admin.: inclu. duties)    VB190
Admiralty Islands        DU520    993.7
Adriatic coast (Yug.)        DR1350.A35
Advanced guard        U167.5.A35
Adventists (WWII)    D810.C53
Aegean islands        DS52-53    949.9
Aegean Sea        DR701.A5
Aegean Sea islands        949.9    DS52
Aerial observations (artillery)        UF805
AERIAL OPS. (Sp. Civil War, 1936-39)        DP269.4
Aerial ops. (WWI: G.B.)        940.44941        D602
Aerial ops. (WWI: gen.)        D600
Aerial ops. (WWI: Ger.)        940.44943        D604
Aerial ops. (WWI: particular countries)        940.449
Aerial ops. (WWI: U.S.)        940.44973    D606, D570.6-7 (squadrons)
AERIAL OPS. (WWII: Australia)    940.544994        D792.A8
Aerial ops. (WWII: by country: inclu. specific craft, units, fliers)        940.5449+
Aerial ops. (WWII: Can.)        940.544971
Aerial ops. (WWII: China)        940.544951        D792.C5
Aerial ops. (WWII: G.B.: R.A.F. etc.)        940.544941-544942        D786
Aerial ops. (WWII: gen.)        D785    940.544
Aerial ops. (WWII: Ger.: Luftwaffe etc.)    940.544943        D787
Aerial ops. (WWII: It.)        940.544945        D792.I8
Aerial ops. (WWII: Japan)        940.544952        D792.J3
Aerial ops. (WWII: misc. countries)        D792.A-Z
Aerial ops. (WWII: particular srvcs.: scouting, artil. supp., bombing, close air supp.,
        antisub. ops., balloon barrage, coast patrols, etc.)        940.5441
Aerial ops. (WWII: Rus.)        940.544947        D792.R9 or .S65
Aerial ops. (WWII: U.S.: Army Air Corps, Navy, Marines, etc.)        940.544973
                                                                                                    D790
Aerial reconnaisance (U.S.)        UG763
Aerial warfare & air forces        358.4 (inclu. naval av. for works prior to 1989--SEE
        359.94 after 1988)        UG622-1425, UG630, UG633-634 (U.S.),
        UG635.A-Z (places besides U.S.), VG90-95 (naval av.)
Aerodynamics    629.1323
Aeronautics    629.13
Aeronautics (principles)        629.132
AFRICA        960-969    DT
Africa (1884-1945: gen.)        DT29    960.23-31
Africa (1900-45)        960.31    DT29
Africa (gen.)        960        DT, DT3 (gen.), DT20 (gen. hist.)
Africa (geog. & travel)        916    DT55 (1901-50)
Africa (lighthouses, beacons, foghorns, etc.)        VK1115-1119
Africa (lighthouses, beacons, foghorns, etc.: lists)    VK1190-1199
Africa (mil. status: gen.)    UA855        355.03306
Africa (naval status)        VA670-700
Africa, Northwest (geog. & travel: Morocco, Canary Islands, etc.)        916.4
                                                                                                    DT165, DT310 (Mor.)
Africa (overall)    DT1-38        960
Africa (post-WWI territorial ?s)        D651.A4
Africa, Southern        968    DT730-990+, DT732-733

Africa (WWII)         D766.8-99
Africa (WWII: by country)     D766.9-99
Africa (WWII: dipl. history)     D754.A34
Africa (WWII: gen.)       D766.8     940.536, .5423, 960.31
Africa (WWII: misc. countries: by name)     D766.99.A-Z
Afro-Americans & American Indians as troops (WWII)     940.5403     D810.N4,
                                                                                    D810.I5
Afro-Americans (armed forces)     UB418.A47
Afro-Americans (U.S. Navy)       VB324.A47
Afro-Americans (WWII)       940.53150396073     E185, D810.N4
Agricultural products (mil. raw materials)     355.245     UA929.95.A35
Agriculture (defense)     UA929.95.A35
Agriculture, forestry, hunting     S       630-639, 574, 581, 799
AIR BASES & fields (U.S.: by name)     UG634.5.A-Z
Air bases (mil. design)     623.6613     UG633-634.5 (U.S.), UG635 (other lands)
Air bases (WWII: by area or place)       940.5443+
Air bases (WWII: in Australia)       940.544394
Air bases (WWII: in China)       940.544351
Air bases (WWII: in Eng.)     940.544342 D786
Air bases (WWII: in Ger.)     940.544343 D787
Air bases (WWII: in Japan)     940.544352 D792.J3
Air bases (WWII: in Rus.)     940.544347
Air bases (WWII: in U.S.)     940.544373 D790
Air battles & campaigns (WWII)     940.5442     D785+
Air defenses (U.S.)       UG733   358.41450973
Air fields & stations, Naval (U.S.: by name)       VG94.5.A-Z
AIR FORCE administration     358.416     UG770-775, UG1100-1135, UG630-635
Air force bombs (by specific type)   UG1282.A-Z
Air force communications & ops.     358.46     UA940-945, UG611-612.5
Air force equipment (gen.: planes, bombs, etc.)     UG1200       358.418, .412
Air force facilities     623.66     UG633-635, UG21-124 (engnrg. by place),
                                     UG360-390 (field engnrg.)
Air force history (G.B.)     DA89.5-6
Air force life & customs     358.411     U750-773, UG770-775, UG1130-1135
Air force manuals & regulations (places except U.S.)       UG675.A-Z
Air force officers (countries except U.S.)     UG795.A-Z
Air force ops. (gen.)     358.414     UG630, UG633-635, UG700-765
Air force ops. (WWI)     D600-607     940.44
Air force ops. (WWII)     D785-792     940.544
Air force ordnance (gen.: U.S.)     UG1273
Air force personnel     358.4161   UG1130-1135
AIR FORCE PLANES (countries besides U.S.)     UG1245.A-Z
Air force planes (Fr.)     UG1245.F8     358.400944
Air force planes (G.B.)     UG1245.G7     358.400941, .414741-414742,
                                     623.740941, .7460941
Air force planes (Ger.)     UG1245.G3     358.400943, .414743, 623.740943
Air force planes (It.)     UG1245.I8     358.400945
Air force planes (Japan)     UG1245.J3     358.400952, .414752, 623.740952
Air force planes (Rus.)     UG1245.R9     358.400947
Air force planes (U.S.: PREFER UG1242 for particular types)     UG1243
                             358.40973, .4140973, .414773, 623.740973, .7460973
Air force radar & electronics (places besides U.S.)       UG1425.A-Z
Air force regulations & manuals (Ger.)       UG675.G3

Air force tactics (gen.)　　UG700
Air force training & education (U.S.)　　UG638-638.8
Air force units (types)　　358.4131
AIR FORCES & air warfare　　UG622-1425　　358.4, 623.74-746
Air forces & warfare (essays & lectures)　　UG627
Air forces & warfare (hist.: gen.)　　UG625　358.4009
Air forces & warfare, Naval　　VG90-95　　359.94, 358.4
Air forces (Australia)　　UG635.A8
Air forces (Fr.)　　UG635.F8
Air forces (G.B.)　　UG635.G7
Air forces (Ger.)　　UG635.G3
Air forces (It.)　　UG635.I8
Air forces (Japan)　　UG635.J3
Air forces, Naval (U.S.: by area or state)　　VG94.A-Z
Air forces (places besides U.S.)　　UG635.A-Z
Air forces (policy & status)　　358.403　　UG630-635, UA
Air forces (Rus.)　　UG635.R9
Air forces (Sov.Un.)　　UG635.S65
Air forces (U.S.: by state)　UG634.A-W
Air forces (U.S.: gen.)　　UG633　　358.400973
Air museums & exhibitions (by country or area)　　UG623.3.A2-Z
Air National Guard (U.S.)　　UG853
Air-raid warning systems (design)　　623.737 (SEE 623.37 for titles prior to 1989)
　　　　　　　　　UG730-735
Air raids (WWI)　　940.442　　D600-607
Air reserves, Naval & marine (U.S.)　　VG94.7.A-Z
Air traffic control (mil. engineering)　　623.666
Air transport, Military　　UC330-335　　358.44
AIR WARFARE　　D437　　358.41409, 358.41447
Air warfare & forces (collected works: gen.)　　UG624
Air warfare & forces (gen.)　　UG630　　358.4
Air warfare & forces, Naval (gen.)　　VG90　　358.4, 359.3255, 623.746
Air warfare (gen.)　　358.41
Air warfare (hist.: gen.)　　358.41409　　UG625
Airborne & parachute troops　　UD480-485　　356.166
Airborne troop battalions etc. (WWII: U.S.: by #)　　D769.346.1st-
Airborne troops (WWII: G.B.)　　D759.6
Airborne troops (WWII: Ger.)　　D757.6
Airborne troops (WWII: U.S.: gen.)　　D769.345
Aircraft (heavier-than-air: mil. engineering)　　623.746　　UG1240-1245,
　　　　　　　　　UG630-635, TL685.3, VG90-95
Aircraft (lighter-than-air: mil. design)　　623.741　　UG1310-1375
AIRCRAFT CARRIERS (as equip.)　　359.94835 (SEE ALSO .8355 on titles
　　　　　　　　　before 1989)
Aircraft carriers (engineering)　　623.8255　　V874-874.5
Aircraft carriers (G.B.)　　V874.5.G7　　623.82550941
Aircraft carriers (gen.)　　V874　　623.8255, 359.3255
Aircraft carriers (handling)　　623.88255　　V874-875
Aircraft carriers (Japan)　　V874.5.J3　　623.82550952
Aircraft carriers (special topics)　　V875.A-Z
Aircraft carriers (U.S.)　　V874.3　　623.82550973, .81255, 359.32550973
Aircraft carriers (units)　　359.3255 (SEE ALSO .9435 for pubns. after 1988)
　　　V874-875, V874.3 (U.S.), V874.5.A-Z (other places), VA65.A-Z (U.S.: by name)

Aircraft components (cabins, engines, fuselages, instruments, wings, etc.)
623.746049    TL672-683
Aircraft guns & small weapons (gen.)    UG1340
Aircraft instrumentation (flight)    629.1352
Aircraft instrumentation (navig.)    629.1351
Aircraft launching & recovery equipment (carriers)    V875.A36
Aircraft, Naval    359.94834
Aircraft parts & components    629.134
Aircraft (types: engineering)    629.133+
Airfields & bases (countries besides U.S.: by name of base)    UG635.x2.A-Z
Airmen & non-commissioned air officers    UG820-825    358.41338
Airplanes    629.13334 (engineering)
Airplanes (air force: by type)    UG1242.A-Z
Airplanes (air force: gen.)    UG1240
Airplanes, Military    UG1240-1245    623.746, 358.418
Airports (engineering)    629.136
Airships or dirigibles (gen.)    UG1220    623.743
Airships, Rigid (mil. engineering)    623.7435
Airships, Semirigid & nonrigid (mil. engineering)    623.7436-7437
Akagi (aircraft carrier: Japan)    VA655.A43
Alabama    F321-335    976.1
Alabama (to 1950)    F326
Alaska    979.8    F901-915
Alaska (1894-1959)    F909    979.803-804
Alaska (1912-59: U.S. Territory)    979.804    F909
Alaska area    F901-951    979.8
ALBANIA    949.65    DR701.S49-86 (known as Scutari for earlier works),
    DR701.S5, DR941-979+ (for later works), DR941 (gen.)
Albania (1912-46)    949.6502    DR701.S6 (1914-17), .S85 (1939-43),
    DR971, DR972 (WWI), DR975 (WWII)
Albania (1912-44)    DR970-975
Albania (1912-44: gen.)    DR971
Albania (1912-18)    DR972, DR46+ (Balkan War etc.)
Albania (1914-17: Kingdom)    DR701.S6    949.6502
Albania (1917-25)    DR701.S7    949.6502
Albania (1925-39)    DR974    949.6501-6502
Albania (1925-39: Zog I)    DR701.S8    949.6502
Albania (1939-44)    DR975
Albania (1939-43: Ital. rule)    DR701.S85    949.6502
Albania (1944-)    DR977    949.6502-6503
Albania (1946-: Republic)    DR701.S86
Albania (gen.)    DR941
Albania (geog. & travel)    914.965    DR701.S5, DR917 (later books)
Albania (post-WWI territorial ?s)    D651.A5
Albania (Scutari) DR701.S49-86 (SEE ALSO DR941-979 for later titles)    949.65
Albania (WWII)    D766.7.A4
Albany, N.Y.    F129.A3
Alberta    F1075-1080    971.23
Aleutian Islands & Bering Sea    F951 (SEE D769.87.A4 for 1939-45 & Jpn.
    occupation)    979.84, 940.096451, 909.096451824
Aleutian Islands & Southwestern Alaska    979.84    F951
Aleutian Islands (WWII)    PREFER D769.87.A4, but sometimes D767.913
Aleuts (WWII)    D810.A53
Alexander, Harold Rupert (G.B.: 20th c. mil. biog.)    DA69.3.A57
Alexandria, Egypt    DT154.A4

Alfonso XIII (Sp.: King, 1886-1931)    DP238
ALGERIA    DT271-299, DT275, DT284    965
Algeria (1900-62: last of Fr. rule)    965.04    DT295 (older titles), DT294.5-295.3
Algeria (1901+)    DT295 (for newer works SEE DT294.5-295.3)    965.04+
Algeria (1901-62)    DT294.5-295.3 (for older titles use DT295)
Algeria (1901-45)    DT294.5-7    965.04 (1900-62)
Algeria (geog. & travel)    916.5    DT280
Algeria (mil. status)    UA858    355.033065
Algeria (WWII)    D766.99.A6
Algiers, Alg.    DT299.A5    965.3
ALIEN ENEMIES (WWI)    D636
Alien enemies (WWII)    D801    940.5315, .53163
Alien enemies (WWII: by country)    D801.A3-Z
Alien enemies (WWII: Fr.)    D801.F8
Alien enemies (WWII: gen.)    D801.A2    940.5315, .53163
Alien enemies (WWII: U.S.: inclu. Japanese relocation centers: SEE ALSO D753.8.
    For alien property custody SEE JX5313.U6)    D769.8.A6    940.5315+,
                                                             .547273, .53163
Alliances, Military    355.031
Allied forces (air)    358.41356    UG625, UG630+
Allied forces (inclu. various multi-nat. & combined ops.)    355.356    UA12 (U.S.),
                                                                    UA15, U260 (comb. ops.)
Allied intervention (Rus. Rev.: by country)    DK265.42.A-Z
Allied naval forces (inclu. various coalition forces)    359.356    VA40-42, VA, U260
ALLIES & Allied military ops (WWI: gen.)    D544    940.412+, .414, .42-3, 944.0814
Allies & anti-Axis exile govs. or nat. groups (WWII: dipl. hist.)    940.5322+    D748
Allies & associates (WWI: dipl. hist.)    940.322    D511, D459 (Triple Entente)
Allies (WWI: gen. particip.)    940.332    D544
Allies (WWI: mil. & naval life & customs)    940.483+    D544
Allies (WWII: mil. & naval life & customs)    940.5483+    U750, U765+,
                                                          V720 (naval), V735+
Allowances & pay (U.S. Navy: tables inclu. interest)    VC54
Almanacs & yearbooks, Nautical (American: inclu. abridged)    VK7
Almanacs, annuals, etc., Military (countries besides U.S.)    U10.A-Z
Almanacs, annuals, etc., Military (G.B.)    U10.G7
Almanacs, annuals, etc., Military (U.S.)    U9
Almanacs, Naval (official)    V9    359.00202
Alpine region (Switz.)    949.47    DQ820-841, DQ823
Alps    DQ820-829    949.47
Alsace, Fr. (WWI)    D545.A55 (SEE ALSO DD801.A57)
Alsace-Lorraine (Ger.)    DD801.A31-69
Alsace-Lorraine (WWII: occupied terr.)    D802.A45
Ambulance services (WWII)    940.54753
Ambulances (mil. design)    623.74724    UH500-505
Ambulances, Military (plus transport)    UH500-505    623.74724
America (1901-)    E18.185    970.05
America & American neutrality (WWII: dipl. history)    D752.8
America & North America (gen.), United States    E    970, 973
America (gen.)    E1-143    970
America (mil. status: gen.)    UA21    355.03301812
Americal Division (WWII: U.S.)    D769.295.A5

AMERICAN literature in English     PS     810-819
American military ops. & U.S. (WWI: gen. unofficial)     D570.A5-Z     940.373,
                                                                     41273, .40973, 327.73
American Red Cross   UH537.A
American Samoa     DU819.A1     996.13
American waters (gen.: pilot & sailing guides)     VK804     623.89297
Americanization, civilization, etc. (U.S.)     E169.1
Americans (in Arg.)     F3021.A5
Americans (in Brazil)     F2659.A5
Americans (in Peru)     F3619.A5
Americas (WWII)     D768-769
Ammunition & other ruinous media (design)   623.45     UF700-770
Ammunition (navies)     359.825
Ammunition, Artillery     UF700     358.825, 623.45
Ammunition, Naval     VF460     359.825, 623.45
Ammunition, Small arms   355.8255
Amphibious ops.     U261     359.83, .96
Amphibious planes   629.133348
Amsterdam, Neth.     DJ411.A5-59
Analysis, Air warfare (real & imagined)   358.4148     UG630-635
Analysis, Military (real & mock events)   355.48     UA719-740+, U161-167+
Analysis, Naval warfare (real & imagined battles, campaigns, etc.)     359.48
                                                                     V25-55, V160-178
Anarchism & anarchists (WWII)     D810.A6
Anarchists (Rus. Rev., 1917-21)     DK265.9.A5
Anchors, cables, etc. (marine engin.)     VM791
Ancient history     930-939     C-F
Andalusia (Sp.)   DP302.A41-55
Andaman & Nicobar Islands     DS491.A5-6
Andes     F2212
Andorra     946.79     DC921-930
Andorra (modern hist.)     DC928
Anecdotes (WWII)     940.5494
Angkor, Cam.     DS558.A6
ANGLO-Egyptian Sudan (1899-1955)   DT108.6     962.403
Anglo-French & Allied military ops (WWI)     D544-549+
Anglo-German naval conflict & blockade (WWII: gen.)     D771     940.545, .5452
Anglo-Italian naval conflict (WWII: gen.)     D775     940.545941, .545945
Anglo-Saxon supremacy     D446
Anglo-Soviet Treaty (26 May 1942)     D749.5.A5
Angola (Portuguese West Africa)     DT591-617     967.3
Animals (WWI: use of)     D639.A65
Animals (WWII: inclu. use of dogs, horses, etc.)   D810.A65
Animals, Military     UH87-100
Animals, Use of (mil. sci.)     355.424
Annam (Fr. protectorate only)   DS559.92.A5
Annam (Vietnam: gen.)     DS556.5
Annapolis (U.S. Naval Acad.: gen. hist's. & other titles)     V415.L1
Annapolis (U.S. Naval Acad.: life & conditions)     V415.P1
Annual registers (20th c.: politics and diplomacy)     D440
Anschluss & WWII Period (Austria: 1938-55)     943.6052     DB99 (1938-45),
                                                     DB99.1 (Allied occup., 1945-55)
Antarctica     998.9

ANTI-aircraft artillery (WWII: Ger.)     D757.4.A-53
Anti-aircraft artillery (WWII: U.S.: gen.)     D769.342
Anti-aircraft artillery battalions (WWII: U.S.: by #)     D769.343.1st-
Anti-aircraft Command (WWII: G.B.)     D759.523
Anti-aircraft, Light Artillery regiments (WWII: G.B.)     D759.527
Anti-guerrilla warfare     U241
Anti-Semitism     DS145
Anti-Soviet propaganda (1925-53: gen.)     DK272.5
Antiaircraft (U.S.: N.Y. army reserves)     UA367.7-75
Antiaircraft artillery (U.S.: Calif. army reserves)     UA97.7-75
Antiaircraft guns & defenses     UF625 (SEE ALSO UG730+)     358.13
Antiaircraft guns, Naval     VF418     359.981
Antilles (Greater: gen. hist. of the chain)     F1741     972.9
Antilles (Lesser: gen.)     F2001     972.9
Antisubmarine & submarine ops. (WWII: gen.)     D780     940.54516
Antisubmarine aircraft     UG1242.A25
Antisubmarine warfare     V214     359.3254, .42-43
Antitank guns     UF628     623.42, .44, .4518
Antwerp area (Bel.)     DH801.A6-69
Antwerp, Bel.     DH811.A55-68
Appliances, Ships' (engin.: gen.)     VM781     623.86
Arabian Desert (Egypt)     DT137.A7
Arabian Penninsula     953     DS201-248+, DS244 (1914-)
Arabian Peninsula (gen.)     DS223
Arabian Peninsula (geog. & travel)     915.3     DS207
Archangel & northern Russia (WWI)     D559
Archangel (Rus.)     DK511.A5
Archangel, Rus.     947.23
Architecture, Military     UG460     623.1
Architecture, Naval (collected, nonperiodical works)     VM7
Arctic areas (WWII: Greenland etc.)     D763.5
Arctic islands     998-998.8
ARGENTINA     F2801-3021+, F2831 (gen.)     982
Argentina (1810-)     F2846     982.03+
Argentina (20th c.)     982.06     F2847-2849+
Argentina (1910-46)     982.061     F2848
Argentina (1910-43)     F2848     982.06
Argentina (1943-: Inclu. Perón regime & biog.)     F2849     982.061-062
Argentina (gen.)     F2831
Argentina (mil. status)     UA613-615     355.033082
Argentina (naval status)     VA416     359.030982
Argentina (WWII: dipl. hist.)     940.532282, .532582 (might ALSO be at .532482
                                   with Axis)     D754.A7
Arizona     979.1     F806-820
Arizona (battleship: U.S.)     VA65.A75
Ark Royal (aircraft carrier: G.B.)     VA458.A7, D772.A66 (WWII)
Arkansas     976.7     F406-420
Arkansas (battleship: U.S.: WWII)     D774.A7
Arkansas (WWII: Reconstruction)     D828.A8-81
Arlington National Cemetery (Arlington, Va.)     F234.A7
Armament (modern: Asia: by country)     U821.A-Z
Armament (modern: Eur.: by place)     U820.A-Z
Armament (modern: gen.)     U815
Armament (modern: U.S.)     U818
Armament, Naval (gen.)     V950     623.8251

Armenia    DK509 (gen. titles), DS161-199 (earlier titles), DK680-689 (later works)    956.62
Armenia (1901-)    DS195    956.6202
Armenian S. S. R. (1920+)    DK687+
Armenians (WWII: U.S.)    D769.88.A7
ARMIES & navies (of the world)    UA15
Armies etc. (WWI: U.S.)    D570.25-.358    940.412+, .44973, .45
Armies etc. (WWII: G.B.: by #)    D759.5.1st-    940.541241-541242
Armies etc. (WWII: U.S.)    D769.25-4
Armies etc. (WWII: U.S.: misc.)    D769.4
Armies (organiz., descrip., & world status)    UA    355
Armies (U.S.: by #/author)    UA27.3.1st-
Armies (WWII: Fr.)    D761.1    940.541244
Armies (WWII: Ger.)    D757.1    940.541343
Armies (WWII: U.S.: by # or author)    D769.26
Armistice (WWII: by country)    D813.A-Z    940.5314, .532+
Armistice (WWII: Fr.)    D813.F7
Armistice (WWII: gen.)    D812    940.5314, .532+
Armistice (WWII: Germ.)    D813.G3
ARMOR & CAVALRY   UE (SEE ALSO UA for specific armies)   357-358.1
Armor & cavalry (Asia)    UE99-113
Armor & cavalry (Australia & New Z.)    UE121-122.5    357.099+
Armor & cavalry (China)    UE101
Armor & cavalry (essays & speeches)    UE149
Armor & cavalry (Eur.)    UE55-95
Armor & cavalry (Fr.)    UE71    357.0944
Armor & cavalry (G.B.)    UE57-64
Armor & cavalry (G.B.: by date)    UE58
Armor & cavalry (gen. hist.: inclu. several countries)    UE15    357.09, .109, 358.1809
Armor & cavalry (Ger.)    UE73    357.0943
Armor & cavalry (It.)    UE79
Armor & cavalry (Japan)    UE105    357.0952
Armor & cavalry manuals (U.S.)    UE153-154
Armor & cavalry (Rus.: Asia)    UE109
Armor & cavalry (Rus.: Eur.)    UE85    357.0947
Armor & cavalry (U.S.)    UE23    357.0973
Armor & weapons, Naval    359.8351
Armor plate (naval sci.)    V900-925
Armor plate (naval sci.: gen.)    V900    623.81821, .8251
Armor, Naval (U.S.)    V903    623.82510973
Armor-piercing shells & devices (design)    623.4518
ARMORED cars & other combat vehicles (land: design)    623.7475
Armored divisions (WWII: U.S.)    D769.305-307
Armored divisions (WWII: U.S.: by #)    D769.3053
Armored divisions (WWII: U.S.: gen.)    D769.305
Armored divisions etc. (WWII: G.B..)    D759.528
Armored forces & warfare (tanks, armored cav., etc.)    358.18   UG446.5, UE147
Armored regiments (WWII: U.S.: by #)    D769.3055.1st-
Armored units & cavalry (Ger.)    UA714    357.10943, .50943, 358.180943
Armored units & cavalry (It.)    UA744
Armored units & cavalry (Rus.)    UA774
Armored units & cavalry (U.S.: inclu. mechanized: gen.)    UA30    357.10973
Armories, arsenals, magazines (gen.)    UF540

ARMS & armor (hist.)    U799-897
Arms & ordnance, Naval (gen.)    VF350-355    359.82, 623.418
Arms (gen.: pubn. dates 1801+)    U800.A3-Z    355.8, 623.4
Arms manuals (infantry)    UD320-325
Arms, Small (infantry: gen.)    UD380
Arms, Small (marines: gen.)    VE360    359.96824, 623.44
Arms, Small (navies: gen. & by place)    VD360-365    359.824, .8242
ARMY artillery (inclu. field & antitank)    358.12    UF400-405, UF15,
            UF21-124 (by place), UF150-157+ (manuals & tactics)
Army corps (WWII: Fr.)    D761.15
Army corps (WWII: Ger.)    D757.2
Army corps (WWII: U.S.)    D769.27
Army hospitals (WWII: U.S.: evacuation: by #)    D807.U722.1st-
Army hospitals (WWII: U.S.: general: by #)    D807.U72.1st-
Army medical schools (U.S.: by region or state)    UH398.5.A-Z
Army posts (Fr.: by place)    UA702.32.A-Z
Army posts (Fr.: gen.)    UA702.3
Army posts (U.S.: by place)    UA26.A7-Z
Army posts (U.S.: gen.)    UA26.A1-6
Army reserves (U.S.)    UA42
Army staffs (U.S.)    UB223
Army War College (U.S.)    U413
Arnhem, Neth.    DJ411.A8
Arras, Battle of (1940)    D756.5.A78
Arsenals, armories, etc. (U.S.: gen.)    UF543
Art (WWII)    D810.A7
Artificers, Military (U.S.: ALSO tech. troops)    UG503
Artificers, Naval (gen.: inclu. carpenters' mates etc.)  VG600
Artificial horizon    VK584.A7
ARTILLERY    UA (for specific armies & units), UF    358.1+, 355.82+
Artillery & rifle ranges    U300-305
Artillery, Antiaircraft (land)    358.13  UF625
Artillery (Asia)    UF99-113
Artillery (Asia: gen.)    UF99
Artillery (Australia & New Z.)    UF121-122.5
Artillery batteries (U.S.: by #/author)    UA33.1st-
Artillery (by place)    UF21-121 (SEE ALSO UA for particular armies)
Artillery (China)    UF101
Artillery, Coast    355.8217, 358.16    UF450-455
Artillery (design)    623.41    UF, UF1-910+, UF15 (gen.), UF144-145 (gen.),
            UF21-124 (by place), UF23 (U.S.), VF320-325 (naval)
Artillery equipment, Naval    VF320-325
Artillery, Field    355.8212    UF400-405
Artillery, Field (U.S.)    UF403-404
Artillery fire control (inclu. instruments: gen.)    UF848  623.558
Artillery (Fr.)    UF71    358.120944
Artillery (G.B.)    UA658    358.10941, .120941
Artillery (G.B.: by date periods)    UF58
Artillery (G.B.: gen.)    UF57    358.120941
Artillery (G.B.: WWII)    UF58.1939-45
Artillery (gen. hist.)    UF15    358.109, .1209, 355.82, .821
Artillery (Ger.)    UA715, UF73    358.120943
Artillery, Howitzer & mortar (places besides U.S.)    UF475.A-Z
Artillery installations (arsenals, depots, target ranges, schools, etc.)    355.73
                            UF540-545

Artillery instruments (misc.)    UF856.A-Z
Artillery (It.)    UA745, UF79
Artillery (Japan)    UF105    358.120952
Artillery, Land missile forces & armored warfare    358.1    UF, UF15,
                                                    UF21-124, UE147, UA32-33 (U.S.), UA
Artillery manuals (U.S.)    UF153-154
Artillery (misc.: design)    623.419 (for space artil. after 1988)
Artillery, Mountain (U.S.)    UF443-444
Artillery museums & exhibitons (gen.)    UF6.A1.A-Z    358.12
Artillery, Naval    359.8218, 355.8218    VF320-325
Artillery (Norway)    UF81
Artillery projectiles (gen.)    UF750
Artillery (pubn. 1801+)    UF145    358.12
Artillery, Railway (U.S.: gen.)    UF493
Artillery range finders (particular types)    UF850.A3-Z
Artillery (Rus.)    UA775
Artillery (Rus.: Eur.)    UF85
Artillery, Seacoast (U.S.)    UF453-454
Artillery services, Naval    359.9812
Artillery shells & other projectiles (design)    623.4513    UF750-760, VF480 (naval)
Artillery, Siege (gen.)    UF460
Artillery (specific pieces)    355.822
Artillery (titles in collections)    UF7
Artillery (U.S.)    UF23    358.120973, .10973, 355.820973
Artillery (U.S.: Calif. reserves: gen., inclu. field)    UA96
Artillery (U.S.: gen.)    UA32    358.10973, .120973
Artillery (U.S.: N.Y. reserves)    UA366-367.75
Artillery (WWII: Fr.)    D761.6
Artillery (WWII: G.B.)    D759.52
Artillery (WWII: Ger.)    D757.4.A-5
Artillery (WWII: Rus.)    D764.52
Artisans, Naval (carpenters' mates, painters, etc.)    VG600-605
Artists (WWII)    940.53157    D810.A7
Arts & architecture (visual, decorative & applied)    N    700-709, 720-769
Arts, architecture, music, sports, & recreation    700-799    N, NB-NX, NA, M, GV
ASIA    DS    950-959, DS5, DS33
Asia (1480-1905)    950.3    DS33
Asia (20th c.)    DS35    950.4
Asia (1905-45)    950.41    DS35
Asia (air war geog.)    358.41475
Asia & the Pacific Theatre    D767-767.99
Asia (biog.: heads of state)    923.15    DS32 (collective)
Asia (geog. & travel) 915    DS9 (1901-50)
Asia (lighthouses, beacons, foghorns, etc.)    VK1099-1113
Asia (lighthouses, beacons, foghorns, etc.: lists)    VK1203-1209
Asia (maps & atlases)    912.5    G2200+
Asia (mil. status: gen.)    UA830    355.03305, .03325, .03355
Asia (naval geog.)    359.475    VA620-639
Asia (naval status: gen.)    VA620    359.03095
Asia, Russian    DK750
Asia, Southeast (20th c.)    959.05    DS526.6-7+
Asia, Southeast (newer titles)    DS521-526+
Asia, Soviet Central    DK845-973    958

ASIAN coasts (pilot & sailing guides: gen.)    VK902
Asian coasts (tide & current tables)    VK702
Asian infantry (gen.)    UD99    356.1095
Asian marines (gen.)    VE99
Asian military law    UB685-710
Asian naval law    VB700-799
ASSOCIATIONS, periodicals, conferences (Russo-Fin. War, 1939-40)    DL1095
Associations, periodicals, societies (U.S.: 20th c.)    E740
Associations, periodicals, societies (U.S.: army reserves)    UA42.A6.A-Z
Associations, societies (U.S.)    E172
Associations, societies (WWII)    D732
Associations, societies (WWII: U.S.)    D769.A1-15
Associations, societies (WWII: Yug.)    D766.6.A1-5
Astor, Nancy W. Langhorne, Viscountess (G.B.: 1910-36 era)    DA574.A8
Astrology (WWII)    D810.A75
Athenia (WWII: steamship)    D772.A7
Athens, Gr.    DF915-936, DF925 (1901-)    949.512
Athens, Gr. (1910-)    DF925
Athens, Gr. (WWII)    D766.32.A8
Athletes (WWII)    940.5315796    D810.E8
ATLANTIC Charter (Newfoundland: 14 Aug. 1941)    D734.A7-8
Atlantic Coast (S.Am.)    F2214    980.009821, .009636
Atlantic Coast (U.S.: Maine to Flor.)    F106    974-975
Atlantic Declaration ('Charter': 14 Aug. 1941)    D735.A7
Atlantic Fleet (U.S.)    VA63.A83
Atlantic Ocean (all & east: pilot & sailing guides)    VK810-880
Atlantic Ocean (all & east: tide & current tables)    VK610-680
Atlantic Ocean (Loran tables)    VK561.A7
Atlantic Ocean (West: pilot & sailing guides)    VK959-992
Atlantic Ocean Islands    997
Atomic bombs    UG1282.A8, U264    358.41825119, 623.45119
Atomic weapons    U264, UG1282.A8
Atrocities (Sp. Civil War, 1936-39)    DP269.5-55
Atrocities, war crimes, trials (WWI)    D625-626
Atrocities, war crimes, trials (WWI: Ger. & Central Powers)    D626.G3
Atrocities, war crimes, trials (WWII)    D803-804
Atrocities, war crimes, trials (WWII: Ger.)    D804.G4
Attachés, Military    UB260
Attachés, Naval    VB240
Attack & defense plans (gen.)    UA920    355.0330+, .0332+, .0335+, .4+
Attack, defense, & siege    UG443-449
Attack planes    UG1242.A28
Auckland, N.Z.    DU430.A8    993.122
Auckland, N.Z. (area)    993.122    DU430.A79
Auschwitz Concentration Camp (Poland)    940.5317438

AUSTRALIA     DU80-398, DU450-480, DU110 (gen.)     994
Australia (1901-45: Commonwealth)     DU116     994.04
Australia (1901-22)     994.041
Australia (1922-45)     994.042
Australia & Anzacs (WWI)     D547.A8
Australia & Australian military ops. (WWII)     D767.8-82
Australia & New Zealand (lighthouses, beacons, foghorns, etc.: lists)
                    VK1211-1212     623.89440993-89440994
Australia & New Zealand (pilot & sailing guides)     VK927-929
Australia. Army (descrip. & hist.)     UA872     355.00994, .30994, .310994
Australia. Army (special branches by name)     UA873.A-Z
Australia, Central     994.2     DU300-330, DU390+
Australia (gen.)     DU110     994
Australia (geog. & travel)     919.4     DU104
Australia (lighthouses, beacons, foghorns, etc.)     VK1121-1122     623.89420994
Australia (mil. geog.)     355.4794     UA995.A
Australia (mil. policy)     355.033594     UA870-874
Australia (mil. status)     355.033094     UA870+
Australia (mil. status)     UA870     355.033094, .033294, .033594
Australia (mil. status: states, territories, localities)     UA874.A-Z
Australia (naval geog.)     359.4794     VA710-719
Australia (naval status: gen.)     VA713.A5-Z     359.030994, .00994, .4794
Australia, New Zealand, Tasmania     DU80-480
Australia, Western     994.1     DU350-380
Australia (WWII: dipl. hist.)     940.532294     D754.A8
Australian aerial ops. (WWII)     D792.A8     940.544994
Australian military ops. & Australia (WWII: gen.)     D767.8     940.532294, .5394,
                    .540994, .541294, .5426, 994.042
Australian naval ops. (WWII)     D779.A8     940.545994
AUSTRIA     DB1-860     943.6
Austria (1801-)     DB38     943.604
Austria (20th c.)     DB91-99+     943.605
Austria (20th c.: gen.)     DB91
Austria (20th c. & 1919-)     943.605     DB91 (20th c.), DB96 (1918-)
Austria (1914-18: WWI era)     DB86.7
Austria (1916-18: Emp. Karl I: gen.)     DB92
Austria (1918-: Republic)     DB96     943.6051
Austria (1938-1945: Ger. annex.)     DB99     943.6052
Austria & Austria-Hungary (mil. status)     UA670     355.0330436
Austria & Austro-Hungarian Empire (gen.)     DB17
Austria, Czechoslovakia, Hungary     DB     943.6-943.9
Austria (geog. & travel)     914.36     DB21-27, DB26 (1901-45)
Austria-Hungary. Army (gen.)     UA672     355.309436
Austria, Hungary, Czechoslovakia     DB     943.6-9
Austria (naval status)     VA470-479     359.2809436
Austria (post-WWI territorial ?s)     D651.A95
Austria (WWII: gen.)     D765.4     940.53436, 943.6052
Austrian question (20th c.)     DB48
Austrian Republic (1919-38)     943.6051     DB96-98
Automatic firearms (rifles, machine guns, etc.)     355.82424     UF620
Automatic pilot (marine navig.)     VK584.A8
Automatic weapons (machine & submach. guns, auto. rifles, etc.: design)
                    623.4424     UD390-395, UF620 (mach. g's.)
Auxiliaries, Army (U.S.)     UA565.A-Z
Auxiliary Territorial Service (WWII: G.B.)     D760.A8

Aviation, Naval (places besides U.S.)    VG95.A-Z
Aviation, Naval (U.S.: gen.)    VG93
Axis (Ger.-Italy: 1919-39)    D728    940.51-52
Axis (WWII: gen. particip.)    940.5334    D743, D748
Axis (WWII: mil. & naval life & customs)    940.5484+    U750, U765+,
        V720 (naval), V735+
Axis Powers (WWII: dipl. hist.)    940.5324+    D748
Azerbaijan S.S.R.    DK690-699
Azerbaijan S.S.R. (1917+)    DK697.3-5
Azimuth instrument (artillery)    UF850.A9
Azores    DP702.A81-99, .A9 (19th-20th c.)    946.99
Azores (19th & 20th c.)    DP702.A9    946.99


BACTERIAL & biological warfare    UG447.8
Bacteriology, Military (inclu. vaccination)    UH450-455
Baden military ops. (WWI)    D533
Badges, brevets, medals of honor, rewards, etc. (navies)    VB330-335
Badges, insignia, etc. (mil.: SEE ALSO UB430+ for decorations)    UC530-535
Badoglio, Pietro (It.: 1900-46 period)    DG575.B2
Baguio, Philip.    DS689.B2
Bahama Islands    F1650-1660    972.96
Bahamas (gen. hist.)    F1656-1657
Bahrein    DS247.B2-28
Baker, Johnston, Palmyra, Midway, & other outlying Hawaiian Islands    996.99
        DU629.M (Midway), DU650
Bakeries (mil.)    UC730-735
Baku (Rus.: prov.)    DK511.B2
Baku, Rus.    DK699.2-39
Balbo, Italo (It.: 1900-46 period)    DG575.B3
Baldwin, Stanley, 1st Earl (G.B.: 20th c.)    DA566.9.B15
Balfour, Arthur James Balfour, 1st Earl of (G.B.: 20th c.)    DA566.9.B2
Bali (Indon.)    DS647.B2    959.86
Balikpapan, Br. N. Borneo    DS646.335.B24
BALKAN conflict (WWI)    D560-565
Balkan Peninsula (inclu. Balkan Wars of 1912-13)    949.6    DR1-48,
        DR45 (20th c.), DR46 (Balkan Wars)
Balkan Peninsula (1913-19)    DR47
Balkan Peninsula (1919-45)    DR48
Balkan Peninsula & Eastern Europe (1901-: gen.)    DR45
Balkan Peninsula, Eastern Europe  DR (titles written prior to about 1978-79)
        949.6-949.8, 943.7-943.9, 947, 947.8, 956
Balkan Peninsula (geog. & travel)    914.96    DR15, DR1221 (later works)
Balkan States (mil. status: descrip. & hist.)    UA822
Balkan States (mil. status: gen.)    UA820    355.0330496
Balkan War (1912-13)    DR46    949.6
Balkans & Near East (WWII: misc. countries: by name)    D766.7.A-Z
Balkans, Near East, Eastern Mediterranean (WWII)    D766-766.79

Ballistic instruments    UF830.A-Z
BALLISTICS    UF820-830    623.51+
Ballistics & gunnery (engineering)    623.5    UF800-830, UF820
Ballistics (engineering)    623.51    UF820-830
Ballistics, Exterior    UF825    623.514
Ballistics, Exterior (environmental)    623.514    UF825
Ballistics, Interior    UF823  623.513
Ballistics, Interior (within bore)    623.513    UF823
Ballistics, Terminal (effects on targets)    623.516
Balloons & kites, Air force    UG1370-1375    623.741-744
Balloons, Military (design)    623.742    UG1370-1375
Baltic provinces (post-WWI territorial ?s)    D651.B2
Baltic Sea (mil. status)    UA646.53    355.033016334, .4716334, 359.4716334
Baltic States    DK502.3-505
Baltic States (gen.)    DK502.7
Baltic States (WWII: occupied terr.)    D802.B3
Bands & music, Military    UH40-45
Bands & music, Naval (SEE ALSO ML1300-1354)    VG30-35
Bandung, Java    DS646.29.B23
Bangkok, Thai.    DS589.B2
Banking services, Military    UH60-65
Baptists (WWII)    D810.C56
Barbary States    DT181-346    961.1-2, 964-965, 966
Barbary States (19th-20th c.)    DT204    961.023-03+
Barcelona, Sp.    DP402.B2-3
BARRACKS & camps, Military (gen.)    UC400    355.412, .7
Barracks & quarters, Air force    UG1140-1145    358.4171
Barracks & quarters, Marine    VE420-425
Barracks & quarters, Marine (U.S.: by place)    VE424.A-Z
Barracks & quarters, Marine (U.S.: Calif.)    VE424.C2    359.967109794
Barracks, quarters, housing (naval)    VC420-425
Barrage balloons & nets (design)    623.744    UG1370-1375, UG730-735,
                                        UF625
Baruch, Bernard (U.S.: 20th c.)    E748.B32
BASES & camps (marines)    359.967    VE21-124, VE23-25 (U.S.), VA67-68,
                                    VG90-95 (marine av.)
Bases & fields, Air force    358.417    UG634.5.A-Z (U.S.: by name),
                                    UG635.A-Z (other countries)
Bases & stations, Naval    359.7    V220 (gen.), VA67-750 (by place),
                  VA69-70 (U.S.), VA459-461 (G.B.), VA516-517 (Ger.),
                  VA576-577 (Rus.), VA656-657 (Japan), VC412-425 (maint.: gen.)
Bases, ports, & docks (naval: gen.: SEE ALSO VA67-750 for specific countries)
                                      V220        359.7
Bases, ports, etc. (G.B. Royal Navy: by place)    VA459.A3-Z
Bases, ports, etc. (U.S. Navy: by place)    VA68.A-Z
Basic training (mil.: inclu. drills, survival exercises, etc.)    355.54    U400-717,
                                    U765-773, U320-325
Basic training (mil. living conditions: ALSO regular quarters)    355.1292
Basic training (naval)    359.54    V260-265
Bataan (Luzon, Philip.)    DS688.B2    959.91
Batavia, Java (Djakarta)    DS646.29.B3
Bath, Eng. (WWII)    D760.8.B3
Batteries, Storage (submarine architec.)    VM367.S7

Battle conditions, Naval          359.1294
Battle of the Atlantic, freedom of the seas, general naval ops. (WWII)    D770
                                                                          940.545
Battlefield guides (WWI: gen.: SEE ALSO specific battles)          D528
Battlefield guides (WWII: gen.: particular battles at D756.5 etc.)          D747
BATTLES & campaigns, Aerial (WWI)          940.44          D600-607
Battles & campaigns, Aerial (WWII: inclu. comb. air & naval ops. as well as
    antiaircraftdefenses)          940.544          D785-792, D785 (gen.)
Battles & campaigns, Naval (WWI)          940.45          D580-595, D580 (gen.)
Battles & campaigns, Naval (WWII)          940.545 (SEE ALSO .542 for ops. by
        theatre)          D770-784, D770 (gen.), D773 (U.S.: gen.), D774.A-Z (U.S.: by
        ship, battle, etc.), D769.45-598 (U.S.: by fleet, squadron, base, etc.)
Battles & campaigns (WWII: by theatre)          940.542          D756-769
Battles & local history (Russo-Fin. War, 1939-40)          DL1103.A-Z
Battles, campaigns, etc. (Sino-Jpn. Confl., 1937-45: by name)          DS777.5316.A-Z
Battles, campaigns, sieges (Russo-Polish, other Polish conflicts, 1918-21: by
        name)                                                  DK4407.A-Z
Battles, campaigns, sieges (Sp. Civil War, 1936-39: by name)          DP269.2.A-Z
Battles, campaigns, sieges (WWII: Rus., Eastern front: by place)          D764.3.A-Z
Battles, campaigns, sieges (WWII: West: by place)          D756.5.A-Z
BATTLESHIPS (as equip.)          359.8352
Battleships (besides U.S.: by place)          V815.5.A-Z
Battleships (engineering)          623.8252          V750
Battleships (G.B.)          V815.5.G7          623.82520941
Battleships (gen.: construc., armament, etc.: SEE V750 for earlier titles)
                                        V815          623.8252, .81252, 359.3252
Battleships (Ger.)          V815.5.G3          623.82520943
Battleships (handling)          623.88252          V750
Battleships (Japan)          V815.5.J3          623.82520952
Battleships (U.S.)          V815.3          623.82520973, 359.32520973
Battleships (units)          359.3252          V750, V765-767, V799-800, VA,
                                        VA65.A-Z (U.S.: by name)
Bavaria          DD801.B31-55          943.3
Bavaria (1939-45)          DD801.B422
Bayonet drill          UD340-345
Bayonet drill (marines)          VE340          359.96547
Bayonet drill (naval seamen)          VD340-345
Bayonets          UD400
Bayonets (marines)          VE380          623.441
Bayonets (navies)          VD380          359.8241
Bayreuth, Ger.          DD901.B4
Bazookas, grenade & rocket launchers, etc. (design)          623.4426          UF628-630
Beacons, buoys, etc. (marine navig.)          623.8944          VK1000-1249, VK1010,
                                        VK1021-1124, VK1023-1025 (U.S.)
Beacons, foghorns, lighthouses, etc. (gen.)          VK1010          623.8942, 387.155
Beacons, foghorns, lighthouses, etc. (lists: gen.: inclu. Br. Admiralty)          VK1150
                                                                          623.8944
Beatty, David Beatty, 1st Earl (G.B.: 20th c. naval biog.)          DA89.1.B4
Beaverbrook, William Maxwell Aitken, Baron (G.B.: 20th c.)          DA566.9.B37
Beck, Josef (Pol.: 1918-45 era)          DK440.5.B4, DK4420.B4
Belfast, N. Ire. (WWII)          D760.8.B4
Belgian Congo          DT641-665          967.5
Belgian Congo (WWII)          D766.95
Belgian military ops. (WWII: gen.)          D763.B4

BELGIUM          DH418-811+, DH521          949.3
Belgium (20th c.)          DH677          949.304
Belgium (1909-)          949.304          DH677 (20th c.)
Belgium (1909-34: Albert I)          949.3041          DH681-685, DH681, DH682 (WWI)
Belgium (1914-18: WWI)          DH682
Belgium (1920-)          DH683
Belgium (1934-51: Leopold III)          949.3042          DH687-689, DH687
Belgium & Belgian military ops. (WWII)          D763.B4-42          940.3493, 949.3
Belgium & Luxembourg          DH401-925
Belgium (geog. & travel)          914.931-934          DH433
Belgium (mil. status)          UA680-689          355.0330493
Belgium (naval status)          VA480-489
Belgium (post-WWI territorial ?s)          D651.B3
Belgium (WWII: dipl. hist.)          940.5322493          D754.B
Belgrade, Serbia (Yug.)          DR2106-2124
Belgrade, Yug.          DR386
Belgrade, Yug. (WWII)          D766.62.B4
Belorussia          947.65          DK511.W5 (White Russia)
Ben-Gurion, David (Palestine: 19th-20th c.)          DS125.3.B37
Benefits, pay, allowances (air forces: U.S.)          UG943
Benes, Edward (Czech.: era of 1918- )          DB2191.B45
Bengal (E. Pak.)          DS485.B39-492
Bengal (W. Pak.)          DS485.B493          954.14
Berchtesgaden, Ger. DD901.B443
Bergen (Nor.: area)          DL576.B4
Bergen, Nor.          DL596.B4
Bering Strait & Alaska coast (pilot & sailing guides)          VK943
BERLIN, Ger.          943.155          DD851-900, DD860 (gen.)
Berlin, Ger. (1914-21)          DD879
Berlin, Ger. (1922-45)          DD880          943.155086
Berlin, Ger. (1933-45)          943.155086          DD880
Berlin, Ger. (districts, sections)          DD883
Berlin, Ger. (gen.)          DD860          943.155
Berlin, Ger. (WWII)          D757.9.B4          943.155086
Bermuda & West Indies (geog. & travel)          917.29          F1611
Bermuda (gen. hist.)          F1636-1637
Bermuda Islands          F1630-1640          972.99
Bern, Swit.          DQ401-420          949.45
Bernadotte af Wisborg, Folke, greve (Swe.: 1907-50 period)          DL870.B47
BIBLIOGRAPHIES (inclu. partic. kinds, subjects, etc.)          010-019, 016 (SEE ALSO
                                     subject #'s like 359+, 940+, etc.)          Z
Bibliographies (G.B.: hist.)          Z2016-2020+          016.941-942, .94109
Bibliographies (Ger.: hist.)          Z2237          016.94309
Bibliographies (Japan: hist.)          Z3306-3308          016.95209
Bibliographies (mil. hist.: Ger.)          Z2241.M5          016.3550943
Bibliographies (mil. hist.: U.S.)          Z1249.M5          016.3550973, .35500973,
Bibliographies (mil. sci. & hist.)          Z6724          016.355, .35509, 355.009, .0009
Bibliographies (naval hist.: G.B.)          Z2021.N3          016.3590941
Bibliographies (naval hist.: Japan)          Z3308.M5          016.3590952
Bibliographies (naval hist.: U.S.)          Z1249.N3          016.3590973, .35900973,
                                     .35930973,   .3593310924
Bibliographies (naval sci. & hist.)          Z6616          016.359, .35909, .35900722
Bibliographies (Rus.: hist.)          Z2506-2510+          016.94709
Bibliographies (specific subjects)          016          Z (sometimes D-F, U-V, or other
                                     subject classes)

Bibliographies (U.S.: hist.)    Z1236-1245+, Z1236    016.97309
Bibliographies (U.S.: hist.: 1900-45)    Z1244    016.9730904, .97309044 (WWII)
Bibliographies (WWI)    Z6207.E8 or .W7    016.9403
Bibliographies (WWII)    Z6207.W8    016.94053-94054, .36
Bibliography    Z (sometimes D-F, U-V, or other subject classes)    010
Bibliography & library science    Z (bibliog's. sometimes classed with A-Z subject #s)
                    010-028+
Bicycle troops (mech. cav.)    357.52    UH30-35
Bicyclists, Military (gen.)    UH30    357.52
Billeting    UC410
Binoculars & telescopes, Military    UF845
Binoculars (naval clothing: inclu. other misc. accessories)    VC340
BIOGRAPHY & genealogy    920-929    CT (gen. or collec.), D-F, other specific
                    classes for specialists or famous people in those areas
Biography (20th c.: collective: gen.)    D412    920.02
Biography (20th c.: individual or memoir by name)    D413.A-Z
Biography (20th c.: memoirs and collective)    D412-412.8
Biography (1945-: collective)    D839.5
Biography (1945-: individual by name)    D839.7.A-Z (SEE ALSO DA-F
                    country & era #s)
Biography, Air force (collective)    UG626    358.400922
Biography, Air force (G.B.: collective)    DA89.6.A1
Biography, Air force (G.B.: inclu. memoirs)    DA89.6.A-Z
Biography, Air force (individual)    UG626.2.A-Z    358.400924
Biography (Australia: 1901-45)    DU116.2 (SEE DU114 for earlier pubns.)
Biography (Australia: by name)    DU114.A3-Z (SEE ALSO DU116.2 for later works)
Biography (Australia: collective)    DU114.A2
Biography (Austria: 20th c.: by name: inclu. memoirs)    DB98.A-Z
Biography (Bel.: 1909-34)    DH685.A-Z
Biography (Bel.: 1934-51)    DH689.A-Z
Biography (Bulg.: 1879-1943: inclu. memoirs)    DR85.5.A-Z
BIOGRAPHY (CHINA: 20th c. & 1912-49: collective: SEE paric. era for indiv.)
                    DS776
Biography (China: 1912-49 period: except Sun Yat Sen)    DS777.15.A-Z
Biography (China: 1928-37 era: collective)    DS777.487
Biography (China: 1928-37 era: indiv. inclu. memoirs)    DS777.488.A-Z
Biography (China: 1937-45)    DS777.5194-5
Biography (China: 1949+)    DS778.A-Z
Biography (collective: WWII)    D736 (for individuals SEE DA-F class numbers for
    person's country: SEE ALSO D811 for personal narratives)
    940.5481-5482 (ALSO country numbers ended sometimes by 0922-0924)
Biography (Czech.: 1918-)    DB2191.A-Z
Biography (Czech.: 1918-39)    DB2200-2201.A-Z
Biography (Czech.: 1939-45: by name)    DB2821.A-Z
Biography (Czech.: 1939-45: inclu. memoirs)    DB2211.A-Z
Biography (Den.: 1912-47)    DL257.A-Z
Biography (divers: marine engin.)    VM980
Biography (Egypt: 1879-1952)    DT107.2.A-Z
Biography (Eur.: group)    940.092    D106-110 (group)
Biography (Fin.: 20th c.)    DK461.A-Z
Biography (Fin.: 1918-39)    DL1088-1088.5
Biography (Fin.: 1939-45)    DL1093-1093.5
Biography (Formosa: 1895-1945)    DS799.72.A-Z

Biography (Fr.: 1871-1940: by name: inclu. memoirs & autobiog.)    DC342.8.A-Z
Biography (Fr.: 1871-1940: collective)    DC342
Biography (Fr.: 20th c.: by name)    DC373.A-Z
Biography (Fr.: 20th c.: collective)    DC371
BIOGRAPHY (G.B.: 20th c.: collective)    DA566.9.A1
Biography (G.B.: 20th c.: inclu. memoirs)    DA566.9.A-Z    941.0820922-24
Biography (G.B.: 1910-36: collective)    DA574.A1
Biography (G.B.: 1910-36: inclu. memoirs)    DA574.A-Z
Biography (G.B.: 1910-36: various royalty)    DA574.A2-45
Biography (G.B.: 1937-52: collective)    DA585.A1
Biography (G.B.: 1937-52: inclu. memoirs)    DA585.A-Z
Biography (G.B.: 1937-52: misc. royalty)    DA585.A5.A-Z
Biography (gen.)    920 (sometimes '92' or 'B' are used, followed by particular
                individuals in alphabetical order by last name. These may ALSO be
                placed in specific discipline number areas followed by the standard
                subdivision, '092'. So, 355.0092 is for mil. biog.)
Biography (Ger.: 1888-1918+: by name)    DD231.A-Z
Biography (Ger.: 1918-48: group)    DD243
Biography (Ger.: 1918-48: inclu. memoirs: by name)    DD247.A-Z
Biography (Ger.: mostly pre-WWI: by name)    DD219.A-Z
Biography (Greece: 20th c.)    DF836.A-Z
Biography (Hawaii: 1891-1959: inclu. memoirs)    DU627.7.A-Z
Biography (Hung.: 20th c.: by name, inclu. memoirs)    DB950.A-Z
Biography (India: 1901-: collective)    DS481.A1
Biography (India: 1901-: inclu. memoirs)    DS481.A-Z
Biography (Iraq: 1919-: by name)    DS79.8.A-Z
Biography (It.: 1871-1947: collec.)    DG574
Biography (It.: 1871-1941)    DG556.A-Z
Biography (It.: 1900-46: by name, inclu. memoirs)    DG575.A-Z
BIOGRAPHY (JAPAN: 20th c.: collective)    DS885.5.A1
Biography (Japan: 20th c.: inclu. memoirs: SEE ALSO DS890)    DS885.5.A-Z
Biography (Japan: 1926-89: collective)    DS890.A1
Biography (Japan: 1926-89: inclu. memoirs: SEE ALSO DS885.5)    DS890.A-Z
Biography (Japan: 1926-89: royal family)    DS889.7-9
Biography (Japan: collective)    DS834
Biography (Japan: Imperial family & rulers)    DS834.1
Biography (Korea: 20th c.: inclu. memoirs)    DS916.5.A-Z
Biography (merch. marine)    VK139-140
BIOGRAPHY, MILITARY    U51-55 (SEE ALSO D-F war & country #s)
                355.0092, .00922-00924, .3310922-0924,
Biography, Military engineering (collective)    UG127
Biography, Military engineering (indiv.)    UG128.A-Z (SEE ALSO UG21-124)
Biography, Military (Eur.)    923.54
Biography, Military (except U.S.: group by place)    U54.A-Z
Biography, Military (except U.S.: individual)    U55.A-Z
Biography, Military (G.B.: 20th c.: collective)    DA69.3.A1
Biography, Military (G.B.: 20th c.: inclu. memoirs)    DA69.3.A-Z  355.3310922-24
Biography, Military (G.B.: collective)    DA54
Biography, Military (Ger.: collective: gen.)    DD100.A2
Biography, Military (Ger.: collective: officers)    DD100.A3-Z
Biography, Military (It.: collective)    DG481
Biography, Military medical (collective, inclu. nurses)    UH341    355.3450922
Biography, Military (Rus.: collective)    DK50.5-8
Biography, Military (U.S.: individual)    U53.A-Z    355.330973
Biography (Montenegro: 1918-45)    DR1890-1891

Biography (N. Viet.: 1945-: inclu. memoirs)     DS560.72.A-Z
BIOGRAPHY, NAVAL     359.0092     V61-64 (SEE ALSO D-F #s for indiv. biog's.
     from particular countries), V63.A-Z (U.S.: by name), V64.A-Z (other countries)
Biography (naval architec.)     VM139-140
Biography, Naval (G.B.: 20th c.: by name)     DA89.1.A-Z
Biography, Naval (G.B.: 20th c.: collective)     DA89.1.A1
Biography, Naval (G.B.: collective)     DA74
Biography, Naval medical (gen.)     VG226
Biography, Naval medical (places besides U.S.)     VG228.A-Z
Biography, Naval (places besides U.S.: by place)     V64.A-Z
Biography, Naval (U.S.: by name)     V63.A-Z     359.00924, .3310924,
     940.410924, .450924, .540924, .5420924, .5450924
Biography, Naval (U.S.: by name)     VB314.A-Z     359.3310973, .3310924
Biography (Neth.: by name)     DJ283.A-Z
Biography (New Z.: inclu. memoirs: by name)     DU422.A-Z
Biography (Nor.: 20th c.)     DL529.A-Z
Biography (Nor.: 20th c.: collective)     DL529.A1
Biography (Palestine: 19th-20th c.)     DS125.3.A-Z
Biography (Palestine: 19th-20th c.: collective)     DS125.3.A2
Biography (Philip.: 1935-46: collective)     DS686.2.A2
Biography (Philip.: 1935-46: inclu. memoirs)     DS686.2.A-Z
Biography (Pol.: 1918-: collective)     DK440.5.A1
Biography (Pol.: 1918-: inclu. memoirs)     DK440.5.A-Z
Biography (Pol.: 1918-45: by name, inclu. memoirs)     DK4420.A-Z
Biography (Pol.: 1918-45: collec.)     DK4419
Biography (Port.: 1910-)     DP676.A-Z
Biography (Royal Naval Coll., Dart.: by name)     V515.M1.A-Z
Biography (Rum.: 1914-27)     DR262.A-Z
Biography (Rus.: 1894-1917: by name, inclu. memoirs)     DK254.A-Z
Biography (Rus.: 1894-1917: collective)     DK253
Biography (Rus.: 1925-53: collective)     DK268.A1
Biography (Rus.: 1925-53: inclu. memoirs: by name)     DK268.A2-Z
Biography (Serbia: 1903-18)     DR2031
Biography (Serbia: 1918-45)     DR2038
Biography (social sciences: gov., law, commerce, etc.)     923
Biography          920-929 (sometimes placed with country #s or topical #s in
     930-999 or 000-999)     C-F
Biography (Sp.: 1886-1931)     DP235-236
Biography (Sp.: 1931-39: collective)     DP260
Biography (Sp.: 1939-)     DP271.A-Z
Biography (Sp.: 1931-39: by name: inclu. memoirs)     DP264.A-Z
Biography (Swe.: 1907-50: by name)     DL870.A-Z
Biography (Swe.: 1907-50: collec.)     DL869
Biography (Swit.: 20th c.)     DQ206-207
Biography (Tur.: 1909-: inclu. memoirs)     DR592.A-Z
Biography (U.S.: 20th c.: by name)     E748.A-Z
Biography (U.S.: 20th c.: collective)     E747
Biography (U.S. Marines)     VE25 (PREFER E #s)
Biography (U.S. Mil. Acad.: by name)     U410.M1.A1-Z
Biography (U.S. Naval Acad.: by name)     V415.M1.A-Z
Biography (Viet.: by name: inclu. memoirs: Ho Chi Minh at DS560.72.H6)
                                                                                    DS558.83.A-Z
Biography (Viet.: collective)     DS558.82
Biography (WWI: collective)     D507     940.3092, .481-2. Also use country #'s

Biography (Yug.: 20th c.)     DR359.A-Z
Biography (Yug.: 20th c.: collective)     DR359.A2
Biography (Yug.: 1918-45)     DR1293-1294
Biography (Yug.: 1918-45: by name, inclu. memoirs)   DR1294.A-Z
Biography (Yug.: 1934-45+)     DR1300-1305
Biological agents (ammunition: design)   623.4594
Biological agents (mil.)     355.82594
Biological warfare     358.38     UG447.8
Birkenhead, Frederick E. S., 1st Earl of (G.B.: 20th c.)   DA566.9.B5
Bisayas (Visayan Islands, Philip.)   DS688.B6     959.95
BISMARCK Archipelago (inclu. New Britain [Rabaul] & New Ireland)
          993.6 (PREFER 995.8 for pubn. dates after 1988), 995.8 (SEE ALSO
          993.6 for books before 1989)     DU550-553, DU553.N35 (New Brit.)
Bismarck Archipelago (1942-45: WWII period)   995.803     DU550-553
Bismarck Archipelago (gen.)     DU550     993.6
Bismarck Archipelago (geog. & travel)     919.36
Bismarck Archipelago (WWII: gen. particip.)     940.53936   DU550-553
Bismarck (battleship: Ger.: WWII)     D772.B5, VA515.B4
Bismarck Islands (naval geog.)     359.47936   VA750.B
Bismarck Islands (WWII)     D767.99.B46
Bismarck Sea, Battle of (1943-44)     D774.B48
BLACK Forest (Ger.)     943.48     DD801.B63-65
Black Sea area (geog. & travel)     914.77   DK511.C7
Black Sea region     DJK61-66
Black Sea region (Rus.)     947.7     DK509
Blacks (in U.S.)   E185     973.0496
Blacks (WWI: Negroes)     D639.N4
Blacks (WWII: Negroes)     D810.N4
Blacks as soldiers & seamen (U.S.)     E185.63
Blamey, Thomas, Sir (Australia)     DU114.B52
Blinkers & electrooptical signal devices (mil. engineering)     623.7314     UG580,
                          UG614- 614.5, VK387
Blitzkrieg (lightning war)     U167.5.L5
Blockades & blockade-running (WWI)     940.452     D581
Blockades & blockade-running (WWII)     940.5452     D770, D771 (Anglo-
                          Grmn.), D773 (U.S.)
Blockades, Naval     V180     355.44, 359.42-43, 940.452, .5452
Blueprints, drawings, designs (naval architec.: laying out)     VM297.5
Blum, Léon (Fr.: 20th c.)     DC373.B5
Boat attack (naval tactics)     V178     359.32, .42
Boatswains     VG950-955
Boatswains' mates (U.S.)   VG953
Boatyards, Small craft (by name)     VM321.52.A-Z
Boatyards, Small craft (gen.)     VM321.5
Boilers, Marine     VM741-750     623.873
Boise (cruiser: U.S.: WWII)     D774.B6
Bolivia     F3301-3359     984
Bolivia (1938-)     F3326     984.051
Bomb disposal & demolition (army engineers)     358.23     UG370, UG550-555
Bomb reconnaissance (WWII)     D810.B66
Bomb shelters (plus other special civil defense topics like psych. aspects)   UA926.5
Bombay, India     DS486.B7

Bomber forces & ops.    358.42       UG1242.B6, UG633-635, UG633 (U.S.),
                 TL685.3, TL686.A-Z (by co. or name)
Bombers & fighter-bombers (mil. engineering)       623.7463        TL685.3,
                 TL686.A-Z (bymanufac. or model), UG1242.B6
Bombers (air force)      UG1242.B6       623.7463, 358.42
Bombing, dog fighting, other air tactics (U.S.)    UG703
Bombs, Air force       UG1280-1285        358.418251, 623.451
Bombs, ammunition, etc.        355.825
Bombs & projectiles, Aircraft (inclu. std. & nuclear)    UF767    623.451
Bonin Islands (Japan)    DS895.B6    952.85 (SEE .28 for works after 1988)
Borneo       959.83       DS646.3-38, DS646.3
Borneo & the Dyaks       DS646.3-38       959.53-55, .83
Borneo (WWII: gen. particip.)       940.535983       D767.7, DS646.3
Bose, Subhas Chandra (India: 1901+ era)    DS481.B6
Bosnia & Bosnia-Herzegovina (20th c.)       DB250
Bosnia & Hercegovina (1914-18: WWI)       DR1732
Bosnia & Hercegovina (1918-45)       DR1733-1741
Bosnia & Hercegovina (1941-45: Axis occup.)    DR1741
Bosnia & Hercegovina (Herzegovina)    DR1652-1785 (SEE ALSO DR357 etc.)
                 949.742

Boston, Mass. (1865-1950)       F73.5
Bougainville (WWII)            D767.982.B5, D767.99.B54
Boxer Rebellion (China: 1899-1901)    DS770-772       951.03
Boy Scouts (WWII)            D810.B7
Boys (armed forces)  UB418.B69
Brandenburg, Ger.    DD901.B65
BRAZIL       F2501-2659, F2521    981
Brazil (1822-)    F2535       981.04+
Brazil (1889-)    F2537       981.05+
Brazil (1930-54)    981.061       F2538
Brazil (1930-54)    F2538       981.06-061
Brazil (gen.)  F2521
Brazil (mil. status)    UA619-621
Brazil (WWII)    D768.3       940.5381, .544381, 981.061
Brazil (WWII: dipl. hist.)    940.532581       D754.B
Breech-loading ordnance       UF560-565... .B.L.
Bremen, Ger.       DD901.B71-79
Bremen (pass. ship)  VM383.B7
Brest, Fr.       DC801.B83
Brest, Fr. (WWI: U.S. training camp)    D570.37.B7
Brest-Litovsk, Russia (WWI: treaty: 3 Mar. 1918)       D614.B6
Brest-Litovsk, Ukraine (WWI: treaty: 9 Feb. 1918)       D614.B5
Brevets, badges, medals, etc. (U.S. Navy: inclu. Navy Cross)    VB333
                 359.13420973

Briand, Aristide (Fr.: 20th c.)    DC373.B7
Bridge troops & sappers (gen.)       UG510
Bridges (London, Eng.: inclu. London Bridge)    DA689.B8
Bridges (mil. engineering)       UG335       623.67
Brisbane, Australia       DU278       994.31
Bristol, Eng. (WWII)       D760.8.B7

BRITAIN (19th c. & Victorian era of 1837-1901)   941.081   DA550-566, DA550 (gen.)
Britain (20th c. & Edward VII era of 1901-1910)                 941.082
                    DA567-570 (Ed. VII), DA570 (gen.), DA566 (20th c.: gen.)
Britain (1910-36: George VI)       941.083           DA573-578, DA576 (gen.),
                                                     DA577 (WWI era), DA578 (1920-39)
Britain (1936-45: WWII era)       941.084             DA580-587, DA586 (gen.),
                                                     DA587 (WWII period)
Britain & British Isles      941      DA
Britain, Battle of (1940)    D756.5.B7
BRITISH aerial ops. (WWI)       D602     940.44941
British aerial ops. (WWII)      D786     940.544941
British air force history (gen.)    DA89.5      358.400941
British armament (modern)       U820.G3
British Central Africa (1901-52)    DT855     968.97
British Columbia      F1086-1089.7, F1089 (gen.)      971.1
British Columbia (gen. hist.)    F1088
British East Africa & East Africa    DT421-435        967.6
British East Indies     DS648 (SEE DS646.3 for Borneo)
British Empire    DA10-18
British Empire & Britain (WWI: by place or name)  D547.A-Z
British Empire (gen.)      DA16     909.824+
British engineering ops. (WWII)     D795.G7
British espionage (gen.)   UB271.G7         327.120941
British (in Arg.)       F3021.B86
British (in S.Am.)      F2239.B8
British (in U.S.)       E184.B7
British infantry (gen.)    UD57     356.10941
British Isles & English Channel (pilot & sailing guides)    VK827-844
                                          623.892916336, .8929422
British Isles (pilot guides)      623.892941-892942      VK827-838.5
British Isles (tide & current tables)     VK627-638
British Isles (WWII: gen. particip.)     940.5341-5342
British marines (gen.)     VE57     359.960941
BRITISH MILITARY education (special time periods)   U511
British military history (gen.)   DA50     355.00941
British military ops. & Great Britain (WWII: gen.)      D759     940.54091, .5341-
                                                     5342, 942.084
British military ops., British Empire, & England (WWI)      D546-547.8+, D547.A-Z+
British military ops. (WWI: gen.)     D546.A2-Z      354.42066, 940.48341, .412+,
                                          941.083
British military ops. (WWII: special by group or region)    D760.A-Z    940.5412
British naval education (special topics)      V511-512
British naval history (gen.)     DA70     359.00941
British naval ops. & Anglo-German naval conflict (WWI: by battle, ship, etc.)
                                          D582.A-Z
British North Borneo      DS646.33-34     959.53
British prisons & prisoners (WWII)     D805.G7
British public opinion (WWII)    D810.P85.G7
British Somaliland      DT406      967.73-7305+
British South Africa      DT751-848      968-968.7
British submarine ops. (WWII: G.B.)     D784.G7
British West Africa      DT491-518      966, 966.4-51, .7, .81, .9
British West Indies    F2131-2133      972.9, .973
Brittany (Fr.)      DC611.B841-915      944.1
Browning machine guns    UF620.B6

Brunei          DS646.35     959.55
Brüning, Heinrich (Ger.: 1918-48 era)     DD247.B7
Brussels, Bel.     DH802-809
Brussels, Bel. (20th c.)     DH807.5
Bucharest, Rum.     DR286          949.82
Budapest, Hun. (20th c.)     DB872
Budapest, Hun. (WWII)     D765.562.B8
Budgets, Naval (G.B.)     VA455
Budgets, Naval (gen.)     VA25     359.622
Budgets, Naval (Ger.)     VA511
Budgets, Naval (U.S.)     VA60     359.6220973
Buenos Aires (Arg.: prov.)          F2861
Buenos Aires, Arg.     F3001     982.11
Buenos Aires, Arg. (area)     982.11          F3001
Buffalo, N.Y.          F129.B8
Buildings (London, Eng.)     DA686-687
Buildings (London, Eng.: by name)     DA687.A-Z
Buildings, Public (Berlin, Ger.)     DD896
Buildings (Washington, D.C.)     F204.A-Z
Bukowina (20th c.)     DB280
BULGARIA     DR51-98     949.77
Bulgaria (1878-1946)     949.7702     DR85-93, DR89 (1918-43)
Bulgaria (1879-1943)     DR85     949.7702
Bulgaria (1912-13: Balkan War period)     DR87.7
Bulgaria (1914-18: WWI)     DR87.8
Bulgaria (1918-43: Boris III era)     DR89
Bulgaria (1943-: inclu. regency of Simeon II, 1943-46)     DR90
Bulgaria (geog. & travel)     914.977     DR60 (1879-1950)
Bulgaria (mil. status)     UA824     355.03304977
Bulgaria (post-WWI territorial ?s)     D651.B8
Bulgaria (WWII)     D766.7.B8
Bulge, Battle of the (Ardennes: 1944-45)     D756.5.A7
Bulletproof clothing, materials, etc.     UF910
Bullets     UF770     623.455
Bullets (navies)     VF500     359.8255, 623.455
Bunkers, caves, shelters (defense engineering: protective construc.)     623.38
Bunks & bedding (mil.)     UC550-555
Burial services, graves registration, & naval military mail     359.69
BURMA     959.1     DS485.B79-892, DS527-530 (newer works), DS528.5
Burma (1851-1947)     DS485.B89     959.104
Burma (1885-1945)     DS530
Burma (1886-1948: British rule)     959.104     DS485.B89, DS530-530.32
Burma & India (WWII)     D767.6
Burma (gen.)     DS527.4
Burma (geog. & travel)     915.91     DS485.B74-892, DS527.6 (later bks.)
Burma (mil. status)     UA853.B9
Buses (mil. design)     623.74723
Bushido (Jpn. custom)     DS827.B98

CABLES (naval supplies)     VC279.C3
Cadiz, Sp.     DP402.C2-3
Caen, Fr.     DC801.C11
Cairo, Egypt     DT139-152     962.16
Cairo, Egypt (gen. hist. & descrip.)     DT143
Caissons, gun carriages, etc. (U.S.: gen.)     UF643

221

Calais, Battle of (1940)    D756.5.C2
Calcutta, India        DS486.C2
Calcutta, India (area)    954.14        DS486.C2
CALIFORNIA        F856-870, F861 (gen.)    979.4
California (1869-1950)    F866 (SEE D570.85.C2-21 for 1914-18 war years &
                D769.85.C2-21 for 1939-45)    979.404-4053
California (1900-)        979.405    F866 (1869-1950)
California (1918-45)    979.4052    F866
California (battleship: U.S.)    VA65.C3
California (gen.)    F861    979.4
California (geog. & travel)    917.94    F859.3, F861, F866 (hist.: 1869-1950)
California National Guard (gen.)    UA90
California (naval geog.)    359.47794    VA100-107
California, Southern    979.49    F867
California (WWII: gen. particip.)    940.53794    D769.85.C2-21, F866
California (WWII: gen.)    D769.85.C2    979.4052
Cambodia        DS554 (newer works), DS554.7, DS557.C2 (older titles)    959.6
Cambodia (1863-1954)    DS554.7-73    959.603
Camel batteries        UF420
Camel troops & camelry        UE500
Camels, elephants, etc. (mil. transp.)    UC350
Cameroon (mil. status)        UA859
Cameroons (German West Africa) & Togoland    DT561-584    966.6695, .81, 967.1
Camouflage  UG449, V215 (naval)  358.3, 623.77
Camouflage, Marine    V215    623.77
Camouflage (WWII)    D810.C2
Camp-making (mil. sci.)    UG365    355.412, .544, .71
Camp Pendleton (Calif.: U.S. Marines)    VE434.C2 or P...
Camps & barracks, Military    UC400-440
Camps, Marine training (U.S.: by place)    VE434.A-Z
Camps, Training (armor & cavalry: U.S.)    UE433-434
CANADA        F1001-1140+    971
Canada (1867+)    F1033    971.05+
Canada (20th c. & 1911-)  971.06    F1034
Canada (1911-21)    971.061
Canada (1914+)    F1034 (SEE ALSO D768.15 for 1939-45 war years)
                971.061+
Canada (1921-35)    971.062
Canada (1935-57)    971.063
Canada (1935-48: 2d prime min'ship. of Wm. Lyon Mackenzie King)    971.0632
Canada (E. coast: pilot & sailing guides)    VK985
Canada (gen.)    F1026
Canada (geog. & travel)  917.1    F1015
Canada (mil. status: gen.)    UA600    355.033271, .033571, .033071
Canada (naval status: gen.)    VA400    359.030971, .4771
Canada (W. coast: pilot & sailing guides)    VK945
Canada (WWI)    D547.C2
Canada (WWII)    D768.15    940.5371, .532271, .540971, .541271, 971.063
Canada (WWII: dipl. hist.)    940.532271    D754.C2
Canadian aerial ops. (WWII)    D792.C2-29
Canadian naval ops. (WWII)    D779.C2-29
Canal Zone & Panama Canal    F1569.C2    972.875
Canary Islands    DP302.C36-51    964.9
Canberra, Australia  994.71    DU145
Canberra, Australia (inclu. Capital Territory)    DU145

Cannons, howitzers, mortars, small rockets, other specific artillery (design)
623.42
Canteens & post exchanges, Military (U.S.)     UC753
Canteens & ship exchanges     VC390-395
Canteens (mil. equip.)     UC529.C2
Canteens (off-post mil. recreation: U.S.)     UH905
Canton, China     DS796.C2
Cape Verde Islands     DT671.C2     966.58
Cape York Peninsula (Queens., Aust.)     DU280.C3
Capital Territory (Australia)     994.7     DU145
Captured nations (WWII: Allied-occup'd.: gen. particip.)     940.5338
Captured nations (WWII: Axis-occup'd.: gen. particip.)     940.5337
Carbines, rifles, etc.     UD390
Career guidance (naval sci.)     VB259
Cargo & personnel transport planes (design)     623.7465     TL685.7
Cargo ships, freighters, & tankers (engineering)     623.8245     VM391-395,
VM455-459, VM455 (tankers)
Caribbean, Mexico, & Central America     972     F1201-1392 (Mex.), F1421-2175
Caribbean Sea & Gulf of Mexico (tide & current tables)     VK771-777
Caribbean Sea & West Indies (pilot & sailing guides)     VK971-973
Caribbean Sea Area     F2161-2175     972.9, 909.096365
Caribbean Sea area (1811-)     F2175     972.904-905
Carol II (Rum.: King, 1930-40)     DR266
Caroline & Mariana Islands (geog. & travel)     919.66-67
Caroline Islands     DU560-568     355.47966, 996.6
Caroline Islands (gen.)     DU565
Caroline Islands (modern hist.)     DU567
Caroline Islands (pilot & sailing guides)     VK933.C27
Caroline Islands (WWII)     D767.99.C3
Carpathian Mts. region     DJK71-75
Carpathian Mts. (Uk.)     DK508.9.C37
Carpenters & other naval artisans (U.S.)     VG603
Carriers, Aircraft (as equip.)     359.8355 (SEE ALSO .94835 with works after 1988)
Carriers, Aircraft (as units)     359.9435 (SEE .3255 for works before 1989)
Carriers, Aircraft (besides U.S.)     V874.5.A-Z
Carriers, Aircraft (design)     623.81255     V874-875
Cartography (WWII)     D810.C26
Cartridges     UF740-745     623.455
Cartridges, Naval     VF470     359.8255
Casablanca, Mor.     DT329.C3     964.3
Casablanca, Mor. (area)     964.3     DT329.C3
Cases (courts of inquiry, naval: U.S.)     VB814.A-Z (PREFER KF #s)
Cases (courts of inquiry: by place: SEE KF7642 etc. for U.S.)     UB867.A-Z
Cases (courts-martial, mil.: by place)     UB857.A-Z (for U.S. SEE KF7642,
7652, etc.)
Cases (courts-martial, naval: besides U.S.: by place)     VB807.A-Z
Cases (courts-martial, naval: U.S.)     VB806 (PREFER KF7646-7650)
Catalonia (Sp.)     DP302.C57-69
Catalonia (Sp. Civil War, 1936-39)     DP269.27.C3
Catholic Church (WWI)     D622
Catholic Church (WWII)     D810.C6
Caucasus area (Rus.)     DK511.C1-35     947.9
Caucasus (geog. & travel)     914.79

CAUSES, aims, results (WWI)    D511-520    940.31-2
Causes, aims, results (WWI: gen.)  D511    940.311, .314
Causes, aims, results (WWII: by country)    D742.A-Z    940.534-539
Causes, aims, results (WWII: gen.)    D741    940.5311, 327+
Causes (WWI)    940.311    D511
Causes (WWI: econ.)    940.3113    D635
Causes (WWI: polit. & dipl.)    940.3112    D610-621, D610
Causes (WWI: psychological & social)    940.3114
Causes (WWII: dipl. & polit.)    940.53112    D741-742, D443, D727, D748
Causes (WWII: econ.)    940.53113    D741-742, D720-728, D421, D800
Causes (WWII: gen.)    940.5311    D741 (gen.), D742.A-Z (by country), D720-728
Causes (WWII: psychological & social)    940.53114    D741-742, D726, D421
Causes of war (economic)    355.0273    HB195
Causes of war (political)    355.0272
Causes of war (psychological)  355.0275
Causes of war (sociological)   355.0274
CAVALRY & armor (Asia: gen.)    UE99    357.095
Cavalry & armor (by place)    UE21-124 (SEE ALSO UA for specific units)
Cavalry & armor (collections)    UE7
Cavalry & armor (Eur.: gen.)    UE55    357.094
Cavalry & armor (G.B.: gen.)    UE57    357.0941
Cavalry & armored regiments (U.S.: by #/author) UA31.1st-
Cavalry (armored & mechanized)    UE
Cavalry (Austria & Austria-Hung.)    UA674
Cavalry divisions (WWII: U.S.: 1st)    D769.308
Cavalry (G.B.)    UA654-657    357.10941
Cavalry groups etc. (WWII: U.S.: by #)    D769.325.1st-
Cavalry, Horse    357.1    UE15, UE21-124, UE150+, UA
Cavalry horses (gen.)    UE460
Cavalry installations (horse)    357.187    UE350, UE430-435, UC400-405, UA
Cavalry, Mechanized    357.5    UE147-149, UE150-155 (manuals), UE159,
        UE160-302 (by place)
Cavalry (WWII)    D794
Cavalry (WWII: G.B.)    D759.54
Cavalry (WWII: Rus.)    D764.54
Cavalry (WWII: U.S.: gen.)    D769.32
Cebu (Philip.)    DS688.C4    959.95
Cebu, Philip. (town)    DS689.C5
Celebes    DS646.4    959.84
Celebrations & commemorations, Military    355.16
Celebrations, memorials, monuments (WWII: U.S.: gen.)    D833    940.546573
CEMETERIES & graves, Military    UB390-397
Cemeteries & monuments (WWI)    940.465    D639.D4 (cem's.), D663-
        680 (mon's.), D675.W2 (Tomb of Unkn. Soldier: Wash. D.C.)
Cemeteries & monuments (WWII)    940.5465    D833-838 (celebrations,
        monuments, etc.), D810.D4 (dead, cemeteries, etc.)
Cemeteries & monuments (WWII: Eng.)    940.546542    D838.G6 (gen.),
        .G7.A-Z (local, by place)
Cemeteries & monuments (WWII: U.S.)    940.546573  D833-836, D833 (gen.),
        D835.A-W (by state), D836.A-Z (by town)
Cemeteries (naval)    VB300-305    351.86, .866
Censorship, news media, etc. (WWII: by country)    D799.A-Z
Censorship, press, publicity (WWI: gen.)    D631 (SEE ALSO D639.P6-7 for
        propaganda)    940.315097

CENTRAL Africa    DT351-364    967
Central America        F1421-1577, F1436    972, 972.8+
Central America (1821-1950)        F1438    972.804-805
Central America (1900-)        972.805        F1438-1439
Central America (mil. status: by country)    UA607.A-Z
Central America (pilot & sailing guides)    VK951-952
Central Asia & Tibet (pubns. to 1950: gen.)    DS785.A5-Z    951.5, 958 (C. Asia)
Central Asia (Rus, Rev., 1917-21)    DK265.8.S63
Central Asian question (19th c.)    D378
Central Asian question (20th c.)    D471-72
Central Asian question (20th c.: by country)    D472.A-Z
Central Asian question (1914-)    D471
Central Australia    DU390    994.2
Central Europe & Germany (geog. & travel)    914.3    DD21-43, DB21-27, D901-980
Central Powers (WWI: dipl. hist.)    940.324    D511, D458 (Triple Alliance)
Central Powers (WWI: gen. particip.)    940.334    D531
Central Powers (WWI: mil. & naval life & customs)    940.484
Cephalonia, Gr. (WWII)    D766.32.C4
Ceremonies, honors, & salutes (navies: gen.)    V310    359.17, .1349
Ceremonies, Military    355.17    U350-355
Ceylon    DS488-490, DS489.5 (gen. hist.)    954.93
Chamberlain, Austen, Sir (G.B.: 20th c.)    DA566.9.C43
Channel Islands (Eng.: WWII: gen. particip.)    940.534234    DA670.C4,
                                             .J5 (Jersey), .G8-9 (Guernsey)
Channel Islands (G.B.)    DA670.C4    942.34
Chaplain Corps (WWII: U.S. Army)    D769.375
CHAPLAINS, Air force    UG1000-1005
Chaplains, Military (U.S.)    UH23    355.3470973
Chaplains, Naval (U.S.)    VG23    359.3470973
Chaplains or religious officials, Military (gen.)    UH20    355.347
Chaplains or religious officials, Naval    VG20-25
Chaplains (WWII: by country)    D810.C36.A-Z
Chaplains (WWII: gen.)    D810.C35    940.5478
Chaplains (WWII: U.S.)    D810.C36.U6 (SEE ALSO D769.375 & D769.59)
Charges, Demolition (destructors, bangalore torpedoes, etc.: design)    623.4544
                                                           UG370, UF860
Charities, refugees, relief work (WWI: gen.)    D637    940.477+
Charities, refugees, relief work (WWII: by country)    D809.A-Z    940.54778+
Chart use, Nautical (plus other misc. topics on naut. instruments)    VK587
Chasseurs & Chasseurs Alpine (WWII: Fr.)    D761.5
Chemical & biological weapons (design)    623.4516    UG447-447.6 (chem.),
                     UG447 (gen.), UG447.5.A-Z (type gas), UG447.8 (bio.)
Chemical & biological weapons (projectiles etc.)    355.82516    UG447-447.8
Chemical Corps battalions etc. (WWII: U.S.: by type, sub-arranged by # if applic.)
                                                           D769.353.A-Z
Chemical Corps (WWII: U.S.: gen.)    D769.35
Chemical industry (defense)    UA929.95.C5
Chemical warfare    358.34    UG447-447.6
Chemical warfare (inclu. flames)    UG447-447.6    623.4516
Chesapeake Bay region (Va.)    F232.C43
Chiang Kai Shek (China: 1887-1975: SEE DS778.M3 for Mao Tse Tung)
                                                           DS777.488.C5
Chicago, Ill.    F548    977.311
Chicago, Ill. (1892-1950)    F548.5    977.31103-033

Children & orphans (WWI)    D639.C4    940.53161
Children & orphans (WWII)    D810.C4
Chile    F3051-3285, F3081 (gen.)    983
Chile (1921-)    F3099    983.063-064+
Chile (gen.)    F3081
Chile (mil. status)    UA622-624
CHINA    DS701-796+    951
China (1861-1912)    DS761
China (1911-12: Rev.: gen.)    DS773.4
China (1912-49 [Republic] & 20th c. overall)    DS773.83-776, DS774 (gen.)
    951.03-04
China (1912-49)    951.04    DS773.83-777.544, DS774
China (1912-28: gen.)    DS776.4    951.041
China (1912-27)    951.041    DS776.4-777.462, DS776.4
China (1913: 2d Rev.)    DS777.2
China (1927-49: Nationalist rule: inclu. Sino-Jpn. conflict of 1937-45)    951.042
    (SEE ALSO 940.53 for Sino-Jpn. War of 1937-45)    DS777.47-544, DS777.47
China (1928-37: gen.)    DS777.47
China (1928-37: Nationalist rule)    DS777.47-514    951.042
China (1937-45)    DS777.518    951.042
China (1945-49: Republic: gen.)    DS777.535    951.042
China (air war geog.)    358.414751
China & Chinese military ops. (WWII)    D767.3    940.5351, .540951, .5425,
    951.042
China. Army (gen.)    UA837    355.30951, .00951
China (biog.: heads of state)    923.151
China (gen.: pubn. 1801+)    DS735.A3-Z 951
China (geog. & travel)    915.1    DS710 (1901-48)
China (lighthouses, beacons, foghorns, etc.)    VK1101-1102
China (mil. capabil.)    355.033251
China (mil. geog.)    355.4751    UA995.C
China (mil. status)    UA835    355.033051, .033251, .033551
China (naval geog.)    359.4751    VA630-639
China (naval status)    VA630-639    359.030951
China (pilot guides)    623.892951    VK902-907
China (plus surrounding areas)    951    DS701-796+, DS706, DS735
China (post-WWI relns.: Japan)    D651.C6
China (post-WWI relns.: U.S.)    D651.C5
China (post-WWI territorial ?s)    D651.C4-7
China (Southwestern)    951.3
China (WWII: causes, aims, results)    D742.C5
China (WWII: dipl. hist.)    940.532251    D754.C5
Chinese Civil War (1945-49: gen.)    DS777.54
Chinese (in other lands: gen.)    DS732
Chinese-Japanese Conflict (1931-33)    DS777.5    951.042, 952.033
Chinese-Japanese Conflict (1937-45: gen.)    DS777.53    940.53, 951.042,
    952.033
Chinese-Japanese War (1894-5)    DS764.4-767.7    951.03, 952.031
Chinese Revolution (1911-12)    DS773.32-6    951.03
Choiseul (WWII)    D767.982.C4
Christchurch, N.Z.    DU430.C5    993.155
Christchurch, N.Z. (area)    993.155    DU430.C5
Christian Scientists (WWII)    D810.C62
Christian X (Den.: 1912-47 period: also gen. histories of time)    DL255

Chronologies, outlines, syllabi, tables, etc. (20th c.)     D427     909.82, 940.28
Chronologies, tables, outlines (WWII)     D743.5     940.530202
Chronologies (U.S.)     E174.5
Chronometers, Nautical (PREFER QB107)     VK575
Chungking, China (plus Szechwan Province)     951.38
Church of the Brethren (WWII)     D810.C63
Churches (WWII: gen.)     D810.C5
Churchill, Winston Leonard Spencer, Sir (G.B.: 20th c.)     DA566.9.C5
Ciano, Galeazzo, Conte (It.: 1900-46 period)     DG575.C51
Civic programs (armed forces: U.S.)     UH723
CIVIL Affairs Division (WWII: U.S. Army)     D769.309
Civil defense (countries besides U.S.)     UA929.A-Z
Civil defense (G.B.)     UA929.G7
Civil defense (gen.)     UA926.A3-Z (SEE ALSO numbers within wars, such as
                D810.C69 for WWII)
Civil defense (Sov.Un.)     UA929.S65
Civil defense (U.S.: gen.)     UA927
Civil defense (WWII)     D810.C69 (SEE UA926-929 for more technical works)
Civil depts. (naval admin.: gen.)     VB170
Civil engineering (navies)     VG590-595 (SEE ALSO VA66.C6+)
Civil liberties & freedom of speech (WWII: U.S.)     D769.8.C4 (SEE UB342.U5 for
                conscientious objectors)
Civilian personnel (mil. admin.: gen.)     UB180     355.23
Civilian personnel (mil. resources)     355.23
Civilian personnel (naval admin.)     VB180-187
Civilian personnel (naval admin.: places besides U.S.)     VB185.A-Z
Civilian personnel (navies)     359.23     VB170-187
CIVILIZATION, customs, social life (20th c.)     D429 (SEE ALSO CB415, GT146)
                940.5,320.904,327.09
Civilization, customs, social life (1919-39: sometimes Europe alone)     D726
Civilization, customs, social life (Australia)     DU107
Civilization, customs, social life (China: 20th c. & 1912-49)     DS775.2
Civilization, customs, social life (China: gen.)     DS721
Civilization, customs, social life (Fr.: 20th c.)     DC365
Civilization, customs, social life (Fr.: 1901-)     DC33.7
Civilization, customs, social life (G.B.: 20th c.)     DA566.4
Civilization, customs, social life (Ger.)     DD67
Civilization, customs, social life (Ger.: 1918-)     DD239
Civilization, customs, social life (It.: 1816-1945)     DG450
Civilization, customs, social life (Japan: 1868+)     DS822.25
Civilization, customs, social life (Japan: 1912-45)     DS822.4
Civilization, customs, social life (Japan: by special topic) DS827.A-Z
Civilization, customs, social life (Japan: gen.)     DS821
Civilization, customs, social life (Palestine & the Jews)     DS112-113
Civilization, customs, social life (Philip.)     DS663-664
Civilization, customs, social life, races (Pacific)     DU28
Civilization, customs, social life (Rus.: 1925-53)     DK268.3
Civilization, customs, social life (Rus.: gen.)     DK32
Civilization, customs, social life (Serbia: 1918-45)     DR2035
Civilization, customs, social life (Swit.)     DQ36
Civilization, customs, social life (U.S.: gen.)     E161
Civilization, customs, social life (Pol.)     DK411
Class histories (Royal Naval Coll., Dart.: by date)     V515.K3
Class histories (U.S. Naval Acad.: by date)     V415.K4
Classification, Military     UB337

Collision & grounding, Nautical (prevention)    623.8884    VK371-378
Collisions & avoidance, High seas    VK371-378
Colombia    F2251-2299    986.1+
Colombia (1904-46)    F2277    986.1062-10631
Colonial troops    UA14
Colonial troops (Fr.)    UA709
Colonial troops (G.B.: inclu. natives: gen.)    UA668
Colonial troops (Ger.)    UA719
COLONIES, British    DA10-18 (SEE ALSO JV1000-1099 for other collective
                        works & D-F for specific colonies)
Colonies, Dutch    DJ500 (PREFER D-F #s for indiv. colonies or JV2500-2599 for
                    collective)
Colonies, French    DC890 (PREFER D-F for individual colonies or JV1800-1899 for
                    collective)
Colonies, German    DD905 (PREFER D-F #s for specific colonies or JV2000-2099
                    for collective)
Colonies, Portuguese    DP802.A-Z (SEE ALSO D-F for indiv. places & JV4200-
                        4299 for collective works)
Colonies (WWI)    D573-578
Colonies (WWI: G.B.: gen.)    D547.A1
Colonies (WWII: Fr.: gen.)    D761.9.A1
Colonies (WWII: G.B.: gen.)    D760.A1
Colorado    F771-785, F776    978.8
Colorado (WWII: Reconstruction)    D828.C6-61
Colors & standards, Military    355.15    UC590-595, U360-365
Colors & standards (navies)    359.15    V300-305
Colors, flags, standards (mil.: U.S.)    UC593-594
Colt machine guns    UF620.C6
COMBAT & support aircraft    358.4183-4184    UG1240-1245, UG1242.A-Z (by
                        type), UG1243 (U.S.), UG633-635, VG90-95 (naval), TL685+
Combat conditions (mil. life)    355.1294
Combat craft, Light (torpedo boats etc.: engineering)    623.8258    V830-
                        835 (p.t.'s), V880
Combat engineers (WWII: U.S.: gen.)    D769.33
Combat units (by service field)    355.35    UA
Combat vessels, Small (P.T.'s etc.: units)    359.3258    V830-840, V880-885
Combined ops. (joint: air, army, navy)    U260
Combined ops., Military (2 or more types of forces)    355.46
Combined ops., Naval (2 or more types of forces)    359.46
Comics, caricatures, humor (WWII)    940.5496-5497    D743.9, D745
Command & control systems    UB212
Command control    UB200-245    355.41, .33, .6
Command of ships (naval admin.: gen.)    VB200    359.33, .6, 158.4, 350.00323
Commandeering, compensation, etc. (naval: by country or place)    VC268.A-Z
Commando ops. (WWII)    D794.5
Commando tactics    U262    355.425
Commemorations & celebrations (navies)    359.16    V310
Commemorations, celebrations, & memorials (WWI: gen.)    940.46    D663-
                        680, D663 (gen.)
Commemorations, celebrations, & memorials (WWII: gen.)    940.546    D830-838
Commencement addresses (U.S. Naval Acad.: by speaker)    V415.F3.A-Z
Commerce, communications, & transport    380-389    HF, HE

Commissioned & warrant officers, Air force   358.41332   UG820-825
Commissioning, draft, examination, registration, other methods of naval personnel
    procurement   359.2236   VB260-275 (enlisted pers.), VB307-315 (officers)
Commissioning, registration, classification, exams, etc. (mil. manpower procure.)
                        355.2236   UB330+, U400+
Commissions, Military (gen.)   UB870
COMMUNICATION & transport (air force resources)   358.4127   UC330-335,
                          UA940-945
Communication & transport (mil. resources)   355.27   UA940-945,
                          UA929.95.T7, UC10+, UC270-275
Communication & transport (naval resources)   359.27   VC530-580 (trans.),
                          VB255, VG70-85, V270
Communication equipment, Military   355.85   UG570-613, UA940-945
Communication equipment, Naval   359.85   VG70-85
Communication routes (except U.S.)   UA955.A-Z
Communication routes (mil. sci.)   UA950-979
Communication routes (U.S.)   UA953-954
Communication systems, Naval (blinkers & electrooptical: design)   623.85614
Communication systems, Naval (flag & semaphore: design)   623.85612
                        V280-285, V300-305 (flags), VK385
Communication systems, Naval (pyrotechnical: design)   623.85613
Communication systems, Naval (radar: design)   623.85648
                        UG612-612.5, UG612.3 (U.S.)
Communication systems, Naval (radar & radiocommun.: design)   623.8564
                        VG76-78, UG610
Communication systems, Naval (radio telegraph: design)   623.85642   VG70-75
Communication systems, Naval (radio telephone: design)   623.85645   VG80-85
Communication systems, Naval (shortwave radio: design)   623.85641
Communication systems, Naval (visual: design)   623.8561   V280-305
COMMUNICATIONS, Military (U.S.)   UA943-944
Communications, Naval (inclu. radio, radar, wireless telegraph: gen.)   VG76
                        623.8564, .734
Communications services, Naval   359.983   VG70-85
Communications, signaling, & cryptography forces (mil. engineers)   358.24
                        UG570-611.5, UA940-945, UB290 (cryp.)
Communications systems, Naval (engineering)   623.856   VG70-85, VB255
Communications technology (mil. engineering)   623.73   UG590-613.5, UG580,
                        UG590, UG570-575
Communications (WWII)   D810.C7
Compasses (sea, air, or land: inclu. gyro type)   VK577   623.82
Compulsory service & exemption (mil.: besides U.S.)   UB345.A-Z
Comrades of the Great War (G.B.)   D546.A12
CONCENTRATION camps & internment centers (WWII: by location)
                        940.53174-53179
Concentration camps, internment centers, labor camps (WWII)   940.5317
Concentration camps (Sp. Civil War, 1936-39: outside Sp.)   DP269.67
Concentration camps (WWII)   D803-805
Concentration camps (WWII: by country)   D804.A-Z
Concentration camps (WWII: gen.: atrocities)   D803
Concentration camps (WWII: Ger.)   D804.G3
Concentration camps (WWII: Jpn.)   D804.J3
Concrete ships (naval architec.)   VM148

Conduct & rewards, Military    355.13    U765+
Conduct & rewards, Naval    359.13    VB840-845, VB843 (U.S.)
Conduct, discipline, & reward (air forces: etiquette, enforcement, punishments, etc.)
                                358.4113    UB790-795, UB430-435
CONFERENCES (1941: Berlin: Potsdam, Ger.)    D734.B4
Conferences (1943: Cairo, Eg.)        D734.C2
Conferences (1943: Casablanca, Mor.)    D734.C25
Conferences (1943: Tehran, Iran)        D734.T4
Conferences (1945: Crimea: Yalta, Rus.)    D734.C7
Conferences (air forces)    UG623
Conferences & treaties (WWI)    940.3141    D642-647
Conferences & treaties (WWII)    940.53141
Conferences (marine navig. & merch. marine)    VK5
Conferences (naval architec.)    VM5
Conferences (naval sci.)    V7    359.0060+, .0063
Conferences (Paris: 29 July-15 Oct. 1946)    D814.565
Conferences (WWII)    D734
Conferences (WWII: gen. & multi.)    D734.A1.A-Z
Conferences (WWII: single)    D734.A2-Z999
Confiscation (WWII)    D810.C8
Congresses, International (relief, sick, wounded, etc.: misc.: by date)    UH534
Conscientious objectors    355.224    UB341-342
Conscientious objectors (by country)    UB342.A-Z
Conscientious objectors (gen.)    UB341    355.224
Conscientious objectors (WWII)    D810.C82
Conscription & exemption (mil. service)    UB340-345
Conscription or draft (navies)    359.22363
CONSTRUCTION & maintenance (army engineers)    358.22    UG360-390+, UG15-124
Construction Battalions (U.S. Navy)    VA66.C6-65    359.33+, .90973
Construction Div. (U.S. Army)    UC45
Construction of warships (1860-1900: armored vessels)    V799
Construction of warships (1901+)    V800    623.825, 359.325+
Construction of warships (materials: besides U.S.)    V805.5.A-Z
Construction of warships (materials: gen.)    V805
Construction of warships (materials: U.S.)    V805.3
Construction, Road (mil. engineering)    623.62    UG330
Contract administration (mil.)    355.6211    UC267
Contract administration (navies)    359.6211    VC267
Contracts & claims, Naval (supplies: by place)    VC267.A-Z
Contracts & procurement, Air force (U.S.)    UG1123
Contracts & specifications (naval architec.)    VM295-296
Contracts, Military (supplies)    UC267
Convoy lanes (N. Atlantic: pilot & sailing guides)    VK813
Convoys, Naval    V182    359.4-43
Cook Islands    DU430.C6    996.23-24
Cookery & diet, Medical (mil.)    UH487
Cookery, Naval    VC370-375    359.81
Cooking (mil.: gen.)    UC720
Coolies (mil. transp.)    UC349
Cooling & heating (naut. craft: engineering)    623.853    VM481
Copenhagen, Den.    DL276
Coral Sea, Battle of (1942)    D774.C57
Corpo Volontari Della Libert`a (WWII: Ital.)    D763.I815-817
Corpo Volontari Della Libert`a (WWII: Ital.: by name)    D763.I817.A-Z
Corpo Volontari Della Libert`a (WWII: Ital.: gen.)    D763.I815

Corporal punishment & flogging (mil. sci.: gen.)     UB810
Corporal punishment (naval)     VB910     364.67, 343.0146, 359.13325
Corregidor (Philip.)     DS688.C67     959.91
Corsica (Fr.)     DC611.C8-839
Corvettes & frigates (besides U.S.)     V826.5.A-Z
Cossacks (Rus. Rev., 1917-21)     DK265.9.C62
Cossacks (Ukr.)     DK508.55
Cossacks (WWII)     D810.C83
Costs, Military     UA17     355.622
Costs, Naval (budgets etc.)     VA20-25
Council of Foreign Ministers (WWII)     D814.4-47
Council of Foreign Ministers (WWII: gen.)     D814.4
Councils of Defense (WWI: U.S.: by state)     D570.8.C8.A-Z
Counterintelligence (mil.)     355.3433
Counterintelligence, Naval     359.3433
Countermining (defense engineering)     623.36 (SEE ALSO .3)     UG490
Course navigation (marine: inclu. celestial)     623.89     VK549-572+
COURTS-martial, Military     UB855.A-Z (besides U.S., for which SEE KF7625-7659)
Courts-martial, Military (gen.)     UB850     343.0146, 355.13325
Courts-martial, Naval (besides U.S.: by place)     VB805.A-Z
Courts-martial, Naval (gen.)     VB800     343.0146
Courts-martial, Naval (U.S.)     VB803 (PREFER KF7646-7650)
Courts of inquiry, Military (gen.)     UB860
Courts of inquiry, Naval     VB810-815     343.0143
Courts of inquiry, Naval (besides U.S.)     VB815.A-Z
Coventry, Eng.     DA690.C75
Coventry, Eng. (WWII)     D760.8.C6
Crete     DF901.C78-89, .C86 (1898-)     949.98
Crete & Aegean Islands (geog. & travel)     914.99     DF901.C8 (Crete),
          .C9 (Cyclades), DS52-53, DS53.A-Z (by island), DS53.R4-6 (Rhodes)
Crete (WWII)     D766.7.C7
Crimea (Rus.)     DK511.C7     947.717
Crimes, Military (gen.)     UB780     355.1334
Crimes, Naval (gen.)     VB850     359.1334
Crippled sailors, Employment of (PREFER UB360-366)     VB278
CROATIA (inclu. Dalmatia, Istria, Slavonia)     DB361-380, DR1502-1645     949.72
Croatia (1914-18: WWI)     DR1582
Croatia (1918-45)     DR1583-1591
Croatia (1918-45: gen.)     DR1584
Croatia (1941-45: WWII)     DR1591
Croatia (gen.)     DR1510, 1535
Croatia (post-WWI territorial ?s)     D651.C78
CRUISERS (as equip.)     359.8353
Cruisers (besides U.S.)     V820.5.A-Z
Cruisers (G.B.)     V820.5.G7
Cruisers (gen.: tech. info.)     V820     623.8253, .81253, 359.3253
Cruisers (handling)     623.88253     V820-820.5
Cruisers (in units)     359.3253     V820-820.5, VA65.A-Z (U.S.: by name)
Cruisers (naval engineering)     623.8253     V820-820.5
Cruisers (U.S.)     V820.3
Cryptography & ciphers     UB290     358.24
Cryptography (WWI)     D639.C75
Cryptography (WWII)     D810.C88

Cuba          F1751-1849, F1758, F1776        972.91
Cuba (1899-)        972.9106        F1787-1788
Cuba (1933-)        F1788        972.91063
Cuba (gen.)        F1776
Cullum's Register (U.S. Mil. Acad.)        U410.H5
Cupolas, Revolving (& other portable gun shelters)        UF660
Curiosities, Military (inclu. collector's hdbks.)        U790
Curiosities, Naval        V745        359.00207, .002
Current & tide tables (Atlantic Ocean: west)        VK759-792
Current & tide tables (gen.: pubn. 1801+)        VK602        623.8949
Current & tide tables (North Pacific)        VK717
Current events yrbks. (20th c.: nonserial: includes pictorial titles: by time then
                author)        D410.5
Customs & laws of war (inclu. treatment of prisoners)        UB485 (SEE ALSO JX)
Customs, Military (gen.)        U750
Customs, Naval (gen.)        V720        359.1
Cyclists, Military        UH30-35
Cylinders, valves, etc. (internal combustion engines: marine engineering)
                                623.87237        VM769
Cyprus        DS54        956.45
Cyprus (1878-1960: British rule)        956.4503        DS54.8
Cyprus (WWII: gen. particip.)        940.535645        DS54.8
Czech military ops. (WWII: gen.)        D765.5
CZECHOSLOVAKIA (inclu. Bohemia, Moravia, Slovakia)        DB191-217 (earlier titles),
                DB2000-3150+ (for most titles cataloged after 1979)        943.7
Czechoslovakia        DB2000-2299        943.7+
Czechoslovakia (1801-1976 pubns.)        DB2062
Czechoslovakia (20th c.)        DB215        943.7024-703+
Czechoslovakia (to 1918)        943.702
Czechoslovakia (1918-)        DB2185-2232+
Czechoslovakia (1918-: gen.)        DB2186
Czechoslovakia (1918-45)        943.703        DB215-215.3, DB2186-2211,
                DB2186 (gen.), DB2196 (1918-39), DB2206 (1939-45)
Czechoslovakia (1918-39)        DB2195-2202        943.703
Czechoslovakia (1918-39: gen.)        DB2196
Czechoslovakia (1939-45: Ger. occup.)        DB215.3, DB2205-2211        943.703
Czechoslovakia (1939-45: Ger. occup.: gen.)        DB2206
Czechoslovakia & Czech military ops. (WWII)        D765.5-55        940.53437, 943.703
Czechoslovakia (gen.)        DB2011
Czechoslovakia (geog. & travel)        914.37        DB191 (titles prior to 1979-80), DB2020
Czechoslovakia (mil. status)        UA829.C95        355.0330437
Czechoslovakia (post-WWI territorial ?s)        D651.C9
Czechoslovakia (WWII: dipl. history)        D754.C95
Czechoslovakia (WWII: gen. particip.)        940.53437        D765.5, DB215.3,
                                DB2205-2211, DB2206
Czechoslovakia (WWII: mil. hist.)        940.5409437        D765.5
Czechoslovakian military ops. (WWI)        D539.5.C8
Czechs (in Pol.)        DK4121.5.C9

DALADIER, Édouard (Fr.: 20th c.)        DC373.D3
Dallas, Texas        F394.D2
Dalmatia (20th c.)        DB420
Dalmatia (Yug.: local Croatia)        DR1620-1630        949.72
Damage control (warships)        V810        623.888

Danube River Valley (gen.)     DJK76
Danube River Valley (Yug.)     DR1350.D35
Danzig          DD901.D2-29
Danzig (19th-20th c.)     DD901.D28
Danzig, Pol. (1919-45: time of free city)     DK4673
Danzig, Pol. (Gdansk)     DK4650-4685
Dardanelles (Tur.)          DR701.D2
Dartmouth (Royal Naval College: Act of incorp.)     V515.A1
Darwin & N. District (Australia)     994.295     DU398.D3
Darwin, Australia     DU398.D3     994.295
Davao (Philip.)          DS688.D3
Dawes Plan (WWI)     D649.G3.A4-5
De Gaulle, Charles (Fr.: 20th c.)     DC373.G3
DEAD reckoning (naut. navig.)     623.8923     VK572
Dead reckoning (naut. navig.)     VK572     623.8923
Dead, Treatment of     UH570
Dead, wounded, decorated (WWI: lists: U.S.)     D609.U6-7
Dead, wounded, decorated (WWII: Australia)     D797.A8
Dead, wounded, decorated (WWII: South Australia)     D797.A83
Dead, wounded, decorated (WWII: U.S.: Calif.)     D797.U62.C2
Dead, wounded, decorated (WWII: U.S.: gen.)     D797.U6     940.546773
Dead, wounded, decorated (WWII: U.S.: special)     D797.U7
Dead (WWI: burial, cemeteries, etc.)     D639.D4
Dead (WWII: treatment, cemeteries, etc.)     D810.D4
Death (Jpn. custom)     DS827.D4
Decorations, Military (gen.)     UB430
DEFENSE & attack plans (U.S.)     UA923     355.033073, .4773
Defense, attack, & siege (gen.: pubn. 1789+)     UG444     355.4+
Defense, Civil (U.S. states, cities, etc.)     UA928-928.5.A-Z
Defense, Industrial (U.S.)     UA929.6-8
Defenses, Air          UG730-735, UF625 (antiaircraft), UA926+ (civil defense)
                    358.4145, .13
Defenses, Air (places besides U.S.)     UG735.A-Z
Defenses, Direct-invasion (barriers, flooding, traps, etc.)     623.31     UG375,
                    UG403, UG407-409, UG448 (coast)
Defenses, Fortified (Eur.: gen.)     UG428     623.194, 355.474
Defenses, Fortified (U.S.: gen.)     UG410     623.1973, 355.4773
Delivery or charge-holding devices (naval ammun.)     359.8251
Demobilization (by country)     UA917.A3-Z
Demobilization (gen.)     UA917.A2     355.29
Demobilization (mil. resources: gen.)     355.29     UA917
Demobilization, Naval (inclu. civil employ.)     VB277     359.29, .1154
Demolition (mil. engineering)     623.27     UG37
Demolition charges     355.82545
Demolitions (mil. engineering)     UG370     623.4545, 358.23
DENMARK     DL101-291+, DL148(gen.)     948.9
Denmark (20th c.)     DL250     948.905
Denmark (1906-)     948.905     DL250 (20th c.)
Denmark (1906-45)     948.9051     DL253-257
Denmark (1912-47: time of Christian X)     DL255-257     948.9051
Denmark (1914-18: WWI)     DL256
Denmark (1919+)     DL256.5
Denmark & Finland     948.9
Denmark (gen.)     DL109     948.9
Denmark (geog. & travel)     914.891-895     DL118

```
Denmark (mil. status)      UA690-699      355.0330489
Denmark (naval status)   VA490-499
Denmark (WWII: gen.)     D763.D4
Dentistry, Military    UH430-435
Dentistry, Naval       VG280-285
Denver, Colo.    978.883     F784.D4
Deportation (WWII)   D810.D5
Depression range finder   UF850.D4
Depth charges    359.8254
Depth charges, Naval     VF509      623.45115, .4517
DESCRIPTION & travel (Africa: 1901-50)    DT12    916.0431-0432
Description & travel (Algeria: 1901-50)          DT280
Description & travel (Arabian Penin.: 1801-1950)        DS207
Description & travel (Arg.: 1806-1950)      F2815    918.2043-2062
Description & travel (Asia: 1901-50)    DS9      915.044
Description & travel (Australia: 1901-50)    DU104    919.4044
Description & travel (Austria: 1901-45)      DB26
Description & travel (Barbary States: 1901-50)   DT190
Description & travel (Bel.: 1831-1945)        DH433
Description & travel (Bel. & Holl.: 1901-50)   DH39
Description & travel (Brazil: 1890-1950)   F2515    918.1045-1061
Description & travel (Brit. Empire)   DA11
Description & travel (Bulg.: 1879-1950)      DR60
Description & travel (Burma: 1824-1945)        DS527.6
Description & travel (Can.: 1867-1950)    F1015      917.1045-1063
Description & travel (Carib. Sea: 1811-)    F2171
Description & travel (Caroline Islands)    DU563
Description & travel (Chile: 1810-1950)    F3063      918.3044-30643
Description & travel (China: 1901-48)      DS710      915.1043-1044
Description & travel (Cuba: 1898-)    F1765      917.291046
Description & travel (Czech.: 1901-45)   DB2020
Description & travel (Den.: 1901-50)    DL118
Description & travel (Dutch E. Ind. & Indon.: 1801-1945)   DS619
Description & travel (E. Eur. & Balkan Penin.: 1901-50)    DR15
Description & travel (Eastern Europe: 1901-50)      DJK17
Description & travel (Egypt & Egyp. Sudan: 1901-50)      DT55    916.2044-2045
Description & travel (Ethiopia: 1901-50)      DT378
Description & travel (Europe: 1901-1950)    D921    914.045
Description & travel (Far East, E. & SE.Asia: 1901-50)    DS508    915.0441
Description & travel (Fin.: 1901-44)    DL1015.2
Description & travel (Fin.: 1945-80)    DL1015.3
Description & travel (Formosa: to 1945)    DS799.15    915.1249044
Description & travel (Fr.: 1871-1945)      DC28
Description & travel (Fr. Indoch.: 1788-1950)    DS534    915.97043
Description & travel (G.B.: 1901-45)      DA630    914.1-2, 914.10482
Description & travel (Ger.: 1919-45)      DD42    914.3009042
Description & travel (Hawaiian Is.: to 1950)    DU623    919.69043
Description & travel (India, pre-1947 Pak.)    DS413
Description & travel (Iran: 1801-1950)        DS251
Description & travel (It.: 1919-44)        DG429
Description & travel (Jam.: 1811-1950)    F1871
Description & travel (Japan: 1901-45)      DS810    915.2043
Description & travel (Java, Indon.: 1801-1945)    DS646.2
Description & travel (Latin Am.: 1811-1950)      F1409    918.042-043
Description & travel (Libya: 1901-50)      DT220
```

```
Description & travel (Lux.: to 1945)          DH906
Description & travel (Mex.: 1867-1950)        F1215      917.2048+
Description & travel (Mid. East, SW. Asia: 1901-50)   DS49    915.6044
Description & travel (Montenegro: 1860-1950)          DR109
Description & travel (Morocco: 1901-50)       DT310
Description & travel (N. Africa: 1901-50)     DT165      916.2043
Description & travel (New. Z.: 1840-1950)     DU411      919.31042-310435
Description & travel (Neth.: 1901-45)         DJ39
Description & travel (Nor.)              DL418
Description & travel (Pacific: 1898-1950)     DU22
Description & travel (Palestine: 1901-50)     DS107.3
Description & travel (Paris, Fr.: ALSO gen. hist.)      DC707
Description & travel (Peru: 1820-1950)        F3423
Description & travel (Philip.: 1898-1945)     DS659      915.99043
Description & travel (Pol.: 1867-1945)        DK407
Description & travel (Pol.: 1867-1944)        DK4070
Description & travel (Port.: 1816-1950)          DP525
Description & travel (Puerto R.: 1898-)          F1965
Description & travel (Rum.: 1866-1950)        DR209
Description & travel (Rus.: 1901-44)          DK27       914.70904
Description & travel (S.Am.: 1811-1950)       F2223
Description & travel (Scan., N. Eur., Fin.: 1901-50)   DL10
Description & travel (SE. Asia: 1901-50)      DS522.4 (for earlier books SEE DS525)
                                              915.9045+
Description & travel (Siberia: 1801-1945)     DK755
Description & travel (Sp.: 1901-50)           DP42
Description & travel (Swe.: 1901-50)     DL618
Description & travel (Swit.: 1901-50)    DQ24
Description & travel (Thai.: 1801-1950)       DS565
Description & travel (Tunisia: 1901-50)       DT250
Description & travel (Tur.: 1901-50)          DR428
Description & travel (Viet.: 1801-1954)       DS556.36   915.97043
Description & travel (W.Ind.: 1810-1950)      F1611      917.29044-045
Description & travel (Yug.: 1860-1944)        DR309
Description & travel (Yug.: 1901-44)          DR1221     914.971+
Description (Rome, It.: 1861-1950)       DG806
Description, travel, civilization, customs (U.S.: 1866-1913)   E168
Description, travel, civilization, customs (U.S.: 1914-45)     E169    917.3049
Desert warfare      U167.5.D4
Desertion (mil.)      UB788
Desertion (naval)      VB870-875   359.1334
Designs, drawings, blueprints (naval architec.)   VM297      623.812
DESTROYER escorts (d.e.'s) & destroyers (naval engineering)    623.8254
                                                               V825-825.3
Destroyer escorts (d.e.'s) & destroyers (units)   359.3254   V825-825.5, VA65 (U.S.)
Destroyers (as equip.)     359.8354
Destroyers (besides U.S.: by place)      V825.5.A-Z
Destroyers (gen.)      V825      623.8254, .81254, 359.3254
Destroyers (handling)      623.88254   V825-825.5
Destroyers (Japan)    V825.5.J3
Destroyers (U.S.)     V825.3
Destruction & pillage (WWII)   D810.D6 (SEE ALSO D785.U58-63 for U.S. Strategic
                                        Bombing Survey)
Deterrence      U162.6
```

Detonators    355.82542
Detonators (design: fuses, percus. caps, primers, etc.)    623.4542    UF780,
                                                            VF510
Deutsches Jungvolk (Nazi Party)    DD253.49
Deutschland (submarine: Ger.: WWI)    D592.D4
Devonshire Regiment (WWII: G.B.)    D760.D4
Dewey, Thomas (U.S.: 20th c.)    E748.D48
Dictionaries (20th c. history)    D419    909.8203, 320.03, 320.904
DICTIONARIES & ENCYCLOPEDIAS (air forces & warfare)    UG628    358.4003
Dictionaries & encyclopedias (artillery)    UF9    358.1203
Dictionaries & encyclopedias (China)    951.003    DS705
Dictionaries & encyclopedias (history: gen.)    903    D9
Dictionaries & encyclopedias (mil. & naut. engineering)    623.003 (SEE ALSO 603)
                                                            UG144-147
Dictionaries & encyclopedias (mil. sci.)    U24-25    355.003
Dictionaries & encyclopedias (naval forces)    359.003    V23
Dictionaries & encyclopedias (naval sci.: gen.)    V23    359.003
Dictionaries & encyclopedias (U.S.)    E174    973.03
Dictionaries & encyclopedias (WWI: includes 'Times' index and chronology)    D510
Dictionaries & encyclopedias (WWII)    D740    940.5303
DICTIONARIES, CHRONOLOGIES, ETC. (Asia)    DS31
Dictionaries, chronologies, etc. (China)    DS733
Dictionaries, chronologies, etc. (G.B.)    DA34
Dictionaries, chronologies, etc. (Japan)    DS833
Dictionaries, chronologies, etc. (military history: world)    D25.A2
Dictionaries, chronologies, etc. (Palestine, the Jews)    DS114
Dictionaries, chronologies, etc. (Rus.)    DK36
Dictionaries, gazeteers, guidebooks (Japan)    DS805
Dictionaries, guidebooks, etc. (Far East, E. & SE.Asia)    DS504
Dictionaries, Military (G.B.)    DA52
Dictionaries, Naval (G.B.)    DA72
Dictionaries (naval sci.: multi-ling.)    V24
Dieppe, Fr.    DC801.D56
Dieppe Raid (1942)    D756.5.D5
Diesel engines (marine engineering)    623.87236    VM770
Diesel, oil, & gas engines (marine engin.)    VM770    623.8723
Dinaric Alps (Yug.)    DR1350.D55
DIPLOMACY (20th c.)    D451-457
Diplomacy (20th c.: gen. special)    D455
Diplomacy (20th c.: gen.)    D453    909.82, 327.3-9, 320.9
DIPLOMACY & POLITICS (Africa: 19th-20th c.: gen.)    DT31.5
Diplomacy & politics (Bel.: gen.)    DH566
Diplomacy & politics (Bulg.)    DR72
Diplomacy & politics (Ger.: 1918-)    DD240-241
Diplomacy & politics (Ger.: gen.)    DD112    320.943, 327.43+
Diplomacy & politics (India, pre-1947 Pak.: 20th c.)    DS448
Diplomacy & politics (Iran)    DS274
Diplomacy & politics (Iraq: gen.)    DS70.95
Diplomacy & politics (It.)    DG491-499
Diplomacy & politics (Japan)    DS840-849    320.952, 327.52
Diplomacy & politics (Lux.)    DH908.5
Diplomacy & politics (Neth.: 1795-20th c.)    DJ147
Diplomacy & politics (Nor.: gen.)    DL458
Diplomacy & politics (Pacific: gen.: inclu. colonial rule)    DU29
Diplomacy & politics (Pol.)    DK418, DK4178.5-4185

Diplomacy & politics (Port.)          DP555-557          320.9469, 327.469+
Diplomacy & politics (Rum.)                      DR226
Diplomacy & politics (Rus.-Jpn. War, 1904-5)          DS517.13
Diplomacy & politics (Saudi Arabia: gen.)       DS227
Diplomacy & politics (Serbia: gen.)          DR1975
Diplomacy & politics (Sp.)                      DP83-86
Diplomacy & politics (Sp.: 1931-39)          DP257-258
Diplomacy & politics (Swe.)                      DL658-659
Diplomacy & politics (Swe.: 1907-50)       DL867.5       948.5051-2
Diplomacy & politics (Swit.)          DQ68-76       320.9494, 327.4940+
Diplomacy & politics (Swit.: 1798-20th c.)          DQ75
Diplomacy & politics (Syria: gen.)       DS95.5
Diplomacy & politics (Tur.: 1918-)       DR477       327.5610+, 320.9561
Diplomacy & politics (Yug.)          DR326
Diplomacy & politics (Yug.: 1918-45)       DR367.A-Z
DIPLOMACY (Arg.: gen.)          F2833
Diplomacy (Australia: gen.)          DU113       327.94
Diplomacy (Brazil: gen.)       F2523       327.81
Diplomacy (Can.: gen.)       F1029       327.71
Diplomacy (Chile: gen.)       F3083
Diplomacy (China: gen.)       DS740.4       327.51
Diplomacy (Cuba: gen.)       F1776.2
Diplomacy (Den.: gen.)       DL159
Diplomacy (Fin.: gen.)       DL1046       327.4897
Diplomacy (Formosa: gen.)       DS799.625
Diplomacy (Fr.: gen.)       DC55
Diplomacy (G.B.: gen.)       DA45       327.41+
Diplomacy (Ger.: 1888-1918: gen.)       DD228.6       327.43+
Diplomacy (Greece: gen.)       DF785
Diplomacy (Hung.: gen.)       DB926
Diplomacy (Ire.: 20th c.)       DA964.A-Z
Diplomacy (Japan: gen.)       DS845       327.52
Diplomacy (Latin Am.: gen.)       F1415       327.8
Diplomacy (Liech.: gen.)       DB893
Diplomacy (Mex.: gen.)       F1228
Diplomacy (N. Viet.)       DS560.68
Diplomacy (Paraguay)       F2682
Diplomacy (Peru: gen.)       F3433
Diplomacy (Rus.)       DK65-69
Diplomacy (Sp.: 1814-20th c.)   DP85.8
Diplomacy (U.S.: gen.)       E183.7   327.73
Diplomacy (Ukr.: gen.)       DK508.56
Diplomacy (Urug.: gen.)       F2722
Diplomacy (Venez.: gen.)   F2321.2
Diplomacy (Viet.: gen.)       DS556.57
Diplomacy (W.Ind.: gen.)   F1621.5

Diplomacy (WWI)        D610-621    940.32
Diplomacy (WWII)       D748-754    940.532+, .5322-5325, 327.+
Diplomacy (WWII: Fr.)       940.532244    D752
Diplomacy (WWII: G.B.)     940.532241    D750
Diplomacy (WWII: gen.)     D748
Diplomacy (WWII: Ger.)    940.532443    D751
Diplomacy (WWII: Ire.)    940.5325415 (could ALSO be at .5322415 with Allies or at
    .5324415 with Axis)    D754.I5-7
Diplomacy (WWII: misc. countries or areas)    D754.A-Z
Diplomacy (WWII: Sweden)    940.5325485    D754.S8
Diplomacy (WWII: U.S.)     940.532273    D753
Diplomacy (WWII: Yug.)    940.5322497    D754.Y
Diplomatic history (WWI)    940.32    D610-621, D610 (gen.)
Directories (naval architec.)    VM12
Dirigibles    629.13324
Dirigibles (Ger.)    UG1225.G3
Dirigibles (mil. engineering)    623.743    TL659, UG1220-1225
Dirigibles (places outside U.S.)    UG1225.A-Z
Disability benefits, pensions, etc. (naval admin.: U.S.)    VB283
Disabled American Veterans of the World War (WWI)    D570.A15.D5
Disabled veterans (U.S.: rehab.)    UB363-364
Disarmament (WWI: Ger.)    D650.D5
Disarmament (WWII)    D820.D5
Disasters, Submarine    VK1265
Discharge, promotion, recruitment, enlistment (mil. sci.: countries besides U.S.)
    UB325.A-Z
Discharge, promotion, recruitment, enlistment (naval sci.: places besides U.S.)
    VB265.A-Z
Discharge, retirement, other termination (mil.)    355.114    UB320+
Discipline & conduct, Military (regulation)    355.133
Discipline & enforcement (naval conduct)    359.1332    VB850-855, VB890-925
Discipline, Military (U.S.)    UB793 (SEE ALSO KF7590)
Discipline, Naval (besides U.S.)    VB845.A-Z
Discipline, Naval (G.B.)    VB845.G7
Discipline, Naval (U.S.)    VB843    359.130973
Disinfection & fumigation (naval engin.)    VM483
Dispensaries, Naval    VG270-275
Distance finders (inclu. tables etc.)    VK579
District of Columbia    975.3    F191-205, F194
District of Columbia (geog. & travel)    917.53    F192.3, F194, F199
Diving (marine engin.)    VM975-989 (SEE GV840.S78 for skindiving),
    VM981 (gen.)    627.72 (gen.)
Diving (marine engin.: hist.)    VM977    627.7209, 623.8257 (subs.),
    359.3257 (subs.-naval ops.), 797.23 (scuba)
Diving (marine engin.: special types)    VM985-989

Division of the Philippines (U.S. Army)    UA27.P5
DIVISIONS etc. (WWII: Australia)    D767.813    940.541294
Divisions etc. (WWII: Bel.)    D763.B41
Divisions etc. (WWII: Czech.)    D765.53
Divisions etc. (WWII: Dutch: by #)    D763.N41.1st-
Divisions etc. (WWII: Fin.)    D765.32
Divisions etc. (WWII: Ital.: by #)    D763.I81.1st-
Divisions etc. (WWII: Ital.: by name or author)    D763.I813.A-Z
Divisions etc. (WWII: Japan)    D767.23
Divisions etc. (WWII: New Z.)    D767.851    940.5412931
Divisions etc. (WWII: Nor.: by #)    D763.N61.1st-
Divisions etc. (WWII: Nor.: by name or author)    D763.N613.A-Z
Divisions etc. (WWII: Pol.)    D765.13
Divisions etc. (WWII: Rum.)    D766.413
Divisions etc. (WWII: Rus.: by #)    D764.5.1st-    940.541247
Divisions etc. (WWII: U.S.)    D769.29-309
Divisions etc. (WWII: U.S.: by #)    D769.3.1st-
Divisions etc. (WWII: U.S.: by name )    D769.295.A-Z
Divisions etc. (WWII: U.S.: gen.)    D769.29
Divisions etc. (WWII: Yug.: by #)    D766.61.1st-
Divisions etc. (WWII: Yug.: by name)    D766.613.A-Z
Divisions (U.S. Army: by place)    UA27.A-Z
Divisions (U.S. Marines: by #)    VE23.22.1st+
Divisions (U.S.: by #/author)    UA27.5.1st-
Divisions (WWII: Fr.)    D761.2
Dnepropetrovsk (Uk.)    DK508.9.D64
Documentary films, slides, etc. (WWI: catalogs)    D522.22
Documentary films, slides, etc. (WWII: catalogs)    D746.3 (older titles),
                                                     D743.22 (newer titles)
Dog fighting, bombing, other air tactics (countries besides U.S.)    UG705.A-Z
Dogs, Military    UH100
Dogs (mil. transp.)    UC355 (SEE ALSO UH100)    355.424
Dollfuss, Englebert (Austria)    DB98.D6
Dominican Republic    F1931-1941    972.93
Don River Valley (Rus.)    DK511.D7
Donovan, William, 1883-1959 (WWII: spy)    D810.S8.D55
Dover, Eng. (WWII)    D760.8.D6
Downing St. (London, Eng.: No. 10)    DA687.D7
Draft & exemption (mil.: Japan)    UB345.J3
Draft & exemption (mil.: U.S.)    UB343-344    355.2236306073
Draft, Military    355.22363    UB340-345, UB343 (U.S.)
Draftsmen & surveyors, Naval (gen.)    VG920
Dreams (WWI)    D639.D7
Dresden, Ger.    DD901.D71-79
DRILL camps, instruction bases, maneuver grounds (gen.)    U290
Drill camps, maneuver grounds, etc. (U.S.: by name)    U294.5.A-Z
Drill regulations (armor & cavalry: U.S. reserves)    UE161
Drill regulations (artillery: U.S. reserves: by state)    UF162.A-W
Drill regulations (infantry: U.S. reserves)    UD161
Drill regulations, Marine (U.S.)    VE160-162
Drill regulations, Naval (U.S. reserves)    VD161
Drills, maneuvers, & tactics (artillery: by place)    UF160-302

DRILLS, MARINE (Asia)    VE270-280
Drills, Marine (Australia)    VE295
Drills, Marine (Eur.)    VE215-269
Drills, Marine (G.B.)    VE234
Drills, Marine (Ger.)    VE231
Drills, Marine (Japan)    VE277
Drills, Marine (U.S.: gen.)    VE160        359.965, .9654
DRILLS, NAVAL (Asia)    VD270-280
Drills, Naval (Australia)    VD295        359.50994
Drills, Naval (China)    VD271
Drills, Naval (Eur.)    VD215-269
Drills, Naval (G.B.)    VD234        359.50941
Drills, Naval (Ger.)    VD231        359.50943
Drills, Naval (Japan)    VD277        359.50952
Drills, Naval (New Z.)    VD298
DRILLS, NAVAL ORDNANCE (Asia)        VF270-280
Drills, Naval ordnance (Australia)    VF295
Drills, Naval ordnance (Eur.)    VF215-269
Drills, Naval ordnance (Fr.)    VF228
Drills, Naval ordnance (G.B.)    VF234
Drills, Naval ordnance (Ger.)    VF231
Drills, Naval ordnance (Japan)    VF277
Drills, Naval ordnance (Rus.)    VF252
Drills, Naval ordnance (U.S.: gen.)        VF160
Drills, Naval (Rus.)        VD252
Drills, Naval (U.S.)        VD160-162
Drills, tactics, & maneuvers (armor & cavalry: Eur.)    UE215-269
Drills, tactics, & maneuvers (infantry: U.S.)        UD160-162
Dry docks, shipyards, etc. (naval engineering)    623.83        VM301
Dunkirk, Battle of (1940)        D756.5.D8
Düsseldorf, Ger.        DD901.D95
DUTCH East Indies & Indonesia    DS611-649
Dutch East Indies & Indonesia (WWII)    D767.7        940.53598, .5425, 959.8022
Dutch East Indies (WWII: Reconstruction)    D829.D8
Dutch military ops. (WWII: gen.)    D763.N4
Dutch New Guinea (West)        DU744-744.5        995.1
Dutch West Indies        F2141    972.986
Dyak Islands & Borneo (gen.)        DS646.3        959.53, .83
Dzerzhinsky, Feliks (Rus.: 1925-53 era)        DK268.D9


EAST Africa        DT365-469        967.6, 963
East Africa (to 1960)        DT431
East Africa (1884-1960: gen.)        DT365.7        967.6
East Africa (Uganda & Kenya)        967.6    DT421-435+ (newer titles), DT431
East Africa (WWII)        D766.84        940.53676, 967.6
East African islands        DT469.A-Z
East Coast (U.S.: Loran tables)        VK561.U53-54
East Coast (U.S.: pilot & sailing guides)        VK981
East Coast (U.S.: tide & current tables)        VK781    623.8949091634
East Downing, Eng. (WWII)    D760.8.E3
East Indies & Indonesia (pilot & sailing guides: from U.S.)        VK931
East Indies (pilot & sailing guides: Eng. to India etc.)        VK881

Eastern Asia (history & foreign relns.: inclu. SE. Asia)    DS518-518.9
Eastern Europe (1815-1918)    DJK48
Eastern Europe (1918-45)    DJK49
Eastern Europe & Balkan Peninsula    DR (SEE DJK for gen. bks. on E. Eur. after
                    about 1977-78)    949.6-8
Eastern Europe    DR (pubns. prior to 1978 & specific countries), DJK (titles after
                    about 1977-78)    943.7-943.9, 947, 947.8, 949.6-949.84
Eastern Front (WWI)    D550-569
Eastern Front (WWII)    D764-766.7
Eastern Orthodox Church (WWII)    D810.C6745
Eastern question (1801-1914/20)    D371-379    949, 320.956, 327.41-42
Eastern question (20th c.)    D461-475    320.95, 956.03, 325.342
Eastern question (20th c.: by country)    D469.A-Z
Eastern question (20th c.: gen.)    D463
Eastern question (general: 19th c.)    D374
Ebert, Friedrich (Ger.: 1918-48 era)    DD247.E2
Economic aspects (Rus. Rev., 1917-21)    DK265.9.E2
Economic factors of war    355.023 (PREFER 355.02)    HB195, HC65, JX1953
Economic matters (Sp. Civil War, 1936-39)    DP269.8.E2
Economic matters (WWI: commerce, finance, mail)    D635 (SEE ALSO HC56,
                    HF3030, HJ236, HJ8011)
Economic matters (WWII: commerce, mail, finance, monetary & fiscal planning, etc.
        in gen.)    D800 (SEE ALSO HC, HF, HJ for specific places)
Economics    330-339    HB-HJ
Ecuador    F3701-3799    986.6
Ecuador (1895-1944)    F3737    986.607-6072
Eden, Anthony (G.B.: 20th c.)    DA566.9.E28
Edinburgh, Scot.    941.34    DA890.E2-4
EDUCATION    L    370-379
Education & employment of veterans (U.S.)    UB357-358    355.1150973
Education & training, Air force    UG637-639    358.415+
Education & training, Military (U.S.)    355.50973
EDUCATION, MILITARY    U400-714    355.07
Education, Military (Asia)    U635-660
Education, Military (Australia)    U700-704    355.0071094
Education, Military (Austria-Hung.: gen.)    U550
Education, Military (Balkan States)    U625
Education, Military (China)    U640-644    355.0071051
Education, Military (Eur.)    U505-630    355.007104+
Education, Military (Fr.)    U565-569
Education, Military (G.B.)    U510-549.3
Education, Military (gen.: pubns. 1801+)    U405
Education, Military (Ger.)    U570-574    355.0071043
Education, Military (It.)    U585-589
Education, Military (Japan)    U650-654    355.0071052
Education, Military (New Z.)    U705-709
Education, Military (Nor.)    U590-594
Education, Military (Rus.)    U600-604    355.0071047
Education, Military (Tur.)    U620-624
Education, Military (U.S.)    U407-439

EDUCATION, NAVAL    V400-695
Education, Naval (Asia)    V625-650
Education, Naval (Asia: misc. countries)    V650.A-Z
Education, Naval (Australia)    V690-694    359.007094
Education, Naval (Can.)    V440-444
Education, Naval (China)    V630-634
Education, Naval (Eur.)    V500-623
Education, Naval (Fr.)    V565-569
Education, Naval (G.B.)    V510-530
Education, Naval (Ger.)    V570-574
Education, Naval (hist.: 20th c.)    V409
Education, Naval (hist.: gen.)    V401
Education, Naval (It.)    V585-589
Education, Naval (Japan)    V640-644
Education, Naval (New Z.)    V694.1-5
Education, Naval (Philippines)    V650.P5
Education, Naval (Rus.)    V600-604
Education, Naval (Turkey)    V650.T9
Education, Naval (U.S.)    V411-438
Education (WWI)    D639.E2-6
EDUCATION (WWII)    D810.E2-5
Education (WWII: gen.)    D810.E2
Education (WWII: Missouri)    D810.E4.M8-81
Education (WWII: U.S.)    D810.E3-46
Education (WWII: U.S.: by state)    D810.E4.A-W
Education (WWII: U.S.: gen.)    D810.E3
Education (WWII: Wisconsin)    D810.E4.W6-61
Edward VII (G.B.: King: 1901-1910)    DA567
Edward VIII (G.B.: King: 1936)    DA580
EGYPT    UA865    355.033062
Egypt (1879-1952)    DT107    962.03-052
Egypt (1882-1922: Brit. protec.)    962.04    DT107-107.8, DT107 (gen.)
Egypt (1914-17: Hussein Kamil)    DT107.7    962.04
Egypt (1917-36: Fuad I)    DT107.8    962.04-051
Egypt (1922-: Independence)    962.05    DT107.8+
Egypt (1922-36: Fuad I)    962.051    DT107.8
Egypt (1936-52: Faruk I)    DT107.82    962.052
Egypt & Sudan    962    DT43-159
Egypt & Sudan (geog. & travel)    916.2    DT55 (Egypt), DT124
Egypt & the Egyptian Sudan    DT43-154    962
Egypt (gen.)    DT43-107, DT77, DT115-154    962
Egypt (lighthouses, beacons, foghorns, etc.: lists)    VK1198
Egypt (naval status)    VA690    359.030962
Egypt (WWI)    D568.2
Egypt (WWII)    D766.9    940.5423, .5362, 962.052
Egyptian Sudan (inclu. Anglo-Egyptian)    DT108, DT154.1-159 (newer titles)    962.4
Eire (Republic of Ireland)    941.7    DA963
Eisenhower, Dwight D. (U.S.: 1953-61)    E836    973.9210924, 940.540973,
                                                                                    355.0024
El Paso, Texas    F394.E4
El Paso, Texas (area)    976.496    F392.E45, F394.E4

ELECTRIC engines (marine engineering)   623.8726   VM773
Electric lighting (naut. craft: engineering)   623.852   VM491-493
Electric plants (defense)   UA929.95.E4
Electric propulsion (marine engin.)   VM773   623.8726
Electrical engineering (mil.)   623.76   UG480, VM471-479
Electrical systems (naut. craft: engineering)   623.8503   VM471-475
Electricians, Military   UG560-565
Electricity (mil. uses)   UG480   623.76
Electricity (naval architec. & engin.)   VM471-479   623.8503, .852, .8726
Electricity (naval architec. & engin.: U.S. Navy)   VM473
Electronic systems (naut. craft: engineering)   623.8504   VM480-480.5
Electronics & radar, Air force (U.S.)   UG1423
Electronics, Marine (radar, radio, sonar, etc.: naval architec. & engin.)   VM480
                                         623.8504, .734+, .8564-85648
Electronics, Marine navigation   VK560   623.893
Electronics, Military   UG485   623.732+
Elephant batteries   UF430
Elizabeth (G.B.:1937-52 royal biog.: Consort of George VI)   DA585.A2
Elks, Benevolent...Order of (WWII)   D810.E6
Ellice Islands   DU590   996.81
Ellice Islands (WWII)   D767.99.E55
Emigrés, Russian (1925-53)   DK269
Employees, Civilian (naval admin.: U.S.)   VB183
Employment & education of veterans (countries except U.S.)   UB359.A-Z
Employment for crippled soldiers & sailors   UB360-366 (PREFER), UH560
                                         355.1154-1156
Encampment & field training (mil.)   355.544   U180-185, UG400-409+
Encampments   355.412   U180-185
Encampments   U180-185   355.412
Encyclopedias & dictionaries (G.B.)   941.003   DA34
Encyclopedias & dictionaries (U.S.)   973.03   E174
Encyclopedias & dictionaries (WWI)   940.4003   D510, D521, D523
Encyclopedias & dictionaries (WWII)   940.54003   D740
Enforcement (naval conduct)   359.13323
Engine auxiliaries (marine engineering: boilers, blowers, pumps, propellers, etc.)
                 623.873         VM753-757 (propellers),
                 VM741-750 (boilers), VM821 (pumps), VM781+
Engine fuels, Marine   623.874   VM779
Engineer battalions etc. (WWII: U.S.: by #)   D769.335.1st-
Engineer battalions etc. (WWII: U.S.: by name)   D769.337.A-Z
Engineer forces, Army   358.2   UG15, UG21-124 (by place), UG23 (U.S.),
                 UG500-620
ENGINEERING   620   T
Engineering facilities, Naval   359.74   VM621-724, VM623 (U.S.), VC590-595
Engineering installations, Military   355.74
Engineering ops. (WWII)   D795
Engineering ops. (WWII: by country)   D795.A3-Z
Engineering ops. (WWII: gen.)   D795.A2
Engineering services (air forces)   358.47
Engineering services, Naval   359.982
Engineering systems (naut. craft: mech., electric, water, etc.)   623.85   VM471-505
Engineering, Camouflage (mil.)   623.77   UG449, UG1240-1245 (air forces),
                 V215 (ships)
Engineering, Civil (navies: gen.)   VG590
Engineering, Defense   623.3   UG400-442

Engineering, Marine (gen.)   VM600-605   623.87
Engineering, Marine (hist.: by place)   VM621-724
ENGINEERING, MILITARY   UG1-620
Engineering, Military & nautical   623   UG, VM (naval), V, UG15 (mil.: gen.),
        UG21-124 (mil.: by place), UG23 (U.S.), V750-895 (vessels)
Engineering, Military & nautical (construction)   623.047   UG460
Engineering, Military & nautical (electronic)   623.043   UG480-485
Engineering, Military & nautical (mechanical)   623.045   UG450
Engineering, Military & nautical (nuclear)   623.044
Engineering, Military & nautical (optical)   623.042   UG476, UG487
Engineering, Military (Asia)   UG99-113
Engineering, Military (Australia + New Z.)   UG121-122.5
Engineering, Military (by country or area)   UG21-124
Engineering, Military (China)   UG101
Engineering, Military (essays & lectures)   UG156
Engineering, Military (Eur.)   UG55-95   358.2094
Engineering, Military (Fr.)   UG71
Engineering, Military (G.B.)   UG57
Engineering, Military (gen. hist.)   UG15   358.2, .209
Engineering, Military (gen.: pubn. 1801+)   UG145
Engineering, Military (Ger.)   UG73
Engineering, Military (Japan)   UG105
Engineering, Military (Rus.: Eur.)   UG85
Engineering, Military (U.S.)   UG23-25   358.20973
Engineers (WWII)   940.531562   D795
Engineers (WWII: G.B.)   D759.55
Engineers (WWII: Ger.)   D757.8
Engines, Aircraft   629.134352-134354+
Engines, Marine (gen.)   VM731   623.872
Engines, Marine (types: design)   623.872   VM731-779, VM731
ENGLAND   DA20-690
England (1485-)   DA300
England (1702-)   DA470
England (1837-1901: Queen Victoria)   DA550-565   941.08
England (20th c.: misc. overall)   DA566-566.9
England (1901-10: King Edward VII)   DA567-570   941.082
England (1910-36)   942.083   DA576
England (1910-36: King George V)   DA573-578   941.083
England (1936-45)   942.084   DA586-587
England (1936: King Edward VIII)   DA580-583   941.084
England (1937-52: King George VI)   DA584-589   941.084
England & Wales   942   DA20-745, DA20-690 (Eng.), DA700-45 (Wales)
England & Wales (WWII: gen. particip.)   940.5342
England (gen.)   DA30   941, 942
England (geog. & travel)   914.2   DA600-668, DA600 (gen.), DA630 (1901-45)
England (WWII: mil. units & ops.)   940.541242   D759.5-63+, D760.A-Z
English Channel (tide & current tables)   VK639-644
English literature   PR   820-829
English poetry, satire, etc. (WWI)   D526.2 (PREFER PR, PS)
English poetry, satire, etc. (WWII)   D745.2 (PREFER PR, PS)

ENLISTED personnel & non-coms, Air force    358.41338    UG820-825
Enlisted personnel & non-coms, Naval   359.338    VB260-275
Enlisted personnel (inclu. non-coms)    355.338    UB320, U765+
Enlisted personnel, Naval (G.B.: by city or other div.)    VD64.A-Z
Enlisted personnel, Naval (gen.: nonperiodical collections)    VD7
Enlisted personnel (naval sci.: Ger.: inclu. enlistment, promotion, etc.) VB265.G3
                                    359.2230943
Enlisted personnel (naval sci.: inclu. recruitment, enlistment, promotion, discharge,
            etc.)    VB260-275
Enlisted personnel, Naval (U.S.: by city)    VD25.A-Z
Enlistment, Military    355.22362    UB320-325, UB323 (U.S.)
Enlistment, recruiting, etc. (air forces: gen.)    UG880
Enlistment, recruitment, promotion, discharge (mil. sci.: U.S)   UB323  355.20973
Enlistment, recruitment, promotion, discharge (Naval sci.: U.S.: by region or state)
                                    VB264.A-Z
Entanglements & misc. fortification    UG407
Enterprise (aircraft carrier: U.S.: WWII)    D774.E5
Entertainers (WWII)    940.5315791-5315793    D810.E8
Entertainment, recreation, hospitality (WWII: civilian services for military)   D810.E8
Envelopment (mil. sci.)    U167.5.E57
EQUIPMENT & clothing, Military (gen.)    UC460
Equipment, Air force (gen.: planes, bombs, etc.: U.S.)    UG1203    358.4180973
EQUIPMENT & SUPPLIES (air force)    UG1100-1425
Equipment & supplies (horse cavalry)    357.188    UE440-445, UC260-267
Equipment & supplies (infantry)    356.186    UD380+, UC260-267, UC460+
Equipment & supplies, Military    355.8    U800+, UC260-267
Equipment & supplies (naval aviation)    359.948
Equipment & supplies, Naval (develop., procure., issue, util., shipping, etc.)
            359.8    VC, VF, VC10, VC20-258, VC20 (U.S.: gen.),
                    VC260-267, VF145,   VF21-124, VF23 (ordnance: U.S.),
                    VF57 (G.B.), VF73 (Ger.), VF105 (Japan), VF71 (Fr.)
Equipment & supplies (naval submarines)    359.938
Equipment & supply procurement (air forces)    358.416212    UG1120-1125,
                                  UG1123 (U.S.)
Equipment, fuel, supplies, etc. (ships)    VC270-279
Equipment, Infantry    UD370-375
Equipment, Lifesaving (marine navig.: gen.)    VK1460-1461    623.865
Equipment (marines)    VE350-355
Equipment, Medical corps    UH510-515
Equipment, Military (countries except U.S.)    UC525.A-Z
Equipment, Military (gen.)    UC520    355.8
Equipment, Military (special: by name)    UC529.A-Z
Equipment, Naval artillery (places other than U.S.)    VF325.A-Z
Equipment, Naval (misc.)    V980
Equipment (naval seamen)    VD350-355
Equipment (submarine boats: special)    VM367.A-Z
Eritrea    DT391-398    963.5
Escort carriers (WWII: U.S.)    D769.52.E7    940.545

ESPIONAGE & spies (mil. admin.)   UB270-271
Espionage & spies (naval admin.)   VB250     359.3432-3433
Espionage & unconventional warfare (mil.)   355.343 (SEE ALSO 327.12)
                                                                        UB250-290
Espionage (by country responsible)     UB271.A-Z (SEE D-F #s for other cases in
                                                                        particular countries or particular wars)
Espionage, conspiracy, propaganda in U.S. (WWII)   D753.3
Espionage, intelligence, & unconventional warfare (WWII: Australia)   940.548694
Espionage, intelligence, & unconventional warfare (WWII: It.)     940.548745
Espionage, intelligence, & unconventional warfare (WWII: Japan)     940.548752
                                                        UB251.J3, UB271.J3, VB230-250
Espionage, secret service, intelligence (WWII: gen.: spies)   D810.S7
Espionage, secret service, spies (WWI)     D639.S7-8
Espionage, spies (Sp. Civil War, 1936-39)   DP269.8.S4
Espionage (U.S.: gen.)   UB271.U6     327.120973
Essen, Ger.     DD901.E75
Essex (aircraft carrier: U.S.: WWII)     D774.E7
Essex, Eng. (WWII)     D760.8.E7
Estonia     DK511.E4-8, DK503 (later pubns.)     947.41
Estonia (1918-40)     DK503.74-746
Estonia (1940+)     DK503.75-77
Estonia (gen.)     DK511.E6, DK503 (later pubns.)
Ethics, religious questions (WWII)     D744.4
Ethics, prophecy, religious questions (WWI)     D524
ETHIOPIA (Abyssinia)     963     DT371-398, DT381
Ethiopia (1889-1928: inclu. 1895-6 conflict w. Italy)   DT387-387.6     963.043-054
Ethiopia (1896-1941 & 20th c.)     963.05     DT386-387.9, DT386
Ethiopia (1928-74: Haile Selassie)   DT387.7     963.055-06
Ethiopia (1930-74: Haile Selassie era)   963.055     DT387.7-387.92
Ethiopia (1935-6: Italo-Eth. War)     963.056 (SEE ALSO 945.091 for Italo-Eth. War of
                                                                1935-6)     DT387.8
Ethiopia (1936-41: Ital. rule)   963.057     DT387.9
Ethiopia (1941-: Independence)   963.06   DT387.9
Ethiopia & Ethiopian military ops. (WWII)   D766.92     940.5423
Ethiopia (geog. & travel)     916.3     DT378
Ethiopia (mil. status)   UA860     355.033063
Ethnic groups (Sp.-Am. War: U.S.: participation)     E725.A-Z
Ethnic or racial groups (WWI)     940.31503
Ethnic or racial groups (WWII)     940.531503
Etiquette, Military     355.1336     U765+
Etiquette, Naval     359.1336     V720-743, VB260-265, VB307-315
EUROPE     940-949     D-DR
Europe (1789-1914)     940.28     D299, D359 (1801-1914)
Europe (1801-1914)     D359     940.28
Europe (20th c.)     D424     940.288-5
Europe (1900-14)     940.288     D424, D443 (pol. & dipl.)
Europe (20th c. or 1918-)   940.5     D424-425, D720 (1919-39), D431-443, D551,
                                                        D720-728
Europe (1918-29)     940.51
Europe (1930-39)     940.52
Europe (1945-)     D1051+     940.55+
Europe (air war geog.)     358.41474
Europe & the World Wars     940-949     D-DR, D501-651, D731-838
Europe and Turkey     DA-DR   940's, 956.1
Europe & W. Eur. (gen.)     940     D-DR

247

Europe (biog.: heads of state)     923.14     D107
Europe, Eastern (gen.)     DJK38
Europe (gen.)     D51-838, D901+     940-949
Europe (geog. & travel)     914     D901-980, D907 (gen.), D921 (1901-50)
Europe (lighthouses, beacons, foghorns, etc.)     VK1055-1096
Europe (lighthouses, beacons, etc.: lists)     VK1151-1185
Europe (maps & atlases)     912.4     G1796+
Europe (mil. geog.)     355.474     UA990, UA995.E
Europe (mil. status)     355.03304
Europe (mil. status)     UA646     355.03304, .03324, .03354
Europe (misc. areas: Iceland, Belg., Switz., Greece, etc.)     949
Europe (naval geog.)     359.474     VA450
Europe (naval geog.: misc. areas: Greece etc.)     359.4749
Europe (naval status: gen.)     VA450     359.03094, .474
Europe, Northern (plus Scandinavia and Finland)     DL1-87+
European aerial ops. (WWII: U.S. bombing survey)     D785.U6
European Gypsies (by place)     DX211-275
European infantry (gen.)     UD55     356.1094
European marines (gen.)     VE55
European military law     UB590-684
European naval law     VB530-699
European War (1914-18)     940.3-.499     D501-680
European War (1914-18: gen.)     940.3     D521
Evangelical and Reformed Church (WWII)     D810.C64
Examinations (G.B. Royal Navy)     V513
Examinations (U.S. Naval Acad.)     V415.R1-4
Examinations, questions, etc. (WWII)     D743.6
Exemption & draft (mil.: Ger.)     UB345.G3
Exercises, problems, etc. (artillery)     UF148
Exeter, Eng. (WWII)     D760.8.E88
Exhibitions & museums, Air force (by place within country)     UG623.3.x2.A-Z
Exhibitions & museums, Military (by country)     U13.A2-Z     355.00740+
Exhibitions & museums, Naval (by country then city)     V13.x2.A-Z
Exhibitions & museums (naval ordnance: by place or country)     VF6.A2-Z
Expeditionary & colonial forces     355.352     UA14, UA668 (G.B.), UA709 (Fr.),
                                                                          UA719 (Ger.), UA849 (Jp.)
Explosions, powder force, etc.     UF870
Explosives     355.8252     UF860-880
Explosives (design)     623.452     UF860-870
Explosives, Military (gen.)     UF860     623.452
Extermination & concentration camps (WWII: prisons & prisoners)     D805


FALKLAND Islands     F3031     997.11
Falkland Islands (S. Atl. Ocean: G.B.)     997.1     F3031
FAR East (1904-45: inclu. Far Eastern question)     DS518 (SEE ALSO DU29)
                                                                          327.5, 950.41
Far East, Eastern & Southeastern Asia     DS501-935+     950-952, 958-959
Far East (WWII: Reconstruction)     D829.E2
FAR EASTERN question (China: 1861-1945)     DS740.63
Far Eastern question (France)     DS518.2
Far Eastern question (G.B.)     DS518.4
Far Eastern question (Ger.)     DS518.3
Far Eastern question (misc. countries)     DS518.9.A-Z (SEE DS845 for Japan,
                                                                          DS740.63 for China)
Far Eastern question (Netherlands)     DS518.5

Far Eastern question (Port.)    DS518.6
Far Eastern question (Russia)   DS518.7
Far Eastern question (U.S.)     DS518.8
Farley, James (U.S.: 20th c.)   E748.F24
Farmers (WWII)      940.531563      HD9006 (U.S.)
Fascism (1919-39)       D726.5 (SEE ALSO JC481 and 'D' numbers for Italy, Ger.)
                320.533, 321.94094
Fashion (WWI)       D639.F3
Ferdinand (Rum.: King, 1914-27: also works on era)   DR261
Ferrying (mil. engineering)     UG385
FIELD & rail artillery (design)     623.412     UF400-405, UF490-495 (rail)
Field artillery (gen.)   UF400   358.12
Field artillery groups etc. (WWII: U.S.: by #)     D769.34.1st-
Field artillery (places besides U.S.)      UF405.A-Z
Field artillery (U.S.: N.Y. reserves: also gen. artil.)     UA366
Field engineering (mil.)    UG360-390
Field engineering (misc. topics)    UG390
Field fortification     UG403
Field hospitals (WWII: U.S.: by #)     D807.U73.1st-
Field kits & equip. (mil.)   UC540-585
Field kits & equip. (mil.: U.S.)    UC543-544
Field ovens (mil.)      UC730
Field service, Infantry     UD440-445
Field service (mil. sci.)   U170-175
Fighter planes     UG1242.F5      623.7464, 358.43
Figureheads, ornaments, decorations on ships     VM308
Fiji Islands     DU600      996.11
Films, lantern slides, etc.: (WWI)     D527.3
Finances & supplies (air force admin.)     358.4162    UG1100-1105, UG1100-1425
Financial administration (mil.)     355.622    UB150-155, UC263-267, UA21-876,
                UA910-915
Financial administration (navies)     359.622    VC20-258, VC500-505, VA
FINLAND     DK445-465 (pre-1970 pubns.), DL1002-1180+ (pubns. from around
                1970 on)    947.1, 948.97 (works after 1970 or so)
Finland (20th c.)       DL1066.5      948.9703
Finland (20th c.: inclu. Revolution, 1917-18)     DK459    948.9703
Finland (1917-)      948.9703    DK459, DL1066.5
Finland (1917-39)      948.97031    DK459, DL1084
Finland (1918-39)      DL1084      948.97031
Finland (1939-)      DK459.45    948.97032
Finland (1939-45)      DL1090-1105+    948.97032
Finland (1939-45: gen.)     DL1092
Finland (1939-45: WWII era: inclu. Russo-Finnish War)     948.97032 (SEE ALSO
                947.0842 for R-F War)    DK459.45-5+, DL1090-1105+, DL1090 (gen.)
Finland (1945-)      DL1125
Finland & Finnish military ops. (WWII)     D765.3-35    940.53471, 534897,
                .54094897, 948.97032
Finland (gen.)      DL1032      948.97
Finland (geog. & travel)    914.897 (SEE ALSO .71 for earlier works)    DK450,
                DL1015.2 (books cataloged after 1969-70)
Finnish military history (WWII)     940.54094897 (SEE ALSO .5409471 for earlier
                works)    D765.3
Finnish military ops. (WWII: gen.)     D765.3

FIRE control, Artillery (inclu. instruments)     UF848-856
Fire control, Naval gunnery (inclu. instruments)     VF520-530
Fire drills, Naval (Fr.: also quarter, watch, station, etc.)     VD228
Fire-fighting equipment, Airport     629.1368
Fire-fighting (mil. airfields)     623.668
Fire-fighting, Nautical (technology)     623.8886     VK1258
Firearms, Portable (design)     623.442     UG520-525, UD380-385+
Firedrake (WWII: destroyer)     D772.F5
Fires & shipwrecks (gen.)     VK1250     910.453
Fires (mil. qtrs.)     UC425
Fires, Nautical (by name of ship)     VK1257.A-Z
FIRING & fire control (mil. engineering)     623.558     UF848-856, UF848 (gen.),
                              UF850.A-Z (range finders), VF520-530 (naval)
Firing (armor & cavalry)     UE400-405
Firing devices (primers, percussion caps, etc.)     UF780
Firing instructions, Artillery     UF670-675
Firing instructions, Naval     VF450-455
Firing or sharpshooting (infantry: gen.)     UD330
Firing tests (artillery)     UF810
First-aid handbooks, Naval     VG466
First-aid manuals, Soldiers'     UH396 (SEE ALSO UH393-395)
First World War (econ., polit., social hist.)     940.31     D443, D453, D511-523, D610
Flag officers, Naval (above captain)     359.331     VB190, VB200-205, VB310-315
Flag signals (merch. marine)     VK385
Flags, colors, standards (mil.)     UC590-595
Flags, Naval & marine (besides U.S.)     V305.A-Z
Flags, Naval & marine (gen.)     V300 (SEE ALSO VK385)     359.15
Flame & chemical weapons (gen.)     UG447     358.34
Flame throwers, tear-gas devices, smoke mortars, other chemical weapons (design)
                              623.445     UG447-447.5
Flanders area (Bel.)     DH801.F4-49
FLEETS (WWII: U.S. Navy: by #)     D769.5.1st-
Fleets, squadrons, etc. (G.B.: by name)     VA457.A-Z     359.310941
Fleets, squadrons, etc. (Ger.: by name)     VA514.A-Z     359.310943
Fleets, squadrons, etc. (Japan: by name)     VA654.A-Z     359.310952
Fleets, squadrons, etc. (U.S. Navy: by name)     VA63.A-Z     359.310973
Fleets, squadrons, etc. (WWII: U.S. Navy)     D769.5-539
Fliers (biog.)     629.13092
Flight decks (aircraft carriers)     V875.F5
Flight (gen. hist.)     629.1309
Flight training, Air force (U.S.: gen.: inclu. other educ.)     UG638     358.4150973
Flights, groups, squadrons, wings, etc. (naval aviation)     359.9434
Floating batteries     V890
Flogging & corp. punish. (countries besides U.S.)     UB815.A-Z
Florence, It.     DG760
FLORIDA     F306-320, F311     975.9
Florida (1865-1950)     F316     975.906
Florida (1918-45)     975.9062     F316
Florida (geog. & travel)     917.59     F309.3, F316
Florida Keys     975.941     F317.M7 (Monroe Co.)
Florida Keys & Strait & Windward Passage (pilot & sailing guides)     VK977
Florida Keys & Strait & Windward Passage (tide & current tables)     VK777
Florida Keys (Monroe County, Fl.)     F317.M7

Florida (naval geog.)     359.47759   VA140-147
Florida (pilot guides: Key West etc.)     623.8929759     VK977
Florida (WWII)     D769.85.F5-51
Flying     629.1325
Fog signals (merch. marine)     VK383
Foghorns, beacons, lighthouses, etc. (hist's.)     VK1015
Food, clothing, & equipment (naval admin.)     359.65-66 (SEE ALSO .81)
            VC280-285+, VC283 (clothing: U.S.), VC350-355 (food etc.), VC353 (U.S.)
Food, cooking, water, etc.     UC700-780   355.65-66, .81
Foot forces warfare     356     UD, U14-43, UA
Forecaster, Weather (navies: U.S.)     VG613
FOREIGN legions     355.359
Foreign participation (Rus. Rev., 1917-21: by country)     DK265.9.F52.A-Z
Foreign participation (Sp. Civil War, 1936-39: by country)     DP269.47.A-Z
Foreign participation (Sp. Civil War, 1936-39: Ger.)     DP269.47.G3
Foreign participation (Sp. Civil War, 1936-39: It.)     DP269.47.I8
Foreign participation (Sp. Civil War, 1936-39: Rus.)     DP269.47.R8-9
Foreign participation (Sp. Civil War, 1936-39: U.S.)     DP269.47.U6-7
Foreign population war effort (WWII: U.S.)     D769.8.F6
FOREIGN RELNS. & politics (1945-)     D843
Foreign relns. & politics (Fr.: 20th c.)     DC369     944.08
Foreign relns. & politics (G.B.: 20th c.)     DA566.7
Foreign relns. & politics (Malta)     DG991-991.6
Foreign relns. & politics (Scan., N. Eur., Fin.: gen.)     DL55
Foreign relns. (Africa-Fr.: 19th-20th c.)     DT33.5
Foreign relns. (Africa-G.B.: 19th-20th c.)     DT32.5     960.23-3, 325.3+
Foreign relns. (Africa-Ger.: 19th-20th c.)     DT34.5
Foreign relns. (Africa-It.: 19th-20th c.)     DT35.5
FOREIGN RELNS. (ARG.-Fr.)     F2833.5.F8
Foreign relns. (Arg.-G.B.)     F2833.5.G7
Foreign relns. (Arg.-Ger.)     F2833.5.G3     327.82043
Foreign relns. (Arg.-It.)     F2833.5.I8
Foreign relns. (Arg.-Japan)     F2833.5.J3
Foreign relns. (Arg.-partic. lands)     F2833.5.A-Z     327.820+
Foreign relns. (Arg.-U.S.)     F2833.5.U6-7
Foreign relns. (Asia-particular other areas or countries)     DS33.4.A-Z
Foreign relns. (Australia-G.B.)     DU113.5.G7     327.94041
Foreign relns. (Australia-Japan)     DU113.5.J3     327.94052
Foreign relns. (Australia-other specific lands)     DU113.5.A-Z     327.940+
Foreign relns. (Australia-U.S.)     DU113.5.U6-7     327.94073
Foreign relns. (Austria: by other country)     DB49.A-Z
Foreign relns. (Bel.-Fr.)     DH569.F8
Foreign relns. (Bel.-Ger.)     DH569.G3
Foreign relns. (Bel.: by country)     DH569.A-Z
Foreign relns. (Brazil-G.B.)     F2523.G7
Foreign relns. (Brazil-Ger.)     F2523.G3
Foreign relns. (Brazil-other lands)     F2523.A-Z
Foreign relns. (Bulg.-Ger.)     DR73.G3     327.4977043
Foreign relns. (Bulg.-Rus.)     DR73.R9
Foreign relns. (Bulg.-specific countries)     DR73.A-Z
Foreign relns. (Cambodia: plus gen. hist.)     DS554.5-58

FOREIGN RELNS. (CAN.-Fr.)  F1029.5.F8  327.71044
Foreign relns. (Can.-G.B.)  F1029.5.G7  327.71041
Foreign relns. (Can.-Ger.)  F1029.5.G3  327.71043
Foreign relns. (Can.-It.)  F1029.5.I8
Foreign relns. (Can.-Japan)  F1029.5.J3
Foreign relns. (Can.-other places)  F1029.5.A-Z  327.710+
Foreign relns. (Can.-Rus.)  F1029.5.R9  327.71047
Foreign relns. (Can.-U.S.)  F1029.5.U6-7  327.71073
Foreign relns. (Chile-Ger.)  F3083.5.G3
Foreign relns. (Chile-Japan)  F3083.5.J3
Foreign relns. (Chile-other places)  F3083.5.A-Z
Foreign relns. (Chile-U.S.)  F3083.5.U6-7
FOREIGN RELNS. (CHINA: 20th c. & 1912-49)  DS775.8
Foreign relns. (China & other lands: by name)  DS740.5.A-Z  327.510+
Foreign relns. (China-G.B.)  DS740.5.G5-6
Foreign relns. (China-Ger.)  DS740.5.G2-3  327.51043
Foreign relns. (China-Hong Kong)  DS740.5.G6.H6
Foreign relns. (China-Japan)  DS740.5.G6.J3  327.51052
Foreign relns. (China-Sov. Un.)  DS740.5.S65  327.51047
Foreign relns. (China-U.S.)  DS740.5.U6-7 (PREFER E183.8.C5)  327.51073
Foreign relns. (Cuba-G.B.)  F1776.3.G7
Foreign relns. (Cuba-Ger.)  F1776.3.G3
Foreign relns. (Cuba-other places)  F1776.3.A-Z
Foreign relns. (Cuba-U.S.)  F1776.3.U6-7
Foreign relns. (Czech.: 1918-: gen.)  DB2189
Foreign relns. (Czech: 1918-39)  DB2199
Foreign relns. (Czech.: 1939-45)  DB2209
Foreign relns. (Czech.: by country)  DB2078.A-Z
Foreign relns. (Den.-G.B.)  DL159.5.G7
Foreign relns. (Den.-Ger.)  DL159.5.G3
Foreign relns. (Den.-other lands)  DL159.5.A-Z
Foreign relns. (Eastern Europe)  DJK43-44
Foreign relns. (Egypt & various countries)  DT82.5.A-Z  327.620+
Foreign relns. (Egypt-G.B.)  DT82.5.G7  327.62041
Foreign relns. (Egypt-Ger.)  DT82.5.G3  327.62043
Foreign relns. (Fin. & other partic. lands)  DL1048.A-Z
Foreign relns. (Fin.-Ger.)  DL1048.G3
Foreign relns. (Fin.-Rus.)  DL1048.R9
Foreign relns. (Fin.-Sov. Un.)  DL1048.S65
Foreign relns. (Formosa-Japan)  DS799.63.J3
Foreign relns. (Formosa-other places)  DS799.63.A-Z
Foreign relns. (Formosa: 1895-1945)  DS799.718
FOREIGN RELNS. (FR.: 19th-20th c.)  DC58
Foreign relns. (Fr.-G.B.)  DC59.8.G7  327.44041
Foreign relns. (Fr.-Ger.)  DC59.8.G3  327.44043
Foreign relns. (Fr.-Rus.)  DC59.8.R9
Foreign relns. (Fr.-Sov.Un.)  DC59.8.S65
Foreign relns. (Fr.: by country)  DC59.8.A-Z  327.440+
Foreign relns. (G.B.-Fr.)  DA47.1  327.41044
Foreign relns. (G.B.-Ger.)  DA47.2  327.41043
Foreign relns. (G.B.-misc. countries: SEE E183.8 for U.S.)  DA47.9.A-Z
Foreign relns. (G.B.-other countries)  DA47  327.410+
Foreign relns. (G.B.-Rus.)  DA47.65  327.41047

FOREIGN RELNS. (GER.: 19th-20th c.)      DD117      327.43+
Foreign relns. (Ger.: 1918-: by country)      DD241.A-Z
Foreign relns. (Ger.-Albania: 1918-)      DD241.A5
Foreign relns. (Ger.-Argen.: 1918-)      DD241.A7
Foreign relns. (Ger.-Austria: 1918-)      DD241.A9
Foreign relns. (Ger.-Bel.: 1918-)      DD241.B4
Foreign relns. (Ger.-Brazil: 1918-)      DD241.B7
Foreign relns. (Ger.-Bulg.: 1918-)      DD241.B8
Foreign relns. (Ger.: by country)      DD120.A-Z      327.430+
Foreign relns. (Ger.-Can.: 1918-)      DD241.C2-29
Foreign relns. (Ger.-Czech.: 1918-)      DD241.C95
Foreign relns. (Ger.-Den.: 1918-)      DD241.D3
Foreign relns. (Ger.-Egypt: 1918-)      DD241.E3
Foreign relns. (Ger.-Fin.: 1918-)      DD241.F5
Foreign relns. (Ger.-Fr.)      DD120.F8      327.43044
Foreign relns. (Ger.-Fr.: 1918-)      DD241.F8
Foreign relns. (Ger.-G.B.)      DD120.G7      327.43041
Foreign relns. (Ger.-G.B.: 1888-1918)      DD228.7.G7
Foreign relns. (Ger.-G.B.: 1918-)      DD241.G7
Foreign relns. (Ger.-Greece: 1918-)      DD241.G8
Foreign relns. (Ger.-Hung.: 1918-)      DD241.H9
Foreign relns. (Ger.-India: 1918-)      DD241.I4
Foreign relns. (Ger.-Ire.)      DD120.I6
Foreign relns. (Ger.-Ire.: 1918-)      DD241.I6
Foreign relns. (Ger.-It.)      DD120.I8
Foreign relns. (Ger.-It.: 1918-)      DD241.I8
Foreign relns. (Ger.-Japan)      DD120.J3      327.43052
Foreign relns. (Ger.-Japan: 1918-)      DD241.J3
Foreign relns. (Ger.-Neth.: 1918-)      DD241.N4
Foreign relns. (Ger.-Nor.: 1918-)      DD241.N8
Foreign relns. (Ger.-Pol.: 1918-)      DD241.P7
Foreign relns. (Ger.-Port.: 1918-)      DD241.P8
Foreign relns. (Ger.-Rum.: 1918-)      DD241.R8
Foreign relns. (Ger.-Rus.)      DD120.R9      327.43047
Foreign relns. (Ger.-Rus.: 1918-)      DD241.R9
Foreign relns. (Ger.-Sov. Un.)      DD120.S65
Foreign relns. (Ger.-Sp.: 1918-)      DD241.S7
Foreign relns. (Ger.-Swe.: 1918-)      DD241.S8
Foreign relns. (Ger.-Swit.: 1918-)      DD241.S9
Foreign relns. (Ger.-Syria: 1918-)      DD241.S95
Foreign relns. (Ger.-Tur.: 1918-)      DD241.T8
Foreign relns. (Ger.-U.S.)      DD120.U6-7
Foreign relns. (Ger.-U.S.: 1918-)      DD241.U6-69+
Foreign relns. (Ger.-Uruguay: 1918-)      DD241.U7+
Foreign relns. (Ger.-Yug.: 1918-)      DD241.Y8
Foreign relns. (Greece: by country)      DF787.A-Z
Foreign relns. (Greece-G.B.)      DF787.G7
Foreign relns. (Greece-Ger.)      DF787.G3
Foreign relns. (Greece-It.)      DF787.I8
Foreign relns. (Hung.-Ger.)      DB926.3.G3
Foreign relns. (Hung.-other lands)      DB926.3.A-Z
Foreign relns. (Hung.-Sov. Un.)      DB926.3.S65
Foreign relns. (India-Ger.)      DS450.G3      327.54043
Foreign relns. (India-Japan)      DS450.J3      327.54052
Foreign relns. (India-other specific places)      DS450.A-Z      327.540+

```
Foreign relns. (Indon.-Japan)        DS640.J3
Foreign relns. (Indon.-other countries)  DS640.A-Z
Foreign relns. (Iran-G.B.)       DS274.2.G7      327.55042
Foreign relns. (Iran-Ger.)       DS274.2.G3      327.55043
Foreign relns. (Iran-other countries)    DS274.2.A-Z     327.550+
Foreign relns. (Iran-Rus.)       DS274.2.R9  327.55047
Foreign relns. (Iran-U.S.)       DS274.2.U6-7    327.55073
Foreign relns. (Iraq-G.B.)         DS70.96.G7
Foreign relns. (Iraq-Ger.)         DS70.96.G3
Foreign relns. (Iraq-other specific places)    DS70.96.A-Z
Foreign relns. (Ire.: 20th c.: gen.)   DA964.A2
Foreign relns. (Ire.-G.B.: 20th c.)    DA964.G7
Foreign relns. (Ire.-Ger.: 20th c.)    DA964.G3
FOREIGN RELNS. (IT.: 1861-1945)      DG498
Foreign relns. (It.-Alb.)        DG499.A5
Foreign relns. (It.: by country)  DG499.A-Z  327.450+
Foreign relns. (It.-Eth.)        DG499.E7
Foreign relns. (It.-Fr.)   DG499.F8
Foreign relns. (It.-G.B.)   DG499.G7
Foreign relns. (It.-Ger.)   DG499.G3
Foreign relns. (It.-Japan)  DG499.J3
Foreign relns. (It.-Rus.)        DG499.R9
Foreign relns. (It.-Sov.Un.)     DG499.S65
Foreign relns. (It.-Swit.)       DG499.S9
Foreign relns. (It.-U.S.)        DG499.U6-7
Foreign relns. (It.-Yug.)        DG499.Y8
FOREIGN RELNS (JAPAN-Asia)    DS849.A75      327.5205
Foreign relns. (Japan-Australia)    DS849.A8        327.52094
Foreign relns. (Japan-Burma)      DS849.B9
Foreign relns. (Japan-Cambodia)    DS849.C15
Foreign relns. (Japan-China)   DS849.C5    327.52051
Foreign relns. (Japan-G.B.)    DS849.G7    327.52041
Foreign relns. (Japan-Ger.)    DS849.G3    327.52043
Foreign relns. (Japan-India)   DS849.I4
Foreign relns. (Japan-Indoch.)     DS849.I45
Foreign relns. (Japan-Indonesia)   DS849.I5
Foreign relns. (Japan-It.)     DS849.I8
Foreign relns. (Japan-Korea)   DS849.K5
Foreign relns. (Japan-Malayas)     DS849.M3
Foreign relns. (Japan-New Zea.)      DS849.N45
Foreign relns. (Japan-other places)    DS849.A-Z       327.520+
Foreign relns. (Japan-Philip.)       DS849.P5        327.520599
Foreign relns. (Japan-Rus.)     DS849.R9    327.52047
Foreign relns. (Japan-Sov. Un.)    DS849.S65  327.52047
Foreign relns. (Japan-Thai.)    DS849.T4
Foreign relns. (Japan-U.S.)     DS849.U6-7      327.52073
Foreign relns. (Japan-Viet.)    DS849.V5
Foreign relns. (Korea-China)    DS910.2.C5      327.519051
Foreign relns. (Korea-Japan)      DS910.2.J3      327.519052
Foreign relns. (Korea-other lands)     DS910.2.A-Z     327.5190+
Foreign relns. (Korea-Rus.)        DS910.2.R9
Foreign relns. (Laos: also gen. hist.)   DS555.5-58
```

FOREIGN RELNS. (LATIN AM. & other places except U.S.)    F1416.A-Z    327.80+
Foreign relns. (Latin Am.-Fr.)        F1416.F8
Foreign relns. (Latin Am.-G.B.)       F1416.G7
Foreign relns. (Latin Am.-Ger.)       F1416.G3      327.8043
Foreign relns. (Latin Am.-It.)        F1416.I8
Foreign relns. (Latin Am.-Japan)      F1416.J3      327.8052
Foreign relns. (Latin Am.-Rus.)       F1416.R9
Foreign relns. (Latin Am.-U.S.)        F1418    327.8073
Foreign relns. (Libya & other particular places)       DT227.5.A-Z
Foreign relns. (Libya-Ger.)            DT227.5.G3
Foreign relns. (Libya-It.)             DT227.5.I8
Foreign relns. (Liech.: by country)    DB894.A-Z
Foreign relns. (Liech.-Ger.)           DB894.G3
Foreign relns. (Lux.: by country)    DH908.6.A-Z
Foreign relns. (Lux.-Ger.)           DH908.6.G3
Foreign relns. (Mex.-Ger.)         F1228.5.G3      327.72043
Foreign relns. (Mex.-Japan)        F1228.5.J3        327.72052
Foreign relns. (Mex.-other places)   F1228.5.A-Z     327.720+
Foreign relns. (Mex.-Rus.)         F1228.5.R9       327.72047
Foreign relns. (Mex.-Sov.Un.)      F1228.5.S65      327.72047
Foreign relns. (Mex.-U.S.)         F1228.5.U6-7     327.72073
Foreign relns. (Mid. East, SW. Asia: by specific country)  DS63.2.A-Z    327.560+
Foreign relns. (Morocco-Fr.)       DT317.5.F8
Foreign relns. (Morocco-Ger.)      DT317.5.G3
Foreign relns. (Morocco-other specific places)    DT317.5.A-Z
Foreign relns. (N. Viet.-other countries)         DS560.69.A-Z
Foreign relns. (N. Zea.-Japan)        DU421.5.J3      327.931052
Foreign relns. (N. Zea.-other specific places)    DU421.5.A-Z     327.9310+
Foreign relns. (N. Zea.-U.S.)         DU421.5.U6-7    327.931073
Foreign relns. (Neth.: by country)    DJ149.A-Z
Foreign relns. (Neth.-Ger.)           DJ149.G3
Foreign relns. (Nor.-G.B.)       DL459.G7
Foreign relns. (Nor.-Ger.)       DL459.G3
Foreign relns. (Nor.-other specific countries)    DL459.A-Z     327.4810+
Foreign relns. (Nor.-Swe.)       DL459.S8
Foreign relns. (Pacific-Fr.)     DU50
Foreign relns. (Pacific-G.B.)    DU40
Foreign relns. (Pacific-Ger.)    DU60
Foreign relns. (Pacific-Sp.)     DU65
Foreign relns. (Pacific-U.S.)    DU30
Foreign relns. (Paraguay-Ger.)        F2682.G3      327.892043
Foreign relns. (Paraguay-other places)      F2682.A-Z
Foreign relns. (Peru-Ger.)       F3434.G3
Foreign relns. (Peru-Japan)      F3434.J3
Foreign relns. (Peru-other places)   F3434.A-Z
Foreign relns. (Peru-U.S.)       F3434.U6-7
Foreign relns. (Philip.: by country)   DS673.A-Z      327.5990+
Foreign relns. (Philip.-Japan)         DS673.J3       327.599052
Foreign relns. (Philip.-U.S.)          DS673.U6-7     327.599073

FOREIGN RELNS. (POL.: 1918-45)      DK4402.5
Foreign relns. (Pol.: by country)           DK418.5.A-Z
Foreign relns. (Pol.-Fr.)          DK418.5.F8, DK4185.F8 (newer titles)
Foreign relns. (Pol.-G.B.)        DK418.5.G7
Foreign relns. (Pol.: gen.)       DK4180
Foreign relns. (Pol.-Ger.)        DK418.5.G3 (earlier titles), DK4185.G3
Foreign relns. (Pol.-Rus.)        DK418.5.R9, DK4185.R9 (later works)
Foreign relns. (Pol.: with particular countries)   DK4185.A-Z
Foreign relns. (Port.-G.B.)       DP557.G7
Foreign relns. (Port.-Ger.)       DP557.G3
Foreign relns. (Port.-other countries: by name)   DP557.A-Z
Foreign relns. (Port.-Sp.)        DP557.S7
Foreign relns. (Port.-U.S.)       DP557.U6-7
Foreign relns. (Rum. & partic. countries)         DR229.A-Z
Foreign relns. (Rum.-Ger.)        DR229.G3      327.498043
Foreign relns. (Rum.-Rus.)        DR229.R9
FOREIGN RELNS. (RUS. & non-U.S. Am. countries)   DK69.3.A-Z
Foreign relns. (Rus.-Asia: gen.: pubns. 1801-)   DK68.A3-Z
Foreign relns. (Rus.-Asian countries by name)    DK68.7.A-Z
Foreign relns. (Rus.-Balkan Penin.)         DK67.4
Foreign relns. (Rus.-Bulg.)       DK67.5.B8
Foreign relns. (Rus.-Can.)        DK69.3.C2-29
Foreign relns. (Rus.-Cath. Church)     DK67.3
Foreign relns. (Rus.-China)       DK68.7.C5        327.47051
Foreign relns. (Rus.-Czech.)      DK67.5.C95
Foreign relns. (Rus.-Europe)      DK67
Foreign relns. (Rus.-Fin.)        DK67.5.F5
Foreign relns. (Rus.-Fr.)         DK67.5.F8
Foreign relns. (Rus.-G.B.)        DK67.5.G7
Foreign relns. (Rus.: gen.)       DK66          327.47
Foreign relns. (Rus.-Ger.)        DK67.5.G3
Foreign relns. (Rus.-Greece)      DK67.5.G8
Foreign relns. (Rus.-Hung.)       DK67.5.H9
Foreign relns. (Rus.-India)       DK68.7.I4
Foreign relns. (Rus.-Iran)        DK68.7.I55
Foreign relns. (Rus.-It.)         DK67.5.I8
Foreign relns. (Rus.-Japan)       DK68.7.J3     327.47052
Foreign relns. (Rus.-Mex.)        DK69.3.M6
Foreign relns. (Rus.: particular areas)   DK67-69      327.470+
Foreign relns. (Rus.-Pol.)        DK67.5.P7
Foreign relns. (Rus.-Rum.)        DK67.5.R8
Foreign relns. (Rus.-specific Eur. countries)    DK67.5.A-Z
Foreign relns. (Rus.-Swe.)        DK67.5.S8
Foreign relns. (Rus.-Tur.)        DK68.7.T8
Foreign relns. (Rus.-U.S.)        DK69 (PREFER E183.8.R9)      327.47073
Foreign relns. (Rus.-Yug.)        DK67.5.Y8
Foreign relns. (Saudi Arab. Penin.: G.B.)   DS228.G7
Foreign relns. (Saudi Arab. Penin.: Ger.)   DS228.G3
Foreign relns. (Saudi Arabia-specific countries)   DS228.A-Z
Foreign relns. (Serbia-other specific places)    DR1976.A-Z
Foreign relns. (Slovakia: 1918-)        DB2809
Foreign relns. (Slovakia: 1939-45)      DB2819

FOREIGN RELNS. (SP.-Fr.: 1931-39)    DP258.F8
Foreign relns. (Sp.-Ger.)                    DP86.G3        327.46043
Foreign relns. (Sp.-Ger.: 1931-39)         DP258.G3
Foreign relns. (Sp.-It.)                DP86.I8
Foreign relns. (Sp.-It.: 1931-39)      DP258.I8
Foreign relns. (Sp.-Port.: 1931-39)  DP258.P8
Foreign relns. (Sp.-Rus.)              DP86.R9        327.46047
Foreign relns. (Sp.-Rus.: 1931-39)       DP258.R9
Foreign relns. (Sp.-Sov. Un.)            DP86.S65
Foreign relns. (Sp.-Sov. Un.: 1931-39)        DP258.S65
Foreign relns. (Sp.-specific lands: 1931-39)    DP258.A-Z
Foreign relns. (Sp.-U.S.: 1931-39)       DP258.U6-7
Foreign relns. (Sp.: with partic. countries)    DP86.A-Z    327.460+
FOREIGN RELNS (SWE.-Fin.)    DL659.F5
Foreign relns. (Swe.-G.B.)        DL659.G7
Foreign relns. (Swe.-Ger.)        DL659.G3
Foreign relns. (Swe.-Nor.)        DL659.N8
Foreign relns. (Swe.-other lands: by name)  DL659.A-Z  327.485+
Foreign relns. (Swe.-Rus.)                 DL659.R9
Foreign relns. (Swe.-Sov. Un.)    DL659.S65
Foreign relns. (Swe.-U.S.)        DL659.U6-7
Foreign relns. (Swe.: 1818-20th c.)     DL658.8
FOREIGN RELNS. (SWIT.-Fr.)    DQ76.F8
Foreign relns. (Swit.-G.B.)        DQ76.G7
Foreign relns. (Swit.-Ger.)    DQ76.G3    327.494043
Foreign relns. (Swit.-It.)    DQ76.I8    327.494045
Foreign relns. (Swit.-Rus.)    DQ76.R9
Foreign relns. (Swit.-specific countries)    DQ76.A-Z    327.4940+
Foreign relns. (Swit.-U.S.)    DQ76.U6-7  327.494073
Foreign relns. (Syria-Fr.)    DS95.6.F8
Foreign relns. (Syria-G.B.)    DS95.6.G7
Foreign relns. (Syria-Ger.)        DS95.6.G3
Foreign relns. (Syria-other countries)    DS95.6.A-Z    327.56910+
Foreign relns. (Thai.-Japan)        DS575.5.J3
Foreign relns. (Thai.-other places)    DS575.5.A-Z
Foreign relns. (Tunisia-It.)    DT257.5.I8
Foreign relns. (Tunisia-other lands: by name)    DT257.5.A-Z
Foreign relns. (Tur.-G.B.)        DR479.G7
Foreign relns. (Tur.-Ger.)        DR479.G3
Foreign relns. (Tur.-particular countries)    DR479.A-Z
Foreign relns. (Tur.-Rus.)        DR479.R9
Foreign relns. (Ukr.: by country)    DK508.57
FOREIGN RELNS. (U.S.: 1865-1900: gen.)        E661.7 (SEE ALSO E183.8.A-Z)
Foreign relns. (U.S.: 1897-1901: gen.)        E713
Foreign relns. (U.S.: 20th c.: gen.)    E744    327.73
Foreign relns. (U.S.: 1913-21)    E768
Foreign relns. (U.S.-China)    E183.8.C5    327.73051
Foreign relns. (U.S.-Fr.)    E183.8.F8    327.73044
Foreign relns. (U.S.-G.B.)    E183.8.G7    327.73041
Foreign relns. (U.S.-Ger.)    E183.8.G3    327.73043
Foreign relns. (U.S.-It.)    E183.8.I8    327.73045
Foreign relns. (U.S.-Japan)    E183.8.J3    327.73052
Foreign relns. (U.S.-other places)    E183.8.A-Z    327.730+
Foreign relns. (U.S.-Russia)    E183.8.R9    327.73047
Foreign relns. (U.S.-Sov.Un.)    E183.8.S65    327.73047

Foreign relns. (Urug. & other partic. places: by name)     F2722.5.A-Z
Foreign relns. (Urug.-Ger.)     F2722.5.G3          327.895043
Foreign relns. (Urug.-It.)               F2722.5.I8
Foreign relns. (Venez. & other places)          F2321.3.A-Z
Foreign relns. (Venez.-Ger.)       F2321.3.G3
Foreign relns. (Viet.-Fr.)        DS556.58.F8
Foreign relns. (Viet.-Japan)      DS556.58.J3
Foreign relns. (Viet.-other countries: by place)     DS556.58.A-Z
Foreign relns. (W.Ind.-G.B.)          F1622.5.G7
Foreign relns. (W.Ind.-Ger.)          F1622.5.G3
Foreign relns. (W.Ind.-partic. places)     F1622.5.A-Z
Foreign relns. (W.Ind.-U.S.)          F1622
FOREIGN RELNS (YUG.: 1918-45)          DR1292
Foreign relns. (Yug.-G.B.: 1918-45)          DR367.G7
Foreign relns. (Yug.: gen.)          DR1257-1258
Foreign relns. (Yug.-Ger.: 1918-45)          DR367.G3
Foreign relns. (Yug.-It.: 1918-45)          DR367.I8
Foreign relns. (Yug.-Rus.: 1918-45)          DR367.R9
Foreign relns. (Yug.-specific countries)          DR327.A-Z
Foreign relns. (Yug.-U.S.: 1918-45)          DR367.U6-7
Forest fighting          U167.5.F6
FORMOSA (Taiwan)          951.249     DS895.F7-77 (books prior to about 1970),
                    DS798.92-799.99+ (many post-1969 pubns.)
Formosa (19th-20th c.)     DS895.F75          951.24903-24904
Formosa (1895-1945)     DS799.69-72     951.24904
Formosa (1895-1945: Japanese period)          951.24904          DS895.F75,
                    DS799.69-72, DS799.7 (gen.)
Formosa (gen.)     DS799.5     951.249
Formosa (WWII: gen. particip.)          940.5351249     DS895.F75,
                    DS799.69-72 (pubns. 1970+)
Fortification     UG400-442
Fortification (gen.: pubn. 1801+)     UG401          355.544, 623.1
Fortification, Permanent          UG405
FORTIFICATIONS (Asia: by country)          UG432.A-Z
Fortifications (by place)     UG410-442          623.19+, 355.45-47+
Fortifications (Eur.: by region or country)          UG429.A-Z
Fortifications (Eur.: by town or place)          UG430.A-Z
Fortifications (mil. engineering)          623.1     UG400-442
Fortifications (mil. engineering: by place)          623.19 (for works prior to 1989 SEE
                    ALSO .109)          UG410-442
Fortifications (U.S.: by state or region)          UG411.A-Z          623.1974-1979+,
                    355.450974+, .4774+
Fortifications (U.S.: by town or place)     UG412.A-Z
FORTIFIED defenses (Asia)          UG431-433          623.195
Fortified defenses (Australia)          UG437-439
Fortified defenses (Can.)     UG413-415
Fortified defenses (Eur.)     UG428-430
Fortified defenses (Ger.)     UG429.G3
Fortified defenses (Japan)     UG432.J3          623.1952
Fortified defenses (Pacific islands)          UG440-442
Fortified defenses (Philip.)     UG432.P5
Fortified defenses (U.S.)     UG410-412          623.1973, 355.4773
Fortified defenses (W. Indies)     UG422-424
Fortress & garrison artillery (U.S.: gen.)          UF483
Foul-weather gear, Naval (plus other special clothing)          VC307          359.81

French (in Arg.)        F3021.F8
French (in Brazil)      F2659.F8
French (in S.Am.)       F2239.F8
French (in U.S.)        E184.F8
French (in Urug.)       F2799.F7
FRENCH INDOCHINA        DS531-560        959.4, 959.6-7
French Indochina (to 1949)        959.703        DS556.8-83
French Indochina (1884-1945)        DS549        959.703
French Indochina & Vietnam        959.7        DS531-558
French Indochina (gen.)        DS541
French Indochina (WWII)        D767.45        940.53597, 959.703
French military history (gen.)        DC45        355.00944, .033044
French military ops. & France (WWI)        D548-549
French military ops. & France (WWII: gen.)        D761        940.5344, .540944,
                944.0815-0816
French military ops. (WWII: misc.)        D761.9.A-Z
French mission to U.S. (WWI)        D570.8.M6.F4
French naval history (gen.)        DC50
French poetry, satire, etc. (WWI)        D526.3
French poetry, satire, etc. (WWII)        D745.3
French prisons & prisoners (WWII)        D805.F8
French Somaliland (Djibouti or Afars & Issas)        DT411        967.71-7104+
French West Africa        DT521-553        966, 966.1-3, .52, .68, .81
French West Indies        F2151        972.976
Friendly Islands (Tonga)        996.12        DU880
Frigates & corvettes (gen.)        V826        623.8254
Frigates (U.S.)        V826.3
Frogmen (navies: gen.)        VG86        359.984
Fronts (WWI: Eur.)        940.414        D521, D530 (W.), D550 (E.)
Fronts (WWI: Rus. & E. in gen.)        940.4147        D550, D551 (Rus.-Ger.-Austrian),
                D556 (Rus.-Austrian), D560 (Balkan)
FUEL & light (mil. qtrs.)        UC420
Fuel, Naval (other than U.S.)        VC276.A5-Z
Fuel, Naval (U.S.)        VC276.A3-49        359.83
Fuel supplies & costs, Naval        VC276
Fuel supplies (WWII)        D810.F83
Fuels, Aviation        629.134351
Fuels, Marine engine        VM779        623.874
Fukien Province (China)        951.245
Furloughs        UB420-425
Furloughs, leaves, etc. (air forces: U.S.)        UG973
Furloughs, leaves, other inactive periods (navies)        359.113        VB260-275,
                VB307-315
Furnishings (mil. qtrs.)        UC415
Furniture (naut. design)        623.866
Fuselages, Aircraft        629.13434

GALICIA (20th c.)        DB500
Galicia (Pol.)        DK4600.G34
Galicia (Pol.: Polish wars, 1918-21)        DK4407.G3
Galleys & equipment (naval sci.)        VC398
Gallipoli & the Dardanelles (WWI)        D568.3
Gallipoli (Tur.)        DR701.G3
Galveston, Texas (area)        976.4139        F392.G25
Gandhi, Mohandas (India: 1901+ era)        DS481.G3

Garand rifle    UD395.G4
Garbage disposal (mil. engineering)    623.754
Garner, John Nance (U.S.: 20th c.)    E748.G23
Garrison & fortress artillery (gen.)    UF480
Gas masks (mil.)    UG447.6
Gas-turbine engines (marine engineering)    623.87233    VM740, TJ778
Gas warfare (by chem. name)    UG447.5.A-Z    623.4516
Gas warfare (WWI)    D607.5 (PREFER UG447)
Gases, poisons, other chemical agents (design)    623.4592
Gatling machine guns    UF620.G3
Gdansk, Pol. (Danzig: gen.)    DK4670
Gear, equipment, & outfitting (nautical: engineering)    623.86    VM781-861,
                                                                        VM781 (gen.)

Genealogy    929
Genealogy (royal houses: G.B.)    929.72 (hist. treatment poss. or in 941+)
                                    DA28.1-.35, CS418-424
GENERAL & flag officers (above army col. or navy capt.)    355.331    UB200, UB210
General officers (air forces)    358.41331    UG790-795
General orders (naval: U.S.)    VB365
General orders (Rus. military: collections)    UB657
General staff & headquarters (WWI: U.S.)    D570.25.A-Z
General staff & headquarters (WWII: U.S.)    D769.25
General works (gen. almanacs, encyclopediae, etc.)    A    000-099
Generals, marshals, commanders (admin.: duties etc.)    UB200    355.331
Geneva & Hague conventions UH531-533 (PREFER JX5136 & JX5243)    341.6+, .65
Geneva, Swit.    DQ441-460    949.45
GEOGRAPHY, Air warfare    358.4147    UG633-635, UA
Geography & history    900-999    G, D-F
Geography & history (gen.)    900-909    G, C-D
Geography & travel    910-919    G, D-F
Geography & travel (by locale)    913-919
Geography, anthropology, sports, & recreation    G    910-919, 301, 790's
Geography, Marine military (strategic & tactical)    359.9647+    VE21-124, VA
Geography, Military (gen. inclu. Eur.)    UA990    355.47
Geography, Military (tactical & strategic)    355.47    UA985-997
Geography, Naval (strategic & tactical)    359.47    UA985-997, VA160-178,
                                                        VA49-750 (by place)
Geology & seismology, Military    UG465-465.5
Geonavigation, Marine    623.892
Geonavigational aids, Marine (misc. non-electronic)    623.894
George V (G.B.: King: 1910-36)    DA573
George VI (G.B.: King: 1937-52)    DA584
Georgia    F281-295, F286    975.8
Georgia (Rus.)    DK511.G3-47 (earlier pubns.), DK670-679
Georgia, Transcaucasia (post-WWI territorial ?s)    D651.G2
Georgian Republic (U.S.S.R.)    947.95    DK511.G3-47, .G47 (gen. hist., 1917-)
Georgian S. S. R. (1801-1921)    DK677.4-6
Georgian S. S. R. (1921+)    DK677.7-9+
Germ warfare (WWII: bacterial)    D810.B3

GERMAN aerial ops. (WWI)    D604    940.44943
German aerial ops. (WWII)    D787    940.544943
German-Anglo naval conflict & blockade (WWII: by battle, ship, etc.)    D772.A-Z
                                                                   940.545941-43

German armament (modern)    U820.G7
German Austria & Bavaria    DD791-800
German culture (in other lands: gen.)    DD68
German East Africa (gen.: later Tanganyika)    DT444
German East Africa (post-WWI territorial ?s)    D651.A41
German East Indies    DS649
German engineering ops. (WWII)    D795.G3
German espionage (gen.)    UB271.G3    327.120943
German field artillery    UF405.G3
German marching (mil.)    UD315.G3
German military education (special times)    U571
German military history (gen.)    DD101    355.00943
German military ops. (WWI: West & overall)    D531-538
German military ops. (WWII: gen.)    D757    940.5343, .54013, .5413, .5421,
                                                943.086
German naval education (main school)    V574.A2-65
German New Guinea (N.E.)    DU742 (SEE ALSO DU550+ for Bismarck Arch.)
                                              993.6, 995
German poetry, satire, etc. (WWI)    D526.5
German poetry, satire, etc. (WWII)    D745.5
German prisons & prisoners (WWII)    D805.G3
German propaganda (1933-45: in other countries: gen.)    DD254
German ski troops    UD475.G3    356.1640943
German Southwest Africa (post-WWI territorial ?s)    D651.A42
German submarine ops. (WWI: gen.)    D591    940.4512
German submarine ops. (WWII: by battle, ship, etc.)    D782.A-Z
German submarine ops. (WWII: gen.)    D781
German West Africa (1884-1916)    967.8202    DT444, DT447 (newer books)
GERMANS (in Arg.)    F3021.G3
Germans (in Bolivia)    F3359.G3
Germans (in Brazil)    F2659.G3
Germans (in C.Am.)    F1440.G3
Germans (in Calif.)    F870.G3
Germans (in Can.)    F1035.G3
Germans (in Chile)    F3285.G3
Germans (in Mex.)    F1392.G4
Germans (in N.Y.)    F130.G3
Germans (in other lands: gen.)    DD119.3
Germans (in Paraguay)    F2699.G3
Germans (in Peru)    F3619.G3
Germans (in Pol.)    DK4121.5.G4
Germans (in S.Am.)    F2239.G3
Germans (in U.S.)    E184.G3
Germans (in Urug.)    F2799.G3

Girl Scouts (WWII)    D810.G57
Gobi (China)    DS793.G6
Goebbels, Joseph (Ger.: 1918-48 era)    DD247.G6
Göring, Hermann (Ger.: 1918-48 era)    DD247.G67
Goriunov machine guns    UF620.G6
Governments in exile (WWII)    D639.G6
Graf Spee, Admiral (armoured cruiser: Ger.: WWII)    D772.G7, VA515.G
Grain industry (defense)    UA929.95.G7
Granada (Sp.)    DP302.G51-65
Graves registration & burial services (navies)    359.699
Graves registration & military burial    355.699
Graydon aerial torpedo thrower    V855.G7
Great Basin & Pacific Coast states    979    F786-915, F786-850 (New S.W.),
                                                                F786-788, F851-915 (Pac. states), F851

GREAT BRITAIN  DA 941-942
Great Britain (1837-1901: gen.)    DA550    941.08
Great Britain (20th c.: gen.)    DA566    941.082
Great Britain (1901-10: gen.)    DA570
Great Britain (1910-36)    DA576
Great Britain (1914-19: WWI era)    DA577
Great Britain (1920-39)    DA578
Great Britain (1936)    DA583
Great Britain (1937-52)    DA586
Great Britain (1939-45: WWII era)    DA587
Great Britain (air war geog.)    358.414741    UG635.G7
Great Britain & British military ops. (WWII)    D759-760
Great Britain & Ireland (geog. & travel)    914.1    DA11, DA600-668, DA969-
                                                                987 (Ire.)
Great Britain & Ireland (lighthouses, beacons, foghorns, etc.: lists)
                                                    VK1153-1159    623.89440941
Great Britain. Army    UA649-668
Great Britain. Army (gen.)    UA649    355.00941, .310941
Great Britain (biog.: heads of state)    923.141-142
Great Britain. Fifth Army (WWI)    D546.5.5th
Great Britain (lighthouses, beacons, foghorns, etc.)    VK1057-1064
Great Britain (mil. geog.)    355.4741-4742    UA995.G7
Great Britain (mil. policy)    355.033541-033542    UA647+,UA647-668
Great Britain (mil. status)    UA647    355.033041
Great Britain (naval geog.)    359.4741-4742    VA452-467, VA454 (gen.)
Great Britain (naval hist.)    359.00941-00942    VA452-467, DA70-89
Great Britain (naval policy & status)    359.030941
Great Britain (post-WWI relns.: countries other than U.S.)    D651.G7
Great Britain (post-WWI relns.: U.S.: inclu. defensive alliance w. Fr., U.S.)    D651.G6
Great Britain (post-WWI territorial ?s)    D651.G5-7
Great Britain (post-WWI territorial ?s: gen.)    D651.G5
Great Britain. Royal Naval College, Dartmouth (admin.)    V515.C1-K3
Great Britain. Royal Navy (gen.)    VA454    359.0309441, .30941,
                                                                .4741-4742, .00941
Great Britain (WWI: causes, aims, results)    D517
Great Britain (WWI: mil. hist.)    940.40941-40942    D546-547
Great Britain (WWI: Reconstruction)    D659.G7
Great Britain (WWII: causes, aims, results)    D742.G7
Great Britain (WWII: dipl. history)    D750    940.532241
Great circle routing (marine navig.)    VK571

Great Lakes & North Central states (geog. & travel)    917.7    F477.3 (Old NW.),
                                                        F551 (Lakes area in gen.), F484.5
Great Lakes (U.S.)          F551-556          977
Great Lakes Naval Training Station (Ill.)    V434.G7
Great Plains & American West (geog. & travel)    917.8    F591
Great War (1914-18)         940.3-.499       D501-680
Greater Antilles (Cuba, Haiti, Puerto Rico, Jamaica, etc.)  F1741-1991  972.9, .91-95
GREECE          949.5          DF, DF757
Greece (1821-1924: Monarchy)          949.506          DF802
Greece (20th c.: gen.)          DF833    949.507
Greece (20th c.: 1924-)         949.507          DF833 (20th c.), DF838 (WWI)
Greece (1914-18: WWI)           DF838          949.506
Greece (1924-35: Republic)          949.5073    DF848
Greece (1935-47: George II era)     DF849          949.5074
Greece (1935-67: Monarchy)          949.5074    DF849
Greece & unredeemed Greeks (post-WWI territorial ?s)    D651.G8
Greece (gen.)          DF751          949.5
Greece (geog. & travel)    914.95          DF726
Greece (mil. status)    UA720-729          355.0330495
Greece (modern)         DF701-951+
Greece (naval status)    VA520-529
Greece (WWII: gen.)    D766.3          940.53495, 949.5074
Greek Isles (WWII: gen. particip.)    940.53499          DF901.C9 (Cyclades)
Greenland          998.2
Grenades          UF765          623.45114
Grenades, Hand & rifle          355.825114  UF765
Grenades, Hand or rifle (design)    623.45114          UF765
Grenades, mines, etc.          355.82511
Grenades, mines, nuclear weapons (design)          623.4511
Grey, Edward (G.B.: 20th c.)          DA566.9.G8
Guadalajara, Battle of (Sp. Civil War: 1937)          DP269.2.G8
Guadalcanal (WWII)          D767.982.G92, D767.99.G88
Guam (Mariana Is.)          DU647          996.7
Guam (WWII)
Guam (WWII)          D767.99.G9, D767.99.M272.G9
Guam (WWII: U.S. naval base)          D769.542.G9
Guernsey (G.B.: island)          942.342
Guerrilla tactics          355.425 (SEE 355.0218 for guer. war)          U240
Guerrilla warfare & small wars          U240    355.02184, 356.15
Guiana (Brit., Dutc, & Fr.)          F2351-2471          988
Guidebooks (Berlin, Ger.)          DD859
Guidebooks (G.B.)          DA650
Guidebooks (Ger.)          DD16
Guidebooks (London, Eng.)          DA679          914.21
Guidebooks (Paris, Fr.)          DC708
Guided aircraft (pilotless: mil. design)          623.7469          UG1310-1315
Guided missile forces (land: gen.)          358.171
Guided missiles (design)          623.4519          UG1310-1315
Guides & marching (mil.)          UD313-314

GULF Coast & South Central states (geog. & travel)   917.6   F296 (Gulf), F396
Gulf Coast (Florida)   F317.G8
Gulf Coast (Texas)   F392.G9
Gulf of Mexico (pilot & sailing guides)   VK975-977
Gulf of Mexico (tide & current tables)   VK775
Gulf states (U.S.: gen.)   F296   976
Gulf states, Mississippi Valley, Middle West, & Texas   F296-395   975.9-976.4,
                                                                 976.7-9
GUN carriages, caissons, limbers, etc. (gen.)   UF640   623.43
Gun carriages, Disappearing   UF650
Gun carriages, Naval   VF430   623.43
Gun carriages, Self-propelled (plus track-layer tractors & other self-contained)
                                                                 UF652
Gun handbooks (U.S.: by mm. or cm. then date)   UF563.A4.1+
Gun mounts   355.823
Gun mounts (design)   623.43
Gun salutes & other military rewards (misc.)   355.1349 (use 355.134 with
                                                1989+ pubn.)
GUNNERY (engineering)   623.55   UF800-805, VF144-302
Gunnery practice, Naval (G.B.)   VF315.G7   623.5530941
Gunnery practice, Naval (U.S.)   VF313   623.5530973
Gunnery, Aircraft (engineering)   623.555
Gunnery, Artillery (gen.)   UF800   623.55
Gunnery, Land (engineering)   623.551   UF800-805
Gunnery, Naval (engineering)   623.553   VF144-302, VF145 (gen.),
                                  VF150-155 (hdbks.), VF160-302 (drill bks.), VF160 (U.S.)
Gunpowder, cordite, & other explosives (design: inclu. propellant types)
                                                  623.4526   UF870
Guns (gen.)   U880   623.4
Guns (misc. types: mil. sci.)   UF630
Guns, Aircraft   UG1340-1345   623.7461
Gustav V (Swe.: King, 1907-50)   DL867
Gvardia (WWII: Rus.: by #)   D764.6.G8.1st-
Gvardia (WWII: Rus.: gen.)   D764.6.G7
Gynecology (WWI)   D639.G8
Gypsies   DX1-301
Gypsies in Czechoslovakia   DX222
Gypsies in Europe (gen. & elsewhere)   DX145
Gypsies in Germany   DX229
Gypsies in Russia (inclu. Poland & Lith.)   DX241
Gypsies (WWII)   D810.G9
Gyroscopic devices (marine navig.)   VK584.G8

HAAKON VII (Nor.: King, 1905-57)   DL530
Hácha, Emil (Czech.: 1939-45 period)   DB2211.H33
Hague & Geneva conventions (official works: by date)   UH531 (PREFER JX5136 &
                                                         JX5243)
Haiti   F1900-1940   972.94
Haiti (1915-50)   F1927   972.9405-9406
Halsey, William F., 'Bull', Admiral (U.S. Navy)   VB314.H25
Hamburg, Ger. (WWII)   D757.9.H3
Hammocks, berths, etc. (naval architec.)   VM511
Hampton Roads Naval Training Station (Va.)   V434.H2
Hancock (aircraft carrier: U.S.: WWII)   D774.H3

Hand signaling (mil.)     UG582.H2
Hand-to-hand combat & self-defense (training: inclu. unarmed & knife fighting)
                                    355.548        U167.5.H3, U262
HANDBOOKS & manuals (marine navig. & merch. marine)     VK155     623.890202
Handbooks & manuals (marines: G.B.)     VE155.G7
Handbooks & manuals (marines: U.S.)     VE153
Handbooks & manuals (mil. hygiene: Eng. & Am.)     UH623
Handbooks & manuals (naval ordnance)     VF150-155
Handbooks & manuals, Soldiers'     U110-145     355.00202
Handbooks & manuals, Soldiers' (by place except U.S.)     U115.A-Z
Handbooks & manuals (U.S. Navy: Pay & allowances)     VC60
Handbooks & tables (naval pay & allowances: U.S.)     VC54-60
Handbooks, Gun (U.S.: artillery)     UF563.A4-8
Handbooks, Gun (U.S.: by class or type)     UF563.A7-8 (sometimes use UF563.A4-
                                    6 with measure. & alphab. symbol: e.g. UF563.A5.12
                                    in.M for 12 in. mortar or ... Mt. for mountain)
Handbooks, Gun (U.S.: by inches)     UF563.A5
Handbooks, Gun (U.S.: by pounds)     UF563.A6
Handbooks, Infantry (U.S.)     UD153
Handbooks, Medical & surgical (navies)     VG460-466
Handbooks, Naval     V110-145
Handbooks, Naval officers'     V130-135     359.3320202
Handbooks, Naval reserve     V140-145
Handbooks, Officers'     U130-135
Handbooks, Petty officers'     V120-125
Handbooks, Seamen's (gen.)     V110     359.00202
Handbooks, tables, etc. (marine engin.)     VM607     623.870202
Handbooks, tables, etc. (ship calculations: naval architec.)     VM151
                                    623.810202, .810212
Handling of nautical craft (gen.)     623.881     VK541
Handling of nautical craft (powered)     623.8814     VK541, VK145, VK205,
                                    VB200-205
Hankow, China     DS796.H3
Hanoi, Viet.     DS558.H3 (earlier titles), DS560.92.H3
Harbor piloting (inclu. approach)     623.8929     VK321-369.8
Harbors & ports     VK321-369+     387.1+
Harbors, canals, dams (mil. engineering)     UG350     623.64
Harvard Univ. (WWII)     D810.E45.H38
Hatchways, ladders, other special fittings (marine engin.)     VM851
Havana, Cuba     F1799.A-Z     972.9123
Havana Province (Cuba)     F1791-1799
Hawaii (1900-59: U.S. Territory)     DU627.5.A6-Z     996.903
Hawaii (island)     DU628.H25-28     996.91
Hawaii (WWII: U.S. naval base)     D769.542.H38
HAWAIIAN ISLANDS     DU620-629     996.9
Hawaiian Islands (1898-1959: U.S. Terr.)     996.903     DU627.5
Hawaiian Islands (annex. to U.S.)     DU627.4
Hawaiian Islands (gen.)     DU620-629, DU625     996.9
Hawaiian Islands (geog. & travel)     919.69     DU623
Hawaiian Islands (mil. geog.)     355.47969     UA995.H
Hawaiian Islands (naval geog.)     359.47969     VA750.H, VA158-158.7
Hawaiian Islands (pilot & sailing guides)     VK933.H3
Hawaiian Islands (WWII)     D767.92, D769.87.H3     940.539969, 996.903
Hazing (U.S. Naval Acad.: Cong. docs.)     V415.E9
Headgear, Naval     VC320

Headquarters, Military     UB230-235
Headquarters, Naval (ops. inclu. aides)     VB210
Heads of state (biog.)     923.1
Health, hygiene, & sanitation (navies)     VG470-475
Health, hygiene, & sanitation (navies: U.S.)     VG473
Heat or other radiations (ammunition: design)     623.4595
Heating, ventilation, & sanitation (naval architec. & engin.)     VM481-482
Heidelberg, Ger.     DD901.H55-59
Helena (cruiser: U.S.: WWII)     D774.H4
Helicopters     629.133352
Helicopters, Military     UG1230-1235     623.746047
Helicopters, Military (design)     623.746047     TL716
Heliograph (mil. signal.)     UG582.H4
Helmets, hats, etc. (mil.)     UC500-505
Helsingfors, Fin. (Helsinki: area)     948.971     DK465.H5, DL1175,
                                                            DL1175.48 (1917-)
Helsinki, Fin.     DL1175     948.971
Helsinki, Fin. (1917-)     DL1175.48
Helsinki, Fin. (gen.)     DL1175.42
Hemp (naval supplies)     VC279.H45
Hercegovina & Bosnia (1918-45: gen.)     DR1734
Hercegovina (Herzegovina) & Bosnia     949.742     DB231-250 (Bos.), DB521-
                                                            540 (Her.), DR1652-1785
Herzegovina (20th c.)     DB540
Herzegovina (Hercegovina) & Bosnia (gen.)     DR1660, 1685
Hess, Rudolf (Ger.: 1918-48 era)     DD247.H37
Hierarchy, Air force     358.4133     UG770-775
Hierarchy (marines)     359.9633
Hierarchy, Military (mil. personnel)     355.33     UA, UB410-415, UB210
Hierarchy, Naval     359.33     V110-145, VA, VB21-124, VB23 (U.S.),
                                        VB257-258.5, VB203
High-explosive devices (torpedoes, blockbusters, etc.: design)     623.4517
                                        V850-855 (torpedoes), UF860-870
High explosives (design: inclu. dynamite, nitro, TNT)     623.4527     TP285,
                                        TP270-295
Highland Division (WWII: G.B.: 51st)     D759.5.51st
Highways (U.S.)     UA963-964
Hilo, Haw.     DU629.H5
Hindenburg, Paul von (Ger.: 1888-1918+ period)     DD231.H5
Hirohito (Japan: Emperor, 1926-89)     DS889.8
Hiroshima, Japan     DS897.H48     952.19
Hiroshima, Japan (WWII)     D767.25.H6
Hispanic-Americans (armed forces)     UB418.H57
Historiography (WWI)     D522.42
Historiography (WWII)     D743.42
HISTORY (1945-)     D839-845+
History & geography     900-999+     G (geog.), D-F
History (auxiliary: civilization, gen. archaeology, heraldry, gen. biography)  C  900-
                                        909, 920-929, 930-939+
History (gen., Eastern Hemisphere, Oceania)     D     909, 930-969, 990-996
History (gen., world wars, Eur. overall, etc.)     D1-1075+     909, 940, 950
History (misc. areas: Oceania, Atlantic islands, Arctic, extraterr. worlds, etc.)
                                        990- 999     C-F, G, Q
Hitler, Adolf (Ger.: 1918-48 era)     DD247.H5
Hitler Youth (Hitlerjugend)     DD253.5

Ho Chi Minh (N. Viet.)        DS560.72.H6
Hobart, Australia (Tasmania)   DU480.H6    994.61
Hokkaido (Japan)        DS895.H6    952.4
HOLLAND (NETHERLANDS)    949.2    DJ, DJ109 (gen.)
Holland (1890-1948: Queen Wilhelmina era)        949.2071        DJ281-287,
        DJ281 (gen.), DJ285 (WWI time), DJ287 (WWII era)
Holland (20th c.)    949.207    DJ216 (19th-20th c.)
Holland (geog. & travel)    914.92    DJ39
Holland (WWII: gen. particip.)    940.53492    DL763.N4-42, DJ287
Holland (WWII: mil. hist.)    940.5409492    D763.N4-41
Holocaust (WWII: inclu. exterm. camps)        940.5318
Holy See (1870-)    DG799
Home defense (coasts, frontiers, other valuable redoubts)    355.45    UA (gen.),
    UG410-442 (fortific's.), UG410-412 (U.S.), UG428-430 (Eur.), UG429.G7 (G.B.)
Home defense, Air force    358.4145    UG730-735, UG630-635
Home defense, Naval    359.45    VA45, V200
Home guard naval forces    359.351    VA45
Home guards & frontier troops    355.351    UA42 (U.S. Nat. Guard)
Homes, Sailors'    VB290-295 (SEE ALSO UB380-385)
Homosexuals (WWII: U.S.: armed forces)    D769.2    940.54097308664
Honan (China)    DS793.H5
Hong Kong    DS796.H7    951.25
Hong Kong (1843-1945)    951.2504    DS796.H757
Hong Kong Naval Base (Royal Navy)    VA459.H55
Hong Kong (WWII: gen. particip.)    940.53512    DS796.H7
Honolulu, Haw.    996.931    DU629.H7
Honolulu, Haw.    DU629.H7    996.931
HONORED & dead (WWI: G.B.: rolls)        940.46741    D609.G7
Honored & dead (WWI: Ger.: rolls)        940.46743    D609.G3
Honored & dead (WWII: Fr.: rolls)    940.546744    D797.F8
Honored & dead (WWII: G.B.: rolls)        940.546741    D797.G7
Honored & dead (WWII: Ger.: rolls)        940.546743    D797.G3
Honored & dead (WWII: Japan: rolls)    940.546752    D797.J3
Honored & dead (WWII: Rus.: rolls)    940.546747    D797.R9
Honored & dead (WWII: U.S.: rolls)    940.546773    D797.U6-7
Honshu (Japan)    952.1
Hood (battle cruiser: G.B.)
Hood (WWII: battle cruiser: G.B.)    D772.H6, VA458.H6
Hoover, Herbert (U.S.: Pres., 1929-33)    E802
Hopkins, Harry (U.S.: 20th c.)    E748.H67
Hornet (aircraft carrier: U.S.: WWII)    D774.H6
Horse artillery    UF410
Horse cavalry (gen. & ops.)    357.184    UE150-475, UE150+, UE157+
Horses & mules, Military    UC600-695
Horses, Artillery    UF370
Horses, Cavalry    UE460-475
Horthy, Miklós (Hung.: 20th c.)    DB950.H6

HOSPITAL corps, Naval     VG310-325
Hospital corps, Naval (places besides U.S.)     VG325.A-Z
Hospital corps, Naval (U.S.)     VG320
Hospital services & hospitals, Naval     VG410-450 (SEE ALSO D #s for
                                                         particular wars)
Hospital services, Military     UH460-485
Hospital services, Naval (gen.)     VG410   359.72
Hospital services, Naval (U.S.)     VG420-425
Hospital ships     VG450     623.8264, 359.3264
Hospital ships (WWII: U.S.: by name)     D807.U74.A-Z
HOSPITALS, medical services, etc. (WWII: gen.)     D806     940.5475
Hospitals, medical services, Red Cross (WWI: gen.)     D628
Hospitals, Military (except U.S.)     UH475.A-Z
Hospitals, Military (gen.)     UH470   355.72
Hospitals, Naval (gen.)     VG420
Hospitals, Naval (U.S.: by town)     VG425.A-Z
Hospitals (WWI: in particular places)     940.4763+     D629.A-Z
Hospitals (WWI: operated by particular countries)     940.4764-4769
HOSPITALS (WWII: in Australia)     940.5476394     D807.A8
Hospitals (WWII: in China)     940.5476351     D807.C5
Hospitals (WWII: in Fr.)     940.5476344     D807.F8
Hospitals (WWII: in G.B.)     940.5476341-5476342     D807.G7
Hospitals (WWII: in Ger.)     940.5476343     D807.G3
Hospitals (WWII: in Japan)     940.5476352     D807.J3
Hospitals (WWII: in particular places)     940.547634-547639     D807.A-Z
Hospitals (WWII: in U.S.)     940.5476373     D807.U6-87
Hospitals (WWII: operated by particular countries)     940.54764-54769   D807.A-Z
Hotchkiss machine guns     UF620.H8
Hotchkiss ordnance     UF560-565... .H.
Housing administration (air forces)     358.4167     UG1140-1145
Housing administration (mil.)     355.67 (SEE ALSO .71 & .12 [gen.])     UC400-440
Housing administration (navies)     359.67     VC420-425
Housing & barracks, Naval (places besides U.S.)     VC425.A-Z
Houston, Texas     F394.H8     976.41411
Howitzers & mortars     UF470-475
Howitzers & mortars (Fr.)     UF475.F8
Howitzers & mortars (G.B.)     UF475.G7
Howitzers & mortars (Japan)     UF475.J3
Hudson River (N.Y.)     F127.H8
Hull, Cordell (U.S.: 20th c.)     E748.H93
Hull design (naval architec.)     623.8144     VM156
Hulls (special construc.: anti-fire & -shock, corrosion-resistant, etc.)     623.848
Human resources (air forces: enlistment etc.)     358.4122     UG880-885
Human resources (mil.)     355.22     UA17.5, UB320+, UB340+
Human resources (navies)     359.22
Humor, comics, pictorials, & miscellanea (WWII)     940.549     D743.9, D745
Hunan (China)     DS793.H7

Hungarian military ops (WWI)       D540
HUNGARY        943.9        DB901-975+, DB906, DB925
Hungary (20th c.)        DB947-957+        943.9043+
Hungary (20th c.: gen.)        DB947
Hungary (1914-18: WWI era)        DB953        943.9043
Hungary (20th c.: 1918-)        943.905        DB947-950, DB947 (gen.), DB950.A-Z (biog.)
Hungary (1918-45)        DB955        943.9051-2
Hungary (1918-41)        943.9051        DB955
Hungary (1942-56)        943.9052        DB956
Hungary (gen.)        DB906        943.9
Hungary (gen.: pubn. dates 1801+)        DB925
Hungary (geog. & travel)        914.39        DB916-917
Hungary, Liechtenstein        DB861-975+
Hungary (mil. status)        UA829.H9        355.0330439
Hungary (post-WWI territorial ?s)        D651.H7
Hungary (WWII: gen.)        D765.56        940.53439, 943.905
Hydrography, Marine        VK588-597
Hydrology, Military        UG468
Hygiene & sanitation, Military        UH600-629
Hygiene & sanitation, Military (besides U.S.)        UH605.A-Z
Hygiene, health, & sanitation (navies: special: tropics, drinking water, alcohol
                        problem, venereal diseases, diet, etc.)        VG471
Hygiene, Mental (besides U.S.)        UH629.5.A-Z


IBERIAN Peninsula        DP        946
Iberian Peninsula & Spain        946        DP, DP1-402+ (Sp.), DP501-900+ (Port.)
Ice excavation, tunnels, rooms, etc. (mil. engineering)        UG343
Icebergs        VK1299
Icebreakers (naval architec.)        VM451        623.828
Iceland        949.12        DL301-398+, DL375 (1918-)
Iceland (1801-1918)        DL365
Iceland (1918-)        DL375        949.1204
Ickes, Harold (U.S.: 20th c.)        E748.I28
Ickes, Harold (U.S.: 20th c.: works)        E742.5.I25
Illinois        977.3        F536-550, F541, F546 (1865-1950)
Illinois (1865-1950)        F546        977.303
Imaginary naval battles & wars        V253        359.47
Imperial War Museum (London, G.B.)        U13.G72.L69
Incendiary bombs (aerial)        UG1282.I6        623.4516
Incendiary weapons        UG447.65
Indemnity & reparations (WWI: gen.)        D648        940.31422
Indemnity & reparations (WWII: gen.)        D818
Indemnity (Sino-Jpn. Confl., 1937-45)        DS777.533.I53

INDIA        954      DS436, DS401-481
India (1761-1947: Brit. rule)     DS463-480.83      954.03
India (1785-1947: British rule)  954.03        DS463-480, DS463 (gen.)
India (1914-19)              DS480.4      954.0356-0357
India (1916-26)              954.0357     DS480.4-6
India (1916-21: Viscount of Chelmsford)      DS480.5
India (1919-47)              DS480.45     954.035+
India (1926-36)              954.0358     DS480.7-8
India (1931-36: Marquis of Willingdon)      DS480.8
India (1936-47: Gov'ships. of Linlithgow, Wavell, Mountbatten)      954.0359
                                                      DS480.82-83
India (1936-43: Marquis of Linlithgow)        DS480.82    954.0359
India (1943-47: Earl of Wavell)          DS480.83    954.0359
India & Burma (WWII)      D767.6-63    940.5425, .5354, 954.0359
India (mil. status)          UA840-844    355.033054
India (overall) & pre-1947 Pakistan          DS401-481      954
India, Pakistan, & Ceylon (geog. & travel)    915.4        DS335, DS413
India, Pakistan, Ceylon, Burma, etc.      DS376-498      954, 959.1
India (WWII: dipl. hist.)      940.532254      D754.I4
INDIAN Ocean islands      DS491.A-Z
Indian Ocean (pilot & sailing guides)      VK885-901
Indian Ocean region & Southern Asia (gen.)  DS335
Indian Ocean (tide & current tables)       VK685-701
Indians as soldiers (WWI: U.S.)       D570.8.I6
Indians (N. Am.)      E77-99    970.00497, .1-5, 973.0497
Indians (U.S. Navy: native-Am's.)  VB324.I5
Indians (WWII)       D810.I5
Indochina            DS521-560      959-959.7
INDONESIA (1602-1945: Dutch period)      959.802      DS642-643
Indonesia (1798-1945)          959.8022    DS643
Indonesia (1798-1942: colonial era)    DS643      959.8022
Indonesia (1942-45: Japanese occupation)    DS643.5      959.8022
Indonesia & Borneo (naval geog.)    359.47598    VA667.I or .B
Indonesia & Malay Archipelago      959.8    DS611-649
Indonesia & Malay Archipelago (WWII: gen. particip.)      940.53598
                          D767.7 (Dutch E. Indies), DS643.5, DS643
Indonesia (geog. & travel)      915.98      DS619
Indonesia (mil. status)      UA853.I5
Indonesia (WWII: mil. hist.)    940.5409598    D767.7
Induction & exemption (mil.)    UB340      355,22363, .225
INDUSTRIAL defense (by specific industry)      UA929.95.A-Z (SEE ALSO H
                                                  industry #s)
Industrial defense (gen.)      UA929.5      355.28, .26
Industrial defense (places besides U.S.)    UA929.9.A-Z
Industrial mobilization (by country)    UA18.A3-Z (SEE ALSO D-F for specific wars)
Industrial resources & raw materials (air forces)      358.4124-4126
                                            UG1100-1105, UG630+
Industrial resources (mil. use)      355.26      UA18, UA929.5+, HC106+
Industrial resources (navies)      359.26
Industry, Shipbuilding (gen.)      VM298.5      338.476238, 387.5+

INFANTRY        356.1        UD, UD15, UD21-124 (by place), UD144-145+, UA
Infantry arms (small: U.S.)        UD383-384
Infantry (Asia)        UD99-113
Infantry (Australia)        UD121        356.10994
Infantry (Austria)        UD65        356.109436
Infantry (Austria & Austria-Hung.)        UA673
Infantry (Can.)        UD26
Infantry (China)        UD101        356.10951
Infantry (collections)        UD7
Infantry (Eur.)        UD55-95
Infantry (Fr.)        UD71        356.10944
Infantry (G.B.)        UA650-653, UD57-64
Infantry (G.B.: by date)        UD58
Infantry (G.B.: gen.)        UA650        356.10941
Infantry (gen.)        356.18        UD160-302, UD160 (U.S.)
Infantry (gen. hist.)        UD15        356.09, 109, 355.009
Infantry (gen.: pubn. 1801+)        UD145        356.1
Infantry (Ger.)        UA713.A1-Z9.A-Z, UD73        356.10943
Infantry (Ger.: by group name)        UA713.Z9.A-Z
Infantry (Ger.: by regiment #)        UA713.Z6.1st-
Infantry (Ger.: gen.)        UA713.A6-Z4
Infantry (hist.: by area or country regardless of specific unit)        UD21-124 (SEE
                                                                                      ALSO UA)

Infantry (It.)        UA743, UD79        356.10945
Infantry (Japan)        UD105        356.10952
Infantry manuals (gen.)        UD150        356.10202
Infantry, Mounted (U.S.)        UD453-454
Infantry (New Z.)        UD122.5
Infantry regiments etc. (WWII: U.S.: by #)        D769.31.1st-
Infantry regiments (G.B.: by name)        UA651.A-Z
Infantry regiments (Sp.-Am. War: U.S.: by #)        E725.4.1st-
Infantry regiments (U.S.: by #/author)        UA29.1st-
Infantry (Rus.)        UA773.A1-Z9.A-Z
Infantry (Rus.: Asian)        UD109
Infantry (Rus.: by group name)        UA773.Z9.A-Z
Infantry (Rus.: by regiment #)        UA773.Z6.1st-
Infantry (Rus.: Eur.)        UD85        356.10947
Infantry (Rus.: gen.)        UA773.A6-Z4
Infantry tactics & maneuvers (Asia: gen.)        UD270
Infantry tactics & maneuvers (Eur.: gen.)        UD215
Infantry tactics & maneuvers (U.S.: gen.)        UD160
Infantry (tactics, use, gen. hist's.)        UD (SEE ALSO UA for specific armies)        356
Infantry (U.S.)        UD23        356.10973
Infantry (U.S.: Calif. reserves)        UA93-94
Infantry (U.S.: gen.)        UA28        356.10973
Infantry (U.S.: N.Y. reserves)        UA363-364
Infantry (WWI: U.S.)        D570.33 (newer bks. may use A1 or #'s as in D570.27)
INFANTRY (WWII: Fr.)        D761.3
Infantry (WWII: G.B.)        D759.53
Infantry (WWII: Ger.)        D757.3
Infantry (WWII: Ger.: by author, division, name, etc.)        D757.32.A-Z
Infantry (WWII: Rus.)        D764.53
Infantry (WWII: U.S.: regiments, combat teams, etc.: by #)        D769.31.1st-
Infiltration, espionage, & unconventional warfare (WWII: Rus.)        940.548647
                                                                              UB251.R9, UB271.R9

Information & recreation, Military (U.S.: gen.)     UH805        355.3460973
Information & recreation services, Naval (U.S.: gen.) VG2025-2026    359.3460973
Information security (mil. data: gen.)     UB246
Inquiry, Courts of (mil.: by country)     UB865.A-Z
Inquiry, Courts of (naval: U.S.)     VB813 (PREFER KF7646-7650)
Insignia & badges (naval clothing)  VC345        359.1342
Insignia, badges, etc. (air force)  UG1180-1185
Insignia, badges, etc. (mil.: U.S.)  UC533
Inspection, Military     UB240-245
Inspection, Naval (inclu. inspectors)     VB220-225
Inspection (small arms: infantry)     UD382
Installations, Infantry        356.187       UC400-405, U180-185
INSTRUCTION camps, maneuver grounds, etc. (U.S.)     U293
Instruction (marine engin.)     VM725-728        623.8707
Instruction (marine engin.: places except U.S.)  VM728.A-Z
Instruction (merch. marine)     VK401-529
Instruction (mil. engineering)     UG157
Instruction (naval architec.)     VM165-276
Instruction (naval architec.: by place)        VM171-274
Instruction (naval medicine)     VG230-235
Instruction (naval ordnance)     VF357
Instruction (ordnance & small arms)     UF527
Instruction (WWII)        D743.4
Instrumentation, Aircraft        629.135
Instrumentmen, Naval        VG1030-1035
Instruments, Artillery (specific types)   UF849-856
Instruments, Nautical        VK573-587
Instruments, Nautical (design)       623.863        VK573-587
Instruments, Nautical (special)       VK575-584
Instruments, Naval gunnery       VF520        623.558
INTELLIGENCE & military espionage (inclu. cryptanalysis, data analysis, etc.)
        355.3432        UB250-251, UB251.A-Z (by country), UB270-271,
        UB271.A-Z (by place), UB271.x2.A-Z (by spy), UB271.R92.S565 (R. Sorge)
Intelligence, espionage, & unconventional warfare (WWI: G.B.)        940.48641
Intelligence, espionage, & unconventional warfare (WWI: Ger.)        940.48743
                                    D619.3-5 (in U.S.)
Intelligence, espionage, & unconventional warfare (WWII: G.B.)        940.548641
                    D810.S7, UB251.G7, UB271.G7, VB230-250
Intelligence, espionage, & unconventional warfare (WWII: Ger.)        940.548743
                        D810.S7+, UB251.G3, UB271.G3
Intelligence, espionage, & unconventional warfare (WWII: U.S.)        940.548673
                    D810.S7+, UB251.U5, UB271.U5, VB230-250 (naval)
Intelligence, Military        UB250-271
Intelligence, Military (by country)        UB251.A-Z
Intelligence, Naval        359.3432        VB230-254, VB230, UB250-271
Intelligence, Naval (by country)     VB231.A-Z        359.343209+
Inter-allied Military Commission of Control in Germany (WWI)        D650.I6
Inter-war period (1919-39: essays, minor works)        D725
Inter-war period (1919-39: gen.)        D720        940.5-.52
Inter-war period (1919-39: special)        D723
Internal combustion engines (marine engineering)     623.8723        VM770
International forces        355.357 (perhaps PREFER 355.356)
International military law   UB481 (PREFER JX areas)        341.6
International naval law   VB353

Internment centers & P.O.W. camps (WWI: in U.S.)   940.47273      D627.U6+
Internment centers, labor & concentration camps (WWII: geog. treatment: by
                          controlling country)      940.531709+ (SEE .5472+ for
                          works prior to 1989 on intern. ctrs.)
Intrenching tools (mil.)      UG380
Invincible (aircraft carrier: G.B.: WWII) VA458.I55
Ionian Sea islands    949.55      DF901.I57-69
IRAN (Persia)      DS251-325      955
Iran (1794-1925: Kajar dynasty: gen.)      DS298
Iran (1906-)        955.05      DS298, DS313-318+
Iran (1906-25)      955.051      DS315-316
Iran (1909-25: Ahmed era)      DS315        955.05-051
Iran (1925-41: Pahlavi family: Reza Shah era)   DS317      955.052
Iran (1941-78?: Pahlavi: Mohammed Reza)      DS318      955.053
Iran (WWII)      D766.7.I55
IRAQ      956.7        DS67-79, DS70.9
Iraq (1517-1918: Turkish period)   DS77      956.703
Iraq (1919-)      DS79      956.704
Iraq (1920-: Mandate & independence)  956.704      DS79
Iraq (1921-33: Faisal I)      DS79.5
Iraq (1933-39: Ghazi I)      DS79.52
Iraq (1939-58: Faisal II)      DS79.53      956.7042
Iraq (geog. & travel)      915.67      DS70.6, DS79+
Iraq (WWII)      D766.7.I57
IRELAND      941.5        DA900-995, DA910 (gen.)
Ireland (19th-20th c.)      941.508      DA950-965+
Ireland (20th c.)      DA959-965, DA959      941.5082
Ireland (1900-20)      941.50821      DA960
Ireland (1901-22)      DA960
Ireland (1914-21)      DA962
Ireland (1921-49)      941.50822      DA963
Ireland (1922-: Irish Free State, Eire, etc.)   DA963
Ireland (WWI)      D547.I6
Ireland (WWII: dipl. history: gen.)   D754.I5
Ireland (WWII: gen. particip.)      940.53415
Irish Free State (WWII: dipl. history)      D754.I6
Irish Guards (WWII: G.B.)      D760.I7
Irish troops (G.B.)      UA665
Irregular troops (guerrillas, brigands, etc.)   356.15      U240, U167.5.A-Z
Israel (inclu. Palestine)      956.94      DS101-131+, DS116-117, DS123
Israel (70 A.D.+)      DS123
Israel (1917-48: Brit. rule)      956.9404      DS126, DS126.3 (WWII era)
Israel & the Jews (1939-45: WWII era)      DS126.3 (PREFER D810.J4 to cover
      titles on ethnicgroup)
Istanbul, Tur. (Constantinople)      DR716-739      956.3

ITALIAN aerial ops. (WWII)          D792.I8
Italian-Anglo naval conflict (WWII: by battle, ship, etc.)    D775.5.A-Z
Italian East Africa & Northeast Africa          DT367          963
Italian military history (gen.)    DG482          355.00945
Italian military ops (WWI: gen.)          D569.A2          940.4145
Italian military ops. (WWII: gen.)          D763.I8
Italian poetry, satire, etc. (WWII)          D745.7.I8
Italian Somaliland          DT416          967.73-7305+
Italians (in Arg.)          F3021.I8
Italians (in N.Y.)          F130.I8
Italians (in Paraguay)          F2699.I8
Italians (in S.Am.)          F2239.I8
Italians (in U.S.)          E184.I8
Italo-Ethiopian War (1935-6)          DT387.8          963.056
Italo-Ethiopian War (1935-6: gen.)    DT387.8.A8-Z          963.056
ITALY          945          DG
Italy (476-)          DG401-579
Italy (1870- & 20th c.)          945.09          DG555-575+, DG555, DG570 (WWI era)
Italy (1871-1947: gen.)          DG555          945.09
Italy (1871-1947: United Italy: Monarchy)          DG555-575
Italy (1900-46: times of Vittorio Emanuele III, Umberto II)          DG566-575
Italy (1914-18: WWI)          DG570          945.0814
Italy (1918-46)          945.091 (SEE ALSO 963.056 for Italo-Eth. War of 1935-6)
          DG566-575, DG571, DG571-572 (Fascist period), DG572 (WWII time)
Italy (1919-45: Fascism)          DG571          945.0815-0816
Italy (1939-45: WWII era)          DG572          945.0816
Italy & Italian military ops. (WWII)          D763.I8-82          940.40945, .41345, 945.091
Italy & Italian neutrality (WWI: dipl. history)          D617
Italy. Army (gen.)          UA742          355.30945
Italy (biog.: heads of state)          923.145
Italy (gen. hist., culture, etc.)          DG417
Italy (gen.: titles dated after 1800)          DG467
Italy (geog. & travel)          914.5          DG428-429
Italy (lighthouses, beacons, foghorns, etc.)          VK1079-1080
Italy (mil. status)          UA740          355.033045
Italy (naval geog.)          359.4745          VA540-549
Italy (naval status: gen.)          VA543.A5-Z          359.030945, .00945, .30945, .4745
Italy (post-WWI relns.: U.S.)          D651.I7
Italy (post-WWI territorial ?s: inclu. Fiume)    D651.I6-8
Italy, Sicily, Sardinia, Malta          DG 945
ITALY (WWI)          D569          940.4145
Italy (WWI: causes, aims, results: includes Treaty of London, 1915)          D520.I7
Italy (WWI: mil. hist.)          940.40945          D569
Italy (WWI: Reconstruction)          D659.I8
Italy (WWII: dipl. hist.)          940.532445          D754.I8
Italy (WWII: dipl. history)          D754.I8
Italy (WWII: religious & ethical ?'s)          D744.5.I8
Iwo Jima (WWII)          D767.99.I9

```
JAMAICA        972.92      F1861-1896, F1881
Jamaica (1810-1953)      F1886      972.92034-9205
Jamaica (gen.)           F1881
JAPAN        DS801-897+      952
Japan (1868+: modern era)      DS881.85+      952.03
Japan (1868-1945: Imperial power)      952.03    DS881.9
Japan (20th c.)        DS885      952.03-04
Japan (1912-26: special topics: inclu. large earthquakes like 1923)      DS888
Japan (1912-26: Taisho or Yoshihito era)      952.032      DS885.8-888, DS886 (gen.)
Japan (1914-18: WWI era)      DS887      952.032
Japan (1926-89: Hirohito rule: collected, non-serial works)      DS888.15
Japan (1926-89: Hirohito rule: gen.)      DS888.2
Japan (1926-89: Showa or Hirohito period: inclu. Sino-Jpn. conflict of 1937-41)
               952.033 (PREFER 951.042 for Sino-Jpn. War of 1937-41)
               DS888.15-890+, DS888.2, DS888.5 (1926-45)
Japan (1926-45)        DS888.5      952.033
Japan (1945+: may ALSO cover 1926+)      DS889      952.04
Japan (air war geog.)      358.414752
Japan & China (mil. policy)      355.033551 (China)-033552 (Japan)      UA830,
                                                      UA835+, UA845+
Japan & Japanese military ops. (WWII)      D767.2-25
Japan. Army (gen.)      UA847      355.00952, .30952, .310952
Japan. Army (service branches by name)      UA848.A-Z
Japan (biog.: heads of state)      923.152
Japan (gen. & cultural)      DS806
Japan (gen. history, descrip., culture)      DS835
Japan (geog. & travel)      915.2      DS810 (1901-45)
Japan (mil. geog.)      355.4752      UA995.J2
Japan (mil. status)      355.033052      UA845+
Japan (mil. status: gen.)      UA845      355.033052, .033252, .033552
Japan (mil. status: states, provinces, etc.)      UA849.A-Z
Japan (naval geog.)      359.4752      650-659
Japan (naval hist.)      359.00952      VA650-659
Japan (naval policy & status)      359.030952
Japan (naval status: gen.)      VA653.A5-Z      359.030952, .00952, .30952, .4752
Japan (pilot guides)      623.892952      VK909
Japan (post-WWI relns.: U.S.)      D651.J4
Japan (post-WWI territorial ?s)      D651.J3-5
Japan (WWI: causes, aims, results)      D519
Japan (WWII: causes, aims, results)      D742.J3
Japan (WWII: dipl. history)      D754.J3      940.532452
Japan (WWII: religious & ethical ?'s)      D744.5.J3
JAPANESE aerial ops. (WWII)      D792.J3-39  940.544952
Japanese-Americans (WWII)      D753.8 (SEE ALSO D769.8.A6)
Japanese armament (modern)      U821.J3
Japanese engineering ops. (WWII)      D795.J3
Japanese (in Brazil)      F2659.J3
Japanese (in Calif.)      F870.J3
Japanese (in Can.)      F1035.J3
Japanese (in Peru)      F3619.J3
Japanese (in U.S.)      E184.J3
```

Japanese Islands (lighthouses, beacons, foghorns, etc.)    VK1105-1106
                                                            623.89420952
Japanese Islands (lighthouses, beacons, foghorns, etc.: lists)    VK1207
                                                            623.89440952
Japanese Islands (pilot & sailing guides)    VK909    623.892952
Japanese Islands (tide & current tables)    VK709
Japanese military education (special periods)    U651
Japanese military ops. & Japan (WWII: gen.)    D767.2    940.5352, .540952,
                                                            .541352, 952.033
Japanese military ops. (WWI: gen.)    D571
Japanese naval ops. (WWII: by battle, ship, etc.)    D777.5.A-Z
Japanese naval ops. (WWII: gen.)    D777    940.545952, .5426
Japanese propaganda (1926-89: in other lands: gen.)    DS889.2
Japanese submarine ops. (WWII: by battle, ship, author, etc.)    D783.7.A-Z
Japanese submarine ops. (WWII)    D783.6, D784.J3
Japanese territories (WWII)    D802.J3
Java (Indon.)    959.82    DS646.17-29, DS646.2, DS646.27
Jeeps (mil. design)    623.74722
Jersey (G.B.: island)    942.341
Jerusalem, Pal.    DS109
Jerusalem, Pal. (1917-)    DS109.93
Jet aircraft (mil. design)    623.746044
Jet airplanes (engineering)    629.133349
Jewish groups (WWII)    940.5315296 (SEE ALSO .531503924)    D810.J4
Jewish question    DS141
JEWS & the Holocaust (WWII)    D810.J4
Jews (by country or area)    DS135.A-Z    Usually 004924 after Dewey place #s
Jews (Central Eur.)    943.0004924
Jews (Eng. and G.B.)    DS135.E5-6
Jews (Eur.)    DS135.E8-9    940.04924 (single '0' after decimal in this case)
Jews (Fr.)    DS135.F8-9    944.004924
Jews (Ger.)    DS135.G3-5    943.004924
Jews (Ger.: 19th-20th c.)    DS135.G33
Jews (Ger.: gen.)    DS135.G3.A5-Z
JEWS (IN Arg.)    F3021.J5
Jews (in Brazil)    F2659.J5
Jews (in Calif.)    F870.J5
Jews (in Chile)    F3285.J4
Jews (in Cuba)    F1789.J4
Jews (in Mex.)    F1392.J4
Jews (in N.Y.)    F130.J5
Jews (in S.Am.)    F2239.J5
Jews (in U.S.)    E184.J5
Jews (in Urug.)    F2799.J4
Jews (It.)    DS135.I8-9    945.004924
Jews, Modern    DS143
Jews (outside Israel: economic, political, social conditions)    DS140-140.5
Jews (outside Israel: gen.)    DS134    909.04924
Jews (outside Palestine)    DS133-151
Jews, Palestine, & Israel (gen. histories)    DS117

Jews (Rus.)        DS135.R9-95    947.004924
Jews (S. Am.)      DS135.S8 (PREFER E #s in most cases)
Jews (Sp.-Am. War, 1898: U.S.)      E725.5.J4
Jews (U.S.)        DS135.U6-7 (PREFER E184.J5 in most cases)        973.004924
Jews (WWI: includes Ukrainian pogroms)      D639.J4 (SEE DS145.P5-7 for Protocols
                                                 of the Wise Men of Zion)
Jews (WWI: peace topic)        D650.J4
Jews (WWII)        940.531503924 (SEE ALSO .5315296)        D810.J4,
                   D804.G4, D829.J4, DS135
Jews (WWII: Reconstruction)        D829.J4
Joffre, Joseph J. (Fr.: 1871-1940 era)    DC342.8.J6
JORDAN        DS153-154        956.95
Jordan (1517-1918: Turkish rule)    DS154.4        956.9503
Jordan (1919-)        DS154.5        956.9504
Jordan River (Pal.)    DS110.J6
Joubert de la Ferté, Philip Bennet, Sir (G.B.: air force biog.)        DA89.6.J6
Journalists & publishers (WWII)    940.5315097        D798 (gen.), D799.A-Z (by place)
Judiciary, Military (by country except U.S.)    UB845.A-Z (for U.S. SEE KF7601-7679)
Judiciary, Naval (U.S.: inclu. overall naval justice)        VB793
Jungle warfare        U167.5.J8
Justice, Naval (gen.: inclu. judiciary)        VB790        343.014, .0146
Juvenile works (WWI)        D522.7
Juvenile works (WWII)        D743.7


KAMCHATKA (Sib.)        DK771.K2
Kansas        F676-690        978.1
Kauai (Haw. Is.)        DU628.K3        996.941
Kemal, Mustafa (Tur.: 'Atatürk': 1909- era)        DR592.K4
Kent, Eng. (WWII)        D760.8.K4
Kentucky        976.9        F446-460
Kenya        967.62        DT434.E2 (older titles), DT433.5-434 (newer books),
                   DT433.522, DT433.557
Kenya (1895-1963: Brit. era)    DT433.57-433.577        967.6203
Kenya (1920-63)        DT433.575
Kenya (mil. status)        UA860.5        355.03306762
Kerensky, Aleksandr (Rus.: 1894-1917: biog.)        DK254.K3
Key West, Fl. (fortifications)        UG412.K4
Khartoum, Egypt        DT154.K63
Kiangsi (China)        DS793.K4
Kiangsi Province (China)        951.222
Kiangsu Province (China: inclu. Nanking & Shanghai)        951.13        DS793.K
Kiel Naval Base (Ger.)        VA516.K4
Kiev, Rus.        DK651.K37
Kiev, Uk. (Kyiv)        DK508.92-939, DK508.95.K54
King's Own Scottish Borderers (WWI)        D547.K47
Kingston, Jam.        F1895.K5
Kiribati (inclu. Gilbert Is.)        996.81        DU615
Klintsy, Rus. (WWII)        D764.7.K5
Knapsacks (mil. equip.)        UC529.K6
Knives, bayonets, swords, etc. (design)        623.441        UD420-425,
        UD400 (bayonets)
Knots & splices (naut. ropes & cables)        623.8882        VM533
Knox, W. Frank (U.S.: 20th c.)        E748.K55
Konoye, Fumimaro, Prince (Japan: 20th. c.)        DS885.5.K6

KOREA        DS901-935+        951.9
Korea (20th c.)        DS916        951.903-904
Korea (1945+)        DS917
Korea (gen.)        DS907
Korea (geog. & travel)        915.19        DS902
Korea (WWII)        D767.255        940.53519
Korea (WWII: gen. particip.)        940.53519        DS916
Krakow, Pol. (Cracow)        DK4700-4735
Krupp armor plating (naval sci.)        V907.K7
Kurile Islands (Japan or Russia)        DS895.K9        957.7
Kuwait        DS247.K8-88
Kwangsi (China)        DS793.K6
Kwangtung (China)        DS793.K7
Kweichow (China)        DS793.K8
Kyoto, Japan        DS897.K8        952.191 (use 952.1864 with books after about 1988)

LABOR camps, internment centers, concentration camps (WWII: Ger.)
        940.53170943
Labor (WWI)        D639.L2
Labrador        F1135-1139
Ladrone Islands (Marianas: gen.)        DU645
Lake Baikal (Sib.)        DK771.B3
Lake Superior & Upper Peninsula (Mich.)        977.49        F572.N8 (N. Penin.),
        F552 (Lake Sup.)
Lanai (Haw. Is.)        DU628.L3        996.923
LAND forces warfare        356-357        UD-UF
Land (mil. bases, reservations, etc.)        355.79
Land (naval bases etc.)        359.79        VC412-416
Land transport (mil. engineering)        623.61
Land vehicles, Motorized (mil. design)        623.747        UC270-275, UC340-345
Landing (aviation)        629.1325213
Landing craft (naval engineering)        623.8256        V895
Landing craft (navies: units)        359.3256        V895
Landing maneuvers & debarkation        U200
Landing ops. & field service tactics (naval: inclu. shore srvc., small arms
        instruc., etc.)        V175        355.41, .422
Language        400-499        P
Languages & literatures        P        400-499, 800-899
Laos        959.4        DS555, DS557.L2 (earlier books)
Laos (1893-1954)        DS555.7-73        959.403+
Laos (WWII: gen. particip.)        940.53594        DS555.36
Lapland (Fin.)        948.977        DL971.L2, DL1170.L2
LATIN AMERICA & the West Indies        F1201-3799+        972, 980-989
Latin America (1898-)        F1414        980.032+
Latin America (gen.)        F1401-1419        980
Latin America (mil. status: gen.)        UA602.3        355.03328, .03308
Latin America (naval status)        VA402.5
Latin America (WWII)        D768.18        940.538, .53228, .53248, .53258, 980.033
Latitude & longitude (marine navig.: inclu. tables)        VK565
Latrines & sewers (mil. qtrs.)        UC430
Lattre de Tassigny, Jean Joseph (Fr.: 20th c.)        DC373.L33

LATVIA      DK511.L15-18 (earlier pubns.), DK504 (later works)      947.43
Latvia (1800-1918)      DK504.73
Latvia (1914-18: WWI)      DK511.L178
Latvia (1918-)      DK511.L18
Latvia (1918-40)      DK504.74-76
Latvia (1940+)      DK504.77-79
Latvia (WWII: occupied terr.)      D802.L3
Laundries, Military      UC440
Laundries, Naval      VC430
Laurel, José P. (Philip.: 1935-46 period)      DS686.2.L3
Laval, Pierre (Fr.: 20th c.)      DC373.L35
LAW      K      340, 342-349
Law, Military (gen.: pubn. 1801+)      UB465      343.01
Law, Military (Rus.: commentaries, digests, etc.)      UB655.A7-Z
Law, Naval (gen.)      VB350      359.13, 343.01+
Law, Naval (U.S.)      VB360      343.7301
Laws (engineer corps)      UG130-135
Laws (engineer corps: U.S.)      UG133 (PREFER KF7335.E5)
Laws, Ordnance      UF130-135
Lawyers (WWII)      D810.L4
Leadership, Military      UB210
Leadership (naval admin.: besides U.S.)      VB205.A-Z
Leadership (naval admin.: U.S.)      VB203
League of Nations Commission of Enquiry (Manchuria: Lytton Commission)
                              DS783.7.L4-45
Leaves, furloughs, etc. (air forces: gen.)      UG970
Leaves, furloughs, other inactive periods (mil.)      355.113
Lebanon      DS80-90      956.92
Lebanon (1861-1918: close of Turkish era)      DS85
Lebanon (1919-)      DS86      956.92034+
Leeward Islands (inclu. St. Thomas, Virgin Islands, etc.)      F2006      972.97
Legislative compendia (WWI: U.S.)      D570.A3
Legislative compendia (WWII: U.S.)      D769.A3
Lend-lease, mutual aid (WWII: U.S.-G.B.)      D753.2.G7
Lend-lease, mutual aid (WWII: U.S.-Rus.)      D753.2.R9
LENIN Vladimir Ilich (Rus.: 1894-1917: biog. & works)      DK254.L3-46
Leningrad area (Rus.)      DK511.L195
Leningrad, Rus.      947.45      DK541-579, DK568 (1801-)
Leningrad, Rus. (Rev., 1917-21)      DK265.8.L195
Leningrad, Siege of (WWII)      D764.3.L4
Leningrad, U.S.S.R.      DK541-579      947.45
Lesser Antilles & Caribbes      F2001-2151      972.9, .97-98
Lesser Antilles (by political group)      F2131-2151
Lesser Antilles (indiv. islands in alphab. order)      F2033-2129
Levant (WWII: dipl. history)      D754.L4
Lewis machine guns      UF620.L5
Lexington (aircraft carrier: U.S.: 1st with name: WWII)      D774.L4
Libraries (WWI)      D639.L5 (PREFER Z675.W2)
Libya      961.2      DT211-239, DT224
Libya (1911-52: Ital. rule)      961.203      DT235
Libya (1912-45)      DT235      961.203
Libya (mil. status)      UA868      355.0330612
Libya (WWII)      D766.93      940.5423, 961.203
Liechtenstein      DB540.5 (older titles), DB881-898      943.648
Liechtenstein (gen. hist. & descr.)      DB886, 891

LITHUANIA        DK511.L2-28 (earlier pubns.), DK505        947.5
Lithuania (1800-1918)        DK505.73
Lithuania (1914-19)        DK511.L26
Lithuania (1918-40)        DK505.74-76
Lithuania (1919-)        DK511.L27
Lithuania (1940+)        DK505.77-79
Lithuania (post-WWII territorial ?s)        D821.L5
Lithuania (WWII: Reconstruction)        D829.L5
Little Entente (1919)        D460
Little Russia (Ukraine)        947.71        DK508
Litvinov, Maksim M. (Rus.: 1925-53 era)        DK268.L5
Liverpool, Eng. (WWII)        D760.8.L6
Living conditions (air forces)        358.4112
Living conditions (marines)        359.9612        VE420-425
Living conditions, Military        355.12        U750-773, U750, U765
Living conditions (navies)        359.12        V720-743, V720 (gen.), V735 (modern),
                                V736 (U.S.), V737 (G.B.)
Living conditions (navies: partic. situations)        359.129
Lloyd George, David (G.B.: 20th c.)        DA566.9.L5
Loading & unloading nautical craft (plus cargo handling)        623.8881        VK235
Local government (WWII: U.S.)        D769.8.L6
LOCAL HISTORY (Algeria: towns etc.)        DT299.A-Z
Local history (Arabian Penin.: cities)        DS248.A-Z
Local history (Arabian Penin.: regions, sultanates, etc.: by place)        DS247.A-Z
Local history (Arg.: provinces, regions, etc.: alphab. order)        F2850-2991
Local history (Arg.: towns etc.)        F3011.A-Z
Local history (Armenian S. S. R.)        DK689
Local history (Australia)        DU145-398
Local history (Bel.: provinces, regions, etc.)        DH801.A-Z
Local history (Bel.: towns except Brussels)        DH811.A-Z
Local history (Bismarck Arch.: islands, groups, etc. by name)        DU553.A-Z
Local history (Br. Colum.: towns, cities, etc.)        F1089.5.A-Z
Local history (Br. N. Borneo)        DS646.335.A-Z
Local history (Brazil: regions, states, etc.)        F2541-2636+
Local history (Bulg.)        DR95-98
Local history (Calif.: regions, counties, etc.)        F868.A-Z
Local history (Calif.: towns etc.)        F869.A-Z
Local history (Caroline Islands: islands, groups, towns, etc.)        DU568.A-Z
Local history (China: cities & towns)        DS796.A-Z
Local history (China: dependencies, provinces, areas, etc.)        DS793.A-Z
Local history (Croatia)        DR1620-1636+
Local history (Den.: counties, islands, regions)        DL271.A-Z
Local history (Den.: towns etc.)        DL291
Local history (Dutch E. Ind.: islands, regions, etc.)        DS647.A-Z
Local history (Egypt: cities, towns, other)        DT154.A-Z
Local history (Egypt: provinces, regions, etc.)        DT137.A-Z
Local history (Eng.: towns besides London)        DA690.A-Z        942.2+
Local history (Ethiopia: kingdoms, regions, towns, etc.)        DT390.A-Z        963.056
Local history (Eur. Russia, Poland: provinces, governments, regions, etc.)
                                DK511.A-Z
Local history (Fin.: regions, provinces, etc.)        DL1170.A-Z
Local history (Fin.: towns except Helsinki)        DL1180.A-Z
Local history (Florida: regions, counties, etc.)        F317.A-Z
Local history (Florida: towns etc.)        F319.A-Z

Local history (Fr. Indoch.: regions: earlier titles: by place)      DS557.A-Z
Local history (Fr. Indoch.: towns: earlier works)      DS558.A-Z
Local history (Fr.: north, east, Riviera, etc.)      DC601-609+
Local history (Fr.: regions, prov.'s, depts., etc.: by name)      DC611.A-Z
Local history (Fr.: towns besides Paris)      DC801.A-Z
Local history (G.B.: counties, regions, etc.: by name)      DA670.A-Z   942+
Local history (Ger.: areas, towns except Berlin)      DD901.A-Z
Local history (Ger.: large areas)      DD701-800
Local history (Ger.: provinces, regions, states, etc.)      DD801.A-Z
Local history (Greece: regions, islands, provinces, etc.)      DF901.A-Z
Local history (Hawaii: islands, counties, etc.)      DU628.A-Z
Local history (Hawaii: towns, volcanoes, etc.)      DU629.A-Z
Local history (Ice.)      DL396-398
Local history (Ice.: towns etc.)      DL398.A-Z
Local history (India, Burma, etc.)      DS486.A-Z
Local history (India, Pak., Burma, Ceylon, Indian Ocean islands, etc.)   DS485-498
Local history (Indian region kingdom, states, etc.)      DS485.A-Z
Local history (It.: large areas, cities)      DG600-980
Local history (It.: non-metro. towns, provinces, etc.)      DG975.A-Z
Local history (Jam.: regions, islands, etc.)      F1891.A-Z
Local history (Jam.: towns etc.)      F1895.A-Z
Local history (Japan: islands, provinces, regions)      DS895.A-Z
Local history (Japan: towns & cities)      DS897.A-Z
Local history (Java, Indon.)      DS646.29.A-Z
Local history (Libya)      DT238-239
Local history (Libya: towns etc.)      DT239.A-Z
Local history (London, Eng.)      DA675-689      942.1
Local history (Malay Penin.: protectorates, regions, settlements)   DS598.A-Z
Local history (Malay Penin.: towns etc.)      DS599.A-Z
Local history (Mariana Is.: islands, towns, etc.)      DU648.A-Z
Local history (Mex.: cities, towns, etc. except for Mex. City)   F1391.A-Z
Local history (Morocco: cities, towns, etc.)      DT329.A-Z
Local history (N. Australia: regions, towns, etc.)      DU398.A-Z
Local history (N. Viet.: cities etc.)      DS560.92.A-Z
Local history (N. Viet.: regions etc.)      DS560.9.A-Z
Local history (N. Zea.: regions, towns, dependencies, etc. except Wellington)
                                                            DU430.A-Z
Local history (N.Y.: cities, towns, etc. except N.Y.C.)      F129.A-Z
Local history (N.Y.: regions, counties, etc.)      F127.A-Z
Local history (Neth.: islands, provinces, regions, etc.)      DJ401.A-Z
Local history (Neth.: towns, cities, etc.)      DJ411.A-Z
Local history (New Mex.: towns etc.)      F804.A-Z
Local history (New S. Wales, Aust.: towns, regions, etc. except Sydney)
                                                            DU180.A-Z
Local history (Nor.: counties, regions, etc.)      DL576.A-Z
Local history (Nor.: towns, villages, etc.)      DL596.A-Z
Local history (Palestine: regions, towns, etc.)      DS110.A-Z
Local history (Pan.: provinces, regions, etc.)      F1569.A-Z
Local history (Paris, Fr.)      DC701-790+      944.36
Local history (Philip.: islands, provinces, regions)      DS688.A-Z
Local history (Philip.: towns & cities)      DS689.A-Z
Local history (Pol.)      DK4600-4800
Local history (Pol.: provinces)      DK4600.A-Z
Local history (Port.: regions, provinces, areas)   DP702.A-Z
Local history (Prus.: provinces, regions, etc.)   DD491.A-Z

Local history (Puerto R.: regions, towns, etc.)    F1981.A-Z
Local history (Queens., Aust.: all except Brisbane)        DU280.A-Z
Local history (Rum.)          DR281-296
Local history (Rus. Rev., 1905-6: by place)    DK264.2.A-Z
Local history (Rus. Rev., 1917-21: by place)    DK265.8.A-Z
Local history (Rus.: towns other than Moscow in Eur., Pol. areas)        DK651.A-Z
Local history (Russia)    DK501-973+
Local history (S. Australia except Adelaide)    DU330.A-Z
Local history (S.Am.: regions)      F2212-2217
Local history (Samoan Is.: partic. islands, towns, etc.)    DU819.A3-Z
Local history (Scotland: counties, regions, etc.)    DA880.A-Z
Local history (Serbia)    DR2075-2125
Local history (Siberia: provinces, regions, etc.)    DK771.A-Z
Local history (Siberia: towns etc.)    DK781.A-Z
Local history (Sp. Civil War, 1936-39: by place name)    DP269.27.A-Z
Local history (Sp.: provinces, regions, etc.)    DP302.A-Z
Local history (Sp.: towns except Madrid)    DP402.A-Z
Local history (Sumatra, Indon.)    DS646.15.A-Z
Local history (Swe.)    DL971-991
Local history (Swit.: cantons, cantonal capitals)    DQ301-800
Local history (Swit.: lakes, peaks, regions)    DQ841.A-Z (SEE ALSO DQ820+ for
                                                                    more Alps #s)
Local history (Swit.: towns except cantonal capitals)    DQ851.A-Z (SEE DQ301-
                                                                    800 for canton capitals)
Local history (Tasmania: regions, towns, etc.)    DU480.A-Z
Local history (Texas: regions, counties, etc.)    F392.A-Z
Local history (Texas: towns etc.)    F394.A-Z
Local history (Thai.)    DS588-589
Local history (Tur.: Eur. regions: by name)    DR701.A-Z
Local history (Ukraine: regions, oblasts, etc.)    DK508.9.A-Z
Local history (Ukraine: towns etc.)    DK508.95.A-Z
Local history (Victoria, Aust.: all except Melbourne)    DU230.A-Z
Local history (Viet.: cities, towns, etc.)    DS559.93.A-Z
Local history (Viet.: regions, protectorates, etc.)    DS559.92.A-Z
Local history (Virginia: regions, counties, etc.)    F232.A-Z
Local history (Virginia: towns etc.)    F234.A-Z
Local history (W. Australia except Perth)    DU380.A-Z
Local history (Washington, D.C.: cemeteries, churches, hotels, statues, parks,
                                    circles, streets, etc.)    F203
Local history (Wash. state: regions, counties, etc.)    F897.A-Z
Local history (Wash. state: towns etc.)    F899.A-Z
Local history (WWI: Calif.)    D570.85.C21.A-Z
Local history (WWI: England: by place)    D547.8.A-Z
Local history (WWI: Ger.: by place)    D538.5.A-Z
LOCAL HISTORY (WWII: Australia: by place)    D767.82.A-Z    994.1-8
Local history (WWII: Austria)    D765.45.A-Z
Local history (WWII: Bel.)    D763.B42
Local history (WWII: Calif.: by place)    D769.85.C21.A-Z
Local history (WWII: Cochin China: by place)    D767.352.A-Z
Local history (WWII: Czech.)    D765.55.A-Z
Local history (WWII: Den.: by place)    D763.D42.A-Z
Local history (WWII: Fin.)    D765.35.A-Z

Local history (WWII: Fr.: by place)    D762.A-Z    944.1-9+
Local history (WWII: G.B.: by place)    D760.8.A-Z    941.084, 942.084,
                                                         942.1-9+, 940.5341-5342+
Local history (WWII: Ger.: by place)    D757.9.A-Z    940.5343+, 943.1-9+
Local history (WWII: Greece)    D766.32.A-Z
Local history (WWII: Hung.)    D765.562.A-Z
Local history (WWII: It.: by place)    D763.I82.A-Z
Local history (WWII: Japan: by place)    D767.25.A-Z
Local history (WWII: Neth.: by place)    D763.N42.A-Z
Local history (WWII: New Britain)    D767.99.N415.A-Z
Local history (WWII: New Z.)    D767.852.A-Z
Local history (WWII: Nor.: by place)    D763.N62.A-Z
Local history (WWII: Pol.)    D765.2.A-Z
Local history (WWII: Rum.)    D766.42.A-Z
Local history (WWII: Rus.: by place)    D764.7.A-Z
Local history (WWI: U.S.: by state)    D570.85.A-W    974-979
Local history (WWII: U.S.: by state)    D769.85.A-W, F1-951+
Local history (WWII: Yug.)    D766.62.A-Z
Local history (Yug.)    DR381-396
Local history (Yug.: provinces, regions, etc.)    DR381.A-Z
Local history (Yug.: regions not limited to partic. sections or old republics)
                                                         DR1350.A-Z
Local history (Yug.: sections & old republics: Slovenia, Bosnia, Montenegro, etc.)
                                                         DR1352-2285+
Lodge, Henry Cabot (U.S.: 1865-1900 era)    E664.L7
Lodz Voivodeship (Pol.)    DK4600.L63
Logistics & support, Air force    358.4141    UG1100-1105
Logistics & troop movement    355.411
Logistics (mil. sci.)    U168    355.411
Logistics, Naval    V179    359.411
Logs, Nautical    VK581
Lombardy & Milan, It.    DG651-662
LONDON, Eng.    942.1    DA675-689, DA677 (gen.)
London, Eng. (1901-50)    DA684    942.1082
London, Eng. (1936-45)    942.1084    DA684
London, Eng. (boroughs, streets, etc.)    DA685.A-Z
London, Eng. (gen.)    DA677    942.1
London, Eng. (WWI)    D547.8.L7
London, Eng. (WWII)    D760.8.L7    942.1084, 940.534421
Long Island (N.Y.)    F127.L8    974.721
Long March (China: 1934-35: Communists)    DS777.5132-5139
Long March (China: 1934-35: Communists: gen.)    DS777.5134
Longitude & time at sea (marine navig.: inclu. tables)    VK567
Looting & other mil. crimes    UB789
Looting & other naval crimes    VB880
Lop-nor (China: lake)    DS793.L6
Loran tables (marine navig.: by region)    VK561.A2-Z
Loran tables (marine navig.: ca. 1932+: gen.)    VK561.A1
Los Alamos, New Mex.    F804.L6
Los Angeles, Calif.    F869.L8    979.494
Los Angeles County (Calif.)    F868.L8    979.493
Louisiana    F366-380, F369    976.3
Low Countries    DH-DJ
Lucerne, Lake (Swit.)    DQ841.L8
Lucerne, Swit.    DQ501-520    949.45

Ludendorff, Erich (Ger.: 1888-1918+ period)     DD231.L8
Lutheran Church (WWII)     D810.C66
LUXEMBOURG     949.35     DH901-925, DH916 (1815-)
Luxembourg (WWII: Grand Duchy)     D763.L9
Luxemburg     DH901-925
Luxemburg (1815-)     DH916
Luxemburg (gen.)     DH908     949.35
Luxemburg (gen. hist., culture, etc.)     DH905
Luzon (geog. & travel)     915.991     DS688.L9
Luzon (Philip.: inclu. Manila & Bataan)     959.91     DS688.L9
Lvov, Siege of (Polish wars, 1918-21)     DK4407.L9
Lyons, Fr.     DC801.L96-988
Lytton Commission (Manchuria: League of Nations Commission of Enquiry: summary
    & var. reports)     DS783.7.L45


M1 rifle     UD395.M17
Macao     DS796.M2     951.26
MacDonald, James Ramsay (G.B.: 20th c.)     DA566.9.M25
MACEDONIA     DR701.M13-42, DR2152-2285+     949.76
Macedonia (1912-45)     DR2230
Macedonia (1912-19)     DR2237
Macedonia (1919-45)     DR2240
Macedonia (1941-45: WWII)     DR2242
Macedonia (gen., descrip., culture, hist.)     DR2160, 2185
Macedonia (WWII: occupied terr.)     D802.M15
Machine-gun warfare     U167.5.M3
Machine guns (gen.)     UF620.A2     623.4424
Machine guns, Naval (gen.)     VF410.A2     623.4424
Machine guns (specific types) UF620.A3-Z
Machinists, Naval     VG800-805
Madagascar     DT469.M21-38     969.1
Madagascar (WWII)     D766.99.M3
Madeira Is.     DP702.M11-23
Madrid, Sp.     DP350-374     946.41
Madrid, Sp. (1801-1950)     DP361
Madrid, Sp. (area)     946.41     DP350-374, DP361
Madrid, Sp. (Civil War, 1936-39)     DP269.27.M3
Magazines & serial pubns. (WWI)     940.4005     D501
Magazines & serial pubns. (WWII)     940.54005     D731
Magazines, armories, etc. (countries except U.S.)     UF545.A-Z
Magazines, Ordnance (navies: gen.)     VF380     359.75
Maginot Line (Fr.: fortific's.: engineering)     623.1944     UG429.F, UG430.M
Mail, Military     355.693
Mail, Military (navies)     359.693
Maine     974.1     F16-30, F19 (gen.), F25 (1865-1950)
Maine (1865-1950)     F25
Maine (gen.)     F19

MAINTENANCE & building devices & procedures, Marine (engin.)   VM901-965
Maintenance & repair (aircraft)     629.1346
Maintenance & repair (naut. engineering)        623.8208 (SEE ALSO .00288 after
                                                 1988)        VM763 (engines)
Maintenance & repair, Naval (yards etc.)     VC417
Maintenance & repair (ordnance)     623.48        UF350-355, UF550-560
Maintenance & repair (small craft)     VM322
MAINTENANCE & TRANSPORT (mil.: Asia)   UC234-245
Maintenance & transport (mil.: Australia)     UC255
Maintenance & transport (mil.: Can.)     UC90-93
Maintenance & transport (mil.: Eur.)     UC158-233
Maintenance & transport (mil.: G.B.)     UC184-187
Maintenance & transport (mil.: Ger.)     UC180-183
Maintenance & transport (mil.: Japan)     UC241
Maintenance & transport (mil.: New Z.)        UC256.5
Maintenance & transport (mil.: Pac. islands)     UC257-258
Maintenance & transport (mil.: Rus.)     UC208-211
Maintenance & transport (mil.: U.S.)     UC20-88
Maintenance & transport (mil.: U.S.: by time period)   UC23
Maintenance & transport, Military     UC
MAINTENENCE, NAVAL        VC        359.6-8
Maintenance, Naval (Asia)     VC230-245
Maintenance, Naval (Australia)     VC255-256   359.60944
Maintenance, Naval (Can.)        VC90-93
Maintenance, Naval (China)     VC235
Maintenance, Naval (Eur.)     VC160-229
Maintenance, Naval (Fr.)     VC176-179
Maintenance, Naval (G.B.)     VC184-187        359.60941
Maintenance, Naval (Ger.)     VC180-183        359.60943
Maintenance, Naval (Ger.: by region or area)     VC183.A-Z
Maintenance, Naval (It.)        VC196-199
Maintenance, Naval (Japan)        VC241        359.60952
Maintenance, Naval (New Z.)        VC256.5
Maintenance, Naval (Rus.)     VC208-211
Maintenance, Naval (U.S.)     VC20-65
Malacca, Malay Penin.     DS599.M3
MALAY Archipelago & Indonesia     DS600-605        959.8
Malay Archipelago (gen.)        DS603
Malay Peninsula, Malaya, & the Straits        DS591-599        959.5
Malay Peninsula (to 1946)     DS596.5        959.503
Malay Peninsula (WWII)        D767.5        959.503
Malaya & Malay Peninsula (gen.)        DS596
Malaya (mil. status)     UA853.M3
Malaya (WWII: occupied terr.)        D802.M2
Malaysia     959.5        DS591-599, DS592, DS596
Malaysia & Singapore (tide & current tables)     VK710
Malaysia (to 1946)     959.503        DS596, DS596.6
Malaysia (WWII: gen. particip.)     940.535951        D767.5, DS596, DS598-
                                                 599 (local, A-Z)
Malaysia (WWII: mil. hist.)     940.5409595        D767.5
Maldive Islands        DS491.M3

MALTA     945.85     DG994
Malta & Maltese Islands     DG987-999
Malta (1798-1964: Brit. era)     DG992.7
Malta (1802-1947)     DG993
Malta (20th c.)     DG994
Malta (gen.)     DG990
Malta (geog. & travel)     914.585     DG989
Malta (WWII)     D763.M3
Manchester, Eng. (WWII)     D760.8.M3
Manchoukuo (1932-45: P'u-i era)     DS784
Manchuria     951.803-804     DS781-784.2+, DS784 (1932-45)
Manchuria (19th-20th c.)     DS783.7
Manchuria (geog. & travel)     915.18     DS784
Manchuria (WWII: gen. particip.)     940.53518     DS784
Manchuria (WWII: occupied terr.)     D802.M25
Mandates (post-WWI)     940.31426     D651
Mandates (post-WWII)     940.531426
MANEUVERS, Air force (training)     358.4152
Maneuvers & tactics (armor & cavalry: Asia)     UE270-280
Maneuvers & tactics (armor & cavalry: by place) UE160-302
Maneuvers & tactics (artillery: Asia)     UF270-280
Maneuvers & tactics (artillery: Eur.)     UF215-269
Maneuvers & tactics (marines)     VE157     359.9642, .9652
Maneuvers, drills, & tactics (artillery: gen.)     UF157
Maneuvers, drills, & tactics (infantry: gen.)     UD157     356.18, 355.42
Maneuvers (mil. engineering)     UG320-325
Maneuvers (mil. sci.)     U250-255
Maneuvers (mil. sci.: gen.)     U250     355.52
Maneuvers (mil. sci.: places besides U.S.)     U255.A-Z
Maneuvers (mil. sci.: U.S.)     U253
Maneuvers, Naval     V245, U260-262 (combined — army, navy, air forces — or
                amphibious warfare ops.)     359.52
Maneuvers, Naval (training)     359.52     V245
Manila, Philip.     DS689.M2     959.91
Mannerheim, Carl (Fin.: 20th c.)     DK461.M32
Manning of vessels (merch. marine)     VK221
Manpower (by country)     UA17.5.A3-Z
Manpower (gen.)     UA17.5.A2     355.22, .61
Manual of arms (infantry: U.S.)     UD323-324
Manual of arms (marines)     VE320     359.968240202
Manual of arms (naval seamen)     VD320     359.5470202, .8240202
MANUALS & handbooks (marines: gen.)     VE150     359.960202
Manuals & handbooks (marines: places besides U.S.)     VE155.A-Z
Manuals & handbooks (mil. hygiene: not Eng. or Am.)     UH625
Manuals & handbooks (naval ordnance: places besides U.S.)     VF155.A-Z
Manuals & handbooks (naval ordnance: U.S.)     VF153
Manuals & handbooks, Soldiers' (U.S.)     U113
Manuals & regulations, Air force (gen.)     UG670
Manuals, Armor & Cavalry     UE150-155
Manuals (artillery)     UF150-155     358.120202
Manuals, Infantry     UD150-155
Manuals, Infantry (places besides U.S.)     UD155.A-Z
Manuals, medical & surgical (navies: besides U.S.)     VG465.A-Z
Manuals (mil. engineering)     UG150-155

Manuals, Naval ordnance (U.S.: by mm., cm., inches, or lbs.)    VF393.A4-6
Manuals (naval seamen: gen.)    VD150, V110+, V120+ (SEE ALSO V110+ &
                                V120+)    359.00202, .40202
Manuals (naval seamen: places except U.S.)    VD155.A-Z
Manuals (naval seamen: U.S.)    VD153    359.402020973
Manuals (U.S. Marines)    VE23.A48
Manufacture (naval ordnance & arms: gen.)    VF370
Manufacture (ordnance & small arms: gen.)    UF530    623.4+, 338.476234
Manufacture (small arms & ordnance: U.S.: by state)    UF534.A-W
Manufacturers (small arms & ordnance)    UF537.A-Z
Manzanar Internment Camp (Calif.)    940.531779487
Mao Tse Tung (China: 1893-1976: SEE DS777.488.C5 for Chiang Kai Shek)
                                                    DS778.M3
Map maneuvers & problems    U312
Mapping & surveying, Military (U.S.)    UG472
Maps & atlases    912    G
Maps & atlases (WWI)    D522.3, G1037 (PREFER)
Maps & atlases (WWII)    D743.3, G1038 (PREFER)
Marblehead (cruiser: WWII)    D774.M3
Marching & guides (countries except U.S.)    UD315.A-Z
Marching & guides (mil.: gen.)    UD310
Marco Polo Bridge Incident (Sino-Jpn. Confl.: 1937)    DS777.533.M3
MARIANA ISLANDS (Ladrones: inclu. Guam)    DU640-648, DU643-5 996.7
Mariana Islands (mil. geog.)    355.47967    UA995.M
Mariana Islands (pilot & sailing guides)    VK933.M27
Mariana Islands (WWII: by specific is.)    D767.99.M272.A-Z, D767.99.A-Z (direct
                                alternatives, e.g. D767.99.G9 for Guam)
Mariana Islands (WWII: gen.)    D767.99.M27
Marianas (Ladrone Islands)    996.7    DU640-648, DU643-645
MARINE barracks & quarters (gen.)    VE420    359.961292, .9671
Marine camps (South Carolina: training)    VE434.S6    359.96709757
Marine Corps divisions (WWII: U.S.: by #)    D769.37.1st-
Marine Corps regiments (WWII: U.S.: by #)    D769.372.1st-
Marine Corps (WWII: U.S.: gen.)    D769.369
Marine drills (Asia: gen.)    VE270
Marine drills (by place)    VE160-302
Marine drills (Eur.: gen.)    VE215
MARINE ENGINEERING    VM600-989
Marine engineering (hist.: Australia)    VM721
Marine engineering (hist.: Eur.)    VM655
Marine engineering (hist.: Fr.)    VM671
Marine engineering (hist.: G.B.)    VM657    623.870941-870942
Marine engineering (hist.: gen.)    VM615
Marine engineering (hist.: Ger.)    VM673    623.870943
Marine engineering (hist.: It.)    VM679
Marine engineering (hist.: Japan)    VM699    623.870952
Marine engineering (hist.: Rus.)    VM685
Marine engineering (hist.: U.S.)    VM623-625
Marine engineering (instruction: U.S.)    VM727
Marine engines    VM731-779
Marine hydrography & surveying (gen.)    VK591
Marine lifesaving (hist's.)    VK1315
Marine military ops.    359.964    VE21-124 (by place)

Marine navigation & merchant marine     VK
Marine navigation & merchant marine (gen.: pubn. 1801+)     VK145     623.89
Marine navigation (instruction: by locale: inclu. merch. marine)     VK421-524
Marine navigation science     VK549-572
Marine regiments (U.S.: by #)     VE23.25.1st+
Marine training camps (U.S.: gen.)     VE432     359.9670973
Marine uniforms (U.S.)     VE403     359.96140973
MARINES     VE     359.96
Marines (Am.)     VE21
Marines & marine warfare     359.96 (add to .96 those #s after 355 in 355.1-.8)
                    VE, VE7-500+,VE15 (gen.), VE21-124 (by place), VE23 (U.S.),
                    VE57 (G.B.), VE145-146, VG90-95 (aviation)
Marines (Asia)     VE99-113
Marines (Australia & New Z.)     VE121-122.5
Marines (by geographic area)     VE21-124
Marines (Can.)     VE26
Marines (collected, nonserial titles)     VE7
Marines (Eng. & Wales)     VE59
Marines (Eur.)     VE55-96
Marines (G.B.)     VE57-64
Marines (gen. hist.)     VE15     359.96, .9609
Marines (gen.: pubn. 1801-1970)     VE145     359.9609
Marines (gen.: pubn. 1970+)     VE146     359.9609
Marines (Ger.)     VE73
Marines (It.)     VE79
Marines (Japan)     VE105     359.960952
Marines (misc. subjects: not A-Z)     VE500
Marines (N. Am.)     VE22
Marines (Rus.)     VE85
Marines (Scot.)     VE61
Marines (WWI: U.S.: inland ops.)     D570.348
Marines (WWII: U.S.: land ops. only)     D769.369-372 (SEE D767, D769.45, D774,
                    D790, U-V for naval or aerial ops.)
Maritime Provinces (Can.: Atlantic coast)     F1035.8     971.5-8
Marksmanship (marines: U.S.)     VE333     359.96547
Marksmanship (naval seamen: U.S.)     VD333
Marquesas Islands     DU700     996.31
Marseilles, Fr.     DC801.M34-38
Marshall Islands (inclu. Kwajalein Atoll)     DU710     996.83
Marshall Islands (WWII)     D767.99.M3
Marshall Islands (WWII: occupied terr.)     D802.M3
Maryland (battleship: U.S.: WWII)     D774.M35
Masaryk, Jan (Czech.: era of 1918-)     DB2191.M37
Masaryk, Tomas G. (Czech.: era of 1918-)     DB2191.M38
Massachusetts     974.4     F61-75, F64
Massachusetts     F61-75     974.4
Massachusetts (1865-1950)     F70 (SEE D570.85.M4-41 for war years, 1914-18
                    & D769.85.M4-41 for 1939-45)     974.404-043
Masters' manuals (merch. marine: inclu. command of ships)     VK205
Material, Naval (U.S. Navy. Office of: reports)     VA52.A68-69
Matériel & equipment (marines)     359.968     VE350-390, VF (ordnance)
Matériel & equipment, Air force     358.418     UG1100-1425+, UG1100-1105
Maui (Haw. Is.)     996.921     DU628.M3
Maui (Haw. Is.)     DU628.M3     996.921
Maurras, Charles M. (Fr.: 20th c.)     DC373.M3

Mauser rifle     UD395.M3
Maxim machine guns     UF620.M4
May 4th Movement (China: 20th c.)     DS777.43
Measurement of ships (naval architec.)     VM155
Mecca, Saudi Arabia     DS248.M4
Mechanical engineering (mil. applications)     UG450
Mechanical systems (naut. craft: engineering)     623.8501
Mechanized & armored cavalry     UE147     357.5, 358.18
Mechanized cavalry (gen. & ops.)     357.58     UE147-155, UE159,
          UE160-302 (by place)
Mechanized cavalry (jeep, truck, other large-motor vehicle troops)     357.54
          UC340-345, UG615-620
MEDALS, badges, brevets, etc. (navies: gen.)     VB330     359.1342
Medals, badges, decorations (WWII: by country)     D796.5.A-Z
Medals, badges, decorations (WWII: inclu. individual s & lists)     D796 (SEE ALSO
          D797 for older works)
Medals, decorations, badges, etc. (mil. rewards)     355.1342
Medals, decorations, etc. (mil.: U.S.)     UB433
Medals, decorations, other reward insignia (navies)     359.1342
Media & public relns. (mil.: gen.)     UH700     070.433, .449, 355.342
Media & public relns. (navies: gen.)     VG500     359.342, 070.433, .439
MEDICAL & health services, Air force     358.41345     UH201-655
Medical & health services, Military     355.345     UH201-629, UH215,
          UH223-225 (U.S.)
Medical & mental examinations (mil. recruits)     UB330-336
Medical & nursing services (navies)     359.345     VG100-475, VG115, VG121-
          224 (overall by place), VG123 (U.S.), VG350-355 (nurse corps)
Medical & relief services, Military     UH201-570
Medical & surgical handbooks (navies: gen.)     VG460     359.3450202,
          610.0202, 617.0260202
Medical biography, Military (indiv.: by name)     UH347.A-Z     355.3450924
Medical biography, Naval (U.S.: collective)     VG227.A1
Medical care for retired military     UB448-449
Medical care of veterans     UB368-369     355.115
Medical corps equipment (gen.)     UH510
Medical facilities, Naval     359.72     VG410-450, VG420 (U.S.), VG430 (G.B.)
Medical installations, Military     355.72     UH470-475
Medical schools, Army (places besides U.S.)     UH399.A-Z
Medical schools, Army (U.S.: gen.)     UH398
Medical services (air forces)     UG980-985     358.41345
MEDICAL SERVICES & RED CROSS (WWI: G.B.)     D629.G7
Medical services & Red Cross (WWI: U.S.: gen.)     D629.U6
Medical services & Red Cross (WWII: Australia)     D807.A8
Medical services & Red Cross (WWII: G.B)     D807.G7
Medical services & Red Cross (WWII: Hawaiian Islands)     D807.H3
Medical services & Red Cross (WWII: U.S.)     D807.U6-89
Medical services & Red Cross (WWII: U.S.: gen.)     D807.U6     940.547673
Medical services, hospitals, Red Cross (WWI)     D628-630     940.475+, .477+
Medical services, hospitals, Red Cross (WWII)     D806-807

MEDICAL SERVICES, MILITARY (Africa)    UH315-319
Medical services, Military (Asia)    UH299-313
Medical services, Military (Australia)    UH321-322
Medical services, Military (Can.)    UH226-227
Medical services, Military (China)    UH301-302
Medical services, Military (Egypt)    UH317-318
Medical services, Military (Eur.)    UH255-295
Medical services, Military (Eur.: gen.)    UH255    355.345094
Medical services, Military (Eur.: WWI)    UH256.1914-18
Medical services, Military (Eur.: WWII)    UH256.1939-45
Medical services, Military (Fr.)    UH271-272
Medical services, Military (G.B.: gen.)    UH257    355.3450941
Medical services, Military (Ger.)    UH273-274    355.3450943
Medical services, Military (hist., statistics, etc.: gen. & by place)    UH215-324
Medical services, Military (Japan)    UH305-306    355.3450952
Medical services, Military (misc. Asian lands)    UH313.A-Z
Medical services, Military (New Z.)    UH322.5
Medical services, Military (Pac. islands)    UH323-324
Medical services, Military (Philippines)    UH313.P5
Medical services, Military (Rus.)    UH285-286
Medical services, Military (Rus.: Asia)    UH309-310
Medical services, Military (Scandin.)    UH286.5
Medical services, Military (Tur.)    UH311-312
Medical services, Military (U.S.)    UH223-225    355.3450973
Medical services, Military (U.S.: official reports)    UH223.A1-49
Medical services, Military (U.S.: unofficial)    UH223.A6-Z
Medical services, Military (U.S.: WWI)    UH224.1917-18
Medical services, Military (U.S.: WWII)    UH224.1941-45
MEDICAL SERVICES, NAVAL    VG100-475 (SEE ALSO UH201-515)
Medical services, Naval (Asia)    VG199-213
Medical services, Naval (Australia)    VG221
Medical services, Naval (Eur.)    VG155-196
Medical services, Naval (G.B.)    VG157
Medical services, Naval (Ger.)    VG173
Medical services, Naval (Japan)    VG205
Medical services, Naval (Rus.)    VG185
Medical services, Naval (U.S.)    VG123    359.3450973
Medical services (WWI: hospitals)    940.476    D628-629
Medical services (WWI: particular countries)    940.4754-4759    D629.A-Z
Medical services (WWI: Rus.)    940.47547    D629.R9
Medical services (WWI: U.S.)    940.47573    D629.U6-8
MEDICAL SERVICES (WWII: G.B.)    940.547541    D807.G7
Medical services (WWII: Ger.)    940.547543    D807.G3
Medical services (WWII: hospitals)    940.5476    D806
Medical services (WWII: hospitals, British)    940.547641    D807.G7
Medical services (WWII: hospitals, German)    940.547643    D807.G3
Medical services (WWII: hospitals, Japanese)    940.547652    D807.J3
Medical services (WWII: hospitals, Russian)    940.547647    D807.R9
Medical services (WWII: hospitals, United States)    940.547673    D807.U6-87
Medical services (WWII: Japan)    940.547552    D807.J3
Medical services (WWII: particular countries)    940.54754-54759    D807.A-Z
Medical services (WWII: Rus.)    940.547547    D807.R9
Medical supplies    355.88    UH440-445
Medical supplies, Naval    359.88    VG290-295

MEDICINE      610-619      R
Medicine, Military (gen., hdbks., etc.)    UH390-396
Medicine, Military (places besides U.S.: manuals etc.)    UH395.A-Z
Medicine, Military (U.S.: official manuals etc.)    UH393
Medicine, Military (U.S.: unofficial manuals etc.)  UH394
Medicine, psychiatry, & nursing    R      610-619, 649
MEDITERRANEAN Region (Eastern)     956.9      DS80-151+, DS62
Mediterranean Sea (lighthouses, beacons, foghorns, etc.: lists)    VK1176
                                               623.8944091638
Mediterranean Sea (mil. status)    UA646.55    355.03301638, 359.471638
Mediterranean Sea (pilot & sailing guides)    VK853-874    623.89291638, .8929448
Mediterranean Sea (tide & current tables)    VK653-674
Mediterranean, Eastern (geog. & travel)      915.69      DS44, DS49, D972-973
MEETINGS (CNCL. FOR. MIN.: Berlin: 1954: 25Jan.-18 Feb.)      D814.47
Meetings (Cncl. For. Min.: London: 1945: 11 Sept.-2 Oct.)            D814.413
Meetings (Cncl. For. Min.: London: 1947: 25 Nov.-16 Dec.)    D814.45
Meetings (Cncl. For. Min.: Moscow: 1945: 16-26 Dec.)        D814.415
Meetings (Cncl. For. Min.: Moscow: 1947: 10 Mar.-24 Apr.)     D814.44
Meetings (Cncl. For. Min.: New York: 1946: Nov.-Dec.)    D814.43
Meetings (Cncl. For. Min.: Paris: 1946: Apr.)          D814.42
Meetings (Cncl. For. Min.: Paris: 1946: 15 June-July)    D814.425
Meetings (Cncl. For. Min.: Paris: 1949: 23 May-20 June)    D814.46
MEETINGS (NAZI PARTY: Ger.: 1923)       DD253.28.1923
Meetings (Nazi Party: Ger.: 1926)      DD253.28.1926
Meetings (Nazi Party: Ger.: 1927)    DD253.28.1927
Meetings (Nazi Party: Ger.: 1929)    DD253.28.1929
Meetings (Nazi Party: Ger.: 1933-38)      DD253.28.1933-38
Meetings (Nazi Party: Ger.: gen.)        DD253.27
MELANESIA     993.2-993.7 (PREFER 995 after 1988)      DU490 (gen.)
Melanesia & New Zealand (mil. geog.)      355.4793
Melanesia (gen)  DU490 (SEE DU520-950 for specific islands, groups, atolls, etc.)
                                               993, 993.2-7, 996.1
Melanesia (geog. & travel)      919.32-37
Melanesia, New Guinea & Oceania      995 (SEE ALSO 993.2-7 for titles on Mel. &
                          New G. before 1989; 990 for gen. titles on Oceania
                          prior to 1989)        DU739-746, DU739
Melanesia (WWII: gen. particip.)     940.5393     DU940
Melbourne, Australia       DU228    994.51
Melbourne, Australia (WWII)     D767.82.M44     994.51
Memorials, monuments, celebrations (WWI: gen.)     D663 (SEE ALSO D503 for
                               museums & NA9325 for fine arts)
Memorials, monuments, celebrations (WWII: G.B.: local: by place)    D838.G7.A-Z
Memorials, monuments, celebrations (WWII: gen.)    D830    940.5465
Memorials, monuments, celebrations (WWII: misc.)    D831
Memorials, monuments, celebrations (WWII: U.S.)    D833-836    940.546573
Mennonites (WWII)      D810.C665
Mental & medical examinations (mil. recruits: gen.)    UB330      355.2236
Mental health, psychiatry, etc. (mil.: gen.)      UH629

MERCHANT MARINE & navigation (20th c.: hist. & conditions)     VK20
Merchant marine & navigation (gen. hist's.)     VK15
Merchant marine & navigation (gen. special)     VK147
Merchant marine & navigation (hist. & conditions: by area or country)  VK21-124
Merchant marine & navigation (instruction: U.S.)     VK423
Merchant marine & navigation (study & teaching: gen.)     VK401
Merchant marine (occupation)     VK160     387.0023
Merchant ships, Powered (engineering)     623.824
Messes & clubs, Naval officers' (gen.)     VC380     359.346
Messing (mil.: cooking: U.S.)     UC723
Metal ships (naval architec.)     VM146-147     623.8182
Metals (mil. raw materials)     355.242
Meteorology, Aviation     629.1324
Meteorology, Military     UG467
Methodist Church (WWII)     D810.C67
Meuse, Battle of the (Monthermé: 1940)     D756.5.M4
Mexican-Americans (WWII: as troops)     D769.88.M4     940.5404
Mexican & Central American coasts (pilot & sailing guides)     VK969-970
MEXICO     F1201-1392     972-972.7
Mexico (1910-46)     F1234     972.081-082
Mexico (1917-64)     972.082     F1234-1235
Mexico & Central America (geog. & travel)     917.2     F1215 (Mexico), F1432 (C.Am.)
Mexico (mil. status)     UA603-605
Mexico (overall)     972     F1201-1392, F1208, F1226
Mexico (WWII)     D768.2     940.5372
Mexico (WWII: dipl. hist.)     940.532572 (could be with Allies at .532272)     D754.M
Mexico City area (Mex.)     F1386     972.53
Miami, Florida     975.9381     F319.M6
Michael (Rum.: regent period, 1927-3; King, 1940-47)     DR265
Michigan (inclu. Lakes Mich. & Huron)     F561-575, F566     977.4
MICRONESIA     996.5     DU500 (gen.)
Micronesia & Polynesia (mil. geog.)     355.4796
Micronesia, Eastern     996.8
Micronesia, Eastern (Ellice, Gilbert, Marshall Is.: WWII: gen. particip.)
                              940.53968          D767.917 (Gilb's.),
                              D767.99.M3 (Marshalls), DU500 (Micro.), DU590 (Ell. Is.),
                              DU615 (Gilb's.), DU710 (Marshalls)
Micronesia (gen.)          DU500 (SEE DU520-950 for particular islands, island
                              groups, atolls, etc.)     996.5-68
Micronesia (geog. & travel)     919.65     DU500
Micronesia (naval geog.)     359.47965     VA750.M
Micronesia (WWII: gen. particip.)     940.53965     DU500
MIDDLE Atlantic states & District of Columbia     F116-205
Middle East (Near East)     956     DS41-326
Middle East (1918-45)     956.03     DS62.4
Middle East & Southwestern Asia     DS41-329     953, 955, 956
Middle East (geog. & travel)     915.6     DS49-49.5
Middle West & Mississippi River Valley (1865-1950)     F354     977.03
Midway, Battle of (1942)     D774.M5
Midway Islands (Haw. Is.)     DU628.M5     996.99
Midway Islands (WWII)     D767.94
Mihailovic, Draza (Yug.: 1918-45 era)     DR359.M5, DR1294.M54
Milan, It.     DG660-662

Militarism & antimilitarism (inclu. mil.-indus. complex)   355.0213   JX1952,
                                          JX1963, UA23, U21.5, JF195.C5
MILITARY ADMINISTRATION         355.6        UB-UC
Military administration (Africa)      UB115-119
Military administration (Asia)        UB99-113
Military administration (Australia)   UB121-122        354.94066
Military administration (Belg.)          UB67-68
Military administration (by country)   UB21-124
Military administration (Can.)           UB26-27
Military administration (China)       UB101-102        354.51066
Military administration (civil sections)    UB180-197
Military administration (Den.)           UB69-70
Military administration (Eur.)           UB55-95
Military administration (Fr.)         UB71-72      354.44066
Military administration (G.B.)        UB57-64
Military administration (G.B.: by time period)       UB58.1900+
Military administration (G.B.: Eng. & Wales)       UB59
Military administration (G.B.: Scot.)            UB61
Military administration (gen.: pubn. 1801-1970)   UB145   355.6
Military administration (gen.: pubn. 1971+)       UB146   355.6
Military administration (Ger.)        UB73-74      354.43066, 355.60943
Military administration (Greece)          UB75-76
Military administration (India)           UB103-104
Military administration (It.)         UB79-80
Military administration (Japan)       UB105-106        354.52066, 355.60952
Military administration (Lat.Am.)     UB27.5-54
Military administration (misc. Asian lands)   UB113.A-Z
Military administration (misc. Eur. lands)   UB95.A-Z
Military administration (New Z.)      UB122.5
Military administration (Norway)      UB81-82
Military administration (Pac. islands)   UB123-124
Military administration (Pol.)            UB95.P7
Military administration (Rus.: Asia & Sib.)   UB109-110
Military administration (Rus.: Eur.)     UB85-86      354.47066
Military administration (Scan.: gen.)    UB86.5
Military administration (Sp.)            UB87-88
Military administration (U.S.)        UB23-25      353.6, 355.60973
Military administration (U.S.: by state)       UB24.A-W
Military air transport (U.S.)                 UC333-334      358.440973
Military & marine engineering       623      UG; VM
Military & nautical engineering (hist. & biog. works: overall)   623.009+   UG400-401
Military & nautical engineering (overall topics)   623.04
MILITARY & NAVAL HISTORY (Arg.)       F2832
Military & naval history (Brazil)        F2522
Military & naval history (Cuba)          F1776.1
Military & naval history (G.B.: 20th c.)       DA566.5
Military & naval history (Mex.)          F1227.5
Military & naval history (Philip.: inclu. battles vs. Sp. & U.S.)   DS682-684 (PREFER
          E717.7 for Battle of Manila Bay [1898] & U.S.-Sp. naval confront.)

MILITARY & NAVAL LIFE & customs (WWI: Ger.)      940.48443        D532-538,
                                                 D581-582 (naval), D604 (aerial)
Military & naval life & customs (WWI: U.S.)   940.48373    D570, D589.U6-7 (naval),
                                                 D606 (aerial)
Military & naval life & customs (WWII: G.B.)      940.548341      U767, V737
Military & naval life & customs (WWII: Ger.)      940.548443      U769, V739
Military & naval life & customs (WWII: Japan)     940.548452      U773, V743.J3
Military & naval life & customs (WWII: Rus.)      940.548347      U771, V741
Military & naval science    355-359     U, V
Military animals (gen.)       UH87       355.24
Military artificers & technical troops (places besides U.S.)      UG505.A-Z
Military barracks & camps (U.S.)         UC403-404        355.70973
Military bases, camps, forts, reservations, etc. (geog. & hist. applic.)      355.709
MILITARY BIOGRAPHY      923.5 (SEE ALSO 355.0092, 940.3+, .53+, etc.)      U51-55
Military biography (Asia)        923.55
Military biography (China)       923.551    DS738 (group)
Military biography (G.B.)        923.541-542      DA54 (collec.), DA69.3.A-Z (20th c.:
                                 indiv.), DA89.1.A-Z (naval: 20th c.: indiv.), U55.G7
Military biography (Ger.)        923.543    DD100 (group)
Military biography (Japan)       923.552    DS838-839
Military biography (Rus.)        923.547    DK50.5-8
Military biography (U.S.)        923.573    E181 (mil.: collec.), E182 (naval:
                                 collec.), U52-53
Military biography (U.S.: collective)    U52
Military bridges (design)        623.67     UG335, UC320-325
Military capability       355.0332+
Military clothing & equipment (U.S.)     UC463-464
Military clubs (U.S.)     U56
Military commissions (by country except U.S., for which SEE KF7661)      UB875.A-Z
Military communications (except U.S.: by country)      UA945.A-Z
Military communications (gen.)      UA940       355.27, .41, .6
Military construction (U.S.: gen.)      UC46 (SEE ALSO UG for engineer., VC420+ &
                                 VG590+ for naval)      358.22
Military crimes (countries outside U.S.)      UB785.A-Z
Military crimes (U.S.)      UB783 (SEE ALSO KF7615-7618)
Military decorations, medals, rewards, etc.      UB430-435      355.1342
Military discipline      UB790-795      343.014, .13325
MILITARY EDUCATION & training (gen.)      U400      355.07
Military education (Asia: gen.)      U635
Military education (Can.)      U440-444
Military education (China: gen.)      U640
Military education (Eur.: gen.)      U505
Military education (G.B.: gen.)      U510
Military education (Ger.: gen.)      U570
Military education (Ger.: special topics)      U572.A-Z
Military education (Japan: gen.)      U650
Military education (U.S.: Command & Gen. Staff Coll.)      U415
Military education (U.S.: gen.)      U408      355.0071073

MILITARY ENGINEERING          623.1-7        UG
Military engineering, air forces, & air warfare   UG    358.2, 623, 358.4 (air forces etc.)
Military engineering & air forces      UG
Military engineering (Asia: gen.)      UG99
Military engineering (collections)      UG7
Military engineering (Eur.: gen.)      UG55
Military engineering (field: gen.)      UG360
Military engineering (G.B.: by #'d regiment)        UG57.Z6.1st+
Military engineering (Japan: by #'d regiment)       UG105.Z6.1st+
Military engineering (misc.)        623.7
Military engineering (U.S.: by #'d regiment)   UG125.1st+
Military engineering (U.S.: gen.)            UG23
Military engineering maneuvers (U.S.)   UG323
Military engineering manuals (U.S.)        UG153
Military enginering (Ger.: by #'d regiment)        UG73.Z6.1st+
Military equipment (U.S.)        UC523-524        355.80973
Military expeditions        U265
Military explosives, unguided rockets, etc.   UF860-880
Military flags, colors, standards (gen.)        UC590        355.15
Military footwear (U.S.)        UC493
Military forces & science        355-358        U
Military fortifications, Permanent (engineering)    623.12 (for titles after 1988 SEE
                                    ALSO .1)    UG405
Military fortifications, Temporary (engineering)    623.15        UG403
Military geography        UA985-997        355.47+, .0330+, 359.47+
Military geography (except U.S.)        UA995.A-Z
Military geography (U.S.)        UA993        355.4773, 359.4773
Military headgear        UC500
Military headquarters ops. (gen.: inclu. aides, adjutants, etc.)        UB230
MILITARY HISTORY (1801-1914/20)        D361        355.033003+
Military history (20th c.)        D431        355.020904, 355.009, 355.033+
Military history (Australia)        DU112.3        355.00994, .033094
Military history (Bel.: 1815-)        DH545
Military history (Bel.: gen.)        DH540
Military history (Bulg.)        DR70
Military history (Can.)        F1028        355.00971
Military history (China: 20th c. & 1912-49)        DS775.4
Military history (Den.)            DL154
Military history (Dutch E. Ind.)        DS636
Military history (Egypt)        DT81
Military history (Fin.)        DL1036-1037        355.0094897
Military history (Formosa: 1895-1945)        DS799.714
Military history (Fr. Indoch.)        DS544
Military history (Fr.)        DC44-47
Military history (Fr.: 1871-1940)        DC339
Military history (Fr.: 19th-20th c.)        DC47
Military history (Fr.: 20th c.)        DC367
Military history (G.B.)        DA50-69.3
Military history (G.B.: 20th. c.: gen.)        DA69        355.00941, .033041, .033241,
                                    .033541
Military history (Ger.)        DD99-105
Military history (Ger.: 20th c.)        DD104        355.00943, .033043, .033242, .033543
Military history (Greece)        DF765
Military history (India: 1901-)        DS442.6

```
Military history (It.)            DG48-84
Military history (It.: 1792-20th c.)   DG484
Military history (Japan: 1868+)    DS838.7   355.00952, .033052, .033252, .033552
Military history (Japan: overall)   DS838    355.00952
Military history (Malta)          DG990.5
Military history (N. Zea.)         DU420.5   355.009931
Military history (Neth.)          DJ124
Military history (Nor.)           DL454     355.009481
Military history (Philip.)         DS671     355.009599
Military history (Pol.)           DK417 (older titles), DK4170-4178
Military history (Pol.: 1795-1918)   DK4173
Military history (Pol.: 1919-)      DK4174
Military history (Port.)          DP547
Military history (Rum.)           DR219
Military history (Rus.: 1917-)     DK54     355.00947, .033+
Military history (S. Afr.)         DT769    355.00968
Military history (Scan., N. Eur., Fin.)   DL52
Military history (Serbia)          DR1970
Military history (Sp.: 1808-20th c.)   DP78.5    355.00946
Military history (Swe.)           DL654
Military history (Swit.)          DQ59
Military history (Thai.)          DS573
Military history (U.S.)           E181     355.00973, .033073
Military history (U.S.: 20th c.: inclu. biog.: more than 1 war)   E745    355.00973,
                                            .033073, .033273, .033573
Military history (Ukr.)           DK508.54
Military history (world)          D25      355.48, 904.7, 909
MILITARY HISTORY (WWI)         940.4    D521 (gen.), D529-608
Military history (WWI: Australia)    940.40994    D547.A8
Military history (WWI: by place)    940.409
Military history (WWI: Can.)    940.409571    D547.C2
Military history (WWI: New Z.)   940.40993 (SEE ALSO .409931 for titles earlier than
                                  1989)    D547.N5
Military history (WWI: U.S.)    940.40973    D570
Military history (WWI: units & ops.: by country: inclu. structure, hist., registers, etc.)
                       940.412-413+      D532-578, D608
Military history (WWI: units & ops.: G.B.)   940.41241    D546-546.55+, D547
Military history (WWI: units & ops.: Ger.)   940.41343    D531-538
MILITARY HISTORY (WWII)        940.54    D743
Military history (WWII: Australia)    940.540994    D767.8
Military history (WWII: Austria)     940.5409436    D765.4
Military history (WWII: Belgium)    940.5409493    D763.B4
Military history (WWII: Bulg.)     940.54094977    D766.7.B8
Military history (WWII: Burma)     940.5409591    D767.6
Military history (WWII: by place)    940.54094-54099    D757-769
Military history (WWII: Can.)      940.540971   D768.15
Military history (WWII: China)      940.540951    D767.3
Military history (WWII: Denmark)    940.5409489    D763.D4
Military history (WWII: Egypt)     940.540962    D766.9
Military history (WWII: Fin.)      940.5409471 (SEE .54094897 for newer titles)
                             D765.3
Military history (WWII: Fr.)      940.540944    D761
Military history (WWII: G.B.)     940.540941-540942    D759-760
Military history (WWII: Ger.)     940.540943    D757
Military history (WWII: Greece)    940.5409495    D766.3
```

Military history (WWII: Hungary)    940.5409439    D765.56
Military history (WWII: India)    940.540954    D767.6, D767.63 (Free India,
                                                                1943-45)
Military history (WWII: It.)    940.540945    D763.I8-817
Military history (WWII: Japan)    940.540952    D767.2
Military history (WWII: Luxemb.)    940.54094935    D763.L9
Military history (WWII: New Z.)    940.5409931 (SEE ALSO .540993 for titles
                                                                prior to 1989)    D767.85
Military history (WWII: Norway)    940.5409481    D763.N6-613
Military history (WWII: Philip. Is.)    940.5409599    D767.4
Military history (WWII: Rumania)    940.5409498    D766.4
Military history (WWII: Rus.)    940.540947    D764
Military history (WWII: S. Africa)    940.540968    D766.97
Military history (WWII: Singapore)    940.54095957
Military history (WWII: Turkey)    940.5409561    D766.7.T8
Military history (WWII: U.S.)    940.540973    D769, D769.25-4 (armies,
                                div's., regt's.), D769.45-598 (naval particip., units, ops.)
MILITARY HISTORY (WWII: UNITS & OPS.: Australia)    940.541294    D767.8
Military history (WWII: units & ops.: Belgium)    940.5412493    D763.B4
Military history (WWII: units & ops.: Burma)    940.5412591    D767.6
Military history (WWII: units & ops.: by country: inclu. structure, history, registers, &
                                                service records)    940.5412-5413+
Military history (WWII: units & ops.: Can.)    940.541271    D768.15
Military history (WWII: units & ops.: China)    940.541251    D767.3
Military history (WWII: units & ops.: Fin.)    940.54134897    D765.3
Military history (WWII: units & ops.: Fr.)    940.541244    D761.1-9
Military history (WWII: units & ops.: G.B.)    940.541241    D759.5-760.A-Z
Military history (WWII: units & ops.: Ger.)    940.541343    D757.1-.85
Military history (WWII: units & ops.: Greece)    940.5412495    D766.3
Military history (WWII: units & ops.: India)    940.541254    D767.6,
                                                                D767.63 (Free India, 1943-45)
Military history (WWII: units & ops.: It.)    940.541345    D763.I81-813,
                                                D763.I815-817 (Corpo Volontari Della Liberta)
Military history (WWII: units & ops.: New Z.)    940.5412931 (SEE ALSO .541293
                                                for works before 1989)    D767.85
Military history (WWII: units & ops.: Norway)    940.5412481    D763.N61-613
Military history (WWII: units & ops.: Phil. Is.)    940.5412599    D767.4
Military history (WWII: units & ops.: Rum.)    940.5413498    D766.4
Military history (WWII: units & ops.: S. Africa)    940.541268    D766.97
Military history (WWII: units & ops.: Scot.)    940.5412411    D760.S
Military history (WWII: units & ops.: U.S.)    940.541273    D769.25-4,
                                D769.5-555 (naval), D769.585-598 (Coast Guard
                                etc.), D769.73-76+ (transport, ordnance, supplies)
Military history (WWII: units & ops.: U.S.: particular areas or states)    940.541274-
                                                541279    D769.85.A-Z
Military history (WWII: units & ops.: Yug.)    940.5412497    D766.61-613
Military history (WWII: units & ops.:Japan)    940.541352    D767.2
Military history (WWII: Yug.)    940.5409497    D766.6-613
Military history (Yug.)    DR319
Military history (Yug.: gen.)    DR1251
Military horses & mules (gen.)    UC600
Military hospitals (U.S.)    UH473-474 (SEE ALSO D629.U6-8 & D807.U6-87 for
                                                WWI & II)
Military hygiene & sanitation (U.S.)    UH603

Military information (security: besides U.S.)     UB248.A-Z
Military information (security: U.S.)     UB247
Military inspection     355.63     UB240-245
Military installations & land (inclu. bases, forts, camps, posts, etc.)     355.7
                                                    UA26+ (U.S.), UC400-405, UA600-876
Military intelligence (G.B.)     UB251.G7
Military intelligence (gen.)     UB250     355.3432
Military intelligence (Ger.)     UB251.G3     355.34320943
Military justice (admin.: gen.)     UB840     343.0143, .133
Military kits & field equip. (gen.)     UC540     355.81
MILITARY LAW     UB461-736
Military law (Asia )     UB685
Military law (Australia)     UB730-734
Military law (Austria)     UB600-604
Military law (Balkan states)     UB680-683
Military law (Can.)     UB505-509
Military law (China)     UB690-694
Military law (Eur.: gen.)     UB590
Military law (Fr.)     UB615-619
Military law (G.B.)     UB625-629 (PREFER KD6000-6355)     343.010941
Military law (Ger.)     UB620-624     343.010943
Military law (Japan)     UB700-704     343.010952
Military law (New Z.)     UB734.5
Military law (Phil. Islands)     UB705-709
Military law (Rus.: gen.)     UB655     343.010947
Military law (Rus.: statutes & compil's.)     UB655.A2
Military law (Tur.)     UB675-679
Military law (U.S.)     UB500-504 (PREFER KF7201-7755)     343.010973,
                                     .0106073
MILITARY LIFE & CUSTOMS     U750-773     355.1
Military life & customs (modern: Fr.)     U768
Military life & customs (modern: G.B.)     U767     355.10941
Military life & customs (modern: Ger.)     U769     355.10943
Military life & customs (modern: It.)     U770
Military life & customs (modern: misc. countries besides U766-771)     U773
Military life & customs (modern: Rus.)     U771     355.10947
Military life & customs (modern: U.S.)     U766     355.10973
Military life, customs, & postmilitary benefits     355.1     U750, U22
Military life (service periods, promotion, vet. benefits, etc.)     355.11
Military living conditions (partic. situations)     355.129     U765+
MILITARY MAINTENENCE & TRANSPORT (Asia: gen.)     UC234
Military maintenance & transport (Eur.: gen.)     UC158
Military maintenance & transport (gen.)     UC10     355.6-8
Military maintenance & transport (U.S.: gen.)     UC20
Military maintenance & transport (U.S.: WWI era)     UC23.1917-1918
Military maintenance & transport (U.S.: WWII era)     UC23.1941-1945
Military maneuvers     355.52     U250-255

MILITARY MEDICAL SERVICES (Asia: gen.)     UH299
Military medical services (G.B.: by period or date)     UH258
Military medical services (gen.: inclu. organization, surgeons, etc.)     UH400
Military medical services (hist., statistics, etc.: includes sanitary services: gen.)
                                                            UH215        355.345
Military medical services (U.S.: by time period or date: SEE ALSO particular wars)
                                                            UH224
Military medical services, Military (Eur.: by date or period)     UH256
Military medicine (gen.: inclu. hdbks., manuals, etc.)     UH390     616.98023
Military missions     UA16
Military missions & attachés     355.032
Military motor vehicles (places besides U.S.)     UG620.A-Z
Military movie services (U.S. Army)     UH826
Military museums & exhibitions (gen.)     U13.A1
Military nursing (U.S.)     UH493
Military observations (collected: 2 or more wars)     U719
Military oceanography (U.S.)     V396.3-4
Military officers (except U.S.: by country)     UB415.A-Z
MILITARY OPS. (hist's. & types of persons)     355.409 (SEE ALSO 355.47 for
                                              geog. treat.)     U27-43
Military ops. (Russo-Fin. War, 1939-40)     DL1099
Military ops. (Sp. Civil War, 1936-39: gen. titles on the war)     DP269.A56-Z
Military ops. (WWI: West: gen.)     D530     940.41+, .421, .424, .4272, .431, .434
Military ops. (WWII: West: gen. special)     D756.3
Military ops. (WWII: West: gen.)     D756
Military personnel (inclu. organization; readiness of partic. groups)     355.3
                                              UA15+, UA23-39+ (U.S.)
Military personnel (WWII)     940.5315355
Military pistols & revolvers (design)     623.443     UD410-415
Military planning     U150-155
Military police & conduct enforcement     355.13323
Military police (gen.)     UB820     355.13323
Military Police (MP's: WWII: U.S.)     D769.775
Military police (WWI: U.S.)     D570.35
Military prison life     355.1295 (SEE ALSO 365.48)
Military prisons     355.13325 (SEE ALSO 365.48)     UB800-805
Military prisons & prisoners (gen.)     UB800     365.48, 355.13325, 344.03548
Military prisons (outside U.S.)     UB805.A-Z
Military quarters & camps (besides U.S.)     UC405.A-Z
Military radar (U.S.)     UG612.3
Military radio (U.S.)     UG611.3
Military radio services (U.S. Army)     UH857
Military railroads & rolling stock (engineering)     623.63     UC310-315, UF490-
                                              495 (r.r. artil.), UG345 (engnrg.)
Military railroads (U.S.: gen.)     UC313     355.830973
Military recreation & information services (gen.)     UH800     355.346
Military research, Aeronautical (U.S.: by state of origin)     UG643.5.A-W
Military research (U.S.)     U393
Military resources (prep., review, preserv.)     355.21

MILITARY SCIENCE 355-358 U
Military science (19th c.) U41
Military science (20th c.) U42 355.00904
Military science & engineering U 355-358, 623
Military science & organization (ALSO armed forces, ground forces, etc.)
          355 (inclu. officers' hdbks.) U, U21+
Military science (gen.) U1-900+ 355
Military science (gen.: pubn. date 1789-) U102 355, .43
Military science (history) U27-45
Military science (history: by country or area) U43.A-Z
Military science (history: gen.) U27 355.009
Military science, military engineering, & air forces U-UH 355-359, 623
Military science (misc. services: medical etc.) UH
Military science (modern: 1800-) U39
Military service as a profession UB147
Military services (misc.) UH
Military signaling (gen.) UG580
Military skill (Indians of N. Am.) E98.M5
Military social & welfare services (countries besides U.S.) UH769.A-Z
Military sports (by place) U328.A-Z
Military staffs (countries besides U.S.) UB225.A-Z
MILITARY STATUS (20th c.) 355.033004 U42
Military status (1900-1919) 355.0330041
Military status (1930-39) 355.0330043
Military status (1940-49) 355.0330044
Military status (Africa) UA855-868
Military status (Asia) UA830-853
Military status (Asia: by country except India, China, Japan) UA853.A-Z
Military status (Australia) UA870-874
Military status (Balkan States) UA820-827
Military status (by area or country) 355.03301-03309
Military status (Can.) UA600-602
Military status (Central Am.) UA606-608
Military status (China) UA835-839
Military status (Eur.) UA646-829
Military status (Fr.) UA700-709
Military status (G.B.) UA647-668 355.033041-033042, .033241, .033541
Military status (gen. hist.) 355.033 D25, U21+, U27, UA15
Military status (gen.: inclu. policy) 355.03
Military status (Ger.) UA710-719
Military status (hist. periods) 355.033001-033005
Military status (It.) UA740-749
Military status (Japan) UA845-849
Military status (misc. Eur. countries) UA829.A-Z
Military status (N. Am.) UA22-602
Military status (New Z.) UA874.3-7
Military status (Norway) UA750-759
Military status (Pacific islands) UA875-876
Military status (Rus. or Sov.Un.) UA770-779
Military status (S.Am.) UA612-645
Military status (U.S.) UA23-585 355.033273
Military staus (W. Hemis.) UA21-645
Military status (world: gen.) UA10 355.03
Military status (worldwide: place by place) UA21-876+ 355.0330+

Military supplies & stores (gen.)     UC260
Military supply ships (freighters, tankers, etc.: units)     359.3265 (SEE ALSO
                                    .9853 after 1988)     VA79
Military surveying, mapping, & topography   UG470-474
Military tactics (partic. kinds: commando, retreats, blitz, landings, attacks &
     counters, etc.)     355.422
Military tactics (special topics: by name)     U167.5.A-Z
Military telegraph & troops (U.S.)     UG603
Military telephone (U.S.)     UG610.3
Military transport engineering     623.6     UC, UC10, UC270-360, UC270-275 (gen.)
Military transport (U.S.)     UC273-274
Military transport vessels & hospital ships (units)     359.3264 (SEE ALSO
                              .9853 for transp. ships on pubns. after 1988)
                              VA79 (transports), VG450 (hosp. ships)
Military tunnels (design)     623.68     UG340
Military uniforms (U.S.)     UC483-484     355.140973
Military units (marines)     359.9631
Military units (types: armies, div's, regiments, co's., mil. districts, etc.)
                    355.31     UA, UA23-39+ (U.S.), UA646-829 (Eur.),
                    UA830-853 (Asia), UA870-876(Australia-Pac.)
Militia (Ger.)     UA717
Militia, Naval (U.S.: state by state)     VA90-387
Militia (U.S.: inclu. Nat. Guard etc.: state by state)     UA50-549
Mindanao (geog. & travel)     915.997     DS688.M2
Mindanao (Philip.)     DS688.M2     959.97-8
Mindoro (Philip.)     DS688.M28     959.93
MINE laying & sweeping (mil. engnrg.: land)     623.262     UG490
Mine sweeping & laying (mil. engineering: marine)     623.263     V856-856.5
Minelayers & minesweepers (naval engineering)     623.8262     V885 (sweepers),
                                    V856-856.5 (both)
Minelaying, minesweeping, submarine mines, etc. (gen.)     V856     623.2, .26,
                         .263, .36, .45115, .8262, 359.825115, .3262
Minerals (non-metal: mil. raw materials)     355.243
MINES (design)     623.45115     UG490, V856-856.5 (naval)
Mines (mil. equip.)     355.825115     UG490
Mines (naval ammun.)     359.825115
Mines, Land (inclu. countermeasures)     UG490     623.45115
Minesweepers     V885 (SEE ALSO V856)     623.8262
Minesweepers & minelayers (navies: units)     359.3262     V885, V856+
Minesweeping, minelaying, sub. mines, etc. (by place)     V856.5.A-Z
Mining & torpedo troops     UG550-555
Minnesota     F601-615     977.6
MINORITIES & women in the armed forces (gen.)     UB416     355.22 (women), .3
Minorities & women in the armed forces (places besides U.S.)     UB419
Minorities & women in the armed forces (U.S.: by group name)     UB418.A-Z
Minorities & women (navies)     VB320-325
Minorities, Ethnic (WWII: as troops)     940.5404     D769.88.A-Z,
                                    D769.88.M4 (Mex.-Am's.)
Minorities (U.S. Navy: by group)     VB324.A-Z
Minsk, Rus.     DK651.M5
Missile forces & warfare (land: may be mostly post-WWII)     358.17     UG1310-1315
Missiles & rockets, Air force (by particular type)     UG1312.A-Z
Missiles, Surface-to-surface (design)     623.45195

Mississippi          F336-350      976.2
Mississippi (WWII)   D769.85.M7
Mississippi Valley & the Midwest   F351-355    976-977
Missouri             977.8         F461-475, F466
Missouri (battleship: U.S.)        VA65.M8      359.32520973
MOBILIZATION         UA910-915
Mobilization (except U.S.: by name of place)    UA915.A-Z
Mobilization (G.B.)  UA915.G7      355.280941
Mobilization (gen.)  UA910         355.28
Mobilization, Industrial (gen.)    UA18.A2      355.28
Mobilization (mil. resources: inclu. requisition, commandeering, voluntary, etc.)
                                   355.28       UA910-915, UA913 (U.S.)
Mobilization, Naval (G.B.)         VA463        359.280941
Mobilization, Naval (Ger.)         VA518        359.290943
Mobilization, Naval (Japan)        VA658        359.280952
Mobilizaton, Naval (gen.)          VA48         359.28
Mobilization (U.S.)        UA913   355.280973
Mobilization (U.S. Navy)   VA77    359.280973
Model ships          623.8201
Models, Military     U311
Models, Ship         VM298         623.8201, 745.5928
Modern history (1453-)       D208         901.93, 909.8+, 940
Modern history (1789-)       D299         909.8+
Modern history (1801-1914/20)       D358      909.81
Modern history (1945-)       D840         909.824-825+
Mohammed V (Tur.: ruler, 1909-18: also titles on era)       DR583
Molokai (Haw. Is.)           DU628.M7     996.924
Molotov, Viacheslav M. (Rus.: 1925-53 era)       DK268.M64
Moluccas         DS646.6         959.85
Monaco           944.949         DC941-947, DC945
Mongolia         DS793.M7 (SEE ALSO DS19-23.1 for Mongols)       951.7
Mongolia (WWII: gen. particip.)       940.53517       DS793.M7
Mongols          DS19-23.1 (SEE ALSO DS793.M7 for Mongolia)
Mons, Bel. (WWI)       D542.M7
Montana          F726-740        978.6
Montego Bay, Jam.       F1895.M6
MONTENEGRO       DR101-196+, DR1802-1928 (SEE ALSO DR357+, DR1214)
                       949.745, .76
Montenegro (1878-1918: Nicholas I)       DR1878-1883
Montenegro (1912-18: Balkan wars & WWI)       DR1883
Montenegro (1914-18: WWI)       DR158
Montenegro (1918-: part of Yug.)       DR159
Montenegro (1918-45)       DR1884-1893
Montenegro (1918-45: gen.)       DR1885
Montenegro (1941-45)       DR1893
Montenegro (gen.)       DR117, DR1810, 1835
Montevideo (steamship: WWII)       D782.M6
Montevideo, Urug.       F2781       989.513
Montgomery, Bernard Law Montgomery, 1st Viscount (G.B.: 20th c. mil. biog.)
                                   DA69.3.M56

Monuments & cemeteries (WWI: Rus.)    940.46547    D680.R
MONUMENTS & CEMETERIES (WWII: Australia)    940.546594    D838.A8
Monuments & cemeteries (WWII: China)    940.546551    D838.C5
Monuments & cemeteries (WWII: Fr.)    940.546544    D838.F8
Monuments & cemeteries (WWII: Ger.)    940.546543    D838.G3
Monuments & cemeteries (WWII: Hawaiian Is.)    940.5465969    D835.H, D838.H
Monuments & cemeteries (WWII: Japan)    940.546552    D838.J3
Monuments & cemeteries (WWII: Rus.)    940.546547    D838.R9 or .S65
Monuments & cemeteries (WWII: U.S.: Wash. D.C.)    940.5465753
                                                                        D835.D6, D836.W
Monuments, memorials, celebrations (WWI)    D663-680    940.46+
Monuments, memorials, celebrations (WWI: G.B.)    D680.G7
Monuments, memorials, celebrations (WWI: U.S.: by city)    D675.A-Z
MONUMENTS, MEMORIALS, CELEBRATIONS (WWII: Australia)    D838.A8
Monuments, memorials, celebrations (WWII: Fr.: gen.)    D838.F8
Monuments, memorials, celebrations (WWII: Fr.: Paris)    D838.F8.P3
Monuments, memorials, celebrations (WWII: G.B.: gen.)    D838.G6
Monuments, memorials, celebrations (WWII: G.B.: London)    D838.G7.L5
Monuments, memorials, celebrations (WWII: Ger.)    D838.G3
Monuments, memorials, celebrations (WWII: memorials dedicated to special divisions
                                classed with them)    D830-838
Monuments, memorials, celebrations (WWII: N.Z.)    D838.N45
Monuments, memorials, celebrations (WWII: outside U.S.: by place)    D838.A-Z
Monuments, memorials, celebrations (WWII: Rus.)    D838.R9
MONUMENTS, MEMORIALS, CELEBRATIONS (WWII: U.S.: by city)    D836.A-Z
Monuments, memorials, celebrations (WWII: U.S.: by state)    D835.A-Z
                                                                        940.546574-54679+
Monuments, memorials, celebrations (WWII: U.S.: Calif.)    D835.C2-21
                                                                        940.5465794
Monuments, memorials, celebrations (WWII: U.S.: District of Columbia)    D835.D6
Monuments, memorials, celebrations (WWII: U.S.: Ill.)    D835.I3-31
Monuments, memorials, celebrations (WWII: U.S.: Los Angeles)    D836.L62
Monuments, memorials, celebrations (WWII: U.S.: N.Y.)    D835.N4-5
Monuments, memorials, celebrations (WWII: U.S.: New York City)    D836.N49
Monuments, statues, memorials (London, Eng.)    DA689.M7
Monuments, statues, memorials (Washington, D.C.)    F203.4.A-Z
Moral & health protection (mil.: alcoholism, drug abuse, prostitution, venereal
                                diseases, etc. & work vs.)    UH630
Morale, Military    355.123    U22
Morale (navies)    359.123
Moravia (20th c.)    DB2415-2421
Moravia (20th c.: gen.)    DB2416
Moreton Bay (Queens., Aust.)    DU280.M7
Moroccan question (20th c.)    D475 (PREFER DT317)
MOROCCO    DT301-330    964
Morocco (19th-20th c.)    DT324    964.03-04
Morocco (1900-56)    964.04    DT324
Morocco (gen.)    964    DT301-330, DT305, DT314
Morocco (mil. status)    UA867    355.033064
Morocco (WWII)    D766.99.M8    940.5364, 964.04
Mortars & howitzers (U.S.: gen.)    UF473
Mortars (U.S.: handbooks)    UF563.A75

Moscow area (Rus.)      DK511.M6
Moscow, Rus.        DK591-609, DK601 (hist. to 1950)        947.31
Moscow, Rus. (to 1950)        DK601
Moscow, Rus. (Rev., 1917-21)      DK265.8.M6
Moscow, Rus. (WWII)        D764.7.M58
Moslems or Muslims (WWII)      D810.M6 or .M8
Mosley, Oswald, Sir, Baronet (G.B.: 1910-36 biog.)      DA574.M6
Moss, Nor.      DL596.M7
Motion-picture services, Military (U.S.: gen.: inclu. armed forces)      UH825
Motor transport, Artillery      UF390
Motor transport (mil. sci.)      UC340-345        355.83
Motor transport (naval sci.)      VC570-575
Motor vehicles, Military (gen.)      UG615        623.747, 355.83, 357.5+
Motorboats & launches (small craft: gen.)      VM341
Motorcycle troops (mech. cav.)      357.53        UC347
Motorcycles (mil. transp.)      UC347        623.7472
Motorized infantry      356.11 (pubns. before 1989 may inclu. regular infan. ALSO)
            U167.5.M6, UD15, UD21-124+, UA
Motorized units (mil. sci.)      U167.5.M6
MOUNTAIN artillery      UF440-445
Mountain guns (U.S.: handbooks)      UF563.A5.2.95in.Mt. (2.95)
Mountain Province (Philip.)      DS688.M5
Mountain troops (WWII: Ger.)      D757.39
Mountain troops (WWII: Ger.: by author, division, name, etc.)      D757.4.A-Z
Mountain warfare & troops      UD460-465        356.164
Mounted forces & warfare      357      UE, UE15, UE21-124, UE23 (U.S.),
            UE57 (G.B.), UE65 (Austria), UD450-455
Mounted infantry (gen.)      UD450
Movie services, Military (by place except U.S.)      UH829.A-Z
Movie services, Military (gen.)      UH820
Movies & movie propaganda (WWII)      D743.23      791.43+, 940.53+
Movies (WWI)      D522.23
Mozambique (Portuguese East Africa)      DT451-465      967.9
Mukden, China      DS796.M8
Mukden, Manch. (Ch.-Jpn. Confl.:1931: incident)      DS783.8
Mules & horses, Military (places besides U.S.)      UC605.A-Z
Munich Four-power Agreement      DB2202
Munich, Ger.      DD901.M71-95
Munich, Ger. (1871-1950)      DD901.M9
Munich, Ger. (gen.)      DD901.M77
Munich, Ger. (WWII)      D757.9.M9
MUSEUMS, Air force (inclu. exhibitions: gen.)      UG623.3.A1      623.74074,
                  358.40074
Museums & exhibitions (marine navig. & merch. marine)      VK6
Museums & exhibitions (mil. engineering)      UG6
Museums & exhibitions (naval architec.)      VM6
Museums & exhibitions (naval ordnance: gen.)      VF6.A1
Museums, Artillery (by city within area, whose 1st letter & shelf # are shown by
                  'x' in 'x2')      UF6.x2.A-Z
Museums, Artillery (by country or region)      UF6.A2-Z
Museums, Artillery (inclu. exhibitions)      UF6

MUSEUMS, EXHIBITIONS, ETC. (arms)    U804
Museums, exhibitions, etc. (arms: by country)    U804.A2-Z
Museums, exhibitions, etc. (WWI)    D503
Museums, exhibitions, etc. (WWII)    D733
Museums, exhibitions, etc. (WWII: by country)    D733.A2-Z
Museums, exhibitions, etc. (WWII: gen.)    D733.A1
MUSEUMS, MILITARY (Fr.)    U13.F8
Museums, Military (G.B.)    U13.G7
Museums, Military (inclu. exhibitions)    U13.A-Z    355.0074
Museums, Military medical (inclu. exhibitions)    UH206
Museums, Military (Sov.Un.)    U13.S65
Museums, Military (U.S.)    U13.U6-7    355.0074073
Museums, Naval (gen.: inclu. exhibitions)    V13.A1    359.0074
Music    M    780-789
Music & bands, Military (gen.)    UH40
Music & bands, Naval (U.S.)    VG33    359.340973, .170973
Musicians (WWII)    940.531578    D810.A7 or .M
Mussolini, Benito (It.: 1900-46 period)    DG575.M8
Mustard gas    UG447.5.M8    623.4516
Muster rolls & accounts, Military (gen.: inclu. gen. corresp.: admin.)    UB160
Mutinies & military offenses    355.1334 (SEE 364.138 for war crimes)    UB780+
Mutiny & other naval offenses    359.1334    VB850-880
Mutiny (mil.)    UB787
Mutiny (naval: except U.S.)    VB865.A-Z
Mutiny (naval: gen.)    VB860    359.1334
Mutiny (naval: U.S.)    VB863
Mutual-aid agreements (WWII: U.S.: by country)    D753.2.A-Z
Muzzle-loading ordnance    UF560-565... .M.L.


NAGASAKI, Japan    DS897.N285    952.2
Nagasaki, Japan (WWII)    D767.25.N3
Nagumo, Chuichi, Vice Adm. (Japan: 1926-89 period)    DS890.N23
Namur area (Bel.)    DH801.N2-29
Nanking, China    DS796.N2
Naples, It. (kingdom & later)    DG840-855
National characteristics (Ger.)    DD76
National Home & Vets' Admin. (U.S.: gen.)    UB383
National security (gen.)    UA10.5
National War College (U.S.: Wash., D.C.)    U412
Nationalities & the war (WWII: U.S.: by name)    D769.8.F7.A-Z (for Indians
                                                                    SEE D810.I5)
Nationalities (WWI: U.S.)    D570.88.A-Z
Nationalities (WWII: population transfers: gen.)    D820.P7
Nationalities (WWII: U.S.)    D769.88.A-Z    940.5315+
Nationalsozialistische Deutsche Arbeiter-Partei (Ger.: 1930-45: gen.)    DD253.25
Nationalsozialistische Frauenschaft    DD253.58
Naturalized subjects in belligerent lands (WWI)    D639.N2-3
Naturalized subjects (WWII: in belligerent countries: by place)
                            D810.N3.A-Z (SEE D753.8 for Japanese-Am's. in
                            U.S., D769.8.A6 for alien enemies in the U.S.)
Naturalized subjects (WWII: in belligerent countries: gen.)    D810.N2
Nauru (Pleasant Island)    996.85

NAUTICAL almanacs & yearbooks     VK7-8
Nautical craft & types        623.82        VM, VM145
Nautical engineering & seamanship        623.8        VM (architec.), VK (navig.)
Nautical instruments (gen.)        VK573        623.894, .863
Nautical instruments (misc.)        VK584.A-Z
Nautical life (merchant marine: pop. titles)        VK149
Nautical lifesaving (by area)        VK1321-1424
Nautical pilots & piloting (gen. hist's.)        VK1515        623.8922, .892209
Nautical tables (gen.: inclu. azimuth)        VK563
NAVAL ADMINISTRATION        VB
Naval administration (Asia)        VB99-113
Naval administration (Australia)        VB121        359.60994
Naval administration (by country)        VB21-124
Naval administration (Can.)        VB26
Naval administration (civil sections)        VB170-187
Naval administration (Eur.)        VB55-96
Naval administration (Fr.)        VB71        359.60944
Naval administration (G.B.)        VB57        359.60941, .30941
Naval administration (gen.: pubn. 1801-1970)        VB145        359.6, .3
Naval administration (Ger.)        VB73        359.60943, .30943
Naval administration (It.)        VB79        359.60945
Naval administration (Japan)        VB105        359.60952, .30952
Naval administration (New Z.)        VB122.5
Naval administration (Rus.)        VB85        359.60947
Naval administration (U.S.)        VB23        359.60973
Naval air forces & warfare        359.94 (SEE 358.4 for titles before 1989)        VG90-95
Naval & military life & customs (WWII: U.S.)        940.548373        U766, V736
Naval & submarine ops. (WWI)        D580-595
Naval & submarine ops. (WWII)        D770-784        940.545
NAVAL ARCHITECTURE & marine engineering        VM
Naval architecture & shipbuilding        VM, VM1-565 (SEE ALSO V750-995+ for
        construction & armament of warships), VM142-148 (gen.)        623.81
Naval architecture (hist.)        VM15-124
Naval architecture (hist.: 19th c.)        VM19
Naval architecture (hist.: 20th c.)        VM20
Naval architecture (hist.: modern: gen.)        VM18
Naval armament (installation)        V960
Naval armor & ordnance        359.3251        V900-905, V950-980, VF, VF23 (U.S.)
Naval armor (places besides U.S.)        V905.A-Z
Naval armor testing (U.S.)        V913
Naval arms & ordnance (gen.: U.S.)        VF353
Naval artillery (design)        623.418        VF320-325, VF323 (U.S.)
Naval artillery equipment (U.S.)        VF323
Naval aviation (Ger.)        VG95.G3
Naval aviation (Japan)        VG95.J3
Naval aviation (U.S.)        VG93-94        358.40973
Naval aviation units        359.943

NAVAL BASES & STATIONS (in Fr.)          359.70944
Naval bases & stations (in G.B.)          359.70941-70942
Naval bases & stations (in Ger.)     359.70943
Naval bases & stations (in It.)     359.70945
Naval bases & stations (in Japan)          359.70952
Naval bases & stations (in New Z.)          359.70993
Naval bases & stations (in Philip.)          359.709599
Naval bases & stations (in Rus.)     359.70947
Naval bases & stations (in U.S.)          359.70973
Naval bases, ports, docks, etc. (Australia)     VA716     359.70994
Naval bases, ports, docks, etc. (G.B.)          VA459
Naval bases, ports, docks, etc. (Ger.: gen.)     VA516.A1          359.70943,
                              940.4530943 (WWI), .54530943 (WWII)
Naval bases, ports, docks, etc. (Japan. Imper. Navy)     VA656          359.70952,
                              940.54530952 (WWII)
Naval bases, ports, docks, etc. (U.S.)          VA67-68
Naval bases (WWI)          940.453+          D581-589
Naval bases (WWI: in G.B.)          940.45341
NAVAL BASES (WWII)     940.5453+     D769.54-542 (U.S.), D770-784 (other lands)
Naval bases (WWII: in Fr.)          940.545344
Naval bases (WWII: in G.B.)          940.545341
Naval bases (WWII: in Ger.)          940.545343
Naval bases (WWII: in It.)          940.545345
Naval bases (WWII: in Japan)          940.545352
Naval bases (WWII: in U.S.)          940.545373
Naval bases (WWII: in U.S.: Calif.)          940.5453794
Naval bases (WWII: in U.S.: Calif.: S.F. Bay Area)          940.54537946
Naval bases (WWII: in U.S.: Calif.: San Diego)          940.5453794985
Naval bases (WWII: in U.S.: Va.)          940.5453755
Naval bases (WWII: U.S.: by location)     D769.542.A-Z
Naval bases (WWII: U.S.: gen.)     D769.54     940.545373
Naval biography (collective)          V61     359.00922
Naval biography (places except U.S.: by person's name after country name)
                              V64.x2.A-Z
Naval biography (U.S.: collective)          V62     359.00922
Naval cemeteries (U.S.)          VB303-304
Naval ceremonies          359.17     V310
Naval Chaplain Corps (WWII: U.S.)          D769.59
Naval chaplains (gen.)          VG20     359.347
Naval clothing & personal equipment (overall)     VC280-285
Naval coaling stations (U.S.: gen.)     VA73     359.70973, .750973
Naval command and leadership          VB200-205
Naval construction battalions (WWII: U.S.)          D769.55-555
Naval construction maintenance (WWII: U.S.: gen.)     D769.554
Naval construction maintenance units (WWII: U.S.:by#)     D769.555.1st-
Naval contracts (supplies: U.S.)     VC267.U6-7
Naval crimes (except U.S.)          VB855.A-Z
Naval crimes (G.B.)          VB855.G7
Naval crimes (Ger.)          VB855.G3
Naval crimes (Japan)          VB855.J3
Naval crimes (U.S.)          VB853
Naval demobilization          359.29     VB277, UA917
Naval desertion (U.S.)          VB873

Naval design                623.81       VM, V750-995 (warships), VM15-20 (hist.),
                            VM21-124 (by place), VM23 (U.S.), VM57 (G.B.),
                            VM146 (metal ships), VM156 (theory), V750, V765, V800
Naval design (components & details)    623.814     VM, VM156
Naval discipline        VB840-845       359.13
Naval districts (U.S.: by #)       VA62.7.1st+
Naval districts (U.S.: gen.)       VA62.5        359.70973
Naval drills (Asia: gen.)          VD270
Naval drills (seamen: by country or area: includes watch, station, quarter, fire)
                                                               VD160-302

NAVAL EDUCATION & training (gen.)      V400       359.007
Naval education (Asia: gen.)       V625
Naval education (Eur.: gen.)       V500
Naval education (G.B.: gen.)       V510       359.0071141, .50941, .550941, .007041
Naval education (Ger.: gen.)       V570       359.007043, .50943
Naval education (Japan: gen.)      V640       359.007052, .0071152, .50952, .550952
Naval education (U.S.: gen.)       V411       359.0071073, .0071173, .50973,
                                              .550973
Naval engineering & seamanship     623.8      VM, VK
Naval engineering (civil: U.S.)    VG593
Naval equipment & supplies (gen.: for ships)     VC270       359.8
Naval facilities (bases, docks, artificial harbors, etc.: design)       623.64
                    V220-230, VA69-750 (by place), VA67-70 (U.S.), VM301
Naval flags (G.B.)      V305.G7
Naval flags (Japan)     V305.J3
Naval flags (U.S.: inclu. marine)      V303
Naval forces & divisions (WWII: U.S.: by name)       D769.52.A-Z
Naval forces & warfare     359      V-VM, V27-55, V101-109
Naval fuel (gen.: ALSO costs etc.)       VC276.A1     359.83, 623.874, .415
Naval gunnery practice (places except U.S.)      VF315.A-Z
Naval handbooks (seamen's: places besides U.S.)      V115.A-Z
Naval health, hygiene, & sanitation (gen.)     VG470
NAVAL HISTORY (1453-)      D215
Naval history (1801-1914/20)       D362
Naval history (20th c.)        D436       359.409, 904.7, 359.47
Naval history (Australia)      DU112.4    359.00994
Naval history (Can.)           F1028.5    359.00971
Naval history (China: 20th c. & 1912-49)       DS775.5
Naval history (Den.: 19th-20th c.)       DL154.7
Naval history (Dutch E. Ind.)      DS637
Naval history (Fin.)       DL1040-1042
Naval history (Fr.)        DC49-53
Naval history (Fr.: 19th-20th c.)      DC53
Naval history (Fr.: 20th c.)       DC368
Naval history (Fr. Indoch.)        DS545
Naval history (G.B.)       DA70-89
Naval history (G.B.: 20th c.)      DA89       359.00941, .4741
Naval history (Ger.)       DD106      359.00943, .4743
Naval history (Greece)     DF775
Naval history (India)      DS443
Naval history (It.: gen.)      DG486      359.00945
Naval history (Japan: 1868+)       DS839.7    359.00952, .4752
Naval history (Japan: gen.)        DS839     359.00952
Naval history (Malta)      DG990.7
Naval history (Nor.)       DL456

Naval history (Philip.)          DS672
Naval history (Pol.)             DK417.7
Naval history (Pol.)             DK4177-4178
Naval history (Port.)            DP551
Naval history (Rum.)             DR225
Naval history (Rus.-Jpn. War, 1904-5)      DS517.1
Naval history (Rus.: 1917-)      DK59      359.00947
Naval history (Scan., N. Eur., Fin.)      DL53
Naval history (Swe.)             DL656
Naval history (Thai.)            DS574
Naval history (U.S.)             E182      359.00973, .4773
Naval history (U.S.: 20th c.)    E746      359.00973, .4773
Naval history (world)            D27       359, 904.7
Naval hospital corps (gen.)          VG310
Naval hospitals (places except U.S.)      VG430.A-Z
Naval hospitals (U.S.: by area or state)  VG424.A-Z
Naval inspection          359.63      VB220-225
Naval installations (hist. & geog. works)      359.709+
Naval intelligence (G.B.)      VB231.G7      359.34320941
Naval intelligence (gen.)      VB230      359.3432
Naval intelligence (Ger.)      VB231.G3      359.34320943
Naval intelligence (U.S.)      VB231.U6-7      359.34320973
Naval justice (admin. of)      VB790-925
Naval justice (places besides U.S.)      VB795.A-Z
NAVAL LAW          VB350-785
Naval law (Asia: gen.)      VB700
Naval law (Australia)      VB775
Naval law (by area or country)      VB360-785
Naval law (Can.)      VB370-379
Naval law (China)      VB710-719
Naval Law (Eur.: gen.)      VB530
Naval Law (FR.)      VB570-579
Naval Law (G.B.)      VB590-599 (PREFER KD6128-6158)      343.4101
Naval Law (Ger.)      VB580-589
Naval law (Japan)      VB730-739      343.5201
Naval law (New Z.)      VB777
Naval law (Rus.)      VB650-659
Naval law (U.S.)      VB360-369 (PREFER KF7345-7375)
NAVAL LIFE & CUSTOMS      V720-743
Naval life & customs (modern)      V735-743
Naval life & customs (modern: G.B.)      V737      359.10941
Naval life & customs (modern: Ger.)      V739      359.10943
Naval life & customs (modern: Japan)      V743.J3
Naval life & customs (modern: misc. countries)      V743.A-Z
Naval life & customs (modern: Rus.)      V741      359.10947
Naval life & customs (modern: U.S.)      V736      359.10973
Naval living conditions (training or perm. bases)      359.1292
Naval machine guns (special by name)      VF410.A3-Z
Naval maintenance (Asia: gen.)      VC230
Naval maintenance (Eur.: gen.)      VC160
Naval maintenance (gen.)      VC10      359.6
Naval maintenance (U.S.: gen.)      VC20      359.60973
Naval medical biography (U.S.: indiv.)      VG227.A2-Z
Naval medical services (by place)      VG121-224
Naval medical services (gen.)      VG115      359.345, .72, 616.98024

Naval mobilization          359.28          VA48, VA77-750, VA77 (U.S.)
Naval museums & exhibitions (by country)   V13.A2-Z     359.00740+
Naval mutiny (by ship)          VB867.A-Z
Naval nurse corps (gen.)          VG350          359.345, 610.7349, .7361, 616.98024
Naval observations (wartime)     V701-716 (PREFER D-F areas)
Naval officers (except U.S.)     VB315.A-Z
Naval officers' clubs (U.S.)     VC383          359.3460973
Naval officers' clubs (U.S.: by state)     VC384.A-W
Naval officers' handbooks (U.S.)     V133
NAVAL OPS. (hist's.: gen.)          359.409          V27-55
Naval ops. (Sp. Civil War, 1936-39)     DP269.3-35
Naval ops. (U.S. Navy. Office of: reports)     VA52.A7-79
Naval ops. (WWI)          D580-595          940.45
Naval ops. (WWI: Australia)     940.45994     D589.A
Naval ops. (WWI: G.B.)     940.45941          D581-582, VA458
Naval ops. (WWI: Ger.)     940.45943          D581-582
Naval ops. (WWI: U.S.)          940.45973          D589.U5-8
NAVAL OPS. (WWII)          D770-784
Naval ops. (WWII: Australia)     940.545994          D779.A8, DU112.4
Naval ops. (WWII: Can.)     940.545971          D779.C2, F1028.5
Naval ops. (WWII: Fr.)          940.545944          D779.F8, DC53, DC368
Naval ops. (WWII: G.B. Royal Navy)          940.545941-545942          D771-772,
          D767 (Pac.), DA89, DA89.1.A-Z (biog's.), DA566.5 (20th c.)
Naval ops. (WWII: Ger.)     940.545943          D771-772, DD106
Naval ops. (WWII: It.)          940.545945          D775, DG486
Naval ops. (WWII: Japan)     940.545952          D777, VA653, DS890.A-Z (biog.)
Naval ops. (WWII: misc. countries: by place)     D779.A-Z
Naval ops. (WWII: New Z.)     940.5459931 (SEE ALSO .545993 for earlier titles
                    prior to 1989)          D779.N45
Naval ops. (WWII: U.S.: U.S.N., Marines, Coast Guard)     940.545973     D773-774,
                    D769.45-598 (fleets etc.), E746
NAVAL ORDNANCE & arms (gen.)          VF350
Naval ordnance & arms (manufacture: U.S.)     VF373
Naval ordnance (Asia: gen.)          VF99
Naval ordnance (by country or place)     VF21-124
Naval ordnance drills (by place)     VF160-302
Naval ordnance (engineering)     623.8251          VF, VF21-124 (by place),
                    VF23 (U.S.), VF350-355
Naval ordnance (Eur.: gen.)          VF55
Naval ordnance material (besides U.S.)     VF395.A-Z
Naval ordnance material (gen.)          VF390          623.418
Naval ordnance (nonperiodical collections)   VF7
Naval ordnance (special overall)     VF147
Naval personnel (admin.: U.S.)     VB258          359.610973
Naval petty officers' handbooks (U.S.)     V123
Naval prisons & prisoners (gen.)     VB890          344.03548
Naval projectiles (gen.)     VF480          359.8251, 623.451
Naval propaganda & psychological warfare   359.3434     UB275-277
Naval provisions & subsistence (countries besides U.S.)     VC355.A-Z
Naval provisions & subsistence (U.S.)     VC353-354          359.810973
Naval quarters & barracks (U.S.)     VC423-424
Naval recreation & information services (gen.)   VG2020     359.346
Naval research (ordnance: places besides U.S.)     VF360.5.A-Z
Naval research (U.S.: by special establishment locale)     V394.A-Z
Naval research (U.S.: by state)     V393.5.A-W

Naval Reserve & Women's Reserve (WAVES: WWII: U.S.)    D769.597
Naval Reserve Officers' Training Corps (U.S.: N.R.O.T.C.)    V426    359.2232
Naval reserves (U.S.: Calif.: gen.)    VA100    359.3709794
Naval reserves (U.S.: gen.)    VA80    359.370973
Naval resources (preparation, eval., preserv.)    359.21
Naval schools (Ger.: by name or place)    V574.A7-Z
NAVAL SCIENCE    359    V
Naval science (19th c.)    V51    359.009034
Naval science (20th c.)    V53    359.00904, .40904
Naval science (ancient hist.)    V29-41    359.00901
Naval science (by region or country)    V55.A-Z    359.47+
Naval science (collected works: monographic)    V15-17
Naval science (gen.)    V, V1-995+    359, 623.8
Naval science (gen.: pubn. thru 1800)    V101
Naval science (gen.: pubn. 1801+)    V103
Naval science (history, antiquities, & biog.: gen., during peace & war)    V25-64 (SEE
                        ALSO D-F #s for specific countries, wars, etc.)
Naval science (medieval hist.)    V43-46    359.00902
Naval science (misc. services: medical etc.)    VG
Naval science (modern hist.: 17th-20th c.)    V47-53+    359.00903
Naval science, navigation, & naval architecture    V    359, 623, 629
Naval science, navigation, & shipbuilding    V-VM
Naval science (pop. works)    V107    359
NAVAL SEAMEN (by area or country)    VD21-124
Naval seamen (G.B.: Eng. & Wales)    VD59
Naval seamen (G.B.: N. Ire.)    VD63
Naval seamen (G.B.: Scot.)    VD61
Naval seamen (gen. hist.: enlisted way of life etc.)    VD15    359.338, .12
Naval seamen (Ger.: by locality)    VD74.A-Z
Naval seamen (U.S.: by state)    VD24.A-W
Naval services (misc.)    VG
Naval shipbuilding (hist.: Asia: gen.)    VM99    623.8095
Naval shipbuilding (hist.: by area or country)    VM21-124
Naval shipbuilding (hist.: Eur.: gen.)    VM55    623.8094
Naval shipbuilding (instruc.: gen.)    VM165    623.8107
Naval signaling (U.S.)    V283
Naval small arms (U.S.)    VD363    359.8240973
Naval stations & shore facilities (countries besides U.S.)    VC416.A-Z
Naval stations & shore facilities (Ger.)    VC416.G3
Naval stations & shore facilities (U.S.: Calif.)    VC415.C2
Naval stations & shore facilities (U.S.: Fl.)    VC415.F5
Naval stations & shore facilities (U.S.: Haw.)    VC415.H2

NAVAL STATUS (Asia)            VA620-667
Naval status (Asia: misc. countries)    VA667.A-Z
Naval status (Australia)    VA710-719
Naval status (Can.)    VA400-402
Naval status (Eur.)    VA450-619
Naval status (Fr.)    VA500-509
Naval status (G.B.)            VA452-467
Naval status (Ger.)    VA510-519
Naval status (It.)    VA540-549
Naval status (Japan)    VA650-659
Naval status (New Z.)    VA720-729
Naval status (Rus.)            VA570-579
Naval status (S.Am.)            VA415-445
Naval status (U.S.)    VA52-395
Naval status (U.S.: gen.)    VA50    359.030973, .4773
Naval status (world: gen.)    VA10    359, .03
Naval status (worldwide: place by place)    VA49-750+
Naval stores & supplies (G.B.)    VC265.G7
Naval strategy (gen. special)    V165
Naval strategy (gen.: pubn. 1801+)    V163    359.03, .43
Naval submarines (diesel- & electric-powered: engineering)    623.82572
Naval submarines (units)    359.3257 (SEE ALSO .933 after 1988)
            V857-859, V858 (U.S.), V859.A-Z (other countries),
            VA65.A-Z (U.S.: by name), VM365-367 (construc.)
Naval supplies & stores (gen.)    VC260    359.8, .62
Naval surgeons (U.S.)    VG263
Naval tactics (gen. particular)    V169
Naval target practice (gen.)    VF310    623.553
Naval telegraph (U.S.)    VG73    359.4150973
Naval telephone (U.S.)    VG83
Naval training ships (U.S.: by name)    V436.A-Z
Naval training stations (U.S.: by place)    V434.A-Z
Naval transport (U.S.)    VC533
Naval underwater teams (U.S.: inclu. demolition)    VG87    359.9840973
Naval uniforms (insignia, service, etiquette, etc.)    359.14    VC300-345
Naval uniforms (U.S.: gen.)    VC303    359.140973, .81
Naval uniforms, badges, shoes, etc.    VC300-345
Naval vessels (auxiliary: fleet trains, repair & supply ships, etc.)    V865
            623.826, 359.326
Naval vessels (misc., non-major: inclu. landing craft)    V895
Naval vessels, Unarmored    V870
Naval War College (U.S.)    V420    359.550973, .0071173
Naval warrant officers (besides U.S.)    VB309.A-Z
Naval weapons systems    VF347
Naval welfare services (places besides U.S.)    VG2005.A-Z
Naval yards & stations (G.B.)    VA460    359.70941
Naval yards & stations (U.S.: gen.)    VA69    359.70973, 623.830973
NAVIES (America)    V55.A65    359.477, .1812
Navies (Asia)    V55.A75    359.475
Navies (Europe)    V55.E8    359.474
Navies (gen. hist.)    V27    359.009, .409, .47
Navies (of the world: gen.)    VA40    359, .03, .009, 623.82509
Navies (organiz. & world status)    VA

NAVIGATION, Aerial    629.13251
Navigation & merchant marine    VK
Navigation, Marine (gen. hist's.: modern: inclu. merch. marine)    VK18
Navigation, Marine (instruction: G.B.: inclu. merch. marine)    VK457
Navigation, Marine (science: hist.)    VK549    527.094, 387.155
Navigational aids, Marine (electronic)    623.893    VK560
Navigational aids, Marine (radar & microwave)    623.8933    VK560-561, VG76-78
Navigational aids, Marine (radio: beacons, compasses, loran, radio, etc.)
                                        623.8932    VK560-561, VG76-85
Navigational aids, Marine (sonar & other sound-ranging)    623.8938    VK388,
                                        VK560, VM480-480.5

Navy base hospitals (WWII: U.S.: by #)    D807.U85.1st-
Navy clubs (U.S.)    V66
Navy frogmen (besides U.S.)    VG88.A-Z
Navy mobile base hospitals (WWII: U.S.: by #)    D807.U87.1st-
Navy yards, shore facilities, stations, etc.    VC412-425
Nazi Party (Ger.: 1930-45)    DD253.2-8    329.43, 324.243+, 943.086
Nazi Party (Ger.: admin. offices)    DD253.29-3
Nazi Party (Ger.: branches or gliederungen)    DD253.46-73
Nazi Party (Ger.: geog. divisions)    DD253.39-45
Nazi Party meetings (Ger.: specific by date)    DD253.28.Date
Near East (1900-18)    956.02    DS62.4
Near East & Southwestern Asia (modern)    DS62.4
Near East, Balkans, E. Mediterranean (WWII: gen.)    D766    940.53495+, 949.5+,
                                        956.03, 962.052
Near East, Turkey, Italy, Greece (WWI)    D566-569
Near East (WWII: dipl. history)    D754.N34
Nebeltruppe (WWII: Ger.)    D757.83
Negros Islands (Philip.)    DS688.N5    959.95
Nehru, Jawaharlal (India: 1901+ era)    DS481.N35
NETHERLANDS (HOLLAND)    DJ    949.2
Netherlands (1890-1948: gen. & biogs. of Queen Wilhelmina)    DJ281    949.2071
Netherlands (1914-18: WWI)    DJ285    949.2071
Netherlands (1939-48: inclu. WWII period)    DJ287
Netherlands & Dutch military ops. (WWII)    D763.N4-42    940.3492071, 949.207
Netherlands (mil. status)    UA730-739    355.0330492
Netherlands (naval status)    VA530-539
Neutral nations (WWII: gen. particip.)    940.5335    D743, D749
Neutrality, other special diplomatic history (WWI)    D611
Neutrality, small states, other special diplomatic history (WWII)    D749
Neutrals (WWI: dipl. hist.)    940.325    D611, D639.N
Neutrals (WWI: gen. particip.)    940.335    D639.N, D615 (Belgium), D611
Neutrals (WWII: dipl. hist.)    940.5325
Nevada    979.3    F836-850
New Britain (Bismarck Arch.: inclu. Rabaul)    DU553.N35
New Britain (WWII)    D767.99.N4
New Brunswick    F1041-1045    971.5
New Caledonia    DU720    993.2 (works before 1989), 993.97
New Caledonia (WWII)    D767.99.N42
New Caledonia (WWII: gen. particip.)    940.53932    DU720
New countries (post-WWI: formation)    940.31425    D651
New countries (post-WWII: formation)    940.531425

NEW ENGLAND (1865-1950)          F9          974.04-042
New England & Middle Atlantic states          974          F1-105 (New Eng.),
                                             F106-205 (Mid. At.), F1-15, F106
New England & Middle Atlantic states (1918-45)          974.042          F9 (New Eng.),
                                             F106 (Mid. At.)
New England & Middle Atlantic states (geog. & travel)          917.4          F2.3, F4,
                                             F9 (1865-1950), F106 (Mid.Atl.)
New England  (gen. hist.)          F4          974
New England (overall)          F1-15, F4          974
New England states          F6-105          974.1-6
New Georgia (WWII)          D767.982.N34, D767.99.N44
NEW GUINEA          DU740-746          995.1-7, 995
New Guinea (geog. & travel)          919.5          DU740
New Guinea (Highlands region: 1942-45: WWII era)          995.603
New Guinea (mil. geog.)          355.4795
New Guinea (Northern coastal region: inclu. Lae, Huon Penin., Madang, Wewak, etc.:
          1942-45: WWII era)          995.703
New Guinea(overall)          995
New Guinea (Papua: naval geog.)          359.4795          VA750.N, VA667.N
New Guinea (WWI)          D578.N4
New Guinea (WWII)          D767.95          940.5426, .5395
New Hebrides          DU760          993.4, 995.95 (books after 1988)
New Hebrides (WWII)          D767.99.N46
New Hebrides (WWII: gen. particip.)          940.53934          DU760
New Ireland (Bismarck Arch.)          DU553.N4
New Ireland (WWII)          D767.99.N47
New Jersey          F131-145          974.9
New Jersey (1865-1950)          F139 (SEE D570.85.N3-31 for 1914-18 war years &
                                             D769.85.N3-31 for 1039-45)
New London Naval Station (U.S.: Conn.)          VA70.N5
New Mexico          F791-805, F796          978.9
New Mexico (1848-1950)          F801
New Mexico (WWII)          D769.85.N33-34
New Orleans (cruiser: U.S.: WWII)          D774.N4
New South Wales (Australia)          DU150-180, DU170          994.4
New South Wales (Australia: 1837-1950: gen.)          DU161
NEW YORK          F116-130, F119          974.7
New York (1865-1950)          F124 (SEE D570.85.N4-5 for 1914-18 war years &
                                             D769.85.N4-5 for 1939-45)          974.704
New York (1918-45)          974.7042          F124 (1865-1950)
New York City area (N.Y.: 1901-50)          F128.5          974.7104-043
New York City (fortifications)          UG412.N5
New York City, N.Y.          F128, F128.3          974.71
New York City, N.Y. (gen.)          F128.3
New York City, N.Y. (sections, suburbs, rivers)          F128.68.A-Z
New York City, N.Y. (streets, bridges, railroads)          F128.67.A-Z
New York (gen.)          F119
New York National Guard (gen.)          UA360
New York (WWI)          D570.85.N4-5
New York (WWII)          D769.85.N4-5          979.7042

NEW ZEALAND        DU400-430   993.1 (PREFER 993 after 1988)
New Zealand (1908-: Dominion)       993.103 (works before 1989), 993.03+ (for titles
                                    after 1988)        DU420-421
New Zealand (1908-18)     993.031, 993.1031 (works prior to about 1989)
New Zealand (1918-45)     993.032, 993.1 (titles before about 1989), 993.1032
New Zealand & Melanesia (overall)        993 (SEE ALSO 995 for Mel. with pubn.
                                    dates after about 1988)        DU400-490+
New Zealand. Army (descrip. & hist.)     UA874.5     355.309931
New Zealand. Army (special sections)     UA874.6.A-Z
New Zealand (gen.)        DU420        993.1-1037+
New Zealand (geog. & travel)    919.31        DU411
New Zealand (lighthouses, beacons, foghorns, etc.)   VK1122.5     623.894209931
New Zealand military ops. (WWII)    D767.85
New Zealand (mil. status: gen.)    UA874.3     355.0330931
New Zealand (naval geog.)        359.4793     VA720-729
New Zealand (naval status: gen.)    VA723.A5-Z        359.0309931, .009931, .47931
New Zealand (WWI)        D547.N5
New Zealand (WWII)        D767.85-852        940.53931, .5409931, .5426, 993.1032
New Zealand (WWII: dipl. hist.)        940.5322931 (titles after 1988 may be at
                                    .532293)        D754.N45
Newfoundland    F1121-1139        971.8, .803 (1934-49)
NEWS & PROPAGANDA (WWI)        940.488        D639.P6-7, D631-633, D619.3
News & propaganda (WWI: in Ger.)        940.488943
News & propaganda (WWI: in Rus.)        940.488947
News & propaganda (WWI: in specific countries)  940.4889+
News & propaganda (WWII)        940.5488        D810.P6 (gen.),
                                    .P7.A-Z (by country)
News & propaganda (WWII: in Australia)        940.5488994
News & propaganda (WWII: in Can.)        940.5488972
News & propaganda (WWII: in China)        940.5488951
News & propaganda (WWII: in Fr.)        940.5488944
News & propaganda (WWII: in G.B.)        940.5488941-5488942
News & propaganda (WWII: in Ger.)        940.5488943
News & propaganda (WWII: in It.)        940.5488945
News & propaganda (WWII: in Japan)        940.5488952
News & propaganda (WWII: in Philip. Is.)        940.54889599
News & propaganda (WWII: in Rus.)        940.5488947
News & propaganda (WWII: in specific places)    940.54889+
News & propaganda (WWII: in U.S.)        940.5488973        D753.3
News media, censorship, etc. (WWII: G.B.)        D799.G7
News media, censorship, etc. (WWII: Ger.)        D799.G3
News media, censorship, etc. (WWII: U.S.)        D799.U6
News media (WWII: gen.)        D798
Newspapers, media, & public relns. (mil.: Japan)        UH705.J3
Newspapers, media, & public relns. (navies: besides U.S.)     VG505.A-Z
Nicaragua (post-WWI territorial ?s)        D651.N5
Nice, Fr. (1860-)        DC989
Nicholas II (Rus.: Czar, 1894-1917)        DK258
Night fighting        U167.5.N5
Nihon Kirisuto Kyodan (WWII: churches)        D810.C674
Nile River (20th c.: descrip. & travel)        DT124        962.044-045
Nitti, Francesco (It. 1900-46 period)        DG575.N5

Noncombat services (air forces)   358.4134
Noncombat services (mil.: inclu. soc. srvcs., dependent srvcs., civil activ's., etc.)
                                                              355.34
Non-combat services, Naval   359.34   VG1-2029+, VC10-580+
Noncombatants, pacifists, sympathizers, etc. (WWI)   940.316
Noncombatants, pacifists, sympathizers, etc. (WWII)   940.5316
Non-commissioned officers, Air force (countries besides U.S.)   UG825.A-Z
Nonexplosive agents (tear gas etc.: design)   623.459   UF780
Nonmilitary use of armed forces   UH720-725
Nordenfelt machine guns   UF620.N8
Nordenfelt ordnance   UF560-565... .N.
Norfolk Navy Yard (U.S.: Va.)   VA70.N7
Norfolk, Va.   F234.N8
Normandie (pass. ship)   VM383.N6
Normandy area (Fr.)   944.2   DC611.N841-899
Normandy (Fr.)   DC611.N841-899
Normandy (Fr.: 20th c.)   DC611.N899
NORTH Africa   961   DT160-346
North Africa (1830-1950: Eur. era)   961.03   DT176
North Africa (19th-20th c.)   DT176   961.023-03+
North Africa (Egypt & Barbary States)   DT160-177   961-962
North Africa (WWII)   D766.82   940.5361, .5423, 961.03
NORTH AMERICA   E-F1392+, E11-45, E31-45   970
North America (1900-)   970.05   E45, E18.85
North America (1900-18)   970.051
North America (1918-45)   970.052
North America & America   970-979   E-F
North America (gen.)   E45
North America (geog. & travel)   917   E41, E27
North America (mil. status: gen.)   UA22   355.03307
North & South America (WWII: gen.)   D768
North Atlantic Fleet (U.S.)   VA63.N8
North Atlantic (pilot & sailing guides)   VK811-814.5
North Atlantic (tide & current tables)   VK611   623.8949091631
North Carolina   F251-265   975.6
North Carolina (1865-1950)   F259
North Central states   977   F476-705, F476-590 (Old N.W.), F476-485, F591-
                                              705 (Trans-Miss.), F591-596
North Dakota   F631-645   978.4
North Dakota (WWII: Reconstruction)   D828.N9-91
North Island (New Z.)   993.12
North Pacific (pilot & sailing guides)   VK917   623.89291644-89291646
North Sea & Baltic (pilot & sailing guides)   VK815-826
North Sea & Baltic (tide & current tables)   VK615-626
North Sea (mil. status)   UA646.6   355.033016336
North Vietnam (1945-75)   DS560   959.7
North Vietnam (gen.)   DS560.6
Northcliffe, Alfred C. W. Harmsworth, 1st Viscount (G.B.: 20th c.)   DA566.9.N7
Northeast Africa (1900-74)   DT367.75   963.05+
NORTHERN Australia   DU392-398   994.29
Northern Australia (gen. & descrip.)   DU395-396
Northern Europe & Scandinavia   948   DL
Northern Europe (mil. status)   UA646.85   355.033048
Northern Europe, Scandinavia, Finland (1901-45)   DL83   948.08
Northern Expedition (China: 1926-28)   DS777.46

Northern Ireland          941.6          DA990.U45-46
Northern Ireland (WWII: dipl. history)          D754.I7
Northern Rhodesia (Zambia), Rhodesia (Zimbabwe), & Nyasaland (Malawi)
                    968.9          DT858-865 (Malawi, Nyasaland, Br. Central
                    Afr. Protec.), DT946-965 (Rhodesia), DT963 (Zambia)
Northern Territory (Australia)          994.29          DU392-398
Northwest Africa, Morocco, & offshore islands          964
Northwest (U.S.: Old)          F476-590          977
NORWAY          DL401-596+, DL448 (gen.)          948.1
Norway (20th c.)          DL527          948.104
Norway (20th c.: 1905-)          948.104          DL527+
Norway (1905-57: Haakon VII era)          DL530-533          948.1041-1045
Norway (1914-18)          DL531
Norway (1939-45)          DL532
Norway & Norwegian military ops. (WWII)          D763.N6-62          940.3481, 948.1041
Norway, Central & Northern          948.4
Norway (geog. & travel)          914.81-84          DL418
Norway (mil. status)          UA750          355.0330481
Norway (naval status)          VA550-559          359.0309481
Norway (WWI: dipl. hist.)          D621.S45
Norway (WWII: dipl. hist.)          940.5322481          D754.N8
Norwegian military ops. (WWII)          D763.N6
Nova Scotia          F1036-1040, F1038 (gen.)          971.6
Nuclear ops., Military (also gen. strategy)          355.43 (use .4 for post-'88 titles on
                    gen. strategy)          U161-163
Nuclear warfare          358.39          UF767, U162, U165, UA
Nuclear weapons          355.825119          UG1282.A8
Nuclear weapons (design)          623.45119          UF767, UG1282.A8 or .H,
                    QC773.A1 or .H
Nuremberg, Ger.          DD901.N91-97
Nuremberg Trial of Major German War Criminals (1945-46)          D804.G42
Nurse corps, Naval          VG350-355
Nurse corps, Naval (U.S.)          VG353
Nurses & nursing, Military (gen.)          UH490          355.345
Nursing & nurses, Military (besides U.S.)          UH495.A-Z
NYASALAND (Malawi, Brit. Cent. Afr. Protec.)          DT858-865

OAHU (Haw. Is.)          DU628.O3          996.93
O'Bannon (destroyer: WWII)          D774.O3
OBSERVATIONS, Military          U719-740+
Observations, Military (Russo-Jpn. War, 1904-5)          U735
Observations, Military (Sino-Jpn. War, 1937-45)          U739.8
Observations, Military (Sp. Civil War, 1936-9)          U739.5
Observations, Military (WWI)          U738
Observations, Military (WWII)          U740
Observations, Naval (Russo-Japanese War, 1904-5)          V713          952.031,
                    359.4752, .4747
Observations, Naval (WWI)          V715          940.45-453
Observations, Naval (WWII)          V716          940.545-5459
Obstacles (mil. engineering)          UG375          355.544
Occupation & government, Military          355.49          D802 (WWII)
Occupation, Military (WWI: Rhineland)          D650.M5
Occupational rehabilitation of veterans (by occup.)          UB366.A-Z

OCCUPIED countries (WWII: gen. particip.)     940.5336     D802.A2
Occupied territories (WWI: by country)     D623.A3-Z
Occupied territories (WWI: gen.: includes laws)  D623.A2
Occupied territories (WWII: by country, area, etc.)   D802.A3-Z
Occupied territories (WWII: events, laws, etc.)     D802
Occupied territories (WWII: gen.)     D802.A2
Oceania          993-996          DU
Oceania, Australia, New Zealand     DU     990-996
Oceania (mil. status)     UA875     355.03309
Oceania or Pacific Islands (WWII)     D767.9-99
Oceania (Pacific Ocean)     DU     990-996, 909.0964
Oceanica & other misc. areas   990 (SEE ALSO 995 for gen. works after about 1988)
                                DU, DU28.3
Oceanography, Military (gen.)     V396     359.982, 551.46, 620.4162
Oceanography, Military (places besides U.S.)     V396.5.A-Z
Odessa & Crimea areas (Rus.)     947.717     DK511.C7
Odessa, Rus.          DK651.O2
Odessa, Uk.          DK508.95.O33
Offenses & crimes, Military     UB780-789
Offenses & crimes, Naval     VB850-880
OFFICERS, Air force (gen.)     UG790     358.41331-41332
Officers, Air force (Ger.)     UG795.G3
Officers, Air force (U.S.)     UG793
Officers' clubs & messes, Military (U.S.)     UC743
Officers' clubs & messes, Naval     VC380-385
Officers, Commissioned & warrant     355.332     UB407-415
Officers, Commissioned & warrant (navies)     359.332     VB307-315
Officers' handbooks, Naval (places besides U.S.)     V135.A-Z
Officers, Military (G.B.)     UB415.G7     355.3320941
Officers, Military (Ger.)     UB415.G3     355.3320943
Officers, Military (inclu. appt., promo., retire.)     UB410-415
Officers, Military (U.S.)     UB412-414     355.3320973
Officers, Naval (G.B.)     VB315.G7     359.3320941
Officers, Naval (inclu. appt., promo., rank, retire., etc.)     VB310-315
Officers, Naval (Japan)     VB315.J3
Officers, Naval (Rus.)     VB315.R9
Officers, Naval (U.S.: gen.)     VB313     359.3320973, .3310973
Officers, Non-commissioned (air: U.S.: inclu. airmen)     UG823
Officers, Warrant (mil.: gen.)     UB407
Officers, Warrant (naval: U.S.)     VB308     359.3320973
Ohio          F486-500, F491     977.1
Okinawa (Japan)     DS895.O4     952.81
Okinawa (WWII)     D767.99.O45
Oklahoma          F691-705     976.6
Old Northwest (U.S.: 1865-1950)     F484.5     977.03
Oman          DS247.O6-68
Ontario (Can.)     F1056-1059.7, F1058 (gen.)     971.3
Operational equipment, Air force (airplanes, bombs, guns, vehicles)     UG1200-1405
Optical instruments & tools, Artillery     UF849
Optimum ship routing     VK570
Oran, Alg.          DT299.O7

Orders, General (Rus. military: offic. compil's.)     UB657.A5
Orders, passes, field correspondence (mil. sci.)     UB280-285
Orders, passes, field correspondence (naval admin.)     VB255
Orders, Special (Rus. military: collec's. & compil's.)     UB657.A6-7
Orders, Transmission of (navies)     V270     359.27, .85
ORDNANCE     355.82     UF520-780, U800-823+
Ordnance, Air force     358.4182     UG1270-1275
Ordnance, Air force (gen.)     UG1270-1275     358.4182, 623.45+
Ordnance, Aircraft (design)     623.7461     UG1270-1275, UF530-537
Ordnance & arms, Naval (in sum)     VF350-375
Ordnance & arms, Naval (manufacture)     VF370-375
Ordnance & small arms     UF520-537     355.82, 623.4+, .44
Ordnance & small-arms research (U.S.)     UF526.3
Ordnance & small arms (U.S.)     UF523     355.820973
Ordnance battalions etc. (WWII: U.S.: by #)     D769.743.1st-
Ordnance battalions etc. (WWII: U.S.: gen.)     D769.74
Ordnance drills, Naval (Eur.: gen.)     VF215
Ordnance (engineering & design)     623.4     UF520-910+, UF520-525 (gen.),
     UF523 (U.S.), VF (naval), VF1-580, VF21-124 (by place), VF23 (U.S.)
Ordnance facilities, Naval     359.73     VF380-385
Ordnance laws (U.S.: PREFER KF7335     UF133
Ordnance magazines & facilities (navies)     VF380-385
ORDNANCE MATERIAL (by type, mark #, ed. date, etc.)
     UF560-565.A-Z.A-Z(II-IV) etc.
Ordnance material (countries besides U.S.)     UF565.A-Z
Ordnance material (Fr.)     UF565.F8
Ordnance material (G.B.)     UF565.G7
Ordnance material (gen.)     UF560     355.82+, 623.4+
Ordnance material (Ger.)     UF565.G3
Ordnance material (Japan)     UF565.J3
Ordnance material (misc.)     VF420
Ordnance material (navies: U.S.)     VF393
Ordnance material (Rus.)     UF565.R9
Ordnance material (U.S.: gen.)     UF563     355.820973, 623.40973
ORDNANCE, NAVAL     VF     359.82, 623.8251
Ordnance, Naval (Asia)     VF99-113
Ordnance, Naval (Australia)     VF121
Ordnance, Naval (Eur.)     VF55-96     359.82094
Ordnance, Naval (Fr.)     VF71
Ordnance, Naval (G.B.)     VF57     359.820941
Ordnance, Naval (gen. hist's.)     VF15     359.8209
Ordnance, Naval (gen. pubns. 1801+)     VF145     359.82
Ordnance, Naval (Ger.)     VF73     359.820943
Ordnance, Naval (handbooks & manuals: gen.)     VF150
Ordnance, Naval (It.)     VF79
Ordnance, Naval (Japan)     VF105     359.820952
Ordnance, Naval (misc. topics)     VF580
Ordnance, Naval (Rus.)     VF85
Ordnance, Naval (U.S.)     VF23     359.820973, 623.82510973
Ordnance proper     UF560-780
Ordnance proper (navies)     VF390-395
Ordnance proper (navies: U.S.: documents)     VF393.A1-3
Ordnance proper (navies: U.S.: gen.)     VF393.A7-Z
Ordnance research, Naval (U.S.)     VF360.3
Ordnance stores, accounts, etc. (gen.)     UF550

Ore carriers     VM457     623.8245, 387.544
Oregon          979.5     F871-885
ORGANIZATION (air forces)     UG770-1045
Organization & personnel (cavalry: inclu. specific units)     357.043
Organization & personnel (infantry)     356.189
Organization & personnel (marines)     359.963     VB21-124
Organization & personnel, Naval     359.3     VA, VA50 (U.S.), VB21-124
Organization (armor & cavalry: gen.)     UE10
Organization (artillery forces)     UF10
Organization (infantry: gen.)     UD10
Organization (mil. maint. & transport: by country)     UC20-258
Organization (mil. medical: inclu. services)     UH400-485
Organization (mil. personnel: hist. & geog. treatment)     355.309
Organization (naval maintenance: by place)     VC20-258
Orientals (in Calif.)     F870.O6
Orientals (in U.S.)     E184.O6
Orkney Islands (Scot.)     DA880.O5-6
Orphans, children, similar noncombatants (WWI)     940.3161     D639.C4
Orphans, children, similar noncombatants (WWII)     940.53161     D810.C4
Osaka, Japan     DS897.O8     952.183
Oslo, Nor. (area)     948.2     DL581
Oslo, Nor. (Christiana)     DL581     948.2
Oxford and Asquith, Herbert Henry Asquith, 1st Earl of (G.B.: 20th c.)     DA566.9.O7
Oxford University (WWI)     D547.O7

P.O.W. CAMPS & internment centers (WWI: in G.B.)     940.47241-47242     D627.G7
P.O.W. camps & internment centers (WWI: in Ger.)     940.47243     D627.G3
P.O.W. camps & internment centers (WWI: in Rus.)     940.47247     D627.R9
P.O.W. camps & internment centers (WWII: run by G.B.)     940.547241     D805.G7
P.O.W. camps & internment centers (WWII: run by Ger.)     940.547243     D805.G3
P.O.W. camps & internment centers (WWII: run by Japan)     940.547252     D805.J3
P.O.W. camps & internment centers (WWII: run by Rus.)     940.547247     D805.R9
P.O.W. camps & internment centers (WWII: run by U.S.)     940.547273     D805.U5-6
P.T. boats (gen.)     V830
PACIFIC aerial ops. (WWII: U.S. bombing survey)     D785.U63
Pacific (air war geog.)     358.41479
Pacific, Asiatic, & other colonies (WWI: Ger.: gen.)     D577
Pacific Coast & Far West (U.S.: geog. & travel)     917.9     F851
Pacific Coast & Great Basin (U.S.: 20th c.)     979.03     F786, F852
Pacific Coast (naval geog.)     359.4779     VA50
Pacific Coast (S.Am.)     F2213
Pacific Coast (U.S.: fortifications)     UG411.P2
Pacific Fleet (U.S.)     VA63.P2
Pacific Islands, German (post-WWI territorial ?s)     D651.P2
Pacific Islands (mil. status: by island or group name)     UA876.A-Z
Pacific Islands (smaller misc.: by name)     DU950.A-Z
Pacific Islands (WWII: gen.)     D767.9     940.5426, .54439, .544952, .54539,
                                            .545952, .5352
Pacific Islands (WWII: misc. by name)     D767.99.A-Z
Pacific (marine mil. geog.)     359.96479+     VE123, VA730
Pacific (naval geog.)     359.479     VA710-750, VA730
Pacific, North Central (inclu. Hawaiian Is.)     996.9
Pacific Northwest (1859-1950)     F852     979.5

PACIFIC OCEAN & islands (lighthouses, beacons, foghorns, etc.) VK1123-1124
                                                          623.8942099+, .894209164+
Pacific Ocean & islands (lighthouses, beacons, foghorns, etc.: lists)
                                         VK1214-1223     623.894409164
Pacific Ocean & islands (pilot & sailing guides)   VK915-956
Pacific Ocean & islands (tide & current tables)   VK715-756
Pacific Ocean & misc. (geog. & travel)   919       DU22
Pacific Ocean area (maps & atlases)   912.9     G2860-3012
Pacific Ocean areas (misc.: geog. & travel)   919.6
Pacific Ocean (Loran tables)   VK561.P3
Pacific Ocean (Oceania: gen.)   DU28.3     990, 990.09, 909.0964
Pacific, Southwest Central (plus isolated S.E. islands)   996.1
Pacific States & Alaska   F851-915+     979
Pacific Theatre & Asia (WWII: gen.)   D767   940.5425-5426
Pacifists (WWI)     940.3162     D613, UB342.A-Z (by place)
Pacifists (WWII)     940.53162     D810.C82, UB342.A-Z (by place)
Packing & shipment (mil. supplies)     UC277
Paderewski, Ignacy Jan (Pol.: 1918-45 era)     DK4420.P3
Page, Walter Hines (U.S.: 1865-1900 era)     E664.P15
Pago Pago, Samoa     DU819.P3
Pakistan (Bengal: East & West)   DS485.B39-493     954.14
Pakistan (pre-1947), India, Ceylon, Burma, etc.   DS401-498   954
Palaces (London, Eng.)     DA689.P17
Palau & Caroline Islands   996.6     DU560-568, DU5630565
Palau Islands (Pelew Is.: WWII)     D767.99.P4
Palawan (Philip.)     DS688.P15   959.94
Palembang, Sumatra     DS646.15.P3
PALESTINE (640-1917)   956.9403     DS124-125, DS125.5 (WWI yrs.)
Palestine (19th-20th c.)   DS125     956.9403-9404
Palestine (1914-18: WWI)     DS125.5     956.9403-9404
Palestine (1919-48: Brit. control)     DS126   956.9404
Palestine (geog. & travel)     915.694     DS107.3
Palestine, Israel, & the Jews     DS101-151   956.94, 909.04924
Palestine (post-WWI territorial ?s)     D651.P3
Palestine (post-WWII territorial ?s)     D821.P3
Palestine (WWI)     D568.7
Palestine (WWII: Israel)   D766.7.I7
Palestine (WWII: Reconstruction)   D829.P3
PAMPHLETS, MINOR WORKS (20th c.)     D416
Pamphlets, minor works (20th c.: diplomacy)     D457
Pamphlets, minor works (20th c.: politics and diplomacy)     D450
Pamphlets, minor works, addresses (Rus.: 1925-53)     DK267.3.1925-1953
Pamphlets, minor works (Jpn. for. relns.)     DS847
Pamphlets, minor works (Jpn. polit. & dipl. hist.)     DS844
Pamphlets, minor works, sermons (Rus. Rev., 1917-21)   DK265.17
Pamphlets, minor works, sermons (Sp. Civil War, 1936-39)     DP269.17
Pamphlets, minor works, sermons (WWI)   D525
Pamphlets, minor works, sermons (WWII)   D743.9
Pamphlets, minor works (WWI: peace)   D646
Pamphlets, minor works (WWI: U.S.)   D570.15
Pamphlets, minor works (WWII: peace)   D816.5
Pamphlets, minor works (WWII: Reconstruction)   D826
Pamphlets, minor works (WWII: U.S.)     D769.15

PANAMA          F1561-1577, F1566          972.87
Panama (1903-52)    F1566.5    972.8705-052
Panama (1904-45)          972.87051    F1566.5
Panama Canal & Zone    972.875    F1569.C2
Panama Canal (fortifications)          UG412.P3
Panama Canal (pilot & sailing guides)    VK970.P2
Panama (mil. geog.)       355.477287 (SEE ALSO .47862)
Panama (mil. status)       UA607.P3
Panama (naval geog.)       359.477287          VA407.P
Panay (Philip.)    DS688.P2    959.95
Panceltism       D448.5
Pangermanism       D447
Panlatinism       D448
Pannonia       DJK77
Panslavism       D449
Panslavism (Eastern question: 19th c.)          D377.3-5
Panzer divisions (by #)          D757.56.1st-
Panzer regiments (by #)          D757.57.1st-
Panzer troops (by author, division, name, etc.)    D757.55.A-Z
Panzer troops (WWII: Ger.)    D757.54-57
Panzer troops (WWII: Ger.: gen.)    D757.54
Papal States       DG791-800+
Papal States (modern)    DG796
Papen, Franz von (Ger.: 1918-48 era)          DD247.P5
Papen, Franz von (WWI: Ger. spy in U.S.)    D619.5.P2
Papua & New Guinea (gen.: inclu. Brit. terr. & Port Moresby, Owen Stanley Mts., Lae,
     Salamaua, etc.)       DU740          995, 995.3
Papua New Guinea & New Guinea region    995.3
Papua New Guinea (inclu. Kokoda Trail, Port Moresby, Owen Stanley Range, etc.:
     1942-45: WWII era)          995.303
Papua Territory (1942-45: WWII period)          995.403
Parachute & airborne troops (gen.)    UD480
Parachute troops (WWII: Brit.)          D759.63
Parachute troops (WWII: Fr.)       D761.7
Parachute troops (WWII: Ger.)       D757.63
Parachute troops (WWII: U.S.)       D769.347
Paraguay       F2661-2699    989.2
Paraguay (1938-)    F2689    989.2071-2072
Paraguay (gen.)       F2681
Paraguay (mil. status)    UA634-636    355.0330892
Paraguay (WWII: dipl. hist.)       940.5322892 (might ALSO be with Neutrals at
                              .5325892)          D754.P
Paratroops       356.166       UD480-485, UD483 (U.S.), UG630-635
Paris, Fr. (1914-21)    DC736
Paris, Fr. (1922-)    DC737+    944.360816
Paris, Fr. (area)       944.36       DC701-790, DC707 (gen.), DC735 (1871-1914),
                    DC737 (1914-)
Paris, Fr. (WWII)    D762.P3    944.360816
Passenger ships (engineering)       623.8243       VM381-385, VM383.A-Z (by ship
                         name), VM385.A-Z (by co.)
Passenger ships (naval architec.)       VM381-383
Passes, orders, field correspondence (mil. sci.: gen.)       UB280
Patrols & reconnaisance, Naval       V190       359.413

PAY & allowances (Ger. Navy)          VC181
Pay & allowances (marines)            VE490          359.9664
Pay & allowances (mil.: G.B.)         UC185
Pay & allowances (U.S. Navy)          VC50-65        359.135, .640973
Pay & benefits (air forces)           UG940-945  358.41135, .4164
Paymaster's Dept. (U.S. Army)         UC70-75
PEACE conferences (WWII: gen.)   D814.56
Peace efforts (WWI: preserve or restore)    940.312     D613, D641-644+ (armistice)
Peace efforts (WWII: preserve or restore)     940.5312     D749, D748-754
Peace (WWI)              D642-651    940.312, .3141
Peace (WWI: gen.)        D644    940.312
Peace (WWII)        D814-821    940.5314, .532+
Peace (WWII: gen.)    D815
Peace (WWII: gen. spec.)      D816
Peace (WWII: special topics)    D820.A-Z
Peiping, China (Peking)        DS795        951.156
Peking, China        951.156        DS795
Penelope (WWII: cruiser)        D772.P4
Pennsylvania            F146-160, F149        974.8
Pennsylvania Ave. (Washington, D.C.)      F203.7.P4
Pennsylvania (1865-1950)        F154
Pensacola, Florida        F319.P4
Pensacola Naval Air Station (Flor.)      VG94.5.P4
Pensions, disability benefits, etc. (naval admin.)      VB280-285   359.115-1156
Pensions, Survivors' (mil.)        UB400-405
Pensions, Survivors' (naval)        VB340-345
Pensions, Veterans'      UB370-375        331.25291355 (PREFER), 355.1151, .64
PERIODICALS & ASSOCIATIONS (air forces)      UG622        358.005-006
Periodicals & associations (armor & cavalry)      UE1
Periodicals & associations (arms & armor: hist.)     U799
Periodicals & associations (artillery)        UF1
Periodicals & associations (Ger.: 1918-)        DD233
Periodicals & associations (infantry)        UD1
Periodicals & associations (marine navig. & merch. marine)      VK1
Periodicals & associations (mil. engineering)      UG1
Periodicals & associations (military: in English)    U1        355.005-006
Periodicals & associations (military medical services)      UH201
Periodicals & associations (military: U.S.)        UA23.A1.A-Z
PERIODICALS & ASSOCIATIONS (NAVAL architec.: Eng.)      VM1
Periodicals & associations (naval medical services)      VG100
Periodicals & associations (naval ordnance)        VF1
Periodicals & associations (naval: G.B.)        VA452
Periodicals & associations (naval: Ger.)        VA510
Periodicals & associations (naval: in English)      V1        359.005, .006+
Periodicals & associations (naval: U.S.)        VA49        359.005-007+
Periodicals & associations (WWI: prisons)        D627.A1      940.472+
Periodicals & associations (WWII: prison)        D805.A1
Periodicals & documents (Ger.: Nazi Party)    DD253.2
Periodicals & yearbooks (U.S.)        E171
Periodicals, associations, collections (Ger.: 1930-45)        DD253.A1
Periodicals, associations, yearbooks (20th c.)        D410
Periodicals, associations, yearbooks (It.: 1919-45)    DG571.A1

Periodicals (mil. admin.)      UB1
Periodicals, serials, collections (WWII)      D731
Periodicals (U.S. Marines)      VE23.A1.A-Z      359.96097305
Periodicals (WWII: by country)      D805.A3-Z.A1-19
Periscopes (submarine architec.)      VM367.P4
Persia (Iran)      955      DS251-325, DS272
Persia (1794-1925: Kajar dynasty)      DS298-316      955.04-051
Persia (geog. & travel)      915.5      DS258
Persia (post-WWI territorial ?s)      D651.P4
PERSONAL accounts, Allied (WWI)      940.481+      D640, D570.9 (U.S.)
Personal accounts, Allied (WWII)      940.5481+      D811
Personal accounts, American (WWII: U.S.)      940.548173
Personal accounts, Australian (WWII)      940.548194
Personal accounts, Axis (WWII)      940.5482+      D811
Personal accounts, British (WWII)      940.548141
Personal accounts, Central Power (WWI)      940.482+      D640, D531-540
Personal accounts, English (WWII)      940.548142
Personal accounts, French (WWII)      940.548144
Personal accounts, German (WWII)      940.548243
Personal accounts, Italian (WWII)      940.548245
Personal accounts, Japanese (WWII)      940.548252
Personal accounts, Russian (WWII)      940.548147
Personal accounts (Russo-Fin. War, 1939-40: collective)      DL1102
Personal accounts (Russo-Fin. War, 1939-40: individual)      DL1102.5
Personal accounts (Russo-Polish War, other Polish conflicts of 1918-21)
                                                                    DK4406.5
Personal accounts (Sino-Jpn. Confl., 1937-45: collections)      DS777.5314
Personal accounts (Sino-Jpn. Confl., 1937-45: indiv. by name)      DS777.5315.A-Z
Personal accounts (Sp. Civil War, 1936-39)      DP269.9
Personal accounts (WWI)  D640 (SEE ALSO D570.9 for U.S. soldiers)      940.481+
Personal accounts (WWII)      D811 (SEE ALSO DA-F country #'s for biographies &
                              memoirs)      940.5481-5482+
Personal accounts (WWII: collections)      D811.A2
Personal accounts (WWII: individual: by name)   D811.A3-Z
Personal accounts (WWII: noncombatants: by name)      D811.5.A-Z
Personal accounts (WWII: U.S.)      D769.9 (PREFER D811)
PERSONNEL administration, Military (civilian & mil.)      355.61      UB160-165,
                              UB180-197, UB410-415 (officers), UB320-338
Personnel administration, Naval (civilian & mil.)      359.61      VB257-258.5
Personnel administration (naval sci.: gen.)      VB257      359.61
Personnel, Air force      UG1130-1185
Personnel & administration (air forces: U.S.)      UG773
Personnel, Civilian (mil. admin.: U.S.)      UB193
Personnel, Civilian (naval admin.: gen.)      VB180
Personnel transport (navies)      VC550-555
Personnel transport vehicles (land: mil. design)      623.7472
Perth, Australia      DU378      994.11
Perth, Australia (area)      994.11      DU378
Peru      F3401-3619, F3431      985
Peru (1919-)      F3448      985.0631-0632
Peru (gen.)      F3431
Peru (mil. status)      UA637-639
Pétain, Henri Philippe (Fr.: 1871-1940 era)      DC342.8.P4

Peter I Karadordevic (Serbia: ruler, 1903-18: ALSO gen. works on period)
DR2030
Peter I (Yug.: King, 1903-21: ALSO covers era)      DR360
Peter II (Yug.: monarch, 1934-45)      DR1297
Petrograd, Rus. (1801-)      DK568
Petroleum industry (defense)      UA929.95.P4
Petty officers' handbooks (gen.)      V120
Pharmacy services, Military      UH420-425
Philadelphia Navy Yard (U.S.: Penn.)      VA70.P5
Philadelphia, Penn.      F158      974.811
PHILIPPINE ISLANDS      DS651-689, DS655, DS668      959.9
Philippine Islands (1898-1946: U.S. era)      959.903      DS679-686.4, DS685
Philippine Islands (1901+)      DS685      959.903
Philippine Islands (1901-35)      959.9032      DS685
Philippine Islands (1935-46: Commonwealth)      DS686-686.4      959.9035
Philippine Islands (1935-44: Manuel Quezon era)      DS686.3      959.9035
Philippine Islands (1942-46: Japanese occup. [1942-45] & Osmeña rule [44-46])
DS686.4
Philippine Islands (gen.: pubn. 1801+)      DS668.A3-Z      959.9
Philippine Islands (pilot & sailing guides)      VK911      623.8929599
Philippine Islands (Sp.-Am. War, 1898: ALSO Battle of Manila Bay)      E717.7
973.8937
Philippine Islands (tide & current tables)      VK711
Philippine Islands (WWII)      D767.4      940.53599, .5409599, .5425-5426, 959.03
Philippine Sea, Battle of (1944)      D774.P55
PHILIPPINES (geog. & travel)      915.99      DS659
Philippines (mil. geog.)      355.47599
Philippines (mil. status)      UA853.P5      355.0330599
Philippines (naval geog.)      359.47599      VA667.P, VA750.P
Philippines (naval status)      VA667.P5      359.0309599
Philippines (WWII: dipl. hist.)      940.5322599 (puppet gov. might be with Axis Powers
at .5324599)      D754.P5
Philosophy & psychology      100-199      B-BD, BH-BJ, BF
Philosophy, Naval (e.g. theory of naval sea power)      V25
Philosophy, psychology, religion      B      100-299
Photographers, Naval      VG1010-1015
Photographic interpretation (navies)      VG1020
Photography, Ballistic (inclu. photochronography)      UF840
Photography, Military      UG476      623.72
Photography, Military (mil. engineering)      623.72      UG476
Photography (WWII)      D810.P4
Physical training (mil. sci.)      U320-325      355.54+
Physical training (navies: U.S.)      V263-264
Pictorial and graphic histories (20th c.)      D426      779.990194, 909.82
PICTORIALS (naval: U.S.)      VA59      359.3250973
Pictorials, satires, etc. (Rus. Rev., 1917-21)      DK265.15
Pictorials, satires, etc. (Sp. Civil War, 1936-39)      DP269.15
Pictorials (ships)      VM307      387.2+
Pictorials (U.S. Mil. Acad.)      U410.L3
Pictorials (U.S. Naval Acad.)      V415.L3
Pictorials (world navies)      VA42
Pictorials (WWI)      D522 (SEE ALSO D527)      940.49
Pictorials (WWII)      D743.2 (SEE ALSO D746)      940.549

Pigeons, Military (for communications: SEE ALSO D639.P45 for WWI & D810.P53
        for WWII)      UH90
Pigeons (WWII)     D810.P53
PILOT & SAILING GUIDES (Atl. Ocean: all & east: gen.)    VK810      623.8929163
Pilot & sailing guides (by area)    VK804-997
Pilot & sailing guides (C. Am.: by locality)    VK970.A-Z
Pilot & sailing guides (E. Pac. & Am. W. Coast: gen.)    VK941
Pilot & sailing guides (Pac. islands: misc.)    VK933.A-Z
Pilot & sailing guides (Pac. Ocean & islands: gen.)    VK915      623.8929164
Pilot & sailing guides (W. Atlantic: gen.)    VK959
Pilot guides & sailing directions (gen.: pubn. 1801+)    VK802     623.8922, .8929+
Pilot guides (geog. treatment)    623.89291-89299    VK804-997
PILOTING, Aerial    629.13252
Piloting & pilot guides, Nautical    623.8922    VK1500-1661, VK1523-1525 (U.S.),
        VK1645 (gen.), VK798-803
Piloting & pilots, Nautical (by area)    VK1521-1624    623.291-89299
Piloting (gen.: mil. engineering)    623.746048 (SEE ALSO .7463 [bombers] or
        other types)    TL710+, UG670-675 (manuals), UG700-705 (tactics)
Piloting, Nautical (Asia)    VK1599-1613
Piloting, Nautical (Australia & the Pac.)    VK1621-1624
Piloting, Nautical (Eur.)    VK1555-1596    623.294
Piloting, Nautical (U.S.)    VK1523-1525    623.2973
Pilots & piloting, Nautical    VK1500-1661
Pilots & piloting, Nautical (gen.)    VK1645-1661
Pilsudski, Joseph (Pol.: 1918+ biog.)    DK440.5.P5
Pilsudski, Jozef (Pol.: 1918-45 time)    DK4420.P5
Pioneer Corps (WWII: G.B.)    D760.P5
Pioneer troops    UG530-535
Pistols & revolvers (gen.)    UD410    355.8243, 623.443
Pistols & revolvers (marines)    VE390    359.968243
Piston & turboprop airplanes    629.133343
Planes, Fighter (design)    623.7464    TL685.3, TL686.A-Z (by manufac.
        or model), UG1242.F5
Planes, Reconnaisance (mil. design)    623.7467    UG1242.R4
Planning, Military (U.S.)    U153
Plans, Attack & defense (countries except U.S.)    UA925.A-Z
Plating, Armor (naval sci.: special type)    V907.A-Z
Plumbing (naval architec. & engin.)    VM501
Poetry, satire, etc. (WWI)    D526-526.7 (PREFER PQ-PT)
Poetry, satire, etc. (WWII)    D745-745.7 (PREFER PQ-PT)
Poetry, satire, etc. (WWII: languages besides Eng., Fr., Ger.)    D745.7.A-Z
POLAND    DK401-441+ (older titles prior to 1976-77), DK414, DK4010-4800
        (titles 1970+?), DK4140    943.8
Poland (1795-1918)    DK434.9 (older), DK4349-4395    943.803
Poland (1795-1918: foreign rule)    943.803    DK434.9, DK4349, DK439
Poland (1864-1918)    DK4380    943.803
Poland (20th c.)    DK4382
Poland (1914-18: WWI)    DK439 (older works), DK4390    943.803
Poland (1915-18: Austrian occupation)    DK4392

Poland (1918-: Republic: inclu. wars of 1918-21)     DK440     943.804
Poland (1918-45)          DK4397-4420          943.804
Poland (1918-45: gen.)     DK4400
Poland (1918-26)          DK4403.5
Poland (1918-21: wars, inclu. Russo-Polish of 1919-20)     DK4404-4409
Poland (1926-39)          DK4409.5
Poland (1926: Coup)        DK4409.4
Poland (1939-)          943.805     DK441
Poland (1939-45: WWII era)     DK441, DK4410-4420 (newer titles)     943.8053
Poland (1939-45: WWII era: gen., inclu. Ger. occup.)     DK4410
Poland (1939-41: Russ. occup.)     DK4415
Poland (1945-)     DK443
Poland & Polish military ops. (WWII)     D765-765.2+
Poland (gen.)     DK4040
Poland (gen. history, culture, etc.)     DK404
Poland (gen.: pubns. 1801+)          DK414.A3-Z, DK4140 (newer works)
Poland (geog. & travel)     914.38     DK407 (1867-1945)
Poland (mil. status)     UA829.P7     355.0330438
Poland (post-WWI territorial ?s)     D651.P7
Poland (WWII: gen. particip.)     940.53438     D765, DK441
Poland (WWII: mil. hist.)     940.5409438     D765
Poles (in other lands)     DK4122
Police, Air force     UG1020-1025
Police, Military (by country)     UB825.A-Z
Police, Naval (besides U.S.)     VB925.A-Z
Policy & status, Naval     359.03+ (country #s follow)     VA
Policy, Military     355.0335+
Policy, Military (gen.)     UA11
POLISH military history (gen.)     DK4170
Polish military ops. (1918-21, inclu. Russo-Polish conflict)     DK4406
Polish military ops. (WWII: gen.)     D765     940.53438, .5409438, 943.8053
Polish question     DK4182
Polish Republic (1918-39)     943.804     DK440, DK4400
Polish troops (WWII: French Army)     D761.9.P6
Political prisoners (WWI: U.S.)     D570.8.P7
Political prisoners (WWII: U.S.)     D769.8.P7 (SEE ALSO D805.U5 for
                                     prisons & prisoners)
Political science     320-329     J
Political science, international law     J     320-329, 341
POLITICS & DIPLOMACY (20th c.)     D440-460
Politics & diplomacy (20th c.: collected works)     D442
Politics & diplomacy (20th c.: gen. special: projected, possible wars, other polit.
                                     events)     D445
Politics and diplomacy (20th c.: gen.: world pol., Triple Alliance & Entente, etc.)
                         D443     940.5, 320.904, 327.09
Politics & diplomacy (1919-39)     D727     327.0904, .4, 909.822-23, 940.51-52
Politics & diplomacy (Africa: inclu. colonialism)     DT31-38     320.96, 327.6
Politics & diplomacy (Asia: gen.)     DS33.3     320.95, 327.5+
Politics & diplomacy (Austria)     DB46-49
Politics & diplomacy (Egypt: gen.)     DT82
Politics & diplomacy (Fr.)     DC55-59
Politics & diplomacy (Ger.)     DD110-120
Politics & diplomacy (Ger.: 1918-)     DD240
Politics & diplomacy (Indon.: gen.)     DS638
Politics & diplomacy (It.: gen.)     DG491     320.945, 327.45+

Politics & diplomacy (Japan: gen.)    DS841
Politics & diplomacy (Korea)    DS910
Politics & diplomacy (Libya: gen.)    DT227
Politics & diplomacy (Middle East, SW. Asia)    DS63    320.956, 327.56+
Politics & diplomacy (Montenegro: 1918-45)    DR1887
Politics & diplomacy (Morocco: gen.)    DT317
Politics & diplomacy (N. Zea.: gen.)    DU421
Politics & diplomacy (Neth.: gen.)    DJ142
Politics & diplomacy (Palestine, Jews)    DS119-119.8
Politics & diplomacy (Philip.: gen.)    DS672.8    320.9599, 327.599
Politics & diplomacy (Pol.: 1918-45)    DK4402
Politics & diplomacy (Port.: gen.)    DP556
Politics & diplomacy (Rus.)    DK60-63
Politics & diplomacy (Rus.: 1894-1939)    DK63
Politics & diplomacy (Rus.: 1939-)    DK63.3
Politics & diplomacy (Rus.: gen.)    DK61    320.947
Politics & diplomacy (Sp.)    DP84
Politics & diplomacy (Sp.: 1931-39: gen.)    DP257
Politics & diplomacy (Swe.: gen.)    DL658.A3-Z  320.9485, 327.485
Politics & diplomacy (Swit.: gen.)    DQ69
Politics & diplomacy (Thai.)    DS575
Politics & diplomacy (Tunisia: gen.)    DT257
Politics & diplomacy (Yug.: 1918-45)    DR1291
Politics & diplomacy (Yug.: 1918-45: gen.)    DR367.A1
POLITICS (China: 20th c. & 1912-49)    DS775.7
Politics (Czech.: 1939-45)    DB2208.7
Politics (Eastern Europe: gen.)    DJK42
Politics (Eng.: gen.)    DA40
Politics (Eng.: modern)    DA42
Politics (Formosa: 1895-1945)    DS799.716
Politics (Georgian S. S. R.: gen.)    DK676.5-6
Politics (Pol.)    DK4179
Politics (Rus. armed forces, 1917-21)    DK265.9.A6
Politics (Serbia: 1918-45)    DR2036
Politics (Serbia: gen.)    DR1972
POLITICS (U.S.: 20th c.)    E743    320.973, .904
Politics (U.S.: 1920 Pres. campaign)    E783
Politics (U.S.: gen.)    E183    320.973
Politics (U.S.: 1932 Pres. race)    E805
Politics (U.S.: 1936 Pres. race)    E810
Politics (U.S.: 1940 Pres. race)    E811
Politics (U.S.: 1944 Pres. race)    E812
Politics (Ukr.: gen.)    DK508.554
Polynesia & other Pacific areas    996    DU510 (Poly.: gen.)
Polynesia (gen.)    DU510 (SEE DU520-950 for specific island groups, individual
    islands, atolls, etc.)    996, 996.1-4, .9
Pomerania (Pol.)    DK4600.P67
Ponape (Carolines)    DU568.P7
Pontoons & pontoon gear (naval architec.)    VM469.5
Popular histories (20th c.)    D422
Popular histories (20th c.: Europe)    D425
Population transfers (WWII)    D820.P7-72
Population transfers (WWII: by nationality)    D820.P72.A-Z
Population transfers (WWII: Jews)    D820.P72.J

PORT Arthur, Siege of (Rus.-Jpn. War, 1904-5)     DS517.3
Port of London (Eng.)     DA689.P6
Port Royal, Jam.     F1895.P6
Ports, bases, docks, etc. (G.B. Royal Navy: gen.)     VA459.A1     359.70941,
                    940.4530941 (WWI), .54530941 (WWII)
Ports, bases, docks, etc. (Ger. Navy: by name)   VA516.A3-Z
Ports, bases, docks, etc. (U.S. Navy: gen.)     VA67     359.70973,
                    940.4530973 (WWI), .54530973 (WWII), .545973 (WWII)
Portsmouth Navy Yard (U.S.: N.H.)     VA70.P8
Portsmouth, Eng. (Royal Naval Barracks)     V522.5.P6
PORTUGAL     DP501-900+     946.9
Portugal (20th c.: gen.)     DP672   946.904
Portugal (1910-)     946.904     DP675
Portugal (1910-: Republic)     DP675     946.904
Portugal (1914-18: WWI)     DP677     946.9041
Portugal (1919-)     DP680     946.9041-9042
Portugal (1919: Revolution)     DP678
Portugal (1926-68)     946.9042     DP680
Portugal (mil. status)     UA760-769
Portugal (post-WWI territorial ?s)     D651.P75
Portugal (WWII: gen. particip.)     940.53469     D754.P8, DP680
Portuguese (in Brazil)     F2659.P8
Position finders (artillery)     UF853     623.46
Possessions of the U.S. (WWI)     D570.87.A-Z
POST exchanges & canteens, Military     UC750-755
Post-war era & Reconstruction (WWI)     D652-659     940.3144, .34-39
Post-WWI reconstruction     940.3144     D652-659, D653 (gen.),
                    D657-658 (U.S.), D659.A-Z (other places)
Post-WWI territorial questions     940.31424     D650, D651.A-Z
Post-WWII reconstruction     940.53144     D824-829, D825 (gen.),
                    D827-828 (U.S.), D829.A-Z (by country, nationality, etc.)
Post-WWII territorial questions     940.531424
Postal service, Military     UH80-85     355.69
Postal service, Naval     VG60-65     359.341
Posters (WWII)     D743.25 (newer works), D746.5 (older works)     769.4994+
Power-driven craft (naut. engineering)     623.823     VM315
Power plants (marine engineering)     623.87     VM600-779, VM600,
                    VM623 (U.S.), VM657 (G.B.), VM673 (Ger.), VM705 (Japan)
Power systems, Electric (naval sci.)     VC418
Powerplants (naval design)     623.8147     VM731+
Prague, Cz. (20th c.)     DB2629
Prague, Cz. (WWII)     D765.55.P7
Presbyterian Church (WWII)     D810.C68
Preservation of maps & charts     UA997
Press & public relns. (mil.)     UH700-705
Press & public relns. (navies)     VG500-505
Press, publicity, censorship (WWI: U.S.)     D632
Press, radio, censorship, propaganda & publicity (WWII: SEE ALSO D746.5 for
                    posters, D753.3 for enemy propaganda in U.S., D810.P6-7
                    for propaganda elsewhere)     D798-799

PRIMARY SOURCES (20th c.: collections)    D411
Primary sources (20th c.: diplomacy)    D451
Primary sources (20th c.: politics and diplomacy)    D441
PRIMARY SOURCES, DOCUMENTS (Australia)    DU80
Primary sources, documents (Australia: military status)    UA871
Primary sources, documents (Bulg.)    DR52
Primary sources, documents (Calif. army reserves)    UA91
Primary sources, documents (China: 20th c. & 1912-49)    DS773.83
Primary sources, documents, collections (WWII: Reconstruction)    D824
Primary sources, documents (Czech.: 1918-)    DB2185
Primary sources, documents (Den.)    DL103
Primary sources, documents (Dutch E. Ind.)    DS613
Primary sources, documents (Eastern Europe: politics)    DJK41
Primary sources, documents (Egypt)    DT43
Primary sources, documents (Eng.)    DA25
Primary sources, documents (Far East, E. & SE.Asia)    DS503
Primary sources, documents (Fin.)    DL1005
Primary sources, documents (Fin.: 20th c.)    DL1066
Primary sources, documents (Fin.: 1939-45)    DL1090
Primary sources, documents (Formosa: 1895-1945)    DS799.693
Primary sources, documents (Fr.)    DC3
Primary sources, documents (Fr.: 1871-1940)    DC334
Primary sources, documents (Fr. Indoch.)    DS532
Primary sources, documents (G.B.: War Dept., Parliament, other re military)
    UA648
Primary sources, documents (Ger. infantry)    UA713.A1-5
Primary sources, documents (Ger.: 1918-)    DD234
Primary sources, documents (Ger.: for. relns. & politics)    DD110
Primary sources, documents (Hawaiian Is.: 1900-59)    DU627.5.A1-5
Primary sources, documents (India, pre-1947 Pak.)    DS403
Primary sources, documents (It.)    DG403
Primary sources, documents (Italo-Eth. War, 1935-6)    DT387.8.A1-7
Primary sources, documents (Japan)    DS803, DS840
Primary sources, documents (Jpn. military)    UA846
Primary sources, documents (Korea)    DS901
Primary sources, documents (N.Y. army reserves)    UA361
Primary sources, documents (naval: G.B.)    VA453
Primary sources, documents (naval: Ger.)    VA512
Primary sources, documents (Nor.)    DL403
Primary sources, documents (Palestine & the Jews)    DS102
Primary sources, documents (Philip.)    DS653
Primary sources, documents (Pol.)    DK402
Primary sources, documents (Pol.: 1918-45)    DK4397
Primary sources, documents (Port.: 20th c.)    DP670
Primary sources, documents (Port.: dipl. & polit. hist.)    DP555
Primary sources, documents (Rum.)    DR203
Primary sources, documents (Rum.: 1881-1914)    DR252
Primary sources, documents (Rum.: 1914-27)    DR260
PRIMARY SOURCES, DOCUMENTS (RUS. military)    UA771
Primary sources, documents (Rus.)    DK3, UA773.A1-5
Primary sources, documents (Rus.: 1894-1917)    DK251
Primary sources, documents (Rus.: 1918-)    DK266.A3
Primary sources, documents (Rus.: for. relns.)    DK65
Primary sources, documents (Rus.: politics & diplomacy)    DK60
Primary sources, documents (Russo-Fin. War, 1939-40)    DL1096

Primary sources, documents (Serbia: 1918-45)      DR2033
Primary sources, documents (Sino-Jpn. Confl., 1937-45)  DS777.52
Primary sources, documents (Sp.: 1931-39)      DP251
Primary sources, documents (Sp.: 1936-39: Civil War)   DP269.A2-55
Primary sources, documents (Sp.: dipl. & polit. hist.)   DP83
Primary sources, documents (Swe.)      DL658.A2
Primary sources, documents (Swit.)      DQ3
Primary sources, documents (Swit.)      DQ68
Primary sources, documents (U.S.)      E173
Primary sources, documents (U.S.: 20th c.)    E740.5
Primary sources, documents (Viet.)      DS556.2
Primary sources, documents (WWI)     D505
Primary sources, documents (WWI: peace: collections)   D642
Primary sources, documents (WWII: collection, preservation)   D735.A1
Primary sources, documents (WWII: peace: collections: gen.)   D814
Primary sources, documents (WWII: sometimes by gov. agency, A-Z)  D735
Primary sources, documents (Yug.)      DR1288
Primary sources, documents (Yug.: 1918-45)    DR364
Prince of Wales (battleship: G.B.)      VA458.P75
Princess (aircraft carrier: WWII)      D774.P7
Prinz Eugen (cruiser, heavy: Ger.)     VA515.P73     359.32530943
PRISONER exchanges     940.473
Prisoner exchanges (WWII)    940.5473   D805
Prisoner-of-war camps & internment (WWI)    940.472   D627
Prisoner-of-war camps & internment centers (WWII)  940.5472+ (SEE ALSO .5317+
                for post-1988 titles on internment camps)   D805
Prisoner-of-war camps (mil. life)   355.1296 (SEE ALSO 365.45)   UB800-805
Prisoners, prisons, punishments (naval)    VB890-910
Prisons, Air force     UG1040-1045
PRISONS & PRISONERS, Naval (except U.S.: by place)   VB895.A-Z
Prisons & prisoners, Naval (G.B.)    VB895.G7
Prisons & prisoners, Naval (Rus.)    VB895.R9
Prisons & prisoners, Naval (U.S.)    VB893     344.035480973
Prisons & prisoners (Sp. Civil War,    1936-39)   DP269.63-65
Prisons & prisoners (WWI: by country)    D627.A3-Z
Prisons & prisoners (WWI: gen.)    D627.A2
Prisons & prisoners (WWII: by country)    D805.A3-Z
Prisons & prisoners (WWII: gen.)    D805.A2
Prisons & prisoners (WWII: inclu. internment camps)   D805   940.5472+
Prisons, Military (U.S.)    UB803 (SEE ALSO KF7675)
Procurement & contracts, Air force (gen.)    UG1120   358.41621
Procurement (mil. supplies)    355.6212   UC263-267, HD3858-3860
Procurement (mil. supplies: countries besides U.S.)   UC265.A-Z
Procurement (naval supples &equip.)    359.6212
Procurement (naval supplies: except U.S.)  VC265.A-Z
Projectile velocities & motions (gen.)    UF820   623.51
Projectiles, Artillery    UF750-770   623.451
Projectiles, Artillery (U.S.)    UF753
Projectiles, Naval    VF480-500
Promotion & demotion (air forces)    358.41112   UB320-325, UB410-415
Promotion & demotion (mil.)    355.112   UB320+
Promotion & demotion (navies)    359.112   VB260-275, VB307-315
Promotion, discharge, recruitment, enlistment (mil. sci.: gen.) UB320  355.2, .61
Promotion, discharge, recruitment, enlistment (naval sci.: enlisted personnel: U.S.)
                VB263   359.2230973, .3380973

Prop-driven aircraft (mil. design)     623.746042
PROPAGANDA, Allied (WWI)     940.4886
Propaganda, Allied (WWII)     940.54886
Propaganda, American (WWI: U.S.)     940.488673     D632, D639.P7.U5+
Propaganda, American (WWII: U.S.)     940.5488673     D810.P7.U6
PROPAGANDA & PSYCH. WARFARE (Ger.)     UB277.G3     355.34340943
Propaganda & psych. warfare (Japan)     UB277.J3     355.34340952
Propaganda & psych. warfare (mil. sci.: gen.: SEE ALSO BF1045.M55 & HM263 for
                    indiv. & social aspects)     UB275     355.3434
Propaganda & psych. warfare (naval sci.: gen.)     VB252     359.3434
Propaganda & psych. warfare (naval sci.: U.S.)     VB253     359.34340973
Propaganda & psych. warfare (Rus.)     UB277.R9     355.34340947
Propaganda & psych. warfare (Sov.Un.)     UB277.S65     355.34340947
Propaganda & psych. warfare (U.S.)     UB276     355.34340973
Propaganda, Anti-Soviet (1925-53: by Ger.)     DK272.7.G3 (SEE ALSO
                    DD255.R9)
Propaganda, Anti-Soviet (1925-53: by Japan)     DK272.7.J3
Propaganda, Anti-Soviet (1925-53: by partic. country)     DK272.7.A-Z
Propaganda, Axis (WWII)     940.54887+
Propaganda, British (WWII)     940.5488641     D810.P7.G7
Propaganda, Central Power (WWI)     940.4887
Propaganda, French (WWII)     940.5488644     D810.P7.F8
Propaganda, French (WWII: Vichy)     940.5488744     D810.P7.F8
PROPAGANDA, GERMAN     DD119.5
Propaganda, German (1933-45: by place)     DD255.A-Z
Propaganda, German (1933-45: France)     DD255.F8
Propaganda, German (1933-45: Gt. Brit.)     DD255.G7
Propaganda, German (1933-45: Rus.: SEE ALSO DK272.7.G3)     DD255.R9
Propaganda, German (1933-45: United States)     DD255.U6-7
Propaganda, German (WWI)     940.488743     D639.P7.G3, D619.3 (in U.S.)
Propaganda, German (WWII)     940.5488743     D810.P7.G3
Propaganda, Italian (WWII)     940.5488745     D810.P7.I8
PROPAGANDA, JAPANESE (1926-89: abroad: by place)     DS889.3.A-Z
Propaganda, Japanese (1926-89: China)     DS889.3.C5
Propaganda, Japanese (1926-89: G.B.)     DS889.3.G7
Propaganda, Japanese (1926-89: Indonesia)     DS889.3.I5
Propaganda, Japanese (1926-89: Philip.)     DS889.3.P5
Propaganda, Japanese (1926-89: U.S.)     DS889.3.U6
Propaganda, Japanese (WWII)     940.5488752     D810.P7.J3
Propaganda, Russian (1925-53: internal)     DK269.5
Propaganda, Russian (WWII: prior to 22 June 1941)     940.5488747     D810.P7.R9
Propaganda, Russian (WWII: after 21 June 1941)     940.5488647     D810.P7.R9
                    or .S65
PROPAGANDA, SOVIET (1925-53: foreign: by country)     DK272.A-Z
Propaganda, Soviet (1925-53: France)     DK272.F8
Propaganda, Soviet (1925-53: G.B.)     DK272.G7
Propaganda, Soviet (1925-53: Ger.)     DK272.G3
Propaganda, Soviet (1925-53: Japan)     DK272.J3
Propaganda, Soviet (1925-53: U.S.)     DK272.U6-7
Propaganda (WWI: by country)     D639.P7.A-Z
Propaganda (WWI: gen.)     D639.P6 (SEE ALSO D631-633 for press)     940.488+
Propaganda (WWII: by country)     D810.P7.A-Z     940.54886-54889+
Propaganda (WWII: gen.)     D810.P6 (SEE ALSO D798-799 for press)
Propellers (marine engin.)     VM753-757     623.81473
Prophecies (WWII)     D810.P75

Propulsion & resistance (marine engin.)    VM751-759
Propulsion (naval architec. & engin.: gen.)    VM521    623.87
Protest movements (WWI)    D639.P77
Protest movements (WWII)    D810.P76
Protocols of the Wise Men of Zion (WWI: anti-Semitism)    DS145.P49-7
Provisions & subsistence, Naval (gen.)    VC350    359.81
Provisions & subsistence, Naval (Ger.)    VC355.G3
Provisions & subsistence, Naval (Japan)    VC355.J3
Provisions & subsistence, Naval (Rus.)    VC355.R9
Provost-Marshall-General's Bureau (WWII: U.S.: gen.)    D769.77
PRUSSIA (1871-1918: gen.)    DD448
Prussia (1918-45)    DD452-454
Prussia (1918-45: gen.)    DD452
Prussia (1918-33)    DD453
Prussia (1933-45)    DD454
Prussia, East & West (post-WWI territorial ?s)    D651.P89-9
Prussia, East (Pol.)    DK4600.P77
Psychiatry, Military (U.S.: inclu. mental health)    UH629.3
Psychical phenomena (WWI)    D639.P8
Psychological warfare & propaganda (countries except U.S.)    UB277.A-Z
Psychological warfare & propaganda (mil.)    355.3434 (ALSO use 355.34 for
        propag.)    UB275-277, UB276 (U.S.), UB277.A-Z (except U.S.)
Psychological warfare & propaganda (naval sci.: places besides U.S.)    VB254.A-Z
PUBLIC administration    350-359    H-J
Public figures (20th c.: collective biog.: men)    D412.6    920.02, 909.82,
                                                                  940.50922
Public figures (Ger.: 1918-48: men)    DD244
Public information & relations (mil.)    355.342    UH700-705, UH703 (U.S.)
Public opinion (WWI: by place)    D639.P88.A-Z
Public opinion (WWI: gen.)    D639.P87
Public opinion (WWII: by country)    D810.P85.A-Z
Public opinion (WWII: gen.)    D810.P8
Public relations & information (navies)    359.342    VG500-505
Public relations & press (mil.: places besides U.S.)    UH705.A-Z
Public utilities (defense)    UA929.95.P93
Publications, Graduate (U.S. Naval Acad.)    V415.K1-4
Puerto Rico    F1951-1983, F1971    972.95
Puerto Rico (1898-1952)    F1975    972.9504-9505
Puerto Rico (gen.)    F1971
Puerto Rico (WWII)    D769.87.P7
Puget Sound area (Wash.)    979.77    F897.P9
Puget Sound (Wash.)    F897.P9
Pumps, Marine (engin.)    VM821
Punishment & enforcement, Military    355.1332
Punishment, Corporal (U.S.)    UB813
Punishments (naval conduct)    359.13325
Pursuit & fighter forces & ops. (air)    358.43    UG1242.F5, UG633 (U.S.),
        UG635.A-Z (places except U.S.), TL685.3, TL686.A-Z (by co. or name)
Pyrenees (Fr.)    DC611.P981-992
Pyrenees region    944.89    DC611.P981-992
Pyrotechnic signal devices (mil. engineering)    623.7313    UG580, UF860

QUAKERS (WWII: Society of Friends)  D810.C65
Qualifications (naval personnel)  359.2234
Qualifications, Service (mil.)  355.2234
Quarter drills, Naval (Can.: also watch, station, other)  VD163
Quartermaster depots (WWII: U.S.: by #)  D769.73.1st-
Quartermaster's Dept. (U.S.)  UC30-34  355.8
Quarters & barracks, Air force (U.S.)  UG1143
Quarters & barracks, Marine (U.S.: gen.)  VE422  359.96710973
Quarters & barracks, Naval (gen.)  VC420-425, VC420  359.71
Quarters, Military (barracks, p.o.w. camps etc. on-site)  355.71  UC400-405
Quebec  971.4  F1051-1055
Queen Mary (pass. ship)  VM383.Q4
Queen's Westminster and Civil Service Rifles (WWI)  D547.Q3
Queens, princesses, etc. (20th c.: collective biography)  D412.8
Queensland (Australia)  DU250-280  994.3
Queensland (Australia: gen.: inclu. descrip.)  DU260-270
Queensland (Australia: inclu. Great Barrier Reef)  994.3  DU250-280
Quick-firing ordnance  UF560-565... .Q.F.
Quisling, Vidkun (Nor.: 20th c.)  DL529.Q5


RABAUL, New Brit. (WWII)  D767.99.N415.R32
Race problems (WWII)  D810.R3
RACES & ETHNOGRAPHY (Australia)  DU120-122
Races & ethnography (China)  DS730-731
Races & ethnography (Ger.)  DD74
Races & ethnography (N. Zea.)  DU423
Races & ethnography (Philip.)  DS665-666
Races & ethnography (Pol.: by specific element)  DK4121.5.A-Z
Races & ethnography (Pol.: gen.)  DK4120
Races & ethnography (Rus.)  DK33
RACES, ETHNOGRAPHY, RELIGIOUS GROUPS (Arg.)  F3021.A-Z
Races, ethnography, religious groups (Arg.: gen.)  F3021.A1
Races, ethnography, religious groups (Bolivia)  F3359.A-Z
Races, ethnography, religious groups (Brazil)  F2659.A-Z
Races, ethnography, religious groups (C.Am.)  F1440.A-Z
Races, ethnography, religious groups (Calif.)  F870.A-Z
Races, ethnography, religious groups (Calif.: gen.)  F870.A1
Races, ethnography, religious groups (Can.)  F1035.A-Z
Races, ethnography, religious groups (Chile)  F3285.A-Z
Races, ethnography, religious groups (Jam.)  F1896.A-Z
Races, ethnography, religious groups (Mex.)  F1392.A-Z
Races, ethnography, religious groups (N.Y.)  F130.A-Z
Races, ethnography, religious groups (Paraguay)  F2699.A-Z
Races, ethnography, religious groups (Peru)  F3619.A-Z
Races, ethnography, religious groups (S.Am.)  F2239.A-Z
Races, ethnography, religious groups (U.S.: gen.)  E184.A1
Races, ethnography, religious groups (Urug.)  F2799.A-Z
Races, ethnography, religious groups (U.S.)  E184.A-Z  973.04+
Races, ethnography, religious groups (W.Ind.)  F1629.A-Z
Races. ethnography, religious groups (Cuba)  F1789.A-Z
Racial minorities (WWI: soldiers)  940.403  D547.N4 (blacks: G.B.),
                    D570.8.I6 (Indians:U.S.), D639.N4 (blacks)

337

RADAR & electronics, Air force (G.B.)        UG1425.G7
Radar & electronics, Air force (gen.)        UG1420        623.7348, .7467
Radar equipment, Naval        VF530        623.557
Radar (mil. engineering)        623.7348        UG612 (gen.), UG612.3 (U.S.),
        UG612.5.A-Z (other places), UG612.5.G7 (G.B.), VG76-78
Radar, Military (G.B.)        UG612.5.G7
Radar, Military (gen.)        UG612        623.7348
Radar, Military (places except U.S.)        UG612.5.A-Z
Radar, radio, & wireless telegraph (navies: besides U.S.)        VG78.A-Z
Radar, radio, etc. (WWII)        D810.R33
Radar, radio, sonar, etc. (naval architec.: U.S. Navy)        VM480.3
RADIO & radar (mil. engineering)        623.734        UG611-612.5
Radio, media, & public relns. (mil.: Ger.)        UH705.G3
Radio, Military (gen.)        UG611
Radio, radar, & wireless telegraph (navies: U.S.)        VG77        623.85640973
Radio, radar, sonar, etc. (naval architec.: G.B.)        VM480.5.G7
Radio services, Military (by place except U.S.)        UH859.A-Z
Radio services, Military (gen.)        UH850
Radiobroadcasting services, Military (U.S.: gen., inclu. armed forces)        UH855
Radiobroadcasting, Military (Fr.)        UH859.F8
Radiobroadcasting, Military (Ger.)        UH859.G3
Radiobroadcasting, Military (Japan)        UH859.J3
Radiotelegraphy (mil. engineering)        623.7342        UG600-607, VG76-78
Raids (mil. sci.)        U167.5.R34
RAILROAD artillery (gen.)        UF490
Railroad troops        UG520-525
Railroads, armored trains, etc. (mil. engineering)        UG345        623.63
Railroads (defense)        UA929.95.R3
Railroads (mil. transp.: gen.)        UC310        623.63, 355.83
Railroads (mil. transp.: U.S. regions or states)        UC314.A-Z
Railroads (naval transp.)        VC580
Railway artillery (countries besides U.S.)        UF495.A-Z
Railway artillery (Fr.)        UF495.F8
Railway artillery (Ger.)        UF495.G3
Railway gun cars        UF655 (SEE ALSO UF563.A76, UF565)        358.22
Railway gun matériel (U.S.: handbooks)        UF563.A76
Rainbow Division (WWI: U.S.)        D570.3.R3
Range finders, Artillery (gen.)        UF850.A2        623.46
Range tables, Artillery        UF857
Range tables, Naval ordnance        VF550        623.5530212
Rangers & commandos        356.167        U262
Ranging & sighting apparatus (ordnance: design)        623.46        UF848-856, VF520
Rangoon, Burma        DS486.R25
Rank, appointment, promotion, retirement, etc. (mil. officers: gen.)        UB410
        355.332
Rank, appointment, promotion, retirement, etc. (naval officers: gen.)        VB310
        359.332, .331
Rasputin, Grigory (Rus.: 1894-1917 biog.)        DK254.R3
Rathenau, Walther (Ger.: 1888-1918+ period)        DD231.R3
Rations (mil.)        UC710-715
Rations, Naval        VC360-365
Raw materials (mil. resources)        355.24        HC110.A-Z, UA18, UA929.5+
Raw materials (naval resources)        359.24        VC260-267, VF390+
Rearguard action        U215
Recoil (mil. engineering)        623.57

RECONNAISANCE & intelligence topography (mil. engineering)     623.71
                                                               UG470-474
Reconnaisance & patrols          U220     355.413, 358.45
Reconnaisance, Aerial            UG760-765       358.45
Reconnaisance battalions (WWII: U.S.)     D769.3058
Reconnaisance, Cavalry           UE360     355.413, 358.45
Reconnaissance forces, Air (inclu. antisub. work)     358.45     UG760-765,
                                                      UG1242.R4
Reconnaissance, Naval    359.413     V190
Reconnaisance planes     UG1242.R4     623.7467, 358.45
RECONSTRUCTION & post-war era (WWI: gen.)   D653
Reconstruction (Fr.: 1919-40)   DC389, D659.F8     944.0815
Reconstruction (WWI: countries outside U.S.)   D659.A-Z
Reconstruction (WWII)            D824-829
Reconstruction (WWII: gen.)   D825     940.53144
Reconstruction (WWII: outside U.S.: by country, nationality, etc.)     D829.A-Z
Records & accounting (marines)          VE480
RECREATION & information services, Military     UH800-910
Recreation & information services, Military (besides U.S.)     UH819.A-Z
Recreation & information services, Military (U.S. Army)   UH810-815
Recreation & information services, Naval     VG2020-2029
Recreation & information services, Naval (places besides U.S.)     VG2029
Recreation, Military (off-post)     UH900-910
Recreation services, Military (inclu. sports, arts, music, libraries, clubs, etc.)
                         355.346     UH800-910, UH800, UH805 (U.S.)
Recreation services, Naval (sports, arts, music, dancing, libraries, etc.)     359.346
                                     VG2020-2029, UH800-910
Recreation, social work, etc. (air forces)     UG990-995
Recruiting, enlistment, etc. (air forces)      UG880-885
Recruiting literature (U.S. Marines: by date)   VE23.A6
Recruitment & enlistment, Military     355.223
Recruitment & enlistment (navies)     359.223     VB260-315
Recruitment, enlistment, promotion, discharge (mil. sci.)     UB320-325
Recruitment, enlistment, promotion, discharge (naval sci.: enlisted personnel: gen.)
                         VB260     359.223, .338, .11+
Recruits, Naval (inclu. medical & mental examinations)     VB270-275     359.2236
RED CROSS & medical services (WWI: by country)   D629.A-Z
Red Cross & medical services (WWII: by country)   D807.A-Z     940.54764-69
Red Cross (by country or region)        UH537.A-Z
Red Cross (gen.: wartime)        UH535     940.4771, .54771
Red Cross (WWII)        940.54771     D806-807
Red Cross at sea        VG457
Red Guard (Rus. Rev., 1917-21: Krasnaia Gvardiia)     DK265.9.K73
Reed, Thomas Brackett (U.S.: 1865-1900 era)     E664.R3
Refrigeration (naval sci.)   VC400     623.8535
Refrigerators, Military          UC760
Refugees (WWI)        940.3159     D637, D638.A-Z (by place)
Refugees (WWII)       940.53159     D808, D809.A-Z (by place)
Refugees, relief work, charities (WWI: by country or area)     D638.A-Z
Refugees, relief work, charities (WWII: gen.)   D808     940.5477

REGISTERS & lists (naval reserves: U.S.: Calif.)          VA102
Registers & lists (WWI: decorated, dead, wounded: by country)     D609.A3-Z
Registers & lists (WWII: dead, wounded, decorated: by country)     D797.A3-Z
Registers & lists (WWII: dead, wounded, decorated: gen.)          D797.A2
Registers, Official & unoff. (Royal Naval Coll., Dart.)          V515.H1-5
Registers, Official (U.S. Mil. Acad.)          U410.H3-4
Registers, Official (U.S. Naval Acad.: annual)          V415.H3-39
Registers (U.S. Marines)          VE23.A33
Regulation of conduct, Naval          359.133
REGULATIONS & manuals, Air force (U.S.)          UG673
Regulations & tactics (mil. engineering: Asia: gen.)          UG270
Regulations & tactics (mil. engineering: Eur.: gen.)          UG215
Regulations, Army (Rus.)          UB655.9-656.5
Regulations, Marine (U.S.)          VE23.A25
Regulations, Naval (U.S.)          VB363
Regulations (U.S. Naval Acad.)          V415.C3-6
Rehabilitation of disabled sailors          VG478 (PREFER UB360+)
Rehabilitation of disabled veterans (gen.)          UB360          355.1156, .1154
RELIEF & WELFARE SERVICES (WWI: in Ger.)          940.477943          D638.G3, D659.G3
Relief & welfare services (WWI: in Rus.)          940.477947          D638.R9, D659.R9
Relief & welfare services (WWII: in China)          940.5477951          D809.C5
Relief & welfare services (WWII: in Fr.)          940.5477944          D809.F8
Relief & welfare services (WWII: in Ger.)          940.5477943          D809.G3
Relief & welfare services (WWII: in Japan)          940.5477952          D809.J3
Relief & welfare services (WWII: in Philip. Is.)          940.54779599          D809.P5
Relief & welfare services (WWII: in Rus.)          940.5477947          D809.R9
Relief associations (besides U.S.)          UH543-545
Relief societies (mil.: inclu. care of sick & wounded)          UH520-560          361.05, .77
Relief societies (mil.: besides U.S.: by place)          UH525.A-Z
Relief societies (mil.: U.S. by state or region)          UH524.A-Z
Relief work, refugees, displaced persons, charities (WWII)          D808-809
Relief work, refugees, displaced persons, charities (WWII: Belgium)          D809.B4
Relief work, refugees, displaced persons, charities (WWII: G.B.)          D809.G7
Relief work, refugees, displaced persons, charities (WWII: U.S.: domestic & abroad)
                                                                       D809.U5
Relief work, refugees, etc. (WWI: U.S.)          D638.U5
Religion          200-299          BL-BX
Religion (Sp. Civil War, 1936-39)          DP269.8.R4
Religion (WWII: churches)          D810.C5-68
Religion, Christianity (WWI)          D639.R4          940.478
RELIGIOUS & counseling services, Military          355.347          UH20-25
Religious & counseling services, Naval          359.347          VG20-25, VG2000
Religious & ethical questions (WWII: by country)          D744.5.A-Z
Religious groups & officials (WWI)          940.3152          D639.R4, D622 (Cath. Church)
Religious groups & officials (WWII)          940.53152          D810.C5-68
Religious officials, Military (countries except U.S.)          UH25.A-Z
Religious officials, Naval (places besides U.S.)          VG25.A-Z
Religious services (WWII)          940.5478          D810.C35-6 (chaplains), .C5 (churches:
                              gen.), .C53-68 (alphab. by denom.)

REPARATIONS & indemnity (WWI: by country)   D649.A-Z
Reparations & indemnity (WWII: by country)   D819.A-Z
Reparations (WWI)                940.31422      D648-649
Reparations (WWI: Ger.)      D649.G3
Reparations (WWII)               940.531422
Reparations (WWII: Ger.)     D819.G3
Reparations (WWII: Jp.)       D819.J3
REPORTS, Congressional (U.S. Military Academy: by date)   U410.E5
Reports, Congressional (U.S. Navy: official & others)   VA53
REPORTS, OFFICIAL & unoff. (U.S. Naval Acad.)   V415.F7
Reports, Official (army reserves: U.S.)   UA42.A1-59
Reports, Official (military medical: U.S.: monographic)   UH223.A3-39
Reports, Official (military medical: U.S.: serial)   UH223.A1-29
Reports, Official (naval maint.: U.S.)   VC25-38
Reports, Official (naval reserves: U.S.: Calif.)   VA101
Reports, Official (Royal Naval Coll., Dart.: annual)   V515.E1-49
Reports, Official (U.S. Army: War Dept., Dept. o/t Army, Adj. Gen., Inspec. Gen.,
                                               etc.: annual)       UA24.A1-7
Reports, Official (U.S. Dept. Defense: formerly War Dept.)   UA23.2
Reports, Official (U.S. Marines)      VE23.A2-79
Reports, Official (U.S. Marines: annual)      VE23.A2
Reports, Official (U.S. Mil. Acad. Superinten.: annual)      U410.E1
Reports, Official (U.S. Naval Acad. Superinten.: annual)   ·V415.E1-4
Reports, Official (U.S. Navy Bur's. of Navigation, Personnel)   VA52.A6-67
Reports, Official (U.S. Navy Dept.)      VA52.A1-89
Reports, Official (WWI: military)         D529
Reports, Unofficial (naval maint.: U.S.)      VC39
Reports, Unofficial (naval pay etc.: U.S.)      VC64
Repression & atrocities (WWI)      940.405      D625 (gen.), D626.A-Z (by place)
Repression & atrocities (WWII)      940.5405      D803, D804.A-Z (by country)
Requisitions, Military        UC15
Rescue aircraft (mil. engineering)      623.7466
Rescue & search ops. (WWII: by country)   D810.S45.A-Z
Rescue ops., Nautical      623.8887      VK1321-1424, VK1323 (U.S.), VK1445 (gen.)
RESEARCH, Aeronautical (mil.: by company or establishment)   UG644.A-Z
Research, Aeronautical (mil.: gen.)      UG640      358.407, .40072+
Research, Aeronautical (mil.: places besides U.S.)   UG645.A-Z
Research & development (air forces equip. & supplies)   358.407
Research & development, Military      355.07
Research & development (naval equip. & supplies)   359.07   V390-395
Research & laboratories, Medical (mil.)   UH399.5-7
Research & laboratories, Naval medical   VG240-245
Research, Military      U390-395      355.07
Research, Naval (countries besides U.S.)   V395.A-Z
Research, Naval (gen.)      V390      359.07
Research (naval ordnance: gen.)      VF360      359.82072
Research, Naval (U.S.: gen.)      V393      359.070973
Research, Ordnance & small-arms      UF526
Research, Physiological (mil. hygiene)   UH627

Reserve Officers' Training Corps (U.S.: R.O.T.C.)      U428.5
RESERVES, Air force          UG850-855      358.4137
Reserves & militia, Infantry      UD430
Reserves, Army          355.37          UA, UA42 (U.S.), UA50-549 (U.S.: by state),
                                        UA661 (G.B.)
RESERVES, ARMY (U.S.: Calif.)      UA90-99
Reserves, Army (U.S.: Hawaii)      UA159.1-9
Reserves, Army (U.S.: Missouri)          UA290-299
Reserves, Army (U.S.: N.Y.: militia, volunteers, Nat. Guard, etc.)      UA360-369
Reserves, Army (U.S.: Nat. Guard, militia, volunteers, etc.)          UA42-560
Reserves, Army (U.S.: Penn.)      UA420-429
Reserves, Army (U.S.: Texas)      UA470-479
Reserves, Artillery          UF356
Reserves, Marine (U.S.)      VE23.3
RESERVES, NAVAL          359.37          VA45, VA, VA80+
Reserves, Naval (G.B.)      VA464
Reserves, Naval (gen.)      VA45      359.37+
Reserves, Naval (Ger.)          VA519          359.370943
Reserves, Naval (Ger.: maint. & organ.)      VC182          359.370943
RESERVES, NAVAL (U.S.)      VA80-390
Reserves, Naval (U.S.: Calif.)          VA100-107
Reserves, Naval (U.S.: Calif.: misc. topics)          VA107
Reserves, Naval (U.S.: Calif.: special groups by #)      VA103.1st+
Reserves, Naval (U.S.: Calif.: special groups by name)      VA104.A-Z
Reserves, Naval (U.S.: Florida)      VA140-147
Reserves, Naval (U.S.: Hawaii)      VA158-158.7
Reserves, Naval (U.S.: Ill.)          VA160-167
Reserves, Naval (U.S.: maint. & organ.)      VC40-41          359.370973
Reserves, Naval (U.S.: Mississ.)          VA240-247
Reserves, Naval (U.S.: Missouri)      VA250-257
Reserves, Naval (U.S.: N.Y.)          VA280-287
Reserves, Naval (U.S.: Texas)          VA350-357
Reserves, Naval (U.S.: Wash.)          VA370-377
Reserves, Naval (U.S.: Wisc.)          VA380-387
Resistance & propulsion (marine engin.: gen.)      VM751
Resistance (Ger. vs. Nazis)          DD256.3
Resistance to projectiles (artillery)      UF900
Resolution of peace (WWI: U.S. Congress by date)      D643.A67
Resources (marines)          359.962      VA-VC
Resources, Air force          358.412      UG630+, UG1100+
Resources, Military          355.2      UA18, UA10
Resources, Naval          359.2      VB, VB21-124 (by place), VB23 (U.S.),
                                        VB144-146, VA49-750 (by place), VA50-80+ (U.S.)
Results (WWI: dipl., econ., & polit.)          940.314 (SEE ALSO specific country #s)
                                        D511-20, D511, D610-611, D643-644+
Results (WWII: dipl., econ, & polit.)          940.5314 (SEE ALSO specific country #s)
                                        D743, D748-754, D825-829 (Reconstruction),
                                        D814-821 (peace, reparations, terr. ?s, etc.), D840+
Retired military          UB440-445          355.1342
Retirement, resignation, other service termination (navies)          359.114
Revolvers & pistols          355.8243      UD410-415
Revolvers & pistols, Infantry (U.S. models)          UD413-414
Revolvers & pistols (navies)          VD390          359.8243

Rewards & privileges, Military    355.134    UB430-435
Rewards, badges, brevets, medals (navies: except U.S.)    VB335.A-Z
Rewards (navies: inclu. privileges, citations, medals, etc.)    359.134    VB330-335
Reykjavik, Ice.    DL398.R5
Reynaud, Paul (Fr.: 20th c.)    DC373.R45
Rhee, Syngman (Korea: 20th c.)    DS916.5.R5
Rhine Province (Prus.)    DD491.R4-52
Rhine River (Ger.)    DD801.R7-76    943.4
Rhine River Valley    943.4    DD801.R7-76
Rhodesia    DT946-965
Ribbentrop, Joachim von (Ger.: 1918-48 era)    DD247.R47
Rifle & artillery ranges (U.S.)    U303
RIFLES    355.82425    UD390-395
Rifles & carbines (design)    623.4425    UD390-395
Rifles, carbines, etc. (infantry)    UD390-395    355.82425, 623.4425
Rifles, carbines, etc. (navies)    VD370    359.82425
Rifles (infantry: by type)    UD395.A-Z
Rifles (marines)    VE370    359.9682425, 623.4425
Riga, Rus.    DK651.R5
Rigging & gear, Nautical (anchors, masts, rope, rudders, sails, etc.: design)
                                623.862    VM791 (anchors), VC279.R6 (rope)
Rio de Janeiro, Br.    F2646    981.53
Rio de Janeiro (Br.: state)    F2611
River & stream crossing (infantry)    UD317
Roads & highways (gen.)    UA960
Roads (mil. engineering)    UG330    623.62
Roads (places outside U.S.)    UA965.A-Z
Robin Moor (steamship: WWII)    D782.R6
Rocket forces (land: types)    358.175
ROCKETS & missiles, Air force    UG1310-1315    623.451, .4519, .4543
Rockets, Air force (Ger.)    UG1315.G3
Rockets, Air force (places except U.S.)    UG1315.A-Z
Rockets, Air force (U.S.)    UG1313
Rockets, signal (marine lifesaving)    VK1479
Rockets, Tactical    355.82543
Rockets, Tactical (design)    623.4543    UF880
Rockets, Unguided (mil. sci.)    UF880 (SEE UG1310-1315 for guided rockets)
                                623.4543
Rocky Mts. area (Mont., Idaho, Wyo., Colo.)    F721-785    978
Rolls of honored & dead (WWI)    940.467    D609, D609.A2 (gen.)
Rolls of honored & dead (WWII)    940.5467    D797
Romania (Rumania)    949.8    DR201-296
Romania (1861-1947: Monarchy)    949.802    DR250-266, DR250,
                                DR263 (1914-18), DR264 (1918-44)
Romania (1944-)    DR267
Rome, It.    945.632    DG803-818, DG808, DG813 (1871-)
Rome, It. (1527-)    DG812
Rome, It. (1871-)    DG813
Rome, It. (476-: gen.)    DG808
Rome, It. (modern era)    DG803-818
Romulo, Carlos P. (Philip.: 1935-46 era)    DS686.2.R6
Roosevelt, Franklin D. (U.S.: 20th c.: works)    E742.5.R5-7
Roosevelt, Franklin D. (U.S.: Pres., 1933-45)    E807
Roosevelt, Franklin D. (U.S.: Pres., 1933-45: family, inclu. Eleanor)    E807.1
Rope (naval supplies)    VC279.R6

Rosenberg, Alfred (Ger.: 1918-48 era)      DD247.R58
Rosters, Officers' (U.S. Mil. Acad.)      U410.H2
Rostov, Rus.      DK651.R7
Rotary International (WWII)      D810.R6
Roten teufel, Die (WWII: Panzer troops)      D757.55.R6
Rowboats, small sailboats, etc.      VM351
ROYAL Armored Corps (WWII: G.B.)      D760.R7
Royal houses (genealogy)      929.7
Royal Military Academy (Woolwich: div'd like U410.A-Z)      U518.A-Z
Royal Military Academy (Woolwich: gen. hist's.)      U518.L1
Royal Military College (Sandhurst)      U520.A-Z
Royal Naval College (Dartmouth)      V515.A1-R1+
Royal Naval College (Dartmouth: hist.)      V515.L1
Royal Naval College (Dartmouth: life, pictorials, etc.)      V515.P1
Royal Naval College (Greenwich: set up like V515)      V520.A1-R1+
Rubber (naval supplies)      VC279.R8
Rudolf (Austria:1848-1916 era: Crown Prince)      DB89.R8
Rulers, kings, etc. (20th c.: collective biography)      D412.7      929.7
RUMANIA (Romania)      DR201-296      949.8
Rumania (1866-1944)      DR250-266
Rumania (1912-13: Balkan War era)      DR258
Rumania (1914-27: Ferdinand)      DR260-263      949.802
Rumania (1914-18: WWI)      DR263
Rumania (1918-44)      DR264-266      949.802
Rumania & Rumanian military ops. (WWII)      D766.4-42      940.53498, 949.802
Rumania (geog. & travel)      914.98      DR209 (1866-1950)
Rumania (mil. status)      UA826      355.0330498
Rumania (post-WWI territorial ?s)      D651.R6
Rumanian military ops. (WWII)      D766.4
Runways, Airport      629.1363
Runways (mil. airfields: design)      623.663
RUSSIA      947 (SEE ALSO DK1-275+)
Russia (1855-)      947.08      DK219+, DK220-221
Russia (1894-1918: NIcholas II)      947.083 (perhaps SEE ALSO 952.031 for Russo-
            Jpn. War)      DK251-264.3, DK258, DK260-262, DS516-517 (R-J War)
Russia (1894-1917)      DK258-260      947.083
Russia (20th c.: gen.)      DK246      947.084
Russia (20th c. & 1917-: Communist period)      947.084      DK246
Russia (1904-17: empire status)      DK262
Russia (1905-6: Revolution: gen.)      DK263
Russia (1914-18: WWI era)      DK264.8      947.083
Russia (1918-: gen.)      DK266.A4-Z
Russia (1925-53: Stalin era: gen.)      DK267      947.0842
Russia (air war geog.)      358.414747
Russia & Eastern Front (WWII: gen.)      D764      940.540947, .532247, .5347,
            .541247,947.0842
Russia. Army (gen.)      UA772      355.30947, .00947
Russia (Asia: lighthouses, beacons, foghorns, etc.)      VK1109-1110
Russia (biog.: heads of state)      923.147
Russia, Eastern & Estonia      DK503 (SEE DK511.E4 for earlier pubns. on Estonia)
            947.41
Russia (Eur.: lighthouses, beacons, foghorns, etc.)   VK1085-1086
Russia, Finland, Poland      DK
Russia (gen.)      DK17

Russia (mil. geog.)          355.4747      UA995.R9
Russia (mil. policy)         355.033547    UA770+
Russia (mil. status)         UA770         355.033047, .033247, .033547
Russia (naval geog.)         359.4747      VA570-579
Russia (naval status: gen.)  VA573.A5-Z    359.030947, .00947, .4747
Russia, Northern             DK501
Russia (pilot guides)        623.892947    VK809, VK821, VK870, VK910 (Siberia)
Russia, Poland, Finland, Soviet Asia    DK
Russia (post-WWI territorial ?s)    D651.R8
Russia, Southern (Black Sea, Caucasus, Armenia, etc.)    DK509
Russia (WWI: causes, aims, results: includes Panslavism)    D514
Russia (WWI: mil. hist.)     940.40947     D550
Russia (WWII: causes, aims, results)    D742.R9
Russia (WWII: dipl. hist.)   940.532247    D754.R9 or .S65 (Sov. U.)
Russia (WWII: occupied terr.)    D802.R8
Russia (WWII: religious & ethical ?'s)    D744.5.R9
RUSSIAN aerial ops. (WWI)    D605
Russian aerial ops. (WWII)   D792.R9
Russian Asia                 DK750-973+    957-958
Russian Central Asia (to 1920)    DK858
Russian espionage (gen.)     UB271.R9      327.120947
Russian military history     DK50-54
Russian military ops. and Eastern Front (WWI: gen.)  D550    940.4147, .40947
Russian military ops. (Rev., 1917-21)    DK265.2
Russian military ops. (WWII: special: by region, name, author)    D764.6.A-Z
Russian mission to U.S. (WWI)    D570.8.M6.R7
Russian naval ops. (Rev., 1917-21)    DK265.3
Russian poetry, satire, etc. (WWII)    D745.7.R9
Russian prisons & prisoners (WWII: SEE ALSO D805.S65 for Soviet)    D805.R9
                                                                    940.547247

RUSSIAN REVOLUTION (1905-6)    DK263-264.3
Russian Revolution (1917-21)    DK265-265.9+
Russian Revolution (1917-21: Allied intervention, 1918-20)    DK265.4
Russian Revolution (1917-21: foreign particip.: gen.)    DK265.9.F5
Russian Revolution (1917-21: gen.)    DK265.A56-Z
Russian Revolution (1917-21: special topics)    DK265.9.A-Z
Russian S.F.S.R. (1917-45)    DK510.7-72
Russian S.F.S.R. (Russia)    DK510
Russians (in U.S.)    E184.R9
RUSSO-Austrian conflict (WWI: gen.)    D556
Russo-Finnish War (1939-40)    DK459.5, DL1095-1105+ (might ALSO try
                               DK459.5)    948.97032, 947.0842
Russo-Finnish War (1939-40: gen.)    DL1097
Russo-Finnish War (1939-40: special topics)    DL1105.A-Z
Russo-German conflict (WWI: gen.)    D551
Russo-German naval conflict (WWII: Arctic areas & Baltic)    D772.3
                                                             940.545947, .545943
Russo-Japanese War (1904-5)    DS516-517    952.031, 947.083
Russo-Polish War (1919-20: plus other Polish conflicts of the time)    DK4405
Ruthenia (post-WWII territorial ?s)    D821.R95
Ruthenia (WWII: occupied terr.)    D802.R95
Ryukyu Islands (Japan: inclu. Okinawa)    DS895.R9    952.81 (try .29 for titles
    after 1988) Ryukyu Islands (WWII)    D767.99.R9

SAAR (Ger.)     943.42     DD801.S13
Saar Valley (post-WWI territorial ?s)     D651.S13
Sabotage equipment (mil. sci.)     UB274
Sabotage, espionage, & unconventional warfare (WWII: Fr.)     940.548644
                    D802.F8 (underground), D810.S7+, UB271.F8
Sabotage, intelligence, & unconventional warfare (WWI: Fr.)     940.48644
Sabotage (mil. sci.: gen.)     UB273     355.3437
Sabotage, Naval     359.3437     VG86-88 (underwater demolition), UB273-274
Sacramento, Calif.     979.454     F869.S12
Safety & sanitation (mil. engineering)     623.75     UH600-629.5, U380-385,
                    VC417.5, VG470-475, VM481-482, V380-386
Safety equipment, Nautical (fire-fighting, life-saving, etc.: design)     623.865
                    VK1258, VK1460-1481
Safety, Marine     VK200
Safety measures, Naval (inclu. educ.)     V380-385
Safety technology, Marine (plus other misc. topics)     623.888
Sahara Desert     DT331-346     966
Sahara Desert & West Africa     966
Sahara Desert (gen. hist., descrip. etc.)     DT333
Saigon, Viet.     DS558.S3 (earlier works), DS559.93.S2 (later titles)     959.7
Saigon, Viet. (WWII)     D767.352.S3
Sailing & pilot guides (official: British)     VK803
Sailing directions & pilot guides     VK798-997
Sailing ships, Modern (engineering)     623.822     VM321, VM351
Sailing vessels (handling)     623.8813     VK543
Sailing vessels (naut. engineering)     623.8203     VM156,
                    VM142-145 (wooden), VM331, VM351
SAILORS, NAVY (Asia)     VD99-113
Sailors, Navy (Australia)     VD121-122     359.3380994
Sailors, Navy (Can.)     VD26-27
Sailors, Navy (China)     VD101
Sailors, Navy (Eur.)     VD55-96
Sailors, Navy (Fr.)     VD71-72     359.3380944
Sailors, Navy (G.B.)     VD57-64
Sailors, Navy (gen.: pubn. 1970+)     VD146
Sailors, Navy (Ger.)     VD73-74
Sailors, Navy (Ire.)     VD76.5
Sailors, Navy (Japan)     VD105-106
Sailors, Navy (New Z.)     VD122.5
Sailors, Navy (Rus.)     VD85-86     359.3380947
Sailors, Navy (U.S.)     VD23-25
Saint Helena (Atl. Ocean)     997.3     DT671.S2
Saint Pierre & Miquelon     F1170     971.88
Saipan (Mariana Is.)     DU648.S35
Saipan (WWII)     D767.99.S3
Sakhalin (Siberia)     DK771.S2
Salaries & wages, Military (admin.)     355.64 (SEE ALSO .135)     UC70-75
Salaries, Military     355.135 (SEE ALSO 355.64)     UC70-75 (U.S.),
                    UC91-258 (other places), UC180-183 (Ger.),
                    UC184-187 (G.B.), UC241 (Japan)
Salary & wage administration, Naval     359.64     VC50-258, VC50-65 (U.S.)
Salvage, Marine     VK1491
Salvation Army (WWI)     D639.S15

Samoa, American          996.13        DU819.A1, DU810-819, DU815
Samoa (modern hist.)     DU817.A6-Z
Samoa, Western           996.14        DU819.A2, DU810-819, DU815
Samoa, Western (post-WWI territorial ?s)    D651.S3
Samoan Islands           DU810-819     996.13-14
Samurai (Jpn. custom)    DS827.S3
SAN Bernardino County (Calif.)         979.495       F868.S14
San Demetrio (WWII: tanker)            D772.S25
San Diego, Calif.        F869.S22      979.498
San Diego, Calif. (fortifications)     UG412.S3
San Diego, Calif. (WWII: U.S. naval base)     D769.542.S345
San Diego County (Calif.)              979.498       F868.S15
San Francisco Bay area                 979.46        F868.S156
San Francisco Bay area (Calif.)        F868.S156          979.46
San Francisco, Calif.    F869.S3       979.461
San Juan, P.R.           F1981.S2
San Marino (Republic)    DG975.S2
Sandhurst (Royal Mil. Coll.: descrip. & life)      U520.L1
Sanitary & medical services, Military     UH201-515
Sanitary control (WWI: med. srvcs.)       940.4752
Sanitary control (WWII)          940.54752
Sanitation & hygiene, Military     UH600
Sanitation & refuse (naval sci.)     VC417.5
Sanitation, health, & hygiene (navies: places besides U.S.)     VG475.A-Z
Sanitation, heating, & ventilation (naval architec. & engin.)     VM481    623.853-854
Sanitation (naut. craft: engineering)     623.8546     VM481-483
Santa Barbara County (Calif.)     F868.S23      979.491
Santa Cruz Islands    DU840      993.5
Sappers & bridge troops (U.S.)     UG503
Saragossa, Sp.        DP402.S3-32
Saratoga (aircraft carrier: U.S.: WWII)     D774.S3, VA65.S28    359.32550973
Sarawak        DS646.36-38      959.54
Sardinia       DG975.S29-33
Satire, caricature (G.B.: 20th c.)     DA566.8
Satire, poetry, etc. (WWI: gen.)     D526
Satire, poetry, etc. (WWII: gen.)     D745     940.5481, .5483, misc. 800 literature #s
Saudi Arabia (1914-: gen.)     DS244      953.04-05
Saudi Arabia (1932-: Ibn Saud)     DS244.53     953.052
Saudi Arabia & Arabian Peninsula     DS201-248     953
Saving life & property (marine navig.)     VK1300-1491
Savo Island (aircraft carrier: U.S.: WWII)     D774.S32
Savo Island, Battle of (1942)     D774.S318
Saxony (Prus.)        DD491.S3-39
SCANDINAVIA        DL
Scandinavia & N. Europe (20th c.: 1905-)     948.08        DL83-87+
Scandinavia & N. Europe (1905-19)     948.081        DL83
Scandinavia & N. Europe (1920-29)     948.082      DL83
Scandinavia & N. Europe (1930-39)     948.083      DL83
Scandinavia & N. Europe (1940-49)     948.084      DL83 (1901-45)
Scandinavia (geog. & travel)     914.8     DL10
Scandinavia (lighthouses, beacons, foghorns, etc.)     VK1086.5     623.89420948

Scandinavia (mil. status)     UA646.7     355.033048, .033248, .033548
Scandinavia (naval geog.)     359.4748     VA619.S, VA590599 (Sweden)
Scandinavia, Northern Europe, Finland     DL
Scandinavia (WWI: dipl. hist.)     D621.S3
Scandinavia (WWII: dipl. history)     D754.S29
Scapa Flow Naval Base (G.B.: Scot.: WWII)     940.5453411
Scenic places (London, Eng.: bridges, parks, etc.)     DA689.A-Z
Schacht, Hjalmar Horace Greeley (Ger.: 1918-48 era)     DD247.S335
Scharnhorst (battle cruisers: Ger.: WWI & II)     VA515.S
Schools (naval architec.: special)     VM275-276
Schools, Naval (Ger.)     V574.A-Z
Schools, Private naval (U.S.)     V430
Schuschnigg, Kurt (Austria)     DB98.S3
Schutzstaffel (SS: Nazi Party: gen.)     DD253.6
SCIENCE & technology (WWI)     D639.S2
Science & technology (WWII)     D810.S2
Science of marine navigation (gen.: pubn. 1801+)     VK555     623.81
Sciences (pure) & math     500-599     Q
Sciences (pure), math, & computer science     Q     500-599, 611-612
Scientists, Applied (WWII)     940.53156
Scientists (WWI)     940.3155     D639.S2
Scientists (WWII)     940.53155     D810.S2
Scotland     941.1     DA750-890, DA760 (gen.)
Scotland (20th c.)     DA821     941.1082
Scotland (1910-36)     941.1083     DA821
Scotland (1936-45))     941.1084     DA821
Scotland (WWII: gen. particip.)     940.53411
Scottish troops (G.B.)     UA664
Scraping, painting, etc. (marine engin.)     VM961
Scutari (Albania: gen.)     DR701.S5
Sea forces & warfare (hist.)     359.009+     VA, D-F, VA10, VA25-55
Seabees or naval construction battalions (WWII: U.S.: gen.)     D769.55
Seabees (WWII: U.S.: by battalion #)     D769.552.1st-
Seacoast artillery     UF450-455
Seacraft, Modern (specific types: engineering)     623.821-829
Seamanship     623.88     VK1-587+, VK541-547
Seamanship (marine navig. & merch. marine)     VK541-547     623.88
SEAMEN, NAVAL     VD
Seamen, Naval (Asia: gen.)     VD99     359.338095, .12095
Seamen, Naval (enlisted personnel in gen.: drill, way of life, etc.)     VD
Seamen, Naval (Eur.: gen.)     VD55     359.338094, .12094
Seamen, Naval (G.B.: gen.)     VD57     359.3380941, .120941
Seamen, Naval (gen.: pubn. 1801-1970)     VD145
Seamen, Naval (Ger.: gen.)     VD73     359.3380943, .120943
Seamen, Naval (Japan: gen.)     VD105     359.3380952, .120952
Seamen, Naval (misc. subjects)     VD430
Seamen, Naval (U.S.: gen.)     VD23     359.3380973, .120973
Seamen's handbooks (G.B.)     V115.G7
Seamen's handbooks (Ger.)     V115.G3
Seamen's handbooks (Japan)     V115.J3
Seamen's handbooks (Rus.)     V115.R9
Seamen's handbooks (U.S. Navy)     V113
Seaplanes     629.133347
Seaplanes (air force)     UG1242.S3     629.133347, 623.7466-7467
Search & rescue ops. (WWII: gen.)     D810.S42

Seattle, Wash.        F899.S4      979.777
Seattle, Wash. (area)      979.777      F897.K4, F899.S4
Seawolf (submarine: WWII)        D783.5.S4
Second Republic (Sp.: 1931-39: gen.)      DP254
Second World War (1939-45)        940.53-5499      D731-838
Second World War (econ., polit., social hist.)      940.531      D421, D443, D720-728,
                                                      D743, D748
Secret service, espionage, military intelligence (WWII: spies)      D810.S7-8
                                                      940.5485-5487+
Secret service, spies (WWI: gen.)        D639.S7
Secretary of the Navy (U.S.: official docs.)        VA52.A2-29
Security (defense info.)        UB246-249
Security, Industrial (defense purposes)        UB249
Security, Naval        V185
Seizure & disposition of German ships (WWI: U.S.)      D570.8.S4
Semaphore, flag signals, & heliograph (mil. engineering)      623.7312      UG582.S4,
                                                      UG580, UG582, VK385, V300-305
Semaphores (mil.)      UG582.S4
SERBIA (inclu. Belgrade)        DR1932-2125+ (SEE ALSO DR301+ & DR1202 areas)
                                949.71-71022
Serbia (1903-18: Peter I Karadordevic)        DR2030-2032
Serbia (1914-18: WWI)        DR2032
Serbia (1918-)      949.7102      DR366, DR2034
Serbia (1918-45: gen.)      DR2034
Serbia (1918-45: part of Yug.)      DR2033-2040
Serbia (1941-45: WWII era)      DR2040
Serbia (gen. histories)      DR1965
Serbia (gen., descrip., culture, history)      DR1940
Serials & periodicals (U.S.)      973.05      E171
Sermons, minor works, pamphlets (WWI)      D525
Sermons, minor works, pamphlets, (WWII)      D743.9
Service flags (WWI: U.S.)      D570.8.S5
Service flags (WWII: U.S.)      D769.8.S5
Service periods (navies)      359.11
Service squadrons (WWII: U.S.: by #)      D769.537
Service squadrons (WWII: U.S.: gen.)      D769.535
Sevastopol, Rus.      DK651.S45
Sevastopol, Uk.      DK508.95.S49
Seville, Sp.      DP402.S36-48
Sewage disposal (mil. design)      623.753      UC430, VM481, VM503
Sex (WWII)      D810.S46
Sextants & quadrants      VK583      527.028, 623.894
Shanghai, China      DS796.S2      951.132
Shanghai, China (Ch.-Jpn. Confl.: 1932: invasion)      DS777.51
Shark protection      VK1481.S4
Sharpshooting (infantry: U.S.)      UD333-334
Shells & shrapnel      UF760      623.4513-4518
Shells & shrapnel, Naval      VF490
Shells, bombs, missiles, other delivery units with charges (design)      623.451
                                                      UF750-755
Shells, Naval artillery      359.82513
Shetland Islands (Scot.)      DA880.S5
Shikoku (Japan)      952.3
Shinto (WWII)      D810.S47

SHIPWRECKS & fires     VK1250-1299 (PREFER D-F 3 #s for specific wars)
Shipwrecks (Asia)          VK1286
Shipwrecks (Australia & Oceania)  VK1289-1294
Shipwrecks (by area)          VK1270-1294
Shipwrecks (by name)     VK1255.A-Z
Shipwrecks (Eur.)          VK1280-1282
Shipwrecks (U.S.)          VK1270-1273
Shipyards & shipbuilding companies (by name)     VM301.A-Z
Shoes & footwear, Naval     VC310
Shoes, footwear, gloves (mil.)     UC490-495
Shooting (marines: inclu. marksmanship, training, etc.)     VE330-335
Shooting (naval seamen: inclu. marksmanship, regs., etc.)     VD330-335
SHORE facilities, yards, stations (navies: gen.)     VC412     359.7, 623.83
Shore patrol (G.B.)     VB925.G7
Shore patrol (gen.)     VB920          359.13323, .34
Shore patrol (Ger.)     VB925.G3
Shore patrol (U.S.)     VB923
Shore service     VF330-335
Shore service (marines)     VE410
Shortwave radio (mil. engineering)     623.7341
Shotguns          UD396
Shrapnel & other antipersonnel devices (design)     623.4514     UF760-765, VF490
Siam (Thailand)     959.3          DS561-589, DS571
Siam (1935-46: time of Rama VIII)     959.3043     DS585
Siam (20th c.)     959.304     DS578
Sian, Ch. (1936: incident)     DS777.514
SIBERIA          DK751-781, DK761          957
Siberia (19th-20th c.)     DK766          957.08
Siberia (Rev., 1917-21)     DK265.8.S5
Siberia & Asiatic Russia (geog. & travel)     915.7     DK755, DK584 (C.Asia)
Siberia (gen.)          DK761
Siberia (gen. hist., exploration, culture, etc.)     DK753          957
Siberia (WWII: gen. particip.)     940.5357 (more likely with Russia at .5347)
                                        D764, D767, DK766
SICILY     945.8     DG869
Sicily (20th c.)          DG869
Sicily (1900-45)     DG869.2
Sicily (geog. & travel)     914.581-582     DG864
Sicily (WWII)          D763.S5
Sicily (WWII: occupied terr.)     D802.S55
Sick & wounded, Care of (mil.: relief societies, etc.: U.S.: gen.)     UH523
Side arms & misc. weapons (design)     623.44     UD380-425
Sidearms, Modern (design)     623.444 (SEE ALSO .441 or .44)     UD420-425,
                                        UD400
Siege artillery     UF460-465
Siege warfare     355.44     UG443-449
Sighting & range apparatus (naval ordnance)     359.826
Sighting apparatus & other ordnance access.     355.826     UF848-856
Sights, Firearm     UF854

SIGNAL corps & troops    UG570-575
Signal corps & troops (U.S.)      UG573
Signal Corps battalions etc. (WWII: U.S.: by #)      D769.363.1st-
Signal Corps (WWII: Ger.: Nachrichten truppen)      D757.65
Signal Corps (WWII: U.S.: gen.)      D769.36
Signal service, Coast (plus coast guard: gen.)      VG50
Signaling, Merchant marine (flags, lights, codes, radio, etc.)    VK381-397
Signaling, Military      UG570-582      358.24, 623.73+, 355.85
Signaling, Military (particular types)      UG582.A-Z
Signaling, Naval (gen.)      V280-285      359.27, .983
Signals, Visual (mil. engineering)    623.731    UG582.V5
Sikorski, Wladyslaw (Pol.: 1918+ biog.)    DK440.5.S55
Sikorski, Wladyslaw (Pol.: 1918-45 period)    DK4420.S5
Silesia (20th c.)      DB660
Silesia Voivodeship (Pol.)      DK4600.S48
Silversides (submarine: WWII)      D783.5.S6
Singapore      DS598.S7    959.52
Singapore (to 1946)      959.5203
Singapore Naval Base (Royal Navy)      VA459.S5    940.5453095952,
                                                    .5453095957 (WWII)
Singapore (WWII)    D767.55    959.5203
Singapore (WWII: gen. particip.)      940.5359527 (SEE .535952 for earlier titles)
                                                    D767.5, DS598.S7
Sino-American Cooperative Organization (WWII)      D769.64 (for aerial ops. such
                                                    as Flying Tigers SEE D790)
Sino-Japanese Conflict (1937-45)    DS777.52-533    940.53, 951.042, 952.033
Sino-Japanese Conflict (1937-45: misc. topics)      DS777.533.A-Z
Sino-Japanese War (1894-5: gen.)      DS765
Ski troops      UD470-475    356.164
Ski troops (by country)      UD475.A-Z      356.16409+
Slaughterhouses, Military      UC770
Slavonia & Croatia (1918-)      DB379
Slavonia (Yug.: local Croatia)    DR1633-1636    949.72
Slavs (WWII)      D810.S5
SLOVAKIA (1800-1945)    DB2795-2822+
Slovakia (1918-: in Czech Republic)      DB2805-2822+, DB2806
Slovakia (1918-45)      DB679-679.3 (PREFER DB2000+)
Slovakia (1918-39)      DB2813
Slovakia (1939-45)      DB2815-2822
Slovakia (1939-45: gen.)      DB2816
Slovakia (1944: uprising)    DB2822
Slovakia (1945-68)      DB2826
SLOVENIA      DR381.S6, DR1352-1485+    949.73
Slovenia (1914-18: WWI)      DR1434
Slovenia (1918-45)      DR1435-1443
Slovenia (1918-45: gen.)      DR1436
Slovenia (1941-45: occupation)    DR1443
Slovenia (gen.)      DR1370, 1376
Slovenia (post-WWI territorial ?s)    D651.S53
Slovenia (WWII: occupied terr.)      D802.S67

SMALL ARMS        355.824        UF520-537+
Small arms (19th-20th c.)        U889
Small-arms ammunition (bullets, bazooka rockets, etc.: design)        623.455
                                    UF700, UF740-745, UF770, TS538, VF500
Small arms & bayonet training        355.547        UD380-415, U169
Small arms & ordnance (besides U.S.: by place)  UF525.A-Z
Small arms & ordnance (gen.)        UF520        355.82
Small arms & ordnance (manufacture: U.S.: gen.)        UF533        338.4762340973
Small-arms & ordnance research (places besides U.S.)   UF526.5.A-Z
Small arms (by region or country)        U897.A-Z
Small arms (gen.)        U884
Small arms (infantry)        UD380-425        355.824+, 623.44
Small arms (infantry: countries besides U.S.)        UD385.A-Z
Small arms (marines)        VE360-390
Small arms (navies)        VD360-390
Small boat service (inclu. armament)        VD400-405        359.3258
Small craft        VM321-349
Small craft (gen.)        VM321
Small craft (naut. engineering)        623.8202        VM320-361, VM321, VM331, VM341
Small craft (naut. handling)        623.8812        VK543, GV811
Smoke screens & tactics        UG447.7
Smolensk, Rus.        DK651.S65
Snipers, bazookamen, machine-gunners, & other special-weapon troops        356.162
                                    U167.5.A-Z, UD390+, UF620
Snowshoeing (WWI)        D639.S5
Snowshoes, skis, skates, etc. (mil. transp.)        UC360
SOCIAL aspects (WWII)        D744.6
Social aspects (WWII: by country)        D744.7.A-Z
Social groups (WWI)        940.315        D639.A-Z
Social groups (WWII)        940.5315+
SOCIAL LIFE & politics (Washington, D.C.)        F196
Social life, culture, customs (Berlin, Ger.)        DD866
Social life, culture, customs (London, Eng.)        DA688
Social life, culture, customs (Moscow, Rus.)        DK600
Social life, culture, customs (Paris, Fr.)        DC715
Social life, culture, customs (Pol.)        DK4110
Social sciences        300-399        G-H, J-L, U-V
Social sciences (economics, commerce, sociology, communism)        H        300-319,
                                    330-389
Social sciences (gen.)        300-309        H1-99
Social services, prisons, & medical services (WWI)        940.47
Social services, prisons, & medical services (WWII)        940.547        D805-809
Social welfare services, Military (U.S. Army)        UH760
Social welfare services, Naval        VG2000-2005
Social work, Military (gen.)        UH750        355.34, .346-347
Social work, Naval (gen.)        VG2000
Social work, recreation, etc. (air forces: U.S.)        UG990
Socialism (WWII)        D810.S6
Societies & associations (WWI)        940.4006        D502, D504 (congresses)
Societies & associations (WWII)        940.54006        D732, D734
Society Islands (inclu. Tahiti, Bora Bora, etc.)        DU870        996.21
Sociological factors of war        355.022 (SEE ALSO 303.66 & 306.2)
Sofia, Bulg.        DR97
Soignes Forest (Bel.)        DH801.S6


353

Soldiers' & sailors' homes      UB380
Soldiers' & sailors' homes (U.S.: state)      UB384.A-W
Soldiers' handbooks & manuals (gen.)      U110
SOLOMON ISLANDS (inclu. Guadalcanal, New Georgia, Choiseul, Savo, Florida,
            Bougainville, etc.)      DU850      993.5 (works prior to about 1989),
                                    995.93 (works dated after 1988)
Solomon Islands (geog. & travel)      919.35
Solomon Islands (mil. geog.)      355.47935      UA995.S
Solomon Islands (naval geog.)      359.47935      VA750.S
Solomon Islands (Northern: inclu. Buka, Bougainville, etc.)      995.92
Solomon Islands (pilot & sailing guides)      VK933.S65
Solomon Islands (WWII: by specific is.)      D767.982.A-Z (SEE ALSO D767.99.A-Z
                                    for alternative #'s)
Solomon Islands (WWII: gen.)      D767.98      940.53935, .5426
Solomons, Battle of the (1942-44)      D774.S45
Somaliland      DT401-420      967.7
Sonar, radio, radar, etc. (naval architec.: places except U.S.)  VM480.5.A-Z
Sound signaling (mil.)      UG582.S68
Sounding apparatus      VK584.S6
SOUTH AFRICA (1909-: Union)      DT779      968.05+
South Africa (1910-61: Union)      968.05      DT779
South Africa (1910-19: Louis Botha)      968.052      DT779.5
South Africa (1914-18: WWI period)      DT779.5
South Africa (1919-39)      DT779.6      968.05-054
South Africa (1939-48: Jan Christiaan Smuts: 2d era)      968.055      DT779.7
South Africa (1939-45: WWII era)      DT779.7      968.055
South Africa & South African military ops. (WWII)      D766.97      940.5368,
                                    .540968, 968.055
South Africa (mil. status)      UA856      355.00968, .033068
South Africa (naval status)      VA700.S52      359.030968
South Africa (overall)      968      DT751-944, DT766
South Africa (WWII: dipl. hist.)      940.532268 D754.S
South Africa (WWII: Reconstruction)      D829.A33
SOUTH AMERICA      F, F2201-3799+      980-989
South America (1830-)      F2236      980.03
South America (1900-18)      980.032      F2236 (1830-)
South America (1918-49)      980.033      F2236, F2237 (1939-)
South America (1939-)      F2237      980.033+
South America & Latin Am. (gen.)      980      F2201-3799+, F2201-2239, F2231 (GEN.)
South America (gen.)      F2231      980
South America (geog. & travel)      918      F2211, F2223, F2236-2237
South America (mil. geog.)      355.478
South America (mil. status: gen.)      UA612      355.03308, .03328
South America (naval status: gen.)      VA415 359.03098
South America (northern: Brazil, Ven., Peru, etc.)      F2216
South America (southern: Arg., Chile, Uru., etc.)      F2217
South American coasts (gen. & east: pilot & sailing guides)      VK961-968
South & South Atlantic states (1865-1950)      F215      975.04, 976.04
South Atlantic states      975      F206-295, F206-220, F209, F215 (1865-)
South Atlantic states & Florida (geog. & travel)      917.5      F106,
                                    F207.3 (S.Atl.), F309.3 (Fla.)
South Atlantic states & the South (U.S.: covers south of Mason-Dixon Line)
                                    F206-220      975-976
South Australia      DU300-330      994.23
South Australia (gen. & descrip.)      DU310-320

South Central states & Gulf Coast          976          F296-475, F296-395 (Gulf),
                                                         F296-301, F396- 475 (Old S.W.), F396
South Dakota (battleship: U.S.: WWII)          D774.S6
South Island (New Z.)          993.15
South Pacific (pilot & sailing guides)          VK925          623.89291646-89291649
South Seas (Oceanica: islands, chains, groups, etc.)          DU520-950
SOUTHEAST ASIA          DS521-689+, DS518 (1904-45: Far E. ?), DS521-605,
                                 DS525, DS541          959
Southeast Asia (1900-45)          DS526.6
Southeast Asia (1900-41)          959.051          DS518, DS526.6 (newer titles), DS549
Southeast Asia (1941-45: Japanese occup.)          959.052          DS549, DS526.6
Southeast Asia, Dutch East Indies, Philippines          DS521-689          959
Southeast Asia (gen. histories: older titles have descrip. & travel)          DS525
Southeast Asia (geog. & travel)          915.9          DS508
Southeast Asia (newer titles: gen.)          DS521          959
Southern Africa          DT730-995          968
Southern Anhui (China: Sino-Jpn. Confl.: 1941: incident)          DS777.534
Southern Asia & India          954          DS335-498+
Southern Asia & Indian Ocean Region          DS335-498          954, 958.1, 959.1
Southern California          F867          979.49
Southwest Africa (German Southwest Africa)          DT701-720          967.1, 968.8
Southwest (New: New Mex., Ariz., Utah, Nev.)          F786-850          978.9-979.3, 979
Southwest (Old) & lower Mississippi Valley (Ark., Tenn., Ken., Missouri)          F396-475
                                                                                          976.7-9, 977, 977.8
Southwestern Asia & Middle East (gen. histories)          DS62
SOVIET Bloc (1945-)          D847
Soviet Central Asia (1920+)          DK859
Soviet prisons & prisoners (WWII: SEE ALSO D805.R9)          D805.S65
Soviet propaganda (1925-53: foreign: gen.)          DK270
Soviet Union & Eur. Russia (geog. & travel)          [SEE ALSO 'Russia' or 'Union of
                                                           Soviet ...']          914.7          DK27
Soviet Union (1917-24: Rev. period & Lenin era)          947.0841          DK265 (Rev.),
                                                                              DK265-266.5+
Soviet Union (1918-)          DK266          947.084
Soviet Union (1918-: special inclu. espionage, sabotage)          DK266.3
Soviet Union (1918-24: Lenin era)          DK266.5          947.0841
Soviet Union (1924-53: Stalin era)          947.0842 (might ALSO try 948.97032 for
                                 Russo-FinnishWar)          DK267-273, DK267 (gen.),
                                 DK459.5 (R-F War), DL1095-1105 (R-F War: later works)
Soviet Union (1925-53: Stalin regime)          DK267-273
Soviet Union (1939-45: WWII period)          DK273          947.0842
Soviets (Rus. Rev., 1917-21: councils)          DK265.9.S6
SPAIN          DP1-402+          946
Spain (1868-)          946.08          DP222 (1868-86), DP233 (1886- & 20th c.)
Spain (1886-20th c.: gen.)          DP233          946.08
Spain (1886-1931: gen.)          DP240
Spain (1886-1931: period of Alfonso XIII)          DP234-247
Spain (1914-18: WWI)          DP246

Spain (1918-31)        DP247     946.08
Spain (1931-39: 2d Repub.: inclu. Civil War, 1936-39)     946.081
              DP250-269, DP254 (gen.), DP269 (Civil War)
Spain (1931-36: Alcalá Zamora y Torres era)    DP267
Spain (1936-39: Azaña period)     DP268
Spain (1936-39: Civil War)    DP269-269.9+    946.081
Spain (1939-75: Franco period)    946.082    DP270
Spain (1939-)        DP270    946.0824
Spain (1939-49)     946.0824
Spain & Portugal (geog. & travel)    914.6    DP42, DP525 (Port.)
Spain (mil. status)       UA780-789    355.033046
Spain (naval status)     VA580-589
Spain (WWII: gen. particip.)    940.5346    D754.S7, DP270-271
SPANISH-American War (1898)    E714-735    973.89-898
Spanish Civil War (1936-39)    DP269    946.081
Spanish Civil War (1936-39: foreign particip.: gen.)    DP269.45
Spanish Civil War (1936-39: special topics)        DP269.8.A-Z
Spanish military ops. (Civil War, 1936-39: Insurgents)    DP269.25
Spanish military ops. (Civil War, 1936-39: Loyalists)    DP269.23
Spanish Morocco    DT330    964.2
Spanish West Africa    964.8
Spark-ignition engines (marine engineering)    623.87234
Spaventa, Silvio (It.: 1871-1945 era)    DG556.S6
Specialist forces & warfare (armored land, technical land, & air)   358   UE-UG
Specialist forces, Naval    359.9
Specifications & contracts (naval architec.: gen.)    VM295
Speeches & essays (naval sci.: gen.)    V19
Speeches (Royal Naval Coll., Dart.: by speaker)    V515.F3.A-Z
Speeches (U.S. Naval Acad.: misc.: by speaker)    V415.F5.A-Z
Speeches (U.S. Navy)    VA54
Speer, Albert (Ger.: 1918-48 era)    DD247.S6-7
SPIES, espionage (WWI: by name)    D639.S8.A-Z
Spies, German (by name)    UB271.G32.A-Z
Spies, intelligence (Sino-Jpn. Confl., 1937-45)    DS777.533.S65
Spies (mil. admin.)    UB270    327.12
Spies, Russian (by name)    UB271.R92.A-Z
Spies, secret service, etc. (Rus. Rev., 1917-21)    DK265.9.S4
Spies, United States (by name)    UB271.U62.A-Z
Spies (WWII: by name)    D810.S8.A-Z
Sports in navies    V267-268
Sports, Military (gen.)    U327
Springfield rifle    UD395.S8
Squadrons, fleets, flotillas, etc. (naval units)    359.31    VA, VA63.A-Z (U.S.),
              VB200-205
Sri Lanka (Ceylon: gen.)    DS489.5
SS (Nazi Party: by Ger. locality)    DD253.62.A-Z
SS (Nazi Party: Ger.)    DD253.6-65
SS (Nazi Party: Ger.: by local #)    DD253.1st-
St. Louis public schools (WWI)    D639.E4.S3
St. Louis, Mo.    F474.S2    977.866
St. Petersburg, Rus. (gen.)    DK561
Staff functions (mil. organiz.)    355.33042
Staff positions (naval hier.)    359.33042
Staffs, Army    UB220-225
Staffs, Military (gen.)    UB220

Stalin, Joseph (Rus.: biogs.)    DK268.S8
Stalin, Joseph (Rus.: works by)    DK268.S75
Stalingrad, Battle of (1942-43)    D764.3.S7
Stalingrad, Rus.    DK651.S7    947.4785
Standards, colors, flags (mil.: places besides U.S.)    UC595.A-Z
Standards (naval architec.)    VM293
'Stars and Stripes' (WWII: periodical)    D731.S73
Statesmen (U.S.: collected works: 20th c.)    E742.5.A-Z (SEE E660 for up to 1921)
Statesmen (U.S.: collected works: inclu. some working through 1921)
                                    E660.A-Z (SEE E742.5 for rest of 20th c.)
Station drills, Naval (Eur.: gen.: ALSO quarter, watch, etc.)    VD215
Stations, shore facilities, yards (navies: U.S.: by state)    VC415.A-W
Statistics (militray medical: U.S.: unofficial)    UH223.A5
Statistics, Official (military medical: U.S.)    UH223.A4-49
Stavanger (Nor.)    DL576.S8, DL596.S8
Steam engines (marine engineering)    623.8722    VM741-749, TJ735-740
Steamship lines (by co. name)    VM385.A-Z
Steel & iron land defenses    UG408-409
Steerage, Nautical    VM565
Steering gear, Marine (engin.)  VM841-845
Sten machine guns    UF620.S8
Stephenson, William, Sir (WWII: spy)    D810.S8.S85
Stepney, Eng. (WWII: Middlesex)    D760.8.S75
Stimson, Henry (U.S.: 20th c.)    E748.S895
Stockholm, Swe.    DL976
Stockholm, Swe. (area)    948.7    DL976
Stores & supplies, Military (U.S.)    UC263-264
Stores & supplies, Naval (U.S.)    VC263-264    359.80973
Stores, Ordnance (U.S.: gen.)    UF553
Strassburg, Ger.    DD901.S81-89
Strasser, Otto (Ger.: 1918-48 era)    DD247.S8
Strategic Bombing Survey (WWII: U.S.: by industry attacked)    D785.U58.A-Z
Strategic Bombing Survey (WWII: U.S.: gen.)    D785.U57
Strategic lines, bases, etc.    UA930    355.43
STRATEGY, Air force    358.4143    U162-163, UG633-635
Strategy & military ops. (plans, attack, defense, etc.)    355.4    UA11,
                                    UA23 (U.S.), U27, U42-43, U102, U161-167
Strategy & naval ops.    359.4 (SEE ALSO .43 for strategic works prior to 1989)
                                    V27-55, V101-107, VA, VA10, VA50-750
Strategy (marines)    359.9643    VE21-124 (by place), VE144-146
Strategy (mil. sci.: pubn. 1789-)    U162    355.43
Strategy, Naval    359.43 (PREFER .4 with titles after 1988)    V160-165
Strategy, Naval (gen.: pubn. thru 1800)    V160
Strategy (WWI)    940.401    D521, D530, D550
Strategy (WWI: Allies)    940.4012    D544, D570
Strategy (WWI: Central Powers)    940.4013    D531
Strategy (WWII)    940.5401    D743
Strategy (WWII: Allies)    940.54012
Strategy (WWII: Axis)    940.54013
Stream & river crossing (artillery)    UF320
Street fighting    U167.5.S7
Streets, bridges, etc. (Berlin, Ger.)    DD887
Stresemann, Gustav (Ger.: 1888-1918+ period)    DD231.S83

Structural design (naval architec.: specific materials)     623.818
Structural design (naval architec.: steel)     623.81821     VM146
Structural theory & design (naval architec.)     623.817     VM156-163
Structure & personnel, Air force     358.413     UG770-775, UG1130-1135
Student publications (U.S. Naval Acad.)     V415.J1-7
Sturgeon (submarine: WWII)     D783.5.S8
Stuttgart, Ger.     DD901.S95-97
Subcaliber guns (U.S.: handbooks)     UF563.A8
SUBMARINE & anti-submarine ops (WWII)     D780-784     940.5451
Submarine boats     VM365-367
Submarine boats (gen.)     VM365     359.3257, 623.8257
Submarine cables (mil.)     UG607
Submarine forces & warfare     359.93
Submarine mines, minelaying, minesweeping, etc. (U.S.)     V856.5.U6-7
SUBMARINE OPS. & submarine chasers (WWI)     D590-595     940.451+
Submarine ops. (WWI: Allies)     940.4513     D590
Submarine ops. (WWI: Ger.)     940.4512     D591 (gen.), D592.A-Z (by ship,
                                                                    battle, etc.)
SUBMARINE OPS. (WWII: G.B.)     940.5451941     D784.G7
Submarine ops. (WWII: Ger.)     940.5451943     D781-782
Submarine ops. (WWII: It.)     940.5451945     D784.I8
Submarine ops. (WWII: Japan)     940.5451952     D784.J3
Submarine ops. (WWII: misc. countries: by place)     D784.A-Z
Submarine ops. (WWII: U.S.)     940.5451973     D783
Submarine warfare (gen.)     V210     359.3257, .42-43
SUBMARINES (besides U.S.)     V859.A-Z
Submarines, Conventionally-powered (navies: as equip.)     359.93832 (SEE .8357 for
                                                                    works before 1989)
Submarines, Diesel & electric (navies: units)     359.32572
Submarines (gen.)     V857 (SEE ALSO V210-14 for sub warfare & VM365-7 for
                                    construc.)     623.8257, .82572, .81257, 359.3257
Submarines (Ger.)     V859.G3     623.82570943
Submarines (Japan)     V859.J3     623.82570952
Submarines, Naval (as equip.)     359.8357 (SEE ALSO .93832 for titles after 1988)
Submarines, Naval (as units)     359.933 (SEE .3257 for titles prior to 1989)
Submarines, Naval (design)     623.81257     V858-859, VM365-367
Submarines, Naval (engineering)     623.8257     VM365-367, V857-859
Submarines (navies: handling)     623.88257     V857-859, V210-214
Submarines (U.S.)     V858     623.82570973, 359.32570973
Submersibles (naut. engineering)     623.8205     VM365-367
Submersibles (naval design)     623.812045
Subsistence & provisions, Naval (inclu. rations, galleys, water, etc.)     VC350-410
Subsistence Dept. (U.S. Army)     UC40-44
Subsistence (mil.: countries besides U.S.)     UC705.A-Z
Subsistence (mil.: gen.)     UC700
Subsistence (mil.: U.S.)     UC703-704
Subversion & sabotage (mil.)     355.3437     UB273-274UB275-277, UB276 (U.S.),
                                                                    UB277.A-Z (except U.S.)
Subversive activities (in U.S.: propaganda, espionage, 5th column, etc.)     E743.5
Sudan     962.4     DT108 (older works), DT154.1-159
Sudan (1900-1955)     DT156.7
Sudan & Anglo-Egyptian Sudan     DT108, (older works), DT154.1-159     962.4
Sudan (gen.)     DT155.6
Suez Canal (Egypt: inclu. Isthmus)     DT154.S9     962.15
Sultan Muhammad Shah, Sir, Agha Khan (India: 1901+ era)     DS481.S8

Sulu Archipelago (Philip.)    DS688.S9    959.99
Sumatra (Indon.)    959.81    DS646.1-15, DS646.129
Sumatra (Indon.: gen.)    DS646.1    959.81
Sun Yat Sen (China: 1912-49 era: autobiography)    DS777.A3
Sun Yat Sen (China: 1912-49 era: biograpy & criticism)    DS777.A597.A-Z89
Sun Yat Sen (China: 1912-49 era: writings of)    DS777.A2-567
SUPPLIES & equipment (air force: gen.)    UG1100-1105    358.418
Supplies & stores, Military (inclu. procure., storage, specs., surplus, etc.)
                                                                                   UC260-267
Supplies & stores, Naval (inclu. stds., procure., storage, etc.)    VC260-268
Supplies & stores, Naval (management methods)    VC266    359.62
Supplies & stores, Naval (misc.)    VC279.A-Z
Supplies, Medical & surgical (mil.)    UH440-445    355.88
Supplies, Medical & surgical (navies)    VG290-295
Supplies, Military (use & disposal)    355.6213
Supplies, Naval (Ger.)    VC180    359.80943
SUPPLY administration (mil.)    355.621    UC260-267
Supply administration (navies)    359.621    VC260-267, VC263 (U.S.)
Supply & administrative services, Military (canteens, post-ex's., messes, etc.)
              355.341 (SEE ALSO 355.6 & .71)    UC, UC750-755, UH80-85
Supply & transport depts. (mil.: G.B.)    UC184
Supply depots, Military    355.75    UC260-269
Supply depots, Naval    359.75    VC260-265
Supply forces & army service forces (WWII: U.S.: gen.)    D769.75
Supply services, Naval (canteens, post exch's, messes, etc.)    359.341
              VC, VC10, VC20-258 (overall by place), VC20-65 (U.S.), VC260-410
Supply ships (naval engineering)    623.8265    V865
Supply transport vehicles (land: mil. design)    623.7474
Supply vessels, transports, service craft, etc. (U.S. Naval Auxiliary Service)
                                                                                   VA79
Support & logistics, Military (logistics, camouflage, p.o.w. care, etc.)    355.41
                                                                      U168, UC260-270
Support & logistics, Naval    359.41    V179, VC10
Support ships (naval engineering)    623.826    V865
Support vessels, Naval (units)    359.326    V865
Surgeons, Naval    VG260-265    359.345, 616.98024, 617.99
Surgical & medical handbooks (navies: U.S.)    VG463
Surrender documents (WWII: Ger.)    D814.1
Surrender documents (WWII: It.)    D814.2
Surrender documents (WWII: Jp.)    D814.3
Surveillance, Military    UG475    355.413, 358.45
Surveying, Hydrographic (gen. special)    VK593
Surveying, mapping, & topography (military: gen.)    UG470    623.71
Surveyors, draftsmen, & engineering aids (navies)    VG920-925
Survival (combat: escape & evasion)    U225
Survival after shipwrecks (plus other misc. lifesaving topics)    VK1445-1447
                                                                                   623.865

SWEDEN            DL601-991+, DL648        948.5
Sweden (20th c.: 1905-)        948.505        DL860+
Sweden (1905-45)              948.5051        DL860-868
Sweden (1907-50: Gustav V)        DL867-870
Sweden (1914-18: WWI era)        DL868
Sweden (1919-)        DL868.5
Sweden (mil. status)        UA790-799        355.0330485
Sweden (naval status)        VA590-599
Sweden (WWI: dipl. hist.)        D621.S5
Sweden (WWII: dipl. history)        D754.S8
Sweden (WWII: gen. particip.)        940.53485        D754.S8, DL868.5-870
Swiss Guards (Papal Guards)        UA745.5
SWITZERLAND        DQ, DQ54        949.4
Switzerland (20th c.)        DQ201        949.407
Switzerland (1918-45)        949.4072
Switzerland (geog. & travel)        914.94        DQ24
Switzerland (mil. status)        UA800-809        355.0330494
Switzerland (WWII: dipl. hist.)        940.5325494        D754.S9
Switzerland (WWII: gen. particip.)        940.53494        D754.S9, DQ201
Sword exercises (cavalry)        UE420-425
Swords        UD420-425
Sydney (cruiser: WWII)        D775.5.S8
Sydney, Australia        DU178        994.41
Sydney, Australia (area)        994.41        DU178
Sympathizers, Enemy (WWI)        940.3163        D570.8.A6 (U.S.), D636.A-Z (by locale)
Sympathizers, Enemy (WWII)        940.53163        D769.8.A6 (U.S.), D801.A2 (gen.),
            D801.A3-Z (by place except U.S.)
SYRIA        DS92-99, DS95.5        956.91
Syria (1516-1920: time of Ottomans)        956.9103        DS97.5-6
Syria (1918-45: French mandate)        DS98        956.9104-91041
Syria (1920-: Mandate & independence)        956.9104        DS98+
Syria (gen.)        DS95
Syria (geog. & travel)        915.691        DS94
Syria (post-WWI territorial ?s)        D651.S9
Syria (WWII)        D766.7.S9-95
Szechwan (China)        DS793.S8
Szechwan Province (China: inclu. Chungking)        951.38        DS793.S8


TABLES, formulae, statistics (marine geonavigation)        623.8920212
Tables, Nautical        VK563-567+        623.8920212
Tables, Nautical navigation (distances etc.)        VK799        623.8920212
Tables, outlines, etc, (WWI)        D522.5
Tables, Tide & current (collections)        VK603
TACTICS, Air force        358.4142        UG700-705
Tactics, Air warfare (bombing, strafing, dog fighting, air mining, etc.)        UG700-705
            358.4142, .43
Tactics & maneuvers, Naval        VD157 (PREFER V167-178 & V245)        359.415,
            .4152
Tactics & operations, Infantry        356.183

TACTICS & REGULATIONS (MIL. ENGINEERING: Asia)     UG270-280
Tactics & regulations (mil. engineering: Australia & New Z.)     UG295-298
Tactics & regulations (mil. engineering: by place)     UG160-302
Tactics & regulations (mil. engineering: Can.)     UG163
Tactics & regulations (mil. engineering: China)     UG271
Tactics & regulations (mil. engineering: Eur.)     UG215-269
Tactics & regulations (mil. engineering: Fr.)     UG228
Tactics & regulations (mil. engineering: G.B.)     UG234
Tactics & regulations (mil. engineering: Ger.)     UG231
Tactics & regulations (mil. engineering: Japan)     UG277
Tactics & regulations (mil. engineering: Rus.)     UG252
Tactics & regulations (mil. engineering: U.S.)     UG160
TACTICS, MANEUVERS, & DRILLS (ARMOR & CAVALRY)     UE157-302
Tactics, maneuvers, & drills (armor & cavalry: Asia: gen.)     UE270
Tactics, maneuvers, & drills (armor & cavalry: Australia)     UE295
Tactics, maneuvers, & drills (armor & cavalry: China)     UE271
Tactics, maneuvers, & drills (armor & cavalry: Eur.: gen.)     UE215
Tactics, maneuvers, & drills (armor & cavalry: Fr.)     UE228
Tactics, maneuvers, & drills (armor & cavalry: Ger.)     UE231
Tactics, maneuvers, & drills (armor & cavalry: Japan)     UE277
Tactics, maneuvers, & drills (armor & cavalry: Rus.)     UE252
Tactics, maneuvers, & drills (armor & cavalry: U.S.: gen.)     UE160
Tactics, maneuvers, & drills (armored & mechanized cavalry)     UE159
TACTICS, MANEUVERS, & DRILLS (ARTILLERY)     UF157-302
Tactics, maneuvers, & drills (artillery: Asia: gen.)     UF270
Tactics, maneuvers, & drills (artillery: Australia & New Z.)     UF295-298
Tactics, maneuvers, & drills (artillery: Can.)     UF163
Tactics, maneuvers, & drills (artillery: China)     UF271
Tactics, maneuvers, & drills (artillery: Eur.: gen.)     UF215
Tactics, maneuvers, & drills (artillery: Fr.)     UF228
Tactics, maneuvers, & drills (artillery: G.B.)     UF234
Tactics, maneuvers, & drills (artillery: Ger.)     UF231
Tactics, maneuvers, & drills (artillery: It.)     UF243
Tactics, maneuvers, & drills (artillery: Japan)     UF277
Tactics, maneuvers, & drills (artillery: Rus.)     UF252
Tactics, maneuvers, & drills (artillery: U.S.: gen.)     UF160
TACTICS, MANEUVERS, & DRILLS (INFANTRY)     UD157-302
Tactics, maneuvers, & drills (infantry: Asia)     UD270-280
Tactics, maneuvers, & drills (infantry: Australia & New Z.)     UD295-298
Tactics, maneuvers, & drills (infantry: Australia)     UD219-221
Tactics, maneuvers, & drills (infantry: China)     UD271-273
Tactics, maneuvers, & drills (infantry: Eur.)     UD215-269
Tactics, maneuvers, & drills (infantry: Fr.)     UD228-230
Tactics, maneuvers, & drills (infantry: G.B.)     UD234-236
Tactics, maneuvers, & drills (infantry: Ger.)     UD231-233
Tactics, maneuvers, & drills (infantry: It.)     UD243-245
Tactics, maneuvers, & drills (infantry: Japan)     UD277-279
Tactics, maneuvers, & drills (infantry: Rus.)     UD252-254
Tactics (marines)     359.9642     VE157
Tactics, Military     355.42     U164-167.5, U165
Tactics, Military (in different terrains, climates, weathers)     355.423
                    U167.D4 (desert), .F6 (forest), .J8 (jungle), .W5 (winter)
Tactics, Military (pubn. 1811-)     U165     355.42
Tactics, Naval     359.42     V167-178
Tactics, Naval (gen.)     V167     359.42

Tailoring (naval clothing)    VC330
Taiwan (1895-1945: gen.)    DS799.7
Taiwan (Formosa: gen. hist., culture, descrip.)    DS799, DS895.F72
Takeoff (aviation)    629.1325212
Tallinn, Rus. (Reval)    DK651.T28
Tanganyika (German East Africa)    DT436-449, DT444    967.82
Tanganyika (to 1960: newer titles)    DT447
Tanganyika (1916-61: Brit. era)    967.8203    DT444, DT447
Tangier Zone, Mor.    DT329.T16    964.2
TANK battalions (WWII: U.S.: by #)    D769.306.1st-
Tank destroyer battalions (WWII: U.S.: by #)    D769.307.1st-
Tank warfare (WWI)    D608    358.18, 940.4+
Tank warfare (WWII)    D793
Tankers (naval architec.)    VM455    623.8245, 387.544
Tanks, armored cars, etc. (attack, defense, & siege: SEE ALSO UE159-302 for
    armored cavalry)    UG446.5    355.422, 357.5, 358.18
Tanks (design)    623.74752    UG446.5
Tarawa (WWII)    D767.99.T3
Target detection & selection (inclu. radar & other methods: engineering)
    623.557 (use .46 for ranging & siting apparatae)
Target practice    UF340-345
Target practice, Naval    VF310-315
Task forces (WWII: U.S.: by #)    D769.53.1st-
Tasmania (Van Diemen's Land)    DU450-480, DU470    994.6
Tatars (in Pol.)    DK4121.5.T3
Teachers (WWII)    940.5315372    D810.E2-5
Technical forces (chem., biol., & radiation warfare: pre-1989 titles may cover
    camouflage construc. & war matériel manufac.)    358.3
Technical forces, Naval (engineering, communic's., etc.)    359.98
Technical intelligence service (WWII: U.S.)    D769.76
Technical troops & artificers (gen.)    UG500    358.2-3
Technical troops & other special corps    UG500-565
Technische Truppen (WWII: Ger.)    D757.855
Technology, medicine, engineering, agriculture, management    600-699
    T, R, QA76, S, H
Technology, photography, manufacturing, handicrafts, home economics    T
    600-609, 620-629, 640-650, 660-699, 770-779
Telecommunication (defense)    UA929.95.T4
Telecommunications, Military    UG590-613.5
Telecommunications, Naval    VG70-85    359.415, .85, 623.856, .73
Telegraph, Military (inclu. telegraph troops)    UG600-605
Telegraph, Naval    VG70-75
Telegraph, radar, & radio communications (navies: wireless)    VG76-78
Telegraphy, Wire (mil. engineering)    623.732    UG600-607
Telemark (Nor.)    DL576.T4
Telephone, Military (gen.)    UG610
Telephone, Military (places besides U.S.)    UG610.5.A-Z
Telephone, Naval    VG80-85    623.85645
Telephone, radio, & telegraph (military: gen.)    UG590    623.732-7345
Telephones, Radio (mil. engineering)    623.7345    UG611 (gen.), UG611.3 (U.S.),
    UG611.5.A-Z (other lands), VG76-85
Telephony, Wire (mil. engineering)    623.733    UG610-610.5
Telescopic sights (artillery)    UF855
Television (mil. engineering)    623.735    UG613-613.5
Tempelhof Airfield (Berlin, Ger.)    UG635.G322.T3

Temperance (WWII)   D810.T4
Tents, Military   UC570-585
Terminals, Marine (bunkers, coal supplies, repairs, etc.)   VK358
Territorial questions (post-WWI: by place)   D651.A-Z
Territorial questions (post-WWI: gen.)   D650.T4 (SEE D651 for specific places)
          940.31424
Territorial questions (post-WWII: by place)   D821.A-Z
Territorial questions (post-WWII: gen.)   D820.T4 (SEE D821 for specific places)
Territories (U.S.: inclu. Alaska & Hawaii)   F965 (SEE ALSO DU620-629 for Haw.)
Territories (U.S.: island types in gen.)   F970 (SEE ALSO DU647 for Guam &
          DU620-629 for Haw.)
Territories (WWII: U.S.: by place)   D769.87.A-Z
Testing (naval armor)   V910-915 (SEE ALSO VF540)
Tests (naval architec.)   623.819
Tests, Ordnance   UF890
Tests, Ordnance & firing (navies)   VF540
Texas   F381-395, F386   976.4
Texas (1846+)   F391 (SEE D570.85.T4-41 for 1914-18 war years & D769.85.T4-41
          for 1939-45)   976.405-406
Texas (1918-45)   976.4062   F391
Texas (geog. & travel)   917.64   F384.3, F391
Texas (WWII: Reconstruction)   D828.T4-41
Thailand (Siam)   DS561-589   959.3
Thailand (19th-20th c.)   DS578   959.303-304
Thailand (1935-46: time of Ananda Mahidol, or Rama VIII)   DS585   959.3043
Thailand (WWII)   D767.47
Thailand (WWII: gen. particip.)   940.53593   DS585
THEATRES, Battle (WWII: Afr. & Mid. E.)   940.5423   D766.8 (Afr.),
          D766 (Balkans, E. Medit., Near E.)
Theatres, Battle (WWII: Am.)   940.5428   D768 (gen.), D768.18-3 (Latin Am.),
          D769 (U.S.)
Theatres, Battle (WWII: E. Ind., S.E. Asian, E. Asia)   940.5425 (SEE ALSO
          951.042 for pre-1941 Sino-Jpn. conflict)
          D767, D767.6 (India-Burma), D767.35 &
          D767.45 (Cochin China, Fr. Indoch.)
Theatres, Battle (WWII: Eur.)   940.5421   D743, D756 (W.), D764 (E.)
Theatres, Battle (WWII: misc.)   940.5429
Theatres, Battle (WWII: Pacific)   940.5426   D767 (gen.), D767.9+ (Pac. Is.)
Theory & philosophy (nautical craft)   623.82001   VM156
Theory & philosophy (naval warfare)   359.001
Theory & principles (naval architec.)   VM156-163
Third Reich (Ger.: 1930+-45: contemporary works)   DD253
Third Republic (Fr.: 1871-1940)   DC335
Thompson machine guns   UF620.T5
Tibet   951.5   DS785
Tibet & Central Asia (1951+ pubns.: gen.)   DS786
Tide & current tables   VK600-794, VK602 (gen.), VK610-650 (Atl.: E.), VK628-
          644 (Brit. Isles & Eng. Ch.), VK653-674 (Medit.), VK702-711 (China, Japan,
          Asian coasts), VK715-756 (Pac.), VK727-733 (Australia & Oceania), VK741
          (Am. W. Coast), VK759-792 (Atl: W., U.S., Carib.)   623.8949
Tide & current tables (Atlantic Ocean: all & east: gen.)   VK610   623.894909163
Tide & current tables (by area)   VK607-794
Tide & current tables (Pac. Ocean & islands: gen.)   VK715   623.894909164
Tide & current tables (South Pacific)   VK725
Tientsin, China   DS796.T5

Timber (naval supplies)    VC279.T5
Time periods (WWII)    D755-755.9
Timor    DS646.5    959.86
Tinian (Mariana Is.)    DU648.ST4
Tinian (WWII)    D767.99.T45
Tiso, Jozef (Czech.: 1939-45 era)    DB2821.T57
Tito, Josip Broz (Yug.: 20th c.)    DR359.T5
Tojo, Hideki, Gen., 1884-1948 (Japan: 1926-89 era)    DS890.T64
Tokyo, Japan    DS897.T6 (earlier works), DS896 (later works),
    DS896.64 (1867-1945)    952.135
Tokyo, Japan (1867-1945)    DS896.64    952.13503
Tokyo, Japan (gen.)    DS896.6
Tokyo, Japan (WWII)    D767.25.T5-6    952.135
Tokyo Trials (1946-48)    D804.J32
Toledo, Siege of (Sp. Civil War: 1936: Alcazar)    DP269.2.A4
Toledo, Sp.    DP402.T7-74
Toledo (Sp.: area)    DP302.T51
Tonga Islands    DU880    996.12
Tonnage tables (naval architec.)    VM153
Tools (naval supplies)    VC279.T6
Topography & mapping, Military (places except U.S.)    UG473.A-Z
TORPEDO & mining troops    UG550
Torpedo boat destroyers    V840    623.8254
Torpedo boat service    V837-838
Torpedo boats    V830-838    623.8258, 359.3258
Torpedo boats (Ger.)    V835.G3
Torpedo boats (places besides U.S.)    V835.A-Z
Torpedo boats (U.S.)    V833
Torpedoes (gen.: inclu. propelling or launching devices)    V850    623.4517,
    359.82517
Torpedoes (types or devices: by name)    V855.A-Z
Torres Strait (Queens., Aust.)    DU280.T7
Traffic control systems, Air    629.1366
TRAINING & EDUCATION, Air force    358.415    UG637-639
Training & education, Air force (gen.)    UG637
Training & education, Air force (places besides U.S.)    UG639.A-Z
Training & education, Military    355.5    U400-717, U400 (gen.),
    U403 (modern), U408 (U.S.), U410 (West Pt.), U510-549 (G.B.)
Training & education, Military (modern hist.)    U403
Training & education, Naval    359.5    V400-695 (by place), V411-438 (U.S.),
    V260-265
Training & education, Naval (G.B.: stations, ships, engin. schools, etc.)    V522-525
Training & education, Naval (modern hist.: gen.)    V404
Training & education, Naval (U.S. Coast Guard)    V437    359.9707
Training camps (armor & cavalry: gen.)    UE430
Training camps (armor & cavalry: places besides U.S.)    UE435.A-Z
Training camps, Marine    VE430-435    359.967+
Training (infantry)    356.184    U400-714 (educ.), U320-325
Training (marine navig. & merch. marine)    VK531-537
Training (marines)    359.965    VE430-435, V411-695, VE422 (U.S.)
Training, Military (Ger.: by school location)    U574.A-Z
Training, Naval reserve    359.2232    V400-695

Training, Officer (air forces)    358.4155
Training, Officer (mil. sci.)    355.55    U400-717 (educ.)
Training, Officer (navies)    359.55    V400-695, V411-438 (U.S.: Annapolis etc.),
                                         VB307-315
Training, Physical (mil. sci.: U.S.)    U323
Training, Physical (navies: countries besides U.S.)    V265.A-Z
Training, Physical (navies: gen.)    V260    359.54
Training planes (design)    623.7462
Training, Reserve    355.2232
Training schools, Naval (misc.)    V425.A-Z
Training ships (U.S. Navy: gen.)    V435
Training (shooting: marines: gen.)    VE330    359.96547
Training, Simulated (navies)    V252
Training stations, Naval (G.B.: by place)    V522.5.A-Z
Training stations, Naval (U.S.: gen.)    V433    359.50973, .70973
Training, Technical (air forces)    358.4156
Training, Technical (mil. sci.)    355.56
Training, Technical (navies)    359.56
Trans-Mississippi & the West (1880-1950)    F595    978.02-033
Trans-Pacific flights    629.130915
Transbaikalia (Sib.)    DK771.T8
Transoceanic flights    629.13091+
Transortation (WWII: inclu. merchant marine)    D810.T8
TRANSPORT & maintenance (mil. sci.: gen. spec.)    UC12
Transport & maneuvers (mil. living conditions)    355.1293
Transport equipment & supplies, Military (vehicles, fuel, trains, etc.)    355.83
                    UC270-360, UC270-275, UC340-345, UC260-267, UG615-620
Transport equipment & supplies, Naval (inclu. fuel, vehicles, ships [gen.], etc.)
                359.83    VC530-580, VC270-279, VC276, V750-895, UC320-325
Transport groups (air forces)    358.44    UC330-335, UG633-635, UG1242.T
Transport planes (air force)    UG1242.T7
Transport ships & hospital ships (naval engineering)    623.8264
                    UC320-325, VG450 (hosp. ships)
Transport, Medical (mil.: gen.)    UH500
Transport, Military    UC270-360    358.25, .44, 355.27
Transport, Military (besides U.S.: by place)    UC275.A-Z
Transport, Motor (mil. sci.: U.S.)    UC343
Transport, Motor (navies: U.S.)    VC573
Transport, Naval    VC530-580
Transport, Personnel (navies: U.S.)    VC553
Transport, Railroad (mil.: places besides U.S.)    UC315.A-Z
TRANSPORTATION Corps battalions etc. (WWII: U.S.: by #)    D769.733.1st-
Transportation Corps (WWII: U.S.)    D769.73
Transportation (defense)    UA929.95.T7
Transportation, Military (gen.)    UC270    358.25
Transportation, Naval (gen.)    VC530-535    359.83, .27
Transportation service (WWII: U.S.: gen.)    D769.72 (PREFER D810.T8)
Transportation services (mil. engineers)    358.25    UC270-275, UG345 (rail)
Transportation (WWI)    D639.T8
Transylvania (1801-1918) DB740 (SEE DR281.T7 for 1918-)
Transylvania (post-WWI territorial ?s)    D651.T8
Transylvania (post-WWII territorial ?s)    D821.T8
Travel & geography    910-919    G (geog.), D-F (descr. & travel)
Travel routes (mil. sci.: gen.)    UA950
Travel routes (misc.)    UA979

TREATIES (Fin.: 1918)        DK459.3
Treaties (Fin.-Rus.: 1920)        DK459.4
Treaties (Pol., 1921: Riga)        DK440.3
Treaties (Russo-Polish, other Polish conflicts: Riga: 1921)        DK4407.3
TREATIES (WWI: Allies-Central powers)        D643        940.3141
Treaties (WWI: Austria: 10 Sept. 1919)        D643.A8-9
Treaties (WWI: Bulg.: 27 Nov. 1919)        D643.B5
Treaties (WWI: countries other than Ger.)        D643.A8-Z
Treaties (WWI: Ger.: 28 June 1919)        D643.A2-A7
Treaties (WWI: Hungary: 4 June 1920)        D643.H7-9
Treaties (WWI: misc. separate)        D614.A-Z
Treaties (WWI: misc. separate: collections)        D614.A2
Treaties (WWI: results)        940.3142        D511-20
Treaties (WWI: Turkey: S`evres: 10 Aug. 1920)        D643.T8
Treaties (WWI: U.S.-Austria)        D643.A83
Treaties (WWI: U.S.-Ger.)        D643.A68
Treaties (WWI: U.S.-Hung.)        D643.H8
TREATIES (WWII: Allies-Bulg.)        D814.9.B9
Treaties (WWII: Allies-Ger.)        D814.6
Treaties (WWII: Allies-It.)        D814.7
Treaties (WWII: Allies-Japan)        D814.8
Treaties (WWII: Allies-misc. Axis powers: by country)        D814.9.A-Z
Treaties (WWII: Axis powers: collections)        D814.55
Treaties (WWII: results)        940.53142
Treaties (WWII: separate: by name)        D749.5.A-Z
Treaties (WWII: with Axis powers)        D814.55-9
Treatment of prisoners (Geneva & Hague conven.: unofficial)   UH533 (PREFER
                                                                JX5136 &JX5243)
TREATY of Neuilly-sur-Seine (WWI: texts)        D643.B6
Treaty of St. Germain (WWI: texts by date)        D643.A8
Treaty of Trianon (WWI: non-U.S. texts)        D643.H7
TREATY OF VERSAILLES (WWI: 28 June 1919: collected texts)        D643.A2
Treaty of Versailles (WWI: official discussions by date)        D643.A6
Treaty of Versailles (WWI: other official by date)        D643.A65
Treaty of Versailles (WWI: preliminary discussions)        D643.A3-4
Treaty of Versailles (WWI: protocol)        D643.A51
Treaty of Versailles (WWI: reservations by date)        D643.A55
Treaty of Versailles (WWI: texts by date)        D643.A5.1919+
Treaty of Versailles (WWI: unofficial talks)        D643.A7.A-Z
Trench artillery (WWI: U.S.)        D570.327
Trench warfare        UG446        355.44
Trepper, Leopold (WWII: spy)        D810.S8.T65
TRIALS (Leipzig: 1921)        D626.G4
Trials, Ship (by name of vessel)        VM881.A-Z
Trials (WWI: atrocities, war crimes: by country accused)        D626.A-Z
Trials (WWII: atrocities, war crimes: by country accused)        D804.A-Z
Trials (WWII: atrocities, war crimes: Germ.: post-Nuremberg before American Military
Tribunals, 1946-49: by main defendant)        D804.G425.A-Z
Trials (WWII: atrocities, war crimes: Germ.: post-Nuremberg: misc. by defendant)
                                                                D804.G43.A-Z
Trials (WWII: atrocities, war crimes: Jp. except Tokyo: by place or defendant)
                                                                D804.J33.A-Z
Trials (WWII: atrocities, war crimes: Jp.)        D804.J3
Trieste (post-WWI territorial ?s)        D651.T85
Trinidad & Tobago        972.983        F2016 (Windward Is.), F2116 (Tob.), F2121 (Trin.)

Triple Alliance (1882)      D458 (SEE ALSO D397, D443, D511)
Triple Entente (1907)      D459 (SEE ALSO D443, D511)
Tripoli, Libya           DT239.T7
Tripolitania (WWII: occupied terr.)      D802.T7
Trondheim, Nor.      DL596.T8
Trondheim (Nor.: area)      DL576.T9
TROOP support (air forces)      358.41415   UG700-705, UG260
Troop support (communication, supply, medical, p.o.w.'s, etc.)      355.415 (ALSO
          use 355.41 for newer titles on p.o.w. care)      UC260-27, UA940-945
Troop support, Naval      359.415
Troops, Airborne (U.S.)      UD483-484      356.1660973
Troops, Ski & mountain      356.164      UD470-475, U167.5.W5
Troops, Special-purpose      356.16      U167.5.A-Z
Troopships & waterways (mil. transp.: gen.)      UC320
Trophies, Military (WWII: U.S.)      D769.8.T8
Tropical hygiene (mil. sci.)      UH611
Trotsky, Leon (Rus.: 1925-53 era)      DK268.T75
Truk (WWII)      D767.99.T89
Truk Islands (Carolines)      DU568.T7
Truk Islands (pilot & sailing guides)      VK933.T79
Truman, Harry S (U.S.: Pres., 1945-53)      E814
Tsinan, Ch. (N. Exped., 1926-28: incident)      DS777.462
Tsingtao, China      DS796.T7
TUNISIA      DT241-269, DT254      961.1
Tunisia (1881-1957: Fr. Protectorate)      DT264      961.104
Tunisia & Egypt (mil. geog.)      355.4761-4762
Tunisia & Libya (geog. & travel)      916.1
Tunisia (mil. status)      UA867.5      355.0330611
Tunisia (WWII)      D766.99.T7-8      940.53611, 961.104
Tunnels (mil. engineering)      UG340      623.68
Turbines, Marine      VM740      623.87233
TURKEY (20th c.)      DR577      956.102
Turkey (1909-18: Mohammed V)      DR583-588      956.101
Turkey (1914-18: WWI era)      DR588
Turkey (1918-45)      956.102      DR589-590
Turkey (1918-22: Mohammed VI)      DR589
Turkey (1923-60: Republic)      DR590      956.1024
Turkey (1923-38: Kemal Ataturk era)      956.1024      DR590, DR592 (biogs.),
                                                    DR592.K4(Ataturk)
Turkey (1938-50: Ismet Inonu rule)      956.1025      DR590, DR592
Turkey & Albania (primarily Tur.)      DR401-741
Turkey & Asia Minor (lighthouses, beacons, foghorns, etc.)      VK1111-1112
Turkey & Cyprus      956.1      DR401-741, DS47-53, DS54 (Cyp.)
Turkey & Cyprus (geog. & travel)      915.61-66      DR428, DS54 (Cyprus)
Turkey (mil. status)      UA810   355.0330561
Turkey (naval geog.)      359.4756      VA667.T9
Turkey (naval status)      VA667.T9      359.0309561
Turkey (overall)      956.1      DR440
Turkey (post-WWI territorial ?s)      D651.T9
Turkey (WWII)      D766.7.T8
Turkey (WWII: dipl. history)      D754.T8
Turkey (WWII: gen. particip.)      940.53561      D766.7.T8, DR590

Turrets & cupolas, Naval        VF440
Turrets, Revolving (naval sci.: inclu. monitors)    V860
Tuscany & Florence, It.        DG731-760
Tuvalu (Ellice Is.)        996.82        DU590
Tyrol & Vorarlberg (20th c.)        DB780
Tyrol (post-WWI territorial ?s)        D651.T95


U.S.        [SEE ALSO 'United States']
U.S. Army        UA24-39
U.S. Army (gen.)        UA25        355.00973, .30973, .310973
U.S. Army (special troops: by name)        UA34.A-Z
U.S. Coast Guard        VG53        359.970973
U.S. Dept. of Defense        UA23.2-6        353.6-7
U.S. Dept. of Defense (gen. hist.)        UA23.6
U.S. Marine Corps        VE23        359.960973
U.S. Marine Corps (gen.)        VE23.A8-Z
U.S. Marine Corps (official hist's.)        VE23.A3-32
U.S. Marine Corps (official monographs)        VE23.A5
U.S. Marine Corps League        VE23.A13-14
U.S. Military Academy (West Point)        U410.A-R3+        355.0071173
U.S. Military Academy (admin.)        U410.C3-H8
U.S. Military Academy (gen. hist.)        U410.L1
U.S. Military Academy (registers, unoff.)        U410.H5-8
U.S. military education (gen. special)        U408.3
U.S. National Guard (gen.)        UA42.A7-Z
U.S. NAVAL ACADEMY (Annapolis)        V415.A1-R4+        359.0071173
U.S. Naval Academy (Act of incorp.: PREFER KF7353.55)        V415.A1
U.S. Naval Academy (admin.)        V415.C3-H5
U.S. Naval Academy (Cong. docs.: gen.: by date)        V415.E5
U.S. Naval Academy (hist. & descrip.)        V415.L1-P1
U.S. Naval Academy (registers, unoff.)        V415.H5
U.S. NAVY        VA52-79 (SEE ALSO E182)
U.S. Navy (distribution: gen.)        VA62        359.4773, .31
U.S. Navy (gen.)        VA55        359.00973, .30973, .4773
U.S. Navy (gen.: 1881-1970 coverage)        VA58        359.00973
U.S. Navy (misc. units: by name)        VA66.A-Z
U.S. Navy (placement & stations)        VA62-74
U.S. Navy Dept. (official docs.: gen.)        VA52.A1-19
U.S. Strategic Bombing Survey reports (WWII)        D785.U57-63
U.S. Veterans' Administration        UB382-384
U.S. War Dept. (ann. reports)        UA24.A1-149
UKRAINE        DK508-508.9+
Ukraine (1917+: earlier pubns.)        DK508.8
Ukraine (1917-44)        DK508.79-835
Ukraine (1917-44: gen.)        DK508.812
Ukraine (Rev., 1917-21)        DK265.8.U4
Ukraine (1921-44)        DK508.833-835
Ukraine (geog. & travel)        914.771
Ukraine (post-WWI territorial ?s)        D651.U6
Ukrainians (in Arg.)        F3021.U5
Ukrainians (in Pol.)        DK4121.5.U4
Ulithi (Carolines)        DU568.U5

UNCONVENTIONAL WARFARE (air forces: intelligence, propaganda, etc.)
358.41343
Unconventional warfare, Allied (WWI: espionage, intell., infilt., sabotage, etc.)
940.486
Unconventional warfare, Allied (WWII: inclu. espionage, infilt., intelligence,
subversion)    940.5486+
Unconventional warfare, Axis (WWII: inclu. espionage, intelligence, infiltration,
subversion)    940.5487+
Unconventional warfare, Central Power (WWI)    940.487
Unconventional warfare (navies)    359.343    VB230-250
Unconventional warfare (WWI: espionage, intell., infilt., sabotage, etc.)    940.485
D639.S7-8
Unconventional warfare (WWII: inclu. espionage, infilt., intelligence, subversion)
940.5485    D810.S7 (gen.), .S8.A-Z (by spy),
D802 (underground), D802.F8 (Fr. undergr.), UB250-
274, UB273-274 (sabo.), UB251.A-Z (intell., by
country), UB271.A-Z (espion., by country respons.),
VB230-250 (naval intell. & espionage)
Underground movements (Sino-Jpn. Confl., 1937-45)    DS777.533.U53
Underwater demolition teams (navies)    VG86-88
Underwater reconnaissance & demolition (navies: inclu. frogmen)    359.984
VG86-88 (demo.), VG190 (recon.)
UNIFORMS, Air force    358.4114    UG1160-1165
Uniforms, Air force    UG1160-1165    358.4114
Uniforms, Infantry    356.1814
Uniforms, Marine    VE400-405    359.9614
Uniforms, Military (besides U.S.)    UC485.A-Z
Uniforms, Military (gen.)    UC480    355.14
Uniforms, Military (inclu. insignia, etiquette of, etc.)    355.14    UC480-535,
UC483 (U.S.)
Uniforms, Naval (besides U.S.)    VC305.A-Z
Uniforms, Naval (gen.)    VC300    359.14, .81
Union of Soviet Socialist Republics (Russia)    [SEE ALSO 'Russia' or 'Soviet
Union']    947    DK, DK1-275, DK501-973+
United Nations (WWII: Allies: gen. particip.)    940.5332    D743, D748
UNITED STATES    [SEE ALSO 'U.S.']    E-F975+, E151-860+, E178 (gen.)
973-979.9+
United States (1865-1900+)    E660-738    973.8-89
United States (1898: Sp.-Am. War)    973.89 (SEE ALSO 946.08 for Sp.-Am. War,
1898)    E714-735, E715
United States (20th c.)    973.9+    E740-749, E741
United States (20th c.: gen.)    E741    973.9
United States (1913-21: gen.)    E766
United States (1913-21: Woodrow Wilson period)    E765-783, E766,
E780 (WWI era)    973.913
United States (1914-18: WWI era: internal)    E780    973.913

United States (1919-33: inclu. Roaring Twenties)     E784     973.913-916
United States (1921-23: Warren G. Harding era)     973.914     E783-786, E785
United States (1921-23: Warren G. Harding era: gen.)     E785 (SEE JX235 ALSO
                    for arms limitation conference, Pacific possessions
                    treaty, etc.)     973.914
United States (1923-29: Calvin Coolidge)     973.915     E791-796, E791
United States (1923-29: Calvin Coolidge period: gen.)     E791 (SEE ALSO JX1952
                    & JX1987 for Kellogg-Briand Pact of 1928)     973.915
United States (1929-33: Pres. Herbert Hoover: inclu. London & 3-Power naval
                    conferences & treaties)     E796-805, E801 (SEE
                    ALSO JX1974)     973.916
United States (1933-45: gen.)     E806
United States (1933-45: Pres. Franklin D. Roosevelt)     E805-812     973.917
United States (1945-53: gen.)     E813
United States (1945-53: Pres. Harry S Truman)     E813-815     973.918
United States aerial ops. (WWI)     D570.6, D606 (gen.)     940.44973
United States aerial ops. (WWII)     D790     940.544973
United States (air war geog.)     358.414773     UG633
United States & U.S. military ops. (WWII: gen.)     D769.A5-Z (SEE ALSO E806 for
                    internal, general U.S. history, 1939-45)
                    940.5373, .540973, .532273, 973.917
United States automatic machine guns     UF620.U6
United States (biog.: heads of state)     923.173     E176.1 (Presidents: collective)
United States engineering ops. (WWII)     D795.U6
United States (gen. & cultural, serials, societies, etc.)     E151
United States (gen. hist.)     E178     973
United States (geog. & travel: overall)     917.3     E169 (1914-45)
United States (geog. & travel: states, areas, & towns)     917.4-9
United States (lighthouses, beacons, foghorns, etc.)     VK1023-1025
United States (lighthouses, beacons, foghorns, etc.: lists)     VK1243
UNITED STATES (LOCAL), Canada, Newfoundland, Mexico, Central & South America
                    F     974-79+, 971-2, 980-89
United States (local history), Canada, Latin America     F     971-972, 974-989
United States (local: regions, states, towns, etc.)     F1-975+     974-979 (note
                    that Hawaii is placed at 996.9)
United States magazine rifle     UD395.U6
United States (maps & atlases)     912.73     G1200+, G1201
United States medical services (WWI: by overseas locale)     D629.U8.A-Z
United States medical services (WWII)     940.547573     D807.U6-87,
                    .U6 (gen.), .U62.A-Z (by state), .U72-73 (Army
                    hospitals), .U85-87 (Navy hospitals)
United States medical services (WWII: by state)     D807.U62.A-W
United States medical services (WWII: Calif.)     D807.U62.C3

UNITED STATES (MIL. capabil.)    355.033273
United States (mil. geog.)    355.473    UA993
UNITED STATES MILITARY OPS. & U.S. (WWI)    D570-570.9+    940.373,
                                            41273, .40973, 327.73
United States military ops. & U.S. (WWII)    D769-769.99    940.532273,
                                            .5373, .540973, .541273, .5428
United States military ops. (WWI: organiz. units: land, sea, air)    D570.2-.79 (SEE
                                            D570.A4-Z, D545 etc. for overall
                                            participation, battles, etc.)
United States military ops. (WWII: gen. special)    D769.2
United States military ops. (WWII: land,air, & sea)    D769.2-799 (SEE D769.5.A5-Z
                                            for gen. works)    940.541273, .544373, .544973
United States military ops. (WWII: organiz. units: land, sea)    D769.2-779 (SEE
                                            D769.A5-Z, D756.5, D767 etc. for overall
                                            efforts, area campaigns & battles)
United States (mil. policy)    355.033573
United States (mil. status)    355.033073 UA23
United States (mil. status: gen.)    UA23.A2-Z
UNITED STATES (NAVAL geog.)    359.4773    VA49-395, VA50 (gen.)
United States (naval geog.: partic. states)    359.4774-4779    VA90-387
United States (naval hist.)    359.00973    VA49-395, VA50-70, E182, E746 (20th c.)
UNITED STATES NAVAL OPS. & Coast Guard ops. (WWII: fleets, squadrons,
                                            bases, etc.)    D769.45-599 (SEE D773-4, D783
                                            for overall works, specific ships & engagements,
                                            submarines)    940.545973
United States naval ops. (WWI)    D570.4-.5    940.45+, .41273
United States naval ops. (WWI: gen.)    D570.4-5, D589.U5-8 (PREFER)
United States naval ops. (WWII)    D773-774 (SEE ALSO D769.45-599 for
                                            specific fleets, squadrons, bases, units)
                                            940.545973
United States naval ops. (WWII: by battle, ship, etc.)    D774.A-Z
United States naval ops. (WWII: gen.: inclu. blockade, patrol)    D773    940.545973
United States naval ops. (WWII: special topics: land batteries, defensive areas,
                                            Marine Corps except land, etc.)    D769.45
United States (naval policy & status)    359.030973
United States ordnance (gen.)    UF563.A9-Z
United States (pilot guides: gen.)    623.892973    VK993
United States (pilot guides: specific areas)    623.892974-892979    VK947-
                                            948 (W. Coast), VK981-982 (E. Coast)
United States propaganda (WWII)    D810.P7.U6
United States submarine ops. (WWII: by battle, ship, etc.)    D783.5.A-Z
United States submarine ops. (WWII: gen.)    D783
United States (WWI: causes, aims, results)    D520.U6-7
United States (WWI: gen.)    D570    940.373
United States (WWI: neutrality & dipl. history)    D619    940.32273, .373
United States (WWI: special topics)    D570.8.A-Z (SEE D639 for outside U.S.)
UNITED STATES (WWII: causes, aims, results)    D742.U5-6
United States (WWII: collections)    D769.A2
United States (WWII: dipl. hist., inclu. neutral years)    D753-753.8
                                            940.532573, .532273, 973.917
United States (WWII: gen.)    D769    940.532273, .5373, .540973,
                                            .541273, .5428
United States (WWII: gen. particip.: by area or state)    940.5374-5379
                                            D769.85.A-Z, D769.87-88, F1-951+
United States (WWII: gen. special)    D769.1

United States (WWII: Reconstruction: by state)   D828.A-W
United States (WWII: Reconstruction: gen.)      D827
United States (WWII: special topics)      D769.8.A-Z (SEE D810.A-Z for outside U.S.)
United States (WWII: states)      D769.85.A-W
Units, Naval air (U.S.: by name: inclu. organizations)      VG94.6.A-Z
Universal service      UB350-355
Universal service & training (mil. resources)      355.225      UB350-355
Ural Mts. region (Rus.)      947.87      DK511.U7
Ural Mts. (Rus.)      DK511.U7      947.87
Ural Mts. (WWII)      D764.6.U82
Urban warfare tactics      355.426      U167.5.S7
URUGUAY      F2701-2799, F2721 (gen.)      989.5
Uruguay (1904-)      F2728      989.5061-5063
Uruguay (1933-51)      989.5063      F2728
Uruguay (gen.)      F2721
Uruguay (mil. status)      UA640-642      355.0330895
Uruguay (naval status)      VA440
Uruguay (WWII: dipl. hist.)      940.5325895 (could ALSO be at .5324895 with Axis)
                  D754.U

V-2 rocket      UG1312.V2
Valencia, Sp.      DP402.V15-25
Valencia (Sp.: area)      DP302.V11-25
Van Diemen's Land (Tasmania: gen. & descrip.)      DU460-470
Vancouver, B.C.      F1089.5.V22      971.134
Vanuatu (New Hebrides)      993.95 (SEE ALSO 993.4 to find works on New
                  Hebrides prior to 1989)      DU760
Vatican City      945.634      DG800
Vatican City (1929-)      DG800
Vatican City (Rome: WWII: gen. particip.)      940.5345634      D763.I82.V or .R,
                  D810.C6, DG800
Vedettes, scout & dispatch boats, other minor craft (gen.)      V880
Vehicles, Military (design: inclu. combat & support v's. & neces. ordnance)
                  623.74      UC270-275+
Vehicles, Motor (air force: ground)      UG1400-1405
Vehicles, Motor (mil.: U.S.)      UG618
Venezuela      F2301-2349, F2321      987
Venezuela (1935-)      F2326      987.0632
Venezuela (gen.)      F2321
Venezuela (mil. status)      UA643-645
Venezuelan coast islands (Aruba, Curaçao, Tobago, Trinidad, etc.)      F2016
                  972.98
Venice, It. (city state & modern)      DG670-679
Verdun, Battle of (WWII: 1940)      D756.5.V3
Verdun, Fr.      DC801.V45
Versailles, Fr. (also Trianon)      DC801.V55-57
Vessels (naval architec.: by use)      VM378-466
Vessels, Naval war (modern period)      V765-767      623.80904
VETERANS' benefits      355.115      UB356-405, UB356-358
Veterans' benefits & services      UB356-405      355.115
Veterans' education, employment, etc. (gen.)      UB356      355.1152, .1154
Veterans' homes & hospitals      UB380-385
Veterans' homes & hospitals (besides U.S.)      UB385.A-Z
Veteran's or Armistice Day addresses, services (WWI: U.S.)      D671
Veterans' rehabilitation (places besides U.S.)      UB365.A-Z

Veterinary service (WWII)     D810.V45
Veterinary services (mil.)     UH650-655     355.345
Vichy France (WWII: dipl. hist.)     940.532444 (perhaps ALSO .532544)
                                     D752
Vickers machine guns     UF620.V4
Victoria (Australia)     DU200-230, DU220     994.5
Victoria (Australia: 1851-1950: inclu. descrip.)     DU212
Vienna, Austria     943.613     DB841-860, DB847 (gen.)
Vienna, Austria (20th c.)     DB855
Vienna, Austria (gen. hist. & descr.)     DB847
Vienna, Austria (WWII)     D765.45.V45
Vietnam (Annam)     DS556     959.7
Vietnam (1802-1954)     DS558.8
Vietnam (geog. & travel)     915.97     DS556.36
Vietnam (mil. status)     UA853.V5
Vietnam (WWII: gen.)     D767.35, DS556.36, DS549 (earlier works)
                        940.53597, 959.703
Views (WWI)     D527 (SEE ALSO D522)
Views (WWII)     D746 (SEE ALSO D743.2+)
Virgin Islands (U.S.)     F2136     972.9722
Virginia     F221-235, F226, F231 (1865-1950)     975.5
Visayan Islands (Philip.: inclu. Cebu, Leyte, Negros, etc.)     959.95
                                     DS688.B6 (Bisayas)
Vistula River & Valley (Pol.: Wisla)     DK4600.V5
Visual signaling (mil.)     UG582.V5
Vittorio Emanuele III (It.: King, 1900-46: gen. inclu. times)     DG566
Vladivostok, Rus.     DK781.V5
Volga River Valley (Rus.)     DK511.V65
Volgograd, Rus. (also Tsaritsyn or Stalingrad)     947.85     DK651.S7
Voluntary enlistment (navies)     359.22362
Volunteers (Nat. Guard, militia, etc.: Illinois)     UA170-179
Vorarlberg, Austria (WWII)     D765.45.V6
Voss, Nor.     DL596.V6


WACS (Women's Army Corps: U.S.)     UA565.W6
WACS (Women's Army Corps: WWII: U.S.)     D769.39
Waffen SS (WWII: Ger.: Waffenschutzstaffel)     D757.85
Wages & salaries, Air force     358.4164     UG940-945, UC74 (U.S.), UC90+
Wagons & carts, Artillery     UF380-385
Wake Is. (WWII)     D767.99.W35
Wake Island     DU950.W28     996.5
Wales     942.9
Wales (19th & 20th c.)     DA722     942.908+
Wallace, Henry A. (U.S.: 20th c.)     E748.W23
Wallace, Henry A. (U.S.: 20th c.: works)     E742.5.W3

373

WAR (aftermath: occupation, reconstruc., etc.)     355.028
War & warfare     355.02     U21, U21.2, U102
War (causes)     355.027     U21.2, HB195, JX1952
War correspondents & public relns. (mil.: U.S.)     UH703
War correspondents & public relns. (navies: U.S.)     VG503
War crimes, atrocities, trials (WWI: gen.)     D625     940.405, .472
War crimes, atrocities, trials (WWII: gen.)     D803
War games     U310     355.5
War games, Naval     V250     359.52
Warfare & military forces (types)     356-359     UD-UG, V
Warfare (summary topics)     355.021     U161-162, UA10
Warning systems (defense engineering)     623.37 (SEE .737 for titles after 1988)
Warrant officers (mil.)     UB407-409
Warrant officers (naval: gen.)     VB307     359.332
Warsaw, Pol.     DK651.W2 (earlier works), DK4610-4645
Warsaw, Pol. (1918-)     DK4633
Warsaw, Pol. (area)     943.84     DK651.W2, DK4610-4645
Warsaw, Pol. (gen.)     DK4630
Warsaw, Pol. (WWII)     D765.2.W3
Warship handling (plus other seamanship topics)     VK545     623.8825
WARSHIPS (as equip.: develop., operation, tech. effectiveness)     359.835-836
                              (SEE ALSO .32+ for ships as units or indiv. ships)
Warships (construction, armament, types, etc.)     V750-995+ (SEE VA for status
                              & organiz. of specific navies around the world)
Warships, Fuel-powered (engineering)     623.825     V750, V765, V797-799
Warships, Fuel-powered (handling)     623.8825     VB200-205
Warships (naval architec.)     VM380 (PREFER V750-995+)     623.825, 359.32
Warships (powered: design)     623.8125     V750, V765-767, V799-800
Warships, Sail-driven (engineering)     623.8225     V750-797, V750, V795
Warships (types)     V815-895     623.825-826, 359.83, .325-326
Washington (state)     F886-900, F891     979.7
Washington (state: to 1950)     F891
WASHINGTON, D.C. (1865-1933)     975.303     F198-199
Washington, D.C. (1933-)     975.304     F199+
Washington, D.C. area (1878-1950)     F199     975.303-304
Washington, D.C. (gen.)     F194
Washington, D.C. (streets, bridges, railroads)     F203.7.A-Z
Washington, D.C. (District of Columbia: WWII)     D769.85.D6
Washington, D.C. (WWII: Reconstruction: Virginia)     D828.V8-81
Watch drills, Naval (U.S.: gen.: ALSO quarter, station, other)     VD160
                              359.50973, .1330973, .133220973
Watch duty (merch. duty)     VK233
WATER & sanitation (naut. craft: engineering)     623.854     VM503-505 (water),
                              VM481-483 (san.)
Water, Potable (naut. craft: engineering)     623.8542
Water, Sea (naut. craft: engineering)     623.8543
Water supplies, Military     UC780
Water supplies, Naval (inclu. preservation, purification, etc.)     VC410 (SEE VM503
                              for onboard storage)     623.854
Water supply (mil. engineering)     623.751     UC780, VC410, VM503-505
Water supply (naval architec. & engin.)     VM503-505     623.854

Waterways        UA970-975
Waterways & troopships (mil. transp.)    UC320-325        359.3264
Waterways (Ger.)        UA975.G3
Waterways (outside U.S.)        UA975.A-Z
Waterworks (defense)        UA929.95.W3
Watkin range finder        UF850.W3
Wavell, Archibald Percival Wavell, 1st Earl of (G.B.: 20th c. mil. biog.)    DA69.3.W37
Waves (U.S. naval reserves for women & other non-local U.S. naval res.)    VA390
Wealthy & upper classes (WWII)        940.5315062        D800
Weapons systems (artillery)        UF500-505
Weapons systems, Naval        VF346-348
Weather forecaster, Naval (gen.)        VG610
Weights & measures (mil. metrology)        UG455
Weimar Republic (Ger.: 1918-33)        943.085        DD233-251, DD237 (gen.),
                            DD251 (Hindenb. era), DD453 (Prussia)
Weizmann, Chaim (Palestine: 19th-20th c.)        DS125.3.W45
Welding & cutting, Underwater (marine engin.)        VM965
WELFARE & RELIEF SERVICES (WWI)        940.477        D637-638
Welfare & relief services (WWI: by G.B.)        940.477841        D638.G7
Welfare & relief services (WWI: in specific places)    940.4779+        D638.A-Z,
                            D657-658 (Reconstruc. in U.S.), D659.A-Z (by place)
Welfare & relief services (WWI: provided by specific countries)        940.4778+
                            D638.A-Z
WELFARE & RELIEF SERVICES (WWII)        940.5477        D808-809
Welfare & relief services (WWII: by Australia)        940.5477894        D809.A8
Welfare & relief services (WWII: by G.B.)        940.5477841        D809.G7
Welfare & relief services (WWII: by U.S.)        940.5477873        D809.U5
Welfare & relief services (WWII: in particular countries)        940.547794-547799
                            D809.A-Z
Welfare & relief services (WWII: provided by specific countries)
                            940.547784-547789        D809.A-Z
Welfare services, Military (U.S.: gen.)        UH755
Welfare services, Naval (U.S.)        VG2003
Wellington, N.Z.        DU428        993.127
Wellington, N.Z. (WWII)        D767.852.W44        993.127
Welsh troops (G.B.)        UA663
WEST Africa        DT471-720        966-967, 968.8
West African islands        DT671.A-Z
West Coast (Am.: plus E. Pac.: pilot & sailing guides)        VK941-956
West Coast (U.S.: Loran tables)        VK561.U57
West Coast (U.S.: pilot & sailing guides)        VK947        623.892916432
West Coast (U.S.: tide & current tables)        VK747        623.8949091643
WEST INDIES        972.9        F1601-2175+, F1608, F1621
West Indies (1898-)        F1623        972.904-905
West Indies (1902-45)        972.9051        F1623
West Indies (gen. hist.)        F1621
West Indies (lighthouses, beacons, foghorns, etc.: lists)        VK1239-1240
West Indies (mil. status)        UA609-611
West Indies (naval geog.)        359.47729        VA409-410
West Indies (pilot & sailing guides: by island[s])        VK973.A-Z
West Point (descrip. & life)        U410.M1.P1
West Point (U.S. Mil. Acad.: official hist's.)        U410.L1.A1-5
West (U.S.) & Trans-Mississippi        F591-705        978

WESTERN Australia        DU350-380        994.1
Western Australia (gen. & descrip.)        DU360-370
Western Europe & Europe (1453+)        940.2    D208, D217
Western Europe (WWII: except Ger., G.B., Fr.)        D763.A-Z
Western Front & Western Europe (WWII)        D756-763        940.5421
Western Front (WWI)        D530-549
Western Hemisphere (gen.) & United States        E        970
Western Samoa (was Ger. Samoa)        DU819.A2    996.14
Western states        978        F591-785, F591-596, F591
Westphalia (Prus.)        DD491.W4-52
White House (Washington, D.C.)        F204.W5
White Russia & Western U.S.S.R. (geog. & travel)        914.76
White Russia (Belorussia)        DK511.W5        947.65
White Russia (Western Russia)        DK507
White Russians (in Pol.)        DK4121.5.W5
Whitehead torpedo        V855.W5
Willkie, Wendell (U.S.: 20th c.)        E748.W7
Wilson, Wilson (U.S.: Pres., 1913-21)        E767
Wilson, Woodrow (U.S.: 1865-1900 era: works)        E660.W7-75
Windward Islands (inclu. Barbados, St. Lucia. etc.)        F2011    972.98
Wings, Aircraft        629.13432
Winter warfare        U167.5.W5
Wireless signals (merch. marine)        VK397
WOMEN (20th c.: collective biography)        D412.5
Women & minorities (navies: gen.)        VB320        359.22
Women & minorities (U.S. Navy: gen.)        VB323
Women & minorities in the armed forces (U.S.: gen.)        UB417
Women & the military (sociology)        U21.75
Women & women's work (WWI)        D639.W7        940.315042
Women & women's work (WWII)        D810.W7
Women (armed forces: U.S.)        UB418.W65
Women (Ger.: 1918-48)        DD245
Women in air forces        358.41348
Women in armed forces        355.0082
Women in naval forces        359.229        VA49-750, VA390.W (U.S. Waves)
Women (Rus. Rev., 1917-21)        DK265.9.W57
Women (U.S. Navy)        VB324.W65
Women's military units        355.348        UA565.W6 (U.S. Wac's)
Women's naval units (gen.)        359.348        VA
Women's reserve, Marine (U.S.)        VE23.4
Women's reserves (U.S.)        UA45
Wooden ships (naval architec.)        VM142-145        623.81
Woodrow Wilson Foundation        E772
WORLD HISTORY (20th c.: collected)        D414-415
World history (20th c.: gen.)        D410-460+, D421-5, D421        909.82
World history (20th c.: several authors)        D414
World history (20th c.: single-author collections)        D415
World history (1919-39)        D720-728
World history, Europe, Africa, Asia, Oceania        D-DX        900-949, 990's
World history (gen.: 1800-)        909.8        D299, D395
World navies (pop. works)        VA41

WORLD WAR I (1914-18)        D501-680      940.3-940.499
World War I (Allies & associates: mil. units & ops.)   940.412+      D544-550, D569-570
World War I & women        940.315042        D639.W7, JX1965
World War I (antisub. ops.)        940.4516      D580-589, D590
World War I (Armistice)        940.439      D641
World War I (Central Powers: mil. units & ops.)   940.413+      D531-540, D566
World War I (gen.)        D521      940.3, 940.4
WORLD WAR I (GEN. PARTICIP.: Australia)        940.394      D547.A8
World War I (gen. particip.: by country: inclu. mobilization)      940.34-39
World War I (gen. particip.: Can.)        940.371      D547.C2
World War I (gen. particip.: Fr.)        940.344      D548, DC387
World War I (gen. particip.: G.B.)        940.341-342      D546, DA577
World War I (gen. particip.: Ger.)        940.343      D531, DD228.8
World War I (gen. particip.: It.)        940.345      D569, DG570
World War I (gen. particip.: New Z.)        940.3931 (SEE ALSO .393 for titles after
                                    1988)      D547.N5
World War I (gen. particip.: Rus.)        940.347      D550, DK264.8
World War I (gen. particip.: U.S.)        940.373-379      D570
World War I (medical srvcs.)        940.475      D628 (gen.), D629.A-Z (by country),
                                    D630.A-Z (biog.)
World War I (mil. units & ops.: gen.)        940.41      D521
World War I (misc. special)        D639.A-Z (SEE D570.8 for U.S.)
World War I (misc. topics)        940.48
World War I (mobilization)        940.402 (SEE .34-39 for particular countries)
World War I (naval ops.: particular countries)        940.459      D580-589
World War I (special topics)        D622-639
World War I (submarine ops.)        940.451      D590-595, D590 (gen.)
WORLD WAR II (1939-45)        D731-838      940.53-940.5499
World War II (1939-45: gen.: inclu. overall works on Sino-Japanese War
                        [1937-45])      940.53      D743
World War II (1940)        D755.2
World War II (1941)        D755.3
World War II (1942)        D755.4
World War II (1943)        D755.5
World War II (1944)        D755.6
World War II (1945)        D755.7
World War II (Allies & United Nations: mil. units & ops.)      940.5412+
World War II & women        940.5315042      D810.W7
World War II (anecdotes)   940.5494      D743.9
World War II (antisub. ops.)        940.54516      D780, D770-784
World War II (Axis Powers: mil. units & ops.)      940.5413+
World War II (collected works)        D739
World War II (dipl. hist.)        940.532      D748-754, D748 (gen.)
World War II (gen.)        D743      940.53, .54

WORLD WAR II (GEN. PARTICIP.: Albania)     940.534965     D766.7.A4,
                            DR701.S8-86, DR974 (later works after 1980?)
World War II (gen. particip.: Algeria)     940.5365     D766.99.A4-6, DT295
World War II (gen. particip.: Asia)     940.535
World War II (gen. particip.: Australia)     940.5394     D767.8-82, DU116
World War II (gen. particip.: Austria & Liech.)     940.53436     D765.4 (Austria),
                            DB99, D765.45.L (Liech.), DB540.5
World War II (gen. particip.: Belgium)     940.53493     D763.B4-42, DH687
World War II (gen. particip.: Bulg.)     940.534977     D766.7.B8, DR89-90
World War II (gen. particip.: Burma)     940.53591     D767.6, DS485.B89,
                            DS530     (later titles post 1970?)
World War II (gen. particip.: by country: inclu. exile govs., undergr. move's., pro- &
                            anti-Axis nat. groups, mobilization, etc.)     940.534-539
World War II (gen. particip.: Can.)     940.5371     D768.15, F1034
World War II (gen. particip.: Caroline Is.)     940.53966     DU565-567
World War II (gen. particip.: China)     940.5351     D767.3, DS777.518-533
World War II (gen. particip.: country groups, inclu. nat. groups, pro- & anti-Axis nat.
                            groups, mobilization)     940.533
World War II (gen. particip.: Crete)     940.534998     D766.7.C7, DF901. C86
World War II (gen. particip.: Denmark & Fin.)     940.53489     D763.D4-42, DL256 (Den.)
World War II (gen. particip.: Egypt)     940.5362     D766.9, DT107.82
World War II (gen. particip.: Finland)     940.534897 (SEE ALSO .53471 for some
                            works before 1980)     D754.F5, D765.3,
                            DK459.45+, DL1090-1105+ (works after about 1980),
                            DL1090, DL1097
World War II (gen. particip.: Fr. & Monaco)     940.5344     D752, D761, DC397
World War II (gen. particip.: G.B.)     940.5341     D750, D759, DA587
World War II (gen. particip.: Ger.)     940.5343     D751, D757, DD253-256.5
World War II (gen. particip.: Greece)     940.53495     D766.3-32, DF726
World War II (gen. particip.: Guam & the Marianas)     940.53967     D767.G or .M,
                            DU647 (Guam), DU645 (Marianas)
World War II (gen. particip.: Hungary)     940.53439     D765.56, DB955
World War II (gen. particip.: India)     940.5354     D767.6, D767.63 (Free India), DS413
World War II (gen. particip.: Iran)     940.5355     D766.7.I55, DS317-318
World War II (gen. particip.: Iraq)     940.53567     D766.7.I57, DS79.53
World War II (gen. particip.: Israel)     940.535694     D766.7.P (Palestine), D766.7.I7
World War II (gen. particip.: It.)     940.5345     D763.I8, DG571-572
World War II (gen. particip.: Japan)     940.5352     D767.2-25, DS888.5-889
World War II (gen. particip.: Libya)     940.53612     D766.93, DT235
World War II (gen. particip.: London, Eng.)     940.53421     D760.8.L7, DA684
World War II (gen. particip.: Luxemb.)     940.534935     D763.L9, DH916
World War II (gen. particip.: Morocco)     940.5364     D766.99.M8, DT324
World War II (gen. particip.: New Guinea)     940.5395     D767.95, DU740-746
World War II (gen. particip.: New Z.)     940.53931 (SEE ALSO .5393 for works after
                            1988)     D767.85-852, DU411
World War II (gen. particip.: Nor.)     940.53481     D763.N6-62, DL532
World War II (gen. particip.: Paris, Fr. area)     940.534436     D762.P3, DC737+
World War II (gen. particip.: Philippines)     940.53599     D767.4, DS686.3-4
World War II (gen. particip.: Rumania)     940.53498     D766.4, DR264-267
World War II (gen. particip.: Rus.)     940.5347     D764, D754.R9 or .S65,
                            DK267-273, DK273

World War II (gen. particip.: S. Africa)   940.5368   D766.97, DT779.7
World War II (gen. particip.: Singapore)       940.535952 (SEE .535957 for later titles)
                                                           D767.5, DS598.S7
World War II (gen. particip.: Solomon Is.)   940.53935   D767.98, DU850
World War II (gen. particip.: Syria)   940.53569   D766.7.S9, DS98
World War II (gen. particip.: Tunisia)   940.53611   D766.99.T8, DT264
World War II (gen. particip.: U.S.)   940.5373   D769, E806-813, E806 (gen.)
World War II (gen. particip.: U.S.: by area or state)       D769.85.A-W,
                                                           D769.87-88, F1-951+
World War II (gen. particip.: U.S.: N.Y.)   940.53747   D769.85.N4-5, F124
World War II (gen. particip.: Yug.)   940.53497   D766.6-62, DR366,
                                       DR1289 (later works after 1980?)
World War II (gen. special: deception, strategy, psychological aspects, world
                                              politics, misc.)   D744
World War II (medical srvcs.)   940.5475   D806-807, D806 (gen.)
World War II (mil. units & ops.: gen.)   940.541   D743
World War II (misc. topics)   940.548
World War II (mobilization)   940.5402 (SEE .534-539 for particular countries)
                       D800, HC, HF, HJ
World War II (naval ops.: particular countries)   940.5459+   D770-784
World War II (Sept. 1939-Dec. 1941)   D755
World War II (Sept. 1939-May 1940)   D755.1
World War II (special topics)   D798-810
World War II (special topics)   D810.A-Z (SEE D769.8.A-Z for U.S.)
World War II (submarine ops.)   940.5451+ (SEE ALSO .542 for ops. by theatre)
                       D780-784, D780 (gen.), D781-782 (Ger.), D783 (U.S.),
                       D784.A-Z (other lands)
World War II (VE Day to VJ Day)   D755.8
Wounded, Care of (mil.: inclu. relief societies: gen.)   UH520   361.05, .77, .9,
                                                           940.477+

Wrecks, Nautical (research)   623.8885   VK1250+
Writers (WWII)   940.53158   D810.A7
Wroclaw, Breslau, Pol. (WWII)   D765.2.W7
Wyoming (WWII)   D769.85.W8-81


Y.M.C.A., Y.W.C.A. (WWII)   D810.Y7
Yachts (small craft: gen.)   VM331
Yalta, Rus.   DK651.Y25
Yalta, Uk. (Jalta)   DK508.95.I24
Yamamoto, Isoroku, Adm., 1884-1943 (Japan: 1926-89 era)   DS890.Y25
Yamato (battleship: Japan)   VA655.Y25   359.32520952
Yangtze River (China)   DS793.Y25   951.2
Yap (Carolines)   DU568.Y3
Yards & stations, Naval (U.S.: by place)   VA70.A-Z
Yards, Navy (gen.)   V230 (SEE ALSO VA67-750 for particular places)   359.7
Yards, stations, shore facilities (navies: U.S.: gen.)   VC414   359.70973
Yearbooks & almanacs, Nautical (non-American)   VK8
Yearbooks, Naval (official: also lists: by country: SEE ALSO VA #s if dept. reports
                              involved)   V11.A-Z   359.0025+, .005
Yearbooks, Naval (unofficial)   V10
Yellow Peril   DS519
Yemen   DS247.Y4-48
Yeomen & clerks, Naval   VG900-905
Young Plan (WWI)   D649.G3.A6-7
Youth (WWII)   D810.Y74

YUGOSLAVIA (Serbia)    DR301-396 (earlier pubns.), DR1214-1307+    949.7-71
Yugoslavia (to 1918)    949.701    DR317, DR1274
Yugoslavia (20th c.)    DR357    949.702, .7102
Yugoslavia (20th c. & 1918-)    949.702    DR357, DR1274, DR1282
Yugoslavia (1903-21: Peter I)    DR360-363    949.701-702
Yugoslavia (1914-18: WWI era)    DR363 (earlier pubns.), DR1280    949.7, .701
Yugoslavia (1918-45)    DR1288-1298    949.702
Yugoslavia (1918-45: gen.)    DR366, DR1289    949.702-7022
Yugoslavia (1918-45: inclu. Croatia, Serbia, Slovenia)    DR364-369
    949.7021-7022, 949.7102 (Serbia)
Yugoslavia (1918-39: Kingdom)    949.7021    DR366, DR1289
Yugoslavia (1918-21: reign of Peter I)    DR1295
Yugoslavia (1921-34: Alexander I)    DR368, DR1296
Yugoslavia (1934-45: Peter II)    DR369, DR1297-98    949.7022
Yugoslavia (1941-45: Axis occup.)    DR1298    949.7022
Yugoslavia (1945-)    DR370
Yugoslavia & Bulgaria    949.7+
Yugoslavia & Yugoslavian military ops. (WWII)    D766.6-62    940.53497, 949.7022
Yugoslavia (central republics: Bosnia, Herzegovina, Montenegro)    949.74
Yugoslavia (gen., descrip., culture, hist.)    DR301-396+ (earlier books),
    DR1202-1307+, DR1214    949.7
Yugoslavia (gen. hist.)    DR317, DR1245-1246    949.7
Yugoslavia (geog. & travel)    914.971-976    DR309, DR1221 (later books)
Yugoslavia (mil. status)    UA827    355.0330497
Yugoslavia (post-WWI territorial ?s)    D651.Y8-9
Yugoslavia (post-WWII territorial ?s: inclu. Trieste)    D821.Y8
Yugoslavia (WWII: collections)    D766.6.A2
Yugoslavia (WWII: dipl. history)    D754.Y9
Yugoslavian military ops. (WWII)    D766.6
Yugoslavia (1939-45: WWII era)    949.7022    DR369, DR1297-1298
Yunnan Province (China)    DS793.Y8    951.35

ZAGREB, Yug. (WWII)    D766.62.Z3
Zanzibar (inclu. time as Brit. colony)    DT434.Z3, DT435, DT449.Z2-Z29 (newer titles)
Zanzibar (island & coast)    DT435
Zanzibar (1890-1963)    967.8103    DT435, DT449.Z2-29 (newer works),
    DT449.Z28
Zionism, Restoration, Judenstaat    DS149-151
Zouaves (WWII: Fr.: infantry)    D761.38
Zurich, Swit.    DQ781-800    949.45

## IV. LIBRARY OF CONGRESS SUBJECT & OTHER HEADINGS

The Library of Congress has constructed a controlled vocabulary system of LC subject, biographical, corporate, and other headings and phrases in order to provide consistent and thorough catalog access to its huge collection. Most academic and public libraries in the United States have adopted LC Subject Headings as the standard for catalog indexing, although some smaller public libraries may use the Sears group of headings. These are based on LC and represent a compact version.

As with the classification systems, change is inevitable in the ongoing subject vocabulary shown in this guide. The Library of Congress deliberately but regularly adds, amends, and drops headings and sub-headings in an attempt to keep pace with a changing world and language. Even corporate and other headings change as, for example, government agencies come into existence and then change names or as people's names finally require death dates. Rather than list only the latest approved descriptors, I have opted to include new and old so as to allow for better entrée in modernized or older catalogs. A richer vocabulary should also help with keyword-searching of entire records for buried terms when using online, optical-disk, or other electronic rosters of the future.

In using the LC subject headings, researchers should note that the network is predominately alphabetic and specialized in nature rather than overarching as with some database thesaurus systems. The latter depend heavily upon cross-references within a controlled framework of broader, narrower, and parallel terms and phrases trying to describe their universe. While LC started in the late 1980's to employ scoped cross-references, the prime character remains particularly alphabetic and diverse rather than attached to any classified verbal skeleton.

Some effort is made to incorporate hierarchical concepts within the alphabetic sequence. Hence, under the many headings that begin with 'World War, 1939-1945', LC has placed assorted subheadings and sub-subheadings in alphabetic suborder. Under 'World War, 1939-1945' may be found '—Aerial operations', '—Campaigns', '—Finance', —Great Britain', '—Naval operations', and numerous other subtopics. Under or after ' World War, 1939-1945— Campaigns' may be found many geographical subdivisions such as '—China', '—France', '—Japan', '—Poland', '—Ukraine', '—Western', and others in alphabetical order. Under some topics one can see historical subdivisions in chronological arrangement. Therefore, under the main heading of 'Japan— History' will be seen the subheadings '—20th century', '—1912-1945', '—Taisho period, 1912-1926', '—1926-1945' and '—March and October incidents, 1931' in that sequence.

The use of subdivisions allows for some gathering of similar subject groups within proximate alphabetic sets. Since the system simultaneously allows specialized descriptors and phrases in isolated positions throughout the alphabet, some confusion as to the best search method is natural. A combination of wider terms and subdivisions along with isolated or pinpoint headings is probably best, given the normal LC policy of assigning several terms of subject access to each cataloged title if warranted.

This division of the guide is organized in alphabetic array by LC term or proper-word heading or subject. Thus, mixed together as in many catalogs may be found historical events, tactical concepts, specific weapons, particular ships, airplane types and models, biographical names, government agencies, etc.

Please note that some electronic library catalogs place proper names of people and organizations into a separate file that encompasses these names as both subjects and authors, while many catalogs of whatever format would place such proper names into either subject or author catalogs depending on specific usage of each term. Also valuable to remember is the idea of searching corporate or government-agency authors as a means of quasi-subject searching. One could, for instance, find pertinent materials under 'United States. War Department' as an author that might not be listed under the subject terms considered for a particular search. I have chosen to keep all headings together so that readers need check only one listing and so as to avoid the separation of terms such as 'United States—History' from 'United States. Army'.

Following some of the headings are Library of Congress and/or Dewey Decimal Classification numbers that might be considered for browsing purposes in the stacks or shelflist. When two or more class numbers are given that begin with the same root, certain abbreviated forms may be seen. For example, LC numbers UG630 through UG670 might appear as 'UG630-70'. In the Dewey system, 358.4183 and 358.440973 could be listed as '358.4183, .440973'.

I have tried to include a large sampling of call numbers. Some of them represent typical range areas, but I have also presented a variety of numbers taken from outside the main historical and military spans that otherwise predominate. I did not discover nor devise numbers in every case. Many terms could be placed in a diverse number of classifications depending on individual library needs, and listing class examples would prove somewhat meaningless in these instances. I have attempted, nevertheless, to include at least representative numbers or ranges for the most important topics or topical groups.

Hopefully, the controlled-term section will help researchers to find more materials through knowledge of more headings and of related subdivision patterns and of classification possibilities. As stated in the class introductions, however, a thorough hunt will utilize both call numbers and regulated headings.

A-5 rocket
Aachen—Siege, 1944          D757     940.5421
Academy War Film Library
Acheson, Dean Gooderham, 1893-1971 [U.S.: Diplomat]        E748.A15-17, E744,
                                   E183.7      973.9180924, 327.73, 353.1
Adachi, Hatazo, 1890-1947     [Japan: Lt. Gen., Commander in New Guinea]
Admirals—Portraits
Adriatic question     D650.T4, D651     940.322497
Aerial gunnery
Aerial reconnaisance      UG760-5     623.72
Aeronautical instruments     TL587     629.135, .15
Aeronautics      TL500-830 (technology)        629.1-13+
    —Biography      TL539-40         926.2913, 629.130922, .1300922
    —History      TL512-32         629.109, .1309, .13009
Aeronautics, Military      UG630-70, JX5124 (int'nal. law), VG90 (naval)
                          623.746, 358.4
        —Germany      UC535, UG635          358.410943, .411094
        —Great Britain      UG653       358.4135
        —History      UG623       358.40074
        —Japan      UG625       355.033052
        —Observations      UG630-70       355.413, 358.45
        —Psychology      RC550, UG632   616.85, 623.746
        —Research      UG633     353.63
        —Russia      UG635       358.400947
        —United States      E746, UG633, VG93 (naval), UC333
                          355.83, 358.400973, .413320924, .4183, .440973, 629.13
            —History      UG633       358.40973, .4130973
            —Statistics      HE9803     387.74
Aeroplane carriers      V895     359.32
Aeroplanes, Military      [This spelling used mostly before 1980, after which SEE
    'Airplanes...']     TL685-6, UG633-5, VG93-5 (naval)       355.6213, 358.407,
                          .4183, 623.740937, .746+, 629.133-134
Afghanistan      DS351-69        915.81+, 958.1+
Africa, North—History—1882-       DT204      916.103, 961.02+
Afro-American seamen
Afro-American soldiers      [For titles before around 1970 SEE 'Negro soldiers—U.S.']
                          E185       355.00917496, .330973, 973.0496073
Afro-American veterans
Agents provocateurs—Germany
Agriculture and state      HD1415, HD1773      338.1091724, .13
Air bases
Air bases, American [British, German, etc.]
Air bases, American
Air bases, British
Air bases, German
Air bases, Japanese
Air bases—United States      UG634     358.417058
Air defenses
Air defenses, Military      UF625 (antiaircraft guns), UG630-5 (mil. aeronautics),
                          U408     358.13, .39
Air forces—History
Air interdiction      UG700

Albania
—History     DR701     949.65
    —1912-1944
—Politics and government
Albert I, 1875-1934     [Belg.: King]     DH514, DH681-2, D615
          949.3040924, 940.3493, 923.1493, .1403, 929.793
Alexander, Harold Rupert Leofric George, 1st Earl, 1891-1969 [G.B.: Field Marshal]
     DA69.3.A43, .A57, D546.A37, D763.I8     942.0840924, 355.3310924
Alfieri, Dino, n.d. [It.: Fascist gov. official]     D811
Algeria—History—1830-1962     DT284, DT294     965, 965.03
Alliances     JX4005, JX1907     341.2, .72, 327.08
Allied and Associated Powers (1914-1920). Treaties, etc.
    .Austria, 1919 Sept. 10     D643.A9
Allied Forces     D756.3
Allied Forces. Southwest Pacific Area. Allied Intelligence Bureau     D810
          940.548673
Allied Forces. Supreme Headquarters. Psychological Warfare Division     D810
          940.54886
Allied Powers (1919-). Reparation Commission     DC59.8.G3, D648-9
Alsace-Lorraine question     DD801     923.544, 944.38308, 320.944383+
Altuzzo, Battle of, 1944
American Cemetery, Manila     D810.D4     940.54655991
American Friends Service Committee
   . Foreign Service Section
American Jewish Joint Distribution Committee
American National Red Cross
American Outpost in Great Britain     D731.O
Amery, Leo, 1873-1955     [G.B.: Conservative politician]     DA566.A, D743.9
          940.5304, 923.242
Amiens, Battle of, 1940
Ammunition     TS538, UF543, UF700     355.415, .621, .82, 623.455, 658.57, 688.7
—Transportation     UC323     359.982
Amphibian planes     TL684     629.133348+
Amphibious assault ships     VC263     658.56
Amphibious warfare     U261, U439, D25     359.83, 355.48
Anarchism and anarchists     HX821-970     320.570922, 335.83+, 923.347, 321.07
Anderson, John, Sir, 1882-1958     [G.B.: Cab. member for domestic affairs, inventor
    of Anderson Shelters, Chanc. o/t Excheq.]
Angary, Right of
Anglo-Russian treaty, 1942
Anschluss movement, 1918-1938     DB48, DB97     320.943085, 943.605
Antiairborne warfare
Anti-aircraft artillery
Anti-aircraft guns     UF625     358.13, 623.41
Anti-comintern pact
Anti-Nazi movement     D802.G3, DD256.3     940.534
Antisemitism     BM535, D5145, DS135, DS145, E184     301.451924,
          .452+, 296.387834+, 909.04924081
    —Germany     DS135, DS145-146     261.8345+, 301.451924+,
          323.11924043, 956.94001
    —History     DS145-147     301.451924, 909.0974+, .04924
    —Russia
    —United States
Anti-submarine warfare

Antitank guns    UF628    358.18, 623.412
Antitank weapons
Antonescu, Ion, 1882-1946    [Rum.: Marshal, Pr. Min.]    DR262.A
                                                        923.5498
Antwerp, Battle of, 1944
Anzio Beachhead, 1944    D763    940.5421, .5338
Arab countries—History-Arab Revolt, 1916-1918    DS223, DS36-39, DS63,
                        D568.4    953.02, 909.04927, .0974927
Arandora Star (Ship)    D801.G7
Archives—United States    CD3021-3022, CD3065, CD6028    025.171
    —Inventories, calendars, etc.    CD3026-3027, CD3041, HE565, Z6027,
                        Z6366    016.32773, .3312973, .910973,
                        .9405488673, 330.973, 350.0914, 387.2097471
Ardeatine Massacre, 1944    D763    945.091
Ardennes, Battle of the, 1944-1945    D756    940.5421
Argentine Republic
    —History—1852-1933    F2848
    —History—1910-1943    F2848    982..06
Armaments    UA10    355.021, .03300+, .0335, 341.6705
    —Yearbooks
Armed forces    U21, U162, UA10, UA15    355.0330+, .0332
Armed forces
    —Appropriations and expenditures    UA17, JX1977    338.47355
    —History
Armed forces in foreign countries
Armed forces
    —Mobilization    UA910
    —Political activity    U21, UH720, JF1820    322.42, .5091724, 355.123094
    —Prayer-books and devotions    BV4588, BV273, BX2170, BM667
                        242.68, .88, 264.093, 296.4
Armed merchant ships
Armed Services Editions, Inc.  [WWII]    Z1039.S6
Armenia—History—1917-1921    DS195    956.62
Armenian massacres, 1915-1923    DS195.5, DS51    361.530924,
                        947.92080924, 956.62, .102
Armenian question    DS194-5, H31    364.15109561, 956.64
Armies    UA10, UA15, UA646    350.895, 355.30944, .3509
    —Equipment    UC460-5    356.186
    —History    U37, UA15    355.0094, .0097
    —Insignia    UC530-5    355.134, .14
    —Officers    UB410-15
    —Organization    UA10, UA15    355.022, 355
    —Staffs    UB220-5    355.33+
Armistices    JX1907    343.31
Armored personnel carriers    UG446.5
Armored trains    UG345
Armored vehicles, Military    UG446    355.83, 623.438, .7475
Armored vessels    V799-800    359.3252, 623.825
Arms and armor    U800-825 (mil.), HD9743 (industry), NK6600-6699 (art)
                        355.82, 623.44, 739.75
Arms and armor, American    U818    355.820973, 623.444
Arms and armor—Bibliography—Catalogs    Z5693 018.1
Army War College (U.S.)    [SEE ALSO 'U.S. Army War College']
Arnaville, Battle of, 1944
Arnhem, Battle of, 1944    D763    940.5421, .54763492

Arnold, Henry Harley ('Hap'), 1886-1950     [U.S.: Gen.]     TL540.A69, D790,
                                            UG633      358.413320924, 940.544973
Arras, Battle of, 1940
Art and war
Art treasures in war     N8750     733.3
Artillery          UF145, UF400, UF560-1     358.109, .12, 623.41, .412
—Bibliography          Z6724     016.35996
Artillery, Coast          UF450-5
Artillery drill and tactics          UF157-302
Artillery, Field and mountain     UF400-45
Artillery—Great Britain          UF57     358.10942, .120941-120942
Artillery, Self-propelled
Artists for Victory, Inc.          NE508.A
Aschaffenburg—Siege, 1945
Asia—Foreign relations          DS33, DS35, JX1569          327.5+
—History—20th century     DS35
Asia, Southeastern
—History          DS511, DS513, DS527, E744          325.5, 915.903, 959.008
Asquith, Herbert Henry, 1852-1928     [G.B.: Prime Min.]          DA566.9.O7
                                            941.0830924, 923.242
Assembly for a Democratic Austrian Republic     [WWII]
Association des Français Libres
Atatürk, Kemal     [SEE 'Kemal Atatürk']
Atlantic Wall
Atlantis (Ship)     [Surface raider]          D772.A74          940.545943
Atomic bomb          D767, D810, HD9698, UF767, QC16, QC773, UG1282
                     355.021708, .2322, .82, 358.39, 539.7, 623.451, 621.483
—History
—Moral and religious aspects          BR115, UF767          261.63, 341.672
—Physiological effect          RA569, RA1231, RC93, U408          614.715,
                                            616.9897, 617.124
Attack and defense (Military science)     UG443-9          355.4
Attlee, Clement, 1883-1967     [G.B.: Pr. Min.]     DA585.A8, DA588, D742.G7
                                            941.08540924,923.242
Attu Island (Alaska), Battle of, 1943
Auchinleck, Claude, Sir ('The Auk'), 1884-1981     [G.B.: Field Marshal]
                     DA69.3.A8-9, D766.82          940.5423, 923.542
Aung San, U, 1915-1947 [Burma: Gen.]          DS485.B8-9, DS503, DS530, DS530.4
                                            320.959104
Auschwitz (Poland: Concentration camp)          [SEE ALSO 'Oswiecim']
Australia
  . Army
    . A.I.F. 2/19 Battalion          D767          940.541294
    . 36th Infantry Battalion          D767.8          940.541294
    . Royal Australian Regiment. 8th Battalion     DS557     959.704342
  . Australian Army
  . Australian Imperial Force (1914-1921)          D520.A9
    . 28th Battalion
—Biography          DU116.2, U55          923.594
—History—20th century          DU110, DU116          994.04
—History, Military          DU112          355.00994, .310994, 940.5394
—History, Naval          VB121          359.00994
  . Navy          [SEE ALSO 'Australia. Royal Australian Navy']
    —History          VA713, VB121          359.00994

Australia
  —Politics and government—1901-1945    DU112, DU116    320.994042,
                                                         994.032
  . Royal Australian Air Force    D792.A8, UG635, UG1242    940.544994,
                                                     358.400994, .4183
  . Royal Australian Army Nursing Corps
  . Royal Australian Navy
Australian Comforts Fund
Austria
  —Foreign relations—Germany
  —History
        —1867-1918
        —1918-1938       DB96      943.605
        —Nazi Putsch, July 1934
        —1938-1945       DB97      943.605
        —Allied occupation, 1945-1955    D802.A9, DB99    943.605
  —Politics and government
        —1918-1938    DB96-7    943.605
        —1938-1945
Austro-Hungarian Monarchy
Automobiles, Military    UG680-5
Averescu, Alexandru, 1859-1938    [Rum.: Lt. Gen., Prime Min.]    DR217, D565.A2,
                                                         D651.R6    949.8

B-17 bomber    [A.k.a. 'Flying Fortress']    D790, TL686    358.42, 623.7463,
                                                         940.544973
B-24 bomber    [A.k.a. 'Liberator']    TL685-6, UG1242    358.4183, 623.7463,
                                                         940.544973
B-25 bomber    ['Mitchell']
B-26 bomber    ['Martin']
B-29 bomber    ['Superfortress']
Babiy Yar Massacre, 1941    D810    940.5405094771
Badoglio, Pietro, 1871-1956    [It.: Field Marshal]    D754.I8, D763    940.5345
Balfour, Arthur James, 1848-1930    [G.B.: 1st Lord o/t Adm'ty, Sec. of State for
                            For. Aff.]    DA566.9.B2, D412.6, D570, VA454
                      942.080924, .0820924, 359.00941, .0942, 920.02, 923.242
Balkan Peninsula
  —History
        —20th century    DR48, DR36, D562.M32, D562    949.6, 914.9603
        —War of 1912-1913    DR46 949.6
  —Politics and government    D463, DJK4, DR10    309.1496, 320.9496
Ballistics    UF820    623.51, .50903
Balloons    TL609-39    629.13322
Baltic States—History—German occupation, 1941-1944
Bao Dai, 1913-?  [Viet.: Emperor of Assam, King]    DS556.83.B3-36
                                                     959.70410924
Baruch, Bernard Mannes, 1870-1965    [U.S.: Fin. adviser and statesman]
                                E748.B32    973.9130924, 923.273
Battle casualties
Battle cruisers
Battles    D25, D210, D431    355.48
  —Europe
  —Germany
Battleships    V765-7, V800, VA58, VA454    359.32+, .3252, .32520973,
                      .83, 623.82530973, .8252

Baum, Herbert, 1912-1942    [Berlin underground participant]    D757.9.B4
Baumbach, Werner, n.d.  [Ger.: Head, Luftwaffe Bomber Command]    D787.B3
                                                                 940.544943
Bautzen (Germany), Battle of, 1945
Bavaria—Politics and government    DD801.B41
Bayerlein, Fritz  [Ger.: Gen.]    D757.55.P35, D757.56.Nr.12, D766.9    940.548
Bazna, Elyesa ('Cicero'), n.d.  [Albania: Highly paid Grmn. spy in Tur.]    D810.S8
                                                        940.548643, .5487430924
Beaverbrook, William Maxwell Aitken, Lord, 1879-1964    [G.B.: Min. of Info. (WWI);
        Min. of Aircraft Produc., Min. of Supply, Lord Privy Seal, Lend-
        Lease admin. (WWII); Press empire lord]    DA566.9.B3, .B37,
        .C4 (Churchill), DA577.B35, UG635.G7    942.083-084,
        .0840924, 940.544, 070.50924, 090.50924, 910.544, 923.242
Beck, Ludwig, 1880-1944  [Ger.: Gen., Anti-Nazi conspir.]    DD247.B38,
                            DD256.3, .5, U55.B    943.0860924
Bedell Smith, Walter ('Beatle'), 1895-1961    [U.S.: Gen., Eisenhower's Chief of
                                        Staff]    Z6300.15.S6
Belgian American Educational Foundation
Belgisch Leger der Partizanen. Korps 034    D802.B4
Belgium
    . Armée. Troupes Coloniales    D766.92
    —History—German occupation, 1940-1945
        —Poetry
Belgrade—Siege, 1944
Belvedere, Battle of, 1944
Belzec (Poland: Concentration camp)
Ben-Gurion, David, 1886-1974    [Isr.]    DS125.3.B3-4    956.9404-9405,
                                        923.2569
Benes, Eduard, 1884-1948    [Aust.-Hung.: Politician, Pres.]    DB217.B3-4, .M3,
        DB2191.B45    943.7020924, 923.1437, .2437, 940.3, .53
Beretta submachine gun    UF620.B45
Bergen-Belsen (Germany: Concentration camp)
Beria, Lavrenty, 1899-1954    [A.k.a. 'Beriia, Lavrentii Pavlovich': Rus.: NKVD chief
        (intelligence)]    DK268.B384-45, .S7-8 (Stalin)    947.08420924
Berlin, Battle of, 1945    D757    940.5421
Berlin—History—1918-1945    DD879-880    914.31550385
Bernadotte af Wisborg, Folke, 1895-1948    [Swe.: Humanitarian]    DL870.B47,
        D808.B, DS126.92    956.042, 940.548, 923.2485
Bernard Leopold, 1911-?  [Neth.: Prince o/t Neth., Consort of Queen Juliana]
                                DJ289.A3    923.1492
Biak Island (Indonesia), Battle of, 1944
Bible—Prophecies
    —Great Britain
    —Jews
    —Russia
    —U.S.
Biddle, Francis Beverley, 1886-1968    [U.S.: Att. Gen., Nuremberg jurist]
                            K60.B473, KF373    340.0924, 923.473
Biography—20th century    CT119-120, D412    070.924, 364.1524,
                            920.00904, 923.2, 920.02
Bir Hakeim, Battle of, 1942    D766 940.5423
Bismarck (Battleship)    D772.B5, DD72    940.545942, .545943,
                            359.32520943
Bismarck Sea, Battle of, 1943

Black market
—Europe
—United States        HF5415 338.526
Black widow (Fighter planes)    [P-61]
Blackouts in war
Blamey, Thomas, Sir, 1884-1951    [Australia: Gen. (G.O.C., Field Marshal]
                    DU114.B65, DU116.2.B54      355.3310924
Blechhammer E/3 (Blachownia Slaska, Poland: Concentration camp)
Blomberg, Werner von, 1878-1943    [Ger.: Field Marshal]
Blum, Leon, 1872-1950        [Fr.: Socialist intellectual, Pr. Min. (1936-7)]
                    DC373.B5-6, D412.6, D410      944.08150924, 923.244
Boatyards
Battice, Battle of, 1940
Bock, Fedor von, 1885-1945    [Ger.: Field Marshal]   D764.3.M6      940.54210924
Boeing airplanes        TL686      629.133340973, 387.7334
Boeing bombers
Bohlen, Charles Eustis ('Chip'), 1904-?   [U.S.: Ambass. to Rus.]      E748.B5-64
                                    327.20924
Bomb reconnaisance      D787      658.47, 940.5412+
Bombardiers            D792.A-Z (by country)
—[country]
Bombardment        JX5117
Bombers    TL685, UG635, UG1242, VG95      358.4183, .420941, 623.7463,
                940.5449+
—Pictorial works      UG635        358.4209+
Bombing, Aerial        UG635        358.409
—Psychological aspects      UG632        363.352
Bombing and gunnery ranges        U300-305
Bombs        TP270, VF373        353.00711, 628.9
Bombsights
Booker T. Washington (Steamship)
Bor-Komorowski, Tadeusz, 1895-1966    [Pol.: Gen., Underground leader]    D802.P6
                                940.53438, .5481
Bordeaux Raid, 1942
Borgo San Dalmazzo (Italy: Concentration camp)
Borneo—History      DS646      919.11, 915.983, 959.83
Boris III, 1894-1943      [Bulg.: King]      DR89
Bormann, Martin, 1900-1945?   [Ger.: Sec. & confidant to the Fuhrer]
                    DD247.B65, .H5 (Hitler)      943.0860924
Bose, Subhas Chandra, 1897-1945        [India: Polit. leader semi-allied with Axis]
                    DS481.B6      954.0350924, 923.254
Bourguébus Ridge, France, Battle of, 1944
Boys anti-tank rifle
Bradley, Omar, 1893-1981    [U.S.: Gen.]   E745.B693, D756.B7      940.54210924
Brain drain—Germany      DD68
Brandt, Willy, 1913-      [Ger.: politician in exile during the war]      DD259.7.B7,
        DD857.B7      943.0870924, 327.430717, 352.043, 940.531
Brauchitsch, Walter von, 1881-1948      [Ger.: Field Marshal]
Braun, Eva, 1912-1945      [Ger.: Hitler's mistress]      DD247.B6-7, .H5 (Hitler)
                                943.0860924
Braun, Werner von      [SEE 'Von Braun, Wernher']
Brazil. Exército. Força Expedicionaria Brasileira, 1944-1945        D768.3, D807.B7
Brazil—History—1930-1954      F2538
Bren machine-gun      UF620.B57

Brereton, Lewis Hyde, 1890-1967   [U.S.: Maj. Gen., aerial commander]
                                   D790.B67        940.544973
Breslau (Cruiser)
Brest (France)—Siege, 1944
Briand, Aristide, 1862-1932   [Fr.: Prem.]        DC373.B7, DC385, DC387, D548,
                                   D568.3          944.08, 940.425
Britain, Battle of, 1940        D756, D785-7, DA89        940.5341, .5421, .5442
British Broadcasting Corporation        D799.G7        621.3841930942
British in Asia        DS35        954, 325.342095
British in foreign countries
British Organization in Rome for Assisting Allied Escaped Prisoners of War
                                   D763.I82.R623        940.547
Brody, Ukraine, Battle of, 1944
Brojce (Poland: Concentration camp)
Brooke, Alan, Sir, 1883-1963   [G.B.: Field Marshal]
Brooke-Popham, Robert, 1878-1953        [G.B.: Air Chief Marshal]
Browning, Frederick ('Boy'), 1896-1966   [G.B.: Lt. Gen. for airborne troops]
Browning automatic rifle
Browning firearms        TS533        683.4
Brzezinka (Poland: Concentration camp)
Buchenwald (Germany: Concentration camp)
Buckner, Simon Bolivar, 1886-1945        [U.S.: Gen.]
Budenny, Semyon, 1883-1973        [U.S.S.R.: Marshal]
Bulganin, Nikolay, 1895-1975   [U.S.S.R.: Polit. Marshal]
Bulgaria
    —History—Boris III, 1918-1943        DR89, DR85-7, DR67        949.77,
                                   940.534977, 949.7702
    —Politics and government—1878-1944        DR85, JN9609        320.9497703
Bullets
Bullitt, William Christian, 1891-1967        [U.S.: Ambass. to U.S.S.R., Fr.]
        E742.5.R5-6, E183.8.R9, D753        940.5378, 973.90924, 327.47073
Bund Deutscher Offiziere        DD256.5
Burma—History—Japanese occupation, 1942-1945        D802, DS485, DS528-9
                                   959.1, 940.53591, 959.103-104
Burma-Siam Railroad        D805.J3        940.547252+
Byrnes, James Francis, 1879-1972        [U.S.: Pres. advis., Sec. of State]        E748.B9,
        E813, D814.4, E183.7.B462, D815        940.531,.53220924, 923.273
Bzura River, Battle of, 1939

C-47: SEE Douglas transport planes
Cables, Submarines        TK5661
Caen, Battle of, 1944        D756        940.5421
Caillaux, Joseph, 1863-1944   [Fr.: Deputy]        DC373.C25, DC371, DC387
                                   944.0810922, .831, 923.244
Calais, Battle of, 1940
California
    —History—1850-1950        F864        979.404
    . National Guard        UA99        355.3510973
California, Southern
    —History—1850-1950        F867-9        979.47-498 917.949035
Cambodia—History        DS554-7        959.6, .704
Cambridge American Cemetery, England        D810.D4        940.5465425
Camouflage (Military science)        UG449, V215 (naval)        358.18, .414
Camp Holmes, P.I. (Concentration camp)        D805.P6        940.547252
Camps (Military)        U180-5, UC400-5, UG635 (camp-making)

Canada
. Army
. . Hastings and Prince Edward Regiment     D768.15
. Canadian Army. Canadian Expeditonary Force
—Claims vs. Italy          JX5486.C16
—Foreign relations—1914-1945        F1034
—History—1914-1945              F1033-4      971.06, .063
—Politics and government—1914-1945      F1034 JL197      320.971,
                                   923.271, 940.540971
Canadian Broadcasting Corporation     D799.C2
Canaris, Wilhelm, 1887?-1945 [Ger.: Adm., Abwehr chief (mil. intell.), anti-Nazi]
        DD247.C16-35, DD253.6, D810.S7      943.086, 940.548743, 923.543
Canteen (British Navy)          VC395.G7
Canteen (United States Army)      UC753
Canteens (War-time, emergency, etc.)
Capitulations, Military          D815-16      940.54012, .5314
Caporetto, Battle of, 1917      D560-4, D569      940.431
Capture at sea      JX5228
Carlson, Evans Fordyce, 1896-1947     [U.S.: Brig.; formed 'Carlson's Raiders']
                          E746.C, DS777.53      923.573
Carol II, 1893-1957      [Rum.: King]      DR266
Caroline Islands      DU563      919.66. 996.6
Carré, Mathilde Bélard ('The Cat'), 1910-?     [Fr.: Double or triple (?) agent]
                          D810.S8.C3      940.5486440924
Cartridges      TS538, UF740-5      355.82, 623.455, .4553, 683.406
Cassino (Italy), Battle of, 1944
Catalina (Seaplanes)
Catholic Church
—Charities      HV530, BX2351 249, 261.83
—Diplomatic service          JX1801-2
—History—Modern period, 1500-      BX1330, BX1396, BV601      270-82,
                                   282.0903
        —20th century      BX1389, BX1746      262.001, 282.0904, .73
Catholic Church in Japan      BX1668      282.52
Catholic Church
—Political activity
—Relations (diplomatic)      BX1790-3, BX850-1691 (hist.), BX1908 (legates
        & nuncios), JX1552 (int'nal. law)      261.87, 262.13, 341.33, 261.7
—Germany      D810.C6, BX1378      262.130924
—Relations (diplomatic) with Germany      BX1378 262.130924
—Relations (diplomatic) with Great Britain      BR750, BX1493, BX2470, DA356
                                   248.894094, 261.7, .87, 282.42
Cavallero, Ugo, 1880-1943      [It.: Marshal, Chief of Gen. Staff]      D766.C3-34
                                   940.548245, 929.214
Cavalry      UE
—History      UE15      357.109
Central Europe—History      DR36-48      940.55
Central Utah Relocation Center      [SEE ALSO 'U.S. Relocation Center, Topaz, Utah']
Cephalonia Massacre, 1943
Chamberlain, Neville, 1869-1940      [G.B.: Pr. Min., War Cabinet member]
                          DA585.C3-5, DA586.C6-7, DA47.2
                941.0840924, 942.084, 327.42043, 923.242, 940.5312
Changkufeng Incident, 1938      DS784 957.7
Channel Islands (Great Britain)—History      DA670      942.34
Charities—History      HV16 361.0209, .73

Chemical warfare     JX1974-7, JX5135, UG447          341.63, .67, .73, 350.895,
                358.34, 363.352
—History—20th century     UG447
Chengtu Incident, 1936
Chennault, Claire Lee, 1890-1958  [U.S.: Maj. Gen., formed the 'Flying Tigers in
                China']     E745.C35-42, D790, DS777.53.S38-42
                940.544973, 358.41332, 923.573
Cherbourg (France), Battle of, 1944
Cheren, Battle of, 1941
Cherkassy, Battle of, 1944
Chiang Kai-shek, 1887 (1886?)-1975     [Ch.: Generalissimo]     DS778.C4-55,
                DS777.47, .488.C5, .518, DS774, D843
                951.0420924, 320.951042, 923.551
Chiang Kai-shek, Madame, 1898?-  [A.k.a. 'Mei-ling Sung, Mme.': Ch.: Wife & advisor
    to Chiang Kai-shek]     DS778.C55, .A1, D743     951.04, 923.551, 940.5304
China
    . Air Force. American Volunteer Group     923.573
    —Description and travel—1901-1948     DS710     915.103-104
    —Foreign relations     DS740     301.291821051, 327.51
        —Japan     DS740, DS777     327.51052, .52051
        —Russia     DK68, DS740     327.47051, .51047
        —United States     E183, DS740     327.51073, .73051
    —History
        —Republic, 1912-1949     DS773-7     951.04
        —1937-1945     DS777-8, UA837     915.138, 951.042
    —Politics and government—1937-1945     DS740, DS774-7, JQ1502-3
                320.951, 327.51, 951.042-05
Chou En-Lai, 1898-1976     [Ch.: Communist liaison to Chiang Kai-shek]
                DS778.C45-593     951.040924, .050924
Chuikov, Vasili, 1900-     [U.S.S.R.: Gen.]     D764.C48515, D765.C46     940.5421
Church work with military personnel     BV4457     253.5
Churchill, Winston Leonard Spencer, 1874-1965  [G.B.: 1st Lord o/t Adm'ty., Min. of
    Munitions (WWI), Pr. Min. (WWII)]     DA566.9.C4-5, D521, D568, D734,
    D743-4, D750, D753, D842, DA69, DA587     941.0820924, 942.084-
    085, 940.425, .45, .5322, .54012, .540942, 359.3310924, 968.040922
    —Addresses, essays, lectures
    —Anecdotes, facetiae, satire, etc.
    —Bibliography
    —Correspondence
    —Fiction
    —Funeral and memorial services
    —Language     PE1421
    —Oratory
    —Poetry
    —Portarits, caricatures, etc.
    —Quotations
    —Views on international relations
Ciano, Galeazzo, 1903-1944     [It.: Count, For. Min.]     DG575.C516, DG571.A2,
                D769     945.091, .0910924
Ciphers     UB290     652.809
Civil defense     UA926-9, JX1907     355.4307, 363.34-35, 353.007-008
    —Warning systems
Civil supremacy over the military     JF195, JF256, DS919, E835 (U.S. hist.),
    JK558, KF27, U410     353.00895, .032, 355.0213+, 322.50904, .5091724
Clark, Mark, 1896-?     [U.S.: Gen.]     E745.C45     940.548373

Clay, Lucius Dubignon, 1897-1978 [U.S.: Gen.]    E745.C47, DD257
                                                  940.531440924, 943.0874
Coast defenses            UG410-48    355.45
Col di Lana, Battle of, 1916    D569.C
Collins, Joseph Lawton ('Lightnin' Joe'), 1896-1963  [U.S.: Lt. Gen.]    E745.C64
                                                  355.3310924
Colt firearms        TS533-7    683.43, 623.443
Combat patrols
Combat
    —Physiological aspects
    —Psychological aspects
Combat survival
Combatants and noncombatants (International law)
Combined operations (Military science)    U260 (allied nations)
Comité Francais de la Libération Nationale
    . Commissariat `a L'information
    . Commissariat `a L'intérieur
Command and control systems    TK5102    621.38
Command of troops    UB210
Commander Islands (R.S.F.S.R.), Battle of, 1943
Commission to Study the Oragnization of Peace
Commodity Credit Corporation [WWII]       HG2051.U5, HD9035-36
                                          353.00825, .81, 338.13, .173
Communications, Military    UA940-5, U408, UG590        355.6, .85, 358.24
Communism        HX626-795, HX36, HX44, HX56, HX134, DK254, DK274
                     320.91717, 321.642, 335.008, .408-409, .413, .42-43
    —China        DS77, DS711, DS740, DS774-8, HX387-8, JQ1519
                     320.951, 335.430951, .4340951, 355.0951, 951.041-05
    —Germany      HX273    335.40943
    —History      DK254, HC101, HX36-56, HX276, HX312, HX628
                     320.5322, 322.42, 330.904, 335.009, .401, .409, .41-43,
                     .438145, 947.0841
    —Russia       B2430, DK254, DK265-8, DK273-6, HC335, HN523, HX312-14,
                  JN6598        142.7, 301.1520947, 320.53220947, .947084,
                  321.642, 329.947, 330.947, 335.413, .430947, 947.083-085
        —History
        —Sources
Communist International    HX11, HX112, HX237, HX387        329.072, .078,
                  335.0094, .4309597, .44, .441
Concentration camps    HV8963, D256, D804-5        341.4, 365.36, 940.5472
    —[geog. regions or countries]
    —California
    —Germany    D256, D804-5, DD256    131.3169, .3469, 940.547243, 943.086
Concentration camps in literature
Concentration camps
    —Pictorial works    NC139        759.13
    —Poland
    —Psychological aspects    RC451    616.8528, .89
    —United States
Conference for Conclusion and Signature of Treaty of Peace with Japan (1951: San
    Francisco)                D814
Conference for the Reduction and Limitation of Armaments, Geneva, 1932-1934
                  JX1974        341.67, .73
Conference on Jewish Material Claims against Germany        D819.G3

Conscientious objectors     UB341-2, BX8128, BX8643     267.23, 289.33, 355.22
—United States          UB342.U5                343.73012, 355.1334, .2240973
Consular reports—United States
Consular service
Contraband of war       JX5231-2, D581          940.452
Convoy              JX5268
Cookery, Marine         VC373           359.81, 641.5753
Cooper, Alfred Duff, 1890-1954      [G.B.]
Cooperative for American Remittances to Europe, Inc.
Coral Sea, Battle of the, 1942      D774        940.5426
Corporate state         HD3611-16 (econ. hist.), JC478, JC481 (fascism)
                301.1832, 330.15, 335.609, .60943
—Italy
Corsair (Fighter planes)    TL686.C45, TL685           623.7464
Corsica—History        DC611       914.49450483
Cossacks—History       D810.C9, DK35       940.5473, 914.70691714
Council of Foreign Ministers    D814.4
Council on Books in Wartime     D810.P7 940.5488673
Courts-martial and courts of inquiry     UB850-67 (mil.), VB800-15 (naval)
                355.9, .133, .1332, 358.411332, 359.1332
—United States      KF26, KF7620, UG633         355.133, .9, 358.41, 359.1
Courts of honor     UB880
Crimes against humanity
Cruisers (Warships)     V820        359.3253+
Crveni krst (Concentration camp: Nis, Yugoslavia)
Cryptographers      UB290       358.24
Cryptography        Z103-4      001.5436, .543609, 358.24, 652.8
Crystal Night, 1938
Cunningham, Andrew Browne, Sir, 1883-1963     [G.B.: Adm., 1st Sea Lord]
                DA89.1.C8, D766.7.C7        359.3310924, 923.542
Curtin, John, 1885-1945     [Australia: Pr. Min.]
Curtis Hawk (Fighter planes)    TL685       623.7464
Curzon, George Nathaniel, 1859-1925     [G.B.: Lord Privy Seal, For. Aff. Sec.]
    DA565.C95, DS480        942.0810924, 327.20924, 923.242, 954.0350924
Curzon Line     D821.P7     327.4380942
Czechoslovak Republic
    —History—1938-1945     DB215       940.5314, 943.703
Czechoslovakia
    . Armáda. Osobitná Part'zánska Brigáda 'Gottwald'    D765.53
    —Foreign relations—Germany     DB205       327.437043
    —History
        —1918-1938      DB215       943.703 (For. relns.)
        —1938-1945      DB215       940.5314, 943.703

Dachau (Concentration camp)     D805        940.54723, .547243
Dachau (Germany: Concentration camp)
Dakar, Battle of, 1940      D766        940.5423
Daladier, Edouard, 1884-1970 [Fr.: Pr. Min.]     DC373.D3, DC389, DC397, D735,
                D761        944.08, 940.5344, 320.9440815, 923.144
Dalmatia (Croatia)—History
Damage control (Warships)       V810        623.888
D'Annunzio, Gabrielle, 1863-1938    [It.: writer, general troublemaker]    DA879.F5,
                DG555, PQ4804.R5        945.09, 949.72, 928.5
Danube Swabian Association of the U.S.A.
Danube Valley—History       DB446       914.9603, 943.48, 949.6

d'Aquino, Iva Ikuko Toguri     [SEE 'Tokyo Rose']
Darlan, Jean Francois, 1881-1942   [Fr.: Adm., Fr. Navy Comm. in Chief]
                                   DC373.D35        940.5344
De Gaulle, Charles, 1890-1970      [Sometimes 'Gaulle, Charles de': Fr.: Gen., Free
    French leader]        DC373.G3, DC404, DC412, DC417, DC420, D843.G2813,
    DS127.85             944.080924, .081-082, .0830924, 923.144, 327.44
De Guingand, Francis, 1900-1979  [G.B.: Major Gen.]     U55.D45, D811.D
                                                       355.3310924
Defense contracts        UC267, UG633, VC267, HC79        338.091724, 353.00713
  —United States         U393, UC263-7, UG633, VC267 (naval), HC110, HD9743
                         338.4735500973, .476234, 343.73013, 346.73023,
                              351.711-712, 355.6210973, .70973, 358.4162110973
Defense information, Classified
Demolition, Military
Denmark
  —Foreign relations—1906-1945
  —History
    —Christian X, 1912-1947        DL148, DL160      948.9
    —German occupation, 1940-1945      D802          940.5421
      —Foreign public opinion
    —Politics and government—1912-1945      JN7013, JN7111, JN7295
                                            301.449209489, 320.09489, .448
Deployment (Strategy)
Depth charges
Desert warfare
Desertion, Military—United States      UB788, KF7618, KF7652        355.1334,
                                       .1330924, .1334
Desertion, Naval—United States
Destroyer escorts
Destroyers (Warships)    V825, VA53, VA454        359.32, .3254+, .6213, 359.83,
                         623.8254
Deterrence (Military strategy)      U162       355.43
Deterrence (Strategy)        U162.6     355.0217, .033+, .033509, .43, .4307
  —Mathematical models       U162       355.03350184
Devastator (Torpedo-bomber)       TL685.3       358.4183
Dieppe Raid, 1942       D756      940.542, .5421
Dietrich, Sepp, 1892-1976     [Ger.: Waffen SS Gen.]     D811.D
Dirksen, Herbert von, n.d.     [Ger.: Diplomat in Tokyo, Moscow, London bet. the
                 wars]  DD247.D54, D735        940.53112, 327.43
Diving, Submarine     D784.G3 (Ger.), D780, GV340, GV840, VM965, VM977,
    VM981+     359.98, 387.55, 623.82+, 627.7, .703, .72+, .7209
Doenitz, Karl, 1891-1980  [A.k.a. 'Dönitz': Ger.: Adm., Ger. Navy chief]
                 DD247.D63, D770.D6, D781.D        943.0860924, 940.545943
Dogs, War use of      UH100
Donovan, William Joseph ('Wild Bill'), 1883-1959 [U.S.: Founder of Office of
                 Strategic Services (intell.)]     E748.D665, D810.S8, .P7,
                 UB271.U52, JK468.I6        940.548673, .5486730924
Doolittle, James, 1896-       [U.S.: Lt. Gen., 1942 Tokyo air raid leader]
                 E746.D664, UG626.2.D66, TL540.D62
                 629.130924, 926.2913
Doorman, Karel, ?-1941       [Neth.: Rear Adm.]
Douglas airplanes        TL686.D      338.476291
Douglas transport planes       TL686.D65, HE9769      387.7334, 629.1333+
Dowding, Hugh Caswell Tremenheere, Sir ('Stuffy'), 1882-1970     [G.B.: Air Chief
    Marshal]      DA89.6.D6       940.54210924

Drancy (France: Concentration camp)
Dresden (Cruiser)        D582.D8
Drvar, Battle of, 1944
Dry-docks        TC361    627.35
Dukla Pass, Battle of, 1944
Dulles, Allen Welsh, 1893-1969    [U.S.: O.S.S. chief in Switz.]    E748.D87,
        JK468.I6    973.90922, 327.12
Dummy warships
Dunkerque (France), Battle of, 1940    [SEE ALSO 'Dunkirk...']    D756    940.5421
Dunkirk (France), Battle of, 1940    [SEE ALSO 'Dunkerque...']    D756
        940.5421, .5756

    —Songs and music

Eaker, Ira Clarence, 1896-1987    [U.S.: Gen. (Air Corps)]    UG626.E24, UG633
        358.400973

Eastern question (Balkan)
Ebert, Friedrich, 1871-1925    [Ger.: Politician]    DD247.E2, DD221, DD248
Economic assistance    D839, E744, HC59-60, HC101, HC106, HC240,
        HC435, HG136, JX1977, HG4517, KF4668    309.2233,
    338.4730154, .90091724, 343.73+, 353.00722, .00825, 358.00892, 387.1
Economic assistance, American
Eden, Anthony, 1897-1977    [G.B.: For. Sec.]    DA566.9.E28, D750
        941.0840924, 940.532241, 923.242
Egypt—History—1919-1952    DT107    962.05
Ehrenburg, Ilia Grigorevich, 1891-?    [U.S.S.R.: Novelist, war correspondent,
    propagandist]    PG3476.E5
Eichelberger, Robert Lawrence, 1886-1961    [U.S.: Lt. Gen.]    D767.E37,
        D769.26.8th    940.54260924
Eichmann, Adolf, 1906-1962    [Ger.: SS col., head of Gestapo's Dept. of Jewish
    Affairs]    DD247.E5, D804.G43, KF211, KF224, E184.J5
        940.5405, 341.410924, 347.91, 363.234, 923.543, .547
Eisenhower, Dwight David, 1890-1969    [U.S.: Gen., Supreme Allied Commander]
        D743.E35, D755-6, E745.E35, E835-6, E863, F689,
        UA23    973.9210924, .920922, 940.5421,
        355.033573, .3310924, 323.40973, 923.173, .573, 978.156
El Alamein, Battle of, Egypt, 1942    [SEE ALSO 'al'Alamayn...']    D766.9
        940.5423
Elections—United States—History    JK97, JK1965, JK171    324.73,
        329.0237302-0237303
Electronic intelligence
Ellice Islands
Emergency communication systems
Emergency medical services    RA645.5-7, RA975, RD81    361.5, 362.11,
        614.875, 940.5475, 344.73041, 362.18
Emergency water supply
Emigration and immigration law—United States    JV6424, JV6507, JV6874,
        JX1977, KF4800, KF4807, KF4819, KF8925    323.60973,
        .6310973, 325.240973, .24580973, 342.73082, 362.8
Émigrés    DC158.1-17    325.244, 942.00441
Enemy property
Enfidaville, Battle of, 1943
Enfield rifle

England     [SEE ALSO 'Great Britain']
   —Civilization—20th century     DA566     914.20382-20384
   —Social life and customs—20th century     DA566    914.2820385, 941.083,
                                              942.0823
Englandspiel
Enterprise (U.S. aircraft carrier)     D774.E5, VA65     940.545973, 623.8255
Espionage     UB270-1     327.120904, 351.74, 355.343, 364.131, 940.548673
Espionage, American [British, German, etc.]
Espionage, American     UB271     327.120973
Espionage, British
Espionage, German     UB271, D810     327.120943
   —United States     D810    940.548743
Espionage, Japanese     UB271     327.120951-120952
Espionage, Russian     DK61, DK266, UB271     327.120947, 355.3432+, 364.13
Estonia
   —History—1918-1940           DK511 947.41
   —Russian occupation, 1940-1941
   —German occupation, 1941-1944
Ethnikon Apeleutherotikon Metopon     D810.S7, DF849
Europe
   —Civilization—20th century        CB53, CB417, D102, D429, D1055
                                     910.03924, 914.031-032, 940.2+
   —Description and travel—1919-1945        D921, D975, G127 914+
Europe, Eastern
      —History     DK440, DR36-8, DR43, DR48     943.804+
        —Autonomy and independence movements     DJK48
Europe
   —Economic conditions—1918-1945     HB501, HC41, HC45, HC240, JX1977
                                   309.1401, 330.94+, .94009, .94028, .94055, .942
   —History
      —20th century     D104, D421, D424, D411     909.82, 940.5
      —1918-1945     D424, D720     909.82, 940.5, .52
   —Politics—1918-1945     D413, D443, D720, D727     320.94051,
                                   940.50924, .51-2
   —Politics and government—1918-1945     D413, D443, D653, D720, D728,
                          D748, JN12     320.9405, 327.11094, .094,
                      .43+, 341.1209+, 940.3142, .509+, .52, .531-2, .5311
   —Relations (military) with the United States     D1065     327.4073
European War, 1914-1918     [Newer term for publications after 1981 or so is 'World
                       War, 1914-1918'. Subdivisions may be found under either]
                       D501-680+, D511, D521, D523, D639, D644
                       940.3-940.499, 940.3+, 940.4+
   —Aerial operations     D600-607, DA89, TL540, UG633     358.43,
                       623.746, 923.542, 940.44, .54
   —Armistices     D641-2     940.434, .439
   —Atrocities     D541, D626
   —Australia     D547.A8     940.394
   —Battlefields     D528     940.46
   —Belgium     D541-2, DH681-2     940.4313, 949.3040924
   —Bibliography     Z674, Z1035, Z6207     016.9403
   —Biography     D507, D570     940.30922, .4, .410922, .46
   —Blockades     D581, D619     940.452

European War, 1914-1918
—Campaigns    D521, D530    940.3, .401, .414, .421
   —Africa    D568, D573    940.4
     —German East    D576    940.41676
     —Tanganyika    D576    940.416, .5423
   —Africa, German Southwest
   —Balkan Peninsula    D561, D569    940.414
   —Belgium    D541    940.4144
   —Eastern    D550-2    940.4326
   —France    D544, D548, DC342, D608    940.4144, .42, .43, .457, .5421
   —Italo-Austrian    D569
   —Maps    G1037    911.09403
   —Mesopotamia and the Persian Gulf
   —Poland
   —Serbia    D561    940.4256
   —Turkey and the Near East    D566-8, D588    940.415, .4153
     —Egypt    D568
     —Gallipoli    D568    940.4143, .425, .4259, .455
     —Mesopotamia    D568    956.7, 940.41567
     —Palestine    D568    940.415, .4291, .438
     —Persia    D568    923.843
   —Western    D509, D530-1, D544-6, DC342    940.4+, .4144,
        .421,.4216, .436
—Causes    CB245, D511, D515, JX1907    940.311, .341
—Censorship    D631-2    940.405
—Chronology    D522
—Church of England    D639    261.873
—Confiscations and contributions—United States    JX5313    341.67
—Conscientious objectors
   —Great Britain    UB342, UB345    355.224, 940.316
   —United States    UB342    355.224, 940.3162
—Diplomatic history    D505, D610-11, D619, JX1906-7    940.3112,
        .314, .32241, .32273,.32443, .45
—Documents, sources, etc.    D505, Z733    940.3082
—Economic aspects    HC56-7, D635    334, 338
   —France    HC56    334+
   —Germany    HC286    940.31, 330.904
   —Great Britain    HC256, HC56, HD8390    330.942, 940.3113, 338.16
   —Russia
   —United States    HC56, HC106, HD8057, JX1416, JX5270    327.73,
        330.973, 338.0973, 341+, 940.37305
—Fiction—Bibliography    Z6207    016.823081
—Finance    HJ8011, HJ8117    940.3144, 336.4, .3094
   —Great Britain    HJ1023    336.42. 940.34205
   —United States    HJ257, HJ8117, HJ8011    336.73
—Food question    D637, HD9007    940.4778
   —Russia    HC56    338.10947
   —United States    HD9005, HD9435
—France    D509, D548    940.344
   —Paris    D544    940.4341
—Germany    D515, D531, DD228, DD231, UA712    355.00943,
        .3310924, 940.32443, .343, .40943, .41343, .4512, 943.084-085
—Great Britain    D517, D546, D651, DA577, DA68-9    320.942, 354.42066,
        923.542, 940.32242, .40942, .342, 942.082
   —London

European War, 1914-1918
—Historiography    D522    940.322
—Hospitals, charities, etc.    D628-9, D638-9, UH537, HV575    360.6273,
        940.47642, .477873, .4779+
—Humor, caricatures, etc.    D526    940.30207, .496-497
—Influence and results    D511, D523, D610, D643, D653, HC56
        940.3144, .3148, 330.9436
—Italy    D523, D560, D640, DG570    940.32, .481, .401245, 945+
—Kansas
—Language (New words, slang, etc.)    D523, PE1689, PE3727    427.09, 428+
—Latin America    D520    940.38
—Law and legislation
—Maps    G1037    912.4
—Massachusetts
—Medical and sanitary affairs    D629-30, UH274, UH400    940.475+,
        .47573 (U.S.),.47634+
—Moral aspects    HQ16    940.3183926
—Museums and libraries
—Naval operations    D580-2, D591-2    940.45+, .459
—Naval operations—Submarine    D568, D581, D589, D591, D593, D595
        940.451+, .4512-13, .459+
—New Zealand    D547
—Norway    D621    940.325481
—Palestine    D568
—Peace    D523, D613, D644-6, D651, JX1906, JX1975    327.4, .73,
        940.312+, .314
—Personal narratives    D602, D628-9, D640    940.343, .48142, .48173
—Pictorial works    D522, D527, NE2012    760.0924, 940.3022, .431, .49
—Poetry    D526, PR610, PR1226-7, PR9900, PS3503, PS3545
        811.52, 821.0080355, 821.912+
—Prisoners and prisons    D627
—Propaganda    D639.P7    940.488+, .5488
—Public opinion    D511, D515, D619, D570, D632    301.15+,
        940.4886+, .3778
—Refugees    D638
—Regimental histories
—Registers, lists, etc.    D589, D609, D639, E186    369.121, 940.412+,
        .41273 (US)
—Religious aspects    D524, D639, BR479, BX5937, BR115    248.4,
        940.3152, .3181331, .53, 230+, 265+, 399
—Russia    D550, D559, D552, D585, D651, DK265    947.084, .08,
        940.3141, .40947
—Secret service    D639.S7-8    940.485-486, .486437
—Serbia    D561
—Siberia    D558
—Sources    D505    940.3082, 940.4
—Sweden    D621.S5
—Switzerland    D621.S    940.3494
—Territorial questions    D650-3    940.314+
—Transportation    D639, HC56, HF56    334+, 385+, 940.41273 (US)
—Treaties    D644
—Turkey    D566, D520    327.430561, 940.32496
—United States    D522, D544, D570, D619-20, E181, E766, E780, E802
    322.440973, 327.172, 355.2120973, 940.32273, .373, .37309, .40973,
    .41273, .4173, .4373, .45973, .314, .46573, 973.91+, 923.273, .573

European War, 1914-1918
—War work                D639-40
—Washington, D.C.        D570+, F199+
—Yugoslavia
European War, 1939-      [Used for books written at the war's beginning. After a
                         time, 'World War, 1939-' was used and, finally after the fact,
                         'World War, 1939-1945' ]          D739-810, D739-44,
                         D741, D743      940.51-58, .53
—Addresses, sermons, etc.        D739, D743      940.5304
—Aerial operations       D786     940.5449+
—American republics      D752     940.537
—Atrocities     D804     940.54056
—Balkan Peninsula        D766     940.53496
—Belgium        D763     940.542
—Bibliography   Z6207    016.94053
—Campaigns      D743     940.542
    —Africa     D766
    —Belgium    D763
    —Norway     D763
—Canada         D745     940.5371
—Causes         D741-2   940.5311+
—Children       D810     940.53161
—Chronology     D743     940.5302
—Dictionaries   D740     940.53
—Diplomatic history      D750, D735, D741        940.531-2
—Documents, etc., sources
—Drama
—Economic aspects        HG2481, JX1907, HC106   308.2, 330.904, 332.1
    —United States       HC106    330.973, 940.531865
—Fiction
—Finance
    —Great Britain       HJ1023   336.42
    —United States       HJ275, HJ258     336.73
—France         D742, D761, DC397      940.5344, .548144
—Germany        D742, D811, DD94, DD256        940.5343, 943.08
—Great Britain  D742, D760, D811, DA566        940.5341-2, .548142, .5497
    —London     D700, D760       940.5342, 636.88
—Greece         D766     940.53495
—Hospitals, charities, etc.      D807     940.54758
—Humor, caricatures, etc.        D745, NC1479    741+, 827.91
—Iceland        D763     940.53491
—Influence and results   D753, D744      940.5373 (US), .5314
—Jews   D810    940.5315296
—Maps   D743-4          940.5499, .53
—Netherlands    D763     940.584
—Norway         D763     940.53481
—Peace  D815
—Personal narratives     D811    940.5481+
—Personal narratives, American   D811     940.53493, .342, .54771, .548,
                                  .5342
—Personal narratives, Dutch      D811     940.5481492
—Personal narratives, English    D811     940.5342, .548142
—Poetry
—Poland         D765, D811       940.544, .5481438
—Prisoners and prisons, French   D805     940.547244

European War, 1939-
    —Propaganda         D753, E744       940.5488, .5488973 (US)
    —Prophecies         D810     940.53
    —Refugees          D809-10     940.53161, .547242
    —Religious aspects  D744    261 940.531
    —Russia            D764     940.542
    —United States      D753, D756, D758      327.73, 940.532, .5373, .5873
    —Women's work     D810     940.5315396
Evacuation of civilians      HV554     355.232
Excess profits tax        HJ4653, KF26-7, KF6471-2     336.243, .274, 343.73052
Executive power—United States     JK501-901, E417, HG2525     328.3456,
                 .73, 342.7306+, 347.7326+, 353.008, .0313-0372, 973.61+
Exiles         CT105 (biog.), JX4261 (int'nal. law)
Expatriation        JX4226
Expatriation and repatriation
Explosive ordnance disposal
Explosives, Military      TP268-99


Falaise Gap, Battle of, 1944         D761     940.5421
Falkenhausen, Alexander von, 1878-1966   [Ger.: Gen.]     DH687.F34
Falkenhorst, Nikolaus von, 1885-1968  [Ger.: Col. Gen.]     D804.G4.F3
Farouk, 1920-1965      [Egypt: King]
Fascism        JC481, D443, D842, D726     320.533, .533019, .94, 321.644,
               .94, 335.6, .60904, 909.82
    —Bibliography     Z2361     016.320533
    —Central Europe    D726     320.943
    —Germany      [SEE ALSO 'National Socialism']    DD259, D424, D445, D726,
                   JC481     320.943, .533094, 321.94094
    —Italy         DG571, DG450, DG575     945.091, .091024,
      309.14509+, 320.5330945, .945091, 321.940945, 330.945, 335.60945
    —Posters
    —Spain        DP257     946.081
    —United States     E743, E806     320.5330973, 335.60973
Fascism and architecture
Fascism and culture
Fascism and literature
Fascism and the Catholic Church
Fascism in art
Fascist ethics
Fascists
Fast attack craft
Ferdinand, King of Rumania, 1865-1927       DR217, DR262.A2, DD120.G7
                949.8020924, 327.430436, 923.1498
Fieseler Fi-156 Storch (Military airplane)
Fighter planes      UG626-626.2
Fighter planes      TL685.3, UG633-5, UG1240, UG1242, VG93
            623.7464+, 629.133, 358.4183+, .43+, .430943 (Ger.),
               .430941-430942 (GB), .430952 (Japan)
    —Piloting     UG633     629.132+
Fighting, Hand-to-hand     U210, GV1111     355.54, 796.8+
Fighting (Psychology)    BF575, BF723     136.727, .7353, 137.33, 158.1, .4245

Finland
   —Foreign relations
      —Germany
      —Russia      DK459, JX1555     327.471047, .470471
   —History—1939-     DK459.45 948.95
   . Maavoimat. 1. Divisioona    D765.32
Fire control (Aerial gunnery)   VG93     623.555
Fire control (Gunnery)      UF848     623.5
Fire control (Naval gunnery)
Firearms      TS535-7 (produc.), UF520, UF800, UF880, UF884, UF897, UD380
      623.44, .4424, .443, 683.4, 355.82+
Firearms, American
Firearms, British
Firearms, German    TS533     683.400943
Firearms
   —History    TS532-5, U818, U884, UD390, UF520     623.4409+,
      355.8209+, 683.4009+
   —Identification    HV8077, VN8077   351.753, 363.33, 364.12+, 683.43012
Firearms industry and trade   HD9743   338.476234, 364.135
      —Great Britain    TS533    338.7683400941
      —United States    TS520, TS535   623.440973, 683.400973
Firearms
   —Maintenance and repair    TS535    683.403
Flame throwers    UG447
Fletcher, Frank ('Black Jack'), 1885-1973   [U.S.: Vice Adm.]
Flight control    TL589.4
Flight crews    TL521    629.1344
Flight engineering     TL671     629.102, .1302, .1325+
Flight—Physiological aspects   RC1075, TL555    616.98, 612.84, 620.13256
Flight training     TL710-12, VG93    623.746, 629.126+, .132+,
      355.622, 358.415
Florida—History—1865-1950    F311, F316     975.906
Focke-Wulf airplanes    TL686.F62    623.7460943
Food relief    HD9000+, HN696, HV696   338.19+, 353.007+, 362.509+, .58, .71
Forced labor    JX1977, HV8900+, HD4800+    331.57, 365.65, 338.09+
   —Germany
   —Russia    HD4875    338.0947, 354.470083
Forrestal, James, 1892-1949  [U.S.: Under Sec. & Sec. o/t Navy]   E748.F68, E813
      973.9170924, .9180924, 353.7, 923.273
Fortification    UG400-409+    355.544
Fortification, Field    UG403
Fortification
   —France
   —Great Britain    DA145    936.22
   —Poland

Franco, Francisco-Bahamonde, 1892-1975  [Sp.: Gen., dictator]      DP254,
    DP264.F7, DP270, DS135.S7      946.0820924, 940.531503924
Franco-German War, 1870-1871      DC285, DC291-3, DC300, DC310, DD219
    943.081-082
Franco-Soviet pact, 1935
Frank, Anne, 1929-1945   [Ger.: Jewish victim]    PT5834.F68, DS135.N5, D810.J4
    940.531503924, .5315055, .53492
Frank, Hans, 1900-1946      [Ger.: Gov. Gen. of Pol.]
Franklin D. Roosevelt Library, Hyde Park, N.Y.      E742, Z733      016.9739,
    027.574733, 026.973917
Fraser, Bruce, Sir, 1888-1981  [G.B.: Adm.]      V64.G72.F73      359.00924
Fraser, Peter, 1884-1950  [New. Z.: Pr. Min.]
Freedom of the seas      JX4423-5 (int'nal. law), JX5203-5268      341.57
Freyberg, Bernard, Sir, 1889-1963  [New Z.: Gen., commander of New Z. troops]
    DA69      923.5931
Frick, Wilhelm, 1877-1946      [Ger.: Min. o.t Inter., Reich Protec. of Bohemia &
    Moravia]
Friends, Society of. American Friends Service Committee      BX7635, BX7747,
    JX1953      172.4, 267.1896+, 289.6
Frigates      V767
Fritsch, Werner von, 1880-1939      [Ger.: Gen.]
Fromm, Friedrich, 1888-1945   [Ger.: Gen., Commander o/t Home Army, lukewarm
    conspirator against Hitler]
Froslevlejren (Froslev, Sonderjyllands amt, Denmark: Concentration camp)
Fuchida, Mitsuo, 1902-?[Japan: Commander, commander of Pearl Harbor attack]
    D774.M5      940.545
Fukuoka 14 (Nagasaki-shi, Japan: Concentration camp)
Fuller, John Frederick Charles, 1878-1966   [G.B.: Tank theorist]      U55.F86
    355.00924
Funk, Walter, 1890-1960  [Ger.]
Fuses (Ordnance)      UF780      353.00712, 623.4542

Galen, Clemens von, 1878-1946    [Ger.: Archbishop of Münster, Nazi critic]
Galland, Adolf, 1912-      [Ger.: Lt. Gen., Luftwaffe fighter ace & chief]
    UG626.2.G35, D787      358.4140924, 940.544943
Gamelin, Maurice Gustave, 1872-1958  [Fr.: Gen.]    D761.G, UA702.G 940.5344
Gandhi, Mohandas (Mahatma) Karamchand, 1869-1948    [India: Spiritual leader]
    DS481.G3, DS423, DS480-1, DS480.45, B133.G4, B5134, DT764,
    H59.G25, HM278, HN687      954.0350924, .040924, 181.4,
    301.15, 320.954035, 322.440954, 370.973, 923.254
Garand rifle      UD395      355.82
Garigliano Valley, Battle of, 1944
Gaulle, Charles de      [SEE ' De Gaulle, Charles']
Gela, Battle of, 1943
Gembloux, Battle of, 1940
Genda, Minoru, ?-1989      [Japan: Commander, fighter pilot & tactician]
    D767.92.G44
General strike      HD5307      331.892, .89201, .8925
General Strike, Germany, 1920
General Strike, Great Britain, 1926      HD5365-8      331.89250941, .892942

Germany
—Foreign economic relations—20th century
—Foreign relations
    —20th century    DD2409, DD247    327.43+
    —1918-1933    DD247
    —1933-1945    DD256
    —Catholic Church    D810.C6
    —France    DD120    327.43044
    —Great Britain    327.43042, .42043
    —Italy
    —Japan    DD120    327.43052, .430952, .52043
    —Poland    DD120    327.430438
    —Russia    DD120, DD241    327.43047
    —Turkey    DD120    327.430561
    —United States    DD247, DD259    327.43073, .73043
. Geheime Staatspolizei    DD253, DD256.5, HV8208    943.086+,
    351.740943
. Heer    DD221, DD240, UA712    355.00943, .30943, 943.08, .085
    —Armored troops    UG446    358.18
. Artillerie    UF495    358.12
    —Biography    D736, D757, CR5327    929.71
. Fallschirmjager    D757, UD485    940.541343, .544943
. Freikorps    DD238    943.085
. Geheime Feldpolizei
. Generalstab    DD101, D757, UA712, UB225    355.00943, .3310943,
    940.541343
. Heeresgruppe Kurland    D764    940.541343
. 250. Jnfanteriedivision (1941-1943)    D757.32, D754, D764    940.5346,
    .541343
. 369. Infanteriedivision (Kroatische) (1942-1945)
    —History    DD103, UA712    355.00943, .30943, .3320943, .3510943
    —Medals, badges, decorations, etc.    UB435    355.1340943
    —Military life
. Oberkommando
    —Officers' handbooks
    —Ordnance and ordnance stores    UF525, UF745    623.40943
    —Organization    UB415.G3, UA712, U165    355.3320943
. Panzerarmeekorps Afrika    D757.55.G4, D766.82    940.5423, .541343
. Panzerdivision 'Grossdeutschland'    D757    940.541343
. Panzergrenadierdivision 'Brandenburg'    D757.55.B7
. LVII. Panzerkorps    D757.56.57th
. Panzertruppen    D757.54, UG446, UG449    358.180943
    —Parachute troops
    —Uniforms    UC485.G3    355.140943
    —Yearbooks    UA710

Ghormley, Robert Lee, 1883-1958  [U.S.: Vice Adm.]
Giap, Vo Nguyen, 1910-1975  [Viet.: Gen.]
Gibson, Guy, 1918-1944  [G.B.: Wing Commander]  D786.G  940.544942
Giffard, George, Sir, 1886-1964
Gilbert Islands  DU615  919.681, 996.81
Giolitti, Giovanni, 1842-1928  [It.: Prime Min.]  DG575.G5, DG555, DG566,
  DG568.5  945.09, .090924, 327.45
Giraud, Henri, 1879-1949  [Fr.: Gen.]  DC373.G5, D766.82.G  940.542,
  923.544
Glaise von Horstenau, Edmund, 1882-1946  [Austria: Gen.]  DB90.G53, D539,
  D569.V5  943.6040924
Glasgow (Cruiser)  [WWI & II: 2 ships]
Glatz (Grafschaft)—History  DD801.G5  943.14
Gliders (Aeronautics)  TL760-769  629.13333
Glomfjord Raid, 1942
Gneisenau (Battleship)
Goebbels, Joseph, Dr., 1897-1945  [Ger.: Min. of Propaganda]  DD247.G6,
  DD256, DD256.5  943.0860924,
  301.15230943, 923.243
Goering, Hermann, 1893-1946  [Also 'Göring...': Ger.: Luftwaffe chief commander,
  Reichsmarschall]  DD247.G67  943.0860922-0860924, 923.243
Gotha gliders
Government and the press
 —Germany
 —Great Britain  PN4748
 —Russia  PN4748  070.449320947
 —United States  PN4738  070.40973
Government, Resistance to
Graziani, Rodolfo, 1882-1955  [It.: Politician]  DG575.G7  355.00924
Great Britain  [SEE ALSO 'England', 'Scotland', 'Ireland']  DA, DA11 941-2
 . Admiralty
 —Air defenses, Military
 . Army
     —Airborne troops  D759  940.544941
     —Eighth Army
     —Biography  DA69.3
     —Black Watch (Royal Highlanders)  UA652.B6  356.110942, 355.31
     —Boys' units  U549.2
     —Coldstream Guards  D760, UA652  940.5421, 356.110942
     —Colonial forces
     —Corps of Royal Engineers. Bomb Disposal Unit  D786
     —East African Rifles  D767.6
     . Field Security Personnel
     —Firearms  UD385  355.82
     —History  UA649, UA853  355.00942, .02130942,
       .30941, .310941
     . 2d King Edward VII's Own Gurkha Rifles
     . 1st King's Dragoon Guards  D760  940.541242
     . Long range desert group  D766.93
     —Military life  DA68, DA566  923.242

Great Britain
—Foreign economic relations   HF1533, HC256     337.9142, 382,0942, .10942
—Foreign relations
    —1910-1936         DA566, DA576-8     327.42, 940.31206342
    —1936-1945         DA566, DA586-7     327.41-2, 940.5312, .532241,
                            942.084+
    —Burma
    —East (Far East)     DA47, DS518     327.4105, .42051
    —Europe     DA47     327.4204, .4042
    —France
    —Germany     DA47     327.42043, .43042
    —Japan
    —Russia
    —Treaties
    —United States     DA47, E183     327.42073, .73042
—History     DA, DA16, DA30-2, DA40, DA45     914.1-2, 941-2
    —Victoria, 1837-1901     DA16, DA536, DA550-4, DA550-4, DA560-6
                            942.08-081, 914.20381
    —20th century     DA16, DA566, DA588     941.082-085, 942.08-082,
                            914.20382, 909.0971242+
        —Edward VII, 1901-1910     DA567-70     941.082, 942.082, 914.20382
        —George V, 1910-1936     DA577-8     942.083, 914.20383
        —George VI, 1936-1952     DA586-8     941.084, 942.085
—History, Military     DA50, DA65, DA68, UA649     355.00942, .30941,
                          .310941
    —20th century     DA69     942.084
—History, Naval     DA70, DA85, DA88, VA454     359.00941-00942,
                        .030941-030942
    —20th century     DA89, D770     359.0942, .33109, .00941
. H.M. Stationery Office     [SEE ALSO 'Great Britain. Stationery Office']
—Kings and rulers     DA28, DA177, JN331     321.60942, 914.2030922-
                        2030924, 942.00922, .09231
. Ministry of Defence
. Ministry of Economic Warfare
. Ministry of War Transport
. Naval Intelligence Division     D771     940.548642
. Navy     [SEE ALSO 'Great Britain. Royal Navy']     V163, V767, V820-5,
    V820, V825, V859, VA454-6, D581     359.00941-00942,
      .0942, .10942, .32520942, .32530942, .32570942, .942,
      623.8250942, .82540942
    —Aviation—History     VG95     358.4183
    —Biography     DA87-8     359.00922, 923.542
    —Bibliography     Z2021     016.35900942
    . British Pacific Fleet     D767     940.5426
    . Fleet Air Arm     VG95     358.40942, 623.746
    —History     DA70-89, V750, V800, V825, VA454-7     359.00941-
                00942, .120941-120942, .13320941, .30942,
                .3250942, .32520942, .32540941, 940.545941
    —Lists of vessels     VA40, VA456     359.320941-320942
    —Regulations     V167     359.00942, .40942, .420942
    —Sea life     DA88     359.10942, .12
—Politics and government
    —20th century
    —1910-1936
    —1936-1945

Great Britain
  —Public Record Office    CD1048    016.95127
  —Relations (military)—Germany
  . Royal Air Force    UG635, UG1245, D568, D602, D756    358.40942,
                    .420941, .430941-430942, 623.7460941, .74630942,
                    940.44942, .5421
      —Biography    D568.4, D602    940.440924
    . Bomber Command    D786    940.544942
    . Fighter Command    UG635    358.414
    —History    DA585, UG635    940.44942, 358.400941-400942,
                  .4135, .4183, .430942
    . 617 Squadron
    . 2d Tactical Air Force    D786    940.544942
  . Royal Navy    [SEE ALSO 'Great Britain. Navy']
    —Aviation    VG695.G7
    —Biography    DA70, DA74, DA88.1
    . Coastal forces
    . Fleet Air Arm    VG95.G7
    —History    DA70, VA454    359.3510942
    —Lists of vessels    VA454-6    359.320942
    —Medals, badges, decorations, etc.    VB335, UB435, CJ6113
    —Officers    VB315.G7    355.220942
    —Records and correspondence
    —Registers    V11.G7
    —Sea life    V737
    —Uniforms    VC305.G7
    —Yearbooks    V10
  . Special Operations Executive    D810.S7, D802    940.548641-
                  548642,.5486492
  . Stationery Office    [SEE ALSO 'Great Britain. H.M. Stationery Office']
  . War Office    D546, D759    942.084, 354.42066
    . General Staff    UB225, UA647    355.3310942, .30924
    . Intelligence Division
    —Manuscripts
Greece—History—Occupation, 1941-1944
Greece, Modern
  —History
    —1917-1944
    —1917-1935    DF845
    —Occupation, 1941-1944    D802    940.53495, 949.507
  —Politics and government—1935-    DF701, DF849, DF852    320.9495,
                  949.507
Gremiashchii (Destroyer)    D779.R9
Grenades    UF765    623.42
Grew, Joseph, 1880-1965    [U.S.: Ambass. to Japan (1932-41)]    E748.G835,
                  DS849.U6    327.20924
Grey, Edward, Sir, 1862-1933    [G.B.: Sec. of State for For. Aff.]    DA566.9.G8, .A1,
                  D517, D546    942.0820924, 940.311, .342, 920.042
Grini (Norway: Concentration camp)
Ground support systems (Ordnance rocketry)
Groupe 'Collaboration'    D731.C    940.5344
Grumman Avenger (Bombers)    TL685    623.7463
Guadalcanal Island (Solomon Islands), Battle of, 1942-1943
Guam    DU647    919.67, 996.7

Henderson, Nevile, Sir   [G.B.: Ambass. to Ger. (1937-9)]   D750.H4   940.531
Herbicides—War use
Heroes
Hess, Rudolf, 1896-1987   [Ger.: Dep. Führer]   DD247.H37   943.0860924,
          940.548243, 923.243
Hewitt, Kent, 1887-1972   [U.S.: Rear Adm.]
Heydrich, Reinhard, 1904-1942   [Ger.: SS Obergruppenführer, Reich Main
     Security Office chief, Reich Protector of Bohemia-Moravia]   DD247.H42,
     DD253.6, DB215, DB215.3        940.43587, .54050924, 923.543
Himmler, Heinrich, 1900-1945   [Ger.: Reischsführer-SS]   DD247.H46, DD256.5
          943.0860924, 923.243
Hindenburg, Paul von Beneckendorf und von, 1847-1934  [Ger.: Field Marshal, Pres.]
     DD231.H5, DD228, D531.H4813        943.0850924, .085,
          923.143, 940.343, .41430922
Hinzert (Germany: Concentration camp)
Hirohito, 1901-1989  [Japan: Emperor]   DS888.5, DS889.8, D767.2
          952.0330924, 940.5352
History, Modern—20th century   D421, D398, D415, D422-9, D443-5, D643, D720
Hitler, Adolf, 1889-1945   [Ger.: Führer]   DD247.H5, DD240, DD253, DD256,
          D741, D751, D757, D811, DB955   943.0840924,
          .0850924, .0860924, 940.5311, .53187, .5324439,
          .540943, .541343, .5482, 309.143086, 320.533, .943085-
          086, 321.940924, 327.140943, 364.131, 923.143
Ho Chi Minh, 1890-1969   [Viet.: Resistance chief]   DS556.8.H6213, DS557,
          DS559.9   959.7040924
Hobart, Percy, Sir, 1885-1957 [G.B.: Maj. Gen.]   DA69.3.H56
Hokkerup, Battle of, 1940
Holocaust, Jewish (1939-1945)   D810.J4, DS135.E83, DS102, D803
          940.5315, .531503+, .5315296, .5405, .546, 956.9404
     —Hungary
Holocaust, Jewish (1939-1945), in art
Holocaust, Jewish (1939-1945), in literature   PJ5012, PN56   809.88924, .93352
Holocaust, Jewish (1939-1945)
     —Psychological aspects   D810.J4   940.5472
     —Statistics   D810.J4   940.531503924
     —Study and teaching
Homma, Masaharu, 1888-1946   [Japan: Gen.]
Hong Kong—History   DS796   951.25, 915.125
     —Siege, 1941
Hopkins, Harry, 1890-1946   [U.S.: Pres. adviser]   E748.H67, E807.S45,
          HV28.H66   973.9170924, 338.54, 362.50924
Horthy, Miklos, 1868-1957   [Sometimes 'Horthy de Nagybánya, Miklos': Aust.-
          Hung.: Vice Adm., Adm., Regent of Hung.]   DB950.H6,
          DB955, D556, D583   943.9050924, .9105, 940.464436, .5324439
Hospitals, Military   UH460-85   355.345, .92, 353.007+, .008+, 362.11+
Hospitals, Naval and marine   RA975, RA980-93, VG410-50, VG463   616.98024
Hot pursuit (International law)
Houston (Cruiser: CL-81)   D774.H65, VA65   940.5425
Howitzers   UF470-5, UF560-5, VF390-5 (naval)
Hull, Cordell, 1871-1955   [U.S.: Sec. of State]   E748.H93, E183.7, D742.U5
          973.9170924, 940.53112, 923.273
Human experimentation in medicine—Germany—History—20th century
          D804.G4   940.5405

Integrated logistic[s] support   UC263      355.621
Intelligence service             UB250     355.3432, 353.0089
    —France
    —Germany
    —Great Britain   D810, JN329        355.34320942, 940.548642
    —Japan
    —Russia
    —Soviet Union
    —United States   D767, UB251, UG633     353.0074, .0081, .00892,
                                        940.5426, .548673
Inter-allied Commission on Mandates in Turkey. American Section   D651     956.102
Inter-allied Games, 1919      GV721
Inter-allied Military Mission to Hungary, 1919-1920      DB955        943.905+
Inter-allied Rhineland High Commission           D650.M5
International Labor Office      HD2755, HD7801      341.5, .763, 658.3
International organization      D815        940.5304
International trusteeships     JX1977, JX4021      321.027, 325.21, .31, 341.132, .27
Intrenchments          UG403 (field fortification), UG446 (trench warfare)
Invincible (Cruiser)
Iran—History—1909-1945      DS315-18        955.05+
Ireland
    —History
        —20th century      DA959-60        941.59
        —1910-1921        DA960-65        941.50821, .59
        —1922-1949        DA963           941.5082
    —Neutrality       D754.I6       940.54874309415
    —Politics and government
        —1910-           DA959        941.591
        —1922-1949       DA963        941.59, 320.9415+, 328.415-417
Ironside, Edmund, Sir, 1880-1959   [G.B.: Field Marshal]      DA69.3.I7, D559
                                        942.0840924, 940.4147
Islands—Japan
Islands of the Pacific        DU17-28        919, 919.65, 990
    —Description and travel       DU15, DU21-3     919.3, .6
    —History        DU28 990
Ismay, Hastings Lionel ('Pug'), 1887-1965    [G.B.: Baron, Gen., Churchill aide]
                                        DA69.3.I8        942.0820924, 940.53
Israel—History—1917-1948       DS126        956.94
Italo-Ethiopian War, 1935-1936      DT387        963.056, .065, 327.44045
    —Causes
    —Diplomatic history
    —Influence
Italy
    . Aeronautica                 D792      940.544945
        —History—World War, 1939-1945        D792.I8
    —Boundaries—Yugoslavia         D821.I or .Y8-9
    —Civilization—20th century      DG451        914.50392, 945.092
    —Description and travel—1901-1944      DG428-9, DG601      914.50491
    —Economic conditions—1918-1945      HC305      330.943086, .945091
    . Esercito   [Army]         D763.I8+, UA742      945.08
        . Alpini
        . XIX Brigata Garibaldi       D763.I813
        . Divisione di Fanteria Acqui

Japan
    —Foreign economic relations
      —Asia
      —United States     HF1602      338.9152073, 382.095201812
    —Foreign opinion, American
    —Foreign relations
      —1912-1945     DS845, DS885-8, JX1975     327.52, 341.2252, 952.033
      —China     327.52051, .51052
      —Germany     DS849     327.52043
      —Philippine Islands     327.520914
      —Russia     DS849     327.52047
      —United States     E183     327.52073, .73052
    —History
      —1868-     DS881-5     952.03+
      —20th century     DS885     952.03
      —1912-1945     DS888     952.033
      —Taisho period, 1912-1926     DS886     952.032, 309.152032
      —Showa period, 1926-     DS888     952.033
      —1926-1945     DS888.5
      —March and October incidents, 1931     DS888.5
      —May Incident, 1932 (May 15)     DS888.5
      —February Incident, 1936 (February 26)     DS888     952.033
      —Allied occupation, 1945-1952     DS889, E745     940.5338, .5352,
               952.04, 915.2034
    —History, Military—1868-
    —History, Naval—1868-
    —Industries
    . Kaigun     [Navy]     VA653, D777, D777.5.A-Z (by ship)     359.030952,
               .052, .3250952, 623.8250952, 940.545952
      —Appropriations and expenditures
      —History     D742, D777, VA653     940.53112, .545952
      . Kamikaze Tokubetsu Kogekitai     D792.J3
      . Kokutai     [Aerial ops.]     VG95     358.4183, 623.74630952
      . Lists of vessels     VA653     359.320952
      . Oka Tokubetsu Kogekitai     D792     940.544952
      . Ordnance and ordnance stores
      . Organization
    —Military policy     UA845, VA50, VA653     355.033552, .33552, 359.030952
    —Politics and government
      —20th century
      —1912-1945     DS845, DS885-9     320.952032-952033, 329.951,
               940.5352, 952.033
      —1926-     DS888.2
    —Relations (general) with the East (Far East)
    —Relations (general) with the Philippine Islands     DS849     301.29520599,
               327.520914
    —Relations (general) with the United States     E183     301.2952073, 327.73052
    —Relations (military) with the United States
    . Rikugen     D767, UA845-7     355.30952, 940.541352, 355.00952
      —Armored troops     UG446     358.180952
      . Kokutai     UG635, UG1242     358.4183, 623.74640952
      —Military life     U773     355.00952
      —Parachute troops—History     UD485     356.1660952
    —Social life and customs—1912-1945     DS821     915.20333
    —Territorial expansion

Japanese American Citizens' League     D753.8
Japanese Americans—Evacuation and relocation, 1941-1945     D769.8.A6, E184
          940.531630973, .547273, 301.451956073, 323.11956073, 341.67
Japanese—Canada—Evacuation and relocation, 1941-1945
Japanese in the Hawaiian islands     D767.92, DU624     940.53969,
          919.6906956, 996.9
Japanese in the United States
     —History     E184     917.306956
     —Personal narratives     D769     940.54727309794
Jasenovac (Croatia: Concentration camp)
Jassy, Battle of, 1944
Java Sea, Battle of the, 1942     D774, VA65     940.5425-5426
Jean Bart (Battleship)     D779.F7-8
Jeep automobile     TL215, TL230     623.74722, 698.28722
Jersey
     —History     DA670     942.34+
     —German occupation, 1940-1944     D802.G72.J467
Jet planes     TL546-7, TL670-1     629.1072, .133+, .14353
Jet planes, Military—History
Jewish Frontier Association     [WWII]     DS149     956.9
Jewish Legion     D568     940.41242, .416
Jewish property in Germany
Jewish question     DS141-51     909.0974924, 910.03924, 956.93-94+
Jewish soldiers
Jews as soldiers     DS119     355.30922
Jews
     —History—1789-1945     DS125-6, DS107, DS140-3     909.0492408,
          956.93-4
Jews in Hungary     DS135     940.5405, .53439
Jews in Europe
     —History     DS135     301.45192404, 914.04
     —Persecutions     DS135, DD247     341.41, 940.5405, 943.086
Jews in France
Jews in Germany
     —History
          —1789-1945     DS135     301.45296043
          —1800-1933
          —1933-1945     DD253, DS135     943.085-086, 323.11924043
     —Political and social conditions     DS135     301.45296043
Jews in Russia—History     DS135     323.11924047, 914.706924, 947.004924
Jews in Poland—History     DS135     301.4519240438, 914.3806924,
          943.8004924
Jews
     —Legal status, laws, etc.
     —Germany
     —Persecutions     DS102, DS116, DS145     301.45192404, 956.93
Jodl, Alfried, 1890-1946     [Ger.: Col. Gen., OKW Chief of Staff]     DD247.J6, D757
Joffre, Joseph Jacques Césaire, 1852-1931     [Fr.: Field Marshal]     DC342.8.J6,
          D507, D511, D530, D545.M3, .V3, D548, D568.3, JN2562
          944.081, 940.410922, .4144, .425, .427, 327.42044
Journalism, Military
Joyce, William ('Lord Haw-Haw'), 1906-1946 [G.B.: Brit. fascist broadcaster from
     Ger.]     DA585.J6, D810.P7, KD8022     364.131, 923.4142
Juin, Alphonse Pierre, 1888-1967     [Fr.: Marshal]     D763.I8     940.542
Jungle warfare     U167.5.J

Junkers airplanes          TL686          623.7463
Junkers Ju-88 (Bomber)          TL685          940.544943
Just war doctrine          B105, BT736          261.873

Kaiser, Henry John, 1882-1967          [U.S.: Shipbuilding industrialist]          HC102.5.K3,
                                                                                                                                          RA413          614.2
Kaiten (Torpedoes)
Kalinin, Battle of, 1941
Kaltenbrunner, Ernst, 1902-1946          [Austria: Austrian SS chief, Reich Main Security
     Office chief]          DD247.K28          943.0860924
Kamenets-Podol´skiy, Battle of, 1944
Kamikaze airplanes          TL685          623.746
Katyn Forest Massacre, 1940          D804          940.5405, .5405094762, .547247
Kawasaki, Japan (Kanagawa Prefecture)—Bombardment, 1945
Keitel, Wilhelm, 1882-1946          [Ger.: Field Marshal, OKW Chief]          DD247.K4
                                                                                                                                  940.548243
Kelly (Destroyer)          D772.K          940.545942
Kemal Atatürk, 1881-1938          [Tur.: Gen., Pres.]          DR592.K4, DR589, D568.3, .7,
                                                                         DK511.C2          956.1, 940.425, .438, 923.1561
Kemal Pasa, Mustafa          [SEE Kemal Atatürk]
Kennedy, John Fitzgerald, 1917-1963          [U.S.: Naval lt., PT commander]
                                             E840-2+, E748.K375, E169, E183, E185
                                             973.9220924, .9228, 301.1543973922,
                          320.943155087, 327.73+, 338.973, 353.030922, 923.273
Kennedy, Joseph Patrick, 1888-1969          [U.S.: Ambass. to G.B. (1937-41)]
                                             E748.K376, E747, E807, E843.K43          973.90924
Kennedy, Joseph Patrick, Jr., 1915-1944          [U.S.: Army Air Corps flyer]
                                             E843.K44          940.54210924
Kenney, George Churchill, 1889-1977          [U.S.: Gen. (Air Corps)]          D767.K4
                                                                                                                         940.5426
Kenya, Mount          [Site of British prison]          D805.G7          940.547242
Kepa Oksywska Island, Poland, Battle of, 1939
Kesselring, Albrecht, 1885-1960          [Ger.: Field Marshal]          DD247.K45
                                                                                                                    355.3310924
Khanka, Battle of, 1936
Kharkov, Battle of, 1942
Kharkov, Battle of, 1943
Khatyn War Memorial (Byelorussian S.S.R.)
Khrushchev, Nikita Sergeevich, 1894-1973 (1?)          [U.S.S.R.: Polit. Commissar]
                                             DK275.K5, DK267, DK268.K, DK274, DK276, DD881
                          947.084, .0842, .085-0852, 320.947085, 338.1847, 923.247
Kido, Koicho, 1889-1977          [Japan: Marquis, Lord Privy Seal, advisor to the
     Emperor]          DS890.K45          952.0330924
Kiev—Siege, 1941
Kimmel, Husband Edward, 1882-1968          [U.S.: Adm.]          D767.92.K54
                                                                                                            940.54260924
King, Ernest, 1878-1956          [U.S.: Adm.]          V63.K56, D773.A, E182          940.5459730924,
                                                                                                                              359.00924
King, William Lyon MacKenzie, 1874-1950          [Can.: Pr. Min.]          F1033.K53, F1034
                                             971.060924, .06220924, 940.5371, 923.271
Kinkaid, Thomas, 1888-1972          [U.S.: Adm.]          E746.K56
Kites (Military and naval reconnaisance)          UG670
Kleist, Paul Ewald von, 1881-1954          [Ger.: Field Marshal]
Klos (Albania: Concentration camp)
Kluge, Gunther von, 1882-1944          [Ger.: Field Marshal]

Knox, W. Frank, 1874-1944    [U.S.: Sec. o/t Navy]
Kock, Battle of, 1939
Kohima, India (City)—Siege, 1944    D767    940.5425
Kolobrzeg, Battle of, 1945
Kommounistikon Komma tes Hellados    D802.G8, DF849-50    320.949507,
          329.9495
Kommunisticheskaia Partiia Sovetskogo Soiuza    JN6598, JA41, HX314, DK273
          320.0947, 329.947, 947.084
    —Party work
Konev, Ivan, 1897-1973    [U.S.S.R.: Marshal]    D755.7.K6+, D764.K    940.5442
Königsberg, Battle of, 1945
Konoye, Fumimaro, 1891-1945    [Japan: Prince]    DS885.5.K6    952.0330924
Kornwerderzand, Battle of, 1940
Korsun'-Shevchenkovskiy, Battle of, 1944
Kosovo Polje, Battle of, 1944
Kozara, Battle of, 1942
Kragujevac, Yugoslavia—Massacre, 1941    D766.62.K7    940.5405094971
Krait (Mine vessel)    D772.K7-85    940.545
Kraljevo, Serbia (City)—Massacre, 1941
Kretschmer, Otto, 1912-? [Ger.: Commander]    D782.U15    940.5451
Krueger, Walter, 1881-1967    [U.S.: Lt. Gen.]    D769.26.6th    940.5426
Krupp von Bohlen und Halbach, Alfried, 1907-1967    [Ger.: Industrialist, munitions-
          maker, chief director & eventual sole owner of Krupp
          industries, War Economy Leader]    HD9523.9.K7,
          UF537.K7    338.7672, 623.4065
Krupp Trial, Nuremberg, 1947-1948
Kuei-lin (China), Battle of, 1944
Kumagaya (Japan)—Bombardment, 1945
Kursk, Battle of, 1943    D764    940.5421
Kutno, Battle of, 1939
Kuznetsov, Vasily, 1894-1964    [U.S.S.R.: Gen.]    D792.R9
Kwajalein Atoll, Battle of, 1944


Lagarde, Battle of, 1940
Lancaster (Bombers)    TL685    623.7463, 940.544942
Landing craft
Landing operations
Langley (Aircraft carrier)    D774.L32
Lanikai (Ship)    D774.L33    940.5425
Last letters before death    D811
Latvia
    —History
        —1918-1940    DK511    947.4384
        —1940-
        —Russian occupation, 1940-1941
Latvian National Foundation
Laval, Pierre, 1883-1945    [Fr.: For. Min., Deputy Head of State during Vichy]
          DC373.L35, D761    944.0810922, .08160924,
          940.5344, 923.5344
Le Paradis Massacre, 1940
Leachman, Gerard, 1880-1920    [G.B.: Lt. Col.]    U55.L347
Leadership    UB210 (mil.), VB203 (naval)    355.4, 359.6
Leaflets dropped from aircraft    HE9739

League of Nations          JX1974-5, D442, D642, D644, D650, D727
                          309.1043, 327.116, .170973 (U.S.), 341.08, .1209,
                          .22, .26, 963.056
 . Covenant       JX4471      341.58
 —Germany        JX1975      341.2243
 —Great Britain     JX1975      341.12
 —Japan          JX1975      341.2252
 . Permanent Mandates Commission      JX1975.A47
 —Russia         JX1975      341.2247
 —Sanctions      JX1975.6
 —United States     JX1975, E744     341.12973
Leahy, William, 1875-1959      [U.S.: Adm.]      V63.L39, E748          359.00924
Leander (Ship)       D779.N45      940.5459931
Lee-Enfield rifle      UD395      623.442
Legates, Papal      BX1908
Legion des Volontaires Francais Contre le Bolchevisme     D764
Leigh-Mallory, Trafford, Sir, 1892-1944  [G.B.: Air Marshal]     D785.L
Leipzig Trials, 1921
Lemay, Curtis, 1906-1990      [U.S.: Gen. (Air Corps)]      E745.L4, D790.L46
                                  940.544973, 358.413320924
Lend-lease operations (1941-1945)      D753.2      338.9147073, 940.5322, .540944
Lenin, Vladimir Ilich, 1870-1924      [Orig. 'Bronshtein, Lev Davidovich': Rus.: Head
   of the U.S.S.R.]      DK254.L4, DK246, DK262, DK265, DK267-8, D412,
                          B4249, HF1028, HX40, HX312, JN6598
                          947.08410924, .8410924, 320.53220947, .947084,
                   322.4209, 329.947, 331.880947, 335.43082, .430947, 923.247
Leningrad—Siege, 1941-1944      D764      940.5421
Lenino, Battle of, 1943
Leonberg (Germany: Concentration camp)
Leopold III, 1901-?      [Belg.: King]      DH687      949.30420924
Leros, Battle of, 1943
Letts        [Latvia: post-WWI terr. ?]      DK511.L17, D561.L4
Lewis machine-gun      UF620.L      355.82
Lexington (U.S. aircraft carrier, 1st of the name)   D774.L4, D790      940.5426, .545
Liberator pistol      UD413      355.82
Libraries and national socialism
Libya—History      DT224-235      961.2-203
Libyan desert       D766.82
Liddel Hart, Basil, 1895-1970  [G.B.: Capt., mil. theorist & author]      U55.L5, U19
                                  355.008, .00924
Lidvard (Motor ship)      D779.N6      940.5459481
Liechtenstein—History      DB540.5      943.648
Liepaja—Siege, 1941      DB540.5      943.648
Lightning (Fighter planes)      [Also known as 'P-38']      TL685-6, UG1242
                                  623.7464,.74640973, 940.544973
Lightning war      U16.5.L5      355.422
Limited war       UA11      355.0215
Lithuania
    —History
        —1918-1945                  DK511      947.5084
        —Russian occupation, 1940-1941      DK511      947.50842
        —German occupation—1941-1944
Little Entente, 1920-1939      D460      341.2

Litvinov, Maxim [Maksim M.], 1876-1952    [U.S.S.R.: Sov. Commissar for For. Aff.,
    Ambass. to U.S. (1941-3), Dep. Comm. for For. Aff.]    DK267.L, DK268.L5,
                          DS145, E183.8.R9        327.73047
Lloyd George, David, 1863-1945    [G.B.: Prime Min.]    D546.L5, D517, DA566,
                     DA577, HN385        941.0830924, .0930924,
        942.0810924, .0830924, 940.341, .40942, 309.142082, 923.242
Lodge, Henry Cabot, 1850-1924    [U.S.: Sen.]        E664.L7, D643, JX1975
                        973.90924, 328.730924, 923.273
Logistics            U168        355.411, .621, 658.7
Logistics, Naval     V179, VE353        359.41, .621+, 355.41
London
  —Air defenses, Military
  —Bombardment, 1917-1918        D547        940.44943
  —Bombardment, 1940-1941        D760        940.5442
  —Bombardment, 1940
  —History—1800-1950            DA683        914.210373
London. Naval Conference, 1930        JX1974        341.2, .67
London Naval Treaty, 1930        JX1974
London Naval Treaty, 1936        JX1974
Longwy (France), Battle of, 1940
Lorraine American Cemetery, France        D810.D4        940.546544
Los Angeles County, Calif. War Service Corps        D769.85.C21.L89
Los Baños (Los Baños, Laguna, Philippines: Concentration camp)
Luger pistol        TS537        623.443, 683.43
Luxembourg    [SEE ALSO 'Luxemburg']        DH916        949.35
Luxemburg     [SEE ALSO 'Luxembourg']        DH916        949.35

M1 carbine        UD395.M17        623.4425
MacArthur, Douglas, 1880-1964    [U.S.: Gen.]        E745.M28-3, D767, D767.4,
                 DS889, DS918,V17.M3        973.910924,
        940.5426, 327.7305, .730924, 355.00924, .0973,
             .3310924, 923.573, 951.9042, 952.04
Macedonia—History—1912-1945        D562.M32
Macedonian question        DR2242, DR381, DR701        320.94976, 949.7
Machine-guns        UF620, VF410 (naval)        355.547, .82+, 623.4424
Madagascar        DT468-9        916.91+, 969.1+
Maginot Line        D756, DC367
Maine—History        F19-20+        974.1+
Maisky, Ivan, 1884-1975    [ALSO 'Maiskii': U.S.S.R.: Ambass. to G.B. (1932-43),
    Dep. Commissar of For. Aff.]        DK268.M3        923.247
Majdanek (Poland: Concentration camp)
Makin, Battle of, 1943
Malaya—History—Japanese occupation, 1942-1945        DS596.6        959.5+
Malenkov, Georgy [Georgii Maksimilianovich], 1902?-?    [U.S.S.R.: Member of
    Comm. for the Defense o/t State, polit. Commissar, Chair o/t Comm. for the
    Restor. o/t Economy]    DK268.M33, DK275.M3        923.247
Malinov, Alexander, 1867-1938        [Bulg.: Min., Pres.]    DR87.7, D20, HD815.S74,
                 JN9609.A8        322.440924, 329.94977
Malmedy Massacre, 1944-1945        D804        940.5405094934, .547243
Malta, Battle of, 1940-1943
Malta—History        DG990        945.85
Mandates        D650, JX4021        341.12, .27
  —Cameroons        DT574
  —Palestine        DS126        956.94
Manila (Philippine Islands)

423

Mannerheim, Carl Gustav Emil von, 1867-1951    [Fin.: Marshal]        DK461.M32,
          DL1067.5.M36              948.97030924, 947.1030922, 923.5471
Mannerheim Cross
Manstein, Erich von, 1887-1973     [Ger.: Field Marshal]        D757.M3213,
          D757.3.M, DD247.M3       940.54013, 355.00924
Mao Tse-tung, 1893-1976 [China: Chairman o/t Chinese Communist Party]
          DS778.M3, DS774-5, DS777, U240        951.040924-
          050924, .90430924, 320.95105, 335.434, 370.951, 923.551
Maps, Military        UA985-97 (mil. geog.), UG470 (topog., surveys), U408, UC30
          526.8, 623.71
—Symbols        UG470-3
Marauder bomber        [A.k.a. 'B-26']
Marco Polo Bridge Incident, 1937
Mariana Islands        DU645        996.7
Maritime law        JX4408-49 (int'nal. law), JX6311 (private), HE585-7 (shipping laws)
          333.9164+, 341.448, .45-762+, 343.096+, 347.75+
Marne, Battle of the, 1914        D544, D545.M3, D515        940.421
Marne, 2d Battle of the, 1918        D544-5
Marseille, Battle of, 1944
Marshall, George Catlett, 1880-1959      [U.S.: Gen.; Army Chief of Staff] Chair, Jt.
          Chiefs of Staff]        E745.M37, D570.9.M37, E183.7.B462, E183.8.C5,
          E836.A42, U53        973.9170924, 940.48173, 355.3310924, 923.573
Marshall, William, Sir, 1865-1939    [G.B.: Gen.]        D521, D546        940.4
Marshall Islands
Martial law        JX4595 (int'nal. law)
—United States        JX343-55, KF223, KF5063        342.73062, 344.0973,
          345.730231
Marzabotto Massacre, 1944        D763        940.5421
Masaryk, Jan Garrigue, 1886-1948        [Czech.: For. Min. o/t gov.-in-exile in Eng.]
          DB217.M3, DB2191.M37        923.1437
Masaryk, Tomas [Thomas] Garrigue, 1850-1937        [Aust.-Hung.: Pres. of Czech.]
      DB217.M3, DB215, DB2191.M38, D521.M43, D558, D619, DS141.M33
      943.7020922-7030922, 940.32273, 320.50924, 923.1437
Mass casualties        355.48
Massachusetts—History—1865-1950
Massaua, Eritrea—Harbor
Matapan, Battle of, 1941        D775        940.5421, .545942
Matsuoka, Yosuke, 1880-1946    [Japan: For. Min.]        DS885.5.M3
Mauser rifle        UD395, TS536        623.44231, 683.42
Mathausen (Mathausen, Austria: Concentration camp)
Mechanization, Military—Germany
Medals, Military and naval        UB430-5 (mil.), VB330-5 (naval), UC530, NK6302
          355.134, .134075, .13409, 737.2
Medicine, Military        RC970-1 (med. practice), UH223 (mil. sci.), UH393
Medicine, Naval        RC981-6, VG228        614.864, 616.98024
Mediterranean region—Strategic aspects
Melanesia—History        DU490
Melitopol, Battle of, 1943
Memorials
Menzies, Robert Gordon, Sir, 1894-1978        [Australia: Pr. Min.(1939-41)]
          DU114.M4        994.040924, 940.5342

Morgenthau, Henry, 1891-1967     [U.S.: Sec. o/t Treasury]
Morocco—History—20th century     DT317, DT324     964.03-04
Mortain (France), Battle of, 1944
Mortars (Ordnance)     UF560-5
Moscow, Battle of, 1941-1942     D764     940.5421
Moscow Trial, 1945
Moscow Trials, 1936-1937     345.470231
Motor-boats     D771, VM341, VM357, VM771     623.8231, .82314-
     82315, .8723, .88, .8823
Motor-trucks, Military     UG615-20     623.7472
Motor vehicles, Amphibious     TL229.A (technology), V880 (naval sci.)     623.747
Motorization, Military     UC340-5
Moulin, Jean, 1899-1943     [Fr.: Fr. Resistance leader]     D762.C45
Mountain guns     UF440-5
Mountain warfare     U240
Mountbatten, Louis, Lord, 1900-1979     [G.B.: Vice Adm.]     DA89.1.M59,
     DS480.84     942.0820924, 954.040924
Moving-pictures in propaganda
Mulberry harbors     D761     940.5421
Munich. Universität—Riot, Feb. 18. 1943     DD256     943.086
Munitions     HD9743 (econ.), JX5390 (int'nal. law), UF530-7 (manufacture),
     JX1907, U102, UF520     338.4735582, .476234,
     382.4535582, .453583
—Germany     UF535     623.0943
—United States     HD9743, UF533     338.476230973, 343.73025,
     355.033573, .62110973, 382.456234, 658.80935582
Murphy, Robert Daniel, 1894-1958     [U.S.: Diplomat, F.D.R.'s N. Afr. envoy (1941-3)]
     E748.M875     327.20924
Music and war
Mussolini, Benito, 1883-1945     [It.: Il Duce]     DG575.M8, DG499, DG571-2,
     DD256     945.0910924, 940.5324, 914.50391, 923.245
Mustang (Fighter plane)     [A.k.a. 'P-51']     TL685.3, TL686, UG1242
     358.4183, .43, 623.7464, 940.544973
Mutiny
—Germany     D639     940.45943
Myitkyina (Burma), Battle of, 1944

Nagas     D767.6     940.542
Nagasaki—Bombardment     D767     940.532452, .5426
Nagumo, Chuichi, 1886?-1944     [Japan: Vice Adm.]
Narvik, Battle of, 1940     D763     940.5421
National cemeteries
—California     353.0086609794
—United States     E160, E494, UB393-4     343.73025, 353.00866,
     355.115, .69, 362.8
National characteristics     CB197, CB203, D443     914.03, 940.5, 901.9
National characteristics, American     E169, E173, E784, B1649, BF755
     917.3039+, .303917-303918, 136.4973, 155.8973, 301.3260973
National characteristics, British     DA110     914.2
National characteristics, English     DA118     914.203+
National characteristics, German     DD76, DD256     914.30631, 155.8943,
     320.943
National characteristics, Japanese     DS821, BF755     915.203+, 136.4952,
     155.8952, 301.2952
National characteristics, Russian     DK32, DK268, DK276     914.7+

National Jewish Welfare Board    D810.J4, UH23    940.5315296, 355.3470973
National security    UA10    355.0335
National Service Board for Religious Objectors    UB342.U5.N2
National socialism    DD253, DD244, DD247, DD256    320.533+,
    .5330943 (Germ.), 914.30386, 943.085-086, 946.086
National socialism and architecture    NA1068.5.N37    720.943
National socialism and art    N6868.5.N37
National socialism
—Biography    DD253    329.943
—History    DD247, DD253, DD256    309.143086, 329.943,
    335.60943,943.086
—Sources
National socialism in literature
National socialism in motion pictures
National socialistische Deutsche Arbeiter-Partei
—Party work
. Waffenschutzstaffel    D757    940.541343
National War College (U.S.)
National War Fund, Inc.    D809.U5.N21-35    940.5477873
Nationalkomitee für ein 'Freies Deutschland'    DD256.5    940.5343
Nationalsozialistische Deutsche Arbeiter-partei    DD236, DD244, DD253,
    DD255-6, DD491, HQ1623, JC481    940.548743, 943.085-086,
    301.4120943, 309.143086, 320.943085-086; .94351208, 329.943
—Biography    DD244    943.0860922
—History    DD253, DD801    301.44420943, 329.943
—Sources    DD256    943.086
. Hitlerjugend    DD253    943.086, 329.943
. Schutzstaffel    DD253, DD256    940.54050943, .547243, 943.086,
    354.430074
. Waffenschutzstaffel    [SEE ALSO 'Waffen-SS' for materials later than 1981
    or so]    D757.85, DD253, UC535    940.541343, 355.14, .140943
    . 28. Freiwilligen-Panzer-Grenadier-Division 'Wallonien'    D757.85
    . 33. Grenadier-Division 'Charlemagne'    D757, D764    940.541244
    . Leibstandarte SS Adolf Hitler    DD253    940.5421, 943.086
Naval architecture    VM, VM15, VM142, VM162    623.8, .81082, .8122, .84,
    .88, .891
—Bibliography    Z6834    623.8016
Naval art and science    V, V103, V107, V143, V163, VA50    359, .03+, .4, .43
—Dictionaries    V23-4    359.003, .03, 387.03, 623.803, .8903
—History    V25-55    359.009, .00904, .009046, .0091822, 623.82
Naval auxiliary vessels    V865
Naval aviation    VG90-5
Naval battles    D27, D436, V163    359.00903, 359.48, 904.7, 940.2
Naval biography    V61-5, D-F (partic. #s by country)    359.09, .33109+
Naval ceremonies, honors, and salutes    V310
Naval convoys—History—20th century    D771
Naval discipline
—United States    359.1334
Naval districts
—United States    VA62.5-7
Naval education    V400-695
—Australia    V691    359.0071194
—United States    V411    359.54
Naval gunnery    VF, VF145, VF160    359.82, 623.418

Naval history               D27, D362, VA573      359.009, 904, 909, 940.2
Naval history, Modern           D27, D215, D436       359, 359.03, .40903, 909
Naval history—Sources—Bibliography      Z6616        016.35900722
Naval law                        VB350-785
—United States        KF7368        343.73019
Naval maneuvers          V245
Naval museums            V13
Naval offenses           VB850-80
—United States             VB853         359.1332
Naval prints
Naval prints, American      NE957         769.49359
Naval reconnaisance        V190
Naval research
—United States        V393       623.808
Naval reserves           VA
Naval stores
Naval strategy           V160-5, V103          359.43
Naval tactics        V167-78        359.42+
Naval War College (U.S.)
Navies            VA10, VA40       359.009+, .03, .1409+, 623.825
Navies and warships        623.825058
Navies, Cost of
Navies
—History—Congresses    V51        359.009
—Officers              VB310          355.33023
—Yearbooks            V10            623.82505
Navigation       VK145, VK149, VK555, VK559, VM341      623.8, .89, .892, 629,
                629.045, .89
Navigation (Aeronautics)       TL586-9, TL507, TL521, TL546          629.125,
                                .1325, .13251, .1351
—Handbooks           TL586         629.13251
Navy-yards and naval stations       V22-40, VA67-7 (by country)
Navy-yards and naval stations, American
Navy-yards and naval stations
—California—San Diego
—United States
Neaux, France, Battle of, 1944
Negro soldiers
—United States   [SEE 'Afro-American soldiers' for titles after about 1969]
                E185        355.00917496, .330973, 973.0496073, .893
Negroes as soldiers
Neretva River, Battle of the, 1943
Netherlands
—History
—Wilhelmina, 1898-1948
—German occupation, 1940-1945       DJ287        940.5337
Neue Bremm (Saarbrücken, Germany: Concentration camp)
Neuengamme (Hamburg, Germany: Concentration camp)
Neurath, Konstantin von, 1873-1956     [Ger.: For. Min. (1932-8), Reich Protector of
    Bohemia-Moravia]           DD247.N4        943.0860924
Neurokopion (Greece), Battle of, 1941
Neutrality          JX5355-97, JA37        341.3, .35, .64, 327.09045, .091716
Neutrality, Armed        JX5383, D295        940.25

Odessa, Battle of, 1941
Odessa, Battle of, 1944
O'Donnell Camp (Luzon, Philippines: Concentration camp)
Offensive (Military strategy)—History—20th century    U162
Official secrets
   —Great Britain    KD8024    345.420231
   —United States    KF26    342.7305
Oflag II C (Dobiegniew, Poland: Concentration camp)
Oflag VI C (Osnabrück, Germany: Concentration camp)
Oflag XIII B (Hammelberg, Germany: Concentration camp)
Oka (Mine layer)    D779.R9
Okino-daito Island, Battle of, 1945
Oksywie Hill (Poland), Battle of, 1939
Oldendorf, Jesse, 1887-?    [U.S.: Rear Adm.]
Onishi, Takajiro, 1891-1945    [Japan: Vice Adm]
Operation Bolero, 1942
Operation Cerberus, 1942
Operation Citadel
Operation Coronet
Operation Dragoon, 1944
Operation Goodwood
Operation Husky, 1943
Operation Jaywick    940.5426
Operation Jericho
Operation Lila, 1942
Operation Long Jump    D734    940.548743
Operation Menace    D766    940.5423
Operation Mercury, 1941
Operation Mincemeat    D810.S7-8    940.548642
Operation Neptune    D770    940.5421
Operation Overlord
Operation Rimau    D767    940.5426
Operation Sea Lion    D771, D786    940.5342, .5421
Operation Sledgehammer, 1942
Operation Stella Polaris, 1944
Operation Sunrise
Operation Torch    D766    940.5423
Operational rations (Military supplies)
Oppenheimer, J. Robert, 1904-1967    [U.S.: Nuclear physicist, led team that built
    1st atomicbomb]    QC16.O62, .L36, HD9698.U52    530.0924,
        323.20973, 353.00183, 358.4182, 364.1310924, 925.3
Oradour-sur-Glane Massacre, 1944    D804    940.5421
Orden Pour Le Merite    D604
Ordnance    UF520-630    355.82+, 356.186+, 623.4
Ordnance, Coast
   —Manufacture    UF530-45    623.4+, .41
Ordnance, Naval    VF15, VF23, VF353    359.82+, 623.4+
Orel, Battle of, 1943
Organisation Gehlen    DD247.G27-37    327.12+
Orion (Auxiliary cruiser)    ['The Black Raider']    D772.O7    940.545943
Orlando, Vittorio Emanuele, 1860-1952 [It.: Pr. Min.]    DG555, DG570, D520.I7,
    D569.I8, .A2, D617, D643.A7    945.09, 940.3141, 327.45

Orphans
Orphans and orphan asylums
Orphans
—Europe
—Great Britain          HV1148          362.73
Oslofjorden, Battle of, 1940
Osmeña, Sergio, 1878-1961    [Phil.: Vice Pres., Pres.]
Ossewa-Brandwag (Organization: South Africa)      DT779.8
Oswiecim (Concentration camp)  [SEE ALSO 'Auschwitz']   D805.G3, D804.G3
                                                         940.547243
Ozawa, Jisaburo, 1896-1966   [Japan: Vice Adm.]

P-38          [SEE 'Lightning (Fighter planes)]
P-40 (Fighter planes)    [A.k.a. 'Kittyhawk', 'Tomahawk', 'Warhawk']    TL685-6,
                         UG1242          358.4183, .43, 623.7464, 940.544994
P-47          [SEE 'Thunderbolt (Fighter planes)']
P-51          [SEE 'Mustang (Fighter planes)']
P-61          [SEE 'Black Widow (Fighter planes)']
Pacifism—History       BX7635, BX7748, JX1938, JX1944, JX1961
                       261.873, 289.6, .673 (US), 327.172+
Painlevé, Paul, 1863-1933      [Fr.: Min. of War, Prem.]    DC342.8.P4, DC373.S3,
                       DC385, D548      944.0810922-0810924, 320.944081
Paléologue, Georges Maurice, 1859-1944   [Fr.: Ambass. to Russia]      DC385,
                       DK265.P255, D453, D741      944.08, 940.311, .3112, 320.94708
Pankrác (Concentration camp)        D805.G3
Papacy—History—20th century         BX1389      262.130904, 282, 327.45634
Parachute troops       UG630-5, UD480-3        356.166, .6
Parachutes             TL750-8          629.134386
Parachuting            TL750-5, GV770, GV761       629.134386, 797.5609
Paraguay—History—1938-      F2681+      989.2+
Paris
   —History—1940-1944        D762, DC737       940.5421, .534436
   —Posters
   . Peace Conference, 1919      D619, D643-7, D651      940.3141+, .3142,
                                 .32273
      . Hungary        D651          940.3142
      . Italy          D651          940.3141
      . Rumania        D651.R6       327.498
      . Russia         D651.R8          940.3141
      . U.S. Territorial Section      D644      940.312
   . Peace Conference, 1919-. Yugoslavia      D651      940.31425
   . Peace Conference (1919-1920)        D647.A2      940.3141
Park, Keith, Sir, 1892-1975      [New Z.: Air Marshal]
Partito nazionale fascista       DG571, JN5657.F3        321.6, .9, 329.945,
                                 .940945
Partizanski spomenik (Mostar, Bosnia and Hercegovina)
Pasic, Nikola, 1845-1926  [Serbia: Pr. Min.]      DR359.P283, DR341, DB91, D741,
                          DJK4      949.71020924, .7101, .6, 940.311, 943.604
Patch, Alexander McCarrell, 1889-1945        [U.S.: Gen.]
Patton, George, 1885-1945       [U.S.: Gen.]      E745.P293-3, D743, D769,
                       D769.26.3d, D805.G3, D811        355.3310924,
                       923.573, 940.5421
Paulus, Friedrich, 1890-1957   [Ger.: Field Marshal]      DD247.P38, DD259.4.P3,
                       D764.3.S7        355.3310924, 923.543

Peace          JX1901-99 (int'nal. law)     172.4+, 309.2206, 320.94+,
          322.43-44, 327.17+, .172+, 341.1+, 355.027, 940.51
Peace treaties        JX5181
Pearl Harbor, Attack on, 1941     D767, D748      940.5426, .5311, .53112,
          .532273, .542, .5426
Pearl Harbor (Hawaii), Attack on, 1941
Peleliu Island (Palau), Battle of, 1944
Pensions, Military      UB370-5 & UB400-5 (army), VB280-5 & VB340-5 (navy),
          E255 (pension rolls)
Pensions, Military and naval—United States
Pensions, Military
—United States      UB373, UB403, KF26-7      355.115, .11510973,
          .11560973, 343.73011, 344.73011
—European War, 1914-1918
—World War, 1939-1945
Penzberg, Germany—Massacre, 1945
Percival, Arthur, 1887-1966   [G.B.: Lt. Gen.]    D767.5.P
Peron, Juan Domingo, 1895-1975  [Argen.: Pres.]  F2849.P48, F2237, F2843,
          F2848, UA613    982.06, 320.98206, 923.182, 980.03
Perth (Cruiser)     D779.A9    940.545994
Peru—History—1919-1968
Pétain, Henri-Philippe Benoni Omer Joseph, 1856-1951   [Fr.: Gen.]  DC342.8.P4,
          DC280.5.B3, DC397, D507, D530, D756.B46, D761
     944.0810922-0810924, .08160924, 940.410922, .4140922, .5344, .544
Petroleum industry and trade     HD9571.5    338.27282+
—Military aspects—History—20th century
Philadelphia Experiment, 1943
Philippine Islands
—History
  —1898-1946     DS685-6      959.903, .9035, 991.4031
    —Japanese occupation, 1941-1945    DS686    915.990335
  —Politics and government—1935-1946    DS685-6     959.9035,
          320.9599032, 309.1599035
Philippine Sea, Battles of the, 1944     D774    940.5426, .545973
Phillips, Tom, Sir, 1888-1941  [G.B.: Adm.]
Photographic interpretation (Military science)    D810.P4 (WWII), UG476    623.72
Photography, Military
Pietransieri di Roccaraso—Massacre, 1943
Pilsudski, Joseph, 1867-1935  [Pol.: War Min.]    DK440.5.P5, DK439
          943.8040924, 320.9438, 923.1438, .5438
Piombino (Italy)—Battle of, 1943
Pistols          UD410-15 (army), TS537 (manufacture), VD390 (naval),
          GV1175 (shooting)    344.7305330262, 623.44+, .442-3,
          683.43, 739.74+, 799.202833, .213
Pistols, American     TS537, UD413    623.44, .4430973, 683.43
Pistols, German     TS537    683.43, .430943
Pistols—History
Pius XII, 1867-1958  [Vatican: Pope]    BX1378, BX1753, BX2250, DD256.3
    261.8, 262.130924, .131, 265.5, 364.131, 922.21, 940.531522, .532545634
Plaszow (Poland: Concentraton camp)
Ploesti, Battles of, 1943-1944
Poincaré, Raymond, 1860-1934    [Fr.: Pres.]    DC385, D511, D650.M5, D741
          944.0810924, 940.311
Point 175, Battle of, 1941

Poland
 . Armia    D765+, U773   940.5412438
  . 2. Korpus    D765   940.5412438
  . Polskie Sily Zbrojne. Armia Krajowa   D802.P6 (Underground)
 —Boundaries
  —Germany   D821.P
  —Russia
 —Foreign relations
  —1918-1945   DK4410    940.53438
  —Russia    DK418, DK441, DK4185   327.438047, 943.805
 —History
  —1918-1945       DK440   914.38, 943.8
  —Occupation, 1939-1945  D802   940.5337
 —Military relations—Soviet Union
 —Politics and government—1918-1945   DK440-1   943.8, 320.9438,
                      .943804-943805
 . Wojsko Polskie. 22. Pulk Artylerii Lekkiej   D765.13
Police
 —Germany
  —Political activity
Police power—Germany
Polish question    D621.P7
Political atrocities
Political crimes and offenses   HV6254-6321    364.13, .132, .154
Political oratory—Germany
Political parties   JF2011-2111   329.02+
  —Germany—History   JN3933   329.020943
  —Great Britain   JN1111-1129   328.42072, 329.020942, .941-2
  —Japan    JQ1698   329.952
  —Soviet Union
Political poetry, American [British, etc.]
Political posters, German
Political posters, Japanese
Political prisoners
  —Russia   HV8959, HV8964, HV9712-13   365.45, .450947, .60924,
          940.5472498, 947.080924, .0842+
Political psychology   BF173, JA74-6, JF2051, JN5651   150.1952, 155.2,
          158.4, 301.592, 320.019, 329.0019
Political purges
  —Germany
  —Japan   940.531440952
  —Russia
Political satire, American [English, German, etc.]
Politics and war
Politics in art—Soviet Union
Polska Partia Robotnicza—History   D802.P62.W26, JN6769   329.9438
Polynesia—History   DU510   996
Popov, Dusko, n.d.   [G.B., Ger.: Double/triple (?) agent]   D810.S8.P6
                         940.5486420924
Popov, Markian, 1902-?   [U.S.S.R.: Gen.]
Population transfers
 —Jews
Portal, Charles, Sir, 1893-1971   [G.B.: Air Chief Marshal]

Portugal
  —Foreign relations    327.4690+
  —History—1910-1974    DP680        946.9042
  —Politics and government
    —1910-1974
    —1933-1974    DP680      320.9469042
Postliminy             JX5187 (int'nal. law)
Potsdam Conference (1945)    D734
Pound, Dudley, Sir, 1877-1943    [G.B.: Adm.]
Powder-magazines         UF540-5, VF380 (naval)
Pozna´n, Poland, Battle of, 1945
Prague, Battle of, 1945
Presidents—United States
  —Archives     CD3029      025.171
  —Biography
  —Election
    —1940     E748, E811     329.0237309, 973.917
    —1944     E812    329.023730917
    —Inaugural addresses    J81    353.03, .035
    —Messages     J81, E173   353.035
    —Press conferences    JK518   353.032, 070.11
Press and politics—Germany
Prezan, Constantine, 1861-1943   [Rum.: Lt. Gen.]    D565.A2, DR262.A2
                              949.8020924, 923.1498
Price regulation     HB236     338.52, .526
  —United States    HB236, HC101, HD1761   338.10973, .5260973,
                            339.50973
Prien, Gunther, 1908-1941    [Ger.: Lt., U-boat Commander (U47)]
              V64.G32.P744, V65.P7   940.54510924, 923.543
Prinz Eugen (Cruiser)    359.32530943
Priorities, Industrial    HD3611-16
  —United States    HD3616, HC106   353.00895, 338.973
Prisoners of war    JX5141 (int'nal. law), UB800   341.33, .6509+, 365.6
  —Germany
  —Japan
  —Psychology    RC451    616.89
  —Russia
  —United States    UB774    365.450973
Prisons, Military    UB800+    355.71
Prize law        JX5245-66    341.36
Profiteering
Projectiles      UF750-70 (mil.), VF480-500 (naval)   355.82, 623.42,
             .451109+, .4513
Projectiles, Aerial    UF767
Propaganda     UB275, HM263, JF1525   301.152-154
Propaganda, American    D632, E744    301.1540973, 327.73,
             940.488673
Propaganda, British    D619     940.488642
Propaganda, German     DD255-6   327.43, .140943, 301.15230943,
             .1540943
Propaganda, Russian   DK270, DK278   327.140947, 947.085

Psychiatry, Military        D807.U6, UB323, UH629        616.8, .89, 355.22
Psychological warfare       UB275-7, U22        355.3434, .42-3, 301.1523
Psychology, Military        U22.3, U15, UH629, HQ797        355.0019, .1156,
                            .22, .6133, 301.593, 155.93
Psychology, Naval
PT boats                    [SEE 'Torpedo-boats']
Public opinion              D810.P85 (WWII)
   —Germany                 DD117, DD228        329.050943
   —United States           D810.P85.U5+        301.1540973
Public shelters
Pyle, Ernest, 1900-1945     [U.S.: War correspondent]        PN4874.P86, D811.5.P
                            070.924, 940.548173, 920.5

Quezon, Manuel, 1878-1944   [Phil.: Pres.]        DS686.3.Q4        959.90350924,
                            991.40350924
Quisling, Vidkun, 1887-1945   [Norway: Head of puppet gov.]        DL529.Q5,
                            DK267        948.1040924, 940.53370924, 947.084

Rab (Concentration camp: Croatia)
Rabaul (New Britain)
Radar                       TK6575-80, UG610        621.38+, .3848
Radar defense networks      UG633        629.437, 358.4145
   —Great Britain
Radar in aeronautics        TL695-6, Q180, TL500        621.3848, 629.1355, .1366
Radio in propaganda         JF1525, HE8696        327.1409+, 301.154
Radio, Military             UG610
Raeder, Erich, 1876-1960    [Ger.: Adm.]        DD231.R17        943.080924, 923.543
Railroads
Railroads and state         HE1051-1081, HE2757 (US), HE2801-3600 (other
                            countries)        385+
   —Italy
Railroads
   —Europe                  HE3004-8        385.094, .2094
   —Germany
   —Great Britain           HE3015-3020, TF57, TF64        385.0941-0942, .142, 625.18,
                            912.138531
   —History—Europe
   —Russia                  HE3135-8        380.50947, 385.0947
Railway artillery           UF490-5        358.12, 623.412
Ramsay, Bertram Home, Sir, 1883-1945        [G.B.: Adm.]
Rapido River, Battle of the, 1944        D763        940.5421
Rationing, Consumer
Ravensbrück (Concentration camp)        D805        940.547243
Rawicz (Leszno, Poland: Concentration camp)
Reconnaisance aircraft
Reconstruction (1914-1939)        D653-9, D638
   —Germany                 D659        330.94308
   —Sources                 E802        940.531440922
Reconstruction (1939-)      D829.A-Z, D826, HC59        940.53144+, 338.91
Reconstruction (1939-1951)  D825, D816, D840        940.5312, .53144,
                            901.944, 909.82, 327.09044
Red Cross        HV560-83, HV568, UH535-7 (army), VG457 (navy)        361.506, .53
   . Germany. Deutsches Rotes Kreuz        D807.G4
   . U.S. American National Red Cross        UC74.R4, HV576-8, HV640        361.506,
                            .77, 362.7

Refugee property
Refugees, Jewish          D810, DS126, HV640, JV8749        940.53159, 956.94,
          909.0492400823, 325.247095694, 361.5309494, 301.451924047
Refugees, Polish
Refugees, Political        JX4292.P6 (int'nal. law), HV640 (relief), D842, JV6477,
          JX1907        325.21, 341.51, 361.53, 940.53159
Reichenau, Walther von, 1884-1942        [Ger.: Field Marshal]        UA712.R4
          940.5497
Reichswald, Battle of,the 1945        D756        940.5421
Relief for Americans in [the] Philippines (New York)        D805.P6        940.5472914
Renunciation of war treaty, Paris, Aug. 27, 1928 [A.k.a. Treaty of Paris (1928)]
          JX1987, E748        341.2, .52, .6, .73, 923.273
Reparations
Repatriation        JX4231
Reprisals        JX4486    341.58
Requisitions, Military        JX5321 (int'nal. law), UC15 (mil. sci.)
Rescue work
Restitution and indemnification claims (1933-)        [for property loss or other injuries]
Retired military personnel—United States
Revolvers        UD410-15 (army), VD390 (navy), TS537 (production), TS535
          623.443, .4434, 683.43
Revolvers, American
Reynaud, Paul, 1878-1966        [Fr.: Pr. Min.]        DC389.R, D761        940.5344
Rhine Valley—History—Separatist movement, 1918-1924
Rhineland (Germany)—History—Separatist Movement, 1918-1924        D650.M5
Ribbentrop, Joachim von, 1893-1946        [Ger.: For. Min.]        DD247.R
Ridgway, Matthew Bunker, 1895-1987        [U.S.: Gen. (airborne infan.)]        E745.R52
          355.3310924
Rifles        UD390-5 (army), VD370 (navy), TS534-5        355.6212, .82,
          623.442-4425, 683.42
Righteous Gentiles in the Holocaust        DS135.R93
Rio de la Plata, Battle of the, 1939        D772        940.545, .545943
Ritchie, Neil Methuen, 1897-?        [G.B.: Gen.]        D766.82        940.5423
Roadblocks (Military science)
Rocket launchers (Ordnance)        UF880, UG633        355.6212, .82
Rocket research—Germany
Rocketry        TL781-2, Q111        629134354, .14353, .4, .409, .42-3, .47509
Rockets (Aeronautics)        TL780-3, UG630, TL732, TL507, QC801        623.451+,
          629.13-14, .133349, .13338, .14353, 629.42
Rockets (Ordnance)        UF767, UF820, UG630-3        623.451, .4519, .54
Röhm, Ernst, 1887-1934        [Ger.: SA chief ('Brown Shirts')]        DD247.R56
          943.086
Rokossovsky, Konstantin, 1896-1968        [U.S.S.R.: Marshal]        D764.R63613,
          D764.3.S7        940.5421
Romania
    . Armata. Divizia Infanterie, 9—History
    —Foreign relations—1914-1944
    —History—1914-1944        DR250, DR266        309.149802, 949.802,
          320.949802
Rome (City)—History—1870-        DG813        945.63209
Rommel, Erwin, 1891-1944        [Ger.: Field Marshal]        DD247.R, U55.R6,
          D756.5.N6, D757, D757.55.A4, D766.32, .82,
          D811.R, D840        940.5421, .5423,
          .54230924, .548142, 923.543
Rooseboom (Ship)        D805.J3 (Jpn. prisoners)        940.548142

Roosevelt, Eleanor, 1884-1962    [U.S.: F.D.R.'s wife, Dir. of Office of Civilian Def.]
    E807.1.R35-572+, E806        973.9170924, 309.175, 362.0924
Roosevelt, Franklin Delano, 1882-1945 [U.S.: Asst. Sec. o/t Navy, Pres.]
            E741-2, E744, E766, E801, E805-7, E811-12, E173, E176.1, E183,
            E183.8, D734.A8, D748, D753, DA566.9.C5 (Churchill)
            973.90924, .9170924, 320.9730917, 327.73+, .7307291,
            329.023730917, .30221, 330.9730917, 338.860973, 353.0313,
                917.303917, 923.173, .573, 940.5320922, .532273
Rosenberg, Alfred, 1893-1946 [Ger.: Nazi philosopher]    DD247.R58, CB425.R74
                                                    320.5330924, 914.30301
Royal Air Force Escaping Society        D805.A2        940.5472
Ruhr Pocket, Battle of, 1945        D756        940.5421
Rundstedt, Gerd von, 1875-1953    [Ger.: Field Marshal]
Russell, Bertrand, 1872-1970 [G.B.: Socialist, pacifist leader]    B1649.R91-4 192.9
Russia  [SEE ALSO 'Russia (1923-   U.S.S.R.)' and 'Soviet Union']    DK1-275+
                                                    947, 914.7
    —Armed forces        UA646, UA772, DK219, D552        355.00947, .30947,
                            940.4147, 947.080924
    . Armiia        UA770, UA772, D550        355.00947, 940.40947
        —Bibliography        Z6725        016.355310947
    —Description and travel—1917-        DK267, DK18-28        914.704842,
                                                    .703-7048
    —Economic conditions—1918-1945        DK266, HC335        330.947084-5,
                                            336.34350947, 338.947
    —Economic policy
        —1938-1942
        —1942-1945
    —Exiles
    —Foreign economic relations
        —Germany
        —United States
    —Foreign relations
        —1917-1945        DK63, DK66, DK265-274        327.09042, .20924,
                            .470+, 341.2247, 940.532247, 947.0841
        —France
        —Germany        327.47043
        —Great Britain        327.47041
        —Japan        DK68.7.J3, DS783, DS849        327.47052
        —United States        E183, JX1555        327.47073, .73047
    —History
        —20th century        DK246, DK268, DK275        947.08+, .084-085,
                            914.7038
        —1925-1953        DK267-8        947.0842, 914.703842
        —1939-1945        DK273        947.0842
        —German occupation, 1941-1944        DK273, D802        940.532443,
                                            .5347, .5337
    —History, Military        UA772, DK268, D550        355.00947, 940.40947,
                            355.4300924
    —Politics and government—1936-1953        DK254-268, JN6598
                                            947.0842, .085, 320.9470842
    —Relations (military) with Germany
    . Voenno-morskoi Flot        VA573, D779.R9        359.00947, .320947, 940.545947

Russia (1923-    U.S.S.R.)          [SEE ALSO 'Russia' and 'Soviet Union']
  . Armiia
    . 5. Armiia          D764.5.5th
    . 97. Gvardeiskaia Strelkovaia Diviziia        D764.6.G8.97th
  . Voenno-Morskoi Flot      [Navy]              VA570, VA573, D779.R9, UA856
                            359.00947, .030947, .30947, .3250947, 940.545947
    . Chernomorskii Flot    [Subs]        D784.R9
      . Severnyi Voennyi Flot
  . Voenno-vozdushnye Sily    [Air force]        UG633, UG635.R9
                                        358.400947, .40947, 940.544947
Russo-Finnish War, 1939-1940        DK459        947.103, 948.95, 941.103
Russo-German treaty, 1939          D749, D751        940.5312, .532443
Russo-Japanese Border Conflicts, 1932-1941        DS784
Russo-Japanese War, 1904-1905        DS517        952.031, .03185
Rydz-Smigly, Edward, 1886-1943    [Pol.: Marshal, head o/t armed forces]
Rzhev, Battle of, 1942-1943


Sachsenhausen (Germany: Concentration camp)
Saint Malo (France)—Siege, 1944
Saint Nazaire Raid, 1942          D756        940.5421
Saint-Lô (France)—Siege, 1944      D756        940.542
Saint-Valery-en-Caux, Battle of, 1940
Saipan, Battle of, 1944
Saipan Island
Sakai (Osaka Prefecture: Japan)—Bombardment, 1945
Salandra, Antonio, 1853-1931  [It.: Pr. Min.]        DG575.S25, DG555, DG568.5,
                            D617, UA742      945.08-09, 327.45, 940.32245, .34502
Salazar, Antonio, 1889-1972    [Port.: Pr. Min.]      DP676.S25, DP680
                                            946.9040924, 320.9469
Salerno, Battle of, 1943          D763        940.5421
San Pietro, Battle of, 1943
Santa Anita Assembly Center, Calif.      D769        940.54779496
Santa Fe, N.M. Relocation Center          D769.8.A6
Santo Tomas Internment Center (Manila, Philippines)
Sapping            UG510-15
Sardinia—History      DG975        945.9
Sauckel, Fritz, 1894-1946        [Ger.: Plenipoten. Gen. f/t Alloc. of Labor]
Saumur, Battle of, 1940
Savez Komunisticke Omladine Jugoslavije        HQ799.V8-9[WWII]
Savo Island, Battle of, 1942      D774        940.5426
Scapa Flow          D581, V65        940.453094112, .5451
Scapa Flow Scuttling, Scotland, 1919
Schacht, Hjalmar Horace Greeley, Dr., 1877-1970    [Ger.: Reichsbank Pres. (1933-
      9), Min. o/t Econ. (1935-7)]        DD247.S33-335        943.085, 332.10924
Scharnhorst (Battleship)    [WWI (armoured cruiser) & II (battle cruiser): 2 ships]
                          D771, D772.S35        940.545, .5459, .545941-3
Schellenberg, Walther, 1911?-1952      [Ger.: SS Gen., Combined Secret Srvcs.
      chief]                DD247.S338        940.548743
Schirach, Baldur von, 1907-1974      [Ger.: Hitler Youth leader till 1940, Gauleiter of
      Vienna]        DD253.S26, DD253.5.S35, DB99        943.605, .086, 329.943
Schleissheim (Displaced persons camp)
Schlieffen Plan
Schmidt, Battle of, 1944
Science and state—Germany—History—20th century      D804.G4        940.5405
Scobie, Ronald, 1893-1969        [G.B.: Gen.]

Scotland—History—20th century
Sea control
Sea-power          V25, V17, VA10, VA50, VA513, VA573          359.0309, .409, .43,
                   355.0308, 327.1109, 325.308
Seamanship—History          VK541          623.809
Seamen          G225, G545          359.109
Seamen
    —[country]—Biography
    —Great Britain—Biography
    —United States—Biography          E207, V63          359.3380924, 973.350924
Seaplanes          TL684          629.13334709, 387.733470904
Search and rescue operations          TL553.8, VG55          353.0075, 359.9709
Search, Right of          JX5268          323.4
Security classification (Government documents)
    —United States          JK468, KF26-7, KF4774, KF7695
                   342.7304, .73068, .73085, 343.73013, .730531,
                   353.00714, 355.61, 364.131, 328.7305-07
Seizure of vessels and cargoes          HJ6645          353.0074
Self-determination, National          JX4054          320.13, .158, 323.1, 341.26, .52
Serbia          DR317, DR360          949.71
    —Foreign relations
        —Europe
        —Russia          DR327          327.4704971
Sevastopol, Battle of, 1944
Sevastopol—Siege, 1942
Seyss-Inquart, Artur von, 1892-1946          [Austria: Reich Commissioner o/t Neth.]
Shawcross, Hartley, Sir, 1902?-          [G.B.: Brit. Chief Prosecutor at Nuremberg trials]
Sherman tank          UG446.5
Ship-building          VM, VM15, VM144-6, VM298          623.8, .823, .809, 387.209
    —United States—History          VM23, VM140, VM299          623.8203,
                   387.50973, 359.830973, 338.4762382
Ship-building workers
Ships—History          VM15-23, VM121, VM307, VK20          387.209, .2074013,
                   .20977, .09687, 623.82009, .821
Ships' stores and Navy exchanges (United States Navy)          VC393          646.024359
Shipwrecks          JX4436 (int'nal. law), G525-30 (narratives), VK1250-99 (reports)
                   910.091636, .45, .453, .45308, 904.5
Shipyards          VM12-124          623.809, .8309+, .830973 (US), 338.476238309
Shooting, Military          UD330-5, UD383          356.162, 623.442, .5, 683.409+
Siberia (R.S.F.S.R.)
    —History          D558
        —Revolution, 1917-1921          DK265          957.084
Sicily—History—1870-1945          945.7
Sidra, Gulf of, Battle of, 1942          D775          940.5423
Sieges          JX5117 (int'nal. law)
Signals and signaling          UG570-82 (mil.), V280-5 (naval), VK385          359.983, 384.9
Signals and signaling, Submarine          VK388
Siiranmäki (Finland), Battle of, 1944
Sikorski, Wladyslaw, 1881-1943          [Pol.: Gen., Free Polish Forces commander]
                   DK440.5.S55, D821.P7          943.8050924, 940.53438
Sikorsky helicopters          TL540, TL714-16          629.13, .133, .13335,
                   380.14562913335
Silesia, Upper (Poland and Czechoslovakia)—History—Partition, 1919-1922
Simovi´c, Dusan, 1882-1962          [Yug.: Gen., Prem. o/t gov.-in-exile]
Singapore—History          DS598          959.5, .52, 915.952

Sino-American Cooperative Organization    D769.64        940.548673, .545
Sino-Japanese Conflict, 1937-1945    DS777-8    940.5312, 951.042, 952.031-033
    —Aerial operations
    —Aerial operations, American
    —Aerial operations, Japanese
    —Anniversaries, etc.
    —Atrocities        DS777        940.540509520951
    —Blockades
    —Campaigns
        —China        DS777        951.042
    —Causes
    —Children
    —Civilian relief
    —Collaborationists    DS777        952.033
    —Destruction and pillage
    —Diplomatic history    DS777        952.033
    —Economic aspects    HC427        330.95143042
    —Education and the conflict
    —Humor, caricatures, etc.
    —Naval operations
    —Naval operations, Japanese
    —Personal narratives, American    DS777        940.53, 951.042
    —Personal narratives, Australian    DS777        951.042
    —Personal narratives, Chinese
    —Regimental histories
    —Underground movements    DS777        951.042
Sirvintà, Battle of, 1941
Sittang River, Battle of the, 1945
Ski troops        UD470
Skorzeny, Otto, 1908?-1975    [Ger.: Lt. Col. (special missions)]    DD247.S54, D756
                        940.54870924, .548743, .548748
Slapton Sands (England), Battle of, 1944        D756.5.S57
Slave labor
    —Germany
    —Soviet Union
Slavic countries—History
Slavs—History        D147        930.04918
Slim, William, 1891-1970    [G.B.: 1st Viscount, Gen.]        DA69.3.S55, D767.6.S55,
                    U55.S54        940.54250924, 355.3310924
Smederevska Palanka (Smederevska Palanka, Serbia: Concentration camp)
Smith, Holland McTyeire ('Howlin' Mad'), 1882-1967    [U.S.: Gen. (Marines)]
                        D769.369.S58        940.541273
Smith, Ian, 1919-    [Rhodesia: Fighter pilot, Pr. Min. of Rhod. after war]
                        DT962    968.91040924
Smith and Wesson firearms        TS537        623.443, .4434, 683.43
Smoke screens        UG447.7
Smolensk, Russia (City), Battle of, 1941
Smolensk, Russia (City), Battle of, 1943
Smuts, Jan Christiaan, 1870-1950    [S.Afr.: Gen., Brit. War Cabinet member (WWI);
    Pr. Min. (WWII)]        DT779.8.S6, D517    968.050924, 923.568, 940.304
Sobibor (Poland: Concentration camp)
Socialist International
Société Nationale des Chemins de Fer Français        D810.T8, TJ603        385.3610944
Society for the Prevention of World War III        D731.P        940.531405
Sociology, Military        U21, UA25        355.009, .022, .1209, .3, .61, 301.593

Sokolovsky, Vasiliy, 1897-1968   [U.S.S.R.: Marshal]     U162.S, UA770
Soldiers                     U1-145, U750-73     355.009, .12, .33809
Soldiers as authors
Soldiers
  —Attitudes
  —Billeting        UC410
Soldiers' bodies, Disposition of     UC34, D810.D4 (WWII)        355.69
Soldiers
  —Conduct of life        U408       174.9355
  —Family relationships      U21      355.135
Soldiers' homes—United States
Soldiers in art           N8260, NX549     704.949355
Soldiers in literature
Soldiers
  —Japan       U43      355.00952, .133
  —Language (New words, slang, etc.)
Soldiers' libraries
Soldiers' monuments      NA9325-55
Soldiers
  —Recreation
  —Religious life      UH23, BV4457, BV4588      355.34, 248.8
  —Sexual behavior
  —Suffrage      JX1876-8 (US)
    —United States     U22, U766, E607     355.100973
  —United States
    —Attitudes
    —Biography     E181, E263    355.3380924, 973.330924
Soldiers' writings, English [French, German, etc.]
Solomon Islands        DU350, DU850     993.5, 919.35
Somerville, James, Sir, 1882-1949 [G.B.: Adm.]
Sonar     VK388, VK560 (navig.), V214, VM480, Q180      621.38953,
        623.73, 359.85
Sorge, Richard, 1895-1944   [U.S.S.R.: Spy in China & Japan]    D810.S8,
    UB271.R92    351.74, 355.34320924, 364.13, 923.547, 952.033
South Africa
 . Air Force. 24 Squadron       D792.S6
 . Army. 6th Mounted Regiment    D766.97
 . Police Brigade        D766.97
South America—History—20th century    F2237      980.03
Soviet Union           [SEE ALSO 'Russia']
 . Armiia
    —Biography
    —History      UA772, DK264
  —Foreign relations
  —History
    —Nicholas, 1894-1917
    —Revolution, 1917-1921
 . Sovetskaia Armiia. Chekhoslovatskii Korpus, 1
 . Voenno-Morskoi Flot
  . Baltiiskii Flot
Sozialdemokratische Partei Deutschlands      D810.G6, DD231, HX274-6,
   JN3946, JN3970-1    320.530943, .943084, 335.00943, 341.242, 943.07
Spaak, Paul Henri, 1899-1972 [Belg.: For. Min.]   DH689.S6    327.493, 923.2493
Spaatz, Carl ('Tooey'), 1891-1974 [U.S.: Gen.]    UG633    358.400973

Spain
—Foreign relations
—1931-1939
—1939-1975          DP270, JX1977          946.082, 341.13946, 327.460+
—Germany
—Russia
—History
—Revolution, 1931
—Republic, 1931-1939          DP254, DP257          946.081
—Civil War, 1936-1939          DP269          946.08-081
—Causes          DP257          946.081
—Foreign participation          DP269          946.08-081
—Foreign participation, German [American, Italian, Russian, etc.]
—Foreign public opinion
—Personal narratives
—1939-1975          DP270-1          946.082
—Politics and government
—1931-1939          DP257          320.94608-081, .446081, 329.946, 946.081
—1939-1975          DP270, JN8221          320.946082, 946.081-082
Special operations (Military science)          VE153          359.9609+
Speer, Albert, 1905-1981 [Ger.: Architect, Min. of Armaments (1942-5)]
                                        DD247.S63, HC286          943.0860924, 338.0943
Speidel, Hans, 1897-?          [Ger.: Gen., anti-Hitler supporter]
Sperrle, Hugo, 1885-1953 [Ger.: Field Marshal (Luftwaffe)]
Spies          JX5121 (int'nal. law), UB270 (mil.), VB250 (naval), UB271-5
              355.34, .342-343, .34309, .3432, 940.5487+, 327.12, .1208,
              .120922, 335.343, 351.74, 364.13
Spitfire (Fighter planes)          TL685          358.43, 940.544
Springfield rifle          UD395          623.4421
Spruance, Raymond, 1886-1969 [U.S.: Vice Adm.]          V63.S68, D767
                                        940.54260924, .5450924
Spy films—Catalogs          PN1998          016.79143
Spy stories [fiction]
Stalag IV B (Mühlberg, Bad Liebenwerda, Germany: Concentration camp)
Stalag 12 D (Trier, Germany: Concentration camp)
Stalag 344 (Lambinowice, Poland: Concentration camp)
Stalag 367 (Concentration camp: Czestochowa, Poland)
Stalag Luft I (Germany: Concentration camp)
Stalag Luft 3 (Zagan, Poland: Concentration camp)
Stalin, Joseph [Iosif] ('Uncle Joe'), 1879-1953          [U.S.S.R.: Dictator, Comm. in Chief
      o/t Armed Forces]          DK268.S8, DK267, DK274, D764, D16,
                                        DS740, HX40          947.080924,
                              .08420924, .085, 940.540947, 320.9470842,
                              335.4, 355.4300924, 923.247, 951.042
Stalingrad, Battle of, 1942-1943          D764, DD247          940.542, .5421, .548243,
                                        355.3310924
—Poetry
Stamboliski, Alexander, 1879-1923          [Bulg.: Politician]          DR88.S77, D643.B6,
      HD815.S74, JN9609.A8          320.94977, 322.440924, 329.94977
Stangl, Franz, 1908?-1971          [Ger.: Treblinka concen. camp commander]
                                        D805.G3          940.54050924, .54724304355
Stark, Harold ('Betty'), 1880-1972          [U.S.: Adm., Chief of Naval Ops. (1939-42),
      Commander of U.S. naval forces in Eur. (1942-5)]
Stauffenberg, Claus von, 1907-1944          [Ger.: Col., planted bomb in attempt on
      Hitler's life]

Sten machine carbine          UF620.S8
Stettinius, Edward Reilly, 1900-1949    [U.S.: War produc. advisor, Lend Lease
                              admin., Under Sec. (1943-4) & Sec. of State (1944-5)]
                              E748, E183.7        973.9170924
Stilwell, Joseph Warren ('Vinegar Joe'), 1883-1946      [U.S.: Gen., Nat. Chinese Chief
                              of Staff (1942-4)]      E745.S68, D767.S76,
                              D767.6.S74, D769      940.54250924, 951.0420924
Stimson, Henry Lewis, 1867-1950    [U.S.: Sec. of War]      E748.S883, E183.7,
              E183.8.J3      973.90924, .910924, .917, 327.73052, 923.273
Stirling, David, 1915-?    [G.B.: Lt. Col., desert commando leader]      D766.82
                                                                940.542, .548642
Stopford, Montagu, Sir, 1892-1971 [G.B.: Gen.]
Storm (Submarine)          D784.G7      940.5451
Strategic materials
   —United States      HC110, UA23        333.80973, 355.240973, .6213, .75
Strategy        U161-3 (mil.), V160-5 (naval), UA11        355.021, .0217, .03, .4,
              .43, .4301-07, 359.43
Stream-crossing, Military      U205, UG335      623.65
Street fighting (Military science)      U167      355.426
Streicher, Julius, 1885-1946    [Ger.: Newspaper ed., Gauleiter of Franconia (till
                              1940), rabid anti-Semite]      DD247.S834,
                              DS146.G4        943.0850924, 305.8924043
Stresemann, Gustav, 1878-1929    [Ger.: Politician]      DD231.S83, DD901
                              943.085, 320.94382, 940.3141, .32443
Stuart (Destroyer)      [Australia]      D779.A9
Student, Kurt, 1890?-1978    [Ger.: Gen. (airborne infan., regular army)]
                              D757.63, UG635      940.541343, .544943
Studzianki, Poland (Kozienice), Battle of, 1944
Stuka (Bombers)        TL685-6        623.7463
Stülpnagel, Karl von, 1886-1944    [Ger.: Gen., Mil. Gov. of Fr., anti-Hitler conspir.]
Submachine guns        UF620.A2        355.82, 623.4424
Submarine boats      V858-9 (by country), VM365 (construc.), V210 (war use), V857
                      359.3257+, .325709, .92, 355.03+, 623.82, .825, .8257,
                      .82572+, .825720943 (Ger.), 940.5451
   —Bibliography      Z6834, V857-9        016.623825
   —History      V857-9, V210, VM365      359.325709, .3257209+, .83, 387.257
Submarine chasers      D590 (WWI)
Submarine disasters      VK1265      613.69
Submarine warfare      V210, VB230, JX1295        359.32, .3257, .4, .83,
                      623.825, .8257, 940.451
Sugiyama, Hajime, 1880-1945 [Japan: Gen.]
Sukarno, Achmed, Dr., 1901-1970 [Indon.: Head of Indon. Nat. Party, worked with
                              Japan most o/t war]        DS644.1.S8, DS643
                              959.8030924, 320.9598022, 991.030924
Sunda Strait, Battle of, 1942      D779      940.545994
Sunderland (Seaplanes)
Suomen Vastarintaliike        [Finn. Underground]      D802.F5
Surgery, Military      RD151-498        617.02, .99
Surgery, Naval      RD151-498
Surplus military property      UC260-5
Surplus military property, American      KF26-7        353.00713, 355.6213
Survival (after airplane accidents, shipwrecks, etc.)  TL553.7, U408, VK1259,
   VK1447, G525-40      613.69, 623.865, 629.13443, 910.091641, .09165, .453
Sutjeska River, Battle of the, 1943
Suzuki, Kantaro, 1867-1948    [Japan: Pr. Min., 5 Apr-Aug 1945]

Sveti Nikola (Concentration camp: Bulgaria)
Sweden
　—Foreign relations—1905-1950　　　DL658　　　327.485
　—History
　　　—1905-　　　　　　　　　　DL658+
　　　—Gustavus V, 1907-1950
　—Politics and government—1905-1950
Switzerland
　—History—20th century
　—Politics and government—20th century


Tacloban (Leyte Island, Philippines: Concentration camp)
Tactics　　　　　　U133, U164-5　　　355.402, .42
　—Bibliography　　　Z6724　　　016.35542
Taiwan—History—1895-1945　　　DS799　　951.24904, 320.95124904, 915.124904
Tallinn, Battle of, 1941
Tanaka, Raizo, n.d.　　　[Japan: Rear Adm.]
Tank gunnery
Tank warfare　　　　UG446, U55, D608　　　358.1809, .180904, 355.331+,
　　　　　　　　　　　　　　　　623.438, 940.412
Tanks (Military science)　　　UG446.5, UF537　　　358.18, .1809+, .180941 (GB),
　　　　　　　.180943 (Ger.), .180973 (US), 623.7475+, 355.621, .8209, .83, 356.5
　—Pictorial works
Taranto, Battle of, 1940　　　　D786　　　940.5421
Tarawa, Battle of, 1943　　　　D767　　　940.542, .5426
Taylor, Maxwell, 1901-1987　　[U.S.: Gen. (airborne)]　　E745.T317　　355.3310924
Tedder, Arthur, Sir, 1890-1967　　　[G.B.: Air Marshal, Dep. Supr. Comm. of
　　　　　　　　　　　　　　Operation Overlord]　　　D785.T4　　　940.544
Telephone—Defense measures
Telescopic sights
Terauchi, Hisaichi, 1879-1945 [Japan: Field Marshal]
Terezin (Czechoslovakia: Concentration camp)
Ternopol (City)—Siege, 1944　　　D764.7.T43
Terrain study (Military science)
Texas (Battleship)　　　　VA65　　　623.82520973
Theater in propaganda
Theater of war
Thompson submachine gun　　　UF620　　　623.4424, 683.4
Thunderbolt (Fighter planes)　　[A.k.a. P-47]　　　TL686.R42 (Republic Co.), UG1242
　　　　　　　　　　　　　　　　623.7464, 358.43
Tibbets, Paul, 1915-　　　[U.S.: Col. (Air Corps), trained atom bomb pilots & flew
　　　　　　　　　　'Enola Gay' on 6 Aug. 1945 over Hiroshima]
　　　　　　　　　　UG626.2.T5　　　940.5449730924
Tiger (Tank)
Tikhvin, Battles of, 1941
Timoshenko, Semyon, 1895-1970　[U.S.S.R.: Marshal]　　DK268.T5　　　923.547
Tinian Island
Tirpitz (Battleship)　　　D772.T5　　　940.5421, .544942, .545
Tiso, Joseph, 1887-1946 [Slovakia: Pres.]　　　DB2821.T57
Tito, Josip Broz, 1892-1980　　[Yug.: Marshal]　　　DR359.T5, DR367.R9, DR370,
　　　　　　　　　　　DR1300, D754, D766.6, D802.Y8　　　949.7020924,
　　　　　　　　　　　940.53497, .542, 327.4970947, 923.1497, .5497
Tizard, Henry Thomas, Sir, 1885-1959　[G.B.: Radar scientist, tech. advisor]
　　　　　　　　　　　Q143.T5, Q127, Q127.G4　　　506.9, 925
Tobruk, Battles of, 1941-1942　　　D766-7　　　940.5423

Togo, Shigenori, 1882-1950    [Japan: For. Min.]    DS886, D742.J3    952.033,
                                                                      940.5352
Tojo, Hideki, 1884-1948    [Japan: Pr. Min. (1941-4)]    DS888.5.T5995,
              DS890.T57, DS890, D804.J    952.030924, .0330924, 940.53452
Tokushima (Japan)—Bombardment, 1945
Tokyo
    —Bombardment, 1942    D790    940.5441-2
    —History    DS896-7    952.135
Tokyo Rose, 1916-    [Also 'Iva Ikuko Toguri d'Aquino': Japan, U.S.: Radio
    propagandist]    CT275.T717    940.54889520924
Torpedo-boat destroyers
Torpedo-boats    V830-8    359.32, .3254, 359.83, 940.5459+
Torpedo bombers
Torpedoes    V850-5    359.4, .82
Totalitarianism    JC481, JC233    320.53-533, 321.6-6082, .64, .9, 335.4-6
Tovey, John, Sir, 1885-1971    [G.B.: Adm.]
Toyoda, Soemu, 1885-1957    [Japan: Adm., Combined Navy Chief (1943-5)]
                                                                      DS885.5.T62
Trading with the enemy    JX5270-1    341.3, 343.73087
    —History—20th century
Transportation and state    HE148-51, HE193    350.87, 380.5, 388.109+
Transportation, Military    UC270-360, UH500-505 (med.), VC550-5    355.27,
                                .341, .8309+, 623.746
    —Cold weather conditions
Treason    HV6275, JC328 (polit. theory)    364.13
    —France
    —Germany
    —Great Britain    343.41
    —South Africa
    —United States    KF9392, E179    343.3, 345.73023108, 351.74, 364.131
Treaties    JX4161-71, JX120-191 (collections), JX235-6, JX351-1195, JA40
              341.026, .2, .273, .2016
    —Catalogs
    —Collections
Treaty of Trianon (1920)    D643.H9
Trench mortars
Trenchard, Hugh Montague, 1873-1956 [G.B.: Air Marshal, R.A.F. founder before
    WWII]                                    DA89.6.T7    923.542
Trepper, Leopold, 1904-? [Pol.: Soviet spy in Belg.]
                        D810.S8    940.54860924, .548647
Trials (Crimes against humanity)
Trials (Genocide)
Trials (Military offenses)    355.1332+
Trials (Naval offenses)
Trials (Political crimes and offenses)    KF221 (US)    345.730231 (US),
                                .47023 (Russia), .023
Trianon, Treaty of, June 4, 1920
Trianon, Treaty of, June 4, 1920 (Hungary)    D651.H7, D643    940.3141-3142
Trieste
    —History    DB321    943.68
    —Politics and government    DB321, DG975    320.945393, 327.450497
Trigger (Submarine)    D783.5.T5-7    940.5451
Troina, Sicily, Battle of, 1943
Trophies, Military

Trotsky, Leon, 1879-1940    [A.k.a. 'Trotskii, Lev': Rus.: Politician]
       DK254.T6, DK265, HC335, HX312       947.083, .0840924, 327.47,
       330.947084, 335.433, 345.470231, 347.9947, 349.4704, 923.247
Trowbridge, Ernest Charles Thomas, 1862-1926   [G.B.: Adm.]      DA565.T7, D580
Truk Island
Truman, Harry S, 1884-1972    [U.S.: Pres.]     E813-15, E176.1, E742.5.T6, E806,
                       HD7293, HD8072, JC599, JK558            973.9180924,
                       301.540973, 323.40973, 329.023, 917.3039, 923.173, .573
Tula, Russia—Siege, 1941
Tule Lake Relocation Center (Calif.)
Tunisia—History—French occupation, 1881-1956       DT264       961.1
Tupolev, Andrey, 1888-1972   [U.S.S.R.: Gen., aircraft engineer]
Turkey
    —Foreign relations
         —Europe
         —Germany
         —Great Britain       DR562       327.4961042
    —History—1918-1960       DR590-2       956.102, 915.61033
    —Politics and government
         —1918-1960       DR590       320.956103
Turner, Richmond Kelly, 1885-1961    [U.S.: Adm.]
Turret ships       V860
Twentieth century       CB425-7 (civiliz.), D401-725 (hist.), D421, D840
                       940.5, 914.035, 901.904, .94, .946, 909.82, 301.24
Twentieth Century Fund. Labor Committee       HD8072       331.0973

U-505 (Submarine)       D782.U12       940.5451
U-977 (Submarine)       D782.U2       940.54512
Udet, Ernst, 1896-1941  [Ger.: Lt. Gen., Luftwaffe tech. chief]      TL540.U3
                                                           940.449430924
Ukraine
    —History       DK508       947.7, .71
         —German occupation, 1941-1944       D764       947.7
Ukrainska Nationlna Armiia       D764.7.U5
Ukraïnska Povstanska Armiia       D802.U4       940.534771
Ulithi, Caroline Islands       DU568.U5       996.6, 919.66
Ultrasonic waves—Military applications
Umezu, Yoshijiro, 1880-1949   [Japan: Gen.]
Underwater demolition teams
Unified operations (Military science)   U260 (jt. ops. of one nation's service branches)
Uniforms, Military       UC480-5, UA712, UE445, VC300       355.14, .1409+,
                                          .14094, .81, 357.1, 359.14094
Union des Femmes Français       D802.F8
United Nations—History       JX1976-7       341.1309, .23, .2309+

448

United States  E, F1-975+  973-9, 917.3
. Adjutant-general's Office  UB173  355.61
—Air defenses, Military  UG633  355.033573, .34320973, .621,
    358.1740973, .403, .4030973, .41450973
. Air Force
 . 8th Air Force  D757  940.544973
 . Historical Division
 —History  UG633  358.40973, .4130973, .4030973
. American Battle Monuments Commission  D528, D570.3, D639  940.41273
. American Commission for the Protection and Salvage of Artistic and Historic
  Monuments in War Areas  D810.A7  940.53187
. American Relief Administration  D637-8, HC335  940.477873, 361.550947
. Armed Services Board of Contract Appeals
—Appropriations and expenditures, 1942 [1943, etc.]  HJ10, HJ2050-2052,
    HC101  336.390973, 338.4750050973, 353.00722
—Archival resources
—Armed Forces  UA23  355.00973, .033073, .30973, 343.73012-73013
 —Afro-Americans  E185  355.3, 323.1196073
 —Airborne troops  UD483
 —Appropriations and expenditures  UA17-24, UC263  355.033573,
        .62120973
 —Barracks and quarters  U15, UC403  355.129, .67, .710973
 —Biography  U52  355.30922-30924, .330922
 —Chaplains
 —Documents
 —Firearms
 —Flags  UC593
 —Foreign countries  355.033273, .1334, .346
 —Fuel  UC263  355.6212, .83
 —Gays—History—20th century  D769.2  940.54097308664
 —Handbooks, manuals, etc.  U113  355.0973, 640.42024355
 —Leaves and furloughs  UB423  355.64, 343.73013
 —Medals, badges, decorations, etc.  UC533, UB433  355.134
 —Messes  UC723  355.65
 —Military police
 —Negroes  D810, E185, U53  940.5403, 355.022, .3320924,
    .5403, 301.4444, .451
 —Nurses
 —Officers  UB147  301.5930973
 —Officers' clubs  U56-7
 —Officers' handbooks  U133, UB210  355.3320973, 332.024024355
 —Organization  UA23, UB23  353.6, 355.0973, .3
 —Parachute troops  UD483
 —Pay, allowances, etc.  UC73-4  331.281355640973,
    343.73012-73013, 355.1156, .1350973, .640973
 —Procurement  UC260-7, UF880  355.6210973, .6211-
    62120973, .82, 338.476234, 339.373, 343.73025
 —Records and correspondence  UB163  355.114
 —Recruiting, enlistment, etc.
  —World War, 1939-1945  UB344  355.22
 —Registers of dead  E181
 —Reserves  UA42  355.370973, 343.73012-73013
 —Uniforms  UC483  355.140973
 —Warrant officers  UB408
 —Women  UB147, UB323  355.0023, .348, 331.48135500973

United States
. Army        U716, UA22-7        355.00973, .033573, .10973, .30973
    . 12th
    —Afro-American troops    [SEE ALSO '...—Negro troops']    D639, E185
                917.80696, 355.330973, .61330973, 356.110973
    . Air Corps    UG633, D606, E745        358.400973, .413320924,
                940.44973, 973.913
    . Army Air Forces    UG633, UG1242, D790        358.4, .4030973, .4140973,
                940.544973
            . 5th Air Force    D785, D790        940.544973
            . 9th Air Force
            . Air Force, 14th    D790    940.544973
            . Air Transport Command    D810.T8    940.5441
            . 312th Bombardment Group    D790    940.5441
            . 885th Bombardment Squadron
            . 5th Fighter Command    D790    940.544973
            . 325th Fighter Group    D790    940.5423
            . Mediterranean Theater of Operations
            —Periodicals
            . Weather Division
    . Army
        —Airborne troops        D769.345-346, UD483        940.544973
        —Ambulances    UH503
        . Americal Division            D769        940.542
        . American Forces in Germany, 1918-1923        D650.M5
        —Anecdotes, facetiae, satire, etc.
. Army and Navy Munitions Board. Industrial Mobilization Plan    UA23, HB195
                355.20973
    . Army
        . 102d Antiaircraft Artillery Battalion    D769.343.102d    940.541273
        . 535th Anti-Aircraft Artillery Battalion    D769.343.535th    940.544973
        —Appointments and retirements    UB413
        —Appropriations and expenditures    UA24.A7, UA25    353.62
        . 1st Armored Division    D769    940.541273
        . 6th Armored Division    D769    940.544973
        . 10th Armored Division    D769    940.542
        . Armored Force    UA30    358.180973
        . 67th Armored Regiment    D769.3055.67th
        —Armored troops
        . First Army    D570.2, D763    940.41273, .53493
        . 2d Army
        . Third Army    D762.26.3d, D769    940.5421
        . Fifth Army    D769.26.5th, D763.I8    940.542
        . Eighth Army    D767.4, D769.26.8th, UG465    940.542, .541273
        . Artillery    UA32-3, UF23, UF153    358.10973, 356.4
            —Drill and tactics    UE160
        —Aviation    [Generally for period after 1947 when U.S. Air Force was
                formed. SEE 'U.S. Army Air Forces' for many titles before that]
                UG633, TL712-16    355.621, .62130973,
                358.400973, .4183, 623.746
        —Barracks and quarters    UC403-4    355.6220973
        . Biarritz American University    D810.E45
        —Bibliography    Z6725    016.35560973, .940540973
        —Biography    E181, E840.5.A-Z, U11, U52    355.30922, .330973

United States
. Army
—Mobilization          UA913          355.280973
—Negro troops   [SEE ALSO '...Afro-Am. troops']     D639, E185, U21
                                940.403, 917.80696, 355.00917496, .30978,
                                .330973, .61330973, 356.110973
—Non-commissioned officers     UB210          355.547
—Officers          UB412-14, UB210     355.0023, .33, .332019,
                                301.1543355332
—Officers' handbooks          U133     355.02, 356.3
—Ordnance and ordnance stores          UF523-63, UF753, U897
                    355.830973, .820973, 343.73025, 623.40973, .440973
—Organization          UA23-33          355.00973, .3
—Parachute troops          D769.347, UD483          356.1660973
—Pay, allowances, etc.     UC70-5, UB403     355.135, .640973
—Physical training          U323, U408
—Pictorial works
—Political activity
—Postal service
—Prisons          KF7675          355.71
—Procurement          UC263-7, UF780          355.62120973, .82, 358.18,
                                .4183, 338.43641371, 343.73013
—Promotions          UB412-14
. 1st Ranger Battalion          D769          940.541273
. Ranger Battalion, 4th
—Records and correspondence     UB163          355.61
—Recruiting, enlistment, etc.     UB323, UB343, UB147, U15     355.220973
          —European War, 1914-1918
          —World War, 1939-1945          UB323          355.22
. Regimental Combat Team, 442nd   [Jpns.-Am's.]
—Registers          U11          940.41273
—Registers of dead          E181
—Regulations          UB501-2, KF7305          355.1
. Reserve Officers' Training Corps     U428     355.2232, .37
—Sanitary affairs          UH223
—Security measures
—Service clubs
United States Army Service Forces
          . Special Service Division
United States Army Service Schools, Fort Leavenworth, Kan. Dept. of
          Military Art   [WWII]
United States
. Army
. Signal Corps     UG573          358.240973
—Signaling     UG573
—Ski troops
—Social services     UH755
—Songs and music     M1629-30
—Sports
—Staffs          UB223          355.330973
—Statistics          UA23-4, D797.U
—Supplies and stores     UC263-7          355.3410973, .6210973,
                                .6212, .80973, 658.78
. Surgeon General's Office
—Surgeons          UH223

452

United States
    . Army
        . 761st Tank Battalion        D769.306.761st
        —Target practice        UD333
        —Test shooting  [Gunnery]        UF810
        —Transport service        UC273        353.62
        —Transportation        UC273, UC333        355.83
        . Transportation Corps        UC323, D769.U        358.250973, 940.541273
        —Uniforms        UC483, UC493        355.14094, .140973
            —Catalogs
        —History        UC483, UC523        355.140973, .140977656, .310973
United States Army War College, Washington, D.C.
        [SEE `ALSO 'Army War College (U.S.)')']
United States
    . Army
        . Western Defense Command and Fourth Army        D769.8        940.547273
        . Women's Army Corps        UA565.W6, D759.U, D769        355.348,
                        940.548173
        —Bibliography        Z1215, Z1236-7        016.917303, .973
        —Bio-bibliography        Z1224
        —Biography        E176, E178, E184, E187, E747, CT215-20        920.073,
                973.0922, 320.0922
            —Bibliography        Z5305        016.920073
            —Dictionaries        E176        920.073
            —Indexes
        —Portraits        E813, N7593, ND1337        920.073, 759.13, 704.9420973
    . Bureau of Aeronautics (Navy Dept.)
    . Bureau of Construction and Repair        [Navy]
    . Bureau of Insular Affairs
    . Bureau of Labor Statistics
    . Bureau of Manpower Utilization
    . Bureau of Naval Personnel
    . Bureau of Naval Weapons
    . Bureau of Ships        [Navy]
    . Bureau of Veterans' Reemployment Rights
    . Bureau of War Risk Insurance
    . Bureau of War Risk Litigation
    . Bureau of Yards and Docks        [Navy]
    . Cadet Nurse Corps
    . Central Intelligence Agency—Officials and employees—Biography
    . Chemical Warfare Service
    —Civil defense        UA927-9        355.232, 353.007232, 363.340973, .350973
    —Civilization
        —1865-1918        E168-9        917.3037-3039, .303911, 301.2973,
                309.173089
        —1918-1945        E169, E806        973.91, .916, 917.30316, .30391+,
                .303916-303917, 309.173
    —Claims        JX238 (int'nal.)        342.73088, 347.7328
    —Claims against Germany        JX238.G
    —Claims against Great Britain
    . Claims Board (War Dept.)
    —Claims vs. Yugoslavia

United States
  —Coast defenses           UG410-12    355.45
  . Coast Guard           VG53, D773      359.970973, 343.7301997, 344.73053,
                                        614.864, 940.545973
  . Coast Guard Reserve. Women's Reserve   ['SPARS']
  . Command and General Staff School, Fort Leavenworth
  —Commerce
      —France
      —Germany
      —Great Britain
      —History           HF3021-3031, HF3003-7, HF3155      330.973,
                              338.0973, .9141073, 380.10973, 381.0973
      —Japan           HF3127        382.0973052, .0952073
  —Commercial policy      HF1455-6, HF1731, HF1756, HF3008, HF3025
                              337.9173, 338.973, 343.7308, 380.130973,
                                  381.0973, 382.06373, .0973+, .30973, .3973
  —Commercial treaties      HF1731-2      337.9173, 341.57
  . Commission to Investigate and Report the Facts Relating to the Attack Made by
      the Japanese Armed Forces upon Pearl Harbor in the Territory of Hawaii on
      December 7, 1941
  . Committee on Public Information      D632      940.488673
  . Congress      JK516, JK570, JK1021      320.97309+, 328.7309, 353.032
    . House          JK1316, JK1323 yr.      328.730+
      . Committee on Military Affairs
      . Committee on Naval Affairs
      . Select Committee Investigating National Defense Migration
      . Special Committee on Un-American Activities
    . Joint Committee on the Investigation of the Pearl Harbor Attack    D767.92
    . Senate         JK1158-70+      327.730+, 328.3690973, .730+, .739
      . Committee on Military Affairs
      . Special Committee Investigating the National Defense Program
                [The Truman Committee]      UA23      328.345
      . Special Committee to Investigate the Munitions Industry      328.345
  . Consulate. Paris
  . Council of National Defense
    . Advisory Comission
    . Committee on Women's Defense Work
    . Dept. of Food Production and Home Economics
    . Field Division. Child Conservation Section
    . General Munitions Board
    . Munitions Standards Board
  —Curiosa      E179      917.30302
  —Defenses      UA23      355.02130973, .033273, .033573, .6220973,
                        358.4030973, 327.730599, 353.00895, .60924
  . Department of State      JK851, JX1293, JX1417, JX1428, JX1705-6
                          327.072073, .6073, .73, 353.00712, .007232
    . Historical Office
    —History
    . Office of Public Affairs
    —Records and correspondence
  . Department of the Army
    . General Staff—History      UB200    355.3310973
    . Office of Military History      D570    940.41273

United States
  —Diplomatic and consular service    JX1705-6, JK851      327.20973,
                                      341.70973, 353.00892, 355.033573
    —Germany
    —Great Britain
    —Italy
    —Japan
    —Russia
  —Economic conditions
    —1865-1918        E661, HC105-6, HD8051       917.3038, 330.97308,
                        .9730913, 309.17308, 333.70973, 339.20973
    —1918-1945        HC106.3-4, HC101, E801     330.973091,
                        339.20973, 309.1730917
  —Economic policy—1933-1945      HC106, HG538       330.9730917,
                        332.4973, 338.973, 309.1730917, 973.917
. Embassy
  . Germany
  . Great Britain
  . Japan
  . Russia
  . Soviet Union
  —Emigration and immigration      JV6403-7127, E158, E184     325.7309,
                      301.3230973, .32845073, .32847073, .4534073,
                      331.880973, 917.30356, .309749162
. Employment Service      HC101, HD5873-5      330.973,
                      331.1106173, .110973, .13770973, 353.008485
  —Executive departments      JK631-821      328.7307+, 342.730602+,
                      .73064, 353.0002-0003, .00722, .008236, .01-09
    —Records and correspondence      CD3030-3041, KF5101
                      342.73066, 353.0372
. Federal Bureau of Investigation      E743, HV6791, HV7914, HV8138-47
                      344.730523, 345.730231, 353.0074,
                      364.1206173, .120924, .120973, .1320973, .973
. Food Administration      D637      940.477873
. Foreign Claims Settlement Commission  [WWII]      KF27      341.55,
                      353.00892
  —Foreign economic relations      HF1455-6, HF73, HC106     330.973,
                      337.9173, 338.9173, .973, 343.73+,
                      353.008, 382.0973, .10973
    —Germany      HF1456      338.9173043, 382.0973043
    —Great Britain      382.0973042
    —Japan      HF1456      338.9173052, 382.0973052
    —Russia
  —Foreign relations      JX1405-28, JX1971, JX1987, E183, E713     320.973,
                      341.2373, 343.73+, 909.82
    —20th century      JX1416-17, JX1916, D413, D570, E173, E744-8, E840
                      327.062073, .20973, .730+, 330.973, 973.92+
    —1933-1945      1416, E173, E742-8, E806-7, E813     327.20924,
                      309.173092, 940.532273, 973.90924, .917
    —Germany      E183, E748      327.73043, .43073, .9613, 943.086,
                      973.917+
    —Great Britain      E183, E664      327.73041-2, .42073
    —Italy      327.73045
    —Japan      E183, DS518, JX233      327.73052, .52073, .5073,
                      301.15439152, 940.5312

United States
—Foreign relations
    —Law and legislation    KF4650-1    328.730765, 342.7306-73064,
        353.00892
    —Russia    E173, E183, E744, E748, JX1974-81, D651, DK69
        327.73047, .47073
    —Speeches in Congress    E173 (collections)
    —Treaties    JX570-3, JX235-6 (texts), JX1407    341.273,
        .762026, .7304, 328.7307+
. General Staff
—Government publications    Z1223 (bibliog.), Z208, Z695, Z7164    015.73,
    016320973, .01573, .309173, .320973, .32873
—Historical geography—Maps
—History    E, F1-975+ (local), E178    973+, 974-9 (local)
    —20th century    E740-2, E173    973.9, .9082, .91, .916
    —1901-1953    E740-1, E766    973.9, .91, .913
    —1913-1921    E766, E780    973.91, .913
    —1919-1963    E784    973.913
    —1919-1933    E741, E784-91, E806    973.91, .914-15, .917,
        .9108, 917.303915, 309.173091
      —Sources    E743, E784-5, E791    973.9108, .914-17
    —1933-1945    E741, E806, E173    973.91, .917,
        917.30391708, .30392, 309.1730917
      —Miscellanea    E806    973.91708
      —Pictorial works    NE1336    769.924
      —Sources    E806, J82    973.91708, 353.035, 320.973, 309.173
    —Addresses, essays, lectures
    —Anecdotes, facetiae, satire, etc.    E178-9    973.08, 917.30308
    —Bibliography    Z1215, Z1236, Z8462    016.9173, .917303
      —Catalogs
    —Chronology    E174.5    973.0202, .03
—History, Comic, satirical, etc.    E178.4, NC1427    973.0207, 741.5973
—History
    —Dictionaries    E174, E18    973.03, 917.30303
    —Fiction
    —Historiography    E175    973.07
—History, Local    E175, E180, F1-970    974-9, 917.303
—History, Military    E181, E183, U133    355.420973, 357.10924, 923.573
    —20th century    E745, E840    901.9
    —Bibliography    Z1249    016.355
    —Chronology    E181    355.00973
—History, Naval    E182, E746, VA58-63    359.00973, .0973, .310973,
        .325, 387.20973
    —20th century    E746-8, E182    359.009, .3310924
    —Bibliography    Z6835    016.35900973, .35930973
    —Sources    E182    359.332+
      —Bibliography—Catalogs    Z1249, Z6616, Z6835
      016.3593310924, .359, .35900973
—History
    —Philosophy    E175.9, E179    973.01, .04, .072, 917.303013
    —Sources    E173, E178, E183    973.08, .082, .908, 917.303,
        .30308, 320.973
      —Bibliography    Z1236, Z6616, CD3027, CD3049    016.9739,
      .917303, .301450973
    —Directories    E175    973.02573

United States
  . International Claims Commission  [WWII]
  . Joint Army-Navy Assessment Committee
  . Mare Island Naval Shipyard, Vallejo, Calif.    VA70.M3
  . Marine Corps      UB210, UG632, VE23, VE422, D570, D767, D769, D821,
                  TL685           359.96, .9609, .960973, 629.1339,
                      940.45973, .5412730952, .5426, .544973, .545
    . Attack Squadron 223—History       D790
    . Aviation—History      VG93, UG633        358.41830973
    —Biography        E182       359.960973, 923.573
    . 1st Division      D767, DS918, DS557      940.541273, 951.9042, 959.704
    . 3d Division      D769.37.3d
    . Division, 4th
    —History      VE23, VE21-3, E746, D767      359.960973, 940.5426
        —Anecdotes      VE500      359.960973
        —World War, 1914-1918
        —World War, 1939-1945      D769      940.541273
    . History and Museums Division
    —Insignia      VE403
    —Medals, badges, decorations, etc.    VE23
    —Military life      VE23      359.96
    . 3d Regiment      D767.98, VE23.25.4th      940.542, 359.96
United States Marine Corps Reserve      VE23.3      359.960973
United States
  . Marine Corps
    —Target-practice      VE333
    —Uniforms      VE403, UC483      359.960973, 355.14, 646.47
    —Women
United States Marine Corps Women's Reserve      UA565.W6      940.541273
United States Marine Fighter Squadron 214  ['Black Sheep']      D790
United States Military Academy, West Point      U408-10
    —Biography      U410      355.0071174731
    —History      U410, U408      355.0071173, .0071174731, .02130973
    . Library
    —Registers
    —Songs and music
United States Military Mission to Russia
United States
  —Military policy      UA23, UA25, UA646, V63, VE23      355.033073,
                  .0330973, .0335182, .033573, .0973, .430973, .820973,
             .02130973, 358.4030973, 359.960973, 327.1740973, .10973
    —Bibliography      Z1215, KF7201      016.3550330973
    —Case studies      UA23      355.033573
    —History      UA23, UA25      355.00973, .033573
    —Militia      UA42      355.35
    . National Archives      CD3028, E179      016.6314, .911777, .91273, 344.73092
    —National Guard      UA42-3, U230      355.3510973, .370973, .4260973, .54,
                  343.73013
    —National security      UA23, JK1051      355.033073, .033573, 328.7307412
    . National War College      355.622, .0711753
    . National War Labor Board      [1942-5]

United States Naval Academy, Annapolis      V415
United States Naval Academy (Annapolis)
    . Alumni Association
    —Buildings
    . Dept. of Engineering and Aeronautics
    . Dept. of Seamanship and Navigation
    —Examinations      V415      359.071175256, 355.071173
    —History      V415, U408
    . Library
    . Museum
    —Registers
    —Songs and music
    .Trident Society
United States Naval Air Station, Pensacola, Fla.      VA70.P44
United States
    . Naval Flying Corps—History      VG93      358.400973
    . Naval History Division. Operational Archives      CD3034      016.940545973
United States Naval Hospital, Norfolk, Va.      VG425.N6
United States Naval Institute, Annapolis
United States Naval Medical Research Institute, Bethesda, Md.
United States Naval Medical School, Bethesda, Md.
United States—Naval militia      VA80
United States Naval Observatory      QB82, Z5156      353.00855
United States Naval Photographic Interpretation Center
United States Naval Postgraduate School, Monterey, Calif.
United States Naval Research Laboratory, Washington, D.C.
United States Naval Reserve      VA80      359.370973
    —Registers
    . Women's Reserve      UA565.W6      355.34
United States Naval Training Station, San Diego, Calif.
United States
    . Navy      V25, V133, V399, V736, V825, V858, V874-80, VA49-58, VB23,
             VM470      359, 359.00973, .030973, .12920973,
             .32520973, .32540973, .32620973, .830973, 623.8250973, .8257,
             .8433, 940.545973
        —Accounting      VC503      359.6223
        —Afro-Americans      [SEE ALSO '...—Negroes']      VB853      359.1332
        —Airmen
        . 7th Amphibious Force      D769.52.7th      940.5426
        —Anecdotes, facetiae, satire, etc.      E182, V736      359.00973, .10973
        —Appropriations and expenditures      VA53, V858      359.83, 343.73013
        —Artificers' handbooks      VG603      535.33
        . Asiatic Fleet      VA63.A78      359.310973
        . Atlantic Fleet      D770, VA63      940.545973, 359.310973
        —Aviation      VG93, TL685, TL721      358.400973, .41, .4183,
                 .4140973, 623.4519, .74607, .7460973, .74640973, 629.130911
            —Job descriptions
        —Aviation electricians      VG93      629.143, .1354
        —Aviation machinists      VG93      623.746, 629.134352
        —Aviation supplies and stores      VG93      355.62120973,
                 358.41621, 359.62120973, 623.746, 629.13443
        —Barracks and quarters      VC423

United States
. Navy
—Bibliography       Z6835, E182        016.35930973, .35900973
—Biography         E182, V23, V62-3     359.310922, .3310922,
                                      .3320922, 923.573
  —Dictionaries
—Boats         V880
—Boatswains        VG953       623.825
—Boatswain's mates
. Bombing squadron 109      D790      940.544
. Chaplain Corps       VG23
. Civil Engineer Corps
—Communication systems    VG77, V283      359.983, 623.8560973
—Congresses
. Construction battalions  [Seabees]    VG597, D769.55     359.982
    —Handbooks, manuals, etc.    VG597
—Demobilization
. Navy Department
     —Appropriations and expenditures
       . Board on Regular and Reserve Aviation Personnel of the Navy and
          Marine Corps
     . Board on Submarine, Destroyer, Mine, and Naval Air Bases
     —History        VB23
     . Office of Industrial Relations
     . Office of Public Relations
     —Officials and employees    VB183
     —Personnel management
. Navy
  . Destroyer Forces        D773      940.545973
  . Destroyer Squadron 23     D769      940.545973
  —Drill manuals      VD160 (seamen), VE160 (Marines), VF160 (ordnance)
  —Engineering aids    VG923      526.9024359
  . Escort Carrier Force     D769.52.E7
  —Examinations      V411, VB273      359.0076, .338076, 371.2640715
  —Facilities
  —Fast Carrier Task Force    V874      359.32550973
  —Fiction
  —Field Service     V175
  —Finance     VA60      359.620973
  —Firearms     VF23 (ordnance), VF353-420, VD363-90 (small arms)
               623.440973, .442
  —Firing regulations      VD333
  —Flags
  . 3d Fleet      D767     940.545973
  . 7th Fleet     V179     359.6210973
  . 10th Fleet
  —Flight officers
  —Fuel     VC276.A47    338.82, 359.83
  —Gunners
  —Gunner's mates
  —Handbooks, manuals, etc.     V113, V123, V133, V143 (officers,
              seamen, etc.), V310 (ceremonies), VA55, VB200, VM605
              359.00202, 623.872

United States
  . Navy
      —History          E182, V767, V833, V874, VA55-8, VB23, D773, E746
                        359.30973, .310973, .32550973, .3320924, .370973,
                        .621, 623.82530973, 940.542, .545973, 973.75
          —Addresses, essays, lectures          VA58    359.070973
          —Bibliography          Z6835          016.35900973
          —World War, 1914-1918
          —World War, 1939-1945
  . Hospital Corps          VG320          359.3450973
      —Hospital Corps—Drill regulations          VG320          359.34, 610.2
      —Illustrations          VA59          359.3250973
      —Indians
      —Insignia          VC345, UC530-3
      —Job descriptions          VB258
  . Judge Advocate General's Corps          KF26          332.6323
      —Lawyers
      —Lists of vessels          VA61          359.32, .320973, .3250973
      —Management          VB203, VG593, VK1474, VM147          359.31, .621,
                        .9820973
      —Maneuvers          V245, V169, VK597          359.5
      —Medals, badges, decorations, etc.          VB333 (medals, decorations),
              VC345 (badges, insignia), UB433, UC533-5, CR4651          355.134
  . Medical Corps          VG425
  . Medical Dept.          VG123, R847, D807.U6          359.3450973, 610.71073
      —Messes          VC383
      —Military construction operations          VA68          341.725
  . Mobile base hospital no. 3          D807.U6-8+          940.547673
  . Motor Torpedo Boat Squadrons          D773, V833          940.545, 359.83
      —Negroes          [SEE ALSO '...—Afro-Americans']          E185, D810
                        325.260973, 940.54516
      —Officers          VB313-14, VB203, UA23          359.3320973, 353.00895,
                        343.73019
          —Classification          VB313          359.332
          —Correspondence, reminiscences, etc.
      —Officers' handbooks          V133, VM600          359.00973, .02, .31, .33, 623.87
      —Ordnance and ordnance stores          VF353-420, VF580, VF160, VF850
                        359.82, .820973, 353.00711, 623.4519
      —Ordnance facilities          VF383
      —Organization
      —Pacific cruise, 1907-1909
  . Pacific Fleet
  . Pacific Fleet and Pacific Ocean areas
  . Pacific Fleet. Submarine Force. U.S. submarine losses, World War II
                        D783.U
      —Painting of vessels          V980
      —Pay, allowances, etc.          VC50-65, UC74          355.135, .64, 353.007232,
                        343.73013
      —Periodicals
      —Personnel management          VB258, VB313          359.341, .61330973
      —Petty officers          V398, VD430, VM147          359.002854, .3380973
      —Petty officers' handbooks          V123          359.00973, .30973, .3380973
      —Physical training          V263          355.12, 358.407, 371.74, 796.4
      —Pictorial works          VA59          359.3250973
      —Postal service          VG63          359.6133

United States Navy Preflight School, St. Mary's College    VG94.5.S
United States. Navy
    —Prisons and prison-ships    VB893
    —Procurement    VC260-7, V214, VG93, VK1474, VM300
            359.6211, .62120973, .82-3, .85, 658.56, 353.007232, 358.4183
    —Promotions    VB313-14
    —Provisioning    VC353, VC373, VC383    359.371, .81, 642.5
    —Public relations    VG503
    —Radarmen    VG77
    —Radiomen    VG77
    —Records and correspondence    VB255, V252, UB163    353.7, 623.746
    —Recruiting, enlistment, etc.    VB263, VB273, UB343    359.22
        —History
        —World War, 1939-1945
    —Registers    V11.U    359.3320973
    —Regulations    VB363, VB793, VB803, KF7345-75    359.13+
    —Religious life
    —Reserve fleets    VA53    353.00895
    —Safety measures    V383
    —Sanitary affairs    VG123, VG463    359.34, 616.98024
    —Sea life    V736, E182    359.332, .345, .98
    —Seamen's handbooks    V113, VD403, VK541
    —Search and rescue operations
    —Service craft
    . Service Squadron 10    D769.537.10th    940.541273
    —Shore patrol    VB923
    —Signaling    V283, V113, VD403, VM493
    —Small-boat service    V113, VD403, VF160
    —Social services
    —Songs and music    M1629-30, PS595
    —Staff corps    VB23
    —Stewards
    . Submarine Forces    V63, D783    359.325709+, 940.5451373
    —Supplies and stores    VC263, VC273    359.341, .3410973,
            .62120973, 353.7, 355.26, 940.5373
    —Surgeons    VG263
    —Target-practice    VF313
    . Task Force 39    D769.53.39th    940.545
    . Task Force 58    D790
    . Torpedo Squadron 8    D790    940.544
    —Tradevmen
    —Transport service    VC553, UC323, D570.72    359.982
    —Transportation    VC553
    —Trails of vessels    VM880-1
    . Underwater Demolition Teams    VG87, D780    359.98, 940.545973
    —Uniforms    VC303, UC483    359.140973, 355.14
    . VF10 Fighter Squadron    D790    940.544
    —Warrant officers
    —Watch duty    V133    359.332
    —Weapons systems    VF347, VG93    358.43, 623.4
United States Navy Yard, Pensacola—History    VA70.P44    359.70975999
United States. Navy—Yeomen    VG903    359.0023

United States
  —Neutrality                    D619, JX1412-16 (int'nal. law), E768          940.32, .373,
                                 .5373, 327.20924, .73, 341.64
. Office for Emergency Management
. Office of Air Force History      D790       940.544973
. Office of Alien Property
. Office of Censorship
. Office of Defense Transportation            HE206
. Office of High Commissioner for Austria
. Office of High Commissioner for Germany
    . Foreign Relations Division
    . Historical Division
. Office of Inter-American Affairs
. Office of Lend-lease Administration          D753       940.5373
. Office of Naval Intelligence                 D810.S8    940.548673
. Office of Naval Operations
. Office of Naval Records and Library
. Office of Naval Research
. Office of Price Administration               HB236.4       338.52606173
. Office of Production Management
. Office of Strategic Services                 D810.S7-8, D802, UB271          940.548673,
                                               .5344, .5485

          —History
          . Research and Analysis Branch
. Office of War Claims Arbiter Under Settlement of War Claims Act of 1928
. Office of War Information
          . Bureau of Overseas Intelligence
          . Bureau of Special Services
          . Foreign Morale Analysis Division
. Office of War Mobilization                   HC106.4       338.91
. Office of War Mobilization and Reconversion  HC106         338.973
. Philippine War Damage Commission
—Politics and government
     —1865-1933                  E660-4, E743, JA84          973.80924, .910924,
                                 320.97308, 328.73071
     —20th century               D743, E742-8, JK261-73, JK411-21, E802, E839
                                 973.9082, .91, .91504, .90924, 320.973, 329.020973,
                                 338.973, 342.739, 923.273, 917.3039,
                                 320.97309, .5130973
     —1901-1953                  E743-8        973.91, 923.273
     —1901-1943                  E748          328.730924
     —1913-1921                  E660, E748, E766-7, E780, E802, JK271, JK1161
                                 973.91, .913, 320.9730913, 328.73071
     —1919-1933                  E743, E784       320.9730915, 973.915
     —1921-1923
     —1923-1929
     —1929-1933

United States
  . War Ballot Commission
  . War Claims Commission   [WWII]
  . War Department          UB23        353.62
    —Appropriations and expenditures
    . Army Pearl Harbor Board       D767.92         940.542
    —Biography
    . Board on Officer-enlisted Man Relationships
    . Bureau of Public Relations
    . Committee on Education and Special Training
    . Conference of Industry, Labor, and Newspaper Leaders,
        Washington, D.C. Sept. 27-28, 1943
    . Division of Insular Affairs
    . Division of Military Aeronautics     UG633
    . General Staff
      —History         UB251       355.34320973
    —History       UB23, UB223    353.6
    —Manuscripts       CD3026       016.9733
    . Military Dictionary Project    U25
    —Records and correspondence    UB163   651.5336
  . War Food Administration
  . War Industries Board         HC106.2    338.0973
    . Price Fixing Committee      HB236.U
  . War Manpower Commission    HD7801    331.152
    . Bureau of Training
    . Employment Service
  . War Policies Commission      HB195     355.210973, 353.0089
  . War Production Board      HC106.4, UA23    338.0973, 353.0912, .26,
                      .2606173, .260973
    . Steel Division        HD9514
  . War Refugee Board       D808.U55-66     940.53159
  . War Relocation Authority    D769.8.A6     940.547273
  . War Relocation Center, Manzanar, Calif.    E184.J3     940.547273
  . War Shipping Administration
  . Wartime Civil Control Administration    D769.1
  . Women's Bureau       HD6093.U    331.406173, 353.008
  . Work Projects Administration
Uruguay—History—1904-1973     F2728    989.506, 918.95036
U.S.S. Arizona Memorial (Hawaii)

V-1 bomb         D785       940.544943
V-2 rocket        D787, UF767, UG635     940.544943, 358.3, 623.451, 926.23
Vågsøy, Battle of, 1941      D756    940.5421
Vandegrift, Alexander Archer, 1887-1972   [U.S.: Lt. Gen.]     E746.V3,
                      VE25.V, D767     355.3320924, 923.573
Vandenberg, Arthur Hendrick, 1884-1951   [U.S.: Sen., isolationist then
    internat'ist.]    E748.V18, E742     973.910924, .9150924, .9170924
Vargas, Getulio Dornelles, 1883-1954   [Brazil: Pres.]     F2538.V33, F2237
                        981.060924, 980.03, 320.98106
Vasilievsky, Alexander, 1895-1977     [U.S.S.R.: Marshal]
Vatutin, Nikolay, 1901-1944    [U.S.S.R.: Gen.]
Vehicles, Military       UC340-3, UG615-18, UG680-5     355.621, .6211,
        .82-3, .830942 (GB), .830943 (Ger.), 623.74, .747, .7409+, .7472
Veluwe (Netherlands), Battle of, 1945

Venezia Giulia (Territory under Allied occupation, 1945-1947)
—Politics and government          DG975.F855
Venizelos, Eleutherios, 1864-1936 [Greece: Pr. Min.]     DF836.V3, DF837-8,
    D569.2, D651.T9          949.5060924, .6, 940.322495, .414, 327.495
Venus (Destroyer)                 D767, D772.V
Verdun, Battle of, 1940          D756.V3
Verona Trial, 1943-1944
Versailles, Treaty of, June 28, 1919 (Germany)     D643.A2-7, D644, D648, D653,
                                  DD231,DD237, DD248, E766, HC57, JV2027, JX1975
                                  940.3141-3142, .31422, .31424, .5314, 943.085,
                                  973.9130924, 320.943, 330.904, 341.69, 344.7301
Veterans          UB356-9          355.115
—California          F868, UB358          355.11509794, 353.979400848
    —Los Angeles County
Veterans, Disabled          UB360-6, HC101          343.73011, 330.973, 362.8
—Rehabilitation          UB360, UB363, HV575, JX1977          362.4, .8
Veterans
—Education          UB357-8          355.1152+, 343.73011
—Employment—United States          UB357, HC101, HD5701          355.11540973,
                                  358.4111540973, 362.85, 330.973, 331.128, 353.00848
—Laws and legislation—United States     KF7703-4, KF7745-9          355.1150973,
                                  .11510973, .1156, 353.979400848, 343.7301102632, 332.720973
—Medical care          UB368-369.5, RA981          355.1154-1156, 362.1109+,
                                  353.00713, .00841-00842
—United States          UB357, UB373          355.1150973
    —Education          UB357          355.11520973, 343.73011
    —Medical care          UB369          355.115
Veterinary service, Military
Vian, Philip, Sir, 1894-1968          [G.B.: Adm., raider]     D771.V45          940.545942
Vickers machine-gun          UF620.V4          355.82
Victor Emmanuel III, 1869-1947          [It.: King]     DG555, DG566, DG570          945.09
Vietnam—History—20th century          DS556          959.703
Vitebsk (City)—Siege, 1944
Viviani, René, 1862-1925 [Fr.: Prem.]
Vlasov, Andrey [Andrei Andreevich], 1900-1945 [1946?]     [U.S.S.R.: Lt. Gen.]
    DK268.V56, D764.6, DK4          947.084, 940.5347, 355.3320924
Volkhov River, Battles of the, 1941-1944
Voluntary aid detachments
Von Braun, Wernher, 1912-1977          [ALSO 'Braun, Werner von': Ger.]     'V'-series
    rocket engineer]          TL781.85.V6          629.409
Voroshilov, Kliment, 1881-1969          [U.S.S.R.: Marshal]
Vosges Mountains (France), Battle of the, 1945
Vrij Nederland          [WWII]
Vyborg, Battle of, 1944


Waffen-SS          [SEE ALSO 'Nationalsozialistische Deutsche Arbeiter-partei.
    Waffenschutzstaffel' for titles earlier than 1982 or so]          D757.85,
                        DD253, UC535          940.541343, 355.14, .140943
    . 12. Panzer-Division Hitlerjugend          D757.85
    . 3. SS-Panzer-Division Totenkopf          D757.85
Wainwright, Jonathan Mayhew, 1883-1953     [U.S.: Major Gen.]     E745.W3-32,
                                  D767.4.W3          940.5426
Wake Island, Battle of, 1941          D767          940.5426
Wallis, Barnes Neville, Sir, 1887-1979     [G.B.: Airplane & bomb designer (bouncing
    bomb, 'Grand Slam', 'Tall Boy')]          TL540          629.1300924

Walther pistols UD415 623.443
War U (mil. sci.), V (naval sci.), U21, U102-5, U750, JX1930-64, JX1291
355, 359 (naval), 355.02+, 327.17+, 341.5-6
War and civilization CB481 901.9
War and crime HV6189
War and education
War and emergency legislation—United States KF26-7, KF5900 342.73062,
343.7301, .7307
War and emergency powers—United States JK558-60, JK339, KF26-7,
KF5060 328.730746, 353.032, .039, 343.73078, .7304, 342.7304
War and literature PN3448.W3 (fiction: hist. & crit.: gen.), PN56.W3 (lit.: h. & c.)
War and morals U21-2, JX4521 172.4
War and religion BL65.W2, BR115.W2 (Christianity), JX1949-52 241.697,
261.63-7, .87308, 301.635
War and society CB401, HM36 301.23, .63, 172.4, 355.02
War—Casualties (Statistics, etc.) D25.5 (mil. hist.), UH215 (mil. med. srvc.), D445
301.322
War correspondents PN4823, PN4871 070.40922, .41, .43, .44990+, .9
War correspondents, American PN4871, PN4874, VG503 070.40922, .9,
359.960973
War, Cost of UA17, HB195 355.023
War crime trials
—Czestochowa, Poland, 1945-1950
—Dachau, 1946
—Dachau—Buchenwald Case, 1947
—Germany D804 364.1380943
—Krasnodar, 1943
—Leipzig, 1921 D626 341.69
—Manila, 1946 D804 341.69
—Nuremberg, 1946-1949 341.41
—Nuremberg
—Einsatzgruppen case, 1947-1948
—Flick case, 1947-1949
—High Command case, 1948-1949
—Hostage case, 1947-1949
—Justice case, 1947
—Milch case, 1946-1947 341.69
—Ministeries case, 1948-1949
—Shanghai, 1946
—Tokyo, 1946-1948 JX1907, JX6731, DS801 341.3, .4, .69
—Indexes DS801 016.34141
—Yokohama, 1945-1949
War crimes JX6731 364.138, 341.3-4, .69
War criminals D804 364.120924
—Germany D804, DD244, DD247 940.547243, 943.086, .0860924,
923.243, 364.1380924
War damage compensation [indemnification to property owners by their gov. for
damage suffered from attacks] 341.3
War damage, Industrial UA929.5-9, HD28 355.26, 658.28, .401
War
—Economic aspects HB195, HC110 330.9, .973092, 338.9, 355.02,
.0273 (US), .027309034, .26, .03, 940.531
—Film catalogs U21 016.35502
War films—History and criticism PN1995 791.4309093, .437

War games        U310, UA673, V250, V253        355.02, .08, .4, .48, .48094, .5, .54,
                356.11+, 904.7, 940.541241
War games, Naval        V250        793.9
War in art        N330, N8260, NC968, NX650        704.949399, .9499047,
                741.65, 769.973
War in literature
War (International law)        JX68, JX1907, JX1916, JX4505, JX4508, JX4511,
                JX4521, JX5001        341.3, .31, .5, .6026, .65-67, .30902
War libraries        Z675.W2
War, Maritime (International law)        JX5203-5268
War—Medical aspects
War memorials        NA9325
        —Europe—Guide-books        D663        914.0455
War neuroses        RC550        616.85, .852109
War (Philosophy)
War poetry        PN6110.W28 (gen.), PR1195.H5 (Eng.), PS595.H5 (Am.)
                808.8193, 821.00803 (Eng.)
War poetry, American
War poetry, English [British]
War Poetry, French
War —Protection of civilians        JX5144 (int'nal' law)        341.481
        —Psychological aspects        U22        355.02019, 150.194, 155.935, 172.4, 301.2
        —Quotations, maxims, etc.        PN6084        808.882
War relief—Case studies        HV639        361.53
War—Relief of sick and wounded        UH201-551
War-songs
War-songs, American        M1628        784.71973, .68973
War-songs, English
War-songs, French
War-songs, German
War stories
War stories, American
War stories, English
War stories, French
War stories, German
War victims
        —Law and legislation
War wounds        RD156        617.1
War—Women's work
Warfare, Conventional
Warlimont, Walther, 1894-?        [Ger.: Gen.]        D757.W38+        940.54013
Warsaw, Battle of, 1945
Warsaw
        —History
                —Uprising of 1943        D765        940.534384, .5405094384, 943.84
                        —Pictorial works        N6999        741.9438
                —Uprising of 1944        D765        940.534384, .5486438, 943.805
Warsaw (Poland)—History—Uprising of 1943
Warsaw—Siege, 1939        D765        940.54763438

Wilson, Henry Maitland, Sir, ('Jumbo'), 1881-1964  [G.B.: Field Marshal]     D766.W,
                                                                                 D811.W
Wilson, Woodrow, 1856-1924  [U.S.: Pres.]     E765-768, E780, D570, D611,
                                      D619, D644, D651, E780     973.0992, .80924,
                                      .912-913, .9130924, 940.3141, .32273, .373, .45,
                                      327.7304+, 378.74967, 923.173
Winant, John, 1888-1947  [U.S.: Ambass. to G.B. (1941-5)]     E183.8.G7
Wingate, Orde Charles, 1903-1944  [G.B.: Maj. Gen., commanded special forces
   ('Chindits') in Burma]     DA585.W6, D767.6     942.082, 940.5426, 923.542
Winter warfare     U167.5.W5     355.423
Wisconsin War Fund, The     D769.85.W75
Witzelben, Erwin von, 1881-1944   [Ger.: Field Marshal]
Wizna (Poland), Battle of, 1939
Wolff, Karl, 1900-?     [Ger.: SS Gen.]
Wood, Kingsley, Sir, 1881-1943     [G.B.: Sec. of State for Air (1938-40), Chanc. o/t
                                    Excheq. (1940-43), econ. innovator]
World politics     D, J, D21, D105, D363, D397, D413, D421, D443, D455, D720,
                 D727,JC251-2, JX1315, JX1395, UA11, UA646     940.28,
                 .51, .55, 301.1523, 327.0904, 341.09, .1818+, 901.9, 909.82
—19th century     D363, D397     327.09034, 320.94028, 335.4, 909.81
—20th century     D440-72, D419, JC252     320.904, 327.0904, 330.15,
                 909.82
—1900-1945     D413, D443, D450     940.531, 901.94, 327.14
—1900-1918     940.312
—1919-1932     D727, DA565, JX1975     940.5311, 327.209+, 341.12,
                 .22+, 309.1
—1933-
—1933-1945     D442-3, D445, JX1395, JX1937, HN17     940.5,
                 .53144, 327.09+, .09043, 341.1, 309.1043
World War II Recorded History Collection     [Gathered by Library of Congress]
World War III     U21.2, U263 (Australia), U313, UA23, D359.7 (world politics:
                 20th C.), D849.5 (world politics: 1975-85)
World War, 1914-1918     [For older books prior to around 1982, SEE 'European
                 War, 1914-1918'. Subdivisions listed in either area may be
                 found under either heading]     D501-680, D511, D521-3,
                 D639, D644, JX1952-3     940.3-940.499, 940.3+, 940.4+
—Addresses, sermons, etc.     B945, D443, PS2120     301.593, .953,
                 940.308, .34208
—Aerial operations     D600-607, D788, DA89, TL515, TL540, UG633     358.43,
                 623.746, 923.542, 940.44, .54
—Aerial operations, American     UG633, D606
—Aerial operations, British     UG635.G7, D786, D602, D545     940.48142,
                 .447
—Aerial operations, German     D546, D604, UG635.G3-4     940.44943
—Africa     D651.A4, DT31-4
—Africa, North     DT204, HC56.C38
—Afro-Americans     D639.N4, D570.33.369th     940.403, .41273
—Arab countries     DA47.9.S4
—Argentina     D621.A8, F2846-8
—Armenia     DS195.5, D651.A7, D638.A7, DS195.3.A65     947.92
—Armistices     D641, D509     940.452, .43, .439
—Atrocities     D625-6, JX1906, DS195.5, DH682, D626.G3 (Ger.),
                 D520.T8 (Turkish), D638.A7 (Armenians)     940.488
—Australia     D520.A9, D568.2-7, DU116, DU212, DU161, D547.A8,
                 D568.A2, DU110, D609.A8     919.4034, 940.41294, .394

World War, 1914-1918
—Causes          D511, D501-515, DD228.5-6, DB89.F7, D465, JX1906,
          DD232.5, DD221          940.3112, .311208, .311, 944.08, 332.09
     —Bibliography          Z6207.E8          016.947
—Cavalry operations
—Censorship          D631-2
—Chemical warfare          UG447          623.45-452
—Children
—China          DS721, D549.C5, DS774-5          940.345102, .32251
—Chronology          D522.5          940.34205
—Civilian relief          BX7635.A, D637-9, D639.W7, D809          940.3144
—Claims          JX5326, JX5483          341.3
—Concentration camps          D627
—Confiscations and contributions
—Conscientious objectors          UB342
—Cryptography          D639.C75
—Czechoslovakia          D558, D539.5.C8, DK265.42-9, DB215-17, DB217.B4
          940.412437
—Destruction and pillage          D626, D626.G3, D639.D55
     —France
—Dictionaries          D510
—Diplomatic history          D509, D505, E183.8, D511, E768, D610-21, D610,
          D645, D453          940.32, .322
—Documents, etc., sources
—Draft resisters          UB343
—Economic aspects          D635, D648, HC54-7, HB171, JX5361, HC276,
          HB195, UA23          330.904, .973, 940.31833
     —Bibliography          Z6464.Z9, Z5074.E3, Z7164.L1
     —Europe
     —France          HD645, HD8430, HC276-8, HD6145.F7          940.31833
     —Germany          UA18.G4, HC285-6, HC286.2          330.943, 940.34305
     —Great Britain          D635, HC56, HC256.2, D505, HJ1023, HB195
          331.0941, 330.19355
     —Russia          HC334-5, HB3607          940.34705, 312.0947
     —United States          D635, HD6095, HD9074, HC106.2, HB236.U5,
          HD9914, HD8072, D619          338.50973, 331.0973, 330.973
—Education and the war          D639.E3
—Egypt          D568.2
—Equipment and supplies          D639.S9
—Europe, Eastern          D639, DJK48, D645
—Fiction
     —Bibliography          Z5917.W33
—Finance          D635, HJ8011, HC56-7, JX1315, HC240          940.31422, 336.3, .34
     —Europe
     —Germany          HJ1119
     —Great Britain          HC256.2, HJ1023, HG1586, D505, HJ8627, D635,
          HB195, HJ1015, HJ2619          336.41-2, .20942,
          330.19355, 940.34205
     —Russia          HJ1207
     —United States          HC56.C33, HC106.2, HJ257, HJ8117, D570.15,
          D570.85          940.37305, 336.73, .30973, 330.973
—Finland          D621.F5, DD120.F49, DK446-59, DK265          327.430471,
          330.9471

World War, 1914-1918
  —Food question    HD9000-9049, D637    940.477873
    —Europe    HD1917
  —Food supply    D570.1
  —France    D516, D548, D520.F8, DC387-9, DC367, DC373    940.405,
      .431, .344, 320.944081, 944.0815
  —German East Africa    D576.G3
  —Germany    D515, D531, D609-13, DD231-232.5, DD221.5, DD228.6-8,
      DD229.8, U738, UA647, UA712    940.53112, .4886,
      .32443, .343, 327.43+
  —Great Britain    D546, D544-7, D517, D521, D547.8, D611, D645,
      DA68.32, DA566.9.A-Z, DA577    942.083, 940.342,
      .31, .41241-41242, .34207, 923.542
  —Greece    DF838, D616, D610, DF833-8
  —Historiography    D515, D522.42, D743.42, DB36.8, DD86, U21
  —Hospitals    D629.G7
  —Hospitals, charities, etc.    D638, D541, D629, D640, D809    360.6273,
      940.47709+, .4771, .34207, 352.047
  —Humor    D526.2, .2-7
  —Hungary    D643.H9, D539-40, D651.H7, DB947-55
World War, 1914-1918, in art    N6888, ND623
World War, 1914-1918, in literature    PR605.W3
World War, 1914-1918, in motion pictures    PN1993.5.U6, D522.33
World War, 1914-1918
  —India    D520.I6, D547.I5
  —Influence and results    D443, D511, D523, D639.D45, D643.A7, D653,
      D741, CB155    940.5, .51, .314, .3149+, 909.82
  —Iran    D640, DS315
  —Iraq    D566
  —Ireland    DA952-62
  —Italy    DG568.5, DG570, DG799, D520.I7, D526.7.I8, D569.A2, D617,
      D621, D640, D651.I6, DB879    940.32245, .345, .34502, .4145
  —Japan    D520.O8, DS518, DS845
  —Jews    DS135.G33, DS135, D609.G3, D639.J4    940.315296
  —Juvenile fiction
  —Language (New words, slang, etc.)    D526.2, PE3727.S6, PC1977.S6,
      PC3747.S6    427.09, 821.04
  —Latin America    D520.S8
  —Law and legislation    JX5003    341.3
  —Libraries (in camps, etc.)    Z675.W2    027.652, .777829
  —Literature and the war    PN56.W1, PN3448, PN3503, PR106, PR478.E8,
      PR605.W3+ (Brit. poetry), PR610, PR888.E9, PR2976.H385,
      PS228.W37 (US), PT405, PT553 (Grmn. poetry), PT772,
      PQ307.W3 (Fr.)    810.9005, 809.33
  —Lithuania    DK511.L2
  —Macedonia    D629.G8
  —Maps    G1037, D521, D540    912.4
  —Medical and sanitary affairs    D628-30    940.5476+, .475+
  —Mexico    F1234, E183.8.M5
  —Monuments    D663
  —Moral and ethical aspects    D523-4
  —Museums

World War, 1914-1918
—Naval operations    D580-9, VA40, VA454    359.3252, 940.45+, .485,
                                             .454-459+
—Naval operations, American    D589.U6    940.45
—Naval operations, Australian
—Naval operations, British    D581-2, D593, DA89.1, VA456, D771
                              359.3320924, 940.455
—Naval operations, German    D581-2, D591, VA513, D639.M82, D640
                             940.45943
—Naval operations, Italian
—Naval operations, Russian    D585, DK265
—Naval operations—Submarine    D580, D589-90, D591-5, D619-21, V210,
                               V859, JX5244.A7    940.451+
—Netherlands    DJ281-5, D621.N4    940.3492
—New York    D570.85.N
—New Zealand    D547.N5, D501.K53, D568.3, D629.N4
—Norway
—Outlines, syllabi, etc.    D522.5    940.302
—Pacific Ocean    D581-2
—Palestine    D568.7, DS125+, DS125.5    956.9
—Participation, Jewish
—Peace    D610-14, D642-50, D443, D523, JX1907, JX5181, JX1952
                               940.31+, .312, .3141, .3162, .318331, 341.1
—Periodicals    D501.A-Z
—Personal narratives    D568.3, D640    940.481+, .476+
—Personal narratives, American    D570+, D570.9, D603, D629, D640
                                   940.48173, .4144, .4771
—Personal narratives, British    D640, D545    940.48141-48142
—Personal narratives, French    D640, D544, D548, D603, D627.G3,
                                D629.F8, DC373.G4    940.48144, .548144
—Personal narratives, German    D640, D581.L96, U738.R6513 (Rommel)
                                 940.48243, 923.543
—Personal narratives, Italian    D640, D569, D569.A2 (Mussolini)
                                  940.48145
—Personal narratives, Jewish    DS125.5, D640
—Personal narratives, Russian    DK188, DK254-65, D640    923.547,
                                  940.48147, 947.084109+
—Pictorial works    D522, D527, D517, D570, D640, N4390, N9150, NC369,
                    NC1115, NE2210.E16    940.497, .3022, .37309
—Poetry    PN6084.W35, PR1195.H5, PR1195.W65 (Eng.)    821.91208,
                    .9108+, 811.52, 940.491
—Poland    DK438-40+, DK417, D651.P7, D640    943.8, 923.5438
—Postal service    HE6184, JX1543, D635
—Posters    D522.25
—Prisoners and prisons    D511, D627, D805, JX5141    940.472
—Prisoners and prisons, British    D627.G7, D576.G5    940.41688
—Prisoners and prisons, German    D627.G3, D640, DK188    940.47243
—Prisoners and prisons, Italian    D627.I8    940.47245
—Prisoners and prisons, Japanese    D627.J3
—Prisoners and prisons, Russian    D627.R8-9    940.47247
—Prizes, etc.    JX5251
—Propaganda    D639.P6-7, D632, UB275    940.4886+, .3152, .322+,
                    .488642
—Prophecies    BF1815.N8, D523
—Protest movements    D639.P77    940.3162

World War, 1914-1918
—Psychological aspects    D523, D525
—Public opinion          D639.P88, .R4, D509, D523, D570.1, D619, D639
                         940.3152, .37+, .4886-4887+
—Quotations, maxims, etc.   PN6084.W35
—Refugees          D637-8        940.3159+
—Regimental histories    D547.A-Z    940.409+, .412+
    —Australia      D547.A8, D568.A2        940.41294
    —Canada        D547.C2    940.40971
    —France
    —Germany      D609.G3, D534.3
    —Great Britain     D547.B74, .G7, D546        940.41242
    —India         D547.I5
    —Ireland       D547.I6
    —Italy         D569.A2
    —New Zealand     D547.N5
    —Russia        UA774, D552
    —United States  D570.3-33. D570-570.9        940.41273
—Registers, lists, etc.    D639.E4, D547, D570.85
—Registers of dead     D609, D639.E
—Religious aspects     D639.R4        940.3152, .3182
—Reparations      D648-9, D644, DC59.8.G3, HG186.F8, HG1997.I6,
                  HG3949, HJ8654, HJ8751, JX1908        940.31422,
                         330.904, 336.309, .30943, .497
—Romania     D520.R8, DR205, D651.R6        940.3498, .482+, 949.8
—Russia      DK265, DK254, D646, D514, D550, D585    940.347, .34705,
                  .4147, 947.08
—Russia, Asiatic     D567.A2
—Science
—Secret service     D639.S7-8, .C75, D619.3, UB250, UB271
                    940.486-487+
    —Germany     D639.S7-8, D619.3    940.48743
    —Great Britain   D639.S7, D616    940.48642
    —Jews         DS125.5
    —United States   D639.S7, D619.3    940.48673
—Siberia     DK265, D558, DB215    940.482
—Social aspects
—Societies
—Songs and music   D526.2, M1646    427.09, 821.04
—Sources     D505-9    940.31412, .4, 943.084 (Ger.)
—South Africa
—Soviet Union    DK254-65, D639.S9, D521
—Spain        D621.S73
—Statistics     D521, D550, D570.1.U
—Study and teaching
—Sweden       D621.S5, DL658
—Switzerland   D621.S8, DQ48, DQ69        940.3494
—Syria        DS98
—Tank warfare   UG446.5

World War, 1914-1918

World War, 1914-1918
—Ukraine          D520.U35, D614.B5, DK188, DK265.8.U3-4, DK508
—Underground movements     DC611
—United States     D570-570.7, D619, D632, D639, E664, E743-5, E766-7,
                   E780, E784, E802, JK464         940.373, .5373, .32273,
                   .3141, .488673, .48743, 973.913, 355.0973
—War work     D570.85, U766
—Washington, D.C.     F199
—Women          D639.W7
—Yugoslavia          DR363, DB215, D651.Y8
World War, 1918-1945
World War, 1930-
World War, 1930-1945
    —Campaigns—Guadalcanal Island
    —Fiction
    —Humor, caricatures, etc.
    —Personal narratives, American
    —Regimental histories—U.S.—Marine Corps. 1st Division
    —Underground movements—France
World War, 1935-1945
World War, 1936-1945
World War, 1939-          [Used for some books written and cataloged before the
                          end of hostilities. SEE 'World War, 1939-1945' for titles penned
                          post-war. Subdivisions listed here under the latter may
                          sometimes be found under the former.]

    —China
    —East (Far East)
    —Mediterranean Sea
    —Naval operations
    —U.S.
World War, 1939-1943
World War, 1939-1945          [For contemporary works early in the period SEE
                              'European War, 1939-' and 'World War, 1939-'. Some titles
                              may ALSO be found under 'World War, 1930-1945',
                              '...1935-1945', '...1936-1945', '...1930-', etc.]
                              D731-838, D741 (overall works), D743-4, D755, D757
                              940.53-5499, .53, .54
    —Addresses, essays, lectures          D742-3, D743.9          940.53, .5304, .54
    —Addresses, sermons, etc.          D742-3, D764          940.53, .5304, .531,
                              .534-5, .5804
    —Aerial operations     [SEE ALSO 'Bombardment' under names of cities]
                   D785-7, D767, D790, D811, TL685.7, UG630          623.746,
                   940.544, .5449+, 358.4+
    —Aerial operations, American [British, German, etc.]
    —Aerial operations, American          D785+, D790, D757.9.A-Z, D767+, D769+,
                   UG633          940.5423-26, .5440973 (US), .544973,
                   923.573, 358.4140973, 338.4762913
          —Chronology
          —Periodicals          D790
          —Sources          D785.U
              —Bibliography—Catalogs
    —Aerial operations, Australian          D792.A8          940.544994
    —Aerial operations
       —Bibliography     Z6207.W8
       —Brazilian          D768.3, D792.B7

World War, 1939-1945
—Aerial operations, British    D785-6, D757.9.A-Z, DA69                940.5421,
                               .544941-544942, .54942, 923.2913, 926.2913,
                               623.7464
—Aerial operations, Canadian    D792.C2        940.544971
—Aerial operations, Chinese    DS777.53    358.413320924, 923.573
—Aerial operations—Chronology    D785
—Aerial operations, Czech    D792        940.544
—Aerial operations—Dictionaries    D743
—Aerial operations, Dutch    D792.N38
—Aerial operations, East Indian    D792.I4
—Aerial operations, English
—Aerial operations, Finnish    D792.F5, DK459.45-5
—Aerial operations, French    D788, D761.9    940.544944
—Aerial operations, German        D787, D757+, D757.63, D811, TL540.A-Z,
                               UD485, UG633, UG635.G3        940.541343,
                               .544943, .544947
        —History        UG630        358.400904
        —Pictorial works
—Aerial operations, Indian    UG635.I3
—Aerial operations, Italian    D792.I8    940.544945
        —Pictorial works
—Aerial operations, Japanese        D792.J3, D767+, D767.2, TL515, UD485,
                               VA653, VG95.J3        940.5425, .544952,
                               356.1660952
        —Periodicals
—Aerial operations—Personal narratives    940.5441
—Aerial operations, Polish    D792.P6, D765.2.W3, D770, D811
        —Fiction
—Aerial operations, Russian    D792.R9, .S65, D764, UD485.S65, UG633, AS36
                               940.544947, .5441
—Aerial operations, South African        D792.S6
—Aerial operations, Yugoslav        D792.Y9
—Aeroplane carrier operations, American        D774        940.545973
—Africa        D739, D753-4, D761, D766, D802, D811        940.548173,
                               .542, .536, 960.4, 355.49
—Africa, Eastern        DT736
—Africa, French Equatorial    DT766.96
—Africa, French-speaking Equatorial    DT766.98
—Africa, French-speaking West        DT766.98
        —Dakar
—Africa, Italian East    D802.A2        940.53635
—Africa, North    D756.3, D766.82, .99.A-Z, D811        940.5322+,
                               .5361, .542, .5423, .54753
        —Fiction
—Africa, Northwest    D753.2.F8
—Africa, South    [SEE ALSO 'World War, 1939-1945—South Africa']
                               D766+        940.5368
—Africa, West        DT494, DT553, D761    916.6
        —Dakar        DT553.D3
—Afro-American troops
—Afro-Americans    D810.N4        940.53150396073, .541273, .5403
        —Sources
—Alabama        F326        917.61
—Alaska        D769.87.A4, DR701, F909        940.5403, .53798, 917.98

World War, 1939-1945
—Albania          D76.7.A4        940.548142
   —Biography    CT1399.8
   —Maps        G2006.S7
—Aleutian Islands     D769.87.A4, F951       940.542, .53798, 917.98
—Algeria          D766.82, .99.A3, DT295      940.5423
   —Algiers (City)
   —Mers-el-Kebir     D766.99.A3, D779.F8
—Alsace-Lorraine     D762.A4, D802.A45, DD801.A35     940.5344, .5404,
                    944.38
—America         D769, E18.85, F1418     355.097
—American republics    D752.8, D742.A5, F1203, F1405-18     940.537-38,
                    972.0082
—Amphibious operations    D744, D756, D761, D767-70, D767.917, D769,
                    D773     940.5421, .5426, .545
—Andorra      D811
—Anecdotes    D743-5, D743.9, D839      940.53082, .542, .548, .5494, 920.5
—Anecdotes, facetiae, satire, etc.
—Anniversaries, etc.
—Anti-aircraft artillery operations
—Arabia        DS63
—Archives
—Arctic Ocean     D771    940.5450916611
—Arctic Regions    D763.5, D771
—Argentina       F2848
—Argentine Republic    D754.A7, F2846-9     940.532582, 982+
—Armenia        D764.7.A7, D779.R9
—Armistices     D812-14, D752, D802     940.5322+, .5314
   —Sources
—Art and the war    D810.A7, N6492.2, N6512, N6918, N6921.F6, N7445,
              N9145, N9165.F8, NC1070     940.53187, .5497,
              704.91, 709.22, 741.9
   —Exhibitions
—Artillery operations
—Artillery operations, American
—Artillery operations, British
—Artillery operations, Japanese
—Asia         DS518
—Asia, Southeastern    D767+, D767.45, .6, D792     940.5359, .548644
—Atlantic Ocean     D770-1, D781, VM395     940.5429, .5459
—Atrocities      D803-5, D804.G3, D805.G3, D810.J4, DD247.E34,
           DD253, DD253.6, DS135.P63     940.54056, .547243,
           .5472475, .54724972, .5405+, 943.086
   —Bibliography    Z6207.W8
   —Fiction
—Atrocities, German
—Atrocities
   —Pictorial works
   —Poetry
   —Psychological aspects    R852.H8
   —Public opinion
   —Sources      D804    940.5405094771
—Audio-visual aids—Catalogs    D743.22.U5

World War, 1939-1945
—Australia  D754.A, D742.A8, D767, D767.8-95, D767.95.A8, D779.A9,
              DU107-110, DU116-17      940.5394, .5304, 330.994
    —Cowra (N.S.W.)  D805.A8
    —Darwin          D767.82.D2      940.5426
    —Darwin (N.T.)
    —New South Wales
    —Sources         D754.A8
    —Sydney (N.S.W.)  D783.7
—Austria  D731, D765.4, D809.G7, D839.3, DB34.5      940.53436
    —Periodicals     DB99.A1
    —Tyrol           DB879.I6
—Austria, Upper      DB169
—Austria
    —Vienna          DB855, D765.45.V
    —Wiener Neustadt  D765.45.W63
—Autographs
—Azerbaijan          D764.7.A93
—Azerbaijan S.S.R.
—Azores              D754.P8
    —Flores Island
—Balkan Peninsula    D750, D754.B3, .R9, DR48, DR2242
                     940.532449+, .5337, 949.6
—Balloons
    —Great Britain
—Baltic Sea          D772.3, D779.R9
—Baltic States       D742.B2, D754.B3, D802.B3, DK511.B3      947.4, 327.474
—Baptists
—Barents Sea         D771, D784.R9      940.545
—Battlefields
    —Guide-books     D747
—Battles, sieges, etc.  [SEE 'World War, 1939-1945—Aerial operations ',
                        '...—Campaigns—{Geog. subdiv.}',
                        '...—Naval operations' and specific battles]
—Bavaria             D757.9.B3      940.5401
—Belgium             D742.B4, D763.B4+, .B42.A-Z (places), D802.B4, DH401,
                     UA680      940.542, .53493, .5404, 949.3
    —Brussels
    —Eupen and Malmédy  D802.A45      940.5404
    —Flanders
    —Gilly           D763.B42.G54
    —Louvain
    —Periodicals
    —Renaix
    —Spa             D763.B42      940.53493
—Berlin              DD256.3
—Berlin (Germany)    D757.9.B4
—Besserabia          DS135.R93
—Bibliography        Z6207.W8, Z6725, D731-838, D734, D746
                     016.94053-94054, .36, 940.52-4
—Biography           D736-7, D769, D797, D507      940.5412, .5413, .5464,
                        .540922, .5481+, .5373, 923.573
    —Bibliography—Catalogs
    —Congresses
    —Dictionaries

World War, 1939-1945
—Campaigns
   —Belgium       D763.B4, D757.54, D755.2     940.54, .542
      —Scheldt      D763.N4
   —Bulgaria       D766.7.B8
   —Burma       D767.6, D769, DS767, UG633     940.5423, .5425,
                                   .544, .548673
   —Byelorussian S.S.R.
   —Caucasus      D764.3.C3
   —China       D767.3
      —Manchuria   D767.2
      —Sources—Bibliography—Catalogs     Z6614.C48
   —Courland
   —Crete       D766.7.C7, D766.3     940.5421, .5423
   —Czechoslovak Republic     D765.5, .55
      —Ostrava region    D765.55.O8
   —Czechoslovakia
   —Denmark      D763.D4, D757, D802.D4     940.5342
   —Dnieper River    D764
   —East Asia      D767
      —Sources
   —East (Far East)    D767, D767.8, D769     940.5412, .542
   —Eastern      D755.1, D757+, D764, D764.6, D765.13, D787-8, DK4185,
               UG633     940.541244, .5421, .54210924
      —Public opinion    D764
   —Egypt
   —England
   —English Channel
   —Estonia
   —Ethiopia    D766.92    940.542
   —Europe     [SEE ALSO 'World War, 1939-1945—Campaigns—Eastern'
                 and '...—Campaigns—Western']     D756.5, D769,
                 D769.31, DD256.5
      —Chronology    D757
   —Europe, Eastern    D764
   —Europe—Sources   D757
   —Finland      D765.3, .32, .35.A-Z
      —Lapin laeaeni   D765.35.L35
   —France       D743, D755.2, D756, D761-2     940.540944, .5421
   —France (1944-1945)    D755.6, D761, E745     940.5421, 944.081
   —France
      —Alps, French   D761.1
      —Moselle      D762.M57
      —Normandy     D756.5.N6    940.5421
        —Chronology
      —Pictorial works
      —Provence
      —Riviera     D762.R5
   —France, Southern   D762 940.5421

World War, 1939-1945
  —Campaigns
    —Germany      D755.7, D757, .9, D769.U      940.5401, .542
      —Addresses. essays, lectures    D755    940.5421
    —Germany (East)
    —Germany
      —Pictorial works
    —Germany (West)
        —Ruhr River Valley      D757.9.R5
    —Gilbert Islands    D767.917, D769.U      940.5426
    —Great Britain
    —Greece      D766.3, .32      940.5421
      —Crete      D766.7.C7
    —Guadalcanal Island      D755, D767.98, D769.A or U (U.S. Army: official)
                            940.541, .5426, 355.3320924
    —Hawaii
    —Hong Kong    D767.3
    —Hungary    D765.56
    —India
    —Indochina    D767, D767.45
    —Indonesia    D767.7
      —Java
    —Iran      D767.6      940.5423
    —Iraq      D766.7.I75, D767.6      940.5423
    —Italy      D763.I8+, D768.15-3, D769.A or U (U.S. Army)
                          940.5421, .548173
      —Literary collections    PR1195.W6
      —Pictorial works
      —Sicily      D763.S5, D810.S7      940.5421
    —Japan      D757
      —Okinawa Island  [SEE ALSO '...Campaigns—Okinawa Island']
                    D767.99.O45
    —Karelia    D757.85
    —Kiribati    D767.917
    —Levant    D766+, D767.8
    —Libya    D766.93, D767.8      940.542
      —Fezzan
    —Lusatia    D765
    —Luxembourg
    —Malay Peninsula    D767.5, .55      940.5425, .547252
    —Malaya
    —Malta    D763.M3
    —Mariana Islands    D767.99.M27, D769.A or U    940.5426
    —Marshall Islands    D767.99.M3, D769.A or U    940.542
    —Mediterranean region
      —Bibliography
      —Historical geography—Maps    G1038
    —Mindoro    D767.4
    —Near East    D766
    —Netherlands    D763.N4, D755.2
      —Limburg    D763.N42.L53
      —Walcheren    D763.N42.W

World War, 1939-1945
—Campaigns
——New Britain (Island)     D767.99.N4     940.542
——New Guinea     D767.94-5, D767.8, D769.A or U, DU740
                    940.5426
——New Guinea (Territory)     U165
——Normandy     D755-6, D756.5.N6, D762, D765     940.5421, .5485
———Congresses
——North Pacific Ocean
——Norway     D763.N6, D779.N6, D757, D802.N     940.5421
——Okinawa Island     [SEE ALSO '...Campaigns—Japan—Okinawa Island']
                    D767.99.O45, D769.A or U (official U.S. Army)     940.5426
——Pacific area     D767     940.5426
——Pacific Ocean     D767+, .9, .98, .99.A-Z (by place: island group etc.),
                    D773-4     940.5425-5426
——Palau—Peleliu Island     D767.99.P4
——Papua New Guinea     D767.95-8
———Guadalcanal Island     D767.98     940.5426
——Pelew Islands     D767.99.P4, D769     940.5426
——Philippine Islands     D767.4, D805.P6     940.5426
———Bataan
———Biscayas     D767.4
———Leyte     D767, D769.A or U     940.5426
———Luzon     D767.4     940.5426, .547252
———Mindanao
———Palawan Island
———Zamboanga (Province)
——Philippines     D767.4, D769.A or U, D805.J3 or P6, DS688
                    940.5426, .547252
———Anniversaries, etc.
———Bataan (Luzon)
———Bataan (Province)
———Corregidor Island
———Luzon
——Poland     D765, D765.13, D765.2, D764.7, UA772, UA829.P7
                    940.542, .5421, .544, 943.804
——Poland (1944-1945)
——Poland
———Bialystok (Voivodeship)     D765.2.B47
———Katowice (Voivodeship)
———Lublin region     D765.2.L8
———Vistula River     D765.2.V57
——Pomerania     D765.2.P6
——Portuguese Timor     D767.7
——Prussia, East     D765.2.E2
——Prussia, East (Poland and R.S.F.S.R.)     D765.2.P68
——Rhine River Valley     D757.9.R5
——Romania
——Russia     D764, D757.32, .85, D764+, DK266-8, UA770
                    940.5421, .5481438
——Russia, Northwestern     UG446.5
——Russia—Pictorial works
——Russian S.F.S.R.—Karelian Isthmus
——Saipan     D767, D769.1.A     940.5426
——Scandinavia     D763.S3

World War, 1939-1945
  —Censorship        D798-9+          940.5405
     —Australia      D810.P7.A84
     —Belgium       D799.B4
     —France         D799.F7
     —Great Britain   D799.G7, Z657
     —Sweden
     —Switzerland    D799.S9
     —United States   D799.U5-6      940.5405
  —Central Europe    D764
  —Cephalonia      D766.32.C3
  —Channel Islands
     —Jersey        UG430.J47
  —Chaplains
  —Chemical warfare   [SEE ALSO '...—Chemistry']
  —Chemistry      [SEE ALSO '...—Chemical warfare']   D769.U, D810.S2
                  358.34, .340973, 940.53185
  —Children        D810.C4, .J4 (Jewish), D811.5, HQ784.W3, HQ792, HV741,
                  LC4069.W3          940.53161, 943.8405+, 362.7061+,
                  .71063+, .74, 371.9

     —Austria
     —Canada
     —Fiction
     —Germany
     —Great Britain
     —Poland
     —Yugoslavia
  —Chile       F3095 983
  —China       D742.C6, D410, D651.C4, D767, D769.A or U (U.S. Army),
             DS710, DS774, DS777.47-53, E183.8.C4, E745.S857 (Stilwell)
             940.5351, .5425, .544973, .548173, .548673, 951.042, .0425,
             915.1, 329.006273, 341.05
     —Periodicals
     —Shanghai    DS796.S2      940.5351
     —Sources      D767      940.54250924
  —Chios (Island)    D766.32.C45     940.53499
  —Chronology     D743.5, D743     940.53, .5302, .5373, .540202,
               .542, .545973 (U.S. Navy)
  —Church of the Brethren   UB342.U5     355.22
  —Churches       [SEE specific denominations or religions as subheads under
              'World War, 1939-1945' and 'World War, 1939-1945—War work']

World War, 1939-1945
—Civilian relief      D808-9, BX7747-9, BX7827, E744, JX1543, JX1977
        940.477873, .53144, .53159, .5342, .54771, .54778494, 266.65
    —Bibliography    Z6207.W8
    —Belgium    D809    940.53159493
    —China    D809.C5, HC101    940.5314451
    —Europe    D809.E, .U5 (by U.S.), HC101    940.53183381, .53144
    —Finland    D809.F5    940.54779471
    —France    D809.F
    —Germany    D809.G3    940.5477943
    —Great Britain
    —Hungary

    —Norway    D809.N6    940.53144481
    —Societies, etc.    D809.U5    940.477873
    —Sources—Bibliography—Catalogs
    —United States    D809.U5    940.5477873
—Claims    [SEE ALSO names of claimants, vessels, etc.]    JX5326,
      JX5486, KF26-7    341.52, .67, 343.7301, .7303153, 940.53144914
    —Periodicals
—Collaboration—France
—Collaborationists    D802.A2+    940.53163
    —Denmark
    —France    D802.F8, D761, D829.F8, DC397    320.944
      —Ariege    D802.F82.A765
    —Germany
    —Netherlands    D802.N4
    —Norway    D763.N6, D802.N, DL529.Q5 (Quisling)    940.53481
      —Drama
    —Philippine Islands    D802.P5    991.4035
    —Philippines    DS686.4
    —Psychological aspects    D802.A2
    —South Africa
    —Yugoslavia
    —United States    D804    940.5487
—Collected works
—Collectibles
—Collections    D731, D739    940.53, .53082, 943.53082
—Colombia
—Commando operations    D794.5
    —Asia, Southeastern    D767
    —Europe
    —France    D802.F8
    —Great Britain
    —United States
—Communications    D810.C7    940.5412

World War, 1939-1945
—Concentration camps    [SEE ALSO names of specific camps]
                        D804 (atrocities), D805.A-Z, D809, D810.J4 (Jews)
    —Albania
    —Australia        D809.A8
    —Austria
    —Bibliography
    —California
    —Canada           D805.C2, D627.C2
    —Czechoslovakia
    —Denmark
    —France
        —Natzwiller
    —Germany          D804.G4, D805.G3
    —Germany (East)
    —Germany
        —Public opinion
    —Germany (West)
            —Baden-Wuerttemberg
    —Greece
    —History
    —Italy
    —Japan
    —Netherlands
    —Norway
    —Philippines      D805.P6
    —Pictorial works
    —Poland
        —Pustkow
    —Spain
    —United States
    —Yugoslavoa
—Confiscations and contributions    D810.C8
    —Argentine Republic    JX5313.A7
    —Germany        D810.C8, HC286.4         330.943
    —Jews           D810.J4
    —Poland
    —United States        JX5313.U5
—Congo, Belgian          D766.92        940.542
—Congo (Democratic Republic)          D766.95
—Congresses        D734
—Congresses, conferences, etc.     D734, D504, E807        940.5314,
                                     .532, .5306373, 973.917
—Conscientious objectors    UB342.C2
    —Great Britain      UB342.G7
    —United States—Finances

World War, 1939-1945
—Conscript—Burma
—Conscript labor         D811
    —Europe, Eastern     D810.J4
    —France—Mayenne (Dept.)     HD4875.F8
    —Germany         D805.G3, D810.J4, DK402, HD8450
    —Hungary         D805.H8, D810.J4, DS135.H9       940.541243
    —Japan       D801.J3
    —Netherlands     D763.N42
    —Poland        D765, D805.P7, DK402
       —Lublin (District)
       —Sources    DK402
    —Russia        D811.5      940.548243
—Corfu        D766.32.C3-4
—Corsica       DC611.C835
—Correspondence
—Cossacks
—Costa Rica       F1547      972.86
—Counterfeit money     D810.C8, HG339, HG339.G3 (Ger.)      940.5488
—Crete       D766.7.C7      940.534998
—Croatia       D804, D411, DB372.P2, DB379     949.7202
    —Baranja       D802.Y82.B37
    —Sources       DR1591
—Cryptography       D810.C88-95, D756.5.N6      940.548641, .5486701
    —Indexes
—Cuba       D742.C9, D754.C92, F1787      940.537291, 972.91
—Czechoslovak Republic     DB215, D765, D802    940.53487, .53437
    —Lidice       D804      940.542
—Czechoslovakia       DB215-17, DB215.3, D754.C95, D802.C95, D804.C9,
                              DD101, DD247.F68      943.7, 940.53437
    —Jihomoravsky kraz
    —Periodicals
    —Prague       D765.55.P7
    —Severocesky kraj       D765.55.S48
    —Slovak Socialist Republic     DB2818-2822
    —Slovakia       DB2822
—Czestochowa, Poland       D804.G4
—Dalmatia       D766.62.D3
—Denmark       D763.D4, D799.D4, D802.D4, D731, DD491, DS135.D4 (Jews)
                   940.53489, .54886, 327.4890943
    —Copenhagen—Fiction
    —Gilleleje       DL291.G46

World War, 1939-1945
—Deportations from Belgium          D810.D5
—Deportations from Bulgaria          D810.J4
—Deportations from Czechoslovakia          DB2742
—Deportations from France          D810.D5, D810.J4 (Jews), D805.G3,
                                  D802.F82, DS135.F8-83 (Jews)          940.5315, .5405
    —Registers
    —Sources          DS135.F8
—Deportations from Hungary          JX5141
—Deportations from Italy          D810.D5, D805.G3
—Deportations from Java (Indonesia)          D805.I55
—Deportations from Latvia          D810.D5
—Deportations from Peru          D769.8.A6
—Deportations from Poland          D810.D5, D805.G3, D805.P7, D802.P62
    —Sources
—Deportations from Seine-Maritime (France)          DS135.F85.S442
—Deportations from the Baltic States          D810.D5
—Deportations from Channel Islands
—Deportations from Yugoslavia
—Desertions
—Destruction and pillage          D810.D6, .A7 (art), .C8 (carillons),
                                D785.U (bombing), N6492.2-3          940.53187
    —Bavaria
    —Belgium—Louvain          D804.G3          027.7493
    —Czechoslovakia—Lidice          D765.55.L43
    —Dresden          D757.9.D7
    —East Asia
    —East (Far East)          D810.D6
    —Europe          D785, D810.D6, N6492.2          940.53187
    —France          D810.D6, D819.F7          940.53187, .5405
        —Rouen          D762.R6          940.5405
    —Germany          D810.D6, D785-6, Z801 (libraries)          940.5442
        —Cologne          D757.9.C6
        —Darmstadt          D757.9.D3          940.5421
        —Dresden          DD901.D78
    —Germany (West)
        —Hamburg          D757.9.H3
        —Wuerzburg          D757.9.W8
        —Würzburg          D757.9.W8
    —Great Britain—London
    —Greece
    —Hungary
    —Italy
        —Florence          D763.I82.F6, N6921.F6          708.5
    —Japan          D785.U          940.544, 621.312
        —Nagoya
    —Periodicals
    —Poland          D810.D6, .D6.P73, D804.G3, NC268.P6
                   940.5405, .53438
        —Warsaw
    —Russia          D829.R8
    —Yugoslavia          DS10          940.5318910453
—Dictionaries          D740, D744          940.53, .5303, 411.5
    —Dutch
    —Polish

World War, 1939-1945
—Diplomatic history        D748-754, D748, D754, D735, DB955, DD256+,
        DD523, DK268, E744, E183.8.A-Z (U.S.-other places)
        940.430+, .520+, .5314, .5322, .5324, .5332, .5373, .542,
        .582, 327.73081
  —Addresses, essays, lectures
  —Congresses
  —Sources
  —Yugoslavia        D754.Y9
—Discography        ML156.2        789.913
—Displaced persons  [SEE ALSO '...—Refugees']        D808-9, DS135, D810.J4,
        D820.P72, JV6416, JV6424, JV9125        940.53159,
        378.12, 301.452309+
  —Case studies        HV43        361.53
  —Registers, lists, etc.
—District of Columbia
—Documents and sources        D734-5
—Documents, etc., sources        D735, DD253        327.43
  —Bibliography
—Documents, sources, etc.        D735        940.53082, .5322, .5332, .52
—Dogs        D810.D        940.541273
—Draft resisters
  —United States
—Drama        PN6120.R2        792+
—Dutch East Indies        DS644, DS889.3.D9, D767.7, D805.J3 (prisons),
        D811.5        940.5391, .547252
—East Asia        D742.J3, D753, D767
  —Bibliography
—East Cameroon        D766.98
—East (Far East)        D767+, D802.A2+, D805.J3, D811.5, DS518,
        E745.C42 (Chennault)        940.5425-5426, .548173,
        .54867+, 915.2, 950+
—Economic appeals
—Economic aspects        D800, HB195, HC58, HC101, HC286.4, D785.U
        940.5485, .53144, .531833, 330.19355, .5452, .904
  —American republics        HF3080
  —Argentina
  —Argentine Republic
  —Asia        HC412        330.95
  —Australia        HC605, HD7957, D767.8.A, D829.A2        331.154, 338.0994
  —Belgium        HC315, DH687
  —Bibliography        Z6207, Z6464.Z9, Z7164.L1, HD6961, JS303
        016.33019355, .331
  —Brazil        HC187
  —California        HC106.4
  —Canada        HC115        330.971, .19355
  —Case studies
  —China        HC427.8, HD3224        334.64
  —Colombia        HC197

World War, 1939-1945
—Economic aspects
    —East (Far East)    HC462
    —Europe    D815    940.531444
    —Finland    HE848.3, HF5415.12.F5
    —France    HB236.F8, HC276, HF5349.F8, HG8055, D742.F7-8, D800
        330.944, 338.50944, 355.23, 940.531833
    —Germany    HC286.4, .5, HD3616.G32-35, HD8450-58, HD9743.G3-
        48, D785.U5-6 (U.S. bombing), D800    330.943,
        331.50943, 338.47621822, .476655, .943, 354.430082+,
        358.30943, 940.5343+, .5310943, .531833
    —Gold Coast    HF5349.G5
    —Great Britain    HA1125 (statistics), HB195, HB236.G7, HC256.4,
        HD1925 (agric.), HD4145, HD6664 & 8390 (unions &labor),
    HD7801, HD9551.5,HD9743.G6-7 (munitions), HJ1023 (public
    finance), D800    330.19355, .942, 331.0942, .1082,
    .137082, .880942, 336.42, 338.942, 355.26, 658.3152,
    690.942, 940.534205
    —Iceland    HC357.I3    330.9491
    —India    HC435, HD7801.I6+    330.954
    —Italy    HC305
    —Jamaica
    —Japan    HC462, D785.U5-6 (U.S. bombing)    330.952,
        338.952, 355.26
    —Latin America    HC163, E744.A2    330.98
    —Maritime provinces, Canada    HC117.M35    330.971
    —Mauritius    HC507.M44, HC517.M5    338.96982
    —Mexico    HC131-5, HF3236    338.526
    —Michigan    HC107.M58
    —Near East    HC410.7    338.956
    —Netherlands    HB236.N4, HD4905.5
    —New Zealand    HB236.N4, HC622    330.9931, 338.526
    —Norway    HC365
    —Periodicals
    —Poland    HC337.P7, HD8538
    —Russia    HC335-335.6, HD6732 (unions), HD8526 (labor),
        HD9735.R92 (manufacturing)    330.947
        —Bibliography    Z7165.R9
        —Maritime Province
        —Siberia    HC487.S5, HD8749.S5
    —South Africa    HC517.S7
    —Soviet Union    HC335.6
    —Spanish America    HC163    330.98+
    —Sweden    HC371-5
    —Switzerland    HF3706

World War, 1939-1945
—Economic aspects
 —United States    HB236.U5 (prices), HC101, HC106.3-6, HD3616
            (industry & state), HD5660.U5, HD6058 (women),
            HD6961 (indus. relns.), HD6983 (costs, wages, profits),
            HD7293 (housing), HD7801 (union-mgt. coop.), HD7833 (labor
            laws), HD8051.A or U (cost of living), HD8072 (labor), HD9105
            (sugar), HG538 (inflation), E173, TX326 (consumers)
            330.973, 331.0973, .8310973, .880973, 332.414, 337.0973,
            338.0973, .476641, .50973, .91, 339.4973, 355.260973,
            940.5315396
  —Bibliography    Z5074.E3 (agric.)    016.6311
  —History    HD5325.A8 (strikes-auto)
 —West (U.S.)
—Education and the war    D810.E3-5, LC4069.W3    940.531537,
            .531837, .5345, 370.973, .61764, .9752, 371.206273,
            .80631, .9, 378.764
 —Congresses
—Egypt    D742, DT70, DT107.82    940.5362, 916.2
—Electronic intelligence—United States    D810.C88
—Emilia-Romagna    D763.I82
—Engineering and construction    D769, D792, D795    940.541273 (U.S.),
            .542, .5459, 359.982
—England
 —Channel Islands    D760.8.C5    940.534234
 —Fiction
 —London
 —Watford—Pictorial works    D760    942.5892084+
 —Westminster
—Equipment and supplies    UC480-5, UG446.5
—Eritrea    D766.84    940.548142
—Estonia    DK511.E45-6, D764.7.E8    947.4
—Ethiopia    D766.92
—Europe    D755-7, D802.A2, D785.U (bombing), D922    940.5337, .544,
            .5308
 —Biography
—Europe, Eastern    D802.E92, DJK49
—Evacuation of civilians    D753.8.U, D768.15 (Jpns. reloc. in Can.),
            D769.8.A6 (Jpns. reloc. in. U.S.), E184.J3 (Jpns.-Am's.),
            D810.C4 (children), HC101    940.53161-
            53163, .5472+, .547273 (U.S.), 330.973
 —Bibliography    Z1361.J2, Z6207.W8
 —Canada    D768.15
 —Great Britain    D801.G7, D809.G7
 —Netherlands
 —Pictorial works    F857
 —Prussia, East (Poland and R.S.F.S.R.)
 —Prussia (Germany)    D809.G3
 —United States—Periodicals    D769.8.A6
—Evangelical and Reformed Church    D810.C64    284.173
—Exhibitions    D733
—Fiction    [Usually classified with individual author within
            nationality/language groups]
 —Collections
 —History and criticism

World War, 1939-1945
—France        D742.F8, D752, D761, D802.F8+ (underground occupied terr.),
                     D811, D819.F, DC340, DC373, DC389, DC396-7
                     940.5344, .540944, .5421, .548144, .5486, .5311, .532244,
                     944.081, 923.544
    —Abbeville         D762.A2
    —Aerial operations    D761.9
    —Allier (Dept.)      D762.A38
    —Alsace            D802.F82.A45 (occup. terr.)
    —Ard`eche (Dept.)     D762.A67, DC611.A67
    —Ariege           D802.F82.A765
    —Arles          D762.A7
    —Arras          DC801.A79       944.27
    —Auvergne       D802.F82.A
    —Beauvais—Pictorial works   D762.B42
    —Biography        DC373
    —Boulogne-sur-Mer    D762.B63
    —Brest
    —Brittany        D802.F82.B745 (underground)
    —Caen          D802.F82.C343
    —Calais          D762.C34
    —Cerizay        DC801.C295
    —Chambon-sur-Lignon (Le)
    —Chartres        D762.C45
    —Children's literature    D743.7
    —Chronology       D761
    —Clermont-Ferrand    D802.F82.C627
    —Cleurie River Valley    DC611.C655
    —Collected works    D761
    —Colonies      D761.9.A1
    —Congresses     D744.4, D765, D802.F8
    —Cote D'Or      D762.C76
    —Cotentin       D756.5.N6      940.5421
    —Eure-et-Loir    D802.F82.E878
    —Finisterre     D802.D82.F567
    —Franche-Comte    D802.F82.F77
    —Granville
    —Guenrouet     D802.F82.G833
    —Haute Savoie
    —Hautes-Pyrenees
    —Havre         D762.H2
    —Juvenile literature
    —La Vallette-du-Var
    —Laon
    —Le-Chambon-sur-Lignon    DS135.F85.L434 (Jews)
    —Literary collections    D745.2
    —Literary questions
    —Loir-et-Cher—Battles, sieges, etc.
    —Lyons region    D762.L93
    —Maillé
    —Manche       D802.F82.M364
    —Marseille     D762.M3
    —Metz         D802.F82.M4378 (occup. terr.)
    —Meurthe-et-Moselle (Dept.)    D762.M4    940.541244
    —Morbihan        D762.M55

World War, 1939-1945
 —France
　　—Moselle　　　　D802.F82.M
　　—Mulhouse　　　 D802.F82.M857
　　—Nantes　　　　　　D802.F82.N362
　　—Naval operations—Sources　　　Z6834.H5
　　—Nord (Dept.)　　　D762.N57
　　—Normandy
　　—Oleron, Ile d'　　　D762.O42
　　—Oradour-sur-Glane　　　D804.G3-4 (atrocities)　　　940.54056
　　—Oullins　　　　　　D762.O94
　　—Pamphlets
　　—Paris　　　　　D762.P2-3, D802.F82.P375-376 (underground),
　　　　　　　　　　D809.F8 (evac. of civilians)　　　940.5344, .534436
　　—Pas-de-Calais (Dept.)　　　D762.N57
　　—Periodicals　　　　　D731
　　—Poetry
　　—Provence　　　D762.P9
　　—Saint Nazaire
　　—Saint-Etienne Region (Loire)　　　D802.F82.S224
　　—Saint-Lô
　　—Sainte-Mere-Eglise　　　D762.S25
　　—Sarreguemines　　　　　D762.S29
　　—Saumur　　　　　D762.S2
　　—Strasbourg　　　D802.F82.S777
　　—Tarentaise　　　D762.T29
　　—Toul　　　　　　D762.T57　　　940.540944382
　　—Toulon　　　　　D779.F8
　　—Toulouse　　　　　　D762.T583
　　—Tournissan　　　　　　D762.T6
　　—Tours　　　　　D762.T6
　　—Tulle
　　—Vercors　　　　D762.V4
　　—Vienne (Dept.)　　　D762.V5
　　—Vincennes
 —Free and resistance movements, Jewish
 —Free India　　　　D767.63　　　940.5354, 954035
 —Friends, Society of　　　D827, BX7635　　　940.53144
 —Friesland (Netherlands)　　　D785, D802.F85
 —Fuel supplies　　　D810.F83　　　940.53
 —Gascony　　　　D802.F8　　　940.5344
 —Georgians (Transcaucasians)

World War, 1939-1945
—German Americans
—German occupation—Netherlands    940.53492
—Germany        D735-7, D741, D742.G3, D751, D757+, D764,
                D781 (naval ops.), D785.U5-6 (bombing of), D804.G3 (atrocities),
                D809.G3 (refugees), D811, D819.G3, D821, DD94, DD232, DD247,
                DD247.H5 (Hitler), DD253, DD256+                940.5314, .5343,
                .54013, .540943, .541343, .5421, .5440943, .5482, .548743,
                943.086, .1087, 355.331, 623.194
    —Addresses, essays, lectures
    —Addresses, sermons, etc.
    —Aerial operations    D787
    —Augsburg
    —Berlin              D757.9.B4, DD256.3, DD880-81
    —Bibliography        Z6207.W8
    —Biography           DD243.A-z, DS135 (Jews)
    —Bremen              D757.9.B67
    —Campaigns    UA713        940.541343
    —Cologne                   D757.9.C6
    —Constance, Lake of        D757.9.C76
    —Dresden                   D757.9.D7
—Germany, East
        —Dresden         D757.9.D7
        —Greifswald
        —Halle (Bezirk)
        —Harz Mountains Region        D757.9.H35
        —Magdeburg (Bezirk)
        —Peenemunde           D757.9.P37 (bombing)
—Germany
    —Fiction
    —Frankfurt am Main        D757.9.F7    940.5343
    —Hamburg             DD901.H28
    —Hanover (City)      D785.U5-6 (U.S. bombing)
    —Heilbronn           D757.9.H36
    —Juvenile literature
    —Kolberg             D757.9.K83
    —Münsterland         D757.9.M78
    —Nuremberg           DD901.N94
    —Oldesloe
    —Periodicals         D731
    —Pictorial works     NC251        741.5943
    —Propaganda
    —Religious aspects
    —Reutlingen (Landkreis)        D757.9.R47
    —Sources             D757, DD247
    —Stralsund           DD901.S8
    —Transportation—History

World War, 1939-1945
  —Hawaii        D767.92, DU623, DU624.7, HC687.H3     940.53969, .5426
  —Hawaiian Islands     D767, D810    940.53969, .5477
    —Pearl Harbor    D767   940.53969
  —Health
  —Health aspects      D805, D807
  —Himalaya Mountains    D790   940.5425
  —Historiography       D742, D743.42, D748, U21     940.53072, .541273
    —Congresses     D743.42, D764
  —History    —Fiction
  —Hongkong        D802.H6, DS796.H75-757     940.5351
  —Horses
  —Hospitals
  —Hospitals, charities, etc.    [SEE ALSO '...—Medical and sanitary affairs.]
  —Humor         D745.2-7
  —Humor, caricatures, etc.    D745.2 (Am. & Eng.), D745.2.P8 ('Punch'),
                D745.3 (Fr.), .5 (Ger.), .7.A-Z (other places), .7.F48 (Finnish),
                D811.Y16-3 ('Yank'), NC1428, NC1429.N ('New Yorker'), NC1479
                940.548141, .548173 (US), .5496-5497, 741.5973, 358.400973
  —Hungary        D742.H9, D754.H9, D765.56, D802.H89, DB950-56,
                DS135.H9 (Jews)     940.534391, .5482439, 943.9105
    —Balatonszarszo    D765.562.B32
    —Budapest    D764, DL870
    —Ujpost    DB999.U54
  —Iceland        D763.I2    940.53491
World War, 1939-1945 in art    ND1442.G76 (G.B.)
World War, 1939-1945 in literature  [SEE ALSO '...—Literature and the war']
                PR605.W3 (Eng. poetry for WWI & II), PG3026.W3 (Russ. poetry)
World War, 1939-1945 in pictures    D743.23, PN1997    940.5300222, 791.437
World War, 1939-1945
  —India        D742.I4, D754.I4, D767.6+, D811.5, DS480.82-3, DS481
                940.548142, .5354, 923.254 (Gandhi)
    —Bengal
    —Bombay
  —Indian Ocean      D767.6
  —Indians      D810.I5, .C95 (cryptography: Navajos)
  —Indochina     DS549
  —Indo-China, French     D767.45, DS549-550     940.5359, .53597, .5425
    —Laos
  —Indonesia     D767.7, DS643.5-644 991
    —Java
    —Sumatra    D805.J3
    —Timor Timor    DS646.5
  —Influence        D727, D741, D744, D749, D753.2
  —Influence and results     D511, D741, D744, D753, CB203, E744, HC58
                940.53, .531, .5314, .531815, .5373, 330.904
  —Influence—Sources
  —Intelligence service
    —France
    —Great Britain
  —International law    JX5144
  —Iran        D766.7.I7, D769, DS318    940.5355
  —Iraq
  —Ireland      D754.I5-6, DA963    941.591
  —Islam

World War, 1939-1945
  —Islands of the Aegean     D766     940.5421
  —Islands of the Baltic     D764.7.B3
  —Islands of the Pacific
  —Italy     D742.I7, D754.I8, D763.I8, D802.I8 (underground), D813.I8,
          D829.I8, DG498, DG571-2, DG575     940.5320924, .5345,
          .5421, 945.091
    —Addresses, essays, lectures
    —Bari (City)     D763.I82.B2-374     940.548673
    —Bibliography
    —Bologna
    —Congresses     DG572
    —Costrignano
    —Emilia Romagna—Periodicals     DG975.E53
    —Exhibitions     D763.I8
    —Finance
    —Florence     D763.I82.F6     940.534551
    —Frascati     D763.I82.F8
    —Gorizia (Province)     D802.I82.G (occup. terr.)
    —Milan     D763.I82.M52
    —Monchio     D763.I82.M65
    —Naples     D763.I82.N36     940.5441
    —Orcia River Valley     D763.I82.O746
    —Ossola Valley     D802.I82.O82
    —Po River and valley
    —Posters     DG571
    —Propaganda     DG571
    —Rome
    —Rome (City)     D763.I82.R6-68     940.5421, .5485 (secret srvc.)
    —Rome—Fiction
    —San Martino Valle Caudina     D763.I82.S267
    —Sicily     DG869-869.2
    —Study and teaching—Congresses
    —Trials
    —Trieste
    —Tuscany
  —Japan     D742.J3, .U5, D754.J3, D767+, D767.2+, D804.J3 (atrocities),
          D810.P7.J352 (propaganda), D814.8 (peace), D821J3, DS503,
          DS530, DS806, DS830, DS843, DS885-90     940.5314+,
          .53452, .5352, .540952, .5412730952, .541352, .542, .5425,
          .5441, .548173, .5488752, 952.03, .033, 915.2
    —Hiroshima     D767.25.H6, D790, UF767.U5-6     940.5425,
          .544, 623.45
    —Hiroshima-shi
    —Nagasaki     D767.25.N3, UF767.U5-6 (atom bomb)     623.45
    —Periodicals
    —Japan, Sea of     D780
    —Supplies     UD446.5, UD485.J3     356.1660952, 358.180952
    —Tokyo     D790
  —Japanese-Americans     D753.8, D769.8.A6 (evacuation)
  —Java     D767.7, D802.J32-38, D805.J3 (prisons), DS646.27
          940.53922, .5337, 992.2
  —Jersey     D760.8.J4, D802.J4     940.5342, .534234

World War, 1939-1945
—Latvia            D742.L3, D802.L3        940.53474, 947.4
    —Courland
    —Riga          D802.L32.R4 (occupied terr.)
—Law and legislation    JX4511 (int'nal. law), JX5270 341.3
    —Africa, North
    —Bombay (State)
    —Canada        KE6818
    —Europe
    —France        D802.F8 (Grmn. occup.), D829.F8 (collaborationists),
                   K25.F84, K50.F8
    —Germany       D802.A2.G7 & JX4514 (occupied terr.),
                   D810.C8 (confiscations)          940.5337
    —Great Britain
    —India         D767.6
        —Bombay (State)
    —Ireland       K25.I68
    —Italy         K25.I8
    —Peru
    —Poland
    —Silesia, Upper (Poland and Czechoslovakia)      DK4600
    —Silesia, Upper (Province)
    —United States    HD3622.U5, J82, JK560, JX5270, UB773 (srvcmen.)
                      353.03, 355.134
        —States       JK2430, KF165
    —Uruguay
    —Virginia      JK3916
—Lebanon           D750
—Levant            D739, D754.L4, D766, D810.J4,(Jews), DS49, DS126.3
                   940.5356, .536, 956+, 915.6
—Libraries         Z665, Z672, Z675.W2      021.93, 027.652, 940.531802
—Libya             DT227        961.2
—Literary collections    PN6071.W75
—Literature and the war    D810.A7, .P7, PN131, PG3026.W3 (Russian),
            PG3096.W67, PQ307.W3 (French),  PR605.W3 (Br. poetry),
            PS228.W37 (Am.)      940.54886+, 029.60621, 808.0668, 810.904
    —Bibliography      Z6519
—Lithuania         D742.L8, D754.L77, D802.L5, DK511.L2-27
                   940.53475, 947.508
—Logistics
—Lutheran Church
—Luxemburg    [SEE ALSO '...—Luxembourg']      D763, D802.A45
                                              940.53493, .5404
—Macedonia         D766.62.M2, D766.6
    —Poetry        PG1189.M289-3, D745.7.M3
—Madagascar        D766.99.M3
—Mainly Peninsula      D767        940.53595
—Malacca, Strait of    D767
—Malay Peninsula       D767.5, D802.M2 (occup. terr.), DS595-8+,
                   DS598.P38 (Penang)    940.53595, .542, .547594, 915.95
—Malaya            D767.5, DS595+      940.5425, 959.5+, 915.95
—Malaysia
    —Malaya        D767.5
—Malta             D763.M3, D768, D784.G7      940.5453, .5442, .5421
—Manchuria         D767.2

World War, 1939-1945
—Manpower    [mil. & econ. discussions]    HD6961, HD8051
            331.061+, .137
    —Belgium    HC315
    —Bibliography    Z6207.W8, HD6961
    —Canada
    —Columbus, Ohio    HD5726.C7
    —Finland    HD8533
    —Germany    HD4813, HD5701, HD7801    331.137082, .57
    —Great Britain    HD5767, HD5917    331.1120942, 355.220941
    —Los Angeles    HD5726.L7-77
    —The West
    —United States    HD5723-5724, HD5873, HD6511 (unions), HD6961,
            HD8072, HB1765.A5.1940, UB343, D769    331+,
            331.06173, .071174967, .112, .152, .880973, 306.27471,
            312.0973, 330.973, 355.220973, .260973
        —History    HD5724
—Manuscripts—Catalogs    Z6611.H5
—Maps    D427, D731, D743, D743.3, D767.4, D820.T4, E744, G1038
        940.53-4, ,5314, .5499, .58
    —Bibliography    Z6207.W8
—Medals
—Medical and sanitary affairs    D806-7, D807.A-Z (by place or by country
            responsible), D807.B8 (Burma), .U5-6+ (U.S. medical work), D629,
            D769, .A or U, D785.U5-6+ (U.S. bombing), D805, D811, R722,
            RA776, RA790, RC971    940.5475+, .54752, .547542 (GB),
            .547547 (Rus.), .547573 (US), .547643 (Ger. hospitals),
            .5476732 (U.S. hospitals)
—Medical aspects
—Medical care    D807
    —Australia    D807.A8, UH321
    —Brazil    D807.B7
    —Netherlands
—Mediterranean region    D731, D766+, D766.82
—Mediterranean Sea    D766, D766.82, D770, D779.A-Z (naval ops.: by
            country: not limited to Med.), D779.A9 (Australian),
            D843, D973    940.542, .5421, .545
    —Congresses
—Mennonites    D810.C665
—Mexico    D754.M6, D769.2, F1203, F1234, F1392.G4 (Grmn. refugees—
            anti-Nazi)    940.5372, 972.0082, .08, .082, 327.72
—Micronesia (Federated States)—Ponape Island    DU568.P7
—Midway Islands    D767    940.545
—Military currency    HG353.5    769.55+, .550216
—Military intelligence
    —Germany    D810.S7
—Mindanao    D767.4.M17-25    940.5426
—Miscellanea    940.504
—Missing in action
—Missouri
—Missouri (Battleship)—Normandy    D769    940.53778
—Moldavia    D764.7.M55
—Montenegro    D766.62.M6

World War, 1939-1945
—Monuments
    —Hawaii
    —Yugoslavia
—Moral and ethical aspects    D744.4, D790 (bombing), UA26
—Moral aspects    D744.4, D810        940.53181781, .5304, .548, 901.9
—Moravia    D765.55.M6
—Moton pictures and the war    D743.23, D810.E8, .P7 (propaganda),
                                PN1995.2.H5
—Mukyokaishugi Shukai
—Museums
—Music and the war    D810.E8
—Muslims    D810.M6
—Naval operations    [SEE ALSO names of individual ships,
            e.g. 'Hotspur (Destroyer)]    D770-784, D767, D769,
            D770, D773, D779, D786, D811, UG1240+ (aviation),
            V767, VA58    940.542, .545+, 359+, 359.32, .3252, .3255+
—Naval operations, American    D773-4, D767, D769, D783+, V833, VA63-5+
                                940.5426, .544973, .545, .5451373 (subs),
                                .545973, .548173, .548673, .54973,387.54

    —Fiction
    —History—Sources—Bibliography—Catalogs        Z6835.U5
    —Pacific    D767    940.545973
—Naval operations, Australian    D779.A9, D767.8.A938, VA715
                                940.545994
—Naval operations
    —Baltic Sea    D764
    —Bibliography    Z6207.W8
    —Brazilian    D768.3
—Naval operations, British    D771, D772.A-Z (ships), D780, D784.G7 (subs),
                            DA89.1.A-Z (biog.), V835, VA454
                            940.545941-545942, .548642, 359.3320922-24

    —Fiction
—Naval operations, Canadian    D779.C2, D770-2, D756.5.D5 (Dieppe Raid)
                            940.545971
—Naval operations
    —Chronology    D770    940.545
    —Congresses    D775
—Naval operations, Dutch    D779.N4        940.5459492
—Naval operations, Finnish
—Naval operations, French    D779.F7-8, D784.F7, D788, DS553.1
                            940.545944
—Naval operations, German    D779.G3, D768.18, D771-3, D772.3,
                            D781 (subs), D781.A-Z, .D6+ (Dönitz), D784.G3,
                            DD770, VA513, VD74        940.545, .545943
—Naval operations, Greek    D779.G, DF775
—Naval operations, Indian    D779.I4
—Naval operations, Italian    D775, D780    940.545945
—Naval operations, Japanese    D777, D777.5.A-Z (by ship), .Y33 (Yamato),
                            D784, D792.J3 (aerial ops.), DS890.A-Z (biog.),
                            .Y25 (Yamamoto), VA653    940.5451, .545952,
                            359.320952
—Naval operations, Mexican    D779.M, D754.M6
—Naval operations, New Zealand    D779.N45        940.5459931

World War, 1939-1945
—Naval operations, Norwegian          D779.N6, D763.N6, D763.5, D802.N8
                                       940.5459481
—Naval operations, Polish          D779.P6, D765.2.G37, D770
—Naval operations, Portuguese          D779.P8
—Naval operations, Russian          D779.R9 or S65 (Soviet Un.),
                                       D784.R9 (subs), VA573          940.545947
—Naval operations, Submarine          D780-4, D782 (Ger.), D782.U15 (U-99),
                              D783 (US), D783.5.A-Z (names etc.), D784.A-Z (misc.
                              countries), .F7 (Fr.), .G7 (GB), D771-3, V859.A-Z,
                              .G3 (Ger.)          940.5451, .54513+, .5451342 (GB),
                              .5451373 (US), .54516, .545943 (Ger.), .5465756
     —Fiction
—Near East          D766, D731, D754, D769.U or A, DS63.2.A-Z          940.542
—Negroes   [SEE ALSO '...—Blacks']   D810.N          940.5403, .541273, .54516
—Netherlands          D754.N4, D763.N4, D793, D802.N4 (occup.), D811+,
                       D829.N2 (reconstruc.), DJ287, DS643
                       940.53144492, .53492, .5481492, 949.2+
     —Arnhem          D763.N42.A75          940.53492
     —Delft          D797.N4
     —Goes          D763.N4.G55-56
     —Gorinchem          DJ411          914.92
     —Heusden          D763.N42.H45-48
     —Leeuwarden          D763.N42.L51
     —Overijssel          D763.N42.O
     —Periodicals
     —Rotterdam          D763.N42.R74
     —'s-Hertogenbosch   D763.N42.H4
     —Twente          D763.N42.T86
     —Walcheren          D763.N42.W3
     —Wisch
—New Britain (Island)          D767.99.N4, D805.J3 (prison)          940.5497, .548173
—New Guinea          D767.95, D792.A8 (Australian air force), D811.5
                     950.542, .544994
—New Ireland (Island)          D767.99.N45          940.5426
—New Jersey
World War, 1939-1945 (New words, slang, etc.)
World War, 1939-1945
—New York
—New York (City)
—New York (N.Y.)
—New York—Oswego
—New York (State)          D769.85.N4
     —New York
—New Zealand          D742.N4-45, D743.9, D754.N45, D767.85
                      940.53931, .542
     —Chronology
—Nigeria          DT296, DT515.75          966.903
—North Carolina
—North Sea          D771, D802.N8

World War, 1939-1945
—Norway        D742.N6, D754.N6, D755.2, D763.N6, D735.G3,
                D802.N7 (underground), DL529, DL532
                940.5082, .532, .53481, .541481, .5459481, 948.1,
                327.7309481 (U.S. dipl. relns.), 387.509481
    —Bergen        D763.N62.B43
    —Bibliography    Z6207.W8
    —Dombas        D763.N62.D
    —Drama
    —Lesja        D763.N62.L475
    —Rjukan        D802.N72.R583
    —Svalbard        D763.N62.S923
—Occupied territories    [collective works: for occupation of single countries,
            SEE '{Name of country}—History—German {Japanese, etc.}
            occupation, {date span}']    D802.A-Z, .A2, D769.A or U (U.S.
            Army)        940.5337-5338, .53144, .54056, 355.4909
    —Congresses    D757, DD257
    —Periodicals
    —Sources
—Oceania        D767+, D767.9
    —Bibliography—Catalogs    Z6207.W8
—Oceanica    D767-9+, D767.9, D810.S7 (coastwatchers), DU29, E847
            940.54099, .5426, .545, .548694 (coastwatchers)
—Oceanics
—Orthodox Eastern Church, Serbian
—Outlines, syllabi, etc.    D427, D743.5, D745    940.5302, .53076, .5373, .54
—Pacific area        D767+, D767.9, D769    940.5425-5426, .544-545
—Pacific Coast        D769.1    940.5428
—Pacific Ocean        D767+, D769+, D769.A or U, D773-4, D777 (Jpns. navy),
            D783 (subs), D790 (air warfare), DS518, DU29, E745,
            E842, VA63.A-Z, VE500        940.5425-5426,
            .5352 (Japan), .542, .54260924 (biog.), .543-545,
            .545973 (U.S. Navy), 923.573 (biog.), 359.960973 (U.S. Navy)
    —Campaigns—Pictorial works
    —Pictorials
    —Sources
—Palestine        DS126.3, DS149, D810.J4 (Jews)        956.9
    —Biography
—Pamphlets
—Papua New Guinea        D767.95
    —Trobriand Islands        D767.99.T76        940.548194
—Participation, Afro-American        D810.N        940.541273
—Participation, Female        D810.W7
—Participation, Jewish
—Participation, Juvenile    [SEE ALSO '...—Juvenile participants']
—Peace        D734, D754.V (Vatican), D814-16+, D821, D825, D829.A-Z,
            DD259.4, E813, JX77, JX1392.5, JX1577, JX1952
            940..5304, .531, .5314, .53141.53144+, .532273,
            .5352 (Japan), .537, .54012, 909.82
    —Bibliography    Z6207.W8        016.940531
    —Collected works    D815.A
    —Periodicals
    —Societies, etc.
    —Sources    D814    940.5312, .5314
—Pechenga region    D765.3    947.103

505

World War, 1939-1945
—Pennsylvania          940.53748
—Periodicals           D731.A-Z (by title), D732, D735
—Persia                DS318
—Personal narratives   [SEE ALSO call number ranges for particular areas,
                       campaigns, topics, etc.]          D811, D811.5, D743,
                       D765, D802 (underground & occupied areas), D810,
                       D810.J4 (Jews)          940.5481-5482, .5449+ (aerial
                       ops.), .542 (battles etc. by theatre), .5315 (social groups)
—Personal narratives, Albanian
—Personal narratives, Alsatian
—Personal narratives, American          D811, D811.5, D761 (Fr.), D763.I8 (Italy),
                       D767 (Pacific), D767.99.I9 (Iwo Jima), .W3 (Wake Is.), D790 (aerial
                       ops.), D805.P6 (Phil. prisons), D811.A2 (group)          940.548173,
                       .44973 (Army air forces), .541273, .544, .545 (Navy), .547243
                       (Ger. prisons), .547252 (Jpns. prisons), .54771, .548673, .5496
—Personal narratives, Australian          D811, D811.5, D766.82 (N. Africa),
                       D767.82.D2 (Darwin), D805.J3 (Jpns. prisons)
                       940.548194, .548394
—Personal narratives, Austrian          D811, D802.A9 (underground),
                       D805.R9 (Rus. prisons)          940.5481436,
                       .5482436, .53159, .5344
—Personal narratives, Belgian          D811, D811.5          940.53493
—Personal narratives, Brazilian          D811, D763.I8 (in Italy), D768.3, D807.B7
—Personal narratives, British   [SEE ALSO '...—Personal narratives, English']
                       D811 & 811.5, D811.A2 (group)
                       940.544942, .548142
—Personal narratives, Bulgarian          D811          940.53496
—Personal narratives, Byelorussian
—Personal narratives, Canadian          D811          940.540971, .544-545, .548171, .594
—Personal narratives, Chinese
—Personal narratives, Collections          D811          940.5481
—Personal narratives, Croatian          D811, D802.Y8
—Personal narratives, Czech          D811, D805.G3 (Ger. prisons), DB215-17
                       940.5482437, .547243
—Personal narratives, Danish          D811, D802.D4          940.5481489
—Personal narratives, Dutch          D811, D802.I52 (Indonesian underground),
                       .N4, D805.J3 (Jpns. prisons)          940.5472492,
                       .5481492
—Personal narratives, East Indian          D767.63, D799.I4 (journalists)
                       940.5354, 355.3510954
—Personal narratives, Ecuadorian
—Personal narratives, English          [SEE ALSO '...—Personal narratives,
                       British']          D811 & 811.5, D756 (Western), D763,
                       D766-767, D766.82 (N. Africa), D767.6 (Burma),
                       D786 (aerial), D805.G3 (Ger. prisons), .J3 (Jpns.
                       prisons)          940.548142, .5342, .5421,
                       .544942, .547243, .548642
—Personal narratives, Estonian
—Personal narratives, Faroese
—Personal narratives, Filipino          D811+, D767.4, DS686.4
                       940.5481914, .5409599, .5426
—Personal narratives, Finnish          D765.3

World War, 1939-1945
—Personal narratives, French    D811+, D761-3, D766+, D766.82 (N. Africa),
    D788 (aerial), D802.F8 (underground), D805.G3
    940.548144, .5344, .5348144 (underground), .544,
    .544944, .547243 (Ger. prisons), 944.0810924
—Personal narratives, German    D811 & 811.5, D757, D763.N6 (Norway),
    D764 (Rus.), D787, D805.F8 (Fr. prisons), .R9 (Rus. prisons),
    .U5 (U.S. prisons), D810.S8 (secret srvc.), DD256, DD259.7
    940.548243, .542, .544943 (aerial), .547244 (Fr. prisons),
    .547273 (Am. prisons), 943.086
—Personal narratives, Greek    D811 & 811.5, D766.3-7,
    D802.G8 (underground)    940.5482495, 949.507
—Personal narratives, Hungarian    D811 & 811.5, D765.56, D805.P7
    940.54814391, .534391, .54814391,
    .547243 (Ger. prisons) & concen. camps)
—Personal narratives, Icelandic
—Personal narratives, Italian    D811+, D754.I8, D763.I8,
    D802.I8 (underground), D805.F8 (Fr. prisons),
    .G7 (Brit. prisons), D807.I8 (medical)
    940.53161, .5345, .547242, .548245
—Personal narratives, Japanese    D811 & 811.5, D767+, D767.25.H6
    (Hiroshima), D767.4 (Philippines), D767.5 (Malay
    Penin.), D767.92 (Pearl Harbor), D767.99.A-Z,
    D767.99.I9 (Iwo Jima), D777 (navy), DS890
    940.548252, .5426+, .547242 (Brit. prisons)
—Personal narratives, Jewish    D811+, D765.2.W3 (Warsaw), D804.G4,
    D810.J4, DS125.5-135, DS135.A-Z, .L5 (Lithuania),
    .R9 (Russia)    940.5315+, .531503, .531503924,
    .53150693, .5315296, .53156, .53159, .53161, .534380924,
    .53492, .535694, .5404-5405, .547243 (Ger. concentration
    camps), .5478, .5481+, .548143, .5481438, 943.805, .8405+
—Personal narratives, Latvian    D811+    940.54814743
—Personal narratives, Lettish
—Personal narratives, Lithuanian    D805.R9 (Rus. prisons)
—Personal narratives, Mexican    D811.5
—Personal narratives, Montenegrin    D811.A2
—Personal narratives, New Zealand    D811 & 811.5, D805.G3 (Ger. prisons),
    .J3 (Jpns. prisons)    940.5481931, .548194, .542
—Personal narratives, Northern Ireland    D770
—Personal narratives, Norwegian    D811+, D779.N6, D802.N8
    (underground), D805.G3 (Ger. prisons), D809.N8
    940.5481481, .547243 (Ger. prisons)
—Personal narratives, Palestinian    D811, D805.G3, D810.J4 (Jews), DS126.3
—Personal narratives, Philippine    D767.2-4
—Personal narratives, Polish    D811+ D811.5, D765-765.2, D792,
    D799.P7 (underground lit.), D802.P6 (underground),
    D804.R9 (Rus. atrocities), D805.G3, .P7, D809.P6
    940.5481438, .547243, .547247 (Rus. prisons)
—Personal narratives, Portuguese    D811.5, D767.7
—Personal narratives, Romanian
—Personal narratives, Rumanian    D811+    940.5481498
—Personal narratives, Russian    D811+, D764+, D792.R9 (aerial ops.),
    D802.U4 (Ukrainian underground), D805.G3
    (Ger. prisons), DK265.7
    940.548147, .540947, .542

World War, 1939-1945
  —Personal narratives, Scottish
  —Personal narratives, Serbian     D811, D766.62.A-Z, D802.Y8 (underground)
  —Personal narratives, Serbo-Croatian
  —Personal narratives, Serbocroatian
  —Personal narratives, Slovenian     D811 & 811.5, D766.62.S45, D802.S63,
                        D810.S7       940.53161
  —Personal narratives, South African     D811, D766.97, D792.S6, D805.A4
                        940.5368, .548168
  —Personal narratives, Spanish     D811, D764, D805 (prisons), DP269.9
  —Personal narratives, Swedish     D811+, D808       940.548
  —Personal narratives, Swiss     D811.5, D754.S9     940.5481494
  —Personal narratives, Ukrainian     D811 & 811.5     940.54814771
  —Personal narratives, Uruguayan
  —Personal narratives, Wendic
  —Personal narratives, Yugoslav     D811+, D754.Y9 (diplomats), D766.62,
                        D802.Y8 (underground)
  —Peru     D769.8.A6
  —Philippine Islands     D767.4, D811, E806     940.5425-5426, .5481914,
               973.917
    —Bataan (Luzon)     D767     940.5426, .547673
  —Philippines     D767.4, D773, D805.J3 (Jpns. prisons), .P6, DS685,
                 DS686.3-4, E806     940.542, .547252, 991.4,
                 919.40335+, 923.1914, 973.917
    —Bataan (Province)
    —Bibliography     DS503
    —Lubang Island
  —Photography     D810.P4     940.5441, .5486, .548173
  —Pictorial works     [SEE ALSO numbers for various specific areas,
            campaigns, etc.]     D731, D743.2, D746, D762, D767 (Pac. &
            Asia), D785 (aerial ops.), UG446, N6512, NC1200, ND1240,
            ND1839, NE2210     940.530222, .53084, .531867+, .5347,
            .540022, .5421, .548173, .5497, 741.91, 743.973, 756, 759.13
    —Catalogs     D743.22
  —Pigeons
  —Poetry     D745+, D745.2, .3, PG3026.W3 (Rus.), PG3488.S692
            (Solzhenitsyn), PQ307.W3 (Fr.), PR1149, PR1195.W66 (Eng.:
            overall), PR1225     820.800912, 821.91082,
            841.91082, 891.7177
  —Poland     D731, D742, D754.P7, D765-765.2, D802.P6 (underground),
            D804.P6 (atrocities), D809.P6 (refugees), D810.G6 (exile gov.),
            DK268, DK440-1, DK4419, DK4600, JK1555.7 (occup.), U773
            940.481438, .5322438, .53438, .5405, .54056, .542, .544, 943.8,
            327.4380943 (for. relns. w. Ger.), .4380947 (w. Rus.),
            .4709438 (Rus. for. relns. w. Pol.)
    —Bialystok (Region)     D765.2.B47
    —Bibliography     Z6207.W8
    —Bydgoszcz region     D802.P62.B98 (underground)
    —Bydgoszcz (Voivodeship)
    —Collected works
    —Czestochowa     D765.2.C9, DS135.P62.C99 (Jews)
    —Drama
    —Fiction
    —Gda´nsk region     D765.2.G37, D802.P62.G375
    —Jaslo (District)     D802.P62.J378, D805.P7.J28-32

World War, 1939-1945
—Poland
    —Kraków          D802.P62.K767-85
    —Lemberg
    —Lód´z
    —Opole region     D765.2.O6
    —Periodicals      D731, DK401.P7+
    —Pictorial works   D765
    —Podlasie        D802.P62.P5886
    —Pomerania      D765.2.P6
    —Pozna´n
    —Rzeszów, Poland (Voivodeship)    D802.P62.R939
    —Siedlce     DS135.P62.S55 (Jews)
    —Sosnowiec   D765.2.S6
    —Sources     DK402
    —Warsaw        D765.2.W3, D765, D799.P7 (underground lit.),
                        D802.P62.W26-32 (underground), D810.J4, DK4633,
                        DS135.P62.W2-3 (Jews)    940.53438, .542,
                        .5481438 (personal narratives)
      —Pictorial works   D802.P62.W33
    —Warsaw region    D802.P62.W3726
      —Sources
    —Wielkopolska    D765.2.W5, D810.D5
    —Zakopane     D804.G4 (atrocities)
    —Zamo´s´c (Region)    D802.P62.Z385
—Pomerania             D802.P62.P62, DD491.P78, DK4410
—Pomerania (Poland and Germany)    DK4410
—Portraits
—Portugal     D754.P8, DP556, DP680     327.469
—Postal service   D800
—Posters       D743+, D743.25, D522.25     769.4994053
    —Catalogs     D522.25 (WWI & II)
    —Exhibitions    D743.25, D527.5 (WWI & II)
—Pribilof Islands    D769     940.542
—Price regulation  [SEE 'Price regulation']
—Prisoners and prisons     D763, D804 (war crimes & atrocities), D805.A2,
                  D806 (Red Cross etc.), D811+ (personal narratives)
                  940.5472+, .547252 (Jpns.), .547243 (Ger.), .5315
—Prisoners and prisons, American [British, German, etc.: prisoners held in
                     {U.S., Brit., Ger., etc.} prisons as well as
                     prisons run by {U.S., G.B., etc.}]
—Prisoners and prisons, American     D769.8.A, D805.U5,
                  DD247.G67 (Goering)     940.547273, .548243
    —Bibliography
—Prisoners and prisons, Australian    D805.A77-8
—Prisoners and prisons, Belgian     D805.B4
—Prisoners and prisons, British     D805.B9, .G7 (GB), D811, DA89
                  940.547242-547243, .5488941
—Prisoners and prisons, Bulgarian
—Prisoners and prisons, Canadian    D805.C2
—Prisoners and prisons—Fiction
—Prisoners and prisons, French     D805.F8, .M8 (Morocco), DC397
                  940.547244

World War, 1939-1945
—Prisoners and prisons, German      D805.G3, .A9 (Austria), .F8 (Fr.),
                .P7 (Poland), D802 (underground), D802.A2,
                D804.G3-4 (concentration camps), D810.J4 (Jews),
                D811-811.5     940.547243, .5405, .541243+,
                .5481+, .54814, .548642
        —Anniversaries
        —Bibliography     Z6207.W8
        —Fiction
        —Pictorial works    D805.A2, .G3
—Prisoners and prisons, Greek
—Prisoners and prisons, Hungarian    D805.H8     940.54724391
—Prisoners and prisons, Italian     D805.I8     940.547245
—Prisoners and prisons, Japanese    D805.J3, .I55 (Indonesia), .J4 (Java),
                .P6 (Philippines), .S5 (Singapore), .T5 (Thailand),
                D767+, D811+, DS485 (Burma), DS644 (Bali), DS796
                940.547252, .547259, .548142, .548194, 951.05
        —Exhibitions
        —War crime trials—Tokyo, 1946-1948    D804    940.547252
—Prisoners and prisons—Kenya—History—Sources    DT387.92
—Prisoners and prisons, New Zealand            D805.N, .A77 (Australian)
—Prisoners and prisons—Periodicals    D805.A1
—Prisoners and prisons, Polish     D805.P, .G3 (Ger.), D804.G
—Prisoners and prisons, Rumanian    [ALSO '..., Romanian']    D805
                        940.5472498
—Prisoners and prisons, Russian     D805.R9, .S65, D810.J4 (Jews), D811+
                940.547247, .547243 (Ger.), .5405094762
—Prisoners and prisons, Soviet
—Prisoners and prisons, Spanish     D805.S7
—Prisoners and prisons—Statistics
—Prisoners and prisons, Swiss     D805.S9
—Prisoners and prisons, Yugoslavian    D805.Y8
—Prizes, etc.
—Propaganda     D639.P7 (WWI & II), D810.P6-7, D810.P7.A-Z (by origin),
        .P7.F73 (Fr.), .P7.G3+ (Ger.), .P7.G7 (Brit.), .P7.J3 (Jpns.),
        .P7.U39-5 (US), DD256.5 (Ger.)    940.4886+, .4889+, .534886+,
        .5486+, .5488, .54886+, .5488642 (Brit.), .5488673 (US), .54887+,
        .5488743 (Ger.), .5488752 (Jpns.), .54889+, .5488973
        —Bibliography     Z6207.W8
          —Catalogs
        —German     D810.P7.G3
—Prophecies     D810.P75, DK254.R3 (Rasputin), BF1815 (Nostradamus)
        940.53181333, .53182201, .53181599613, 159.9613, 133.3
—Protest movements
—Protestant churches     D810.C5
—Prussia, East (Poland and R.S.F.S.R.)
—Prussia, East (Province)     DD491.O66    940.53159
—Psychological aspects     D810.P6-7, .P7 (propaganda), BF698, HM263,
        HM291, RC602     940.53019, .54886+ (propaganda),
        .5488642 (GB), 301.1522+, 355.115, 616.8
        —Bibliography—Catalogs     Z6207.W8

World War, 1939-1945
—Public opinion        D810.P85, .P7+, HM261        940.5342
    —Canada
    —France        D810.P85.F72-8
    —Germany        D810.P85.G3
    —Great Britain        D810.P85.G7
        —Congresses
    —Switzerland        D810.P85.S95
    —United States        D810.P85.U5-56        940.5373
—Quebec (Province)        D754.C2, D768.15
—Quotations, maxims, etc.
—Radar        D810.R33        940.5421
—Radio, radar, etc.        D810        940.5318621384, .545942
—Railroads        [SEE '...—Transportation']
—Rationing        [SEE 'Priorities, Industrial' or 'Rationing, Consumer']
—Reconnaisance, American
—Reconnaisance, Japanese
—Reconnaisance operations        D785
—Reconnaisance operations, American [German, etc.]
—Reconstruction        [SEE 'Reconstruction (1939-1951']
—Red Cross        HV579
—Refugees        [SEE ALSO '...—Displaced persons']        D809.A-Z (by place),
        .C2 (Canada), .E8+ (Europe), .F7 (Fr.), .G3 (Ger.), .S65 (Sov. Un.),
        .S9 (in Switz.), D806, D808, D810.J4 (Jews), D820.P72.A-Z (pop.
        transfers by country), JV6601        940.53159+, .5315943 (Ger.),
        .5315944 (Fr.), .5344, .5486+, .548673, 301.3284
    —Archival resources        Z6207.W8
    —Bibliography        Z6207.W8
    —Pictorial works
—Regi-Esercito. Divisione di fanteria Acqui        D766.32.C3
—Regimental histories        [Subdivided by country, regiment, division, etc.: SEE
                ALSO names of individual units by country, branch,
                then specific unit name as alternative entries]
    —Africa, South—Engineer Corps        D766.97
    —Australia        D767+, D767.8, .813, .99        940.541294
        —2/7th Cavalry Regt.        D767.813
        —14th Infantry Battalion
        —2/28th Infantry Battalion
        —36th Infantry Battalion        D767.8        940.541294
    —Belgium—Troupes coloniales        D766.92
    —Brazil        D768.3
        —Batalhão Carlos Camisão
        —Força Expedicionaria Brasileira        D768.3
        —Força Expedicionaria Brasileira, 1944-1945
        —11. Regimento de Infantaria
    —Canada        D768.15
        —West Nova Scotia Regiment        D768.15
    —Croatia
    —Czechoslovakia        D765.53
        —1. cs partyzanská brigáda Jana Zizky
    —Finland        D765.32
        —Raateen pataljoona
        —Sissipataljoona 3.
    —Forca Expedicionaria Brasileira, 1944-1945        D768.3

World War, 1939-1945
—Regimental histories
——France         D761-761.9       940.541244
———7. armée
———9. armée     D761.1.9th
———Bataillon des volontaires du Pacifique    D761.9.F7
——France combattante
————2. division blindée     D761.9.F7
——France
———Corps expéditionnaire français     D761.15
———4e division cuirassée     D761.2.4th
———3. division d'infanterie algérienne     D761.9.A4
———3. Groupement de choc     D761.9.G7
———6. régiment d'infanterie     D761.3
——Germany      D757-757.85+, D757.55, .57, .85, D764, D766+
               940.541343, .5423
———12. Armee
———12. Armee (1945)
———28. Freiwilligen-Panzer-Grenadier-Division 'Wallonien'    D757.85
———Geheime Feldpolizei
———Grenadier Regiment 67     D757.57.67th
———Heer.1.Panzerarmee     D757.56.Nr.1
———Heeresgruppe Afrika
———Heeresgruppe Süd     D757.1
———12. Infanteriedivision (1935/36-1944)     D757.33.12th
———Infanterie-Regiment 67     D757.57.67th
———97. Jäger Division     D757.32.J3
———Nationalsozialistische Deutsches Arbiter-Partei. Waffenschutz-
        staffel. III. (Germanisches) SS-Panzer-Korps    D757.55.G31
———Oberkommando. Abteilung Fremde Heere Ost
———Panzerarmee, 3
———Panzerarmeekorps Afrika     D757.55.A4, .G4
———Panzerdivision 'Grossdeutschland'
———Panzer-Division Hitlerjugend
———Panzer-division nr. 11     D757.55.11th
———17. Panzergrenadier-Division. Aufklärungsabteilung
———Panzer-Grenadier-Regiment 67     D757.57.67th
———Panzergruppe 3     D757.54
———XIV. Panzerkorps
———LVII. Panzerkorps     D757.56.57th
———Panzerlehrdivision     D757.55.P19
———Panzertruppen     D757.54
———SS-Gebirgs-Division Nord
———Sturmartillerie
———Technische Truppen     D757.855
———Waffenschutzstaffel
———Waffenschutzstaffel. 33. Grenadier-Division 'Charlemagne'
———Waffenschutzstaffel. 3. SS-Panzer-Division Totenkopf    D757.85

World War, 1939-1945
—Regimental histories
  —Great Britain      D759-60, D766-67, D766.82, .9, D767.6, UA652.A-Z
                    940.541242, .5421, .5423, .548642
    —Airborne Troops
    —First Army
    —Eighth Army      D766.82
    —Black Watch (Royal Highlanders)      D760.B57
    —Coldstream Guards
    —Combined Operations Command      D760.C63      940.5421
    —Duke of Cornwall's Light Infantry      D760.D88      940.541242
    —East African rifles
    —Long range desert group      D766.93
    —Manchester Regiment      UA652.M3
    —Princess Victoria's Royal Irish Fusiliers
    —Queen's Own Royal West Kent Regiment      UA652.Q4 D760.Q4
    —Royal Natal Carbineers      D760.R75
    —Royal Regiment of Artillery      D547.R5
    —77th Indian Infantry Brigade      D767.6
    —Worcestershire Regiment      UA652.W6
  —India      D767.6      940.540954
    —4th division
    —7th division
  —Italy      D763.I8+
    —Corpo di spedizione italiano in Russia
    —Corpo Italiano di liberazione      D763.I813
    —Divisione Partigiana Italiana Garibaldi (1943-1945)      D802.I82
    —XIX Brigata Garibaldi      D763.I813
  —New Zealand      D767.85+, D767.85.A (official)      940.54129931,
                    .5412931
    —2nd Division
    —2nd New Zealand Divisional Artillery      D767.851.2d   .
    —3rd Division      D767.85
  —Poland      D765, D765.13, D802.P6 (underground)      940.5412438
    —Armia Krajowa      D765.13, D802.P6
    —Armia Lódz
    —Bataliony Chlopskie—Congresses      D802.P6
    —Kierownictwo Dywersji      D802.P62
    —2. korpus      D765
    —22. Pulk Artylerii Lekkiej      D765.13
    —7. Pulk Piechoty
    —18. Pulk Piechoty
  —Romania
  —Russia      D764, D764.5-6
    —5. Armiia
    —38. Armiia
    —1. Chekhoslovatskii korpus
    —53. gvardeiskaia Fastovskaia tankovaia brigada      D764.6.G8.53d
    —97. gvardeiskaia Strelkovaia diviziia      D764.6.G8.97th
    —4. gvardeiskeii Stalingradskii mekhanizirovannyi korpus
                    D764.6.G8.4th
    —Sissiprikaati 1.      D765.32

World War, 1939-1945
—Regimental histories
　　—South Africa　　　　　D766.97　　　940.5449
　　　　—Police Brigade
　　　　—6th Division
　　　　—6th Mounted Regiment
　　—Soviet Union　　　　　D764.6, D765.32
　　　　—Chekhoslovatskaia Brigada, 1
　　—United States　　[Numerical entries may be filed or listed in some catalogs such that Arabic numbers precede spelled-out versions {e.g. '3d Cavalry', '5th Army', 'Second Army'}. The present guide—for simplicity—tries instead to place entries in alphabetical order by army, division, or other unit type regardless of the preceding specific unit number except in the case of units with distinctive, non-numerical names. Note that histories of units may ALSO be classified or have subject headings assigned pertaining to particular or general campaigns or geographical areas.]
　　　　—535th Anti-Aircraft Artillery Battalion　　　　D769.343.535th
　　　　　　　　　　　　　　　　　　　　　　　　940.544973
　　　　—3d Armored Division　　　　　D769.305.3d
　　　　—6th Armored Division
　　　　—67th armored regiment　　　　D769.3055.67th
　　　　—Third Army　　　　D769.26.3d　　　940.5421
　　　　—Sixth Army
　　　　—Seventh army
　　　　—8th Army　　　　D769.26.8th
　　　　—Eighth Army
　　　　—113th Cavalry
　　　　—1st cavalry division
　　　　—79th Cavalry Reconnaisance Troop
　　　　—5307th Composite Unit (Provisional)
　　　　—102d Construction Battalion
　　　　—IV corps　　　　D769.27.4th
　　　　—VII Corps
　　　　—Corps of Engineers　　　D769.U5+ or A5+
　　　　—1st Division
　　　　—10th Division
　　　　—78th Division
　　　　—102d Division　　　　D769.3.102d
　　　　—104th Division
　　　　—2d Engineer Special Brigade
　　　　—141st Field Artillery
　　　　—36th Infantry
　　　　—305th Infantry
　　　　—550th Infantry Airborne Battalion
　　　　—329th Infantry Regiment　　　　D769.31.329th
　　　　—Marine Corps　　　D767+, D769+　　　940.541273, .5426
　　　　　. 3d Division
　　　　　. 6th Division
　　　　　. 9th Regiment
　　　　—Mars Task Force
　　　　—Quartermaster Corps

514

World War, 1939-1945
—Regimental histories
—United States
—727th Railway Operating Battalion
—3d Ranger Battalion
—Ranger Battalions      D769     940.541273
—Signal Corps
—19th Tank Battalion
—771st Tank Battalion      D769.306.761st
—Transportation Corps
—Yugoslavia      D766.613.A-Z
—Druga prekomorska brigada      D766.613.D
—Gubceva brigada      D766.613.G8
—Presermova brigada      D766.613.P75
—Registers
—Registers, lists, etc.      D797.A-Z (by place), D810.J4 (Jews)
               940.5467+, .546773 (US), .5404, .541273
—Registers of dead    [SEE ALSO 'Registers of dead' as subdiv. of military
         branches {e.g. 'U.S. Army—Registers of dead'}]      D797.A-Z
—Germany
—Netherlands
—Poland
—Krakow (Voivodeship)      D797.P72.K76
—Warsaw      D797.P62.W2
—Soviet Union      D810.D4
—United States      D797.U6
—Religious aspects      D744.4, D810.C35-36 (chaplains), D816, BR479
               940.5304, .531+, .53152+, .53182, .5478, 248+, 264.1
—Reparations      [In general, SEE ALSO 'War damage compensation' and
         'Restitution and indemnification...']      D818-19, D819.A-Z (by place),
         .G3 (Ger.), .J3 (Japan), D821, HC337      940.531422, .53144,
            .5315296 (Jews), 330.9471, 338.943
—Resistance movements      [SEE 'World War, 1939-1945—Underground
         movements']
—Rhine River Valley
—Rhine Valley
—Rhodesia, Southern      D766.99.R346        940.536891
—Riverine operations
—Riverine operations, American [British, etc.]
—Romania      D766.4, DR264
—Ploesti
—Transylvania      DR280.7
—Rome      D763.I82.R6
—Rumania      D766.4, .6, DR262-6        940.53497-53498
—Ploesti

World War, 1939-1945
 —Russia  [SEE ALSO '...—Soviet Union']  D735.R9, D736,
       D742.R9,D753.2.R9, D764+, DK265-8, DK273, UA772+
       940.5347, .540947, .548147, .532, .5322, .5421+, 947.084,
       327.47+ (for. relns.), 330.947 (econ. conditions)
   —Addresses, sermons, etc.  D742.R9
   —Bibliography
   —Caucasus
   —Congresses  D764
   —Crimea  D764.7.C
   —Donets Basin  D764.7.D65
   —Fiction
   —Kerch Peninsula  D764.7.K35
   —Kiev  D764.7.K43
   —Kiev (Province)
   —Leningrad  D764.7.L54, D764.3.L4
   —Liudinovo  D764.7.L7
   —Moscow  D764.7.M6, DK601  940.5347, .542
 —Russia, Northern  D764.N6
 —Russia, Northwestern
 —Russia
   —Odessa  D764.7.O38
   —Pictorial works
   —Sevastopol
   —Societies, etc.
   —Stavropolskii  D764.3.S78
   —Ternopol (City)  D764.7.T43
   —Vitebsk  D552.V83
   —Yasnaya Polyana  DK651.Y3
 —Russian S.F.S.R.
   —Leningrad  D764.3.L4
   —Murmansk  D771
 —Saipan  D767.99.S3  940.542
 —Scandinavia  D742.S29, .B2 (Baltic States), D754.S29, DL83
 —Science  D810.S2  940.53156, .53185, .541242
 —Search and rescue operations
   —United States
 —Secret service  D810.S7-8, .S7 (gen.), .S8.A-Z (by biog. name),
       D810.C88(cryptography), D802.A-Z (underground),
       DD247 (Ger.), E748.D665 (Donovan, Wm.), UB250
       940.5485-5487+, .548642 (Brit. spies), .548644 (Fr.),
       .548647 (Rus.), .548673 (US), 940.548743 (Ger.),
       .548752 (Jpns.), .485, 327.120924 (biog.), 351.742, 355.34
   —Africa, North  D766.82
   —Asia  DS10 351.74
   —Australia  D810  940.5485, .548694
   —Bibliography  Z6724.I7
   —Brazil
   —Burma
   —Czechoslovakia
   —Egypt
   —Europe
   —France  D810.S7, .S8.A-Z

World War, 1939-1945
—Secret service
   —Germany     D810.S7-8, .S8.P815 (Popov), .S8.S63 (Skorzeny), D754,
                        D754.I6 (Ireland: I.R.A.), DD247.C16-35 (Canaris),
                        .S54 (Skorzeny)           940.548743
   —Fiction
   —Great Britain     D810.S7-8, .C88 (cryptography),
                        D802.F8 (Fr. underground), D756.5.N6 (Normandy
                        planning)       940.548641-2
     —Indexes    D810.S7.U (Ultra)
   —Greece
   —Iran
   —Italy
   —Japan       940.548752
   —Malagasy
   —Netherlands
   —Norway      D810.S8, D802.N7 (underground)       940.5486481
   —Oceania
   —Poland      D810.S7-8   940.5486438
   —Russia      D810.S7-8   940.548647
   —Scandinavia
   —Soviet Union    D810.S7, .S8.A-Z, .S8.R623 (Roessler)
   —United States   D810.S7-8      940.548673, .5485
   —Yugoslavia
—Serbia       D766.62.S4
   —Fiction
   —Prijepolje    D766.62.P8
—Senegal
—Sermons
—Siam        D805.J3 (Jpns. prisoners)
—Siberia
   —Congresses
—Sicily        D763.S5, .I8       940.542+
—Silesia       D757.9.S5    940.534314
—Silesia, Lower (Province)
—Silesia, Upper
—Silesia, Upper (Poland and Czechoslovakia)   D802.P62.S567 (underground)
—Silesia, Upper (Province)
—Singapore     D767.5, .55, DS598.S7     940.535952, .5425
—Slavonia      D766.62.S43
—Slovakia     D765.55.S55, D802.S62, DB679.3
—Slovenia     D766, D802.S63 (underground), DB361, DB381.A-Z
               940.54050949, .53497, 949.7
   —Ljubljana Region—Sources
   —Poetry
—Social aspects
   —Europe
   —United States   HQ1420 (women)
   —West (U.S.)    HC107.A17
—Solomon Islands   D767.98, .85     940.542, .545, .541273
—Songs and music   D810.E8, M1648, M1740, ML410.S55 (Shostakovich)
—Songs and music, American
—Songs and music, British
—Songs and music, English
—Songs and music, French

World War, 1939-1945
—Territorial questions    D820-1, D821.A-Z (by place), D644 (WWI), D734.A-Z,
                          D748      940.531, .5314, .531424, .31412 (WWI)
    —Aosta, Valley of        DG975.A6
    —Austria—Tyrol     D821.T9
    —Eritrea            D821.E7-8        940.531424
    —Ethiopia           D821.E8          940.531424
    —Europe             D820       940.5314
    —France—Alsace        D821.F8
    —Germany            D821.G4, D748, DD94, DD801.A-Z        940.5322
        —Bibliography     Z2240.3
    —Germany, Eastern
    —Glatz        DD801.G5    943.14
    —Greece       D821.G     940.53144496
    —Hungary      D765.56
    —Italy         D821.I8, DB321 (Trieste), DG975.F855
        —Trieste      DG975.T825-89
    —Japan         D821.J3
    —Kuril Islands
    —Levant        D821.L4     949.6
    —Netherlands   D819.N4, D821.N4        940.531422
    —Poland            D821.P7, DD801.O35 (Oder-Neisse Line), DK403,
                       DK418.5.R9        940.531424, 943.805
    —Prussia, East        DD491.O45       943.11
    —Rumania           D821.R8          940.531424
    —Saar Valley       DD801.S13        943.42
    —Transylvania       D821.T7          940.531424
    —Trentino-Alto Adige, Italy
    —Trieste         D821.Y9 or T, DB321, DG975.T89        940.531424
    —Tyrol         D821.T9
    —Venezia Giulia      D821.Y8-9
    —Yugoslavia        D821.Y8-9, .I8 (Italy), DB321, DG975.F855
                       940.531424, 327.450497
—Thailand        D754.T3-4, DS578
—Theater and the war    D810.E8        940.548
—Timor, Portuguese    D767.99.T47    940.541294
—Timor Timur, Indonesia    D767.99.T47, DS646.5
—Transportation        D810.T8, HE823 (merch. marine: G.B.),
                   HE2751 (railroads: U.S.), HE3018 (r.r.'s: G.B.), TF23, UG523
                   940.531838+, .5318385, .5412+, .5425, .5441, .545, 356.95,
                   358.2, 385, 387.5
—Treaties        D814 (peace), D814.55, D735, JX1963        940.53141, .5322
—Trench warfare
—Trophies
—Truk Islands      D785.U58-63 (U.S. bombing)
—Tunis         D766.99.T8    940.542
—Tunisia—Campaigns      D766.99.T8
—Tunnel warfare        DS559.8.T85
—Turkey        D754.T8, DR477
—Tuscany       D763.I82.T8

World War, 1939-1945
—U.S.      [SEE ALSO '...United States']
—Ukraine      D764.7.U5, D802.U4 (underground), DK508.8
      940.534771
  —Kiev    D764.7.K43
  —Krasnodon
  —Starobelsk    D804.S65
—Underground
  —Cuneo, Italy
—Underground literature    D798, D799.A-Z (by place), D799.D4 (Denmark),
    .F7 (Fr.), .I8 (It.), D731 (periodicals), D802.A-Z
    —Bibliography    Z6514.U5, Z6941.P41 or U5, Z6207.W8
      —Catalogs
      —Union lists
    —Byelorussian S.S.R.    D799.R9
    —Czechoslovakia    D799.C95
    —Denmark    D802.D4
    —France    D799.F7
    —Italy    D799.I8
      —Venice
    —Poland    D799.P7
      —Kielce (Region)
—Underground movements    D802, D802.A2 (gen.), .A3-Z (by place),
    D756, D810.S7-8 (secret service)
    940.5315, .5337, .534, .5485, .548743
  —Albania
  —Africa, West    D761.9.F7
  —Alessandria, Italy (Province)    D802.I8    940.5345
  —Alps, French    D802.A43
  —Alsace    DD801.A58, DC610.A58    944.383
  —Austria    D802.A9, DB97-9    943.6, .605
    —Bibliography
    —Biography
    —Carinthia    D802.A92
  —Auvergne    D802.F82.A953    940.534459
  —Balkan Peninsula    D802.B29, D766    940.53496
  —Belgium    D802.B4    940.5486493
    —Biography
    —Hainaut
  —Belgrad    D766.62.B4
  —Berlin
  —Berlin (Germany)    D757.9.B4
  —Bialystok, Poland (Voivodeship)    D802.P62.B47
  —Bibliography    Z2241.A53 (anti-Nazis), Z6374.H6 (Holocaust),
    Z6724.I7 (intelligence)
  —Bohemia    D802.B6
  —Bologna    DG975.B64    940.534541
  —Borneo    D802.B65
  —Bosnia and Herzegovina    D802.Y82.B665, D766.62.B6
  —Bouches-du-Rhône    D802.F8
  —Brescia (Province)    D802.I82.B75
  —Bryansk, Russia (Province)    D802.R82.B71
  —Bulgaria    D802.B77-78

World War, 1939-1945
—Underground movements
—Burma        D802.B92
—Byelorussian S.S.R.     D802.S752.B948
—Minskaia Oblast
—Camonica Valley    DG975.C167
—China            D802.C, D769.64      940.548673, 951.04258
—Congresses    D802.A2, D734
—Crete          D802.C6
—Crimea
—Croatia         D802.C7, .Y82.C77
—Nova Gradiska    D802.Y82.N682
—Okucani
—Periodicals
—Czechoslovakia      D802.C95, D799.C95, D765.5
—Karlovy Vary region    D802.C952.K374
—Moravia         D802.C952.M67
—Slovak Socialist Republic    D802.C952.S676
—Poetry      D745.S7.S5
—Sources      DB2822
—Denmark      D802.D4      940.534, .53489
—Fiction
—Emilia-Romagna, Italy    D802.I82.E447
—Estonia       D802.E6
—Europe       D802.E9, .A2, D805.A2      940.534
—Addresses, essays, lectures     D802.A2      940.534
—Sources—Bibliography—Catalogs    Z6207.W8
—Fiesole—Drama
—Finland       D802.F5
—Flanders     D802.F
—Florence
—France        D802.F8, .A2, D761, D811, DC373.A-Z (by person),
                  DC397, DS135.F83 (Jews)      940.5344, .5485,
                  .548644, 944.081

—Artois
—Aude         D802.F82.A92
—Auvergne     D802.F82.A953-956
—Bibliography
—Bigorre       D802.F82.B536
—Biography     D802.F8, DC373.A-Z
—Calais         D802.F82.C253
—Calvados      D802.F82.C343
—Charente     D802.F82.C52
—Congresses    D802.F8, D765
—Cote d'Or     D762.C76
—Dabo
—Dauphine     D802.F82.D388
—Eure-et-Loire    D802.F82.E878
—Finistere      D802.F82.F566
—Franche-Comte
—Is`ere (Dept.)     D802.F82.I838
—Jura          D802.F82.J87
—Lorraine
—Lot (Dept.)—Biography    D802.F82.L676
—Lyon         D802.F82.L9477-948

World War, 1939-1945
—Underground movements, Jewish   D810.J4, DS135.A-Z (by country),
                               .G33 (Ger.)
     —Algeria                   DS135.A3
     —Bibliography          Z6374.H6
     —Byelorussian S.S.R.—Nesvizh     DS135.R93.N453
     —Congresses           D810.J4
     —France               DS135.F83
     —Greece              DS135.G7
     —Hungary
     —Lithuania
     —Poland              D805.P7
     —Sobibor
—Underground movements
   —Jews       D810.J4, DS135.A-Z (by place)     940.531503924, .534,
                                .5405, .5485
     —Congresses
   —Karelia     D802.K36
   —Kaunas
   —Kosovo-Metohija (Albania)
   —Krakow
   —Leningrad (Province)    D802.R8, .L4
   —Lithuania        D802.L5, .S752.L573     940.53475
     —Vilnius
   —Ljubljana      D802.Y82.L7, .S63-67.L46-762
   —Loiret           D802.F82.L
   —Lower Styria     D766.613.S7
   —Luxembourg     D802.L9
   —Lyons
   —Macedonia     D802.M15, D766.62.M2-3
   —Macedonia (Modern Greece)
   —Malay Peninsula
   —Malaya      D802.M2
   —Malopolska     D802.P62.M3822
   —Masovia
   —Milan (Province)     D802.I82.M545
     —Chronology
   —Minsk (Province)    D802.M5, .R82.M66
   —Montenegro     D766.62.M6
   —Moravia      D802.C952.M67
   —Moscow (Province)    D802.R8.M6-85
   —Museums     D733
   —Naples          D763.I82.N36
   —Negros Occidental, Philippines (Province)     D802.P5
   —Negros Oriental, Philippines (Province)
   —Netherlands     D802.N4, D799.N4     940.5486492
   —New Britain (Island)   D767     940.5395
   —Norway        D802.N7-8, D809.N8, DL532     940.5481481,
                           .54860481, .5486481
     —Biography
     —Finnmark Fylke—Fiction
   —Nova Gradiska, Croatia    D802.Y82.N682
   —Oder-Neisse area     DK4600.O33
   —Okucani, Croatia
   —Ossola Valley     D802.I82.O82

World War, 1939-1945
—Underground movements
——Panay (Island)              D802.P5          940.5486914
——Parczew Forest, Poland     D802.P62.P377
——Pavlograd, Ukraine (Dnepropetrovsk Province)    D802.U4
——Periodicals—Indexes      D731
——Philippine Islands       D802.P5         940.53599, .53914,
                                      .5483914, .5486914
——Philippines         D767.4.U
———Negros Island
——Piacenza
——Piedmont         D802.I82.P2
——Poland          D802.P6, D805.P7 (prisons, concentration camps)
                 940.53438, .547247, .5481438
———Bialystok region       D802.P62.B4838
———Bibliography
———Biography        DK4419-20
———Congresses
———Fiction
———Katowice (Voivodeship)     D802.P62.K37
———Krakow         DS135.P62.K8 (Jews)
———Krakow (Voivodeship)     D802.P62.K75-8
———Lodz (Voivodeship)       D802.P62.L624
———Masovia         D802.P62.M365
———Opatow (Powiat)       D802.P62.O635
———Parczew Forest       D802.P62.P377
———Podhale      D802.P62.P582
———Podlasie
———Radomsko (Powiat)     D802.P62.R336
———Sandomierz (Powiat)
———Siedlce region      D802.P62.S546
———Sources       DK4400-4410
———Warsaw      D802.P62.W26-3736
————Biography     D802.P62.W26
———Warsaw (Voivodeship)
———Western and Northern Territories   DK4600.O33
——Zawiercie (Powiat)     D802.P62.Z3
——Polish
——Pyrenees (France and Spain)    D802.F82.P973
——Rablow, Poland
——Radomsko (Powiat), Poland    D802.P62.R336
——Rizal, Philippines (Province)
——Rome        D802.I82.R6+, D763.I82     940.5345
——Ronchi, Italy     D802.I82.R67
——Russia      D802.R8, D764, JN6598.K785    940.5347, .548647
——Rzeszow region      D802.P62.R938
——Savoie, Haute    D802.F8
——Serbia        D802.S47, D766.62.S4, DR369.5
——Siam        D802.S5       940.53593
——Skopje, Yugoslavia   D802.Y82.S525
——Slavonia      D766.62.S43-45
——Slovakia     D802.C952.S6535-675, D745.7.S5
——Slovenia     D802.S63-67, D766.62.S45, D802.Y82.S5826
——Slovensko Primorje
——South Africa

World War, 1939-1945
—Underground movements
    —Soviet Union    D802.R8, .S6+
    —Srem (Region)    D766.62.S7
    —Thailand    D802.T32
    —Trento (Province)    DG975.T72
    —Turin
    —Tuscany    D802.I82.T87-922
    —Ukraine    D802.U4
        —Personal narratives
        —Volhynia    D802.R82.V642
    —Vercors, France    D762.V4
    —Vilna
    —Volhynia    D802.R82.V642, .U4
    —Warsaw    D802.P62.W26+
    —Warsaw (Voivodeship)
    —White Russia    D802.R8, .W5
    —Yugoslavia    D802.Y8, D766.6, DR367.A-Z, DR369.5
                        940.5342, .53497, .54864209497
        —Biography
        —Bosnia and Herzegovina    D802.Y82.B665
        —Croatia    D802.Y82.C76946, D766.62.C7
        —Ljubljana    D802.S63.L762
        —Ljubljana (Slovenia)    D802.Y82.L7
        —Montenegro
        —Periodicals    DR367
        —Serbia    D802.Y82.S466, DR369.5
        —Slovenia    D766.62.S45
        —Tuzla (Bosnia and Hercegovina)    D802.Y82.T887
    —Zagreb    D766.62.Z3
    —Zamosc, Poland (Region)    D802.P62.Z15
—Underground printing plants
    —Belgrad    D799.Y8
    —France
—United States    [SEE ALSO '...—U.S.]    D769+, D731, D742-3, D742.U5,
                        D753+ (diplomacy), D749, D761, D767, E173, E744,
                        E806-7    940.5312, .532, .532273, .5373, .53973,
                                .540973, .541273, 973.917, .92, 327.73 (for. relns.)
    —Addresses, essays, lectures    D753    940.532273, .5373
    —Bibliography    Z6207.W8    016.3552, .94053
    —Biography
    —Collected works    D753    940.5373
    —Economic aspects
    —Periodicals    D731, D790
    —Societies, etc.    D570.A (WWI or II)
    —Sources    D769, D769.1    940.5373
        —Bibliography—Catalogs    CD3031 (Dept. of State archives)
—Unknown military personnel
—Unknown military personnel, American [British, etc.]
—Uruguay    D754.U8, F2726
—Vatican City    D754.V4
—Veterinary service    D810.V45
—Vienna    D811.5.P7495.A3
—Virginia    D769.85.V8    940.53755
    —Hampton Roads    D810.T8, HC107.V82.H48 359.7

World War, 1939-1945
  —Vis Island         D766     940.547642
  —Wake Island
  —War work     [Civilian participation]    D769.85.A-Z (U.S.: by state),
                D807-810, BX7749 (Am. Friends)     940.5477-5478,
                .5477873 (US), .5481497
    —American Legion   D769.8.A
    —Boy Scouts       D810.B7
    —Catholic Church     D810.C6
    —Christian Science    D810.C45     940.53152895
    —Churches        D810.C6
    —Elks           D810.E 940.54777
    —England—London
    —Friends, Society of    BX7747-49
    —Girl Scouts
    —Great Britain
    —Jeunesse ouvri`ere chrétienne     D802.F8       940.531522
    —London
    —Methodist Church    D810.M
    —Presbyterian Church
    —Red Cross        D806-7, D805.G3, UH535     940.54771,
                .54824563, 361.53
    —Russia
    —Salvation Army    D810.S15
    —Schools         D810.E3+     940.531537, 355.071173
    —Seventh-Day Adventists    D810.S   940.53152867
    —Society of Friends    BX7747
    —Soviet Union       DK273
    —Unitarian churches
    —Y.M.C.A.         D810.Y7      940.54774
    —Y.W.C.A.         D810.Y7+     940.54774
    —Young Men's Christian associations
    —Young Women's Christian Association    D810.Y7
  —Washington, D.C.     F199      917.53034
  —Weapons  [SEE '...—Supplies', names of classes of weapons, and names of
              particular ones as well]
  —West Indies, French     D754.W4     940.537297
  —White Russia       D764.7.W5
  —Wisconsin        D769.85.W6
  —Women          D810.W7, DK4419 (underground: Poland), HQ1420,
                HQ1623      940.53161, .5485
    —Bibliography
    —Congresses
    —France          D802.F8
    —United States      HQ1420
  —Women's work      D810.W7, D769, HD6093-5     940.5315396,
           .5318396, .541273, 306.27471, 331.112, .406173 (US), .48219
    —Great Britain
    —United States      HD6093.U     331.406173
  —Wyoming

World War, 1939-1945
—Yugoslavia          D735, D754, D766.6+, D802.Y8+ (underground),
                     DR327.A-Z (for. relns.: by country), .B9 (with Bulgaria),
                     DR359.A-Z (biog.: by person), .M5 (Mihailovic), DR366-70,
                     DR1294.A-Z (biog.: by person)          940.5349, .53497,
                     .54056, .5409497, 949.7, .702, 914.97, 923.5497
     —Addresses, essays, lectures
     —Belgrade       D766.62.B4
     —Bibliography   Z6207.W8
     —Bihac          D766.62.B6
     —Cacak          D766.62.C3
     —Collected works
     —Crepaja        D766.62.C67
     —Crna Trava     D766.62.C68
     —Croatia        D802.Y82.C76958 (underground)
     —Drugovac       D766.62.D75
     —Dubrovnik      D766.62.D8
     —Fiction
     —Karlovac region           D766.62.K28
     —Kokevski Rog Mountain region        D766.62.K56
     —Kozara Mountains          D766.62.K65
     —Leskovac       D766.62.L4
     —Lower Styria
     —Luznica        DR381.L8
     —Maps           G2011.S54
     —Maribor        D766.62.M35
     —Montenegro     D802.Y82.M656 (underground)
     —Paracin, Serbia           DR396.P24-33
     —Prekmurje      D797.Y82.P7-92
     —Salek Valley   D766.62.S3          940.53497
     —Serbia                    D802.Y82.S435 (underground), DR2038.5
     —Slavonia (Croatia)        D766.62.S43
          —Sources
     —Slovenia       D802.Y82.S5824, DR361        940.534973
     —Smartno ob Paki           D766.62.S
     —Sources        D766.6.A, D802.Y8 (underground), DR1298
     —Spodnje Gorje             D766.62.S63
     —Srem (Region)             D766.62.S7
     —Styria, Lower (Slovenia)
     —Sutjeska       D766.62.S9
     —Urosevac       D766.62.U7
     —Valjevo, Serbia           DR396.V28
     —Veliki Kupci              D766.62.V4
     —Vipava Valley             D766.62.V48
     —Voivodina (Serbia)        D766.62.V6
     —Zgornje Gorje  D766.62.S63
  —Zaire
Wormhout (France), Battle of, 1940
Wronki (Pila, Poland: Concentration camp)
Wuhlheide (Berlin, Germany: Concentration camp)

# ABOUT THE AUTHOR

BUCKLEY BARRETT earned his M.S. in Library Science at the University of Southern California in 1973, and began his career as a librarian in the same year. He has served in a number of faculty positions at California State University, San Bernardino since joining the staff in 1982. He was Head of Technical Services from 1987 to 1994, and now serves as Head of Automation Services. Prior to his term at CSUSB, Barrett worked as Library Director at Marymount College in Rancho Palos Verdes, while providing part-time reference services at CSU Dominguez Hills and CSU Fullerton. Earlier, he held professional posts at the California State Library and the South Dakota State Library.

With Mary Bloomberg, Barrett co-authored *Stalin: An Annotated Guide to Books in English* (Borgo Press, 1993) and *The Jewish Holocaust: An Annotated Guide to Books in English* (Borgo Press, 1995). On his own, he wrote *World War I: A Cataloging Reference Guide* (Borgo Press, 1995) and *The Barstow Printer: A Personal Name and Subject Index to the Years 1910-1920* (Borgo Press, 1985). Forthcoming are annotated bibliographies on Sir Winston Churchill and Adolf Hitler.

The author has two children, and lives in San Bernardino with his long-suffering and patient wife, Nette Bricker-Barrett, also a librarian.

www.ingramcontent.com/pod-product-compliance
Lightning Source LLC
Chambersburg PA
CBHW020356100426
42812CB00001B/80